THE EVOLUTION of LANGUAGE

THE EVOLUTION of LANGUAGE

Proceedings of the
9th International Conference (EVOLANG9)

Kyoto, Japan 13 – 16 March 2012

Editors

Thomas C Scott-Phillips
University of Edinburgh, UK

Mónica Tamariz
University of Edinburgh, UK

Erica A Cartmill
University of Chicago, USA

James R Hurford
University of Chicago, USA

World Scientific

NEW JERSEY • LONDON • SINGAPORE • BEIJING • SHANGHAI • HONG KONG • TAIPEI • CHENNAI

Published by

World Scientific Publishing Co. Pte. Ltd.
5 Toh Tuck Link, Singapore 596224
USA office: 27 Warren Street, Suite 401-402, Hackensack, NJ 07601
UK office: 57 Shelton Street, Covent Garden, London WC2H 9HE

British Library Cataloguing-in-Publication Data
A catalogue record for this book is available from the British Library.

THE EVOLUTION OF LANGUAGE
Proceedings of the 9th International Conference (EVOLANG9)

ISBN-13 978-981-4401-49-4
ISBN-10 981-4401-49-8

Printed in Singapore by B & Jo Enterprise Pte Ltd

Preface

This volume collects the refereed papers and abstracts of the 9th International Conference on the Evolution of Language (EVOLANG 9), held in Kyoto on 13-16 March 2012. Submissions to the conference were solicited in two forms, papers and abstracts, and this is reflected in the structure of this volume.

The biennial EVOLANG conference is characterised by an invigorating, multi-disciplinary approach to the origins and evolution of human language, and brings together researchers from many fields including, but not limited to: anthropology, archeology, artificial life, biology, cognitive science, genetics, linguistics, modeling, paleontology, physiology, primatology, and psychology The multi-disciplinary nature of the field makes the refereeing process for EVOLANG very challenging, and we are indebted to our panel of reviewers for their conscientious and valuable efforts. A full list of the panel can be found on the following page. Further thanks are also due to:

- The EVOLANG central organizing committee: Rudie Botha, Angelo Cangelosi, Erica Cartmill, Jean-Louis Dessalles, Ramón Ferrer i Canchó, Tecumseh Fitch, Jim Hurford, Chris Knight, Luke McCrohon, Kazuo Okanoya, Maggie Tallerman, Natalie Uomini
- The local organising committee: Kazuo Okanoya, Koji Fujita, Tao Gong, Takashi Hashimoto, Masayuki Ike-uchi, Roger Martin, Masumi Matsumoto, Luke McCrohon, Ayumi Osawa, Hajime Yamauchi
- The workshop organizers: Johan Bolhuis, Koji Fujita, Tomomi Fujimura, Takashi Hashimoto, Roger Martin, Hajime Ono, Kazuo Okanoya, Reiji Suzuki, Noriaki Yusa
- Our sponsors: The Kyoto University Foundation, The English Linguistic Society of Japan, The Linguistic Society of Japan, RIKEN Brain Science Institute, and JST ERATO Okanoya Emotional Information Project. The conference has also received financial support from a number of grants from the Japan Society for the Promotion of Science (#23242025, #23300085, #21320078, #23520458, #21120011, #23240033, #23118003)
- The plenary speakers: Minoru Asada, Cedric Boeckx, Noam Chomsky, Terrence Deacon, Simon Fisher, Russell Gray, Tom Griffiths, Simon Kirby, Tetsuro Matsuzawa, Rafael Núñez, and Jenny Saffran.
- The invited speakers: Kazuo Fujita, Tao Gong, Atsushi Iriki, Noriko Osumi. Charles Yang
- Finally, and most importantly, the authors of all the contributions collected here.

Thom Scott-Phillips, Mónica Tamariz, Erica Cartmill, Jim Hurford
December 2011

Panel of Reviewers

Christian Abry
Stephen Anderson
Michael Arbib
Kate Arnold
Mark Aronoff
Thomas Bak
Andrea Baronchelli
Mark Bartlett
Teresa Bejarano
Tony Belpaeme
Bob Berwick
Richard Blythe
Ted Briscoe
Greg Bryant
Christine Caldwell
Josep Call
Angelo Cangelosi
Ronnie Cann
Andrew Carstairs-McCarthy
Erica Cartmill
Matt Cartmill
Morten Christiansen
Fred Coolidge
Marie Coppola
Michael Corballis
Hannah Cornish
Tim Crow
Robert Damper
Bart de Boer
Dan Dediu
Jean-Louis Dessalles
Tom Dickins
Marietta Dindo
Shimon Edelman
Mark Ellison
Nicolas Fay
Ramón Ferrer i Canchó
Jacob Foster
Roland Frey
Bruno Galantucci
Simon Garrod
Les Gasser
Peter Gärdenfors
Tim Gentner
Laleh Ghadakpour
Kathleen Gibson
David Gil
Bruno Gingras
Tao Gong
Nathalie Gontier
Tom Griffiths
Steven Harnad
Martin Haspelmath
John Hawks
Bernd Heine
Stefan Hoefler
Jean-Marie Hombert
Jim Hurford
Takashi Ikegami
Gerhard Jäger
Sverker Johansson
Fiona Jordan
James Kirby
Simon Kirby
Chris Knight
Bob Ladd
Marion Laporte
David Leavens
Simon Levy
Phil Lieberman
Elena Lieven
David Lightfoot
John Locke
Gary Lupyan
Erkki Luuk
Heidi Lyn
Dermot Lynott
Michiru Makuuchi
Luke McCrohon
Adrien Meguerditchian
James Minett
Richard Moore
Juan-Carlos Moreno Cabrera
Makoto Nakamura
Jason Noble
Mieko Ogura
Kazuo Okanoya
Irene Pepperberg
Camilla Power
Ljiljiana Progovac
Shannon Pruden
Greg Radick
Sonia Ragir
Anne Reboul
Gareth Roberts
Hannah Rohde
Tamsin Saxton
John Schumann
Thom Scott-Phillips
Robert Seyfarth
Barbora Skarabela
Katie Slocombe
Andrew Smith
Kenny Smith
James Steele
Nina Stobbe
Samarth Swarup
Maggie Tallerman
Mónica Tamariz
Natalie Uomini
Remi van Trijp
Jacques Vauclair
Arie Verhagen
Marilyn Vihman
Paul Vogt
Slawomir Wacewicz
Bill Wang
Stuart West
Mike Wheeler
Stephanie White
Hajime Yamauchi
Jordan Zlatev

Contents

Part II: Abstracts

Papers

EVOLUTIONARY PARALLELS BETWEEN LANGUAGE AND TOOL USE

MICHAEL A. ARBIB
Computer Science, Neuroscience, and the USC Brain Project
University of Southern California, Los Angeles, CA 90089-2520, USA

Brain evolution of ancestral primates came to support simple imitation (shared with the common ancestor of humans and great apes) prior to complex imitation (unique to the hominid line). Apparent drawbacks of over-imitation (exhibited by humans but not by chimpanzees) are essential to human skill transmission. It is argued that Oldowan tool making corresponds to simple imitation and ape gestural communication, Acheulean tool making corresponds to complex imitation and protolanguage, while the explosion of innovations in tool making and social organization of the last 100,000 years correlate with the emergence of language.

1. Introduction

The Mirror System Hypothesis (MSH; Arbib, 2005a, 2012; Rizzolatti & Arbib, 1998) for the evolution of the human-language-ready brain was developed in the light of the following data sets (and more):

1) Comparison of brain mechanisms in macaque monkeys and humans, based primarily on single-cell recordings in the former and brain imaging in the latter.
2) Comparison of human capacities for imitation with those of non-human primates, especially chimpanzees.
3) Comparison of the communication systems of non-human primates (both vocalizations and manual gestures) with the human capacity for language.

The present paper extends the Hypothesis to incorporate the evolution of tool use, taking into account:

4) The archeological record of the evolution of tool use in *Homo.*

2. Varieties of Imitation

Action level imitation (Byrne & Russon, 1998) involves reproduction of details of the manual actions another individual uses. The human capacity for action level imitation surpasses the capability of great apes in at least two ways: (i) We can perceive – more or less immediately and with more or less accuracy – that a novel action may be approximated by a composite of known actions associated with appropriate subgoals. (ii) We can learn deeper hierarchies. I refer to what apes can do (but monkeys cannot) as *simple imitation*, using *complex imitation* to name the extended range of human abilities (Arbib, 2002).

The contrast between humans and chimpanzees can be illuminated by the study of *over-imitation*. Here we look at immediate imitation, but the presumption is that this is a crucial precursor for addition of the skill to the observer's long-term repertoire. In a study by Horner & Whiten (2005), young wild-born chimpanzees and 3- to 4-year-old children observed a human demonstrator use a tool to retrieve a reward from a puzzle-box. The demonstration involved both causally relevant and irrelevant actions, and the box was presented in each of two conditions: opaque and clear. When chimpanzees were presented with the opaque box, they reproduced both the relevant and irrelevant actions, thus imitating the overall structure of the task. When the box was presented in the clear condition, they ignored the irrelevant actions. In contrast, children imitated all the demonstrated actions to solve the task in both conditions, at the expense of efficiency. This is *over-imitation*.

Although at first glance over-imitation seems maladaptive, we view it as quintessential to the development and transmission of human culture (cf. Horner & Whiten, 2005; Nielsen & Tomaselli, 2009). I argue (Arbib, 2011) that over-imitation evolved to support complex imitation; social discriminability is a consequence, not a cause, of this ability.

3. From Primate Gesture to Protosign

In primate communication (Arbib, Liebal, & Pika, 2008), we may contrast (i) the closed set of calls based on innate motor patterns seen in all primates; (ii) the limited set of communicative gestures, seen in different groups of each species of great apes, which depend on learning based on social interaction; and (iii) human languages which enjoy open-ended expansion of the lexicon and employ a rich grammar to support the construction of utterances expressing novel meanings. Most theories of language evolution now accept that a set of increasingly complex "protolanguages" intervened between the time when our common ancestors with the great apes had capabilities (i) + (ii) and the time when they first had true languages (Bickerton, 1995; Hewes, 1973). During this extended period, vocabulary increased and constructions were at first more or less absent.

4. Tool Making as a Hierarchical Skill

We now use data on stone tools from the archeological record to calibrate the Mirror System Hypothesis. We sample the record of Paleolithic stone tool making, focusing on Stout's (2011) analysis of the hierarchy of processes apparently involved in Oldowan and Acheulean tool making, developing suggestions from a recent review (Arbib, 2011).

4.1. *Oldowan Tool Making*

The earliest known stone tools are assigned to the Oldowan Industry (ca. 2.6 - 1.4 mya) and consist of sharp stone flakes struck from cobble "cores" by direct percussion with another stone (the "hammerstone"). They consist of choppers, bone breakers, and flakes that may have been used to break open the bones of animals to extract the protein-rich marrow. The key innovation lay in flaking stones to create a chopping or cutting edge. Typically, many flakes were struck from a single core stone.

Oldowan stone making includes: (i) *procurement of raw materials* (both core and hammerstone – though one may start with a hammerstone retained from a previous occasion, and then either select a core from a pile at hand or conduct the preliminary search and evaluation until a suitable core is found), and (ii) the repetition of *flake detachment* as often as is desired or possible with the given core and hammerstone (Stout, 2011).

The stasis of Oldowan tool making suggests transmission of a few basic discoveries rather than emergence of a general skill for tool making. Here we see a parallel with the limited call set of any group of chimpanzees, as distinct from the situation in protolanguage once the ability to create protowords becomes explicitly available to the community. The range of Oldowan tools seem comparable to those of modern chimpanzees (Boesch & Boesch, 1990).

4.2. *Acheulean Tool Making*

The Acheulean tool industry consisted of axes, picks, and cleavers. It first appeared around 1.5 mya, and is associated with *H. erectus*. The key innovations are the shaping of an entire stone to a stereotyped tool form, as well as chipping the stone from both sides to produce a symmetrical (bifacial) cutting edge. This activity required manual dexterity, strength, and skill. However, the same tools were also used for a variety of tasks such as slicing open animal skins, carving meat, and breaking bones. The Early Acheulean (ca. 1.6 - 0.9 mya) can be characterized by elaborate flake production and by the emergence of large

cutting tools, while Late Acheulean (ca. 0.7 - 0.25 mya) sees production of blanks as the basis of more sophisticated shaping to achieve different tool forms. For Stout (2011), all the Early Acheulean forms of elaborate flake production reflect the key innovation of modification of the core to enable subsequent flake detachments as an explicitly preparatory action, rather than as a byproduct of primary flake detachment. The production of "blanks" suitable for shaping into a hand axe was a key innovation of the Early Acheulean, and involves elaboration of raw material procurement, and the largest cores need to be supported on the ground instead of in the hand. These requirements on perceptual-motor organization make Acheulean production qualitatively different from Oldowan.
This coordination of production elements requires that the tool maker develop the skills of not only (i) selecting a cobblestone from (a fragment of) which, a tool of a given type could be produced (e.g. a hand axe or pick – both these forms can occur at a single site), but also (ii) forming a stable visual representation of the shape of the tool to be produced on this occasion. and associated lower-level actions. The crucial point is that the choice of affordances for each blow would now be based on this imagined final shape, rather than the independent judgment a place on the cobble as offering a suitable affordance for striking off a flake. The challenge lies in the ability to maintain the visual goal even as one rotates the cobble to find new affordances then changes it by removing further flakes. The core itself, as it changes, structures behavior by its relation to a visualized final form of much greater specificity than "a decent core" or "a decent flake". Note that even in Oldowan tool making, the perceptual side – judging a suitable affordance with respect to the current goal – goes "hand in hand" with exercising the motor side, the appropriate effectivity.
As Stout (2011) emphasizes, this technology shows substantial variation, but given the great separation in space and time between, e.g., Olduvai 1.33 mya and West Turkana 400,000 years earlier, the evidence points to *very* slow cultural evolution rather than variations of a shared technique in any one community.

4.3. *The Emergence of Homo Sapiens*

By 200 kya, the technology was in place to create a variety of tools, since the rough blank could follow a pattern that ultimately became either cutting tools, serrated tools, flake blades, scrapers, or lances. Further, these tools could be used with other components to form handles and spears, and as tools to make other tools such as wooden and bone artifacts. McBrearty & Brooks (2000) downplay the European provenance of much of the relevant archeology. They document that many of the components of the "human revolution" are found in the African Middle Stone Age tens of thousands of years earlier and occur at sites that are widely separated in space and time. They thus argue for a gradual assembling of the package of modern human behaviors in Africa, and its later export to other regions of the Old World, so that the origin of our species can be linked with the appearance of Middle Stone Age technology at 250-300 kya, following the late Acheulean.

This view is consonant with the Mirror System Hypothesis if we offer the following equations:

- The Oldowan was period in which our ancestors were still limited to simple imitation and communicated with a limited repertoire of vocal and manual gestures akin to those of a group of modern great apes;
- The early Acheulean was *transitional* between simple and complex imitation, with the transfer of skills being limited in depth of hierarchy and exhibiting little if any ratcheting. At this stage, protohumans communicated with a limited repertoire of vocal and manual gestures larger than those of a group of modern great apes but still very limited;
- By the late Acheulean, complex imitation was fully established, and communication gained an open-ended semantics through the expanded use of pantomime with a reliance on increasingly rich memory structures capable of holding hierarchical plans for both praxis and communication.

Note the emphasis on the expansion of memory in the evolution of brain mechanisms supporting language offered by Francisco Aboitiz and colleagues (Aboitiz & García, 2009; Aboitiz, García, Brunetti, & Bosman, 2006).

Homo sapiens was the first species of *Homo* with a language-ready brain. However, it took more than 100,000 years for the developing power of protolanguage to yield the first true languages with their consequent impact on the acceleration of cultural evolution.

5. Response to Reviewers

The reviewers made a number of excellent points. Rather than rewrite the paper, I have instead abridged the previous draft to make room for a listing of those points, together with brief replies.

1. Explain more about what MSH brings to our understanding of the paleolithic record, and make explicit predictions about how the development of complex tool manufacture and gestural imitation interacted with one another.

MAA: The key hypothesis is that the development of complex skills – not just tool use, let alone tool manufacture (cf. Hansell & Ruxton, 2008) – was linked in a virtuous circle with manual gesture, and that complex imitation then combined with pantomime and conventionalization to support the fractionation and complementary formation of constructions that marked the lengthy transition from protolanguage to language. MSH shows how we may use primatology and comparative neurobiology to make up for the lack of hard data on hominid brain evolution and its behavioral correlates; the present paper indicates how such an approach may enrich and be enriched by attention to the archeological record.

3. The author concludes that only with (early) Homo sapiens, "complex imitation emerged, and communication gained an open-ended semantics" But then very little evolutionary time is left for the adaptations on vocalization, assumed by Arbib's model to follow both the "pantomime" and the "proto-sign" stages.

MAA: Actually, I asserted this of the late Acheulean, but I agree with the reviewer that the wording in the draft was ill-considered and now say "The late Acheulean was the period by which complex imitation was fully established." According to the doctrine of the expanding spiral (Arbib, 2005b) and the view that there was a spectrum of protolanguages (Arbib, 2008b), I offer for debate that the primitive protosign of the early Acheulean was enough to provide scaffolding for limited protospeech (i.e., adaptive pressure for some expansion of voluntary control of the vocal apparatus); that this process continued into the late Acheulean; but it required a great increase in memory capacity for complex imitation to support the emergence of languages with hierarchical depth.

4. The archaeological argument depends largely on Stout's recent review, which is simply given a new interpretive spin.

MAA: The paper is not a re-interpretation of Stout; it is an attempt to see how a deep analysis of the evolution of imitation which is relevant to language evolution can be enriched by linkage to the archeological record. Clearly, the research of others must be assessed in future development of this theme.

5. The lack of novel hypotheses that might lead to new archaeological work or programs of tool-use related neurophysiological observation is disappointing.

MAA: (a) Yes. Future work should suggest new programs of tool-use related neurophysiological observation, building on, e.g., the work of Stout & Chaminade (2007) and Ramayya, Glasser, & Rilling (2010), but it should also build on our prior analyses of the relation of mirror systems to imitation (Arbib & Bonaiuto, 2008) and tool use (Arbib, Bonaiuto, Jacobs, & Frey, 2009). (b) Another strand to develop is to constrain studies linking working memory to archeological data (Coolidge & Wynn, 2005) – with less emphasis on Baddeley's phonological loop (2003) – by more detailed neural analyses of working memory in relation to language evolution (Aboitiz & García, 2009).

A general point: While many people are now aware of MSH, relatively few have read recent work. The new volume (Arbib, 2012) integrates many different strands that deepen the Hypothesis and extend its reach.

Acknowledgements

This material is based in part upon work supported by the National Science Foundation under Grant No. 0924674 (M.A. Arbib, PI). Any opinions, findings, and conclusions expressed in this material are those of the author and do not necessarily reflect the views of the National Science Foundation. The discussion of tool making was heavily influenced by the research on stone tools conducted and reviewed by Dieter Stout (Stout, 2011)

References

Aboitiz, F., & García, R. (2009). Merging of Phonological and Gestural Circuits in Early Language Evolution. *Reviews in the Neurosciences, 20*(1), 71-84.

Aboitiz, F., García, R., Brunetti, E., & Bosman, C. (2006). The Origin of Broca's Area and its Connections from an Ancestral Working Memory Network. In Y. Grodzinsky & K. Amunts (Eds.), *Broca's region* (pp. 3-16). Oxford: Oxford University Press.

Arbib, M. A. (2002). The mirror system, imitation, and the evolution of language. In K. Dautenhahn & C. L. Nehaniv (Eds.), *Imitation in Animals and Artifacts. Complex Adaptive Systems* (pp. 229-280). Cambridge, MA: The MIT Press.

Arbib, M. A. (2005a). From monkey-like action recognition to human language: an evolutionary framework for neurolinguistics. *Behav Brain Sci, 28*(2), 105-124; discussion 125-167.

Arbib, M. A. (2005b). Interweaving Protosign and Protospeech: Further Developments Beyond the Mirror. *Interaction Studies: Social Behavior and Communication in Biological and Artificial Systems, 6*, 145-171.

Arbib, M. A. (2008). Holophrasis and the Protolanguage Spectrum. *Interaction Studies: Social Behavior and Communication in Biological and Artificial Systems, 9*(1), 151-165.

Arbib, M. A. (2011). From Mirror Neurons to Complex Imitation in the Evolution of Language and Tool Use. *Annu Review Anthro, 40*, 257–73.

Arbib, M. A. (2012). *How the Brain Got Language: The Mirror System Hypothesis*. New York & Oxford: Oxford University Press.

Arbib, M. A., & Bonaiuto, J. (2008). From Grasping to Complex Imitation: Modeling Mirror Systems on the Evolutionary Path to Language. *Mind & Society, 7*, 43-64.

Arbib, M. A., Bonaiuto, J., Jacobs, S., & Frey, S. H. (2009). Tool use and the distalization of the end-effector. *Psychol Res, 73*(4), 441-462. doi: 10.1007/s00426-009-0242-2

Arbib, M. A., Liebal, K., & Pika, S. (2008). Primate Vocalization, Gesture, and the Evolution of Human Language. *Curr Anthro, 49*(6), 1053-1076.

Baddeley, A. D. (2003). Working memory: looking back and looking forward. *Nat Rev Neurosci, 4*(10), 829-839.

Bickerton, D. (1995). *Language and Human Behavior.* Seattle: University of Washington Press.

Boesch, C., & Boesch, H. (1990). Tool use and tool making in wild chimpanzees. *Folia Primatologica, 54*, 86-99.

Byrne, R. W., & Russon, A. E. (1998). Learning by imitation: a hierarchical approach. *Behav Brain Sci, 21*(5), 667-684; discussion 684-721.

Coolidge, F. L., & Wynn, T. (2005). Working Memory, its Executive Functions, and the Emergence of Modern Thinking. *Cambridge Archaeological Journal, 15*(01), 5-26.

Hansell, M., & Ruxton, G. D. (2008). Setting tool use within the context of animal construction behaviour. *Trends in Ecology & Evolution, 23*(2), 73-78. doi: 10.1016/j.tree.2007.10.006

Hewes, G. W. (1973). Primate communication and the gestural origin of language. *Current Anthropology, 12*(1-2), 5-24.

Horner, V., & Whiten, A. (2005). Causal knowledge and imitation/emulation switching in chimpanzees (*Pan troglodytes*) and children (*Homo sapiens*). *Animal Cognition, 8*(3), 164-181.

McBrearty, S., & Brooks, A. S. (2000). The revolution that wasn't: a new interpretation of the origin of modern human behavior. *J Hum Evol, 39*(5), 453-563.

Nielsen, M., & Tomaselli, K. (2009). Over-Imitation in the Kalahari Desert and the Origins of Human Cultural Cognition. *Nature Precedings*, http://hdl.handle.net/10101/npre.12009.13049.10101.

Ramayya, A. G., Glasser, M. F., & Rilling, J. K. (2010). A DTI Investigation of Neural Substrates Supporting Tool Use. *Cereb Cortex, 20*(3), 507-516.

Rizzolatti, G., & Arbib, M. A. (1998). Language within our grasp. *Trends Neurosci, 21*(5), 188-194.

Stout, D. (2011). Stone toolmaking and the evolution of human culture and cognition. *Philosophical Transactions of the Royal Society B: Biological Sciences, 366*, 1050-1059.

Stout, D., & Chaminade, T. (2007). The evolutionary neuroscience of tool making. *Neuropsychologia, 45*(5), 1091-1100.

CORTICO-CORTICAL AND CORTICO-CEREBELLAR COMPUTATIONS IN LANGUAGE CHANGE

GIORGOS P. ARGYROPOULOS

Solodkin/Small Brain Circuits Laboratory, University of California, Irvine, Basic Core: Room 3224 Biological Sciences III Irvine, CA 92697, USA

gargyropoulos@gmail.com

The computations performed by cortico-cortical and cortico-cerebellar circuits are argued to support psycholinguistic mechanisms underlying distinct types of language change. Associative cortico-cerebellar computations participate in idiomatization, coalescence, and metonymic inferencing, while categorical cortico-cortical ones underlie schematization, analogical reanalysis, and metaphorical extension. The paper contributes to the much-needed construction of a neurolinguistics of language change.

1. Introduction: Neurolinguistics of Language Change

Despite several pleas for studying language change in terms of properties of the mind (e.g. Bybee *et al.*, 1994; Aitchison, 2003), interdisciplinary discourse with psycholinguistics demonstrates but a few attempts (e.g. Bybee & Scheibman, 1999; Kempson & Cann, 2007; Rosenbach & Jäger, 2008), and discourse with neurolinguistics even fewer (e.g. Argyropoulos, 2008; Givón, 2009). This paper will enrich such discourse by exploring the distinct contributions of cortico-cortical and cortico-cerebellar computations in language change.

2. Cortico-Cortical and Cortico-Cerebellar Computations

Current neurocomputational research promotes the idea that cortico-cortical circuits implement unsupervised, while cortico-cerebellar ones implement supervised learning algorithms (e.g. Doya, 1999). Cerebral algorithms abstract rules from the input data with no pre-specified output and flexibly apply them to different contexts. They may assign, for instance, a set of observations into clusters, so that observations in the same cluster are similar according to some criterion (e.g. Pothos & Chater, 2002). On the other hand, cortico-cerebellar circuits are considered to simulate re-occurring cortico-cortical processes with greater speed, accuracy, and automaticity, yet with poor capacities to generalize across situations (Ramnani, 2006). If a rule is deterministically applied to the same context, cortico-cerebellar algorithms may arbitrarily replicate these reoccurring input-output mappings, providing faster solutions with fewer resources as ''a short-cut circuit or a look-up table for a mapping [...] originally developed by [...] cortico-cortical processing' (Doya, 1999, p. 970).

3. Associative and Categorical Neurolinguistic Computations

This neurocomputational tradeoff has been argued to underlie the 'associative/categorical' distinction (Townsend & Bever, 2001) in language processing (Argyropoulos *et al.*, submitted). Evidence for cerebellar associative learning ranges from classical conditioning to higher cognitive aspects (Timmann *et al.*, 2010). This supports the proposal that linguistic associative, and not categorical relations strongly involve neocerebellar circuitry (Argyropoulos, 2009), since associative relatedness (e.g. 'gift-horse') ''relies on temporal contiguity'', while semantic-categorical relatedness (e.g. 'duck-chicken') ''reflects the similarity in meaning or the overlap in featural descriptions'' (Thompson-Schill *et al.*, 1998, p. 440). Argyropoulos (2011) demonstrated selective effects of neocerebellar stimulation on associative and not categorical priming. Abnormal associative priming is also found in schizophrenia (Nestor *et al.*, 2006, p. 142), where neocerebellar pathology is involved (e.g. Okugawa *et al.*, 2007). In Argyropoulos *et al.* (2011), neocerebellar stimulation was shown to disrupt the access to associative memories of re-occurring pairs of letter strings. Cerebellar damage is also shown to impair verbal fluency by affecting phonemic rule-based word generation, sparing semantic categorical rule-based performance (Leggio *et al.*, 2000). These findings are opposite to those on temporal cortical pathology in semantic dementia and Alzheimer's disease, where deficits in semantic categorical, but not associative priming are reported (e.g. Rogers & Friedman, 2008). Lexical priming studies in Broca's and Wernicke's aphasia also show no impairments in automatic access to lexical or semantic information (Hagoort, 1997), suggesting that associative priming does not rely on these structures.

Moreover, neuropsychological research employing artificial grammar learning (e.g. Christiansen *et al.*, 2010; Petersson *et al.*, 2010) implicates Broca's area in the acquisition of abstract structures, but not the cerebellum (Witt *et al.*, 2002). Furthermore, unlike left perisylvian lesions, cerebellar ones are only exceptionally related with aphasias, suggesting that the cerebellum is not integral to syntactic processing (Desmond & Fiez, 1998). In Pickett (1998), the performance of cerebellars in the comprehension of active- and passive-voice constructions was qualitatively the reverse of that often shown by healthy controls and, to a larger extent, agrammatic aphasics (e.g. Saffran *et al.*, 1998): controls erred in 4% of actives and 10% of passives, while cerebellars made errors in 11% of both actives and passives. The explanation was that cerebellars ''can perform the full range of linguistic processing, but their mental shortcuts have been disrupted, so that processing 'easy' sentences requires more conscious effort and is performed less automatically'' (Pickett, 1998).

4. Brain Circuits in Language Change

The discussion now turns to the impact of these mechanisms on distinct types of language change. The following considerations are summarized in table 1.

4.1. *Constrained Search in Language Processing and Change*

Grammaticalization changes have been argued to involve the introduction of constrained search mechanisms. In sentence processing, Kempson and Cann (2007) distinguish between ''a generally available tree-growth process'' (*ibid*, p. 76) and a ''lexical look-up mechanism'' (*ibid*, p. 95). A shift from the former to the latter accounts for the procliticization of object pronouns in the transition from Medieval to Renaissance Spanish (1); it involves the calling up of ''[...] actions associated with the verb together with those associated with the clitic with a single lexical look-up mechanism'' (Kempson & Cann, 2007, p. 95).

(1) mas los rompan luego (in Kempson & Cann, 2007; from Bouzouita, 2002)
but CL break.3PL afterwards
'But break them afterwards.'

Substantial evidence implicates neocerebellar circuitry in linguistic constrained search. In an fMRI covert word-stem completion task (Desmond *et al.*, 1998), stems with many (MANY condition; e.g. 'STA_') or few possible completions (FEW condition; e.g. 'PSA_') were presented. Prominent increases in activation in the MANY (relative to the FEW) condition were observed in the middle and inferior frontal gyri and anterior cingulate, while neocerebellar compartments showed increases in the FEW (relative to the MANY) condition. A clinical study on schizophrenics (Marvel *et al.*, 2004) replicated these findings, showing selective deficits in stem completions of the FEW condition. Moreover, in Gebhart *et al.* (2002), the range of appropriate responses in the antonym- (e.g. 'kind'-'rude') and verb-generation tasks (e.g. stimulus: 'CHEF', response: 'cook'), in which cerebellar patients showed deficits, was more constrained than that in the subordinate term-generation task (e.g. stimulus: 'MONEY', response: 'dollar'), where they showed spared performance. This suggested that ''the element of constraint in semantic association responses may be a key factor in eliciting a right cerebellar language deficit'' (*ibid*, p. 332).

4.2. *Prefabrication vs Schematization, Coalescence vs Analogical Leveling*

While constructional schemata guarantee productivity, novel expressions are computationally costly (Diessel, 2004). Prefabricated utterances, however, are accessed without schematic activation and provide ''processing short-cuts'' (Wray & Perkins, 2000, p. 17). For instance, the frequent expressions 'I don't know __', 'I don't think __', and 'Why don't you __' (Bybee & Scheibman, 1999) have gained in their syntagmatic bondedness (Lehmann, 2004) and have become prefabrications. The cerebellum has been independently discussed as important for processing rote-memorized sequences, such as childhood jingle or multiplication tables (Thach, 1997, pp. 91-2), providing ''access to relatively automatic word-sequence subroutines'' (Deacon, 1997, p. 275).

Reversely, schematization involves analytical processes where formulae are categorized on the basis of featural overlaps (Wray & Perkins, 2000; Diessel, 2004), and depends, as such, on cortical circuitry. Accordingly, reanalysis and analogical leveling pertain to categorical phenomena, whereby more productive schemata absorb instances of weaker ones according to their specifications (Haspelmath, 1998; Lehmann, 2004; Argyropoulos, 2010). This is the case for the assimilation of the past-tense morphology of low frequency verbs (e.g. weep, creep) into the strong '-ed' schema.

4.3. *Metaphorical Extension and Metonymic Inferencing*

The cognitive-semiotic properties of metaphorical and metonymic changes provide another intersection for historical linguistics and neurolinguistics. Grammatical items are often derived from lexical items expressing temporal concepts that are metaphorically extended (e.g. Hopper & Traugott, 1993) spatial source concepts, as in the transition from (2a) to (2b) in Kwaio.

(2a)	na'o-na 'ifi	'in front of the house'	(Keesing, 1991, p. 335)
(2b)	na'o-na omea	'before the mortuary feast'	

Another mechanism is the semanticization of ''(conceptual) metonymy'', involving ''pragmatic associations that arise in the flow of speech'' (Traugott & Dasher, 2005, p. 58). If the activation of the semantic properties (3a) of an expression routinely co-occurs with a certain inference (3b), the latter is gradually incorporated in the meaning of the expression (3c; Bybee *et al.*, 1994).

(3a) I have done quite a bit of writing since we last met. (temporal meaning)
(3b) Since Susan left him, John has been very miserable. (temporal meaning + causal inference)
(3c) Since you are not coming with me, I will have to go alone. (causal meaning)
(Bybee *et al.*, 1994, pp. 196-7)

Metonymy represents ''semantic transfer through contiguity'' and is ''indexical'', while ''metaphor is semantic transfer through a similarity of sense perceptions'' and is analogical and iconic (Antilla, 1989 [1972], pp. 141-2). This immediately promotes the cerebellum as a strong foundation for processing an indexical sign, which “refer[s] to individuals, single units, single collections of units, or single continua” and “refers to its object not [...] because of any similarity or analogy with it [...], but because it is in dynamical [...] connection [...] with the individual object” (Peirce, 1931-58, Vol. 2, pp. 305-6). Temporal contiguity and non-generalizability are defining properties of cortico-cerebellar associative memory traces. In the transfer from the source to the target concept, the change does not occur on the grounds of shared categorical properties between the two (Bybee *et al.*, 1994, p. 289). On the contrary, metaphor operates on the basis of similarity and analogy, i.e. by featural overlaps between concepts of different semantic domains, as the feature of ‘serial order’ in the mapping from SPACE to TIME in (2) above. Mechanisms of similarity-based learning were seen above to reflect cortical algorithms of unsupervised learning.

The cerebellum is indeed involved in semantic associations, such as those in verb generation (Fiez *et al.*, 1992; Gebhart *et al.*, 2002; Frings *et al.*, 2006). Cerebellars notably provide inappropriate yet categorically related responses (e.g. ‘small’ instead of ‘take’ in response to ‘pill’), and are also able to generate appropriate subordinate terms (e.g. ‘apple’) in response to superordinate ones (‘fruit’), suggesting that “[t]he right posterolateral cerebellum may be more involved in associative semantics than in categorical semantics” (Gebhart *et al.*, 2002, p. 332). Cerebellar stimulation has also been shown to affect associative (e.g. ‘chef’-‘cooking’), and not categorical (e.g. ‘theft’-‘stealing’) noun-to-verb priming (Argyropoulos & Muggleton, submitted).

Table 1. A series of simplified multi-level binary distinctions illustrating the involvement of cortico-cerebellar and cortico-cortical computations in qualitatively different psycholinguistic processes underlying distinct types of language change.

Circuitry	**Cortico-Cerebellar**	**Cortico-Cortical**
Learning Algorithm	**Supervised**	**Unsupervised**
	(Doya, 1999; Ramnani, 2006)	
Learning Criterion	**Temporal Contiguity**	**Featural Overlap**
	(e.g. Thompson-Schill, 1998)	
Lingua Mentis	**Associative**	**Categorical**
	(Townsend & Bever, 2001)	
Processing Modality	**Holistic**	**Analytic**
	(Wray & Perkins, 2000)	
Processing Mechanism	**Constrained search**	**Default Inheritance**
	(Kempson & Cann, 2007; Diessel, 2004)	
Semiotics	**Indexical**	**Symbolic**
	(Peirce, 1931-58; Deacon, 1997)	
Language Change	**Syntagmatic Coalescence**	**Analogical Leveling-Reanalysis**
	(Haspelmath, 1998; Lehmann, 2004; Argyropoulos, 2010)	
	Prefabrication	**Schematization**
	(Diessel, 2004; Wray & Perkins, 2000)	
	Metonymic Inference	**Metaphorical Extension**
	(Antilla, 1989 [1972]; Bybee *et al.*, 1994)	

5. Conclusion

This paper presented evidence for the view that cortico-cortical and cortico-cerebellar computations support psycholinguistic processes underlying distinct types of language change. This approach should be extended to a broader range of circuitry and types of language change. Overall, cognitive neuroscience can now shed ample light on the neurolinguistics of language change.

References

Aitchison, J. (2003). Psycholinguistic perspectives on language change. In B. Joseph & R. Janda (Eds.), *Handbook of historical linguistics* (pp. 736-43). Oxford: Blackwell.

Antilla, R. (1989 [1972]). *Historical and comparative linguistics* (2nd ed.) Amsterdam: John Benjamins.

Argyropoulos, G. P. (2008). The subcortical foundations of grammaticalization. In A. D. M. Smith, K. Smith, & R. Ferrer i Cancho (Eds.), *The evolution of language: Proceedings of the 7th international conference on the evolution of language* (pp. 10-7). Singapore: World Scientific.

Argyropoulos, G. P. (2009). Neocerebellar emulation in language processing. In K. Alter, M. Horne, M. Lindgren, M. Roll, & J. von Koss Torkildsen (Eds.), *Brain Talk: Discourse with and in the brain. Papers from the first Birgit Rausing language. program conference in linguistics* (pp. 193-206). Lund: Lund University, Media Tryck.

Argyropoulos, G. P. (2010). Is grammaticalization glossogenetic? In A. D. M. Smith, M. Schouwstra, B. de Boer, & K. Smith (Eds.), *The evolution of language: Proceedings of the 8th international conference on the evolution of language* (pp. 3–10). Singapore: World Scientific.

Argyropoulos, G. P. (2011). Cerebellar theta-burst stimulation selectively enhances lexical associative priming. *The Cerebellum, 10*(3), 540-50.

Argyropoulos, G. P., Kimiskidis, V., & Papagiannopoulos, S. (2011). Theta-burst stimulation of the right neocerebellar vermis selectively disrupts the practice-induced acceleration of lexical decisions. *Behavioral Neuroscience, 125*(5), 724-34.

Argyropoulos, G.P., & Muggleton, N. (submitted). *Effects of cerebellar stimulation on processing semantic associations.*

Argyropoulos, G.P., Small, S., Solodkin, A., Bak, T.H., & Sturt, P. (submitted). *Neocerebellar computations in language comprehension.*

Bouzouita, M. (2002). *Clitic placement in Old and Modern Spanish: A dynamic account.* Unpublished Master's thesis. King's College London.

Bybee, J., Perkins, R., & Pagliuca, W. (1994). *The evolution of grammar. Tense, aspect, and modality in the languages of the world.* Chicago: University of Chicago Press.

Bybee, J., & Scheibman, J. (1999). The effect of usage on degrees of constituency: the reduction of *don't* in English. *Linguistics, 37*(4), 575-96.

Christiansen, M. H., Kelly, L., Shillcock, R., & Greenfield, K. (2010). Impaired artificial grammar learning in agrammatism. *Cognition*, *116*(3), 382-93.
Deacon, T. (1997). *The symbolic species: The coevolution of language and the brain.* New York: Norton.
Desmond, J. E., & Fiez, J. A. (1998). Neuroimaging studies of the cerebellum: Language, learning, and memory. *Trends in Cognitive Sciences*, *2*(9), 355-62.
Desmond, J. E., Gabrieli, J. D. E., & Glover, G. H. (1998). Dissociation of frontal and cerebellar activity in a cognitive task: evidence for a distinction between selection and research. *NeuroImage*, *7*, 368-76.
Diessel, H. (2004). *The acquisition of complex sentences.* Cambridge: Cambridge University Press.
Doya, K. (1999). What are the computations of the cerebellum, the basal ganglia and the cerebral cortex? *Neural Networks*, *12*, 961-74.
Fiez, J. A., Petersen, S. E., Cheney, M. K., & Raichle, M. E. (1992). Impaired non-motor learning and error detection associated with cerebellar damage. A single case study, *Brain*, *115*, 155-178.
Frings, M., Dimitrova, A., Schorn, C. F., Elles, H.- G., Hein-Kropp, C., Gizewski, E. R., Diener, H. C., & Timmann, D. (2006). Cerebellar involvement in verb generation: An fMRI study. *Neuroscience Letters*, *409*, 19-23.
Gebhart, A. L., Petersen, S. E., & Thach, W. T. (2002). Role of the posterolateral cerebellum in language. *Annals of the New York Academy of Science*, *978*, 318-333.
Givón, T. (2009). *The genesis of syntactic complexity.* Amsterdam: John Benjamins.
Hagoort, P. (1997). Semantic priming in Broca's aphasics at a short SOA: No support for an automatic access deficit. *Brain and Language*, *56*, 287-300.
Haspelmath, M. (1998). Does grammaticalization need reanalysis? *Studies in Language*, *22*, 315-51.
Hopper, P., & Traugott, E. C. (1993). *Grammaticalization.* Cambridge: Cambridge University Press.
Keesing, R. M. (1991). Substrates, calquing and grammaticalization in Melanesian Pidgin. In E. C. Traugott & B. Heine (Eds.), *Approaches to grammaticalization. Vol. 1* (pp. 315-42). Amsterdam and Philadelphia: John Benjamins.
Kempson, R., & Cann, R. (2007). Dynamic Syntax and dialogue modelling: preliminaries for a dialogue-driven account of syntactic change. *Current Issues in Linguistic Theory*, *284*, 73-101.
Leggio, M.G., Silveri, M.C., Petrosini, L., & Molinari, M. (2000). Phonological grouping is specifically affected in cerebellar patients: a verbal fluency study. *Journal of Neurology, Neurosurgery, and Psychiatry*, *69*, 102–6.
Lehmann, C. (2004). Theory and method in grammaticalization. *Zeitschrift fur Germanistische Linguistik*, *32*(2), 152-87.
Marvel, C. L., Schwartz, B. L., & Isaacs, K. L. (2004). Word production deficits in schizophrenia. *Brain and Language*, *89*(1), 182-91.

Nestor, P., Valdman, O., Niznikiewicz, M., Spencer, K., McCarley, R., & Shenton, M. (2006). Word priming in schizophrenia: Associational and semantic influences *Schizophrenia Research*, *82*(2), 139-42.

Okugawa, G., Nobuhara, K., Takase, K., & Kinoshita, T. (2007). Cerebellar posterior superior vermis and cognitive cluster scores in drug-naïve patients with first-episode schizophrenia. *Neuropsychobiology*, *56*, 216-19.

Peirce, C. S. (1931-58). *Collected Writings* (Vol. 1-8). C. Hartshorne, P. Weiss, & A. W. Burks (Eds.). Cambridge, MA: Harvard University Press.

Petersson, K. M., Folia, V., & Hagoort, P. (2010). *What artificial grammar learning reveals about the neurobiology of syntax. Brain and Language*. Article in press. DOI:10.1016/j.bandl.2010.08.003.

Pickett, E. R. (1998). *Language and the cerebellum*. Unpublished doctoral dissertation, Brown University, Providence, Rhode Island.

Pothos, E. M., & Chater, N. (2002). A simplicity principle in unsupervised human categorization. *Cognitive Science*, *26*, 303-43.

Ramnani, N. (2006). The primate cortico-cerebellar system: anatomy and function. *Nature Reviews Neuroscience*, *7*, 511-22.

Rogers, S. L., & Friedman, R. B. (2008). The underlying mechanisms of semantic memory in Alzheimer's disease and semantic dementia. *Neuropsychologia*, *46*, 12-21.

Rosenbach, A., & Jäger, G. (2008). Priming and unidirectional language change. *Theoretical Linguistics*, *34*(2), 85-113.

Saffran, E. M., Schwartz, M. F., & Linebarger, M. C. (1998). Semantic influences on thematic role assignment: Evidence from normals and aphasics. *Brain and Language*, *62*, 255-97.

Thach, W. T. (1997). Context-response linkage. *International Review of Neurobiology*, *41*, 599-611.

Thompson-Schill, S. L., Kurtz, K. J., & Gabrieli, J. D. E. (1998). Effects of semantic and associative relatedness on automatic priming. *Journal of Memory and Language*, *38*, 440-58.

Timmann, D., Drepper, J., Frings, M., Maschke, M., Richter, S., Gerwig, M., *et al.* (2010). The human cerebellum contributes to motor, emotional and cognitive associative learning. A review. *Cortex*, *46*, 845–57.

Townsend, D., & Bever, T. G. (2001). *Sentence comprehension: The integration of habits and rules*. Cambridge, Massachusetts: MIT Press.

Traugott, E. C., & Dasher, R. B. (2005). *Regularity in semantic change*. Cambridge: Cambridge University Press.

Witt, K., Nushman, A., & Deuschl, G. (2002). Intact artificial grammar learning in patients with cerebellar degeneration and advanced Parkinson's disease. *Neuropsychologia*, *40*(9), 1534-1540.

Wray, A., & Perkins, M. R. (2000). The functions of formulaic language: An integrated model. *Language and Communication*, *20*, 1-28.

TOWARDS LANGUAGE ACQUISITION BY COGNITIVE DEVELOPMENTAL ROBOTICS

MINORU ASADA
Adaptive Machine Systems, Osaka University,
Suita, 565-0871, Japan
asada@ams.eng.osaka-u.ac.jp

One of the big issues of human cognitive development is language acquisition process, and constructive approaches have been attacking the issue to understand this process by building vocal robots. This talk gives a survey on these approaches. First, cognitive developmental robotics is briefly introduced to show a general idea of these approaches. Then, learning of vowel vocalization by parrot-like teaching is shown as one of the model of the interaction between an infant and a caregiver. Next, caregiver's anticipation during the interaction process is analyzed , and as a result, it is shown how caregiver shapes the infant vowels. Finally, future issues are discussed towards language acquisition by cognitive developmental robotics.

1. What's Cognitive Developmental Robotics?

Cognitive developmental robotics (CDR) aims to provide new understanding of how human's higher cognitive functions develop by means of a synthetic approach that developmentally constructs cognitive functions. The core idea of CDR is "physical embodiment" that enables information structuring through interactions with the environment, including other agents. The idea is shaped based on the hypothesized development model of human cognitive functions from body representation to social behavior (Asada et al., 2009). The approach of CDR is as follows:

A: construction of computational model of cognitive development

1. hypothesis generation: proposal of a computational model or hypothesis based on knowledge from existing disciplines
2. computer simulation: simulation of the process difficult to implement with real robots such as physical body growth
3. hypothesis verification with real agents (humans, animals, and robots), then go to 1)

B: offer new means or data to better understand human developmental process $\rightarrow$ mutual feedback with A

1. measurement of brain activity by imaging methods
2. verification using human subjects or animal ones
3. providing the robot as a reliable reproduction tool in (psychological) experiments

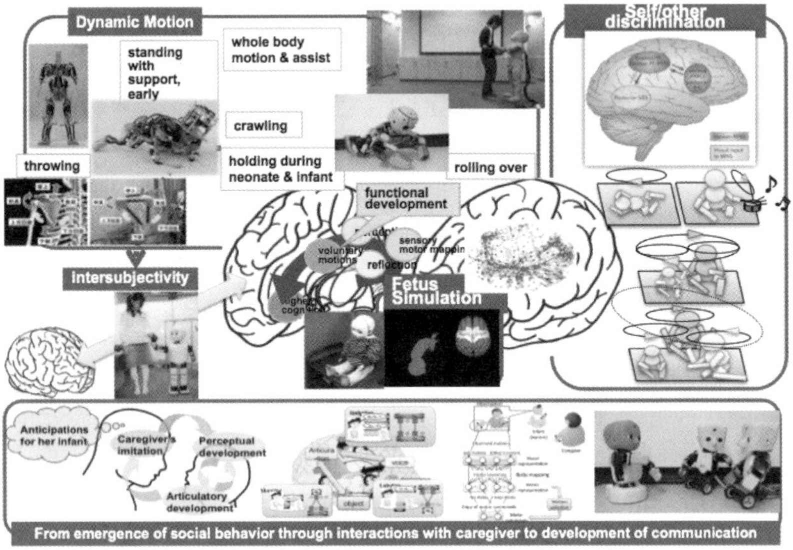

Figure 1. An overview of the achievements by JST ERATO Asada Project

Figure 2. Platforms developed by JST ERATO Asada Project

Based on the idea of CDR, the author's group has started JST ERATO Asada Synergistic Intelligence System Project (www.jeap.jp) in 2005 as totally 6.5 years project. A small part of the achievements is summarized in Figure 1 and also in (Asada et al., 2009). In this project, a variety of robot platforms have been developed, and utilized for the studies of different aspects of human cognitive development. Figure 2 shows these robots. From the left to the right, CB^2 (Child robot with Bio-mimetic Body: 1.3m, 33kg, 56 DoFs, air cylinder type actuators, vision, auditory, and tactile sensors), Neony (top: .5m, 3.5kg, 22 DoFs, 90 tactile sensors), Synchy (bottom: .3m, 2.3kg, LED, 17 DoFs), Kindy (1.1m, 27kg, 42 DoFs), Noby (Nine month Old BabY: .75m, 9kg, 30 DoFs), and Pneuborn 7 and 13 (PMA (Pneumatic Muscle Actuator) robots: 7: .8m, 4kg, 30 DoFs).

One of the social interactions we have been attacking is vowel imitation towards language acquisition with an aspirational vocalization mechanism based on the idea of physical embodiment. In the following sections, an artificial vocal system with learning methods through the interaction with a caregiver and the analysis of the caregiver's bias are introduced and discussed towards language acquisition.

2. Vowel acquisition through mother-infant interaction

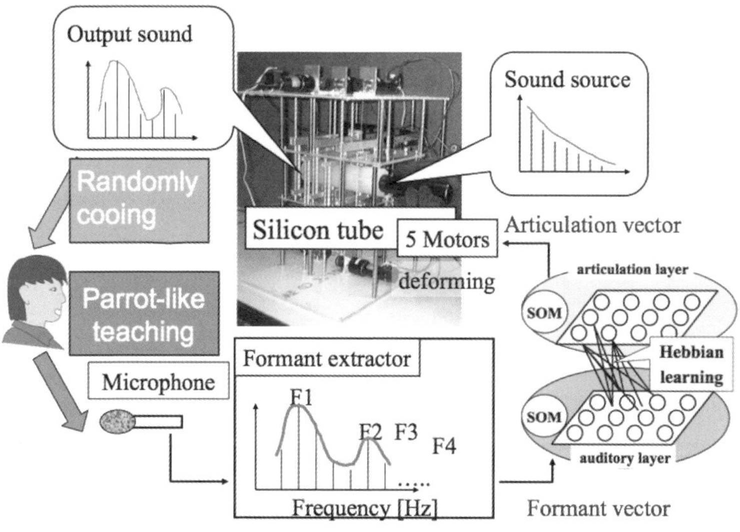

Figure 3. An overview of the system

Inspired by the observation that infants acquire phonemes common to adults without having the capability to articulate, nor having a prior knowledge about the relationship between the sensorimotor system and phonemes, Yoshikawa et al. (Yoshikawa, Asada, Hosoda & Koga, 2003) took a constructivist approach to building a robot that reproduces a similar developmental process. Two general issues are addressed: what are the interactive mechanisms involved and what should be the behaviour of the caregiver/teacher? Based on findings in developmental psychology, it is conjectured that: (a) the caregiver's vocalization in response to infants' cooing reinforces the infant's articulation along the caregiver's phonemic categories; and (b) the caregiver's repetition with adult phonemes helps to specify the correspondence between cooing and the caregiver's phonemes as well as determining the acoustic properties of the phonemes. The robot consists of an artificial articulatory system with a five-degrees of freedom mechanical system deforming a silicon vocal tract connected to an artificial larynx, an extractor of formant, and a learning mechanism with self-organizing auditory and articulatory layers. Starting off with random vocalizations, the system uses the caregiver's repetitive utterances to bootstrap its learning. In order to resolve the arbitrariness in determining proper articulations, the torque to deform the tract and its resultant deformation are minimized.

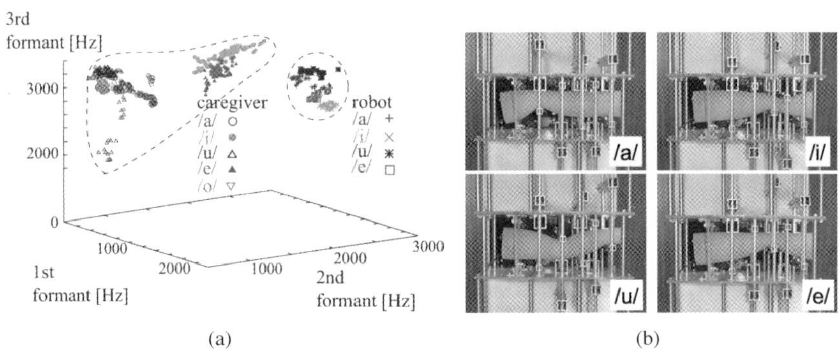

Figure 4. Formant distributions of the robot and the caregiver (a), and the acquired shapes of the vocal tract (b)

Figure 3 shows a vocal robot system which consists of an articulation part and an auditory one with their corresponding layers, respectively. Both layers are self-organized and connected by Hebbian learning through parrot-like teaching by a caregiver. Figure 4 (a) shows formant distributions of the robot and the caregiver which indicate how different each other phonemically. Figire 4 (b) show the resultant vocal tract shapes obtained by learning methods (SOM and Hebbian) through the parro-like teaching of the caregiver.

3. How Caregiver's Anticipation Shapes Infant's Vowel Through Mutual Imitation

The mechanism of infant vowel development is a fundamental issue of human cognitive development that includes perceptual and behavioral development. Ishihara et al. (Ishihara, Yoshikawa, Miura & Asada, 2009) modeled the mechanism of imitation underlying caregiver-infant interaction by focusing on potential roles of the caregiver's imitation in guiding infant vowel development. Proposed imitation mechanism is constructed with two kinds of the caregiver's possible biases in mind. The first is what we call "sensorimotor magnets," in which a caregiver perceives and imitates infant vocalizations as more prototypical ones as mother-tongue vowels. The second is based on what we call "auto-mirroring bias," by which the heard vowel is much closer to the expected vowel because of the anticipation being imitated. Computer simulation results of caregiver-infant interaction show the sensorimotor magnets help form small clusters and the auto-mirroring bias shapes these clusters to become clearer vowels in association with the sensorimotor magnets.

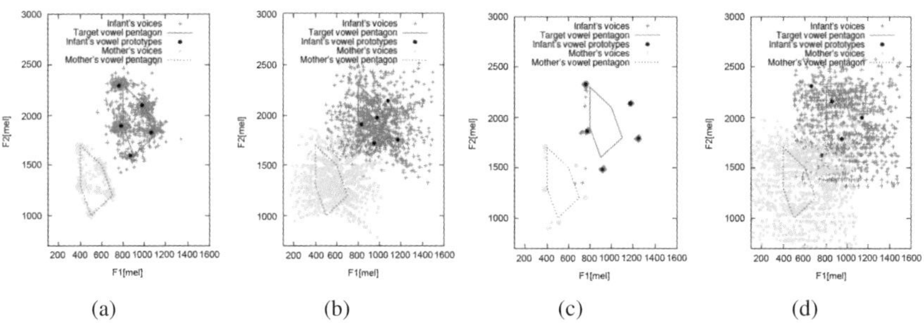

Figure 5. Difference of learning results under several conditions. Apexes of red pentagons represent target vowels of infant, in other words, clearest vowels in her vowel region, and black dots represent infant vowel prototypes after learning.

Figure 5 (a) shows the learning result with two well-balanced biases, where blue and red dots indicate the caregiver and the infant voices, respectively, apexes of red pentagons represent target vowels of the infant, in other words, clearest vowels in her vowel region, and black dots represent infant vowel prototypes after learning. In (a), the infant vowels are almost correctly converged, while (b) - (d) do not seem to be. In (b), the sensorimotor magnet is missing, therefore not convergence but rather divergence of infant vowels and the caregiver's imitated voices is observed. On the other hand, in (c), auto-mirroring biases is missing, and as a result, there is fast convergence but three of five vowels converged onto wrong locations. In the case of no biases, nothing happened, as shown in (d).

4. Towards Language Acquisition

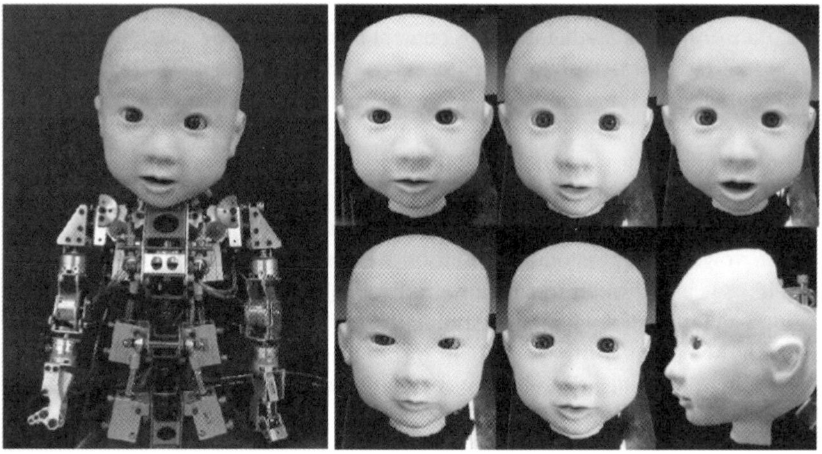

Figure 6. Affetto head with the internal mechanical structure of the upper torso (left), and examples of the facial expressions (right))

The above two studies dealt with an issue of vocal development based on physical embodiment (aspirational vocalization) and social interaction (caregiver's anticipation). Not yet language which is "symbolic" in twofold. One is in the sense of contrast: signal v.s. "symbol," and the other one is "symbolic" faculty among higher cognitive functions, and also means to support themselves. By the latter sense, language acquisition means to acquire almost everything cognitive in humans, and language development is a whole picture of human's cognitive development starting from sensorimotor mapping and generation of dynamic movements, and then self/other concept acquisition, theory of mind, imitation, (joint) attention, emotion, communication, and so on. We have partially attacked the lexicon acquisition problem by multimodal simultaneous mapping with vocal imitation ((Sasamoto, Yoshikawa & Asada, 2010)), or based on curiosity ((Ogino, Kikuchi, & Asada, 2006)). These studies should be integrated into one robot platform which is capable to learn and develop for ever to verify how language can be acquired through the interaction with caregiver (or any other persons). We may need to consider physical development of vocal system, such as down of the larynx from childhood to adulthood. This is one direction of our future work. The other one is to study much deeper issues at each stage of development. One of such issues is emotional interaction with caregiver since emotion or intrinsic motivation is a strong driving force for behavior generation. In case of mother-infant interaction, we need much more realistic infant robot to derive emotional states from the caregiver. Ishihara et al. (Ishihara, Yoshikawa, & Asada, 2011) developed such an infant robot, Affetto, to study how the caregiver-child attachment heavily affects the children's developmental pathway. Figure 6 shows its appearance whose head can generate various facial expressions. Currently, Affetto does not have any vocal system, but in future it will have as unified platform.

Acknowledgements

The author would like to appreciate the following persons for their supports of the achievements introduced in this talk. Profs. Koh Hosoda (Osaka Univ.), Yasuo Kuniyoshi (Univ. of Tokyo), Hiroshi Ishiguro (Osaka Univ.), and Toshiro Inui (Kyoto Univ.), Drs. Yuichiro Yoshikawa (Osaka Univ.), Masaki Ogino (Ksanai Univ.) Katsushi Miura (Currently, Fujitsu), and Ph.D candidates Hisashi Ishihara and Yuki Sasamoto (Osaka Univ.).

References

Asada, M., Hosoda, K., Kuniyoshi, Y., Ishiguro, H., Inui, T., Yoshikawa, Y., Ogino, M., & Yoshida, C. (2009). Cognitive developmental robotics: a survey. *IEEE Transactions on Autonomous Mental Development*, *1*(1), 12–34.

Ishihara, H., Yoshikawa, Y., & Asada, M. (2011). Realistic child robot gaffettoh for understanding the caregiver-child attachment relationship that guides the child development. In *Ieee international conference on development and learning, and epigenetic robotics (icdl-epirob 2011)* (p. CD-ROM).

Ishihara, H., Yoshikawa, Y., Miura, K., & Asada, M. (2009). How caregiver's anticipation shapes infant's vowel through mutual imitation. *IEEE Transactions on Autonomous Mental Development*, *1*(4), 217–225.

Ogino, M., Kikuchi, M., & Asada, M. (2006). Active lexicon acquisition based on curiosity. In *The 5th international conference on development and learning (icdl'06)*.

Sasamoto, Y., Yoshikawa, Y., & Asada, M. (2010). Mutually constrained multimodal mapping for simultaneous development: modeling vocal imitation and lexicon acquisition. In *The 9th international conference on development and learning (icdl'10)* (p. CD-ROM).

Yoshikawa, Y., Asada, M., Hosoda, K., & Koga, J. (2003). A constructivist approach to infants' vowel acquisition through mother-infant interaction. *Connection Science*, *15*(4), 245–258.

PROTOLANGUAGE, DISCRETE INFINITY AND INTERFACES: INVESTIGATING THE EVOLUTION OF THE LANGUAGE AND MUSIC FACULTY WITHIN THE MINIMALIST PROGRAM

RIE ASANO

Department of Systematic Musicology, University of Cologne, Albertus-Magnus-Platz Cologne, D-50923, Germany

'Syntax' of language and music are represented similarly in terms of asymmetrical headed hierarchy yielded by MERGE, the capacity underlying *discrete infinity*, but encode different objects, which are determined by their unique *interface systems*. Therefore, it is suggested that both language and music as human cognitive systems and their evolution can be investigated within the *Minimalist Program* focusing on MERGE and *interface systems*.

1. Introduction

Language and music regarded as *the Faculty of Language* (*FL*) and *the Faculty of Music* (*FM*) are similar but different human cognitive systems. Partial aspects of language and music can also be found in some systems of other animals, but both as such are only available to human beings. That is, both systems are based on some kind of creative capacity which is not accessible for animals other than humans. Is there any shared uniquely human capacity underlying these two different cognitive systems? If so, what makes language differ from music and vice versa? In this paper, I will discuss some aspects related to these two questions and show a possible way to approximate an answer to the central question asked in modern language and music inquiry, "Why is language the way it is?" and "Why is music the way it is?", which can be also interpreted in terms of the investigation of language and music evolution.

2. Comparative research on *FL* and *FM*

2.1. *Different formal representations of language and music*

The foundation of the comparative research on formal aspects of language and music was provided by Lerdahl and Jackendoff (1983) in *A Generative Theory of Tonal Music* (*GTTM*). The goal of *GTTM* is specifying a *structural description* of an experienced listener's mental representation of a heard musical piece of the classical idiom (Lerdahl & Jackendoff, 1983). In *GTTM*, two *reduction systems*, *time-span reduction* and *prolongational reduction*, are relevant for the issues of this article. These two systems provide tree structures that express the relative importance of the pitch-events of a piece differently in hierarchical fashion: the *time-span reduction* organizes them symmetrically into a rhythmically governed hierarchy and the *prolongational reduction* arranges them asymmetrically into a headed hierarchy expressing harmonic and melodic tension and relaxation (Lerdahl & Jackendoff, 1983; Jackendoff, 2009). Here, "asymmetry" means that some elements are regarded as *head* and the others as modifiers or elaborations of the *head* (Jackendoff, 2009). This asymmetrical relation between elements is based on *tonal pitch space* (*TPS*) introduced by Lerdahl (2001). In the tonal system of Western music, every tone is heard in relation to a particular fixed pitch perceived as most stable, the tonic, and the *TPS* is arrayed in relation to this tonal center (Jackendoff & Lerdahl, 2006). In comparing language and music, Jackendoff (2009) emphasized the difference of linguistic syntactic structure and musical prolongational structure because what they encode is completely different. However, concerning the asymmetrical headed hierarchy, which is also a crucial property of syntactic structure of language represented as *head-complement structure* (Jackendoff, 2011), there are reasons to say that they are based on some shared principles. What are these principles? Are they completely identical?

2.2. *Language = MERGE + interfaces? Music = MERGE + interfaces?*

Concerning uniquely human components of language, syntax taking discrete structural elements and combining them in certain ways (but potentially unboundedly) to form hierarchically organized sequences is assumed to make language special. Moreover, music also possesses this kind of 'syntax', which is different from the linguistic one in several ways (Patel, 2012). The *Minimalist Program* (*MP*) is one of different theoretical approaches in linguistics and it seems to provide a promising starting point to develop a general theoretical framework for a comparative approach to language and music. In the following it will be argued that *MP* investigating the mechanism yielding *discrete infinity* in language can be adapted to research on music. *MP* takes MERGE as a minimal condition for linguistic *discrete infinity*. MERGE takes two already formed structures like X and Y, and combines them hierarchically into a new structure A = {X, Y} (Chomsky, 2010). Further, there are two subcases of

MERGE: Given A, we can merge an element to it from outside of A (*external* MERGE) or from within A (*internal* MERGE; *displacement*). That is, *external* MERGE creates a structure like {B, {X, Y}} and *internal* MERGE creates a structure like {X, {X, Y}}. In this way, MERGE yields *discrete infinity* in language.

However, MERGE alone cannot yield the whole aspects of language. Language keeps to some simple operation, MERGE, and is perfectly designed to satisfy *interface conditions* (*strong minimalist thesis*; *SMT*) (Chomsky, 2010). That is, the expressions generated by MERGE should be 'read' at *interfaces* (Chomsky, 2000). These *interface conditions* are given through two linguistic *interface systems*: a *sensory-motor* (*S-M*) and a *conceptual-intentional* (*C-I*) *interface system* (Chomsky, 2000). In other words, *interface systems* give some constraints (or rather rules) to MERGE. The hierarchical aspect of expressions generated by MERGE appears to be affected by these *interface conditions*. These *interface systems* are specific to language and include the phonological system at the *S-M interface* and the semantic system at the *C-I interface* (cf. Hauser et al., 2002). The phonological system is understood in this context as a mechanism of externalization and the semantic system as some interpretative mechanism (Chomsky, 2010).

Katz and Pesetsky's (to appear) well-known identity thesis for music and language, which states that the computational operations underlying language and music are the same, has been developed within the Minimalist Program using essential concepts of this approach. As *interface systems*, Katz and Pesetsky (to appear) introduced *time-span reduction* on the S-M side and *tonal-harmonic component* (*THC*) interpreting key membership and harmonic properties on the C-I side. That is, the core of computation is shared in language and music, but the way how it is put into use by the *interface systems* is quite different.

2.3. *Unique interface systems*

Recently, the nature of *interface systems* becomes revealed in comparative studies of human and other animals. Some empirical studies show that many properties of *interface systems* of language and music can be explained by means of homologue or analogue traits (cf. Hauser et al., 2002; Hauser, & McDermott, 2003). However, there are a few components of *interface systems* that seem to be human specific. For example, *phonemes*, the smallest meaning differentiating elements, seem to exist only in language. The ability to perceive *phonemes* includes more than the ability of categorical perception present in

primate cognition. Further, propositional meaning is unique to language. Although other animals make use of *functionally referential signals* like alarm or food calls, they cannot be regarded as precursor of linguistic reference system (Hinzen, 2009). The fact that primates are not able to use declarative deictic gesture provides also evidence that such a reference system is specific to humans (Tomasello, 2003). Both phoneme perception and a reference system are specific linguistic properties of the *S-M* and *C-I interface systems* that emerged in the course of evolution only in the human communication system.
In music, the systematic patterning of sound in terms of timing, accent, and grouping in regular periodic pulse called *isochronic rhythm* plays a central role (for a definition of "periodicity" and "isochronic rhythm", see also Patel, 2008). Rhythm is a common phenomenon in language and music in which elements are organized hierarchically in a metrical prominence structure (Jackendoff, 2002; Jackendoff, 2009). An important difference is that the linguistic rhythm can be recognized by other animals than humans (Hauser & McDermott, 2003), but there is only little evidence that animals can recognize the rhythmic structure of music (Jackendoff & Lerdahl, 2006). This essential distinction comes from human's specific musical ability to *beat perception and synchronization* (*BPS*) (Patel, 2006). This is a property of *S-M interface system* unique to music which distinguishes music from language.

2.4. *Asymmetry of interface systems and lexicon*

Concerning the relation between such unique *interface systems* and MERGE, some kind of asymmetry in such *interface systems* can be found comparing language and music: Concerning language the *C-I interface system* seems to be primary (Hinzen, 2009; Chomsky, 2010). There are mainly two kinds of evidence for this asymmetry. First, both kinds of MERGE, *external* and *internal* MERGE, appear to correlate closely with the dual aspect of semantics: *external* MERGE correlates with (propositional) argument structure and *internal* MERGE with scopal or discourse related properties like information structure (Chomsky, 2010). That is, *external* MERGE relates with the propositional meaning of linguistic expressions and *internal* MERGE enables humans to 'reinterprete' this meaning in a certain context without any loss of referential precision (*non-degrading recursivity*) (Deacon, 2003). The second evidence is that phonology consists not only of sensory-motor components, an encoding of sound per se (cf. Jackendoff, 2011). For example, *phonemes*, the basic elements of phonology unique to language, bear their discreteness by means of the *C-I system* accounting for thought, interpretation, and organizing action.

On the contrary, the *S-M interface* seems to be primary in music. For example, *Isochronic rhythm*, the unique property of music on the S-M side, seems to be primarily independent from components on the C-I side which are assumed to be essential in terms of MERGE. Further, the asymmetrical structure based on *TPS* which is apparently yielded by *external* MERGE depends on the perception of pitch stability which is largely affected by sensory property. Concerning *internal* MERGE, the fact that a certain pitch can be 'interpreted' through *THC* in several ways seems to be important. For example, pitch D can be interpreted as *tonic* in D major, but as *dominant* in G major. This property is apparently based on *internal* MERGE in terms of 'reinterpretation', and characterized very often as uniquely human (see, for example, Fitch, 2006; Katz & Pesetsky, to appear).
The consequence of this kind of asymmetry in *interface systems* seems to have an effect on the *lexicon* in language and music. Katz and Pesetsky (to appear) tend to see the key factor differentiating language and music in the presence of a *lexicon*, defined as a set of linguistic objects stored in long-term memory or a structured list of assemblies of features, in language and the absence of a lexicon in music. This intuition is to some extent correct. The *lexicon* of language must contain *atoms* or word-like elements characterized by *features* such as phonological components, semantic components and 'something more' like *uninterpretable features* and *Extended Projection Principle* (*EPP*) *features* which are in close relation to *internal* MERGE (Chomsky, 2000). Intuitively, such a rich *lexicon* cannot exist without a rich conceptual system in language. However, this intuition doesn't exclude the possibility that a *lexicon* also exists in music. A *Musical lexicon*, tentatively specified as a memory system containing all representations of the specific musical phrases to which one has been exposed during one's lifetime, seems to be important in processing music (Peretz & Coltheart, 2003). That is, some kind of *musical lexicon* considered as a set of musical objects stored in long-term memory should exist. Jackendoff and Lerdahl (2006) assumed also a stock of musical formulas thought of as similar to the *lexicon* in language in spite of some differences. I propose, therefore, that the key difference between language and music comes from the relation between MERGE and specific *interface systems* which have a strong effect on the distinct construction of the *lexicon* in language and music: unique linguistic and musical *interface systems* provide distinctive building blocks and give rise to diverse representations like syntactic structure of language and prolongational structure of music as emphasized by Jackendoff (2009).

2.5. *What does it say about the Evolution of FL and FM?*

One challenge to explain the evolution of language in terms of *SMT* is introduced by Hauser, Chomsky and Fitch (2002). The main idea in this paper is that *the Faculty of Language* (*FL*) as a whole (*the Faculty of Language in the broad sense*; *FLB*) including the abstract linguistic computational system (*the Faculty of Language in the narrow sense*; *FLN*) relies on some uniquely human capacities that have evolved recently in approximately 6 million years since our divergence from a chimpanzee-like common ancestor (Hauser et al., 2002). Considering the discussions above, the emergence of the capacity underlying MERGE, especially *internal* MERGE, seems to be one of these uniquely human capacities which played a key role in the evolution of *FL*. However, the evolution of *FL* as such cannot be fully explained by investigating the emergence of this capacity alone because, as already discussed above, this core capacity yielding *discrete infinity* is not only used in language but also in music. It is uniquely human, but not domain-specific.

To clarify the relation between *FL* and *FM*, investigations of the evolution of *interface systems* concerning their uniqueness is needed. Thereby, considering various *protolanguage theories* might be a good starting point, which will deliver insights into such aspects related to the evolution of *interface systems*. For example, the evolution of the phonological system in language could be considered with the help of *musical or prosodic protolanguage theories*. The phonological system might be compared with system for animal songs because they are independent of (propositional) meaning, but include rich 'prosodic structures' and require learned complex vocal control (e.g. Fitch, 2006, 2010). Concerning semantic systems, some ideas of *gestural protolanguage theories* are often discussed to show the evolution of a rich (discourse-unrelated) semantic system regarded as responsible for syntactic argument structure (e.g. Rizzolatti & Arbib, 1998). Further, *lexical protolanguage theories* (e.g. Jackendoff, 2002; Bickerton, 2010), in which *interface systems* already exist without syntax, still not makes it possible to consider the emergence of a modern *lexicon* in language which seems to have a close relation to the emergence of modern syntax. Do such *protolanguages* already include the unique components of *interface systems*? How does the emergence of MERGE relate to such *protolanguages*? These are questions which can be investigated in considering the nature of MERGE and *interface systems* within *MP*.

3. Conclusion

Language and music share an asymmetrical headed hierarchical structure in their 'syntactic' representation generated potentially unboundedly by combining discrete structural elements in hierarchically organized sequences. This human-specific property called *discrete infinity* of language and music is investigated in the *Minimalist Program* in terms of MERGE. In language, MERGE generates (propositional) argument structures by *external* MERGE, which are 'reinterpreted' by *internal* MERGE in a certain context without any loss of referential precision. (Western tonal) Music makes use of *external* MERGE in generating asymmetrical structures based on *TPS*, which can also be 'reinterpreted' in other tonal contexts. That is, language and music are very similar in relation to MERGE. However, they differ from each other in their *interface systems*, i.e. the *S-M* and *C-I interface systems*, which affect conditions how MERGE is *put into use*. These unique *interface systems* in language (phonological and semantic system) and music (time-span reduction and *THC*) also contain some human-specific components: phoneme perception and propositional meaning in the *interface systems* of language, and *isochronic rhythm* in those of music. Moreover, such *interface systems* show some kind of asymmetry in relation to MERGE: the *C-I interface system* seems to be primary in language and the *S-M interface system* in music. As consequence language and music have a different *lexicon*. That is, the key difference of language and music comes from the relation between MERGE and unique *interface systems*, which have a strong effect on the distinct construction of the *lexicon*. This idea that both MERGE and *interface* account for language and music as such might be also useful in the research on their evolution and in particular, as a starting point, by comparing *protolanguage theories*.

Acknowledgements

Special thanks to Prof. Uwe Seifert, Prof. Jürgen Lenerz, Son-Hwa Chang M.A., Andrea Ravignani, and Florian Römer for any helpful comments.

References

Bickerton, D. (2010). On two incompatible theories of language evolution. In R. K. Larson; V. Déprez and H. Yamakido (Eds.), *The Evolution of Human Language: Biolinguistic Perspectives* (199-210). Cambridge, MA: Cambridge University Press.

Chomsky, N. (2000). *New Horizons in the Study of Language and Mind.* Cambridge, MA: Cambridge University Press.

Chomsky, N. (2010). Some simple evo devo theses: how true might they be for language? In R. K. Larson; V. Déprez and H. Yamakido (Eds.), *The Evolution of Human Language: Biolinguistic Perspectives* (45-62). Cambridge, MA: Cambridge University Press.

Deacon, T. W. (2003). Universal Grammar and Semiotic Constraints. In M. Christiansen, & S. Kirby (Eds), *Language Evolution* (111-139). Oxford: Oxford University Press.

Fitch, W. T. (2006). The biology and evolution of music: A comparative perspective. *Cognition*, *100*, 173-215.

Fitch, W. T. (2010). *The Evolution of Language.* Cambridge, MA: Cambridge University Press.

Hauser, M. D., Chomsky, N., & Fitch, W. T. (2002). The Faculty of Language: What Is It, Who Has It, and How Did It Evolve? *Science*, *298*, 1569-1579.

Hauser, M. D., & McDermott, J. (2003). The evolution of the music faculty: a comparative perspective. *Nature Neuroscience*, *6*(*7*), 663-668.

Hinzen, W. (2009). The Successor Function + LEX = Human Language? In K. K. Grohmann (Ed.), *InterPhases* (25-47). New York, NY: Oxford University Press.

Jackendoff, R. (2002). *Foundations of Language. Brain, Meaning, Grammar, Evolution*. Oxford: Oxford University Press.

Jackendoff, R. (2009). Parallels and Nonparallels between Language and Music. *Music Perception*, *26*(*3*), 195-204.

Jackendoff, R. (2011). What is the human language faculty? Two views. *Language*, *87*(*3*), 586-624.

Jackendoff, R., & Lerdahl, F. (2006). The capacity for music: What is it, and what's special about it?". *Cognition, 100*, 33-72.

Katz, J., & Pesetsky, D. (to appear). The Identity Thesis for Language and Music. In: http://ling.auf.net/lingBuzz/000959 (Date of retrieval: May 18. 2011).

Lerdahl, F. (2001). *Tonal Pitch Space*, New York: Oexford University Press.

Lerdahl, F., & Jackendoff, R. (1983). *A Generative Theory of Tonal Music.* Cambridge: MIT Press.

Patel, A. D. (2006). Musical Rhythm, Linguistic Rhythm, and Human Evolution". *Music Perception, 24*, 99-104.

Patel, A. D. (2008). *Music, Language, and the Brain*, New York: Oxford University Press.

Patel, A. D. (2012). Language, music, and the brain: a resource-sharing framework. In P. Rebuschat, M. Rohrmeier, J. A. Hawkins, & I. Cross (Eds.), *Language and Music as Cognitive Systems* (204-223), New York: Oxford University Press.

Peretz, I., & Coltheart, M. (2003). Modularity of music processing. *Nature Neuroscience*, *6*(*7*), 688-691.

Rizolatti, G., & Arbib, M. (1998). Language within our grasp. *Trends in Neurosci*. *21*(*5*). 188-94.

Tomasello, M. (2003). On the Different Origins of Symbols and Grammar. In M. Christiansen, & S. Kirby (Eds), *Language Evolution* (94-110). Oxford: Oxford University Press.

LANGUAGE AND FRIENDSHIPS: A CO-EVOLUTION MODEL OF SOCIAL AND LINGUISTIC CONVENTIONS

MARTIN BACHWERK & CARL VOGEL
Computational Linguistics Group
School of Computer Science and Statistics
Trinity College, Dublin 2, Ireland
{bachwerm,vogel}@tcd.ie

Human social networks are dynamic, yet the majority of computational models of language evolution operate with either fixed or random interaction patterns between agents. This paper presents a model of lexicon formation in which agents can adjust their social ties based on the success of performed interactions. Simulation results show that different levels of 'friendship' between agents co-evolve with a system of linguistic conventions, with the observed social network formation processes largely resembling those of modern humans.

1. Introduction

In most computational models of language evolution, agents can be represented as vertices that are connected by predefined, and usually equally weighted edges. In some cases, these agents would be divided into two or more 'age' groups, whereby the vertices in some groups, e.g. the 'child' agents would not be connected among themselves (see Gong, 2010, for a review of such models). However, the common trait of nearly all such models is that the social ties between agents remain fixed throughout the simulation, i.e. agents can neither become 'friendlier' with some agents, nor break off all contact with others. This lack of dynamic social networks has been identified by Gong and Wang (2005) as one of the major issues with the majority of computational models of language evolution to date. In order to address this, Gong and Wang (2005) and Bachwerk and Vogel (2010) have introduced varying inter- and intra-group communication rates into their models of syntax and lexicon formation, respectively. Allowing dynamics in interaction patterns has proven to affect most aspects of the emerging communication system.

However, even the introduction of more sophisticated social structures into models of language evolution is not sufficient as the ties between (groups of) agents in such models remain fixed from the start of a simulation, whereas it has been observed by e.g. Panzarasa, Opsahl, and Carley (2009) that humans constantly re-evaluate their relationships with their interlocutors depending on the obtained feedback and the partner's reciprocity. In effect, apart from contributing to the question of the emergence of language *per se*, a computational model with dynamic ties between agents should also shed light on how agents' decisions during individual interactions influence the overall social structure of the population, i.e. how the very first language-induced friendships were made in human evolution. The following section 2 will provide a short overview of the model that was employed for the presented experiment on dynamic social ties in language evolution, the setup of which is described in section 3. We conclude with a discussion of obtained results in section 4 and suggestions for future work in section 5.

2. Model Overview

The experiments presented in this paper have been performed with the help of the Language Evolution Workbench (LEW) (for a more detailed description of the model see Bachwerk & Vogel, 2010). This workbench provides over 30 adjustable parameters and makes as few *a priori* assumptions about the agents' cognitive skills and their awareness of the possibility of a conventionalized communication system as possible. The few cognitive skills that are assumed can be considered as relatively widely accepted (see Christiansen & Kirby, 2003, for a review) as the minimal prerequisites for the emergence of language. These include the ability to observe and individuate events, the ability to engage in a joint attention frame fixed on an occurring event, and the ability to interact by constructing words and utterances from abstract symbols[a] and transmitting these to one's interlocutor.[b] Finally, the model assumes an infinite space of both meanings and utterances, recursively formed from a finite set of events/entities and symbols respectively.

The simulations of the LEW consist of consecutive rounds of interactions between pairs of agents, during which one of the agents is assigned the intention to comment on an observed event, while a second agent assumes that the topic of the utterance relates in some way to the event and attempts to decode the meaning of the encountered symbols accordingly. The agents' goal is ultimately to agree on a sufficiently broad and reliable lexicon that will enable them to consistently understand each other in the future. Importantly, there is no telepathy built into the model, neither in the form of direct meaning-form transmission, nor in the form of explicit feedback (see Smith, 2005, for further discussion). The lack of a telepathic ability means that the agents need to resort to alternative information sources in order to learn the meaning-form mappings that are being utilized by others. Here we make the assumption that if communication evolved out of the need for cooperation in certain tasks (see Bickerton & Szathmáry, 2011) then successful communication would lead to clearly perceivable payoffs during such

[a]While we usually refer to such symbols as 'phonemes', there is no reason why these should not be representative of gestural signs.

[b]The hearers are not assumed to know the word boundaries of an encountered utterance. For simulations with synchronized transmission the reader is referred to Vogel (2010).

cooperation. By making this assumption, we can define a learning strategy for our agents, according to which an agent's propensity $q_m(t)$ to utilize a lexical mapping *m* in an interaction at time *t* is updated for every lexical mapping *m* employed in an interaction according to the following rule (cf. Barrett & Zollman, 2009):[c]

$$q_m(t+1) = \begin{cases} q_m(t) + \pi(t) & \text{if mapping } m \text{ was utilized} \\ q_m(t) & \text{otherwise} \end{cases} \quad (1)$$

Where $\pi(t)$ represents the payoff of the interaction performed between two agents at time t and is the difference between the *actual communicative success of an interaction* $s(t)$ and the predefined *level of minimum success* s_{min} (see also Bachwerk & Vogel, 2011, for an alternative use of these parameters):[d]

$$\pi(t) = s(t) - s_{min} \quad (2)$$

Communicative success of an interaction $s(t)$ is defined as the level of agreement between the meanings that the agents were observed to have denoted in what was spoken and what was heard (independently of whether they segmented the sound stream identically). In particular, for communicative agreement to be achieved, the agents need to agree on two things: what entities are being spoken about and what are the relations between these entities. Hereby, the relations between the entities are considered to be understood if the ordering of the meanings is sufficiently similar between the two agents. Note that communicative success can be meaningfully measured without subscribing to omniscience: cooperative tasks may be completed, for example, without knowing which parts of which expressions were understood as intended.[e]

3. Experiment Design

The current experiment has been largely inspired by a model of language evolution presented by Gong and Wang (2005), in which the agents continuously updated the strengths of their relationships, i.e. the probabilities of future interactions with other agents based on the success of preceding communication bouts. Furthermore, if the tie connecting a pair of agents exceeded a certain weight threshold, the agents were considered as 'friends' (the labelling had no additional implications in the model). The results of experiments performed with this model have exhibited friendships to be established between agents, as well as a certain amount of clustering occurring throughout the population. Interestingly, the model introduced no limit on how many 'friends' an agent may have and considered agents

[c]In the LEW, q_m values represent the weights and thus the usage probabilities of competing meaning-form mappings an an agent's lexicon, whereby $q_m(0)$ is effectively equal to 0.

[d]As defined, a negative value of $\pi(t)$ will result in a meaning-form mapping being punished.

[e]This approach agrees with Skyrms (2010) in saying that complete understanding is not a requirement for the emergence of conventionalized communicative mechanisms.

who were 'friends' with every other agent simply extremely popular. We believe that the ability of an agent to become friends with every other agent as described above is a severe limitation of the model by Gong and Wang (2005). It does not seem fitting that the definition of 'friendship' is local for every pair of agents and does not take into consideration the strengths of an agent's ties with other agents.[f]

In order to address the above issue, we have adjusted the equations (1,2) to perform updates of the strengths of agent relationships r for every agent $i, j \in \{1, .., n\}$ in a population of $n = 10$ agents based on the communicative success of their interaction, with the level of minimum success s_{min} kept at 0.25, as follows:[g]

$$r_{ij}(t+1) = \begin{cases} r_{ij}(t) + \alpha\pi(t) & \text{if agents } i \text{ and } j \text{ were involved} \\ r_{ij}(t) & \text{otherwise} \end{cases} \quad (3)$$

Notably, when updating the connection strengths between agents, the payoff value is multiplied by a scaling parameter α that essentially defines the ratio between the speed of social and lexical learning (cf. Santos, Pacheco, & Lenaerts, 2006). In the presented experiments, the value of the social update rate α was varied between $1, 0.5$ and 0.1, i.e. the agents were always at least as efficient in updating their lexical mappings as they were in adjusting their social ties.

The evaluation of experimental results was performed with an emphasis on two particular aspects: the communicative properties of the evolving language and the emergent social structures within the population. Even though the agents in the LEW are not endowed with any telepathic abilities, it is still possible for an observer to quantify their communicative success, e.g. by computing the precision and recall rates between a speaker's intended meaning and the hearer's decoded one. These two values can be then summarized with the help of a statistical measure that represents their harmonic mean, defined as $F1 = 2 * \frac{precision*recall}{precision+recall}$. In addition to the success measure, we also consider such statistics as lexicon use and lexicon precision, which give an indication of respectively how broad and reliable are the lexicons of the agents. Finally, we can also evaluate how some of the more general properties of the emergent lexicons compare to those of current human languages by assessing lexicon synonymy and homonymy levels.[h]

The dynamic connection strengths between agents in the presented experiment have been introduced with the goal of observing what kinds of social ties will evolve in a population which is not bound by a predefined network structure, but where its members are capable of becoming more familiar with some, and more

[f] An agent who has a connection to every other agent with $w = 0.0001$ is as likely to communicate to any of these as an equally interconnected agent, but with $w = 1.0$, making the latter agent's 'friendship' ties no different from the former agent's weak ties.

[g] If an agent's connection strength with another agent reaches 0, the former will avoid the latter in all future interactions.

[h] Modern languages seem to tolerate homonymy much more so than real lexical synonymy.

distant with others. In order to be able to evaluate the results on a per-agent basis, we define three types of social connections that an agent i might end up having with a second agent t based on the connection's relative weight $w_{it} = \frac{r_{it}}{\sum_{j=1}^{n} r_{ij}}$, i.e. the actual probability of i selecting t as a partner in an interaction: an acquaintance ($w_{it} \geq 0.1$), a friend ($w_{it} \geq 0.25$) and a best friend ($w_{it} \geq 0.5$).[i] In particular, we observed if and how many connections of any given type were established by the agents, given any particular value of α, with the goal of determining how the first language-induced friendships could have been established in human evolution.

4. Results and Discussion

In total, 600 simulations runs were performed for each of the three different values of α, with 500 rounds of 10 interactions each within every such simulation. The evolution of communicative success rates from these interactions are summarized in figure 1(a), which exhibits that a nearly equivalent amount of learning occurs for all four types of agents, regardless if they are dynamically adjusting their ties to others or not. The only significant exception are agents who are very efficient at adjusting their social ties ($\alpha = 1$) who not only achieve higher understanding levels overall ($t = 6.919, p < 0.0001$), but also have significantly less synonymy in their lexicons ($t = -7.745, p < 0.0001$), as can be seen from figure 1(b). However, the difference between the various agent types is not extremely large even for the two observational values mentioned above, while it does not reach significance levels at all for such properties as lexicon size, lexicon use, or lexicon precision.

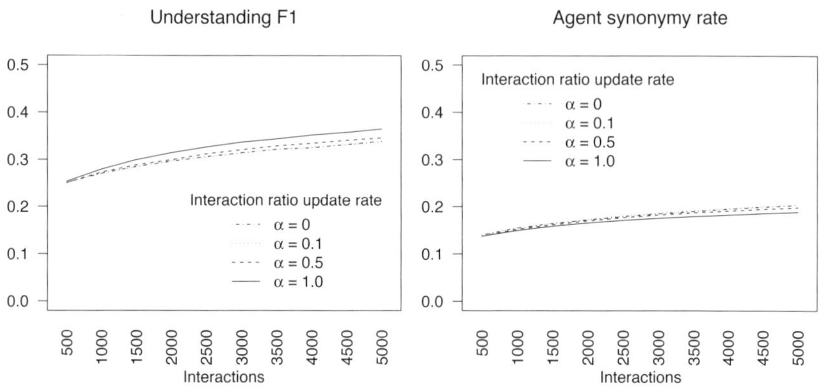

Figure 1. Evolution of (a) understanding (F1 measure) and (b) agent lexicon synonymy.

[i]Given this definition, the analytical limit for any particular agent is to have 2 best friends, 4 friends and 10 acquaintances, population size permitting.

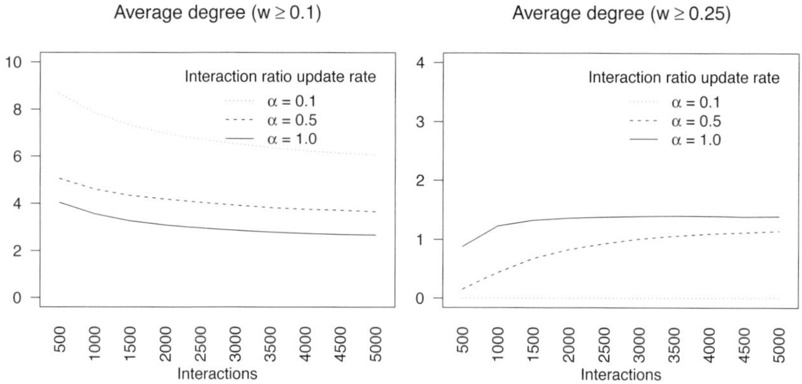

Figure 2. Evolution of average number of agent social ties with (a) $w \geq 0.1$ and (b) $w \geq 0.25$.

Having observed that agents do not seem to perform too differently even when allowed to adjust their interaction preferences throughout the simulations, we ask ourselves if the social structure of the corresponding groups is significantly evolving at all. The connection strengths between every pair of agents i, j were set to $r_{ij} = 1$ at the beginning, i.e. every agent started out with nine social ties whose relative weights $w_{ij} = 1/9$, i.e. $w_{ij} > 0.1$. From figure 2(a), one can see that this does not remain the case for long as the average number of connections per agent with $w \geq 0.1$ steadily decreases throughout the course of the simulations. In particular, for higher values of α, one observes a radical drop in the number of 'acquaintances' from the initial 9 to 5 for $\alpha = 0.5$ and 4 for $\alpha = 1$ by the end of the first 500 interactions (i.e. after around 100 interactions per agent).

The shrinking number of 'acquaintances' observed for all values of α suggests that the interaction weights are being redistributed more densely between the more popular communication partners of an agent, which leads to the establishment of first 'friendships'. Figure 2(b) confirms that this is the case for agents with $\alpha \geq 0.5$ who on average make at least 1 'friend' by the end of the simulations runs. However, agents with $\alpha = 0.1$ do not achieve a connection weight $w \geq 0.25$ with any of their conspecifics due to their 'unwillingness' to give up on other partners too hastily. In effect, the different social update rates model different human characters, ranging from patient pragmatics who are always cautious and thus end up having very practical friendships, if any at all, to the more impulsive types who are ready to become friends with anyone quickly. Finally, figure 3(a) shows that more than half the agents with $\alpha = 1$ end up having a 'best friend' by the end of the simulations, which is also the main reason why these agents outperform other agents in terms of communicative success.

When comparing the social structures that emerge in our simulations to empirical studies of human networks, we have observed two striking similarities in their

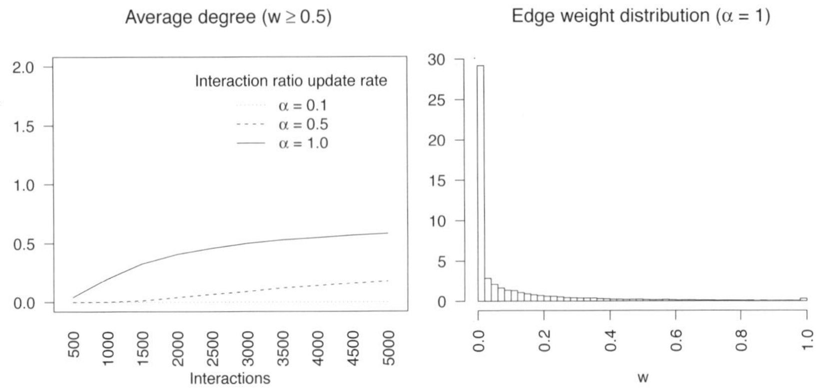

Figure 3. (a) Evolution of average number of agent social ties with $w \geq 0.5$ and (b) frequency distribution of edge weights for $\alpha = 1$.

construction and organization. First of all, the two-stage process of establishing social relationships that was observed for agents with a higher social update rate (in particular for $\alpha = 1$) has been also reported by Panzarasa et al. (2009) among others, who observed that social relationships were established at the very onset of group formation and were then slowly reinforced afterwards. Additionally, it appears that for these agents, the frequency distribution of edge weights, i.e. the connection strengths between agents, depicted in figure 3(b), has a distinct scale-free character (with the exception of an increase in $w = 1$ ties at the tail), which Barabási (2009) considers to be typical of most dynamic networks.

5. Conclusions and Future Work

In summary, it appears that in order for a non-random social structure to emerge, agents need to make their decisions in a decisive and resolute manner. In effect, the fact that social dynamics of agents in our model so closely resemble those of modern humans for certain parameter levels certainly suggests that, if our predecessors were anything like us socially, it is likely that one dominant characteristic of early hominids was a quickness to bond based on successful communication. However, one issue that arises with such individuals who become ‘friends’ with a few of their conspecifics and mainly ignore the majority of the population is that it is hard to imagine how they could have agreed on a highly conventionalized communal communication system such as language.

Future work should look further into the limits of lexicon formation in a population of socially aware agents, while making sure that the group does not evolve into pairs of exclusive ‘best friends’ who do not communicate with others. In particular, one should also investigate the possibility of the existence of either universally esteemed and popular agents or simply variably ‘social’ agents, as well as the effects that the more influential agents could have on the decisions of others, including both their friend-making and language learning strategies.

References

Bachwerk, M., & Vogel, C. (2010). Modelling Social Structures and Hierarchies in Language Evolution. In M. Bramer, M. Petridis, & A. Hopgood (Eds.), *Research and Development in Intelligent Systems XXVII* (pp. 49–62). Springer.

Bachwerk, M., & Vogel, C. (2011). Establishing Linguistic Conventions in Task-Oriented Primeval Dialogue. In A. Esposito, A. Vinciarelli, K. Vicsi, C. Pelachaud, & A. Nijholt (Eds.), *Analysis of Verbal and Nonverbal Communication and Enactment: The Processing Issues* (pp. 48–55). Springer.

Barabási, A.-L. (2009). Scale-Free Networks: A Decade and Beyond. *Science*, *325*(5939), 412–413.

Barrett, J. A., & Zollman, K. J. S. (2009). The Role of Forgetting in the Evolution and Learning of Language. *Journal of Experimental & Theoretical Artificial Intelligence*, *21*(4), 293–309.

Bickerton, D., & Szathmáry, E. (2011). Confrontational scavenging as a possible source for language and cooperation. *BMC Evolutionary Biology*, *11*(1), 261.

Christiansen, M. H., & Kirby, S. (2003). Language evolution: consensus and controversies. *Trends in Cognitive Sciences*, *7*(7), 300–307.

Gong, T. (2010). Exploring the Roles of Horizontal, Vertical, and Oblique Transmissions in Language Evolution. *Adaptive Behavior*, *18*(3-4), 356–376.

Gong, T., & Wang, W. S.-Y. (2005). Computational Modeling on Language Emergence: A Coevolution Model of Lexicon, Syntax and Social Structure. *Language and Linguistics*, *6*(1), 1–42.

Panzarasa, P., Opsahl, T., & Carley, K. M. (2009). Patterns and Dynamics of Users Behaviour and Interaction: Network Analysis of an Online Community. *Journal of the American Society for Information Science and Technology*, *60*(5), 911–932.

Santos, F. C., Pacheco, J. M., & Lenaerts, T. (2006). Cooperation Prevails When Individuals Adjust Their Social Ties. *PLoS Computational Biology*, *2*(10), 1284–1291.

Skyrms, B. (2010). *Signals: Evolution, Learning, and Information.* Oxford University Press.

Smith, A. D. M. (2005). The Inferential Transmission of Language. *Adaptive Behavior*, *13*(4), 311–324.

Vogel, C. (2010). Group Cohesion, Cooperation and Synchrony in a Social Model of Language Evolution. In A. Esposito, N. Campbell, C. Vogel, A. Hussain, & A. Nijholt (Eds.), *Development of Multimodal Interfaces: Active Listening and Synchrony* (pp. 16–32). Springer Berlin Heidelberg.

CAMPBELL'S MONKEYS ALARM CALLS ARE NOT MORPHEME-BASED

LLUÍS BARCELÓ-COBLIJN

Department of Philosophy and Social Work, University of the Balearic Islands, ctra. de Valldemossa km 7,5, Palma, 07122, Spain

ANTONI GOMILA

Department of Psychology, University of the Balearic Islands, ctra. de Valldemossa km 7,5, Palma, 07122, Spain

Since Hockett's (1958) characterization of human language, *duality* has been considered a distinctive feature of human language. However, Ouattara's et al. (2009) description of Campbell's monkeys alarm calls challenges this assumption. They claim that such calls exhibit affixation, hence a morphemic level, hence duality.

We reexamine the nature of their arguments. We contend that: 1) the traditional definition of morpheme has to be updated in order to avoid cross-field confusions; 2) Campbell monkeys alarm calls exhibit linear order, but no hierarchical combination, as required by lexicalization; 3) the lack of hierarchical combination prevents non-human primates of reaching productive morpheme-based structures.

1. Introduction

In 1980 Seyfarth et al. described the alarm call system (henceforth, ACS) of *vervet* monkeys *(Chlorocebus aethiops*[1]*)*. Those monkeys made an oral communicative performance using three kinds of calls, each of them bounded to a particular predator (snakes, eagles and leopards). Despite initial proposals, several reasons made it clear that these calls are not truly homologous to human words: i) they cannot be learned, as human words, which are culturally transmitted; ii) ACS is stimulus-bound: the calls are elicited by the presence of that threat; and iii) monkeys cannot use such calls in order to "reflect" about that threat, or to interchange impressions about it. Thus, while such calls may convey meanings, rather than being expressive of emotional activation, they come short of the structural and functional properties of words.

---

[1]At that time – and still today by some authors – this species was classified as *Cercopithecus aethiops*.

Now, a similar debate has arisen as regards whether the ACS of another species exhibits *duality of patterning*, a property thought to be exclusive of human language according to Hockett's classical proposal (Hockett, 1958). New data about the ACS of Campbell's monkeys – *Cercopithecus campbelli* – (Ouattara, et al., 2009a), reveal a more sophisticated ACS than that of vervets. The results are very interesting: they have up to six calls, and more important, these calls can be modulated by changing their finals, thus modifying their meaning. The authors interpreted this feature as an example of *affixation*.

Affixation is a well-known basic procedure we find in *H. sapiens'* linguistic morphology: a mechanism that intervenes in word building, as part of the alleged duality of patterning that characterizes human language. From the point of view of linguistics, then, such results are very challenging: morphology is considered a "human only" feature.

The paper is structured as follows: in the second section we introduce Campbell's monkey ACS and the morphemic interpretation. In the third section we point out the necessity to avoid the risk of a stipulatory notion of morpheme, which excludes in principle the possibility of morphemes in non-human communication systems. We propose that a notion of morpheme has to be grounded in the structural and functional requirements of this lexical unit. Next, hierarchical structure is singled out as the basic natural property of language governing morpheme concatenation in lexical composition. We argue, in the fifth section, for a notion of *lexicalization* property of morphemes. Finally, we argue that the evidence on Campbell's monkeys ACS falls short of exhibiting such a property, and cannot really be said to be morpheme-based.

2. *Campbell's monkey alarm call system*

Campbell's monkeys, according to the authors, have up to six differentiated calls (Table 1). It is argued that, in an implicit analogy to *H. sapiens* morphemes, the addition of "*-oo*" to the call modifies the call, being this segment an affix. To this end, the authors have borrowed the standard definition of morpheme, which has not suffered substantial changes since its formulation in 1881 by Baudouin de Cortenay: "the smallest linguistic unit that has semantic meaning". Just as the *vervet* monkey ACS was interpreted as exhibiting lexical semantics, these ACS is claimed to exhibit morphology, because this "-oo" unit has a semantic effect on the "lexical root", giving rise to a different meaning.

Table 1. Alarm call system of Campbell's monkeys.

Call	*Possible meanings*	Extended call	*Possible meanings*
krak	"leopard"	Krakoo	"Almost any disturbance"
hok	"crowned eagle"	Hok-oo	"Any disturbance: eagle, neighbouring groups, flying squirrel"
boom	Non-predatory call; falling tree, movement	Wak-oo	"Eagles, flying animals, Diana monkey *eagle* calls"

The contribution of Ouattara and colleagues is important for various reasons: it is the description of the perhaps most sophisticated ACS found until now, but it also invites to an important reflection about the nature and characteristics of natural language morphemes. In Ouattara et al. (2009b) it has also been shown that these monkeys produce ordered strings of calls, suggesting a possible kind of ordering capacity. In Table 2 we have selected four of the nine sequences identified by the authors, where a particular order can be inferred.

Table 2. Some call compositions from Ouattara et al. (2009b)

Composition	*Argued meanings*	*n*
B - K+ boom - krak-oo	[falling-initiate-halt] - [Any disturbance]	53
B - K+ - H+ boom - krak-oo – hok-oo	[falling-initiate-halt]-[Any disturbance]–[range of disturbances-eagle-group]	76
K+ - H – W+ krak-oo - Hok - wak-oo	[Any disturbance]-[crowned eagle]–[eagles]	5
K+ - H – H+ - W+ krak-oo - Hok – Hok-oo - Wak-oo	[Any disturbance]–[crowned eagle]-[range of disturbances–eagle–group]-[eagles]	28

We think that such ordering could be described in terms of Markovian chains: a particular call appears after the precedent one, roughly following a rule-type like [n] > [n+1] … > [n+1], and so until the system halts [STOP].

Now, the question we want to address is whether these evidences really provide support for the conclusion that Campbell's monkey ACS really is morpheme-based, as claimed by these researchers. First of all, we need to reconsider what a morpheme is.

3. *A notion of morpheme for biolinguistics*

It would be possible to reject Ouattara's et al. conclusion by strengthening the notion of morpheme so that it is restricted to human language. It could be said, for instance, that a morphological structure requires the possibility of distinguishing between derivational and inflectional morphology. However, such a stipulative strategy, with the goal of excluding in principle, the possibility of morphology in non-human ACS, illustrates an *ad hoc* strategy. What is required is a notion of *morpheme* that it is not biased to make it "human only" by definition, so that it can be useful for cross-species comparisons and evolutionary approaches.

There is no need to go that far: the standard definition of morpheme as a minimal unit of meaning, composed in its turn of non-meaningful sound categories, is enough to be skeptical of Ouattara's conclusion. That's because Ouattara and coworkers fail to show that the phonemic extension "-oo" has a constant meaning of its own. The way such a final modulation of a common root works, does not seem to be compositional, modifying in a rule-based way the meaning of a morpheme playing the role of a lexical root. From this point of view, it is not clear that "-oo" can be said to be a "minimal unit of meaning", nor that the meaning of the complex signal is the outcome of the combination of the respective meanings of each claimed "morpheme". The case for a morphological understanding of this final modulation of the alarm calls, then, turns out to be defective on its own grounds. This does not exclude the acknowledgement of the Campbell's monkey ACS as highly complex and sophisticated. Thus, it seems clear that these monkeys do differentiate sounds categorically, and that they can emit chains of calls which systematically follow a *prima facie* ordered pattern and that they probably share with us several – if not most – characteristics of phonology (Samuels et al., in press; Endress et al., 2009).

However, it could also be claimed that such alarm calls exhibit duality in that the minimal meaningful signals are composed of phonological units which lack meaning on their own. While this is so, it doesn't follow that these units can be termed "morphemes". In order to argue for this conclusion, though, these results can also be seen as a motivation to revise the classical notion of *duality*[2], and particularly the critical upper level for such a notion: the morpheme. Thus, we will argue that the typical understanding of it as the minimal unit of meaning is incomplete; attention should also be paid to the other dimension: that morphemes are the building blocks of sentences (or larger meaningful units). In other words, morphemes are not just minimal units of meaning (that is to say, a pairing of sound and meaning), but also involve "valence" information regarding how they can be combined to form higher level meaningful units.

This is clear in the case of human language in a way that it is not

---

[2] Hockett was also interested in animal communication; therefore he found that "the terms "phonological" and "grammatical" make too direct a reference to human language", therefore "it will be better to introduce two new terms of general applicability: *cenematic* and *plerematic*. [...] Phonemes are linguistic *cenemes*; morphemes are linguistic *pleremes*." (1958: 575)

stipulative. Affixation, for instance, can be considered a form of inflectional morphology at the service of grammatical coordination; or a form of derivational morphology that affects grammatical category. Thus, either a morpheme plays the role of a lexical root, or it plays a role of modifying it according to a syntactical role. Thus, a closer look to the structure of combined morphemes reveals that their main characteristic is *hierarchical structure*, which restricts how they are formed, how they can be combined and how such combinations affect meaning. As long as ACS's alleged "morphemes" do not also play such role at the other level of the lexicalization process, they should not be considered proper morphemes.

Contemporary, minimalist linguistics is beginning to take into account this "integrative" view of morphology, by which we mean a view of lexical items that pays attention not just to them as pairings of sound and meaning, but also in terms of their syntactic structure (Boeckx, 2008; 2011; Ott, 2009). From this point of view, a clear distinction is to be set between the lexicalization process, by which concepts turn lexical units – a process that takes place as part of the FLN –, and the process by which the lexical unit gets externalized, that is, receives a phonological form and is added to the lexicon. The former process is conceived in terms of the merging of morphemes in terms of their "edge features" (Chomsky, 2008) – a term to capture semantic compositionality and syntactic valence. The latter process generates a phonological form to this complex lexical item, at the sensory motor interface, thus creating a public lexicon. Regardless of the details of the theoretical approach proposed to explain it, though, this integrative view of morphology is well supported.

4. *Information theory considerations*

Further support for this approach can be obtained with the help of information theory. Information theory showed many years ago that hierarchy is maybe the most important aspect of human language, and a property of *nearly decomposable systems*, a class of complex systems (Simon, 1962). We contend that language can be described in such terms so that the main difference between a chain of morphemes and the strings of calls in Table 2 is that morphemes form a hierarchical structure, while alarm calls components just follow a serial order. Corominas-Murtra et al. (2011) have shown that there are different kinds of hierarchical structures and that "the richer the structure [...] the more hierarchical is". Among the possible ones, the pyramidal hierarchy of binary trees seems to be quite suitable for the description of human language. The calls of Campbell's monkeys, however, follow the *linear chain*, which results a perfectly predictable system but without richness. As a consequence, it cannot be seen as morpheme-like.

On the other hand, though, information theory also provides a rationale for duality of patterning (Fortuny, 2009): it is a way to enlarge a limited repertoire of basic signals, when there is pressure to communicate a number of meanings that exceeds the available repertoire. An alternative possibility would be to enlarge the number of basic units, but this may not be an easily available possibility, given the anatomical constraints on operation in this regard. Thus, if we stick to Hockett's classical definition of duality, as the fact that the minimal meaningful units are "made of" non-meaningful sound (or sign) units, it can be said of Campbell monkeys that they exhibit duality. Given that Hockett claimed that duality was a "human-language-only" property, Ouattara's et al. work is to be seen as highly relevant. The meanings that are expressed by these calls, though, cannot be seen as morphologically structured, as they are paired to their meanings in a list-like way.

Information theory inspired approaches to language, then, help make clear some peculiarities in the transmission of information that have consequences in the signals available. When we apply them to an evolutionary and ecological context, morphemes – as cognitive entities – appear to integrate both phonemes and (compositional) meaning, but also hierarchical structure. Another way to put the point is by saying that morphemes are not just minimal units of meaning, but also that they establish the combinatorial possibilities of such units within the higher level of semantic integration.

5. *Conclusions*

The fieldwork made by Ouattara et al. (2009a, 2009b) has revealed an important new example of complexity in animal communication. By arguing that these monkeys make use of affixation, a human linguistic capacity, the authors confer to the monkeys' signals the status of morphemes. As we have argued, the definition of morpheme they rely on is too loose. Therefore we have re-examined the properties of morphemes, insisting upon their hierarchical structure. From this point of view, morphemes are the minimal units of meaning that compose the public lexicon, and they integrate phonological, semantic and syntactic information. These units are organized according to a pyramidal hierarchic binary structure, which is the most robust and richest regarding information properties. By contrast, monkeys' calls seem to be different regarding two important aspects: First, these signals are made of a linear chain of elements. Second, the alleged affix does not seem to contribute a meaning of its own, nor it contributes to the meaning of the whole in a compositional way. However, these calls can still be described to exhibit duality of patterning, as classically defined by Hockett: they are composed of non-meaningful phonetic units. We have made reference to work in information theory that shows that duality of patterning is the way to broaden the repertoire of signals (either oral or signed) when the set of communicative units is very limited. There is no principled reason for it to be a human-language-only property. And Campbell's monkeys, along with cotton-top tamarins (*Saguinus oedipus*), seem to share with humans the rudiments for ordering sounds in a similar way to human affixation (Endress et al., 2009). However, it comes short to provide the rudiments of a hierarchical structure, to be considered an evolutionary precedent of human language.

Acknowledgements

This work has been supported by the BES-2008-003607 grant and the project FFI2010-20759 from the Ministerio de Ciencia e Innovación (Spain).

References

Corominas-Murtra, B., Rodríguez-Caso, C., Goñi, J., & Solé, R. (2011). Measuring the hierarchy of feedforward networks. *Chaos*, 21, 016108.

Boeckx, C. (2011). Some reflections on Darwin's problem in the context of Cartesian Biolinguistics. In di Sciulo, Ana Maria & Boeckx, Cedric (Eds), *The Biolinguistic enterprise: new perspectives on the evolution and nature of the human language faculty* (pp 42-64). Oxford: Oxford University Press.

Boeckx, C. (2008). *Bare Syntax*. Oxford: Oxford University Press.

Chomsky, N. (2008). On Phases. In R. Freidin, C. P. Otero, & M. L. Zubizarreta (Eds), *Foundational Issues in Linguistic Theory: Essays in Honor of Jean-Roger Vergnaud*. The MIT Press.

Endress A.D., Cahill, D., Block, S., Watumull, J., & Hauser, M. D. 2009. Evidence of an evolutionary precursor to human affixation in a non-human primate. *Biology Letters*, 5(6):749-51.

Fortuny, J. (2010). On the duality of patterning. In Zwart, Jan-Wouter & De Vires, Mark (Eds), *Structure Preserved: Studies in syntax for Jan Koster.*, LinguisticAktuell/ Linguistics Today (Vol. 164, pp 131–140). Amsterdam/Philadelphia: John Benjamins Publishing Company.

Hockett, C. F. (1958). *Course in Modern Linguistics* (later Printing.). Prentice Hall College Div.

Ott, D. (2009). The Evolution of I-Language: Lexicalization as the Key Evolutionary Novelty. *Biolinguistics*, 3(2), 255-269.

Ouattara, K., Lemasson, A., & Zuberbühler, K. (2009a). Campbell's monkeys use affixation to alter call meaning. *PloS One*, 4(11), e7808.

Ouattara, K., Lemasson, A., & Zuberbühler, K. (2009b). Campbell's monkeys concatenate vocalizations into context-specific call sequences. *Proceedings of the National Academy of Sciences of the United States of America*, 106(51), 22026-22031.

Samuels, B., Hauser, M., & Boeckx, C. (To appear) "Do animals have Universal Grammar? A case study in phonology." In I. Roberts (ed.), *The Oxford Handbook of Universal Grammar*. Oxford: OUP.

Seyfarth, R. M., Cheney, D. L., & Marler, P. (1980). Monkey responses to three different alarm calls: evidence of predator classification and semantic communication. *Science* (New York, N.Y.), 210(4471), 801-803.

Simon, H. A. (1962). The Architecture of Complexity. *Proceedings of the American Philosophical Society*, 106(6), 467-482.

ON THE INFERENCE 'NEANDERTHALS HAD *FOXP2* = THEY HAD COMPLEX LANGUAGE'

ANTONIO BENÍTEZ-BURRACO

Dpto. de Filología Española y sus Didácticas, Universidad de Huelva, Campus de El Carmen, 21071, Huelva, Spain

VÍCTOR M. LONGA

Dpto. de Literatura Española, Teoría de la Literatura y Lingüística General, Universidad de Santiago de Compostela, Avda. Castelao s/s., 15782, Santiago de Compostela, Spain

This paper makes the point that caution is needed when trying to draw inferences about cognition from fossil DNA analyses. We illustrate such a point by discussing the recent discovery of the modern *FOXP2* gene version in Neanderthals. Many scholars have taken that discovery to be the definitive proof of the existence of complex language in that species. We will aim to show that such an inference cannot be automatically established, because it is based on a simplistic view that assumes, among other aspects, that genes are simple causal agents, and that a direct link exists between genes and traits.

1. Introduction

The recent appearance on stage of fossil DNA analyses can become an important source of indirect evidence for language evolution, as argued for by Fitch (2009) among others. However, fossil DNA evidence should be dealt with caution, for the inferences drawn from it can be equivocal. Our paper illustrates this point with the discussion raised by the recent discovery of the modern *FOXP2* gene version in Neanderthals (Krause *et al.*, 2007). Many scholars have taken this discovery to be the definitive piece of evidence in order to show that Neanderthals had complex (modern-like) language (section 2). However, we will show (section 3) that the inference 'modern *FOXP2* in Neanderthals ⇒ possession of complex language' is untenable (actually, the same would apply to any other human-like sequence of any other language-related gene, if ultimately attested in other extinct hominids), for it is based on a simplistic view of how genes behave.

2. Some examples of the inference

A wide consensus exists about the fact that anatomically modern humans (henceforth, AMH) had complex language since early stages (Botha & Knight eds., 2009). However, disagreement arises on the nature of the communicative system of other species, especially Neanderthals. Many scholars have taken the discovery of modern *FOXP2* in the Neanderthal genome to be the definitive proof that this species had the same type of language than AMH:[1]

> Neanderthals must have had a communication system at least equivalent to the one we can infer for Aurignician moderns. This is consistent with recent genetic evidence [...] indicating that a critical gene known to underlie speech —namely *FOXP2*— was present in the Neanderthal genome (d'Errico & Vanhaeren, 2009:38)
>
> Up to date behavioural and anatomical studies of Neandertal fossils and the recent discovery of their possession of the *FOXP2* gene indicate Neandertals [...] had linguistic capacities similar to living humans (Frayer *et al.*, 2010: 113)

Although we will focus on the genetic and molecular premises that make that inference untenable, the rejection of the inference fits with our interpretation of the available paleoanthropological and archaeological evidence, which is compatible with the possibility that modern language can be an AMH innovation (Balari *et al.*, 2011; in press). Anyhow, Neanderthals could have complex language, but if so, the reasons would go far beyond their mere possession of modern *FOXP2*. As Fisher & Scharff (2009: 173) write, "because language is clearly underpinned by multifactorial influences, the status of a single gene in ancient DNA is insufficient to resolve long-standing debates over linguistic capacities of our extinct ancestors". While this polygenic nature of language is generally recognized, two other, more essential, reasons make the inference problematic (and ultimately, any inference of the sort 'modern 'language gene' in Neanderthals ⇒ possession of complex language'). Firstly, a direct link between genes and traits should be questioned. Secondly, as gene function is always context-sensitive, any gene placed in two different contexts will plausibly fulfill two different biological functions.

3. Why the inference "Neanderthals had *FOXP2* ⇒ they had complex language" cannot be automatically accepted

We shall not consider here the key issue of the (controversial) relationship between *FOXP2* and the Faculty of Language (henceforth, FL) in our own species. Notice, however, that there exists a hot debate on the actual nature of

[1] See also Trinkaus (2007) or d'Errico (2008), among many others.

the deficit/s linked to the mutation/s of the gene, and especially on the possibility that only FL (not other cognitive domains, or even motor functions) is impaired (Watkins *et al.*, 2002; Vargha-Khadem *et al.*, 2005; Shriberg *et al.*, 2006). In addition, as pointed out by Bateson and Mamelli (2007: 821), while a correlation between a genetic mutation and a linguistic impairment could suggest that the mutation is responsible for the impairment, "the correlation by itself does not tell us whether (and in what way) that region of the genome plays a role in normal linguistic development". Certainly, many structural, functional, and physiological data support the hypothesis that the wild version of *FOXP2* plays a key role in our species in the regulation of the ontogeny (plausibly phylogeny as well) of certain neural devices involved in language; however, that role has to be fully characterised (Vargha-Khadem *et al.*, 2005; Fisher & Scharff, 2009).

A second controversy concerns the possibility that the gene (i) is involved in learning and executing motor routines related to vocalization (White, 2010), or, instead, (ii) is a major component of the regulatory network/s related to the computational system of language (Lieberman, 2000; Balari *et al.*, in press). Such two possibilities entail two different evolutionary scenarios. If (i) is correct, the presence of modern *FOXP2* in Neanderthals could be related to the development and/or execution of some kind of quasi-musical vocalizations (Mithen, 2005), but not necessarily to the possession of a modern FL. If (ii) is accurate, a direct relationship between complex language and modern *FOXP2* would not be evolutionary obligatory, as discussed below. Finally it should be noted that the inference 'modern *FOXP2* ⇒ complex language in Neanderthals' only relies (at present) on information about the exonic and intronic regions of the homologue Neanderthal gene (Krause *et al.*, 2007). For instance, we do not know whether the remaining regulatory factors necessary for the expression of the gene, are identical to the human ones (at least functionally).

Ultimately, the inference '*FOXP2* ⇒ complex language' is untenable if we consider the real nature of genes and how developmental processes take place. Such an inference would be accurate only if a direct causal link between genes and traits exists. A number of reasons strongly argue against this possibility:

1. *FOXP2* is post-transcriptionally and post-translationally modified, thus giving rise to diverse functional isoforms with (perhaps) different physiological roles (Vernes *et al.*, 2006). The main isoform is translocated to the nucleus, and also assembled into a multimeric complex (Li *et al.*, 2004). These events could take place in Neanderthals in a similar way, but no information is available.

2. The way how *FOXP2* contributes to the biological processes it is related to depends on the specific times and places the gene is expressed during growth,

and also on the synthesis of a proper amount of protein(s) (the disorders linked to the mutation of *FOXP2* are due to a reduced protein dosage, not to an interfering mutated version). Those parameters are only partially determined by the gene sequence, for other many regulatory elements (transcriptional or translational factors, ncRNAs, etc.) are also involved. However, the nature of such elements in Neanderthals is, again, unknown: if some differences existed at this level, the spatio-temporal expression patterns of modern human and neanderthal genes and/or the properties of the corresponding proteins could have been different, in spite of the identical nature of the exonic and intronic regions.

3. *FOXP2* is a pleiotropic gene; accordingly, it plays a number of roles in different developmental places and times. We cannot rule out the possibility that some of the evolutionary modifications of the gene have been maintained in Neanderthals given their relevance for some role not related to language.

4. FOXP2 does not work in isolation: as already pointed out, it must be assembled with other proteins to make up functional multimeric complexes. More crucially, it works as a part of a complex regulatory network (Spiteri *et al.*, 2007; Konopka *et al.*, 2009). Notice that the mutation of other components of the network also gives rise to cognitive disorders in which language is impaired, as exemplified by *CNTNAP2*, a gene related to autism (Vernes *et al.*, 2008). At the same time, some of these genes have been positively selected (like *FOXP2* itself) in the human clade (Spiteri *et al.*, 2007). It is plausible that the evolutionary emergence of (complex) language has also been the consequence of other modifications affecting other components of this kind of network/s. As White (2010: 26) writes, *FOXP2* is just "a fortuitous entry point of discovery into molecular networks that, in the human brain, contribute to the language phenotype". However, the sequence and the functional properties of the other components of the network in which Neanderthal *FOXP2* was plausibly integrated remain largely unknown.

5. As pointed out in 2, language is a polygenic trait: dozens of genes have been currently identified whose mutation impairs FL, thus plausibly emerging as alternative entry points (to *FOXP2*) to the molecular networks needed for language (Benítez-Burraco, 2009). Some of these genes (like *FOXP2*) have also been positively selected in the human lineage, as *DYX1C1* (a candidate for dyslexia) illustrates (Taipale *et al.*, 2003). Nevertheless, we do not know the sequence of these genes (and their work during growth) in Neanderthals.

6. *FOXP2* expression (and ultimately its physiological role) is modulated by multiple endogenous and exogenous factors, which are, to a large extent, also unknown in Neanderthals. Moreover, for any phenotypic trait to emerge, the cell transcriptional state becomes much more important than the gene sequence. In

fact, it is the transcriptome, rather than the genome, that has undergone more evolutionary changes in our lineage as regards the molecular machinery involved in regulating brain development (Vallender *et al.*, 2008). Again, the transcriptional state of *FOXP2* (and of the remaining 'language genes') in Neanderthals is unknown.

7. Finally, developmental processes also rely on basic physicochemical properties (viscoelasticity, differential diffusion, etc.) (Newman *et al.*, 2006); in addition, they are, to some extent, stochastic phenomena. Consequently, two identical proteins in two identical cellular environments can work in two slightly different ways, thus triggering two different phenotypes (Balaban, 2006).

The reasons discussed so far show that genes cannot be the primary cause of ontogenetic processes; they are just one of the many involved regulatory factors, all of them being equally relevant for the final phenotype to emerge (*parity*) (Oyama *et al.*, 2001). Accordingly, the evolutionary modification of any phenotypic trait cannot be explained as the result of changing the gene frequencies of a population (Müller, 2007), but as the evolution of developmental systems as a whole. Such an evolution can be prompted by any change in the involved parameters, most of which are unknown in Neanderthals (currently, we have only a partial access to their genomes; Green *et al.*, 2010). Therefore, we cannot accurately predict the reaction norm of their genotypes (i.e., the whole set of possible phenotypes they could give rise to in diverse environments), and thus, infer the presence of a modern FL. For instance, as Neanderthals and AMH evolved in different environments (Finlayson, 2005), the reactions norms of their respective "linguistic genotype" (in the basic sense of genes related to language) could have been dissimilar, even if those genes were identical (but this possibility is unlikely; see Green *et al.*, 2010).

It should also be realized that the regulatory mechanisms to which *FOXP2* contributes establish the basic histological organization and interconnection patterns of the neural substrate of language. Nevertheless, such neural structures cannot be directly equated to (the neural substrate of) linguistic features, categories, elements, or operations. On the one hand, neural structures only come to be fully operative computational devices when they undergo additional structural and functional changes through the feedback effect exerted by the neural activity upon developing cells, and ultimately of the interactions (i) among different brain regions, and (ii) between those regions and the environment (Johnson, 2003; Ramus, 2006). On the other hand, neurobiological data suggest that such operative neural devices cannot be confidently correlated in a univocal way with (the neural substrate of) linguistic components, because they seem to be responsible for more basic types of computations or representations that can be recruited for language and other diverse functions.

Finally, only neural structures (and their activities) are the final output of developmental processes, and hence, the only evolutionary *loci*. By contrast, functions emerge as the output of (i) interconnections among diverse structures and of (ii) their relationships with the environment in which development takes place (Love, 2007). This is the reason why the relationship between (neural) structures and (cognitive) functions is not obligatory. Different structures (with distinctive developmental paths) can give rise to a single function, while the same structure can contribute to two (or more) different functions (Wagner & Altenberg 1996; Winther, 2001). More relevantly, some functions that can be regarded as evolutionary novelties can arise in the absence of specific gene mutations, due to the dynamics and generative properties of developmental systems (Müller, 2007). As West-Eberhard (2005: 6547) suggests, "phenotypic novelty is largely reorganizational rather than a product of innovative genes". If so, the presence of modern *FOXP2* in Neanderthals would still be compatible with the hypothesis that FL is an evolutionary innovation specific to AMH. This hypothesis fits in well with the currently available paleoanthropological and archaeological evidence (Balari *et al.*, 2011; in press).

Acknowledgements

This work has been carried out through the project "Biolingüística: evolución, desarrollo y fósiles del lenguaje" (FFI2010-14955/FILO) of the Spanish Ministry of Science and Innovation and partially co-funded by FEDER funds.

References

Balaban, E. (2006). Cognitive developmental biology: history, process and fortune's wheel. *Cognition*, 101, 298-332.

Balari, S. & Lorenzo, G. (2009). Computational phenotypes. Where the theory of computation meets evo devo. *Biolinguistics*, 3, 2-61.

Balari, S., Benítez-Burraco, A., Camps, M., Longa, V. M., Lorenzo, G. &. Uriagereka, J. (2011). The archaeological record speaks: Bridging Anthropology and Linguistics. *International Journal of Evolutionary Biology*, 2011: ID382679.

Balari, S., Benítez-Burraco, A., Longa, V. M., & Lorenzo, G. (in press). The fossils of language: What are they, who has them, how did they evolve? In C. Boeckx & K. K. Grohmann (Eds.), *Handbook of Biolinguistics*. New York: Cambridge University Press.

Bateson, P. & Mamelli, M. (2007). The innate and the acquired: useful clusters or a residual distinction from folk Biology? *Developmental Psychobiology*, 49, 818-831.

Benítez-Burraco, A. (2009). *Genes y lenguaje: aspectos ontogenéticos, filogenéticos y cognitivos*. Barcelona: Reverté.

Botha, R., & Knight, C. (Eds.) (2009). *The Cradle of Language*. New York: Oxford University Press.

d'Errico, F. (2008). The archaeology of language origins. In A. Smith, K. Smith & R. Ferrer i Cancho (Eds.), *The evolution of language. Proceedings of Evolang7* (pp. 413-414). Singapore: World Scientific.

d'Errico, F. & Vanhaeren, M. (2009). Earliest personal ornaments and their significance for the origin of language debate. In R. Botha & C. Knight (Eds.), pp.16-40.

Finlayson, C. (2005). Biogeography and evolution of the genus *Homo*. *Trends in Ecology and Evolution*, 20, 457-463.

Fisher, S. E. & Scharff, C. (2009). *FOXP2* as a molecular window into speech and language. *Trends in Genetics*, 25, 166-177.

Fitch, W. T. (2009). Fossil cues to the evolution of speech. In R. Botha & C. Knight (Eds.), pp. 112-134.

Frayer, D. W., Fiore, I., Lalueza-Fox, C., Radovčić, J., & Bondioli, L. (2010). Right-handed Neandertals: Vindija and beyond. *Journal of Anthropological Sciences*, 88, 113-127.

Green, R. E., Krause, J., Briggs, A. W., Maricic, T., Stenzel, U., Kircher, M. *et al.* (2010). A draft sequence of the neandertal genome. *Science*, 328, 710-22.

Johnson, M. H. (2003). Development of human brain functions. *Biological Psychiatry*, 54, 1312-1316.

Konopka, G., Bomar, J. M., Winden, K., Coppola, G., Jonsson, Z. O., Gao, F., *et al.* (2009). Human-specific transcriptional regulation of CNS development genes by *FOXP2*. *Nature*, 462, 213-217.

Krause, J,, Lalueza-Fox, C., Orlando, L., Enard, W., Green, R. E., Burbano, H. A. *et al.* (2007). The derived *FOXP2* variant of modern humans was shared with Neandertals. *Current Biology*, 17, 1908-1912.

Li, S., Weidenfeld, J. & Morrisey, E. (2004). Transcriptional and DNA binding activity of the Foxp1/2/4 family is modulated by heterotypic and homotypic protein interactions. *Molecular and Cellular Biology*, 24, 809-822.

Love, A. C. (2007). Functional homology and homology of function: Biological concepts and philosophical consequences. *Biology & Philosophy*, 22, 691-708.

Mithen, S. (2005). *The singing Neanderthals*. London: Weidenfeld & Nicholson.

Müller, G. B. (2007). Evo–devo: extending the evolutionary synthesis. *Nature Reviews Genetics*, 8, 943-949.

Newman, S. A., Forgacs, G. & Müller, G. B. (2006). Before programs: the physical origination of multicellular forms. *International Journal of developmental Biology*, 50, 289-299.

Oyama, S., Griffiths, P. E. & Gray, R. D. (Eds.) (2001). *Cycles of Contingency. Developmental Systems and Evolution*. Cambridge: MIT Press.
Ramus, F. (2006). Genes, brain, and cognition: a roadmap for the cognitive scientist. *Cognition*, 101, 247-269.
Shriberg, L. D., Ballard, K. J., Tomblin, J. B., Duffy, J. R., Odell, K. H. & Williams, C. A. (2006). Speech, prosody, and voice characteristics of a mother and daughter with a 7,13 translocation affecting *FOXP2*. *Journal of Speech, Language, and Hearing Research*, 49, 500-525.
Spiteri, E., Konopka, G., Coppola, G., Bomar, J., Oldham, M., Ou, J., *et al.* (2007). Identification of the transcriptional targets of *FOXP2*, a gene linked to speech and language, in developing human brain. *American Journal of Human Genetics*, 81, 1144-1157.
Taipale, M., Kaminen, N., Nopola-Hemmi, J., Haltia, T., Myllyluoma, B. *et al.* (2003). A candidate gene for developmental dyslexia encodes a nuclear tetratricopeptide repeat domain protein dynamically regulated in brain. *Proceedings of the National Academy of Sciences*, 100, 11553-11558.
Trinkaus, E. (2007). Human evolution: Neandertal gene speaks out. *Current Biology*, 17, R917-R918.
Vallender, E. J.; Mekel-Bobrov, N. & Lahn, B. T. (2008). Genetic basis of human brain evolution. *Trends in Neuroscience*, 31, 637-644.
Vargha-Khadem, F., Gadian, D. G., Copp, A. & Mishkin, M. (2005). *FOXP2* and the neuroanatomy of speech and language. *Nature Reviews Neuroscience*, 6, 131-138.
Vernes, S. C., Newbury, D. F., Abrahams, B. S., Winchester, L., Nicod, J. *et al.* (2008). A functional genetic link between distinct developmental language disorders. *New England Journal of Medicine*, 359, 2337-2345.
Vernes, S. C., Nicod, J., Elahi, F. M., Coventry, J. A., Kenny, N., Coupe, A. M., *et al.* (2006). Functional genetic analysis of mutations implicated in a human speech and language disorder. *Human Molecular Genetics*, 15, 3154-3167.
Wagner, G. P., & Altenberg, L. (1996). Complex adaptations and the evolution of evolvability. *Evolution*, 50, 967-976.
Watkins, K. E., Dronkers, N. F. & Vargha-Khadem, F. (2002). Behavioural analysis of an inherited speech and language disorder: comparison with acquired aphasia. *Brain*, 125, 452-464.
West-Eberhard, M. J. (2005). Developmental plasticity and the origin of species differences. *Proceedings of the National Academy of Sciences* Sup. 102: 6543-6549.
White, S. (2010). Genes and vocal learning. *Brain and Language*, 115: 21-28.
Winther, R. G. (2001). Varieties of modules: kinds, levels, origins, and behaviors. *Journal of Experimental Zoology*, 291, 116-129.

THE IMPACT OF L2 SPEAKERS ON THE EVOLUTION OF CASE MARKING

CHRISTIAN BENTZ

Dept. of Theoretical and Applied Linguistics, University of Cambridge, Cambridge, 9 West Road, CB3 9EU, UK

BODO WINTER

Dept. of Cognitive and Information Sciences, University of California, Merced, Merced, CA, 95343, USA

This paper is a summary of a research project addressing the question of how L2 speakers in linguistic communities can shape the structure of languages. We present evidence in support for the view that L2 speakers have an impact on the future development of grammar, namely, that languages with more L2 speakers tend to lose abundant case marking systems. This is in line with the idea that language structure is predominantly the outcome of the processes of cultural evolution, language contact and language learning rather than biological evolution.

1. Introduction

While biolinguistic accounts of language evolution have focused on the evolution of the genetic underpinnings of language, functional linguistics and the Language as Shaped by the Brain Hypothesis (Christiansen & Chater, 2008) focus on seeing language as the product of cultural evolution. Rather than assuming a biological adaptation towards language, language itself is viewed as an adapting structure (see also, Beckner et al., 2009). The general idea is that there are functional and pragmatic pressures that shape languages through repeated interactions, i.e. pressures that arise from the learning constraints of language learners. Language structures are viewed as entities that are more or less suitable for the minds of speakers, and that are more or less suitable for being used by speakers (see also Deacon 1997: 328-333; Johansson 2005: 190).

A version of this general idea is the Linguistic Niche Hypothesis (Lupyan & Dale, 2010), which emphasizes the interaction between social structure and language structure. Languages are considered to be adapting to specific ‘niches’. In particular, there are languages that are used by large speaking communities that interact a lot with surrounding communities and have many second language learners (so-called 'exoteric languages'), and there are languages that are used by small communities with less contact and less L2 learners (so-called 'esoteric languages'). In support of this view, Lupyan and Dale (2010) show that languages in the exoteric niche seem to exhibit less morphosyntactic complexity than languages in the esoteric niche. Bentz and Christiansen (2010) discuss the evolution of case systems in the Latin and Romance languages from this perspective, arguing that Latin exhibited the strongest degree of case reduction when there was the largest influx of L2 learners of Latin. A similar argument for the case of English and German is reviewed in Bentz and Christiansen (submitted).

In this paper, we present further evidence for the Linguistic Niche Hypothesis, focusing on the role of L2 learners and how languages adapt to fit the learning constraints of these learners. We demonstrate that languages that are spoken by a relatively large amount of L2 speakers tend to exhibit less case paradigms, suggesting that the learning constraints of L2 learners shape the evolution of case systems. This evidence can be linked to research on L2 acquisition of case, which suggests that case is difficult to acquire for adults.

2. The impact of L2 speakers on case systems

The question whether population size does enhance or slow down language change in general has been scrutinized by different researchers (Trudgill, 1994; Nerbonne & Heeringa, 2006; Wichmann & Holman, 2009), and both affirmative and negative evidence has been presented. There are different reasons to suppose that population size should be associated with faster or lower rates of change. The hypothesis we address here is that population size indirectly reflects potential language contact situations of the past and therefore might enhance the loss of grammatical markers. This hypothesis has been tested by Lupyan and Dale (2010), where population size was used as shorthand for assessing the role of language contact in a quantitative way. We want to go one step further and provide an even more direct test of the Linguistic Niche Hypothesis by correlating the number of L2 speakers with linguistic structure.

Here, we consider the association between L2 learning and case. There is experimental evidence showing that nominal morphology, and case marking in particular, is difficult to acquire by adult learners of a second language (Parodi, Schwartz & Clahsen, 2004; Gürel, 2000; Haznedar, 2006; Papadopoulou et al., 2011; Jordens, De Bot & Trapman, 1989). Note that these difficulties seem to be independent of whether the native language of the learner itself uses case marking or not. We believe that the difficulty of L2 learners to acquire case paradigms probably poses structural pressures against case marking in languages that have a high proportion of L2 speakers. We want to test this idea quantitatively with a cross-linguistic sample.

Using a variety of sources such as the SIL Ethnologue (Lewis, 2009), the WorldLingo website[1], the Rosetta project website[2], the UCLA Language Materials Project[3], as well as the countries' censuses, we were able to collect the numbers of L2 speakers for 226 languages. We linked this data to Iggesen's (2011) chapter on "Number of Cases" in the *World Atlas of Language Structures* (WALS). Iggesen (2011) adopts 8 ranked case categories to describe a total of 261 languages. For 66 (28%) of these languages, we had the respective information about the number of L1 and L2 speakers. These languages form the dataset that we analyzed. Although the dataset is relatively small compared to other typological samples, it features a wide range of language families (25 families) from a diverse set of geographic areas such as Europe, Southeast Asia, Southern Africa, Greater Abyssinia, Greater Mesopotamia, NE South America, Alaska-Oregon and others (15 areas).

We used linear mixed effects models with the ratio of L2 speakers and L1 speakers (henceforth L2/L1 ratio) as the predictor variable and the number of case categories as the dependent variable. In order to control for specific language areas or families having particular baselines with respect to the number of case paradigms (e.g. South East Asia tends to have languages that have no case), we included language area and language stock as random effects.[4] Controlling for areal and genealogical effects is crucial for typological research in general (e.g. see Dryer 1989), but for case paradigms in particular, because strong areal effects in this domain have been demonstrated by Bickel and Nichols (2009).

The results of the analyses for the relationship between ratio L2/L1 and case marking categories can be seen in figure 1. The figure shows that languages with fewer L2 speakers (smaller log L2/L1 ratios) tend to have larger case inventories (the numbers on the x-axis represent the ranks of categories in Iggesen's WALS chapter). This pattern is significant (p=0.0002) and generalizes over language families and language areas. On the other hand, taking only the number of L1 speakers as a predictor does not produce a significant effect (p=0.51, for the sample of 66 languages) suggesting that the restricted L2 learning abilities

[1] www.worldlingo.com
[2] www.rosettaproject.org
[3] www.lmp.ucla.edu
[4] For a detailed description of the statistical methods applied see (Bentz & Winter, submitted).

discussed in the literature actually 'shaped' the languages of our sample towards using less abundant case marking paradigms.

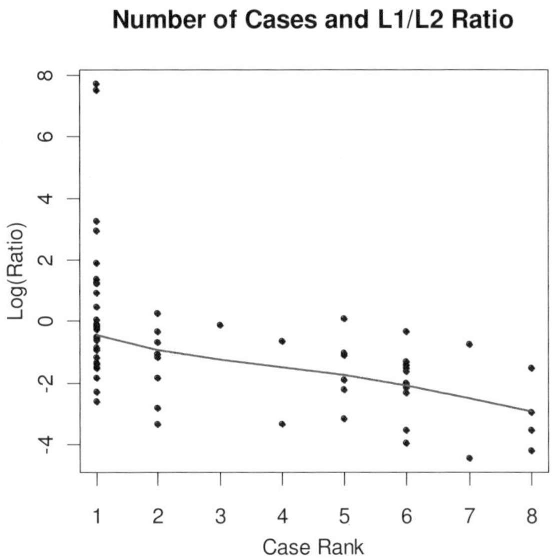

Figure 1. The correlation between number of nominal cases and the ratio L2/L1 in 66 languages; the numbers on the x-axis represent ranks as in Iggesen (2011) with higher ranks indicating more case paradigms. The ratio on the y-Axis was transformed logarithmically in order to reduce distances to outliers.

3. Conclusion

In this paper, we presented the effect of the presence of L2 learners on case systems: languages with more L2 speakers tended to exhibit less complex case systems. This pattern is reminiscent of Lupyan and Dale (2010). However, we provide more direct evidence for the role of L2 speakers. This data only makes sense when we assume that a large part of language is shaped by cultural evolution with the cognitive capacities of language learners constraining language structure, a view that in this particular example seems much in line with the experimental evidence for the difficulty of acquiring case as L2 speakers. Different societies have different social structures, and these social structures in turn interact with the learning constraints, i.e. a society with many L2 learners potentially poses selective pressures against overabundant nominal morphology. From this perspective, every society is a new niche to which language adapts.

References

Beckner, C., Ellis, N.C., Blythe, R., Holland, J., Bybee, J., Ke, J., Christiansen, M.H., Larsen-Freeman, D., Croft, W., & Schoenemann, T. (2009). Language Is a Complex Adaptive System: Position Paper. *Language Learning*, 59, 1-26.

Bentz, C. & Christiansen, M. H. (2010) Linguistic adaptation at work? The change of word order and case system from Latin to the Romance languages. In Andrew D. M. Smith, M. Schouwstra, B. de Boer & K. Smith (Eds.). *Proceedings of the 8th International Conference on the Evolution of Language*, pages 26--33. World Scientific.

Bentz, C. & Christiansen, M.H. (submitted). Linguistic Adaptation: The trade-off between case marking and fixed word orders in Germanic and Romance languages.

Bentz, C., & Winter, B. (submitted). Languages with more second language learners have fewer nominal cases.

Bickel, B., & Nichols, J. (2009). The Geography of Case. Malchukov, A.; Spencer, A. (Eds.). *The Oxford Handbook of Case*. 479-493.

Christiansen, M. H., & Chater, N. (2008). Language as shaped by the brain. *Behavioral and Brain Sciences*, *31*, 489–509.

Deacon, T. W. (1997). *The Symbolic Species: The Co-evolution of Language and the Brain*. New York & London: W.W. Norton & Company.

Dryer, M. S. (1989). Large Linguistic Areas and Linguistic Sampling. *Studies in Language*, 13, 257-292.

Dryer, M. S., & Haspelmath, M. (Eds.) (2011). *The World Atlas of Language Structures Online*. Munich: Max Planck Digital Library. Available online at http://wals.info/. Accessed on 2011-05-19.

Gürel, A. (2000). Missing Case inflection: Implications for second language acquisition. In C. Howell, S.A. Fish, & T. Keith-Lucas (Eds.), *Proceedings of the 24th Annual Boston University Conference on Language Development* 45 (pp. 379-390). Somerville, MA: Cascadilla Press.

Haznedar, B. (2006). Persistent problems with case morphology in L2 acquisition. In: Lleó, Conxita (ed.), *Interfaces in multilingualism*, pp. 179-206.

Iggesen, O. A. (2011). Number of Cases. In M. S. Dryer & M. Haspelmath (Eds.). *The World Atlas of Language Structures Online*. Munich: Max Planck Digital Library, chapter 49.

Jordens, P., De Bot, K. & Trapman, H. (1989). Linguistic aspects of regression in German case marking. *Studies in Second Language Acquisition 11*. 179-204.

Lewis, M. P. (Ed.) (2009). *Ethnologue: Languages of the World*, Sixteenth edition. Dallas, Tex.: SIL International. Online version: http://www.ethno logue.com/.

Johansson, S. (2005). *Origins of Language: Constraints on hypotheses.* Amsterdam: John Benjamins.

Lupyan, G., & Dale, R. (2010). Language Structure Is Partly Determined by Social Structure. *PLoS ONE 5*:1, e8559-e8559.

Nerbonne, J., & Heeringa, W. (2006): Geographic Distributions of Linguistic Variation Reflect Dynamics of Differentiation. In: *Roots: Linguistics in Search for its Evidential Base*, S. Featherston and W. Sternefeld (eds.), Mouton de Gruyter, Berlin, 267-297.

Papadopoulou, D., Varlokosta, S., Spyropoulos, V., Kaili, H., Prokou, S., & Revithiadou, A. (2011). Case morphology and word order in second language Turkish: Evidence from Greek learners. *Second Language Research 27*. 173-205.

Parodi, T., Schwartz, B. D., & Clahsen, H. (2004). On the L2 acquisition of the morphosyntax of German nominals. *Linguistics 42*-3. 669-705.

Trudgill, P. (1974): Linguistic Change and Diffusion: Description and Explanation in Sociolinguistic Dialect Geography. In: *Language in Society*, Vol.3, No. 2, Cambridge University Press, pp. 215-146.

Wichmann, S., Müller, A., Velupillai, V., Brown, C. H., Holman, E. W., Brown, P., Sauppe, S., Belyaev, O., Urban, M., Molochieva, Z., Wett, A., Bakker, D., List, J.-M., Egorov, D., Mailhammer, R., Beck, D., & Geyer, H. (2010): *The ASJP Database* (version 13).

Wichmann, S., Holman, E. W. (2009): Population Size and Rates of Language Change. *Human Biology*, Vol. 81, No. 2-3, Wayne State University Press, Detroit, pp. 259-274.

INTRODUCING PRESSURE FOR EXPRESSIVITY INTO LANGUAGE EVOLUTION EXPERIMENTS

ALEKSANDRS BERDICEVSKIS

Department of Foreign Languages, University of Bergen, Postboks 7805 Bergen, 5020, Norway

I present a language evolution experiment that integrates two evolutionary pressures (for learnability and for expressivity) and two directions of language transmission (vertical and horizontal). Members of each generation of a diffusion chain are given a communication task. The experiment shows that the compositionality of their languages increases over generations, but the reproduction fidelity does not. Moreover, the compositionality of the input language is a good predictor for the compositionality of the output language, but not for the reproduction fidelity. These results, together with the analysis of intragenerational alignment, allow to estimate the contribution of each kind of pressure and each transmission way.

1. Introduction

In a well-known laboratory experiment on language evolution by Kirby et al. (2008) structure emerges in initially unstructured languages, as they are transmitted over generations of a diffusion chain, obviously adapting to the pressure for learnability. The same experiment, however, shows that this pressure alone is not enough.

Only when homonyms were removed by experimenters from every input language, did the languages develop a compositional structure (otherwise they became strongly underspecified). This removal of ambiguity acted thus as a pressure for expressivity, preventing the languages from losing their expressive power. While efficient, this model is artificial. My primary aim is to test whether the pressure for expressivity can be implemented in a more natural way, by using a communication task. This can increase the role of intentional design, but it is likely that the task to adhere to the learned language will temper it.

Introducing communication into iterated learning experiment also answers another call of the developing field (Garrod et al. 2010; Theisen-White et al. 2011): to take into account both horizontal and vertical transmissions and to estimate their roles in the evolution of language.

2. Methods

2.1. *Model of vertical transmission*

48 secondary school students participated in the experiment, all native speakers of Russian, mean age 15.4 years. Participants were rewarded with candies for successful rounds (see below).
Participants were asked to learn an "alien" language and to communicate in it in pairs. During the learning stage the alien language was presented to the participants on a computer screen as a set of string–picture pairs. The members of a pair were trained on the same language: the first pair in a chain on the randomly generated one, and the following pairs on the output of the preceding pair (see below). The training took place simultaneously, but in different rooms.

2.2. *Language*

The meaning space was determined by three parameters: shape (four possible values); colour (two); background (three). The design was made asymmetrical (4x3x2) in order to keep the meaning space less predictable[1]. The strings for the input language of the first pair were generated randomly in lowercase Cyrillic letters (given here in Latin transliteration).

2.3. *Model of horizontal transmission*

After the learning stage, the communication stage took place. Two participants were seated in the same room at different sides of a screen, so that they could not see each other. The only thing they knew was that their partner was an "earthian" who had received the same training. Voice communication was forbidden.

One of the participants (A) was shown a random picture on the screen of a laptop. She wrote a name for it on a paper card. The card was passed to the participant B who depicted on it a picture that, in her opinion, corresponded to that name. If the depiction coincided with the original stimulus, this round was considered successful and the participants were awarded a point. The original stimulus was then shown to B, and the card with the depiction was shown to A, so that they both knew their result. When writing a name for a figure, participants used a black pen, when drawing a picture, they could use any of four coloured pencils (red, blue, green, yellow).

For the next round, the roles were exchanged, and the next picture was

---

[1] The meaning space was indeed poorly predictable: participants often used green and yellow pencils (see below); at debriefings, very few were able to answer how many stimuli they saw.

shown. Such rounds were held for all the 24 stimuli (presented in random order, each stimulus once). Thus, each of the participants performed 12 operations of naming a picture and 12 operations of drawing a picture for a given name.

The communication system shared by A and B was considered to consist of the signs used in successful rounds. In other words, if the participants won a round, the name on the card was considered a word of their shared language, its meaning being the picture on the same card. This output language (E-language, as opposed to each participant's I-language) served as input for the next pair.

2.4. *Bottlenecks and failures*

If the number of signs in an E-language (n) was larger than 12, then n-*12* signs (chosen randomly) were removed. This rule was applied to the first input language as well. If n did not exceed 12, no bottleneck was applied. If n was smaller than 2, then language was considered extinct (evolutionary dead-end), since the pilot experiments showed that in this case the participants were unable to perform the communication task. Thus, the number of signs in the input languages was not fixed and could range from 2 to 12.

2.5. *Data analysis*

I analyze changes in the compositionality of E-languages and the fidelity of their reproduction. The expectation is that the cumulative evolution should lead to the increase of both parameters over generations.

The fidelity of reproduction shows how many signs of the E-language of the previous generation were correctly reproduced. It is calculated as transmission error substracted from one. The transmission error was measured as a mean normalized Levenshtein distance between the signals in E-language of generation n and the corresponding signals in E-language of generation n-*1*. If in the language of generation n a signal was present, but in the language of generation n-*1* it was missing, this was not considered to be an error (the signal had not been part of the input language, there was no name to reproduce), and distance was equated with 0. If in the language of generation n-*1* a signal was present, but in the language of generation n it was missing, distance equaled 1 (the name that had existed was lost).

Compositionality was measured using two different methods. One was the *RegMap* metric as in Tamariz et al. (2010) (originally suggested by Tamariz&Smith 2008). *RegMap* allows to quantify how regular the mappings between signals and meanings are. Partial *RegMaps* estimate how confident a learner can be that a meaning compone,nt (e.g. shape) is associated with a signal component (e.g. first morpheme). Full *RegMap* tests whether these associations are biunique, returning one value for the whole language. This value ranges from 1 (there is a biunique association for every component of both spaces) to 0 (there is no trace of such associations)[2].

Another measure was that of Kirby et al. (2008: 10686), the Mantel test. Here, the structure is measured as the Pearson's product-moment correlation between the matrix of the distances between all pairs of strings in the language (Levenshtein distance) and the matrix of the distances between all pairs of meanings[3] in the language. Significance is measured by Monte Carlo method (1000 randomizations or as many as possible for smaller languages). The variable number of signs in the languages, however, constitutes a problem: smaller languages often have high correlation coefficient, but low significance. If p-value was larger than 0.05, the matrices were considered not correlated and the measure of structure thus equal to 0. This makes the measure blind to changes in structure in these languages, so I consider RegMap as the basic measure.

Expressivity is also reported, measured as a number of signs in an E-language (the score obtained by the pair in the game).

3. Results

3.1. *Vertical transmission*

Three chains (2, 4 and 5) ended up at the first round, since the pairs produced E-language consisting of one sign only. This shows that the tasks offered to the participants were really difficult. Since the results of these pairs are not indicative of the cumulative evolution of language, they are not included into further analysis, which is thus limited to the "successful" chains.

Three pairs struggled successfully through the first round, which resulted into three chains (1, 3 and 6) of seven generations each (Fig. 1). In these chains, there is an increase of compositionality over generations within a chain, as confirmed by Page's trend test (m=3, n=8; using RegMap: L=559, p<0.01; using Mantel test: L=541, p<0.05). There is, however, no significant increase of reproduction fidelity (L=365, m=3, n=7, p≈0.44).

If we look at the dependence of different parameters of an output

---

[2] *RegMap* in its current form relies on the assumption that the language has no "empty cells", that all possible meanings are expressed. This is not the case with my data, and smaller languages receive lower score, even if the signs they include are perfectly regular. I do not adjust for that, since the inability of language to express certain meanings (often present in morphosyntax of natural languages) might also be viewed as irregularity that affects the learner's perspective.

[3] The meaning distance is the number of differences between the two stimuli (0, 1, 2 or 3).

E-language on the compositionality (measured using RegMap) of the input E-language, the picture is as follows. Full *RegMap* of the output language correlates strongly with the full *RegMap* of the input language of the same generation (Pearson's r=0.61, n=19, p<0.01).

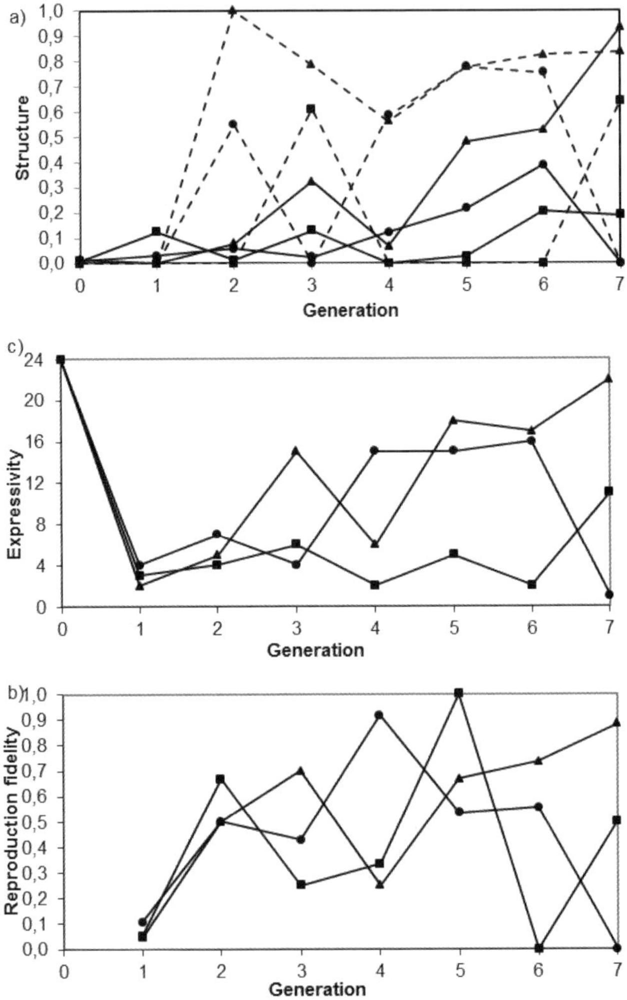

Figure 1. Parameters by generation: a) structure (solid line – RegMap, dashed line – Mantel test); b) reproduction fidelity; c) expressivity. Circles – chain 1, squares – chain 3, triangles – chain 6.

Partial *RegMaps* of the output language also correlate with the corresponding partial *RegMaps* of the input language quite strongly (r=0.53, n=175, p<0.001), thus showing that associations between meaning and signal components are rather stable. The performance of a pair (the expressivity of their E-language) is also correlated with the compositionality of their input language (r=0.45, n=19, p<0.05). The reproduction fidelity of a language, however, does not correlate with its compositionality (r=0.18, n=19, p=0.45).

Mantel test gives a similar picture: performance is correlated with structure (r=0.50, n=19, p<0.05), while fidelity is not (r=0.19, n=19, p=0.42). The only difference is that correlation between the structure of the output language and the structure of the input language is not significant (r=0.36, n=19, p=0.11).

3.2. *Horizontal transmission*

It would be reasonable to expect that within a pair an alignment of the I-languages of the individuals takes place, and they gradually converge on the same language. In other words, participants should agree upon the stimuli appearing towards the end of interaction stage better.

To test this, I calculate the meaning distances between the figure shown to one participant and the one drawn by the second participant for all the moves. If the hypothesis is correct, the distances should decrease towards the end of the chain. Linear mixed model fit confirms this is the case: t=-2.956, p<0.01, degrees of freedom (502) determined as recommended by Baayen (2008:270).

3.3. *Linguistic phenomena*

It is also interesting to look at various linguistic phenomena and types of structure that emerge. The output of the pair 6:7 (Fig. 2a) is an unambiguous agglutinative language: the first letter denotes shape, the second denotes colour. The rest denotes background in a way which may be called hypercompositional: *-hovo* is a combination of *-ho* and *-vo*, and its meaning ('filled') may also be viewed as a superposition of the meanings 'striped' and 'polka dot'. The diachrony confirms this: first, *-ho* and *–vo* became associated with resp. 'striped' and 'polka dot'. Later, 'filled' became associated with *-hovo*, while the association of *–vo* and 'striped' was lost. It resurrected after three generations of variation (*-bi*, *-vi*, *-hi*), obviously under the influence of *-ho* and *-hovo*.

The E-language of the pair 1:4 (Fig. 2b) is also agglutinative. Each syllable denotes a meaning component, 'filled' is expressed by zero morpheme. Irregularity can be observed: for example, the order of morphemes is inverted in the names for all but one filled figures: colour comes first, shape comes second.

The output language of pair 6:7 (Fig. 2c) is more unusual. It resembles the communication systems of monkeys as described e.g. by Ouattara et al. (2009): a limited number of unchangeable signs are combined in long sequences.

a)		square	triangle	circle	rhomb	b)	square	triangle	circle	rhomb
filled	red		tohovo	hohovo	bohovo		kapa	vuka	kale	kape
	blue	vihovo	tihovo	hihovo	bihovo		lepa	levu	lele	lepe
striped	red	vovo	tovo	hovo	bovo					
	blue	vivo	tivo	hivo	bivo			vunape	lenapa	penape
polka dot	red	voho	toho	hoho	boho			vukale		
	blue		tiho	hiho	biho		palele		lelele	pelele

c)		square	triangle	circle	rhomb
filled	red				no-no: l-l-l-l-l
	blue	l-no-no: l-l-l-no-no	l-no: l-l-l-no-no		no-no: l-l-l-no-no
striped	red				
	blue	l-no-no: l-no-no	l-no: l-no-no	l-l: l-no-no	
polka dot	red	l-no-no: no-no-no-no-no	l-no: no-no-nu-nu-nu	l-l: no-no-no-no-no	
	blue	l-no-no: l-no			

Figure 2. E-languages: a) chain 6, generation 7; b) chain 1, generation 4; c) chain 3, generation 7. The words are shortened: *l* stands for *levu*, *no* for *nepopo*, *nu* for *nepopu*.

4. Discussion

My results are in agreement with those of Kirby et al. (2008) with one salient exception: in my experiment, there is no significant increase of reproduction fidelity, given the increase of compositionality.

One explanation for this is that the analyzed seven generations represent the early stages of language evolution, when languages have to change in order to become more structured. It is possible that should chains 3 and 6 be continued, the reproduction fidelity will grow.

Alternative explanation can be sought in the interplay of horizontal and vertical transmissions. While vertical transmission is affected by the learning bottleneck, horizontal transmission is affected by the gap between the participants' I-languages. In order to communicate effectively, they have to bridge this gap by converging on a compositional language (and they gradually do that, as shown in Section 3.2.). The more compositional their input is, the smaller the gap is, the faster the alignment is achieved. In this case, it is possible that the participants succeed in reaching compositionality and expressivity, but still reproduce the input language poorly. It is less likely that they fail to reach compositionality, get a low score, but reproduce the input language well.

This is understandable: in this model, as well as in the real world, speakers' *main* goal is successful communication, not the reproduction of what they learned. People are remarkably effective in quickly establishing communication even in the unfavourable conditions, as shown both by experiments (Scott-Phillips et al., 2009; de Ruiter et al., 2009) and observation of emerging new languages (Sandler et al., 2005, Senghas et al. 2005). It might be that while compositional input makes this process more efficient, faithful reproduction of this input is less necessary. After all, languages do change.

Acknowledgements

I am extremely grateful to Eugenia Kuznetsova, Esther Sheynkman, Fedor Vinokurov and Liudmila Zaydelman for their help in conducting the experiments, and to Dmitry Logvinov for creating the necessary software.

References

Baayen, R.H. (2008). *Analyzing linguistic data: a practical introduction to statistics using R.* Cambridge University Press.

De Ruiter, J.P., Noordzij, M.L., Newman-Norlund, S., Newman-Norlund, R., Hagoort, P., Levinson, S.C., Toni, I. (2010). Exploring the cognitive infrastructure of communication. *Interaction Studies, 11(1)*, 51–77.

Garrod, S., Fay, N., Rogers, S., Walker, B., & Swoboda, N. (2010). Can iterated learning explain the emergence of graphical symbols? *Interaction Studies, 11(1)*, 33–50.

Kirby, S., Smith, K., and Cornish, H. (2008) Cumulative cultural evolution in the laboratory: an experimental approach to the origins of structure in human language. *Proceeding of the National Academy of Sciences, 105(31)*, 10681–10686.

Ouattara, K., Lemasson, A. Zuberbьhler, A. (2009). Campbell's monkeys concatenate vocalizations into context-specific call sequences. *Proceeding of the National Academy of Sciences, 106 (51)*, 22026–22031.

Sandler, W., Meir, I., Padden, C. and Aronoff, M. (2005). The emergence of grammar: Systematic structure in a new language. *Proceeding of the National Academy of Sciences, 102(7)*, 2661–2665.

Scott-Phillips, T.C., Kirby, S. and Ritchie, G.R.S. (2009). Signalling signalhood and the emergence of communication. *Cognition 113(2)*, 226–233

Senghas, R.J, Senghas, A. and Pyers, J.E. (2005). The emergence of Nicaraguan Sign Language: questions of development, acquisition and evolution. In J. Langer, S.T. Parker and C. Milbrath (Eds.), *Biology and Knowledge revisited: From neurogenesis to psychogenesis*. Lawrence Erlbaum Associates.

Tamariz, M., Brown, J.E. and Murray, K.M. (2010). The role of practice and literacy in the evolution of linguistic structure. In A.D.M. Smith, M. Schouwstra, B. de Boer and K. Smith (Eds), *Proceedings of the 8th International Conference on the Evolution of Language*, 313–320. World Scientific.

Tamariz, M., and Smith, A.D.M. (2008). Regularity in Mappings Between Signals and Meanings. In A.D.M. Smith, K. Smith and R. Ferrer-i-Cancho (Eds), *Proceedings of the 7th International Conference on the Evolution of Language*, 315–322. World Scientific.

Theisen-White, C., Kirby, S. and Oberlander, J. (2011). Integrating the horizontal and vertical cultural transmission of novel communication systems. *Proceedings of Cognitive Science Society Conference*, 956–961.

THE EVOLUTION OF THE GREENBERGIAN WORD ORDER CORRELATIONS

JEREMY COLLINS

The University of Hong Kong, Pok Fu Lam Road, Hong Kong

Recurring traits across languages have been argued to relate directly to constraints imposed by the brain. A particular case is Greenberg's word order universals (Greenberg 1966), which have been argued to reflect the demands of language acquisition (Baker 2001, Chomsky 2010) or of processing sentences (Hawkins 1983, Kirby and Hurford 1997). This paper argues that typological universals are indeed relevant to the study of the biological basis of language, but for a different reason, that they are created by the process of grammaticalisation. Recent historical evidence for the grammaticalisation explanation will be presented, concluding that explanations invoking processing or acquisition are misguided. Grammaticalisation involves the use of metaphor and the 'chunking' of constructions similar to the chunking of motor sequences (Bybee 2002), and hence the origin of language universals is argued to be in these properties of the mind rather than those proposed by innatist or functionalist linguists.

1. Explaining Language Universals through Grammaticalisation

1.1 *Greenberg's Word Order Correlations*

Language universals refer to properties common to all languages, or more loosely referring to properties commonly found in unrelated languages.
Greenberg (1966) formulated word order universals such as SOV languages tending 'with overwhelmingly greater than chance frequency' to have noun-adposition and possessor-noun ordering, and for VOS languages to have adposition-noun and noun-possessor ordering. Patterns such as these require an explanation, and attempts to explain them have consequences for our view of what is adaptive in language. Kirby and Hurford (1997) summarises two views which are still widely held today: either these correlations are 'economical' in the grammar and make language acquisition easier (e.g. Pinker 1992, Baker 2001); or they are there because sentences made up of constructions obeying these correlations are easier to process (Hawkins 2004, Kirby and Hurford 1997). The former theory is found regularly in syntax textbooks and research (Roberts (2007), Chomsky (2010)) and the latter theory in prominent functionalist linguistics writing such as Evans and Levinson (2009) and several computer simulations in the evolutionary literature (see Van Everbroek 1999), showing that these hypotheses are still influential.

There is growing historical evidence from a number of language families that these hypotheses are redundant, and arguably incorrect. Instead, these patterns are remnants of a historical process, grammaticalisation, as argued for by Aristar (1991) and others. In brief, the argument is this: the ordering of adpositions and the nouns they modify often correlates with the ordering of genitive and noun simply because adpositions often derive etymologically from nouns. This process is **grammaticalisation**, the process of grammatical elements developing from lexical words. Heine and Kuteva (2007) give numerous examples, such as Chinese *li* 'in' etymologically meaning 'interior' or 'village': hence *fangzi li* 'in the house' might be glossed more literally as 'the house's inside'. The ordering of elements is Noun (*fangzi*)-Postposition (*li*) simply because it derives from a construction which is Genitive (*fangzi*)-Noun (*li*). Similarly for many languages in Ghana such as Moore *nyingri* 'on' < 'sky', and numerous other examples in languages all over the world (Heine and Kuteva 2007). An alternative source of adpositions is verbs, such as Chinese *gen* 'with' from a verb meaning 'to follow'. *Gen* is a preposition because verbs precede objects in Chinese, and *gen* has inherited that ordering even while undergoing category change. Chinese hence has a mixture of prepositions and postpositions, the former systematically deriving from verbs and the latter from nouns. In each case the ordering of the adposition is inherited from a construction which it evolved from, because Chinese has verb-object order and genitive-noun order. Similar remarks apply to the Gbe languages in Ghana which also show typological mixing.

Grammaticalisation can also explain the ordering of verb and object correlating with genitive and noun ordering for at least some languages. Certain types of verb phrase derive from noun phrases made up of a nominalised verb and its object in a possessive case. An example is Ewe, which expresses 'I am seeing him' literally (or etymologically) as 'I am on his seeing': *Me-le e kpe dzi* (1Sg.-be.at his see on) (Claudi 1994).

Ewe is normally SVO but employs the genitive-noun ordering here 'his seeing', creating a construction which is SOV. Nominalisations of this kind are used cross-linguistically for expressing aspect (such as the continuous aspect in Ewe), for subordinate clauses (expressing 'I was surprised that he saw me' as 'I was surprised at his seeing of me' in Javanese, e.g. Adelaar and Himmelmann 2005:61) for voice marking (in Austronesian languages, *ibid.*), or for infinitives (Heine and Kuteva examples of all of these are given in the next section. These verb phrases can become the most frequently used and unmarked verb phrases in the languages, thus the basic verb-object order of a language can evolve from a genitive-noun construction, even if the nominal origins of the verb form are no longer transparent. If this process is sufficiently common across language families, this explains why the ordering of elements in the verb phrase reflects that of the ordering of elements int the noun phrase.

The correlations between constructions can thus be explained almost banally as the accidental product of a historical change. The arguments by Hawkins (1983) and Kirby and Hurford (1997) that these correlations might be easier to process are redundant, and also probably inaccurate in the context of grammaticalisation. The next two sections attempt to strengthen the evidence for this view, which has grown in the last few years of historical linguistic work, and answer possible objections. The final section attempts to make this view more than a negative result by discussing the cognitive basis of grammaticalisation.

1.2 *Grammaticalisation Cross-Linguistically*

How widespread are such examples of grammaticalisation, and to what extent can they explain the correlation? This was asked by Hawkins (1983), dismissing the historical explanation because it seemed to 'lack generality' (p.131). Since the extensive work on grammaticalisation by Heine and Kuteva (2007) among others it is now no longer possible to argue that these patterns of change are exceptional: they seem to happen in every language family, to the point of being true universals of language.

The pattern of adpositions inheriting the ordering of the noun or verb they derive from is borne out in different families, such in many Oceanic languages (Lynch et al 2002:51) where adpositions are transparently nouns and reflect whatever ordering of genitive-noun the language has (hence can be either prepositional, as in Hawaiian, or postpositional as in Motu); Indo-European languages where reconstructible, such as English *across* < 13 c. Anglo-French *an cros* 'on cross' (Bordet et al. 2010:16); Japanese (e.g. *kara* 'from' < 'way', *si* restrictive particle < 'do', Frellesvig 2010); Australian languages in which adpositions are morphologically still nouns (Dixon 2002); Tibetan and Burmese (DeLancey 1997); and so on. Heine and Kuteva (2007:62) even remark that 'we are not aware of any language that has not undergone such a process'.

The pattern of verb phrases evolving from nominalised verbs with a possessor object is also common, although more complicated to reconstruct. A typical example is the evolution of VOS ordering in Proto-Austronesian, which has been inherited by over a thousand Austronesian languages or evolved further into SVO or VSO (Adelaar and Himmelmann 2005:7). It is now accepted that verb phrases in Austronesian languages evolved from nominal verbs, with a sentence such as 'The children are looking for the house' derives from a Proto-Austronesian construction meaning 'The children are the searchers of the house', when in the active voice: *humanap ng bahay ang mga bata'* (searcher GEN house the PL child) (Starosta et al. 1982). The evidence in favour of this hypothesis as presented in Starosta et al. (1982) and Kaufman (2009) is as follows: that the voice markers on verbs derive from nominalising markers, cognates of which still exist in Tagalog and other languages, such as the locative voice marker *an* which is also used for deriving place names, *aklatan* 'library'<*aklat* 'book'; that the direct object of the verb is marked with the genitive marker *ng* or put into the genitive case if a pronoun; that both nominalisation and the use of equational sentences of the form AB 'A is B' are extremely common in conservative Austronesian languages and presumably in Proto-Austronesian, allowing this frequently used construction to become a standard form of predication (Starosta et al.1982); and that the 'subject-only' restriction on relativisation in Tagalog is straightforwardly predicted (for details see Kaufman (2009)). Thus the verb-object ordering in Austronesian languages derives simply from the noun-genitive ordering of Proto-Austronesian which is still retained in these languages. At a stroke this word order correlation is accounted for in roughly a sixth of the world's languages.

As Sasse (2009) noted in a comment on Kaufman (2009), the situation in Austronesian is 'not as exotic as appears at first sight, especially for a Semiticist or Afroasiaticist.' He notes that the Cushitic languages also replaced their finite verb forms with participles and are used with dative marking on the agent, in effect saying 'I hear it' as 'To me was hearing' (Sasse 2009); and that the dative pronouns eventually grammaticalised further to finite verbal morphology. This change also took place in the Iranian and Indo-Ayran languages, and that this process of replacing finite verbs with nominal forms is over a large linguistic area. Sasse also notes that Ancient Egyptian independently shows evidence of this development, in that agents are marked with genitive case. This is in fact a feature of many languages; Sasse cites Mayan and Inuit languages as examples. Gildea (1997) made a similar reconstruction for the Cariban language family, of which the famous OVS language Hixkaryana is an example; it has genitive marking on the object, effectively expressing 'the enemy will destroy the city' as 'it will be the city's destruction by the enemy' (Gildea 1997:153, explaining among other things why the subject is placed last, and why it has ergative marking).

One can add to this list many languages in Asia, as described in Yap et al. (2011), such as Tibeto-Burman languages that often use nominalised forms as sentences (e.g. 'goat-killing exists' for 'he is killing a goat': DeLancey 2011 p.349), and even Japanese in which argument markers such as *ga* were originally genitive markers (Shinzato 2011:462). Examples of Niger-Congo languages such as Ewe were given earlier and are discussed by Claudi (1994), while Heine describes how many Nilo-Saharan and Chadic languages such as Angas express the sentence 'Musa wants to harvest corn' as *Musa rot dyip ke shwe* (Musa want harvest POSS corn) 'Musa wants the harvesting of corn' (Heine 2009 p.31).

These are examples of languages whose basic verb phrases show evidence of evolving from nominalisations with a genitive object. There are further examples of this grammaticalisation pathway in subordinate clauses: Yap et al. (2011) extensively documents this phenomenon in Asia, and Heine (2009) in various African families as well as in some North American languages such as Quechua. Deutscher (2009) documents this is Akkadian, and even argues, following earlier work by Lehmann, that nominalisation may be the origin of subordination in Germanic languages.

There is thus work on a number of language families showing that these processes of grammatical change are widespread. This is a prerequisite for the grammaticalisation explanation of word order patterns to work: a strong prediction which need not have been verified but which seems increasingly borne out by historical linguistic work. The next section discusses whether this makes alternative hypotheses invalid.

1.3 *Against Explanations invoking Processing*

Word order correlations are often argued to make sentences easier to parse in real time. Is it possible that these factors play a role alongside grammaticalisation, for example, if processing demands 'filter out' certain difficult-to-process constructions, as Kirby and Hurford (1997) suggest? It would seem that there is something to explain, why grammaticalisation happens to produce orderings that are easy to parse.

We should be open to the possibility that this is merely a theoretical coincidence. There happen to be two possible explanations available for word order correlations, but that does not mean that they are both correct: it could be that grammaticalisation happens anyway without any guidance by processing, and the result - the illusion of economy or efficiency - would be the same. One would need independent historical evidence that processing concerns do in fact guide historical change. There are some attempts to show this in Old English, for example (e.g. Fischer 1992, Clark et al. 2008) in which the language appeared to converge on the word order correlations after a period of free word order. This would be evidence for word order correlations emerging at least in part out of processing; but there are other possibilities in this case which need to be investigated further, such as it being related to to the rise of analytic verb forms and periphrastic *do,* the loss of inflections (Fischer 1992) or as a result of contact from French. The historical role of processing is unclear even in this case, and there is little conclusive cross-linguistic evidence for it. Additionally it seems to be falsified by the considerable number of mixed languages such as Chinese and the Gbe languages. In these languages grammaticalisation has gone ahead and produced a mixture of prepositions and postpositions, seemingly disregarding whether or not the resulting grammar is 'economical' or 'efficient'. Typologically mixed languages have also survived for thousands of years, without showing inclination to change, a problem for a theory such as Kirby and Hurford (1997)'s that says such inconsistencies should die out (that is their explanation for why languages are so consistent).

2. Implications for Language Evolution

Word order correlations are often invoked as evidence for universals of language acquisition or use. It is hence important to understand their historical background, which standard interpretations do not. The most pernicious abuse of Greenberg's word order correlations is perhaps in Pinker (1994) and Baker (2001), two books which popularised the Universal Grammar account of these patterns. It is still common to invoke parameters relating constructions of different kinds, in literature on language acquisition (e.g. Sugisaki 2008) and typology and syntax (e.g. Roberts 2008). The alternative processing account does not in itself have a negative influence, but is an example of a broader trend of the '*ad hoc* search for functions that match the universals to be explained',as Kirby (1993) put it (Clark et al. 2008). Attempts in the evolutionary literature to simulate processing or learning with computers, thus deriving Greenberg's word order universals (e.g. Van Everbroek 1999, Livingstone 2000), have a particularly 'just-so' flavour: all computer simulations can do is show that processing/learning preferences of individuals *can* cause these correlations to emerge over time, all other historical factors being equal, not that they are actually responsible.

The historical evidence for the grammaticalisation hypothesis by contrast is growing as different language families are investigated. The word order correlations arise during the creation of new constructions by extending old constructions, and are not in themselves functional, but a byproduct. The process these residual patterns reflect is grammaticalisation: an important process first because it seems to be instrumental in creating complex grammar, as argued in Givon and Shibatani (2009), and underlies other universals such as syntactic categories, as argued in Heine and Kuteva's (2007) book. And second, because grammaticalisation seems to be ubiquitous, and therefore is likely to reveal true universals of the language faculty, as argued in Bybee (2002).

The basic mechanisms of grammaticalisation are clear, even if it is possible that there are additional guiding factors yet to be demonstrated (processing concerns being a possibility, but unsubstantiated so far). Two processes are involved: one is semantic, whereby a new meaning is created either by metaphor (body-parts for adpositions, e.g. 'face' for 'opposite', 'back' for 'behind') or by pragmatic inference (the future reading of 'going to' arose in ambiguous sentences such as 'I am going to buy milk') (Bybee 2002). The other is syntactic, with a larger and more complex construction being created by combining smaller constructions: in this case, forming a new lexical unit *going to* + verb, out of the originally independent elements *go,* continuous affix *-ing* and *to*. This latter process has been referred to as *chunking* by Bybee (2002), describing the process by which 'sequences of units which were previously independent come to be processed as a single unit or chunk'. This may subsequently lead to reduction in the form of the unit, as in *gonna.* This process of forming larger units through repetition is argued by Bybee to be part of the production of fluent speech, and resembles chunking in other complex motor skills such as tool-making or playing the piano: and this is supported by evidence for the relationship between language and dexterity from neurology (e.g. Ramachandran 2011:182). Dexterity and the capacity for metaphor have been suggested to be two aspects of the mind crucial to the biological evolution of language in any case, Dawkins (1999:301-10) and Ramachandran (2011) being two popular accounts that stressed these: but they gain an additional importance because of their role in a fundamental part of the cultural evolution of language, grammaticalisation.

If typological universals emerge from grammaticalisation, they thus ultimately reflect the universal cognitive skills of metaphor and chunking. This is an alternative picture of the biological basis of universals, lent support by the known importance of these skills to language evolution, and supported in this paper by historical linguistic evidence.

References

Adelaar, A. and Himmelmann, N.P. eds. (2005). *The Austronesian Languages of Asia and Madagascar*. New York: Routledge.

Bordet, L. and Jamet, D. (2010). Are English prepositions grammatical or lexical morphemes? *Cercles* Occasional Papers Series (2010).

Bybee, J. (2002). Cognitive processes in grammaticalization. In Tomasello, M. ed. *The New Psychology of Language,* vol.2. New Jersey: Lawrence Erlbaum Associates Inc.

Clark, B., Goldrick, M., and Konopka, K. (2008). Language change as a source of word order generalizations. In Eckardt, R., Jaeger, G. and Veenstra, T. eds. *Variation, Selection, Development: probing the evolutionary model of language change.* Berlin: Mouton de Gruyter. 75-102.

Claudi, U. (1994). Word order change as category change. In Pagliuca, W. ed. *Perspectives on Grammaticalization.* Amsterdam: John Benjamins. 191-231.

Croft, W. (1990). *Typology and Universals.* Cambridge: Cambridge University Press.

Dawkins, R. (1999). *Unweaving the Rainbow: Science, Delusion and the Appetite for Wonder.* London: Penguin Books.

DeLancey, S. (1997). Grammaticalization and the Gradience of Categories: Relator Nouns and Postpositions in Tibetan and Burmese. In Bybee, J., Haiman, J, and Thompson, S.A. eds. (1997). *Essays in Language Form and Language Type: Dedicated to T.Givon.* Amsterdam: John Benjamins. 51-70.

Deutscher, G. (2009). Nominalization and the origin of subordination. In Givon and Shibatani (2009): 199-214.

Dunn, M., Greenhill, S.J., Levinson, S.C., and Gray, R.D. (2011). Evolved structure of language show lineage-specific trends in word-order universals. *Nature* 473:79-82.

Evans, N. and Levinson, S. (2009). The myth of language universals: language diversity and its importance for cognitive science. *Behavioral and Brain Sciences, 32:5*, 429-448.

Fischer, O. (1992). Syntax. In Blake, N. ed. (1992). *The Cambridge History of the English Language.* Cambridge: Cambridge University Press.

Frellesvig, B. (2010). *A History of the Japanese Language.* Cambridge: Cambridge University Press.

Gildea, S. (1997). Introducing ergative word order via reanalysis: word order change in the Cariban family. In Bybee, J., Haiman, J, and Thompson, S.A.

eds. (1997). *Essays in Language Form and Language Type: Dedicated to T.Givon.* Amsterdam: John Benjamins. 145-163.
Givon, T. and Shibatani, M. eds. (2009). *Syntactic Complexity: Diachrony, acquisition, neuro-cognition, evolution.* Amsterdam: John Benjamins Publishing.
Greenberg, J. ed. (1966). *Universals of Language.* Cambridge, MA: MIT Press.
Haspelmath, M. (1989). From purposive to infinitive - a universal path of grammaticalization. *Folia Linguistica Historica* 10(1/2): 287-310.
Hawkins, J. (1983). *Word Order Universals.* New York: Academic Press.
Hawkins, J. (2004). *Efficiency and Complexity in Grammars.* Oxford: Oxford University Press.
Heine, B. and Kuteva, T. (2007). *The Genesis of Grammar.* Oxford: Oxford University Press.
Heine, B. (2009). From nominal to clausal morphosyntax. In Givon and Shibatani (2009): 23-51.
Kaufman, D. (2009). Austronesian nominalism and its consequences: a Tagalog case study. *Theoretical Linguistics* 35:1-49.
Kirby, S. and Hurford, J. (1997). Learning, Culture and Evolution in the origin of linguistic constraints. In Husbands, P. and Harvey, I. eds. (1997). ECAL97: 493-502. Cambridge, MA: MIT Press.
Livingstone, D. (2000). A modified-neural theory of the evolution of linguistic diversity. Paper presented at The Evolution of Language: Third International Conference. Paris, France.
Lynch, J., Ross, M., and Crowley, T. eds. (2002). The Oceanic Languages. London: Routledge Publishing.
Pinker, S. (1994). *The Language Instinct.* London: Penguin Publishing.
Pinker, S. and Jackendoff, R. (2009). The reality of a universal language faculty. *Behavioral and Brain Sciences, 32:5*, 465-466.
Ramachandran, V.S. (2011). *The Tell-Tale Brain.* London: William Heinemann.
Roberts, I. (2008). *Diachronic Syntax.* Oxford: Oxford University Press.
Sasse, H-J. (2009). Nominalism in Austronesian: A historical typological perspective. *Theoretical Linguistics* 35:167-181.
Starosta, S., Pawley, A. and Reid, L. (1982). The evolution of focus in Austronesian. In Halim, A., Carrington, L. and Wurm, S.A. eds. *Papers from the Third International Conference in Austronesian Linguistics 1: Tracking the Travellers*, 145-170. Canberra: Pacific Linguistics.
Sugisaki, K. (2008). Early acquisition of basic word order in Japanese. *Language Acquisition* 15:183-191.
Van Everbroek, E. (1999). Language type, frequency and learnability: a connectionist appraisal. In *Proceedings of the Twenty-first Annual Cognitive Science Society Conference.* 755-760.
Yap, F-H., Grunow-Harsta, K. and Wrona, J. eds. (2011). *Nominalization in Asian Languages: Diachronic and Typological Perspectives.*

SEMIOTIC INVESTIGATIONS INTO EARLY FORMS OF SYMBOLISM AND LANGUAGE

CHRISTOPHE COUPE

Laboratoire Dynamique du Langage, CNRS – University of Lyon
14 avenue Berthelot, Lyon, 69007, France

Understanding early traces of symbolism and the origins of language is challenging given the material nature of the archaeological record. In order to address the psychological and cognitive operations which underlay them, we propose a semiotic framework based on the notion of representational medium. This concept helps bridge the gap between ancient and modern semiotic activities by extending analyses of modern media. It also leads us to highlight a possible evolutionary trajectory to modern symbols.

1. Understanding early traces of symbolism

1.1. *Material signs and their hidden cognitive roots*

A clear division between humans and animals has long been advocated on the basis of the symbolic capacity of the formers, despite variations in the definition of symbols, and debates regarding the cognitive capacities they require (Willhelm, 1974). Recent years have seen an increase in the number of archaeological studies pointing toward early use of symbolic representations in *Homo sapiens* (d'Errico et al., 2001; Vanhaeren et al., 2006; d'Errico et al., 2010). They are based on the discovery of engraved pieces of ochre or bones, or collections of perforated and colored shells; their demonstration relies on ruling out all explanations to the properties of these items but a symbolic usage. When it can be evidenced that shells were brought from a distant site, were deliberately collected or perforated, or show residues of pigments, the most likely explanation is that they were worn as ornaments. This means that the humans who owned them had collectively agreed on attributing them specific meanings, likely related to the expression of social identity (Kuhn & Stiner, 2007a).
Like other past behaviors such as ritual burials, parietal art or sea-crossings, early symbols point to the lives, words and thoughts of our ancestors. Understanding their social and cognitive environment however proves to be challenging. The materiality of the archaeological record indeed requires chains

of speculative inferences to go from artifacts to behaviors to cognitive representations. Cognitive archaeologists have followed several lines of reasoning to better assess putative symbolic objects. One is to investigate the function of similar objects in modern populations (Wiessner, 1984). Another is to relate their understanding to generic cognitive components – e.g. working memory (Coolidge & Wynn, 2005) – or abilities – e.g. the capacity to simulate how objects look from conflicting viewpoints (Henshilwood & Dubreuil, 2009) - with attention paid to their neurophysiology, ontogeny and phylogeny. Yet another approach consists in going into semiotic details, and considering how different categories of signs apply to archaeological artifacts (Rossano, 2010).

Most approaches build on the assumption that humans since at least 100,000 years share similar cognitive abilities with us (d'Errico & Stringer, 2011); such abilities were gradually given more adaptive advantage and archaeological visibility by environmental and social changes. Links are proposed with the emergence of language, highlighting its symbolic nature but also the role of syntax and especially recursion in the transmission of symbolic codes (Henshilwood & Dubreuil, 2009).

This paper follows one of the previous lines of research, namely the investigation into the semiotic properties of archaeological artifacts. Its goal is to define a theoretical framework in which to think of symbolic objects in a more generic way. We aim to diverge from the classical Peircian distinction of icons, indexes and symbols (Peirce, 1935), and get insights from a variety of fields, from photography to philosophy to media studies.

2. Representational media and their human comprehension

2.1. *The notion of representational medium*

Our framework revolves around the notion of representational medium –R-medium for short. Conceived in an abstract fashion, R-media carry information between entities that are able to process it, whether they are actually human beings, other organisms or computers. In our species, they convey representations of the world we all experience, with cultural and technological dimensions born from the human mind and continuously shaping it. A watch displays a visual representation of time; roadmaps mediate knowledge about the spatial organization of transport systems; words mediate the entities they refer to, either as acoustic signals or written units. As human beings, our lives lie deeply embedded in a large number of diversified R-media, on which our cognition relies to build inferential processes and take decisions.

Such a broad definition of R-media allows considering prehistoric situations meaningfully. Either colored shells, engraved bones, painted bodies or walls can be considered as R-media, since they conveyed information and meaning between those who produced or wore them, and those who witnessed them.
The previous examples point mainly toward artifacts and more generally human achievements, anchored in the social and technical dimensions which characterize all human societies. However, considering as R-media other elements that do not fall into these categories does not seem unreasonable: footprints in a way mediate the past presence of an animal or a human being where they appear on the ground. Such an extension of the notion actually hints at a more careful semiotic reading, as proposed below.

2.2. *A semiotic reading of the notion of representational medium*

Extracted from the framework of individual cognition, representations escape from their mental substrate, and therefore the properties attached to it. They then get closer to their etymological status of substitute of an entity to an interpreter, and therefore display an intuitive proximity with the notion of sign, defined by Peirce (1935) as '*something which stands to somebody for something in some respect or capacity*'. Through the notion of representation, a semiotic reading can thus be applied to R-media, which can be considered as *carriers of signs*.
From then on, semiotic typologies can help classify R-media according to their properties and usage. For example, Eco (1988) operates a distinction between artificial and natural signs based on the intentionality of the emission process. Complementarily, signs may fall into two categories: entities which primary task is to signify, and entities that primarily serve a different function, but which display a secondary function of signification.
Some R-media carry artificial signs with a primary function of signification. Shell beads were likely worn to primarily express social identities or situations, just as modern neckties do (Kuhn & Stiner, 2007a). In this case, the signification relies on an established, "symbolic", convention. Other R-media may convey artificial signs with a secondary function of signification, like weapons which come to signify the power of their owners. Others yet may convey natural signs with a secondary function of signification, like bones allegedly belonging to the Buddha becoming meaningful relics. Natural signs with a primary function of signification are more difficult to conceptualize, unless one extends the notion of intentionality to encompass a more biological acceptation: the tail of the male peacock primarily and unintentionally 'signifies' the quality of its genes.

This diversity of R-media and the notion of intentionality highlight the central role played by the process of *semiosis* - the process of "meaning making" - and more importantly how it can be understood by animate beings. Artificial signs can only be produced by creatures who understand the role an entity can play as meaning something for someone else. A semiotic rereading of Von Uexküll's notion of *Umwelt* states that all organisms live in a dense web of relationships of signification and processes of semiosis (Sebeok & Umiker-Sebeok, 1992). However, although each species, through its senses and cognitive apparatus, builds its own world of signification and infers its behavior from it, only human beings seem capable of understanding the nature of these ubiquitous processes.

2.3. *Primary and elaborated properties of representational media*

To further understand how the process of semiosis takes place along R-media, it makes sense to investigate their properties. Each R-media is indeed characterized by various features; they relate to which information is carried, or in other words the kind of semiotic mediations it is more or less susceptible to perform.

On the one hand, *primary* properties of the R-medium can be defined independently of any potential interpreter; they strongly impact on the conveyed representations. An intuitive classification derives from our sensorial modalities, but semioticians like Sebeok have put forward broader classifications of signs according to the channel they take - either material or energetic - with subdivisions such as between acoustic, optical or electrical energies (Eco, 1988). These different channels carry representations according to their spatial and temporal properties. Acoustic media do not require the source to be in contact with the receiver and visual ones perform their task only within a distance, contrary to tactile and gustative signs. Acoustic, tactile and visual channels carry much more structured information than flavors and smells etc.

Early symbolic R-media can be analyzed along such lines, with notions such as disruption and stability through time of the representations they convey. Being acoustic, language can be disrupted if noises cover the emission of signals. Visual R-media can be disrupted by darkness. Words uttered basically don't last; material media last longer and can be further distinguished: as markers of social identity, scarifications and tattoos live much longer than body paintings or ornaments, and don't suffer "disruption". Engravings can go past human life, possibly forming external memories and allowing cumulative knowledge.

In addition to these primary properties of R-media, others relate to the way we conceptualize R-media, and how we derive *elaborated* attributes from primary

ones, whether intentionally or not. As humans, we build our comprehension of R-media as much as we extract from their primary nature.
Hence, the choice of shells as body ornaments and the signification they became to express were perhaps motivated by an aesthetic feeling for their 'primary' shapes and colors. However, such conceptualizations are uneasy to derive from primary features, and may actually be partly independent from them. As they do not link directly to the medium but rather coexist with it for some interpreters, they prove difficult to investigate without direct account from these interpreters. Resorting here to more recent, better known proxies can then prove useful.

We have introduced the main lines of a framework in which to analyze processes of semiosis. Additional ideas cannot be presented for lack of space but a coherent context can be assembled which provide rich conceptual tools to analyze past situations. We will now see how some of these tools may be borrowed from studies of modern R-media, and how they can inform us regarding a possible evolutionary and historical scenario for semiotic systems.

3. From the analysis of modern R-media to early semiotic systems

3.1. *Elaborated features in studies of modern R-media*

An interesting proxy for the emergence of early semiotic systems is the long lasting and evolving relationship between painting and photography. Entering into its details exceeds the limited scope of this paper, but the main argument can be summarized as follows. In addition to the quest for a precise and conform representation of reality, photographs have very early been looking for ways to grant the durability of the pictures taken. The achievement of virtually infinite mechanical reproducibility has been seen by Benjamin (1936) as a major evolution or even revolution in Art. The core issue is the divorce that takes place with photography between the *truth* of a representation and its *authenticity*. The cause lies in the displacement induced first by the autonomous process of production of the photographic picture, and then by the cheap mechanical reproduction of this initial image. Such a procedure shifts the value granted by the unicity of the painted masterpiece, its *hic* and *nunc* and the aura it provides to it, to a different domain; the talent of the painter cannot be transferred to the photograph. In other words, it is not because a picture is a true representation that it is felt as authentic; its value has to come from elsewhere.

In this framework, truth and authenticity can be interpreted as elaborated features of the photographic medium, and further details could show how they shaped the various directions taken by photography in the 20th century.
Does it make sense to consider *elaborated* features such as truth or authenticity when it comes to prehistoric R-media? We argue that our ancestors had indeed similar judgments in mind. A first step to assess this idea is to describe known symbolic manifestations, before looking for possible test beds.
If one looks for example more specifically at the symbolic expression of social identity, language seems to be a strong competitor given its productivity and internal consistency. However, language shares with photography the cheap reproducibility of its content, and therefore a low degree of authenticity. Since faking with words is easy, it is difficult to grant authenticity to someone's speech, however articulate its content. Contrastively, irreversible and painful body alterations can be granted more authenticity given these primary features. In between, the time needed to collect and prepare necklaces made of rare shell beads gives value to these ornaments. Given that various aspects of social identity exist on different time scales – inclusion into a group for a brief time period, long-term affiliation to a clan or family –, it makes sense to distribute their expression along R-media depending on their primary and elaborated features. A consequence would be that different archaeological remains reflect varying temporal degrees of group membership. This could perhaps be tested in terms of spatial distribution with respect to known group sizes.

3.2. *An evolutionary road to modern symbols and R-media*

It is difficult to envisage the symbolic ability as something else than a nothing-or-all capacity, as reflected by the broad category of symbols used in many publications. However, the continuous evolution of modern media and earlier glimpses into the typology of signs point to the possibility of a gradual trajectory leading to modern semiotic capacities.
A plausible scenario could start with the endowment of natural signs with a secondary function of signification. This can be the case with untransformed perforated shell beads, where a secondary signification is 'simply' applied to a natural object. Intentionally perforating the shells, applying coloring pigments or performing other alterations would then be a step further, with a modification of the primary features of the medium in relation to its secondary signification.
An evolving evaluation of the primary and elaborated features of R-media could also explain some evolutions. Kuhn & Stiner (2007b) have for example made some proposals regarding the use of colorants and ornaments during prehistory,

and the shift in predominance that occurred from the firsts to the seconds. This is explained by the fact that colorants were unconstrained, fugitive, hard to assess in quality and uneasily transferable, while ornaments were standardized, durable, transferable, and showed varying degrees of investment.

A significant change may have taken place with the first productions of artificial signs. According to this distinction, geometric engravings on ochres or bones differ significantly from the previous elements, a semiotic distinction not commonly operated by prehistorians. The degree of complexity in the production of these R-media would then have increased, from simple engravings to refined parietal art. Primary features may also have been better conceptualized, as exemplified by how the volumes of cave walls were used to create more 'alive' animals.

Interestingly for a scenario fitting the gradualness of natural selection, individuals with differing degrees of mastery of signs can be considered. It is indeed enough to have some people producing signs for them to be used in a group where not all understand the nature of semiosis. Experiments with a variety of animals, from apes to parrots to dolphins, have demonstrated that animals can learn symbols, manipulate and even transmit them (Savage-Rumbaugh et al., 2001; Fouts, 1973), even if they are not able to produce them in the first place – something our ancestors did with language. Natural selection could thus have gradually favored individuals with a refined understanding of semiosis, until it became ubiquitous in human populations (as today).

4. Conclusions

We have outlined a semiotic framework to consider early symbolic activities in the light of modern ones. This approach calls for refined analyses and more concepts related to R-media, like Bolter & Gruisin (1988)'s *immediacy* and *hypermediacy*. All in all, it highlights the complexity of the processes of semiosis which continuously takes place in human societies. It also suggests that the development of a semiotic capacity was a crucial step in human evolution, but that it matured only gradually. Investigating the semiotic nature of archaeological remains is hence a useful window to human cognitive evolution.

References

Benjamin, W. (1935). L'oeuvre d'art à l'ère de la reproductibilité technique. In A. Rouillé (Ed.), *La photographie : texte et controverse*. Macula.

Bolter, J. D. & Gruisin, R. (1999). *Remediation: Understanding New Media*. Cambridge & London: MIT Press.

Coolidge, F. L. & Wynn, T. (2005). Working memory, its executive functions, and the emergence of modern thinking. *Cambridge Archaeological. Journal* 15(1):5-26.
d'Errico, F., Henshilwood, C., & Nilssen, P. (2001). An engraved bone fragment from ca. 75 kyr Middle Stone Age levels at Blombos Cave, South Africa: implications for the origin of symbolism and language. *Antiquity, 75*, 309-18.
d'Errico F., & Stringer, C. B. (2011). Evolution, revolution or saltation scenario for the emergence of modern culture. *Philosophical Transactions of the Royal Society B, 336*, 1060-1069.
d'Errico, F., Vanhaeren, M., & Wadley, L. (2008). Possible shell beads from the Middle Stone Age layers of Sibudu Cave, South Africa. *Journal of Archaeological Science, 35*, 2675-2685.
Eco, U. (1988). *Le Signe*. Bruxelles, Belgium: Labor.
Fouts, R. (1973). Acquisition and testing of gestural signs in four young chimpanzees. *Science, 180*, 978-980.
Henshilwood, C. S., d'Errico, F., & Watts I. (2009). Engraved ochres from the Middle Stone Age levels at Blombos Cave, South Africa. *Journal of Human Evolution, 57(1),* 27-47.
Henshilwood, C. S. & Dubreuil, B. (2009). Reading the artifacts: gleaning language skills from the Middle Stone age in southern Africa. In R. Botha & C. Knight (eds.), *The cradle of language vol.2* (pp. 61-92). Oxford: OUP.
Kuhn, S. L. & Stiner, M. C. (2007a). Paleolithic Ornaments: Implications for Cognition, Demography and Identity. *Diogenes* 214:40-48.
Kuhn, S. L. & Stiner, M. C. (2007b). Body Ornamentation as Information Technology: Towards an Understanding of the Significance of Early Beads. In P. Mellars et al. (eds.), *Rethinking the Human Revolution: New Behavioural and Biological Perspectives on the Origin and Dispersal of Modern Humans* (pp. 45-54). Cambridge: McDonald Institute for Archaeological Research.
Peirce, C. S. (1935). *Collected Papers*. Harvard University Press.
Rossano, M. J. (2010). Making Friends, Making Tools, and Making Symbols. *Current Anthropology* 51(S1):S89-S98.
Savage-Rumbaugh, E. S., Shanker, S. G., & Taylor, T. J. (2001). *Apes, Language, and the Human Mind*. Oxford: Oxford University Press.
Sebeok, T. A. & Umiker-Sebeok, J. (eds.) (1992). *Biosemiotics. The Semiotic Web 1991*. Berlin & New York: Mouton de Gruyter.
Vanhaeren, M., d'Errico, F., Stringer, C., James, S.L., Todd, J.A., & Mienis, H. K. (2006). Middle Paleolithic Shell Beads in Israel and Algeria. *Science, 312*, 1785-1788.
Wiessner, P. (1984) Reconsidering the Behavioral Basis for Style: A Case Study among the Kalahari San. *J. of Anthropological Archaeology* 3: 190-234.
Willhelm, S. M. (1974). On Leslie A. White's Concept of the Symbol: A Reinterpretation. *Current Anthropology* 15(4): 463-466.

SEA CROSSINGS ARE AN UNRELIABLE INDICATOR OF LANGUAGE ABILITY IN HOMINIDS

CORY CUTHBERTSON[1]

Flat 5, 12-14, Queen Victoria Street, Reading, RG1 1TG, United Kingdom
corystade@gmail.com

LUKE MCCROHON[1]

Graduate School of Information Science and Technology, The University of Tokyo, Hongo, Bunkyo-Ku, Tokyo, 113-0033, Japan
luke.mccrohon@gmail.com

Sea crossings are among the indicators researchers have used to infer language ability in prehistoric hominid populations; however, in order for a sea crossing to be a reliable indicator of the presence of language, researchers must show that it was not accidental, and that an intentional crossing in fact requires language. We will make the case that to date, neither of these criteria has been sufficiently demonstrated, and that sea crossings remain, at best, an unreliable indicator of language ability in hominids.

1. Ocean Crossings and Language

A central problem facing language evolution researchers is the lack of direct evidence concerning the linguistic abilities of our ancestors. Researchers are forced to rely on indirect evidence such as traces of behaviours observable in the archaeological record. It has been argued that evidence of behaviours requiring symbolic thought or complex planning can be used as indicators of language ability. For example perforated shell beads found at Blombos Cave in South Africa have been argued to demonstrate a communal understanding of symbols, which is claimed to require a common linguistic medium (Henshilwood, d'Errico, Vanhaeren, van Niekerk & Jacobs, 2004). Another example taken as evidence for the presence of linguistic ability is the migration of hominid populations across open water, the canonical example of this being the migration of modern humans to Australia roughly 40,000 years ago (Balme, Davidson, McDonald, Stern, & Veth, 2009). This migration is generally interpreted as

[1] Both authors contributed equally to the preparation of this paper.

having been a planned sea crossing by a group of watercraft using individuals. It has been argued that language is a prerequisite for both the high level of social coordination and the degree of long term planning this would require (Davidson & Noble, 1992; Coupé & Hombert, 2005; Morwood & Cogill-Koez, 2007), and that therefore the first migrants to Australia must have possessed language.

The archaeological record prior to the invention of writing can provide, at most, indirect evidence of language use, and so its interpretation is conditional on a number of assumptions. In the case of interpreting the evidence from sea crossings, these assumptions include a) that these crossing were intentional, and b) that intentional sea crossings require language. We will make the case that neither of these assumptions has been justified for the Australian crossing. Our central aim will be to show that evidence of sea crossing alone, regardless of the distances or species involved, is not a reliable indicator of any particular degree of linguistic ability.

2. Rafting Events

As mentioned, one of the key assumptions underlying claims that certain prehistoric sea crossings required language is that these crossings were purposeful. While this may be the case, it cannot simply be assumed. In this section we review a number of "accidental" ways in which species have crossed water barriers, and explore whether these methods would also have been available to prehistoric humans and other hominid species.

Species can cross water barriers in many ways, such as by swimming, getting swept out to sea by extreme weather or a tsunami, or drifting across on floating debris (Houle, 1999). If enough individuals make the crossing, a species could establish a new breeding population on the other side of the barrier. Another possibility is transport on "floating islands", masses of decaying vegetation that become host to the growth of plants and the occasional animal species (Trivedy, Sharma, Goel, & Gopal, 1978). As floating islands can reach significant sizes, it is thought that a single island could be washed out to sea, transporting with it a viable breeding population.

New World monkeys (Platyrrhines) have African origins. The founding population is thought to have been carried across the Atlantic Ocean to South America on such a floating island or islands (Houle, 1999). Madagascan mammals, such as lemurs and fossas, also have African origins; Madagascar has been separated from the African mainland since long before the arrival of these mammals, and an over-sea route is their only possible origin (Simpson, 1940). We mention these examples of accidental rafting on floating islands because it has been suggested that early hominids may have crossed water barriers in just this way (Smith, 2001), which would say nothing of the linguistic ability of the individuals involved.

3. Viable Population Sizes

While a floating island may have been able to transport a sizeable population, other types of unintentional crossings are unlikely to transport many individuals at a time. Two questions to ask are then, how many individuals would need to be transported to form a genetically viable population, and are any of the above-mentioned methods capable of transporting such a population?

A number of difficulties exist in determining the minimal viable population (MVP) size for any species, let alone for one in which whose behaviour in its natural environment is unobservable (such as prehistoric hominids). Harcourt (2002) studied the MVP of a number of primate species based on empirical data of their distribution across island environments of varying sizes, and produced estimates ranging between tens of individuals for some lineages to tens of thousands for others. His data also suggested that large species on average require a larger MVP, and it is thus likely that the minimum isolated viable hominid population size was at least in the hundreds, if not the thousands.

MVP may not however be the correct measure to determine the initial size of a viable founder population, as it assumes the complete isolation of that population. If there was continued immigration, this reduces the required population size needed to maintain viable genetic diversity. The immigration required to maintain a certain level of variation is actually independent of the population size (Mills & Allendorf, 1996). Furthermore, even low levels of immigration can have a great effect; in what is called the One-Migrant-per-Generation-Rule, an addition of a single individual per generation is sufficient to maintain approximately 80% of species wide genetic variation (ibid.).

If we assume a single individual was transported across a water barrier to the new population every generation, we no longer need to assume a particular minimum initial population size. So long as an initial breeding population could be established, the subsequent immigration of one individual per generation would keep the population viable. This makes the scenarios for unintentional migration far more likely than they would first appear. Adding to this, Lacy (1987) has shown that the inflow of immigrants need not be regular; a larger number of immigrants every few generations would have had the same effect as a regular flow of one individual per generation. In the seismically active Southeast Asian region, a tsunami every century or so, carrying four or five individuals seems plausible. Also, while it may seem unlikely that subsequent raftings would deposit individuals in close enough geographic proximity to join existing settlements, the fact that all groups would have been subject to similar tidal and meteorological forces makes this significantly more likely.

Having dealt with the question of genetic viability, we now turn to the question of population size physically required to found a new settlement. The historical example of the colonization of Pitcairn Island suggests that only a small population may be necessary. The island was colonized in 1790 by the Bounty mutineers (Young, 2003), who comprised a population of only 26 individuals (15 men and 11 women). Despite their small number, they managed to survive in an isolated, unfamiliar and relatively harsh environment for several generations in complete isolation from the outside world. Anecdotal as this evidence may be, it suggests that an initial population need not be that large to successfully form a community capable of surviving for multiple generations.

Although at first glance it seems improbable that a viable population could be accidentally transported across a water barrier, the fact that individuals need not be transported at once makes this scenario far more plausible. Considering this and the various modes of unintentional sea crossing identified in the previous section, we have shown that there is a real alternative to a sea crossing being the result of intentional actions.

4. Ocean Crossings in Earlier Hominid Species

Stone tools dated to 880,000 years ago have been found on the island of Flores in Indonesia, which would have required a sea crossing of several kilometers to reach. This crossing has often been explained in the literature as accidental, even by the same researchers that claim the Australian crossing must have been intentional: "Currently the best guess may be a series of freakish events, such as a tsunami washing a group out to sea on flotsam, and sea currents then depositing this group on islands "downstream". Far-fetched though this may seem, the time-frames involved make statistically vanishingly-rare events a possibility." (Morwood & Cogill-Koez, 2007, p. 56).

The reluctance to infer intentionality (and hence linguistic abilities) to Flores hominids, in the same way it is inferred to modern humans and their crossing to Australia, is due to other differences observed in the archaeological record such as their comparatively primitive tool kit (Davidson & Noble 1992, Morwood & Cogill-Koez, 2007). Some researchers, though, namely Bednarick (Bower, 2003), maintain that H. erectus did possess seafaring capabilities and arrived on Flores by raft.

On the island of Crete in the Mediterranean Sea, a number of Lower Paleolithic sites have been identified which date to at least 130,000 years ago, and potentially much earlier (Strasser et al., 2010). As Crete has been an island for circa 5,000,000 years, this would have necessitated a sea crossing of some kind, as with Flores, or modern humans' arrival in Australia. Europe's own colonization route by archaic Homo has also been questioned (Bailey, 2009). While the main theory is that hominids first entered Europe through the Levant, with evidence at sites like Dmanisi in Georgia (Anton & Swisher, 2004), the earliest European sites are actually centered around Spain, at sites such as Atapuerca (Cameron & Groves, 2004). This raises the possibility of a short sea crossing from Morocco to Gibraltar, although whether this route, if used, was intentional or not, would be as open to debate as with the rest of the examples of sea crossings discussed above.

Davidson and Noble (1992) point out that H. erectus was present in Java for over a million years, yet there are no signs that erectus or any other primates migrated to Australia, and therefore it is unlikely that Flores was reached in this way. However, this could speak more to the lifestyle of modern Homo sapiens without any hint at their language capacity. If modern humans were exploiting marine resources, and spent more time close to the water than Homo erectus, there would have been significantly more opportunity for them to be washed out to sea. With more knowledge of the sea, they might have known not to drink salt water, and resisted poisoning better if washed away. And finally, they might have simply been better swimmers. None of these skills or behaviours necessarily indicates language use.

The archaeological record provides evidence that several other hominid species were able to successfully migrate across water barriers, but these crossings have generally been dismissed as accidental on the basis of other archaeological indicators. If, however, we are to conclude that water crossings are conclusive evidence of language ability, then we cannot apply this reasoning selectively. Either these earlier crossing also demonstrate language ability, or we have to admit the possibility that later H. sapiens crossings were also accidental.

5. Do Intentional Sea Crossings Require Language?

If we do accept that a particular sea crossing was intentional, it still needs to be demonstrated that this implies language ability. Gil (2006, p. 124), in his analysis of colloquial Malay/Indonesian, argues that, "much of the observational complexity of contemporary human grammar has no obvious function pertaining to the development and maintenance of modern human civilization." This raises the possibility that language is not necessary for endeavors such as raft building. Davidson and Noble (1992) make the case that raft construction requires forward planning and social coordination, and that raft builders would have therefore required language; this however is an untested, and quite possibly untestable, claim. We do not know which aspects of our cognition depend on language, and cannot prove that a language-less hominid would have been incapable of building a raft.

Hominids are thought to have utilized marine resources well into the past, as can be seen by Neanderthals' exploitation of marine mammals at Gibraltar (Stringer et al., 2008), and early modern humans in South Africa (Marean et al., 2007). It is conceivable that their food procurement strategies included the use of rafts, which would imply a shorter time depth of intentionality for raft construction, weakening arguments that the usage of rafts implies language. If coastal populations possessed knowledge of raft construction and navigation, they could be capable of an intentional sea crossing.

6. Explaining Gene Dispersal

In the particular case of the migration to Australia, we do believe this constitutes strong evidence that the original colonizers possessed language, but not because the migration involved a sea crossing. Rather, we think that because of Australia's geographical isolation, combined with the linguistic abilities of its modern indigenous populations, the original migrants must have also been capable of language. If the original population had not possessed language, then we would have to explain how their decedents do. The only two possibilities would be that the language of modern indigenous Australians is the result of parallel evolution, or that the genes for language were introduced into Australia at a later date. If language were dependent on only a single gene, then these scenarios would be plausible, but given its apparent dependence on multiple genes, we consider both scenarios highly unlikely and conclude that the original migrants must have thus possessed fully modern language before their arrival.

The above argument ignores the theoretical possibility that the original migrants were biologically capable of language but did not have access to language culturally. There are two reasons why we think this is unlikely; first there is no known example of a Homo sapiens population observed to have lost any significant degree of its cultural linguistic endowment (it is even generally accepted that all observed languages are of a similar level of complexity). Second, the example of Nicaraguan Sign Language shows that complex cultural language can emerge very quickly from a state of languagelessness, suggesting it is unlikely that a genetically capable population would have existed for any prolonged period of time without language.

7. Conclusion

We do not dispute that the original migrants to Australia were capable of language; we just do not believe that this conclusion can be reached solely based on evidence of sea crossings alone. Australia's geographic and genetic isolation, combined with the language ability of its modern populations, is far stronger evidence that the initial migrants were language users.

Rafting has been offered as an explanation of "accidental" sea crossings in other species. To date, nothing in the literature has ruled out this as a possible means of the introduction of early humans into Australia. The fact that this was a crossing by modern humans, and therefore more likely intentional, is poor reasoning. If sea crossings are evidence of language capabilities, then other species must be treated in the same way, and not simply discredited. For sea crossings to be used as evidence of language ability, it has to be determined that particular crossings were intentional, and that intentional crossings are only possible with language use. Until researchers sufficiently demonstrate these two criteria, sea crossings will remain an unreliable indicator of language ability.

References

Anton, S. C., & Swisher, C. C. (2004). *Early dispersals of Homo from Africa. Annual Review of Anthropology, 33,* 271-296.

Bailey, G. (2009). The red sea, coastal landscapes, and hominin dispersals. In Petraglia, M. D., and Rose, J. I. (Eds.), *The Evolution of Human Populations in Arabia. Vertebrate Palaeobiology and Palaeoanthropology* (pp. 15-37). London: Springer.

Balme, J., Davidson, I., McDonald, J., Stern, N. & Veth, P. (2009). Symbolic behaviour and the peopling of the southern arc route to Australia. *Quaternary International,* 202, 59-68.

Bower, B. (2003). Erectus Ahoy. Science News, 164, 248+250.

Cameron, D. W., & Groves, C. P. (2004). *Stones, bones and molecules: "Out of Africa" and human origins.* London: Elsevier.

Coupé, C. & Hombert, J. (2005). Les Premières Traversées Maritimes. In J. Hombert (Ed.), *Aux Origines des langues et du langage* (pp. 118-161). Fayard.

Davidson I., & Noble, W. (1992). Why the first colonization of the Australian region is the earliest evidence of modern human behaviour. *Archaeology in Oceania, 27*, 135-142.

Gil, D. (2006). How much grammar does it take to sail a boat? (Or, what can material artefacts tell us about the evolution of language?). In Smith, A. D. M., Smith, K., Ferrer-i-Cancho, R. (Eds.), *The evolution of language: Proceedings of the 7th international conference.* Singapore: World Scientific Press.

Harcourt, A. H. (2002). Empirical estimates of minimum viable population sizes for primates: Tens to tens of thousands? *Animal Conservation, 5*, 237-244.

Henshilwood, C., d'Errico, F., Vanhaerin, M., van Niekerk, K. & Jacobs, Z. (2004). Middle Stone Age shell beads from Africa. *Science*, 304, 404.

Houle, A. (1999). The origin of platyrrhines: An evaluation of the Antarctic Scenario and the Floating Island Model. *American Journal of Physical Anthropology 109*, 541-559.

Lacy, R. C. (1987). Loss of genetic diversity from managed populations: interacting effects of drift, mutation, immigration, selection and population sub-division. *Conservation Biology, 1*, 143-158.

Marean, C. W., Bar-Matthews, M., Bernatchez, J., Fisher, E., Goldberg, P., Herries, A., I., R., Jacobs, Z., Jerardino, A., Karkanas, P., Minichillo, T., Nilssen, P., J., Thompson, E., Watts, I., & Williams, H., M. (2007). Early human use of marine resources and pigment in South Africa during the Middle Pleistocene. *Nature 499*, 905-909.

Morewood, M. J., & Cogill-Koez, D. (2007). Homo on Flores: Some early implications for the evolution of language and cognition. In Schalley, A. C., and Khlentzos, D. (Eds.) *Mental States. Volume I: Evolution, function, nature* (pp. 43-73). Amsterdam: John Benjamins.

Simpson, G. G. (1940). Mammals and land bridges. *Journal of the Washington Academy of Sciences, 30*, 137–163.

Smith, J. M. B. (2001). Did early hominids cross sea gaps on natural rafts? In Metcalfe, I., Smith, J. M. B., Morwood, M., & Davidson, I. (Eds.) *Faunal and Floral Migrations and Evolution in SE Asia-Australasia* (pp. 409-416). Lisse: Balkema.

Strasser, T. F., Panagopoulou, E., Runnels, C. N., Murray, P. M., Thompson, N., Karkanas, P., McCoy, F. W., & Wegmann, K. W. (2010). Stone age seafaring in the Mediterranean: Evidence from the Plakias region for Lower Palaeolithic and Mesolithic habitation of Crete. *Hesperia, 79*, 145-190.

Stringer, C. B., Finlayson, J., C., Barton, R., N., E, Fernández-Jalvoe, Y., Cáceres, I., Sabin, R., C., Rhodesi, E., J. (2008). Neanderthal exploitation of marine mammals in Gibraltar. *PNAS 105*, 14319-14324.

Trivedy, R. K., Sharma, K. P., Goel, P. K., & Gopal, B. (1978). Some ecological observations on floating islands. *Hydrobiologia 60*, 187-190.

Wise, J. E. (1994). *Sole survivors of the sea.* Annapolis: Naval Institute Press.

Young, R. A. (2003). *Mutiny of the Bounty and the story of Pitcairn Island, 1790-1894.* Honolulu: University Press of the Pacific.

OVERGENERALIZATION OF VERBS
-
THE CHANGE OF THE GERMAN VERB SYSTEM

MARISA DELZ, BENJAMIN LAYER, SARAH SCHULZ, JOHANNES WAHLE
Seminar für Sprachwissenschaft, Universität Tübingen, Wilhelmstrasse 19, Tübingen, 72072, Germany
{marisa.delz; sarah.schulz; johannes.wahle}@student.uni-tuebingen.de
b-s-layer@gmx.de

In this paper we aim to show that the change in the German verb system from Middle High German to Modern High German can be simulated and partially explained within an Iterated Learning Model. We claim that the German verb system change is in part due to the frequency of usage and the process of overgeneralization. This is the first application of an Iterated Learning Model to simulate the change in real German language, so we are also able to test the quality of the Iterated Learning Model as an explanatory model for language change.

1. Introduction

The computational simulation of processes in natural language is a frequently discussed topic in current linguistics. The phenomenon debated here is the simplification of the German verb inflection system over time. In Middle High German the past tense forms were either strong, weak, or irregular. The strong verbs are divided into seven classes. Each of these classes is based upon a change pattern which allows us to determine which verb belongs to which class.

Our analysis of Modern High German is that the former strong and irregular classes have merged, leaving only two classes: the regular – formerly the weak – and the irregular verbs. The regular verbs form the major category, whilst the irregular verbs are far fewer. We claim that the loss of the ablaut classes was not a spontaneous occurrence in the language but a regular evolutionary process. We simulate this change using an Iterated Learning Model (ILM), similar as Kirby and Hurford's (2002). Our model could also be applied to other languages.

2. The Middle High German verb system

Middle High German verbs were either strong, weak, or irregular in the past tense. The strong verbs formed the past with *ablaut* (see Table 1) and the the weak verbs with the "*-(e)te*" suffix. For our purposes the verbs which have another past tense form were not taken into account.

The ablaut is a qualitative and/or quantitative change of the vowel. All of the seven classes originated in the Indo-European *e/o*-ablaut which were differentiated by sound change phenomena on the way to Middle High German. The regularities characterizing these ablaut classes are dependent upon the phonological environment of the stem vowel. The verbs belonging to the first class, for example, are characterized by the stem vowel /î/. There were two subclasses. If the vowel is followed by any consonant except /h/, /r/ or /w/, then an /ei/ is the stem vowel in the past form and the verb belongs to the first subclass (see Table 1). For the second subclass the stem vowel /î/ is followed by /h/, /r/ or /w/ and the stem vowel changes to /ê/ (see Table 1).[a]

Table 1. ablaut class I

	present		past			
class	*infinitive*	*1. Pers. Sing. Ind.*	*1. Pers. Sing. Ind.*	*1. Pers. Pl. Ind.*	*participle*	*translation*
I a	rîten	rîte	reit	riten	geriten	to ride
I b	zîhen	zîhe	zêch	zigen	gezigen	to blame

The past tense form of the weak Middle High German verbs was formed by adding the dental suffix *-(e)te* to the verb stem, e.g. legen - leg*ete* (to lay). The verbs which belong to this group are mostly formed secondarily, i.e. they were derived from strong verbs, adjectives or nouns; others are already primarily in the group of the weak verbs (c.f. Paul, 1989). The *-(e)te* suffix was probably the result of the cliticalization of the past tense form of *tuon* (to do) which was used before for a periphrastic past form (c.f. Hennings, 2003).

3. The Modern High German verb system

In Modern High German there are only two main categories of verbs: the irregular and the regular verbs, with the regular verbs forming the major category. The regular verbs form their past tense with the suffix *-(e)te* (c.f. Eisenberg, 2009, p. 449), like the weak verbs in Middle High German. This rule facilitates the German grammar and makes it easier for learners to learn the verbal inflection. The irregular verbs are far fewer. This category is actually divided into two subcategories, the strong verbs and the irregular verbs. The irregular verbs have an ablaut and the same suffix as the regular verbs in the past tense, namely the suffix *-(e)te*, e.g. denken (to think)- d*a*ch*te*. These verbs are also called mixed conjugations (c.f. Eisenberg, 2009, p. 454). The strong verbs are verbs with a clearly different past tense form, e.g. reiten (to ride)- *ritt*. We do not include this distinction in our analysis. Both subcategories belong to the category of irregular verbs. Unlike the

[a]Paul (1989) uses a different characteristic feature for each class to build the ablaut classes but the results are the same.

regular verbs, the past tense forms of the irregular verbs need to be saved in the mental lexicon.

Over time, the group of the regular verbs has increased and the group of the irregular verbs decreased. One reason for this change is the frequency of usage. Irregular verbs have a higher frequency of usage than regular verbs (c.f. Nübling, 2008, p. 57): most of the irregular verbs belong to the basic vocabulary of the language (c.f. Eisenberg, 2009, p. 440). Although they need to be saved in the mental lexicon, it is worthwhile for a learner to memorize the morphological forms of these high frequency verbs. The regular verbs are often less frequent; it is therefore more economical to form them via a rule (c.f. Pinker & Prince, 1994). One more reason for this development is the frequency of types. The regular verbs have a higher type frequency than the irregular verbs, because new verbs in a language are mainly derivations of nouns, adjectives, or names and inflected regularly, e.g. voll (full)- füllen, füll*te*. Adopted verbs from French or English are inflected regularly, e.g. to jog- joggen, jogg*te*. Less frequent irregular verbs have mostly moved to the category of weak verbs (c.f. Eisenberg, 2009, p. 456).

These factors have caused the increase in the regular verbs and the decrease of the irregular ones. Although the irregular verbs have become fewer, they will never disappear, because they belong to the basic vocabulary and their high frequency of usage thus protects them. There is a statistic illustrating this reduction. In Old High German, there are 349 irregular verbs, in Middle High German 339, and in Modern High German just 169 irregulars left (c.f. Nübling, 2008, p. 213).

4. The Iterated Learning Model

Our account of this phenomenon is based on the idea of iterated learning. The central element of every ILM is a learning algorithm allowing generalization over learned forms. There are two competing mechanisms: the holistic one, just looking at the data and saving it, and the generalizing one, comparing the data and calculating a probability for each inflection form. To provide such learning, different algorithms have been used. The most frequent ones are based on neuronal networks (c.f. Kirby & Hurford, 2002; Smith, Kirby, & Brighton, 2003) and grammar induction (c.f. Kirby & Hurford, 2002).

The ILM was invented to show that languages are shaped, rather than by an inborn, specialized language capability, by the way they are passed from generation to generation. The teachers learn the language the preceding generation uses and pass this learned language on to the next generation and so on. The crucial term in this context is that of the *bottleneck*. The bottleneck describes the narrow connection between the languages of the teacher and the learner, i.e. the language of a population to which new learners are exposed and the language internalized by a certain learner. The language of the teacher influences the learner's language and the learner's language will become a teacher language, so every language state adopts both teacher and learner roles.

Neither reception nor production is complete: no speaker produces all possible phrases and none perceives all phrases he will possibly produce. For example, a speaker of a language is able to inflect several thousand verbs correctly, even if he has never heard all of the possible forms. He will abduct rules from forms he knows and will try to build the required form by using these rules. During the process of passing over the language from one generation to another, regularities may develop (c.f. Dowman, Kirby, & Griffiths, 2006) and even compositionality (c.f. Smith et al., 2003), irregularity (c.f. Kirby, 2001) and recursion (c.f. Kirby & Hurford, 2002).

5. Statistical Database

To get a realistic simulation of the development of the German verb system we strove to construct an adequate database. Ours is based on an analysis of the digitized Lexer (Burch, 2002) and Ruoff (1981). The search engine of Burch (2002) provides a mechanism which permits the classification of verbs by ablaut classes. The values for the verb classes are shown in the statistics in Table 2. The proportions of the ablaut classes were maintained in the input file of our model. We took the verbs and their frequency values of Ruoff (1981) and added the historically correct ablaut class.

Table 2. Statistic of Middle High German verbs

		absolute	relative
complete		10879	100%
regular		9727	89.41%
irregular (strong)		1152	10.59%
of these	ablaut class		
	1	238	2.19%
	2	171	1.58%
	3	288	2.65%
	4	99	0.91%
	5	115	1.06%
	6	96	0.88%
	7	145	1.33%

6. The model

We developed a simulation of the process of overgeneralization (Onnis, Roberts, & Chater, 2002). The model simulates the change of verb classes from Middle High German to Modern High German. It includes three main parameters: the frequency of the verbs, the degree of restriction at the bottleneck and the number of iterations, i.e. the number of generations. Furthermore, the population at any one time consists of just one agent teaching the language and one agent learning the language.

The overgeneralization mechanism relies mainly on the frequency of the inflection classes, so that the frequency of a verb has a strong influence on its evolution. We keep the verb list and the frequency values for simplicity constant over the generations. We start off with a database containing 327 verbs. Every learner has to assign an inflection class to every verb. A final verb inflection distribution for the whole database is to be found in every generation. The whole vocabulary must be learned before a learner becomes a teacher. That means that the teacher's vocabulary consists of two parts: a part that was learned by hearing a verb and saving it into the memory and another part compiled by overgeneralization.

The assignment to an inflection class is the only dynamic structure in this model. We start with a realistic distribution of verb inflection classes and update it every generation. Every teacher can only teach what he has learned including the inflection that was learned by overgeneralization. This model first runs through the process of one generation and iterates over it. The procedure of one iteration step is shown in Figure 1. It provides the results of every iteration step as its output. The output shows the distribution of the verb inflection class of every learner generation after the overgeneralization.

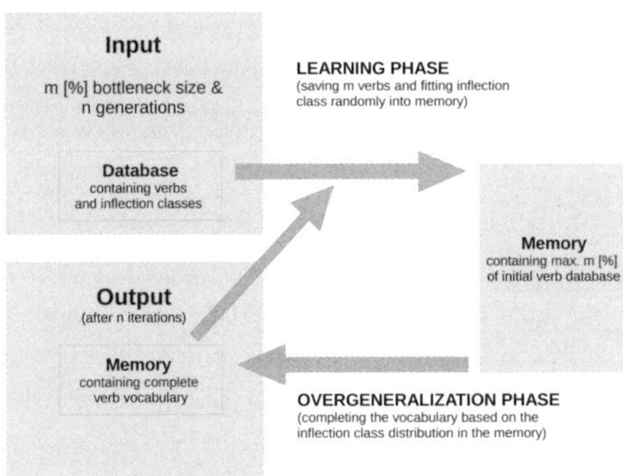

Figure 1. Architecture of the ILM of verb overgeneralization.

Once a word was heard it is put into the learner's memory, which is the basis for the calculation of the probability of an inflection class for the overgeneralization step. Verbs were selected at random (with replacement) out of the pool of 327 for transmission from the teacher to the learner. A bottleneck size is defined by the number of verbs taught. A value of 100% means that exactly 327 randomly chosen verb tokens were taught in a given generation. After the learning step a distribution of the inflection classes is calculated dependent on the already learned vocabulary. This distribution builds the foundation for the overgeneralization probabilities. That means that the heard verbs are learnt by being saved into memory but the missing verbs and their inflection classes are extrapolated on the basis of the verb distribution saved in memory.

At this point reference should be made to the structure of the database and the implementation of inflection classes. The memory is structured in such a way that it does not contain inflected verbs, but the information about the inflection class a verb belongs to. These inflection classes are in turn related to the verb database via parallelism. The database is only used as a reference list. The computation itself is abstracted from a specific language.

7. Analysis

Running the algorithm over our data set of 327 different verbs, the output graph (see Figure 2)[b] shows the tendency that one can expect considering the development in the actual German language. Each individual result is however subject to probabilistic fluctuation. To eliminate these we averaged over 100 different outputs. While several of the strong inflection classes die out, others remain stable after some time of decrease, and the class of weak inflected verbs grows and approaches some threshold depending on the bottleneck size. Due to the the size of the database the seven ablaut classes are all fairly small (see Table 2), so that no clear boundaries can be seen in our output at the beginning. But nonetheless the graph shows the general development of the German verb system, the increase of the class of the weak verbs and the decrease of the others.

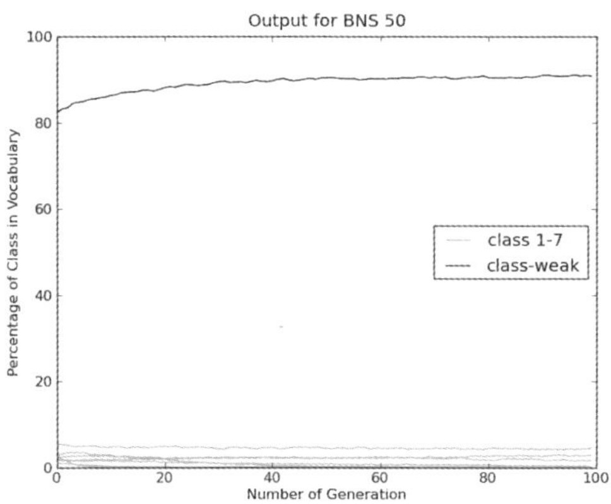

Figure 2. Example output with a bottleneck size of 50% .

The size of the bottleneck provides a way to influence the resulting graph. Augmenting the bottleneck size results in more stable plots, particularly when raising it above 100%, as this means that 327 verbs are drawn from the pool. In practice this means that only slightly above 100 different verbs are taught. Reducing the size of the bottleneck leads to a rapid disappearance of classes, see

[b]We used the same color for the seven abalut classes, because they form a single class in Modern High German (see Section 3).

Figure 3. Outputs that produced realistic graphs were created for bottleneck sizes between 50% and 100%. Taking a look at the actual verbs in the last generations it stands out that mainly the frequent verbs persist in the strong inflection classes over the generations while the rare ones tend to change their classes.

8. Conclusion

The ILM seems to offer an adequate framework to replicate the development in the German inflection system over the last 800 years. The learning and generalization mechanism we used is based on the simple assumption that there is a tendency to inflect unknown verbs in the same way as most others. The model reflects the fact that high frequency verbs can be learned whereas low frequency verbs are derived by generalization. Thus frequency seems to play an important role in the change of the German verb inflection system:[c] although our model is too simple to simulate the actual processes because it is just based on this one parameter, it was nevertheless able to reflect the historical facts. The partiality of learning through a bottleneck creates space for a similarity effect, a quasi-magnetic attraction of forms from smaller classes to bigger ones. The complex inflection system based on verb classes disappears and changes to a system with only regular and irregular forms, whereby the irregular forms are remnants of the Middle High German ablaut classes. The model is not only able to illustrate the massive rise of regular verbs in the German verb inflection system but also provides an explanation for the switch of a few verbs from one strong verb class to another. For the preterite-present 'wizzen' (to know) which has different possible past tense forms, today's strong form prevails. That could be due to the influence of high frequency words of the same inflection class. As time passes, the distribution of verbs levels off. Our model predicts no further crucial changes in the German verb inflection system. Frequency keeps the current class of strong verbs relatively constant. Our model can be used as a basis for further research on this topic.

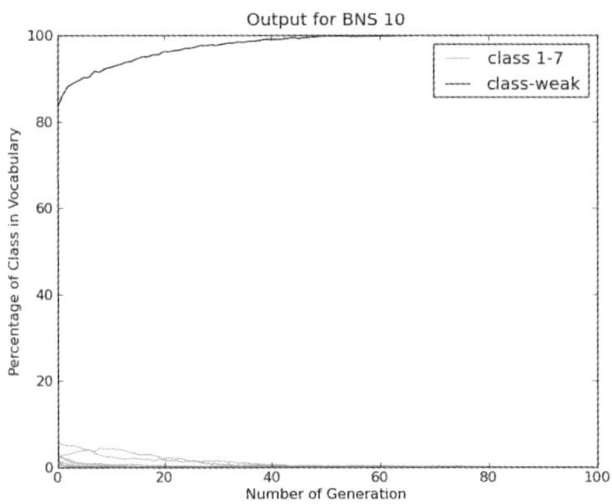

Figure 3. Example output with a bottleneck size of 10% .

[c]Hare and Elman (1994) shows the same effect for the English verb system.

Acknowledgements

The authors would like to thank Michael Franke, Sam Featherston and three anonymous reviewers for their helpful comments and corrections. Remaining mistakes are ours. Furthermore the Authors would like to thank Gerhard Jäger, Detmar Meurers and Erhard Hinrichs for their financial support which enabled us to take part at the conference.

References

Burch, T. H. (Ed.). (2002). *Mittelhochdeutsche Wörterbücher im Verbund.* Stuttgart: Hirzel [u.a.].

Dowman, M., Kirby, S., & Griffiths, T. L. (2006). Innateness and culture in the evolution of language. In *Proceedings of the 6th international conference on the evolution of language* (p. 83-90).

Eisenberg, P. (Ed.). (2009). *Duden - Die Grammatik.* Mannheim: Dudenverl.

Hare, M., & Elman, J. (1994). Learning and morphological change. *Cognition*, 61-98.

Hennings, T. (2003). *Einführung in das Mittelhochdeutsche.* Walter de Gruyter.

Kirby, S. (2001). Spontaneous evolution of linguistic structure: an iterated learning model of the emergence of regularity and irregularity. *IEEE Transactions on Evolutionary Computation*, *5*(2), 102-110.

Kirby, S., & Hurford, J. (2002). The emergence of linguistic structure: An overview of the iterated learning model. In A. Cangelosi & D. Parisi (Eds.), *Simulating the evolution of language* (p. 121-148). London: Springer Verlag.

Nübling, D. (Ed.). (2008). *Historische Sprachwissenschaft des Deutschen: eine Einführung in die Prinzipien des Sprachwandels* (2. überarb. Aufl. ed.). Tübingen: Narr.

Onnis, L., Roberts, M., & Chater, N. (2002). Simplicity: A cure for overregularizations in language acquisition? In *Proceedings of the 24th conference of the cognitive science society.* (p. 720-725). Mahwah, NJ: Lawrence Erlbaum.

Paul, H. (1989). *Mittelhochdeutsche Grammatik.* Niemeyer.

Pinker, S., & Prince, A. (1994). Regular and irregular morphology and the psychological status of rules of grammar. In S. D. Lima (Ed.), *The reality of linguistic rules.* Amsterdam [u.a.]: Benjamins.

Ruoff, A. (1981). *Häufigkeitswörterbuch gesprochener Sprache: gesondert nach Wortarten, alphabetisch, rückläufig alphabetisch und nach Häufigkeit geordnet.* Max Niemeyer Verlag.

Smith, K., Kirby, S., & Brighton, H. (2003). Iterated learning: a framework for the emergence of language. *Artificial Life*, *9*.

WAS THE INTRODUCTION OF WRITING AN EVOLUTIONARY TRANSITION?

JAN TERJE FAARLUND

Centre for the Study of Mind in Nature, University of Oslo, NO-0315 Oslo, Norway

The origin of human language has been considered a major transitions in evolutionary history. One fundamental property of human language is recursion, which may be considered part of Universal Grammar. Recursion as a universal property of language has been challenged by practitioners of various branches of linguistics and philology, who tend to consider complex sentence structure and subordination a recent development, connected to the introduction of writing and literacy. In this paper I will defend the hypothesis of a Language Faculty and a UG, of which recursion is a fundamental element, and which has remained a part of the biological endowment of *homo sapiens* since its origin as a separate species.

1. *Introduction*

The origin of human language has been considered one of the major transitions in evolutionary history, on a par with for example the transition from prokaryote to eukaryote cells, from solitary individuals to colonies, and from primate societies to human societies (Maynard Smith & Szatmáry 1999:16-18). As far as we know, this transition has taken place only once in the biological history of our planet, and it was unique to our own species. The main change involved in this transition was the externalization of cognitive and mental processes, human thinking, and the result was a discrete computational system including abstract symbols. That is, human language the way we know it today.

2. *Recursion*

Recursion is a fundamental property of human language, constituting a part of the human Language Faculty - conventionally represented as Universal Grammar (UG; Hauser et al. 2002). Recursion may take the form as in (1), where a complex unit X contains a unit of its own kind.

(1) $_X$[Y … X … Z]

The operation Merge takes as its input two elements, at least one of which may be a complex unit, a phrase, and yields a phrase as its output. Repeated application of this operation then yields *general recursion*. Merge is category-neutral, therefore every case of a phrase contained in a larger phrase is an instance of recursion (Nevis et al. 2009:366, n.11). Recursion must be distinguished from iteration or simple concatenation; being the result of the operation Merge, it involves a dependency relation.

Sentence embedding is a case of *specific* recursion, (2a) (Hulst 2010). Finite subordinate clauses are a special cases of embedding, (2b).

(2) a. $_{CP}$[...$_{VP}$[V CP]]
b. $_{CP}$[...TP... [$_{VP}$[V $_{CP}$[... TP]]]

Recursion as a universal property of language has been challenged by people skeptical to or opposed to the generative enterprise. One type of challenge comes from descriptions of the languages of present-day hunter-gatherers. Some such studies may give the impression that those languages lack recursion. In particular, the Amazonian language *Pirahã* has been claimed to lack recursion and grammatical subordination (Everett 2005, 2009). This claim is based on the misconception that the lack of finite subordinate clauses is evidence of lack of recursion. (Besides the more general fallacy of taking absence of evidence to constitute evidence of absence!) But as I have shown, sentence embedding is just a special case of recursion. In order to show that a language, e.g. Pirahã, lacks recursion, it must also be shown that it lacks any hierarchical structure, including c-command and scope relations. In fact, hierarchy and scope relations are easy to find in Everett's material, consider (3).

(3) kohoai-kabáob-áo ti gí 'ahoai-soog-abagaí
eat-finish-TEMP I you speak-DESID-FRUST.INIT
'When [I] finish eating, I want to speak to you'
(Everett 2005, 2009)

Here the suffix *-soog* 'want' has scope both over the verb stem 'speak', and over a temporal clause, marked by the suffix *-áo* (Nevis et al. 2009:379).
Another challenge to the theory of recursion as part of UG comes from practitioners of traditional grammar and philology, where there is a tradition of considering complex sentence structure and clausal subordination to be a recent development in the history of human language, connected to the introduction of writing and literacy. Therefore we should not expect to find recursion and

complexity in non-literate or preliterate languages. On this view, such languages would typically employ simple conjunction or concatenation where literate languages use subordination (Deutscher 2000, Sampson 2009). I suspect that this view is based on the fact that our earliest Indo-European written documents are renditions of orally transmitted narratives, with very few embedded clauses. But this view is based on the same misconception as in the previous case, namely that the lack of finite subordinate clauses is evidence of lack of recursion. In addition, there is an even more serious problem with this reasoning, namely the confusion of grammar with usage, and the failure to recognize that usage is heavily genre dependent. Grammar and usage are two different phenomena (Newmeyer 2003). Frequency of use is irrelevant to the description of the I-language. Thus an increase in the occurrence of a certain construction does not mean that a grammatical change has taken place. If we are discussing the human Language Faculty we are interested in the internalized grammar, the I-language of speakers and writers. We want to know whether their grammars have or have not, say, the possibility of finite embedded clauses. Whether or not they are used, and how frequently they are used, in a given context (and it always 'a given context' in ancient literature) is a different question altogether. Therefore, a statement like 'Biblical Hebrew made strikingly little use of subordinate clauses' (Sampson 2009:6-7) is not a statement about the grammar of Hebrew, and it is totally irrelevant to the question of recursion as a property of grammars. It follows that an increase in the frequency of a certain construction is not in itself an indication of a grammatical change. (It may frequently be the *cause* of grammatical change, but that is a different matter altogether.)

3. Complexity

The controversy over the possible or impossible universality of recursion, embedding and other features, is linked to the more general question of complexity in language. The idea that linguistic complexity, such as the use of subordinate clauses, is connected to literacy, culture, or degree of social complexity is not compatible with a hypothesis of UG as a species specific property of *homo sapiens*, nor with standard versions of the innateness hypothesis. According to this hypothesis, recursion, and thereby complex structures, have always been part of the human language faculty, and languages at all stages of civilization have had the opportunity of using complex structures. Opposite, the idea that complexity in grammar, not only in usage, is a function of literacy, would mean either that there is no universal language faculty in humans, or that recursion is not part of it. A third possibility is of course that an evolutionary change has taken place in some human communities since the invention of writing (ca. 5,000 years ago, which is a very brief period in evolutionary terms), possibly by epigenetic or horizontal cultural transmission rather than genetic. We know that some genetic changes have taken place in evolutionarily recent time, such as the development of lactose tolerance and immunity to certain diseases. I have neither the time nor the competence to discuss this further, and I don't know whether it is at all an interesting idea from a genetic perspective, making it at all be worth pursuing.

However we view the origin or universality of complexity, the major problem seems to be to define it. Since we here are concerned mainly with recursion and sentence embedding, it may be relevant to compare different degrees of embedding in different languages. A diagnosis of a high degree of complexity may be the degree of cohesion between the matrix and the embedded clause, or the degree of integration of the embedded clause into the matrix clause.

Time does of course not permit a close examination and comparison of different languages, instead I will offer a brief illustration in the form of a comparison between a language with a long literary tradition and a high degree of literacy among its speakers, namely English, and one with a very recent history of literacy, where very few of its speakers are literate in their own language, namely *Zoque*, a Mesoamerican language of Southern Mexico. The examples (4-9), where the a-sentences are from Zoque and the b-sentences from English, demonstrate the similar degrees of complexity in the two languages.

(4) Juxtaposition, coordination

a. wüj-pa ju'ki-'isñe'-se ket-pa
3ABS.stink-ICL vulture-GEN-SIM 3ABS.see-ICP
'It stinks, seems like that of a vulture'

b. It stinks. I can't stand it

(5) Juxtaposition, complementation

a. mit-u y-man-e nü-am y-koks-yaj-u aŋduŋ
INC-CP 3ERG-heard-DEP PRG-PERF 3ERG-knock-3PL-PG door
'She suddenly heard somebody knock on the door'

b. She suddenly heard someone knock on the door

(6) Conjunction

a. koraje-'aj-u te' pün i ymoka-u y-wijt
3ABS.angry-INCV-CP DET man and 3ERG.hang-CP 3POSS-self
'The man got angry and hanged himself'

b. The man got angry and hanged himself

(7) Free word complementizer

a. sun-pa-t wa'a m-wej-jay-u üj
1ERG.want-ICP-1 COMP 2ERG-call-APP-SUB PRO1.GEN
n-kabay
1POSS-brother.in.law
'I want you to invite my brother-in-law'

b. I hope that you will invite my brother-in-law

(8) Bound subordinator

a. maŋ-pa-'k-am pün'aj-e te' n-komi
FUT-ICP-TEMPSUB-PERF 3ABS.be.born-DEP DET 1POSS-lord
'when our Lord is going to be born'

b. I prefer inviting my brother

(9) Monoclausal construction

a. yempe i-'is-uŋ-te y-'is-pa-pü
any some-ERG-EV-PRED 3ERG-see-ICP-REL
'There were many who saw her'

b. the arriving train (< the train which is arriving)

As we can see, the two languages exhibit the same degrees of complexity in this grammatical domain. The structure and complexity of Zoque can be assumed to be that of a non-literate language. The language has - and has had since the time of colonization - syntactic resources for various degrees of sentence embedding. It exhibits a wide variety of subordination strategies, from simple juxtaposition with no overt complementizer, through independent complementizer words and *wh*-words, to cliticized complementizers (Faarlund 2012). None of this variety can be shown to be due to influence from the colonizer language, Spanish. There has been a certain Spanish influence in parts of the grammar of embedding, mainly in terms of lexical items, but it is not possible to say that this influence has led to a higher degree of complexity. The Spanish influence on Zoque dependent clause constructions has not significantly changed already existing patterns.

4. Conclusion

Based on theoretical considerations and on a careful analysis of historical and contemporary data, I will conclude that the answer to the question in the title of this paper must be in the negative; there is no grounds for assuming that the introduction of literacy and complex societies have had any impact on the human Language Faculty and Universal Grammar.

References

Deutscher, G. (2000). *Syntactic change in Akkadian: the evolution of sentential complementation.* Oxford: Oxford University Press.

Everett, D. (2005). Cultural constraints on grammar and cognition in Pirahã: Another look at the design features of human language. *Current Anthropology, 46,* 621-46.

Everett, D. 2009. Pirahã culture and grammar: A response to some criticisms. *Language, 85,* 405-442.

Faarlund, J. T. (2012). *A Grammar of Chiapas Zoque*. Oxford: Oxford University Press.

Hauser, M.D., Chomsky, N. & Fitch, W.T. (2002). The faculty of language: what is it, who has it, and how did it evolve. *Science, 298*, 1569-1579.

Hulst, H. van der (2010). Re Recursion. In H. van der Hulst (Ed.), *Recursion and Human Language. Studies in Generative Grammar* 104. (pp. xv-liii). Berlin: Mouton De Gruyter.

Maynard Smith, J. & Szathmáry, E. (1999). *The Origins of life: from the birth of life to the origin of language*. Oxford: Oxford University Press.

Nevis, A., Pesetsky, D. & Rodrigues, C. (2009). Pirahã exceptionality: A reassessment. *Language, 85*, 355-404.

Newmeyer, F.J. (2003). Grammar is grammar and usage is usage. *Language, 79*, 682-707.

Sampson, G. (2009). A linguistic axiom challenged. In G. Sampson, D. Gil, & P. Trudgill (Eds.), *Language Complexity as an Evolving Variable* (pp. 1-18). Oxford: Oxford University Press.

MEDIUM AND LONG-RUN PROPERTIES OF LINGUISTIC COMMUNITY EVOLUTION

MICHAEL J. FOX, GEORGIOS PILIOURAS, & JEFF S. SHAMMA
School of Electrical and Computer Engineering, Georgia Institute of Technology
777 Atlantic Drive NW, Atlanta, GA 30332-0250 USA
{mfox, georgios, shamma }@gatech.edu

We analyze a novel model of the co-evolution of linguistic community structure and language. Intuitively, agents want to communicate well with others in their linguistic community, and similarly, linguistic communities consist of those agents that can communicate effectively amongst themselves. Absent the effects of comunity structure, the model suffers from poor efficiency in the medium-run. Over the long-run, efficiency is attained, but diversity vanishes. When effects of homophily are added to the model we find a more nuanced picture. When the population size is large relative to frequency of stochastic shocks then both diversity and efficiency are observed in the medium-run, but diversity does not survive in the long-run. If stochasic shocks are more frequent then diversity and efficiency can survive the long-run.

1. Introduction

The stunning diversity of the modern language lanscape provokes curiosity as to its origins and persistence. Models of language evolution have tended to consider in isolation mechanisms accounting for either efficiency or diversity. Nominally, a model of the former phenomenon attempts to find conditions leading to a population state where a single, sensible language predominates— a circumstance that is clearly at odds with the latter. Indeed, a differential equation model of language competition has been suggested as evidence that linguistic diversity is a transient phenomenon destined to die out (Abrams & Strogatz, 2003).

Exogenous factors such as geographic isolation (Patriarca & Leppnen, 2004) and language's role as an in-group marker (Dunbar, 1998) have been suggested to account for this discrepancy. More recently, researchers have proposed homophily, the tendency to associate with similar others, as a mechanism to account for the persistence of diverse linguistic communities (Quillinan, Kirby, & Smith, 2010). However, the model views languages as abstract feature vectors. In this framework, the desirability of a language is based soley on similarity with neighbors. In contrast, game-theoretic models of language evolution (Trapa & Nowak, 2000), (Nowak, Plotkin, & Krakauer, 1999) have represented languages explicitly as signalling systems (Lewis, 1969). These systems' symbols and meanings can possess homonymy and symonymy, so that languages have varying degrees of intrinsic ambiguity. However, linguistic communities are not modelled.

In Section 2 we review the so-called language game. It is known that under replicator dynamics, the population can converge to a distribution of languages that is inefficient (Pawlowitsch, 2008), (Huttegger, 2007). We prove a tight lower bound on this efficiency loss, establishing that a particular example from the literature is representative of the worst-case. While diversity can persist in this model, low levels of efficiency can too. This model considers infinite populations— the mass action approach. Infinite populations approximate the behavior of large, finite populations over short time-horizons (Benaim & Weibull, 2003).

In order to account for the inefficiency, researchers have considered mutation-selection dynamics (a perturbation of the replicator dynamics) (Hofbauer & Huttegger, 2008), or finite-population versions of the model (Pawlowitsch, 2007), (Fox & Shamma, 2011a). It is shown in (Fox & Shamma, 2011a) that replicator-like dynamics converge to efficient states in the sense of stochastic stability (Young, 1993). That is, the system spends almost all its time in efficient language states as a parameter describing the frequency of stochastic shocks is made small. We show that the finite-population version of the game is a potential game, which suggests that similar results should exist for most sensible dynamics. These results indicate that, in the long-run, agents overcome inefficient states, but in doing so press out diversity.

We attempt to explain the observed persistence of diversity by suggesting an augmentation of the model that introduces linguistic community structure to agents' interactions. Our model is inspired by a model of opinion formation (Krause, 1997). Similarly, our agents define their linguistic community to be those other agents with whom they can communicate above a certain threshhold. At each time step a randomly selected agent updates to the language within her community that achieves the highest utility within that same community. Intuitively, such a model ought to be friendly to diversity because disparate languages can coexist in different communities.

We are able to perform an exact analysis of this model for a restricted set of parameters. In this case we find that only monomorphic[a] language states survive in the long-run. However, this analysis is relevant only when stochastic shocks are extremely rare. Disruptive events with profound implications for the language landscape, such as the reintroduction of Modern Hebrew in the 20th century, would seem to betray such assumptions. Simulation results are provided for higher levels of randomizing behavior, which suggest a strong tendency towards the formation of distinct linguistic communities. Linguistic coherence is high within these communities, but not between them. Alternatively, we make recourse to convergence rates. It has been shown in a closely related setting that systems

[a]A language state is monormophic when everyone uses the same language.

like our own may require time to convergence that is exponential in the population size (Shah & Shin, 2010). However, such systems may linger in metastable states over the medium-run (Nimwegen, Crutchfield, & Mitchell, 1997). We present simulation results that suggest efficient but distinct communities can persist in this manner even when they should be expected to vanish over the long-run. A final simulation study shows that the threshhold parameter defining the linguistic community structure has substantial effects on the relative sizes of the communities observed.

2. The language game

We consider a simple language game, first proposed in a substantially similar form in (Lewis, 1969), and reformulated more recently in (Nowak et al., 1999). An agent's speech strategy is an $m \times n$ binary, row-stochastic[b] matrix and her hearing strategy is an $n \times m$ binary, row-stochatic matrix. The linguistic coherence of a particular speaking strategy P against a particular hearing strategy Q is given by $\mathrm{trace}(PQ)$. To see why, expand out

$$\mathrm{trace}(PQ) = \sum_{k=1}^{m} \sum_{j=1}^{n} P_{kj} Q_{jk}. \tag{1}$$

The outer summation considers each of m rows of P. These rows corresponds to the m objects, with the single one in each row indicating the symbol from among the n available that a speaker using P associates with that object. The inner summation for a fixed k equals one if P maps k to the symbol that Q associates with the object k, and zero otherwise. We will consider this basic model of communication from two different perspectives, taking up the infinite-population setting first.

2.1. *Infinite populations*

Suppose that there is a single population of mass equal to one. Each member of the population must choose both speaking and hearing strategies. We confer any ordering on the set of speaking and hearing matrix pairs, or *languages*. There are $m^n n^m$ languages so that the *population state* $\mathbf{x}$ is an element of the $m^n n^m$-dimensional simplex

$$X = \{\mathbf{x} \in \mathbb{R}^{m^n n^m} : x_i \geq 0, \sum_i x_i = 1\}, \tag{2}$$

[b] A matrix is binary and row stochastic if and only if every row has a single element equal to one and all other elements zero.

where x_i indicates the proportion of agents utilizing the i'th language. The fitness of agents speaking the i'th language, (P_i, Q_i), is

$$f_i(\mathbf{x}) = \text{trace}(P_i(\sum_j x_j Q_j)) + \text{trace}((\sum_j x_j P_j)Q_i). \tag{3}$$

In words, an agent's fitness is her coherence achieved from both speaking and hearing, assuming random matching with the population. We study the replicator dynamics

$$\dot{x}_i = x_i(f_i(x) - \sum_j x_j f_j(x)). \tag{4}$$

A population state $\mathbf{x}$ is a *Neutrally Stable State* (NSS) if

$$\mathbf{x}' f(\mathbf{x}) \geq \mathbf{y}' f(\mathbf{x}) \quad \forall \mathbf{y} \in X, \tag{5}$$

and if $\mathbf{x}' f(\mathbf{x}) = \mathbf{y}' f(\mathbf{x})$ then $\mathbf{x}' f(\mathbf{y}) \geq \mathbf{y}' f(\mathbf{y})$. It has been shown (Pawlowitsch, 2008), (Huttegger, 2007) that the replicator dynamics converge to states not maximizing average fitness from a set of initial conditions with positive measure. Indeed we may converge on NSS with average fitness of four for any value of m or n (Hofbauer & Huttegger, 2008). This fact is particularly unsettling taking into account that the maximum average fitness is $2\min\{m, n\}$. We find that this is the worst-case.

Theorem 1: *If* $\mathbf{x}$ *is an NSS then* $\sum_i x_i f_i(\mathbf{x}) \geq 4$ *and the bound is tight for all* $m, n \geq 2$.

An NSS may include multiple languages, prompting researchers to view such states as providing opportunities for language diversification (Pawlotisch, Mertikopoulos, & Ritt, 2011). However, the accompanying possibility of such a large efficiency gap prohibits the model from providing a holistic account of languages evolving into a diverse landscape.

The mass-action heuristic can be shown to approximate sufficiently large populations over limited time spans (Benaim & Weibull, 2003). In order to understand the long-term behavior of the model we must represent the finite population explicitly.

2.2. *Finite populations*

We consider N agents, each utilizing a particular language. Let $(\mathbf{P}, \mathbf{Q})$ be an vector of N languages, one for each agent. Then the fitness of agent $i \in \{1, ..., N\}$ is

$$f_i(\mathbf{P}, \mathbf{Q}) = \text{trace}(P_i \frac{1}{N-1} \sum_{j \neq i} Q_j) + \text{trace}(\frac{1}{N-1} \sum_{j \neq i} P_j Q_i), \tag{6}$$

analogous to the infinite-population model. The long-run behavior of this game under various dynamics is taken up in (Fox & Shamma, 2011b) and (Fox &

Shamma, 2011a). Each of these dynamics assume that at each time step an agent will with probability $\epsilon > 0$ switch to a different language at random. The states that are observed with positive probability in the limit as ϵ is taken to zero are called *stochastically stable* (Young, 1993). For each dynamic it is shown that the stochastically stable states correspond to monomorphic states maximizing average fitness. We next argue that such outcomes should be expected very generally for this game.

A game is *a potential game* (Monderer & Shapley, 1996) if there exists a function $\Phi : \mathcal{A} \rightarrow \mathbb{R}$ (the domain being the set of joint strategies) such that for any player i, any joint strategy $\mathbf{s}$, and any strategy s of player i we have

$$f_i(s, \mathbf{s}_{-i}) - f_i(\mathbf{s}) = \Phi(s, \mathbf{s}_{-i}) - \Phi(\mathbf{s}), \tag{7}$$

where $\mathbf{s}_{-i}$ is the vector of strategiess for players other than i. The implication of this definition is that individual optimizing activity is tantamount to optimization of the potential function Φ.

Theorem 2: *The finite-population language game is a potential game with potential function* $\Phi \equiv \frac{1}{2}\sum_{i=1}^{N} f_i$.

Since the potential function is proportional to average fitness, it is not suprising that stochastic evolutionary dynamics tend to maximize average fitness. An intriguing question is how this model can be augmented to account for diversity, while preserving some measure of efficiency. Towards this end we propose a dynamic model that assumes the formation of linguistic communities.

3. Linguistic communities

At each time t we select an agent uniformly at random. This agents neighborhood

$$\begin{aligned} h_i(\mathbf{P}[t], \mathbf{Q}[t]) \equiv & \{j \neq i : \text{trace}(P_i[t]Q_j[t] + P_j[t]Q_i[t]) > r\} & (8)\\ & \cup \{j \neq i : (P_j[t], Q_j[t]) = (P_i[t], Q_i[t])\}, & (9)\end{aligned}$$

is precisely the agents with whom she can communicate at a level above some fixed threshold $r \in (0, 2\min\{m, n\})$ along with those sharing her language. If she cannot communicate with anyone above the threshhold she picks a new language at random uniformly. Otherwise, with probability $1 - \epsilon$, she selects the language of an agent within her neighborhood that achieves maximum performance relative to her neighborhood, i.e. from amongst the set

$$\arg \max_{j \in h_i(\mathbf{P}[t], \mathbf{Q}[t])} \sum_{k \in h_i(\mathbf{P}[t], \mathbf{Q}[t])} \text{trace}(P_j[t]Q_k[t]) + \text{trace}(P_k[t]Q_j[t]). \tag{10}$$

Or, with small probability $\epsilon > 0$ she chooses a random language instead. All other agents continue with their previous language and a new agent is selected for revision as above.

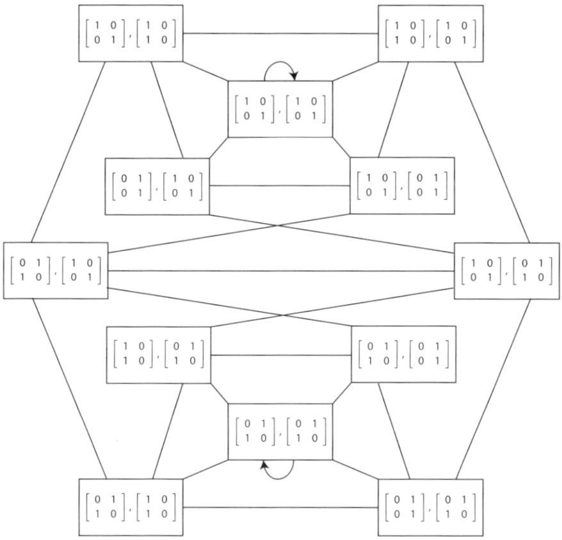

Figure 1. The network structure for $m = n = 2, r = 3$.

Different values of $m, n,$ and r will give a range of possible network structures. As an example, we illustrate the structure for $m = n = 2, r = 3$ in Fig. 1. An agent's neighbors are the agents who use the languages that her own language is linked to in this graph. Notice that for these parameters only 12 of 16 languages possess links, and only two are linked to themselves.

The model appears contrived because an agent that can communicate effectively within her community will with high probability eschew the opportunity to revise her language in order to communicate effectively with a larger community. We are altogether ignoring the advantages of incumbency that models of language competition concentrate on. It turns out that for small ϵ, even this is not enough.

Theorem 3: *Let* $m = n \geq 2$ *and* $r \in (2(n-1), 2n)$. *Then the stochastically stable states of the linguistic community model are the monomorphic states maximizing average fitness.*

Recall that the stochastically stable states are almost all we will see in the long-run. For these parameters, the elaborate linguistic community structure has thus made no difference at all from the viewpoint of stochastic stability . Our analysis does not preclude diversity over the medium-run or for larger values of ϵ, perspectives we now take up.

Stochastic stability characterizes long-run behavior, but such predictions may only become relevant after extraordinary lengths of time. Under more reasonable timescales states that are not stochastically stable may "appear" stable, a phenomenon referred to as metastability. Simulation results illustrated in the leftmost plot of Fig. 2 indicate this can occur for parameter values covered by our theorem.

Two languages satisfy $\text{trace}(PQ) = m = n = 2$, these are the *aligned* languages and are represented with dotted lines. The wider dots indicates the more prevalent of the two[c]. The solid line sums over all other languages. Despite eventually settling into monmorphic states, the simulations indicate a metastable epoch where diverse communities thrive.

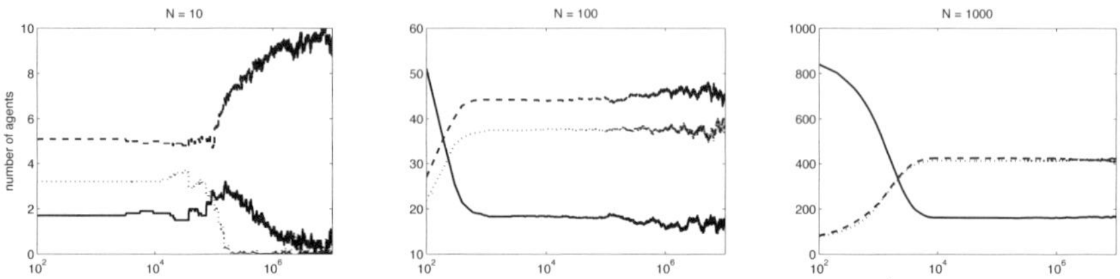

Figure 2. Stability of diversity varies with N; $r = 3, m = n = 2, \epsilon = 10^{-4}$, average of 10 runs.

When ϵ is not small relative to the population size, we observe diverse, efficient linguistic communities even over long time-horizons . The impact of increasing the population size with ϵ fixed is illustrated in Fig. 2. For $\epsilon = 10^{-4}$ we eventually observe monomorphic states for small N, consistent with stochastic stability analysis. As N grows we observe two equally sized internally efficient linguistic communities[d]. Interestingly, the relative community sizes are related to the particular choice of threshhold as illustrated in Fig. 3.

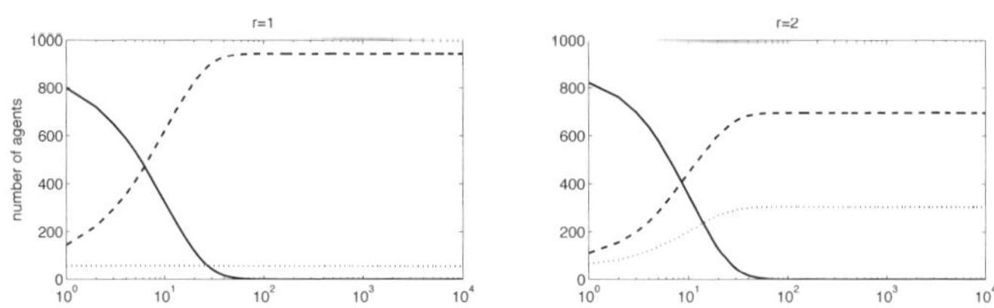

Figure 3. Community sizes vary with r; $m = n = 2, \epsilon = 10^{-4}, N = 1000$, average of 10 runs.

Acknowledgements

Supported by AFOSR projects #FA9550-09-1-0538 and FA9550-09-1-0420, and DARPA project #HR0011-10-1-0009.

References

Abrams, D. M., & Strogatz, S. H. (2003). Modelling the dynamics of language death. *Nature*, *424*, 900.

[c] The identity of the more prevalent language is allowed to change. Either of the two states that is monomorphic in an aligned language can begin to dominate so, absent our convention, averaging over many runs would give the misleading appearance of diversity for large t

[d] Readers should exercise caution in drawing conclusions from these simulations when N is large because convergence rates generally increase with N. However, even simulations initiated from monomorphic states (not shown) behaved similarly

Benaim, M., & Weibull, J. W. (2003). Deterministic approximation of stochastic evolution in games. *Econometrica*, *71*(3), 873–903.

Dunbar, R. (1998). *Grooming, gossip, and the evolution of language.* Harvard University Press: Cambrdige, MA.

Fox, M., & Shamma, J. (2011a). Language evolution in finite populations. *50th IEEE Conference on Decision and Control*.

Fox, M., & Shamma, J. (2011b). Stochastic stability in language evolution. *22nd International Conference on Game Theory*.

Hofbauer, J., & Huttegger, S. M. (2008). Feasibility of communication in binary signaling games. *Journal of Theoretical Biology*, *254*(4), 843 - 849.

Huttegger, S. M. (2007). Evolution and the explanation of meaning. *Philosophy of Science*, *74*(1), 1-27.

Krause, U. (1997). Soziale dynamiken mit vielen interakteuren. eine problemskizze. *Modellierung Simul. von Dynamiken mit vielen interagierenden Akteuren*, 37-51.

Lewis, D. (1969). *Convention: A philosophical study.* Harvard Univ. Press, Cambridge, MA.

Monderer, D., & Shapley, L. (1996). Potential games. *Games and Economic Behavior*, *14*, 124–143.

Nimwegen, E. V., Crutchfield, J. P., & Mitchell, M. (1997). Finite populations induce metastability in evolutionary search. *Physics Letters A*, *229*.

Nowak, M., Plotkin, J., & Krakauer, D. (1999). The evolutionary language game. *Journal of Theoretical Biology*, *200*(2), 147 - 162.

Patriarca, M., & Leppnen, T. (2004). Modeling language competition. *Physica A: Statistical Mechanics and its Applications*, *338*(1-2), 296 - 299. (Proceedings of the conference A Nonlinear World: the Real World, 2nd International Conference on Frontier Science)

Pawlotisch, C., Mertikopoulos, P., & Ritt, N. (2011). Neutral stability, drift, and the diversification of languages. *22nd International Conference on Game Theory*.

Pawlowitsch, C. (2007). Finite populations choose an optimal language. *Journal of Theoretical Biology*, *249*(3), 606 - 616.

Pawlowitsch, C. (2008). Why evolution does not always lead to an optimal signaling system. *Games and Economic Behavior*, *63*(1), 203 - 226.

Quillinan, J., Kirby, S., & Smith, K. (2010). Co-evolution of language and social network structure through cultural transmission. *8th International Conference on the Evolution of Language*, 475-476.

Shah, D., & Shin, J. (2010). Dynamics in congestion games. In *Sigmetrics.*

Trapa, P., & Nowak, M. (2000). Nash equilibria for an evolutionary language game. *Journal of Mathematical Biology*, *41*, 172-188.

Young, H. (1993). The evolution of conventions. *Econometrica*, *61*(1), 57-84.

SCALES, SALIENCE AND REFERENTIAL SAFETY: THE BENEFIT OF COMMUNICATING THE EXTREME

MICHAEL FRANKE

Institute for Logic, Language & Computation
Universiteit van Amsterdam

On an abstract level, this paper tries to show how formal semantics can contribute to theories of language evolution and vice versa. More concretely, the paper argues that signaling games fail to account plausibly for a general preference to use gradable adjectives to communicate *extreme values*. The reason is that these models focus too narrowly on *descriptive language use*. Numerical simulations show that the choice of extreme values is pragmatically beneficial in situations of *referential language use* under possible noise. Bringing evolutionary modeling back to formal semantics, this yields a functional explanation for otherwise rather puzzling patterns in the use of gradable adjectives.

1. Sim-Max Games & Voronoi Languages

Lewisean signaling games (Lewis, 1969) have developed into a leading model of meaning evolution that is theoretically very well understood and has proven its value in many academic disciplines (Crawford & Sobel, 1982; Grafen, 1990; Steels, 1995; Nowak & Krakauer, 1999). More recently, a particular kind of signaling game, called *sim-max game*, has come into the focus of the linguistic community, because of its special theoretical interest to questions relating to the interface between formal semantics and pragmatics, on the one hand, and the cognitive sciences, on the other hand (Jäger & van Rooij, 2007; Jäger, 2007; Franke, Jäger, & van Rooij, 2011). A sim-max game is essentially a cheap-talk signaling game with shared preferences, where communicative success is proportional to a measure of similarity of the sender's intended meaning and the receiver's interpretation. Intended meanings and interpretations come from a metric space T with a numerical similarity measure $sim : T \times T \rightarrow \mathbb{R}^{\geq 0}$. One might think of this as, for example, a space of possible sense perceptions being more or less similar to one another. The sender observes a state $t \in T$, sampled from a prior distribution $\Pr(\cdot) \in \Delta(T)$, and selects a message $m \in M$. The receiver then selects an interpretation $t' \in T$. The exchange is successful proportional to the similarity of t and t', i.e., utilities for sender and receiver satisfy: $U_{S,R}(t, m, t') \propto sim(t, t')$.

Jäger, Metzger, and Riedel (2011) prove that the evolutionarily stable states of these games give rise to so-called *Voronoi languages*. (Caveat: this short exposition cannot possibly pay due respect to all mathematical detail.) A Voronoi language is a pair $\langle \sigma, \rho \rangle$ consisting of a sender strategy $\sigma : T \to M$ and a receiver strategy $\rho : M \to T$ such that: (i) the set $\{\{t \in T \mid \sigma(t) = m\} \mid m \in M\}$ of *declarative meanings* constituted by σ is a (quasi-)partition of T into convex regions, and (ii) the *imperative meaning* $\rho(m)$ of m given ρ, is the Bayesian estimator for the cell $\{t \in T \mid \sigma(t) = m\}$. For example, if the state space is given as the unit interval $T = [0; 1]$, the prior distribution is uniform, and $\mathrm{U}(t, m, t') = -|t - t'|$, then for $|M| = 2$ there are only two isomorphic Voronoi languages which structure the state space as follows (see Figure 1): the sender will use one message for all values below ½, the other for those above; the receiver will interpret the former as ¼, the latter as ¾. For higher-dimensional spaces the resulting structure similarly is a tessellation, with T, $\Pr(\cdot)$ and $\mathrm{U}(\cdot)$ influencing the shapes and location of declarative and imperative meanings. In general, this technical result is conceptually highly interesting, because it demonstrates how evolutionary pressure on effective communication can explain certain natural properties of conceptual meaning space, namely the convexity of natural concepts and the centrality of prototypical interpretations (cf. Gärdenfors, 2000).

Although the Voronoi-predictions of sim-max games line up neatly also with previous results from related models on, for example, the formation of color categories (cf. Belpaeme & Bleys, 2005; Steels & Belpaeme, 2005; Baronchelli, Gong, Puglisi, & Loreto, 2010), from a linguistic point of view they are not entirely satisfactory. A case in point is the use and interpretation of *gradable adjectives*. These are adjectives like *tall*, *closed*, or *pure* which allow for comparative uses and gradual degree modification (e.g. "He is *taller* than her" as opposed to non-gradable, hence awkward "This is *more perfect* than that"). A prominent line of current semantic theorizing relates gradable adjectives to degrees on scales in a way that *prima facie* seems directly applicable to the basic set-up of sim-max games. However, it turns out that Voronoi languages do *not* capture some of the linguistically relevant subtleties in the use of gradable adjectives. This has theoretically interesting repercussions for evolutionary modeling. In order to appreciate this, a short excursion into formal semantics is necessary.

2. Degree Semantics for Gradable Adjectives

According to scale-based formal semantics of gradable adjectives the denotation of a gradable adjective A is a function $g_A : \mathrm{Dom(A)} \to D$ that maps any ap-

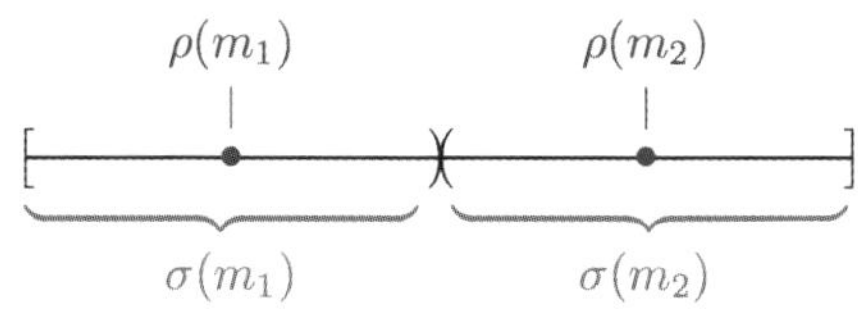

Figure 1. Simple Voronoi language on a one-dimensional state space

plicable arguments of A to a degree $d \in D$, where, crucially, $\langle D, \preceq \rangle$ is a suitably ordered *scale of degrees* (see Rotstein & Winter, 2004; Kennedy & McNally, 2005). As different adjectives may be associated with different kinds of degree scales, a simple classification scheme is obtained. Standardly, one-dimensional scales are assumed and a distinction is made as to whether these are: (i) totally open (*tall*, *short*), (ii) totally closed (*closed*, *open*), or (iii) half-open (*bent*, *pure*). Scale types explain a number of otherwise puzzling observations, such as which adjectives can combine with which modifiers. E.g., the expression *completely A* is felicitous only if A has a totally or upper-closed scale with a maximal element: compare the felicitous *completely closed* with the awkward $^{?}$*completely tall*.

Scale types also influence the licensing conditions of utterances involving gradable adjectives in positive form. Generally speaking, a simple positive sentence like "object x has property A" is considered true whenever the contextually supplied minimal degree of A-ness, $c(A)$, is no higher than $g_A(x)$. However, the contextual standard of applicability $c(A)$ is also affected by the scale type (c.f. Kennedy, 2007): if there is a $\preceq$-maximal or -minimal degree contained in $\langle D, \preceq \rangle$, then $c(A)$ is bound to this; otherwise it is to be retrieved more flexibly from the context of utterance. In more tangible terms, "*Kennedy's observation*", as we may call it here, says that adjectives which are associated with a closed scale of degrees are used rather inflexibly to denote the respective minimal or maximal values on the associated scale (modulo the usual pragmatic slack where lack of precision is conversationally harmless), whereas adjectives associated with totally open scales allow more contextual variability. In effect, this means that open-scale adjectives are more contextually variant and more prone to exhibit vagueness than closed-scale adjectives. For example, the contextual standard for the applicability of open-scale *tall* can vary considerably from one context (talking about jockeys) to another (talking about basketbal players), whereas that of closed-scale *closed* seems glued to the denotation of a minimal (zero) degree of openness.

3. The Extreme-Value Puzzle

Sim-max games fail to satisfactorily explain Kennedy's observation. The main problem, I suggest, is a more general one: sim-max games fail to explain why gradable adjectives are predominantly used to denote *extreme values*. A general preference for extreme values would explain Kennedy's observation. Suppose speakers would, for some reason or other, preferentially communicate those properties that lie at the extremes of a (one-dimensional) scale, no matter whether the absolute values of that scale may shift from context to context. In that case, it would be a mere concomitant of an extreme-value preference that closed-scale terms preferentially bind to their minimal/maximal terms (no matter what their contextually-specified actual value might be), but not so for open-scale terms. However, sim-max games fail to predict a preference for extreme values in general, and Kennedy's observation in particular, unless we make quite implausible assumptions about how to implement different scale topologies. Here is why:

Since endpoints on a one-dimensional scale have Lebesgue-measure zero, it is clear that whether T is an open, closed or half-open interval has no bearing on the structure of the resulting Voronoi language. The most natural idea is to express a difference in scale topology by a combination of T, the prior distribution $\mathrm{Pr}(\cdot)$ and, possibly, the utility function $\mathrm{U}(\cdot)$. Indeed, by tweaking these parameters, it is possible to set up a sim-max game in which at least the *imperative* meanings of the resulting Voronoi language take extreme values. This could be achieved by either assuming that (i) the prior distribution is convex (i.e., the more extreme a value, the more likely it is to occur), or that (ii) the utilities favor more extreme values over less extreme ones. Both assumptions are, however, inadequate. The latter assumption would stipulate exactly what ideally we want to explain, and the assumption of convex priors is simply not true in general: e.g., most people are of around average height, the chance of meeting dwarfs or giants is marginal.

It is an obvious idea to try to explain differences in usage conditions of gradable adjectives with reference to a notion of (perceptual) *salience* (e.g. Fernández, 2009). Kennedy (2007) also tries to explain the influence of scale topology on contextual usage conditions in terms of the salience of endpoints on closed scales and a principle called *Interpretive Economy* which demands that pragmatic interpretation ought to make maximal use of the available semantic resources. Since endpoints on a closed scale are salient elements of the semantic structure, these ought to be used for pragmatic interpretation. Potts (2008) rightly criticizes that *Interpretive Economy* should really be motivated by an evolutionary argument, and therefore looks at a strategic game in which speaker and hearer try to coordinate on the mutually assumed contextual standard for the use of closed-scale adjectives. Potts suggests that the endpoint convention is selected by the replicator dynamic because, by psychological salience, we may assume a (however) slight majority of extreme-value players already initially.

Salience undoubtedly plays a big role in perception and categorization. Moreover, relying on a mutual understanding of what is salient *can* increase performance, e.g., in one-shot coordination games. But not so in sim-max games where the use of extreme values would lead to strictly less effective communication. In other words, salience and the affordances of sim-max games pull in opposite directions. Consequently, just adding salience to sim-max games is *not* a sufficient explanation of an extreme value preference, because this does not explain the evolutionary *cui bono*, viz., why salient values may have adaptive linguistic value.

4. Minimal Risk of Referential Confusion

I suggest that the main reason why sim-max games fail to explain a preference for extreme values is that these games capture too narrow a notion of what language is used for. Sim-max games only model *descriptive language use*: e.g., the speaker says "John is tall" and the hearer forms a mental image of John's height. But we should also consider *referential language use*: e.g., the speaker says "John is the tall guy over there" and the hearer tries to guess who the intended referent may have been. In the latter situation, given a shared but possibly noisy context of potential referents, the speaker should ideally describe an intended referent by a property that is *minimally confusing* to the addressee. The driving intuition of this paper is that minimizing the chance of referential confusion leads to selective pressure for the communication of extreme values.

In corroboration of this intuition, consider the following simple model. Sender and receiver observe a context C that consists of n different objects. Each object is an m-tuple of values, one for each relevant property (height, thickness, ...), sampled randomly from distributions corresponding to open, closed and half-open (lower-closed) scales (see the light gray lines in Figure 2 for example distributions modeling different types of scales). A context is an $n \times m$ matrix, with C_{ij} the value of property j of object i. The sender knows the *designated object* C_o that she wants to communicate, but the receiver does not. The sender selects a property j (supposing for simplicity that there is a common code for that already), and the receiver responds with choosing an object C_i. Communication would be successful iff $i = o$. But if the receiver possibly only perceives a noisy version of context C, the sender should ideally choose that property j for which the desig-

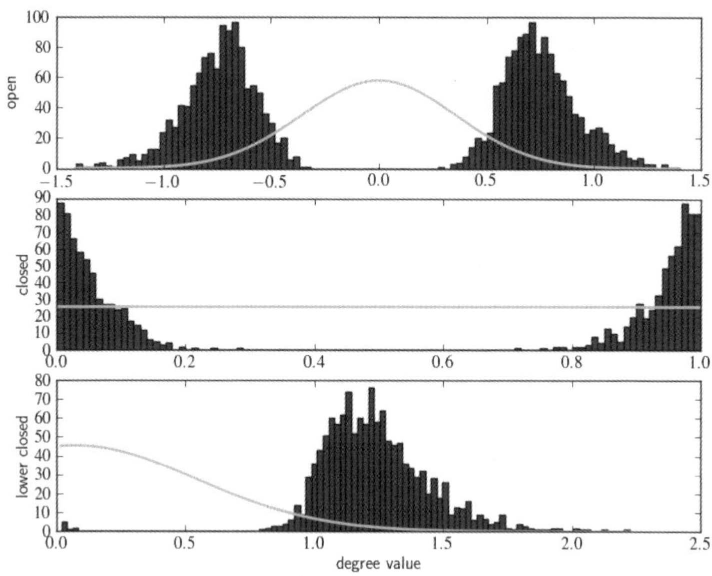

Figure 2. Frequency of values C_{oj} selected by the "optimally non-confusing" choice rule over 5000 randomly sampled contexts with $n = 30$ and $m = 24$ (8 properties each for open, closed, and half-open scales with prior distributions indicated by the light gray lines).

nated object is maximally distinct from the other objects in context. What would count as maximally distinct, and hence an optimal speaker choice, of course, depends on many different factors: noise distributions, players' knowledge thereof etc. To keep matters simple, let us assume that the probability that C_o is confused with C_i is anti-proportional to the difference $|C_{oj} - C_{ij}|$ in the respective values of the property j that is used to describe C_o. In that case, the sender's "optimally non-confusing" choice rule would be to choose arbitrarily from:

$$\arg\max_j \sum_{i=1}^{n} |C_{oj} - C_{ij}| \,. \tag{1}$$

(For clarity, this is not the only reasonably conceivable choice rule, but, perhaps, the simplest. Others have been tested with basically identical results.)

The choice rule in (1) does not yield a preference for extreme values necessarily. But if we look at the values C_{oj} that are selected by this rule for a large number of randomly sampled contexts, then indeed we see that extreme values are preferentially selected, irrespective of whether these are sampled from open, closed or half-open scales (see Figure 2). (The results in Figure 2 also indicate that our referential choice rule improves on the predictions of Voronoi languages in yet further respects: we see (distributional) *vagueness*, but also *non-complementarity*, i.e., values which would be expressed neither by a term nor its antonym.) This suggests that a preference for extreme values, and with it Kennedy's observation, can be explained as a concomitant of the speaker's strategic choice of which property to describe a referent with in a possibly confusing environment.

5. Relating Descriptive and Referential Language Use

If correct, these considerations raise a number of technical and conceptual questions concerning the relation between descriptive and referential language use: is either one to be considered primordial? how can we study their conjoined effect on language evolution in a single model? As a partial answer to the latter issue, I suggest to look at the results of a simple but instructive model of *iterated learning* (cf. Smith, Kirby, & Brighton, 2003) in which each new generation learns its language from a finite sample of how the previous generation actually used its language. By parameterizing the proportion of descriptive/referential use, we find that descriptive and referential language use give rise to diametrically opposed selective pressures on language evolution.

The model assumes that each teacher generation is presented with contexts of objects, as above. With probability α speakers choose the property of the designated object that best matches their own (previously acquired) interpretation strategy $\rho : M \rightarrow \mathbb{R}$, as in sim-max games, and with probability $(1-\alpha)$ speakers choose in accordance with the choice rule in (1). Learners form their interpretations $\rho(m)$ by averaging over all values expressed by the teacher generation for

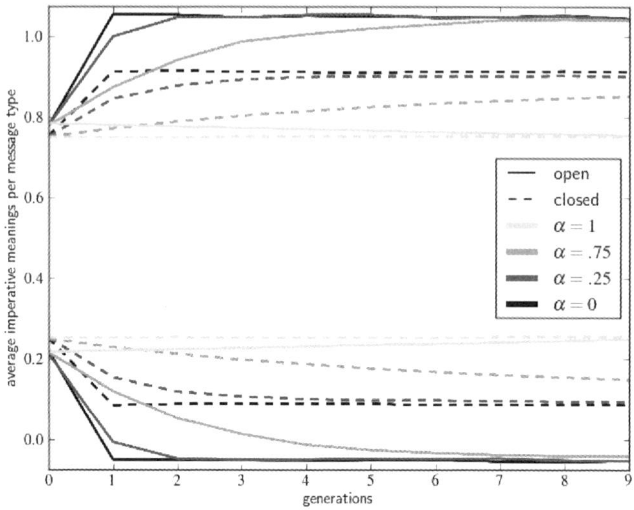

Figure 3. Temporal development of imperative meanings over 10 generations of iterated learning. Plotted are averages over 10 runs, each for different values of α. Each learner generation observed the teacher generation's output for 800 randomly sampled contexts, each containing 10 objects with 4 open- and 4 closed-scaled properties. Here, open-scale values were sampled from a normal distribution with $\mu = {}^1\!/_2$ and $\sigma = {}^1\!/_3$, closed-scale values from a uniform distribution over $[0; 1]$.

message m. (For simplicity, the initial teacher generation used a Voronoi language as interpretation strategy.) Averaged results of 20 runs of such iterated learning are plotted in Figure 3 and clearly indicate that the more prevalent referential use is, the more (and the faster) imperative meanings shift towards extreme values. For purely descriptive use ($\alpha = 1$), closed-scale terms are stuck at the Voronoi language interpretation, while open-scale interpretations even shift to less extreme values (drawn in by the higher *a priori* probability of more median values).

This shows that if the speaker has a choice which scalar property to communicate, then descriptive language use selects for less extreme, while referential language use selects for more extreme values. Hence, in order to account for a preference for extreme values (and with it Kennedy's observation), we should look rather at the affordances of referential communication, rather than descriptive communication. Though negative, this is a conceptually valuable result, in that it quite nicely charters some of the limits of signaling games as a faithful base model of linguistic communication.

In sum, I propose that taking insights from formal semantics more seriously into account, as done here, can fruitfully guide the conceptual debate and the synthetic modeling of language evolution. Formal semantics may likewise profit from evolutionary considerations, as shown here by providing a functional explanation for some otherwise perplexing patterns in the use of gradable adjectives.

References

Baronchelli, A., Gong, T., Puglisi, A., & Loreto, V. (2010). Modeling the emergence of universality in color naming patterns. *PNAS*, *107*(6), 2403–2407.

Belpaeme, T., & Bleys, J. (2005). Explaining universal color categories through a constrained acquisition process. *Adaptive Behavior*, *13*(4), 293–310.

Crawford, V. P., & Sobel, J. (1982). Strategic information transmission. *Econometrica*, *50*, 1431–1451.

Fernández, R. (2009). Salience and feature variability in definite descriptions with positive-form vague adjectives. In *Proceedings of pre-cogsci*.

Franke, M., Jäger, G., & van Rooij, R. (2011). Vagueness, signaling & bounded rationality. In T. Onoda, D. Bekki, & E. McCready (Eds.), *Jsai-isai 2010* (pp. 45–59). Springer.

Gärdenfors, P. (2000). *Conceptual spaces: The geometry of thought*. MIT Press.

Grafen, A. (1990). Biological signals as handicaps. *Journal of Theoretical Biology*, *144*, 517–546.

Jäger, G. (2007). The evolution of convex categories. *Linguistics and Philosophy*, *30*(5), 551–564.

Jäger, G., Metzger, L. P., & Riedel, F. (2011). *Voronoi languages: Equilibria in cheap-talk games with high-dimensional types and few signals*. (To appear in *Games and Economic Behavior*)

Jäger, G., & van Rooij, R. (2007). Language structure: Psychological and social constraints. *Synthese*, *159*(1), 99–130.

Kennedy, C. (2007). Vagueness and grammar: The semantics of relative and absolute gradable adjectives. *Linguistics and Philosophy*, *30*, 1–45.

Kennedy, C., & McNally, L. (2005). Scale structure, degree modification, and the semantics of gradable predicates. *Language*, *81*(2), 345–381.

Lewis, D. (1969). *Convention. a philosophical study*. Harvard University Press.

Nowak, M. A., & Krakauer, D. C. (1999). The evolution of language. *PNAS*, *96*, 8028–8033.

Potts, C. (2008). *Interpretive Economy, Schelling Points, and evolutionary stability*. (Manuscript, UMass Amherst)

Rotstein, C., & Winter, Y. (2004). Total adjectives vs. partial adjectives: Scale structure and higher-order modifiers. *Natural Language Semantics*, *12*(3), 259–288.

Smith, K., Kirby, S., & Brighton, H. (2003). Iterated learning: A framework for the emergence of language. *Artificial Life*, *9*, 371–386.

Steels, L. (1995). A self-organizing spatial vocabulary. *Artificial Life*, *2*(3), 319–332.

Steels, L., & Belpaeme, T. (2005). Coordinating perceptually grounded categories through language: A case study for color. *Behavioral and Brain Sciences*, *28*(4), 469–529.

NON-HUMAN PRIMATES CANNOT DECONTEXTUALIZE AND OBJECTIFY THE ACTIONS OF THEIR CONSPECIFICS

TOM FROESE, TAKASHI IKEGAMI

Department of General Systems Studies, University of Tokyo, Japan

MIKE BEATON

Centre for Research in Cognitive Science, University of Sussex, UK

We argue that all primates primarily perceive the actions of conspecifics as meaningful expressions of agency. Social understanding is a perceptual capacity that does not require human reason or imagination. Conversely, only humans have an additional, sophisticated ability to decontextualize and objectify actions into abstract movements. We thereby turn the traditional consensus on its head: what distinguishes humans from other primates is *not* the ability to perceive other agents. Humans are different because they can detach from the goal-oriented and meaning-laden presence of their natural and social world in order to bring abstract physical details into focus. This objectifying stance is necessary for genuine innovation and fine-grained imitation, especially of opaque instrumental and symbolic gestures, and therefore has implications for the origins of tool use and language.

1. Introduction

The fields of primatology and comparative psychology are undergoing a 'social revolution'. Just over a decade ago it was still widely believed that non-human animals, including our closest primate relatives, are unable to comprehend that conspecifics are intentional agents like themselves (Tomasello, 1999). However, in subsequent years this longstanding consensus has been subjected to drastic revisions based on new empirical evidence. Today the key question is no longer whether chimpanzees understand the mental states of others, but which ones and to what extent (Tomasello, Call & Hare, 2003; Call & Tomasello, 2008).

For example, there is evidence that chimpanzees are sensitive to human attentional states (Hostetter et al., 2007), as well as to the perceptual and social relevance of human body and face orientation, respectively (Kaminski et al., 2004). They have some understanding of what others have perceived in the past and what they have knowledge of (Kaminski et al., 2008). More impressively, they have some grasp of the rationality of others' actions, and they use this understanding to decide whether to imitate or emulate others (Buttelmann et al., 2007), and to distinguish between intentional actions and accidental behavior (Wood et al., 2007), as well as to distinguish between when a human observer is unwilling or unable to act (Call et al., 2004). In addition, it has been found that chimpanzees spontaneously offer altruistic help to human observers (Warneken & Tomasello, 2006) as well as to conspecifics (Warneken, et al. 2007), and they help each other upon request (Yamamoto et al., 2009).

Furthermore, this growing body of evidence is not limited to our nearest primate relatives. There is evidence that rhesus macaques correctly understand communicative gestures (Hauser et al., 2007) and rational, goal-direction actions (Wood et al., 2007). Japanese macaques have been taught joint attention through training in eye contact and pointing (Kumashiro et al., 2002), and this ability has facilitated their imitation of arbitrary body movements (Kumashiro et al., 2008). Even cotton-top tamarins, a more distant primate relative, appear to be able to understand rational, goal-directed actions of humans (Wood et al., 2007). This indicates that social understanding in primates is likely to have arisen at least as far back as the New World monkeys, some 40 million years ago.

Nevertheless, not everyone is convinced that the new evidence is sufficient to overturn the traditional, skeptical consensus concerning the ability of non-human primates to perceive intentional states (e.g. Penn & Povinelli, 2007; Povinelli & Vonk, 2003). For instance, evidence for false-belief understanding has yet to be found (Kaminski et al., 2008; Call & Tomasello, 2008). And even if we accept that the evidence shows that non-human primates can understand others as intentional agents, there still remains the problem of what form a new hypothesis should take, as to the similarities and differences in intentional perception between humans and other primates (Tomasello, et al. 2003; Call & Tomasello, 2008). We argue that the root of the dilemma is that the skeptical hypothesis continues to be logically forced on the field by a set of questionable assumptions. It is largely the commitment to these assumptions, and not a lack of evidence as such, which prevents an alternative theory from taking shape.

2. A logical proof of the skeptical hypothesis

An important first step toward developing a new theory of social understanding in non-human primates is to notice the logical force of the theoretical framework from which the skeptical hypothesis has traditionally been derived. Indeed, on the basis of its seemingly reasonable starting assumptions, it is possible to give a *logical proof* of the idea that non-human primates are *unable* to understand that their conspecifics are intentional agents like themselves.

To begin with, we note that cultural learning was believed to be a difficult achievement for non-human animals precisely because it is "made possible by a single very special form of social cognition, namely, the ability of individual organisms to understand conspecifics as beings *like themselves* who have intentional and mental lives like our own" (Tomasello, 1999: 5). Thus, social understanding, which is often called a 'theory of mind', was thought to be a uniquely human ability. This skeptical hypothesis is logically proved in Table 1.

Table 1. A logical proof of the skeptical hypothesis.

	Propositions
Premise 1	*Homo sapiens* is the only primate capable of cumulative cultural evolution.
Premise 2	Cumulative cultural evolution requires (i) innovation and (ii) imitation.
Premise 3	Non-human primates are capable of innovation by trial and error.
Conclusion 1	*Homo sapiens* must be the only primate capable of genuine imitation.
Premise 4	Imitative learning requires perception of intentional behavior.
Premise 5	Perception of intentional behavior requires (i) perception of physical behavior plus (ii) theory of mind.
Premise 6	All perception provides information about physical aspects of the world.
Conclusion 2	Non-human primates are capable of perceiving others' physical behavior.
Conclusion 3	*Homo sapiens* must be the only primate species capable of theory of mind.

The logical argument begins with the relatively uncontroversial proposition that only humans are capable of giving rise to cumulative cultural evolution (Premise 1). In order to explain this unique ability we need to posit the conditions that enable cumulative cultural evolution to take place. Useful new behaviors must be invented and then retained by a 'ratchet effect' (Tomasello et al., 1993). This necessity of creative innovation and faithful imitation (Premise 2) could explain the essential difference between *H. sapiens* and other primates. Evidence from ethology appears to demonstrate the key factor: "Perhaps surprisingly, for many animal species it is not the creative component, but rather the stabilizing ratchet component, that is the difficult feat" (Tomasello, 1999: 5). In other words, it is assumed that other primates are capable of creative innovation (Premise 3). We have now followed the argument to a specific claim. If we accept that non-human primates are capable of innovation (Premise 3), and that cumulative cultural evolution requires both innovation and imitation (Premise 2), then given that only humans are capable of such cultural evolution (Premise 1), it logically follows that *only humans are capable of imitative learning* (Conclusion 1).

We can now inquire about the necessary conditions of imitative learning to find out why it appears to be uniquely human. Firstly, we note that true imitation requires the perception of *intentional* behavior (Premise 4): if one does not see a behavior as aimed towards a purpose, then one cannot copy it in order to achieve that same purpose for oneself. Traditionally, it is supposed that two conditions have to be fulfilled for perception of intentional behavior, namely the agent must perceive the physical aspects of behavior, and have an additional capacity for a 'theory of mind' (Premise 5). Now, it is also traditionally assumed that the basic function of perception is to provide information about objective properties of the physical world (Premise 6), in which case we should certainly grant this ability to non-human primates, too (Conclusion 2). Therefore, we are in a position to deduce precisely what must make humans unique. If we accept that non-human primates can perceive the physical aspects of the behavior of others (Conclusion 2), and that imitative learning requires both perception of the physical behavior and a theory of mind (Premise 5), then given we have already accepted that only humans are capable of such imitation (Conclusion 1), it logically follows that *only humans are capable of a theory of mind* (Conclusion 3). This final conclusion corresponds to the traditional assumption that the uniqueness of human cumulative cultural evolution is explainable by appealing to a single factor: our capacity for a 'theory of mind', i.e. understanding others as social agents like themselves. Given this logically consistent framework, it is easy to see why there has been such a persistent negative bias against the very possibility of social understanding in non-human species: *uncovering empirical evidence against the presence of a theory of mind in other primate species was the only logically acceptable outcome given the traditional set of assumptions.*

The full extent of the current dilemma is now clear: considering there is a growing body of empirical evidence demonstrating that chimpanzees (and other non-human primates and animals) understand conspecifics as other intentional agents like themselves, then, given the argument's logical structure, some of the premises leading to the skeptical hypothesis must be false. Given that each of the premises seems to be intuitively plausible, the problem now is to determine which of them must be rejected and for what reason.

3. What is wrong with the premises? Uncovering cultural bias

We agree with Povinelli and Vonk (2003) that current research in comparative psychology is distorted because humans have a strong tendency to a biased view of the mind of other creatures. However, we disagree that the main challenge in this regard is to reject an assumed *evolutionary bias* for humans to perceive other creatures as intentional beings. On the contrary, we suggest that what needs to be overcome is a *cultural bias* for scientists to conceive other creatures as mere automata, a view that was popularized by Descartes. In this section we make this cultural bias explicit and criticize its methodological assumptions.

3.1. *Methodological physicalism*

First, there is the overarching assumption of *methodological physicalism*, which holds that the faculty of perception is in the business of manufacturing 'mental representations' of bare physical reality. These representations are conceived as informational statements about objects in the world, and are thus assumed to correspond to the abstract descriptions produced by modern physics (e.g. about a set of particulars with coordinates in a three-dimensional space). But the very idea of treating the world as a set of independent objects located in an abstract space devoid of meaning is a cultural product of the scientific revolution. The assumption that methodological physicalism is a valid description of perceptual experience (Premise 6) is therefore highly questionable; most animals do not in general perceive the world as it is described by physics. It is more likely that they primarily live in an *Umwelt*, i.e. a meaningful situation of Gestalten and affordances relevant to their body plans, skills, and drives.

Methodological physicalism demands both too much and too little of the faculty of perception. On the one hand, it imputes to animal perception an advanced capacity for decontextualization and abstraction. On the other hand, it ignores the possibility that animals live in a meaningful situation shaped by various affordances for social and instrumental action. To be sure, humans are good at bringing abstract physical details into focus, which turned out to be a technological and scientific virtue, but it is a cultural bias to assume that this is the primary role of perception. In nature, meaning comes first, abstraction later.

3.2. *Methodological solipsism*

When methodological physicalism is applied to the case of social understanding we get the assumption of *methodological solipsism,* which holds that perception of another animal's behavior is the same as perception of a moving or changing *object.* It is assumed that animals perceive each other as meaningless physical forms with shifting coordinates in an abstract space, and for them to know that some moving objects could be other agents requires additional effort. Thus, it is believed that most of the actual work supporting interaction with others is done by processing 'mental representations' of a "behavioral code (abstracted spatio-temporal invariances)" (Povinelli & Vonk, 2003: 157). But this is posing a false problem that, again, demands too little and too much of perception. Primarily, perception of others is about making sense of social affordances, which does not require objective analysis of physical properties. On the contrary, the presence of social meaning may prevent the physical medium from coming into view.

3.3. *Methodological dualism*

A further crucial consequence of methodological solipsism is the assumption of *methodological dualism*, which holds that there is a need "to go beyond the surface appearance of behavior to draw inferences about an individual's mental states" (Wood et al., 2007: 1402). If an animal's perceptual (natural and social) world is assumed to contain nothing but meaningless objects, but other agents are assumed to exist as well, then we are forced to assume that there is a dualist split between other agents' purely physical 'surface behavior' and their 'hidden' mind, whereby the being of the latter can only be ascertained by an additional process of reasoning or imagining by analogy (often called 'mind-reading').

However, as the history of philosophy makes abundantly clear, the idea that there is an absolute dichotomy between mind and behavior is another relatively recent socio-cultural bias. The assumption that mindedness cannot be directly perceived in the expressive bodily actions of others was first popularized in the European intellectual climate of the 17th century. Descartes' famous philosophy of mind-body dualism set up the well known 'problem of other minds' and its tentative solution in a 'theory of mind'. In fact, the assumption of mind-body dualism has become so ingrained that evidence to the contrary, such as provided by our own experience, is widely neglected (indicating a socio-cultural version of Kant's categories of perception). Worse, it is even actively suppressed (e.g. Povinelli & Vonk, 2003). However, when we leave this cultural bias aside and carefully attend to our lived experience we find that we directly *perceive* other humans as other minded beings without having to reflect at all on the fact of the matter (and the same is true when we perceive other primates). Instead of seeing mere 'surface behavior', the presence of others minds is immediately visible in their living embodiment. Of course, we can make use of abstraction, reasoning, and imagination as well, but *only* with additional mental effort and *only* on the basis of a preexisting intuitive insight into the existence of other mental lives.

In sum, after leaving these traditional cultural biases aside, it is reasonable to assume that non-human primates are situated in a social milieu and directly perceive conspecifics as other embodied agents. This claim is strongly supported by empirical, philosophical, and phenomenological arguments. What remains debatable is to what extent they can spontaneously decontextualize and objectify aspects of their *Umwelt* in order to analyze its abstract physical properties.

4. Concluding remarks: Steps toward an alternative framework

Animals perceive a meaningful *Umwelt*, and not an abstract physical universe devoid of meaning. Humans are set apart by their objectifying stance, i.e. their capacity for decontextualizing elements of their natural and social *Umwelt* into abstract objects whose physical properties can then be scrutinized. We conclude by highlighting the explanatory value of this alternative hypothesis with respect to the origins of cumulative cultural evolution, tool-use, and language.

Cumulative cultural evolution depends on innovation and imitation, and it is now generally accepted that non-human primates can partially fulfill both of the requirements. We suggest that it is the lack of a sophisticated objectifying stance that accounts for the crucial differences with human cultural evolution. First, if the perceptual presence of the *Umwelt* is defined by the existing affordances of the organism, then it will be difficult to innovate practices and tools based on previously unexploited properties of the environmental medium, since those will not make a direct perceptual appearance as such. Second, non-human primates may have problems in imitating complex gestures, because they cannot objectify them into a specific arbitrary sequence of movements. In both cases the physical medium itself is hidden by the expression of natural and social affordances.

Conversely, we hypothesize that the evolution of an incipient objectifying stance will be facilitated by a medium that is not already saturated with existing signification. In the case of the natural world, normally negligible aspects, such as stones, sticks, and other scattered materials, best serve this requirement of neutrality. They are the most accessible foundation for the invention of tools that go beyond natural affordances. In the social world, the living body itself is not a suitable medium because it is already the vehicle of natural expressions and instrumental action. Vocal production has the advantage that it is mostly hidden from view, and its neutrality is further enhanced by arbitrary vocalizations such as singing. The voice, perhaps aided by materials, creates a new medium for the ritualization of meanings that go beyond existing social affordances. These final remarks cast doubt on 'gesture-first' and 'animal call-first' theories of the origin of language, but support a 'song-first' theory (e.g. Merker & Okanoya, 2007).

Acknowledgements

Froese was supported by a Grant-in-Aid awarded by the JSPS. We thank David Leavens and three anonymous reviewers for their helpful comments.

References

Buttelmann, D., Carpenter, M., Call, J., & Tomasello, M. (2007). Encultured chimpanzees imitate rationally. *Developmental Science*, *10(4)*, F31-F38.

Call, J., Hare, B. H., Carpenter, M., & Tomasello, M. (2004). Unwilling or unable: chimpanzees' understanding of human intentions. *Dev. Sci.*, *7*, 488-9

Call, J., & Tomasello, M. (2008). Does the chimpanzee have a theory of mind? 30 years later. *Trends in Cognitive Sciences*, *12(5)*, 187-192.

Hauser, M. D., Glynn, D., & Wood, J. (2007). Rhesus monkeys correctly read the goal-relevant gestures of a human agent. *Proc. R. Soc. B*, *274*, 1913-1918

Hostetter, A. B., Russell, J. L., Freeman, H., & Hopkins, W. D. (2007). Now you see me, now you don't: evidence that chimpanzees understand the role of the eyes in attention. *Anim. Cogn.*, *10*, 55-62.

Kaminski, J., Call, J., & Tomasello, M. (2004). Body orientation and face orientation: two factors controlling apes' begging behavior from humans. *Anim. Cogn.*, *7*, 216-223.

Kaminski, J., Call, J., & Tomasello, M. (2008). Chimpanzees know what others know, but not what they believe. *Cognition*, *109*, 224-234.

Kumashiro, M., Ishibashi, H., Itakura, S., & Iriki, A. (2002). Bidirectional communication between a Japanese monkey and a human through eye gaze and pointing. *Curr. Psychol. Cogn.*, *21*, 3-32.

Kumashiro, M., Yokoyama, O., & Ishibashi, H. (2008). Imitation of Body Movements Facilitated by Joint Attention through Eye Contact and Pointing in Japanese Monkey. *PLoS ONE*, *3(11)*, e3704.

Merker, B., & Okanoya, K. (2007). The Natural History of Human Language: Bridging the Gaps without Magic. In C. Lyon, C. L. Nehaniv and A. Cangelosi (Eds.), *Emergence of Communication and Language* (pp. 403-420). London, UK: Springer-Verlag.

Penn, D. C., & Povinelli, D. J. (2007). On the lack of evidence that non-human animals possess anything remotely resembling a 'theory of mind'. *Phil. Trans. R. Soc. B*, *362*, 731-744.

Povinelli, D. J., & Vonk, J. (2003). Chimpanzee minds: suspiciously human? *Trends in Cognitive Sciences*, *7(4)*, 157-160.

Tomasello, M. (1999). *The cultural origins of human cognition*. Cambridge, MA: Harvard University Press.

Tomasello, M., Call, J., & Hare, B. (2003). Chimpanzees understand psychological states – the question is which ones and to what extent. *Trends in Cognitive Sciences*, *7(4)*, 153-156.

Tomasello, M., Kruger, A. C., & Ratner, H. H. (1993). Cultural learning. *Behavioral and Brain Sciences*, *16*, 495-552.

Warneken, F., Hare, B., Melis, A. P., Hanus, D., & Tomasello, M. (2007). Spontaneous Altruism by Chimpanzees and Young Children. *PLoS Biology*, *5(7)*, e184.

Warneken, F., & Tomasello, M. (2006). Altruistic Helping in Human Infants and Young Chimpanzees. *Science*, *311*, 1301-1303.

Wood, J. N., Glynn, D. D., Phillips, B. C., & Hauser, M. D. (2007). The Perception of Rational, Goal-Directed Action in Nonhuman Primates. *Science*, *317*, 1402-1405.

Yamamoto, S., Humle, T., & Tanaka, M. (2009). Chimpanzees Help Each Other upon Request. *PLoS ONE*, *4(10)*, e7416.

HOW DID PREDICATION EVOLVE?

DAVID GIL
Max Planck Institute for Evolutionary Anthropology
Leipzig, 04103, Germany

This paper proposes an emergent definition of predication as a composite notion involving the convergence of two more basic properties, thematic role assignment and headedness. This definition makes it possible to construct a scenario in which predication evolves gradually over the course of time. Evidence for such a scenario is provided by a contemporary human language, Riau Indonesian, in which the convergence of thematic role assignment and headedness is not grammaticalized.

Predication is a fundamental feature of human language and conceptual structure. Accordingly, the development of predication must have played a central role in the evolution of human language.

In most semantic theories, as also in logical systems such as the predicate calculus, predication is generally taken to be a primitive irreducible notion. For example, abstracting away from additional semantic features such as tense-aspect-mood, thematic roles, number, definiteness and the like, the basic meaning of English sentence (1) is typically represented in terms of a formula such as that in (2):

(1) The chicken is eating

(2) EAT (CHICKEN)

Following conventional usage in linguistics if not mathematical logic, the meaning of (1) is represented in (2) above in terms of a predicate EAT applying to an argument CHICKEN. The syntax of the formula in (2) reflects the received view of predication as a simple atomistic notion, not reducible to smaller building blocks. As such, there is not really much than can be said about its evolution other than the obvious fact that at some earlier stage it is absent while at some latter stage it is suddenly present.

In contrast, this paper argues that predication is not a primitive irreducible notion but rather a composite emergent entity derived from the coming together of independent elements of conceptual structure. Its emergent nature makes it possible to construct a plausible story accounting for the evolution of predication as a gradual and continuous process taking place over a potentially extended period of time.

In order to trace the emergence of predication, it is first necessary to define the base out of which it arises: a language without predication. This is the simple and abstract language type introduced in Gil (2005) as *Isolating-Monocategorial-Associational* (IMA). The three defining properties of IMA Language pertain to three different linguistic domains, morphology, syntax and semantics, representing the limiting points of maximal simplicity within each of these domains. The first property, *morphologically isolating*, asserts that in IMA language there is no word-internal structure: every word contains exactly one morpheme, and every morpheme constitutes a word. The second defining property, *syntactically monocategorial,* says that in IMA language, all words belong to the same syntactic category: there is no distinction between categories such as noun, verb, adjective and preposition, or between lexical categories and their phrasal projections. The third defining property, *semantically associational*, pertains to the compositional semantics, the ways in which the meanings of complex expressions are derived from the meanings of their constituent members, and makes reference to the *Association Operator*, defined in Gil (2005). In Gil (2006) it is argued that IMA Language can be mastered by captive apes, and therefore must have been part of the cognitive abilities of our common ancestors some 13 million years ago, even if they did not manifest this ability in actual linguistic behaviour. While resembling Bickerton's "protolanguage" in several respects, IMA language also differs from it in a number of ways, among others by having recursion.

To see how IMA language might work, imagine a simple sentence corresponding to English sentence (1):

(3) **chicken eat**

In (3) above, by assumption, the bold-face words ***chicken*** and ***eat*** mean the same as *chicken* and *eat* in English. However, since the language is isolating, each of the above two words is monomorphemic; there is no marking of number or definiteness, tense, aspect or mood, or thematic roles. Moreover, since the language is monocategorial, the above two words belong to the same category, which means that they exhibit the same grammatical behaviour: the above construction is thus a juxtaposition or coordination of like elements. Finally, since the language is associational, the meaning of the above construction is the output of the Association Operator applying to the two constituent terms, as represented in (4) below:

(4) A (CHICKEN EAT)

The above formula may be read as 'entity associated with chicken and eat'.

As represented in (4) above, the meaning of (3) is thus more general than that of (1) in several ways, of which two are of particular relevance here. First, whereas in (1), the morphosyntactic properties of English ensure that *chicken* is understood as the agent of *eat*, the construction in (3) is vague or underspecified with regard to thematic roles. All we know is that the chicken is involved in the eating in some way, but this could be as agent or as patient, or, if an appropriate context were to offer itself, in any other role. Secondly, whereas in (1), the grammatical rules of English entail that the construction is understood as denoting an activity, the construction in (3) is vague or underspecified with respect to ontological category. In particular, it could refer to either an activity 'The chicken is eating' or a thing 'the chicken that is eating'. Indeed, in an appropriate context, it could also be understood as denoting a time 'when the chicken is eating', place 'where the chicken is eating', manner 'the way the chicken is eating', or entities belonging to other ontological categories.

Unlike the English sentence in (1) and its interpretation in (2), the construction in (3) and its semantic representation in (4) are perfectly symmetrical. In (3), both words are monomorphemic and belong to the same syntactic category. That ***chicken*** happens to occurs before ***eat*** in (3) is an artifact of the modalities of writing and speech and not an intrinsic property of the construction. Similarly, in contrast to (2), the formula in (4) affords identical status to each of the two constituent meanings: A (CHICKEN EAT) is logically equivalent to A (EAT CHICKEN). Given that predication involves an asymmetric relationship between a predicate and its argument or arguments, the symmetry of (4) underscores the complete absence of any notion of predication from the meaning represented in (4). Thus, as illustrated by (3) and (4) above, IMA language is language without predication.

Although lacking predication, a construction such as (3) can still be used to describe a situation in which a chicken is eating; it can thus serve as a possible translation for (1). However, as pointed out above, its meaning is actually much broader than that of (1). More generally, IMA language, without predication, can be used for a wide range of communicative functions, while still lacking much of the specificity of English; this is argued in more detail in Gil (2009).

In order to bridge the gap between IMA Language and English, IMA Language must be enriched by, among others, two additional semantic properties, *thematic role assignment* and *headedness*. Each of these two properties draws upon conceptual structures that are independently motivated and not specific to language. Together, these two properties set the stage for an emergent definition of the notion of predication.

A formal definition of predication along these lines is provided in Gil (to appear). Less formally, predication may be said to involve the convergence of thematic role assignment and headedness in a particular configuration involving the identification, within a single meaning element, of the two notions of thematic role assigner and head; and hence also by default of the identification, within other meaning elements, of the notions of thematic role bearer and modifier. Thus, a predicate is a thematic-role-assigner head, while its arguments are its thematic-role-bearing modifiers. Predication is thus contrasted with attribution, in which thematic role assignment and headedness fail to align.

For example, taking as a starting point the IMA language sentence in (3), if ***eat*** were to assign a thematic role to ***chicken***, and if ***eat*** were understood as the head of the construction, projecting its denotational identity up to the entire construction, then the construction as a whole would merit the characterization as predicational, with ***eat*** constituting the predicate and ***chicken*** its argument.

The above definition of predication thus characterizes it as a composite, derivative notion, resulting from the coming together of two more basic notions, thematic role assignment and headedness. In doing so, it sets the stage for the construction of scenarios accounting for the gradual development of predication. For this purpose, however, it is necessary to distinguish between two manifestations of predication: *ad hoc* and *systematic*. Ad hoc predication is when thematic role assignment and headedness just happen to align as one of many alternative configurations equally available for these two features. In contrast, true or systematic predication is when the alignment of thematic role assignment and headedness is grammaticalized, or, in other words, expressed in rule-governed ways by means of dedicated morphosyntactic configurations. With this distinction, it becomes possible to describe the development of predication in terms of a continuous transition from no predication through ad hoc predication culminating in true systematic predication.

But how do we know that this is how predication actually evolved? It is often said that phylogeny may be recapitulated in ontogeny. Invoking this dictum, Gil (to appear) observes that the first-language acquisition of English and other similar languages by young children appears to traverse a similar path from IMA language through instances of ad hoc predication all the way to systematic grammaticalized predication, thereby suggesting that a similar evolutionary path does enjoy at least prima facie plausibility.

An additional argument is based on the observation that phylogeny may also be reflected in typology, via the presence of contemporary languages which, with respect to some features, resemble the presumed language of our pre-human ancestors; see, for example, several of the papers in Sampson, Gil and Trudgill eds. (2009) and also chapter 5 of Hurford (2011). (A disclaimer is necessary here: while phylogeny is a directional process, cross-linguistic variation is non-directional; thus, a contemporary language might share a particular feature with the languages of hominins where the feature in question is a recent development from a prior stage of the language in which that feature is absent. In other words, displaying such a feature does not mean that the language is in any sense "primitive".)

As argued extensively in Gil (2005, 2011) and elsewhere, Riau Indonesian presents an example of a language that comes closer than many other, more familiar languages, to exhibiting the array of properties characteristic of IMA Language. Consider, for example, the counterpart of (3) in Riau Indonesian:

(5) Ayam makan
chicken eat
'entity associated with chicken and eat'
A (CHICKEN, EAT)

Sentence (5) instantiates all three IMA properties: isolating, in that both words are monomorphemic; monocategorial, in that both words belong to the same syntactic category, Sentence; and associational, in that the meaning of the whole sentence is adequately represented by the association operator, as in (4). Semantically, then, sentence (5) resembles IMA language sentence (3) in that it is vague with respect to thematic roles and ontological categories: *ayam* 'chicken' can bear any thematic role with respect to *makan* 'eat', and the construction as a whole can refer to a chicken, an eating, or an entity belonging to any other ontological category. This suggests that Riau Indonesian may be characterized as a language without true predication.

The absence of predication in Riau Indonesian becomes more clearly evident when sentences such as (5) are examined in their naturalistic contexts, as for example in the following utterance, produced by a man standing on a balcony and looking down to the street:

(6) Mobil rusak
car broken.down
'entity associated with car and broken down'
A (CAR, BROKEN.DOWN)

Example (6) is completely parallel to (5), exhibiting isolating, monocategorial and associational structure. However, its broad associational meaning is substantially narrowed down by the context, which limits the interpretation to present tense and a single car bearing the thematic role of theme with respect to the property word 'broken down'. But what, one might ask, is the ontological category of the utterance's meaning? The question may be recast from the perspective of a would-be translator of the utterance into English: should it be translated as 'That car out there is broken down' or as 'There's a broken down car out there'? Adopting the former translation would seem to suggest that (6) denotes a property, in which the property expression *rusak* 'broken down' is predicated of *mobil* 'car'. Alternatively, opting for the latter translation would appear to indicate that (5) refers to a thing, *mobil rusak* 'broken down car', where the property *rusak* 'broken down' is attributed of *mobil* 'car'. So which is the most appropriate translation? The answer is neither. Speakers of Riau Indonesian have no reason to be concerned with the possible translations of their sentences into English. In particular, it is implausible to suppose that the speaker who uttered (6) in the given context had in mind one of the two meanings corresponding to the two possible translations into English, to the exclusion of the other. Rather, what he intended was a single underspecified interpretation represented in terms of the association operator, as indicated in (6). Thus, utterance (6) is most appropriately described as being vague or underspecified with respect to the ontological categories of property and thing. Correspondingly, it is also indeterminate with regard to headedness and the distinction between predication and attribution: *rusak* 'broken down' is neither predicated of *mobil* 'car'' nor attributed of it, but instead the two words stand in an associative relation with respect to each other. Thus, utterances such as (6), when considered in their naturalistic contexts, underscore the IMA character of Riau Indonesian as a language without systematic expression of predication.

Nevertheless, as argued in Gil (2005), Riau Indonesian is not a pure IMA language; while approaching each of the three defining characteristics of IMA language, it doesn't quite get there. Accordingly, Riau Indonesian is characterized as a *relatively* IMA language. Many of the ways in which Riau Indonesian fails to be purely associational involve preference rules of a kind similar to those discussed in detail in another cognitive domain, tonal music, by Lerdahl and Jackendoff (1983): such preference rules apply to representations couched in terms of the association operator, partition them into subinterpretations, and then characterize some subinterpretations as more readily available than others. Of interest to us here are the ways in which such preference rules affect thematic role assignment and headedness.

Consider, for example, sentence (5) above. Although its range of possible interpretations, as represented in terms of the association operator, is extremely broad, it is certainly not the case that all subinterpretations are obtainable with equal ease. If presented with sentence (5) in isolation, the first interpretation that is likely to come to the mind of a speaker of Riau Indonesian is one in which the sentence denotes an activity in which the chicken bears the thematic role of agent — in other words, and abstracting away from number, definiteness, tense, aspect and so forth, an interpretation resembling that of English sentence (1) *The chicken is eating.* This may be accounted for by preference rules making reference to features such as ontological categories, semantic frames, and iconicity — see Gil (to appear) for details. Observe, now, that the preferred interpretation of (5) is one in which thematic role assignment aligns with headedness, with the thematic role assigner, *makan,* also the head of the construction, projecting its denotational identity up to the sentence as a whole. Thus, the preferred interpretation of (5) exhibits the convergence of thematic role assignment and headedness characteristic of predication. In doing so, it presents a case of ad hoc predication. However, it fails to constitute an instance of systematic predication for two reasons: first, because it is not associated with any particular morphosyntactic configuration; secondly, because there is no clear-cut boundary between preferred interpretations upholding the alignment between thematic role assignment and headedness and dispreferred interpretations failing to do so. Or, in other words, because it is not grammaticalized. Nevertheless, from the perspective of pure IMA language, as instantiated in ontogeny and phylogeny, the occurrence of ad hoc predication makes it look as though Riau Indonesian has at least taken a first step or two on the path towards developing true systematic predication

Alongside preference rules such as those mentioned above, another factor playing an important role in the emergence of predication is utterance context. Although, as pointed out in the discussion of (6) above, utterance context often allows for a large degree of vagueness, including indeterminacy between predicative and attributive interpretations, in other cases, utterance context narrows down the possibilities, in many instances restricting them to interpretations of a predicational nature.

In conjunction, then, preference rules and discourse contexts result in the frequent occurrence of utterances in which thematic role assignment and headedness align in a predicational manner. The emergent definition of predication proposed here makes it possible to characterize such utterances as ad hoc predications. Although clearly distinct from instances of systematic predication in languages such as English, they can be viewed as occupying a way station on the path towards the development of true predication.

Thus, as a relatively IMA language, Riau Indonesian provides us with a window into our evolutionary past, by showing us an intermediate stage in the emergence of predication. First there was IMA language, with no predication whatsoever. Down the line, a pre-human population with IMA language but also cognitive abilities including thematic role assignment and headedness produces utterances such as in (3). Such a language gives rise to occasional instances of ad hoc predication. Increasingly, in actual production over time, a tendency emerges for thematic role assigners to align with heads, and for thematic role bearers to align with modifiers. Eventually, this tendency becomes conventionalized and is awarded morphosyntactic expression by various grammatical devices. This, then, is how predication evolves.

References

Gil, David (2005) "Isolating-Monocategorial-Associational Language", in H. Cohen and C. Lefebvre eds., *Categorization in Cognitive Science*, Elsevier, Oxford, 347-379.

Gil, David (2006) "Early Human Language Was Isolating-Monocategorial-Associational", in A. Cangelosi, A.D.M Smith and K. Smith eds., *The Evolution of Language, Proceedings of the 6th International Conference (EVOLANG6)*, World Scientific, Singapore, 91-98.

Gil, David (2009) "How Much Grammar Does It Take to Sail a Boat?", in G. Sampson, D. Gil and P. Trudgill eds., *Language Complexity as an Evolving Variable*, Oxford University Press, Oxford, 19-33.

Gil, David (2011) "Riau Indonesian: A Language without Nouns and Verbs", in J. Rijkhoff and E. van Lier eds., *Flexible Word Classes*, Oxford University Press, Oxford.

Gil, David (to appear) "Where Does Predication Come From?", *Canadian Journal of Linguistics*.

Hurford, James R. (2011) *The Origins of Grammar, Language in the Light of Evolution*, Oxford University Press, Oxford.

Lerdahl, Fred and Ray S. Jackendoff (1983) *A Generative Theory of Tonal Music*, MIT Press, Cambridge.

Sampson, Geoffrey, David Gil and Peter Trudgill eds. (2009) *Language Complexity as an Evolving Variable*, Oxford University Press, Oxford.

INDIVIDUAL AND SOCIAL EFFECTS ON LINGUISTIC DIFFUSION

TAO GONG
Department of Linguistics, University of Hong Kong, Pokfulam Road, Hong Kong

MÓNICA TAMARIZ
Department of Linguistics and English Language, University of Edinburgh Charles Street, Edinburgh, UK

GERHARD JÄGER
Department of Linguistics, University of Tübingen, Wilhelmstraße, Tübingen, Germany

Using a Pólya urn based diffusion model, we examine linguistic diffusion in a population of individuals with different types of social networks. Simulation results and statistical analyses show that individual factors, such as who (speakers or hearers) introduce preference for certain types of variants, and network structural features, e.g., level of centrality, collectively modulate the degree of diffusion. This work shows different diffusion efficiencies of speaker's and hearer's preferences for variants, evaluates the effect of individual learning and social factors on linguistic diffusion, and modifies previous diffusion theories focusing exclusively on individual or social factors.

1. Introduction

Language is a socio-cultural phenomenon that undergoes constant changing (Hruschka et al., 2009). Many changes are achieved via diffusion of various types (phonetic, lexical, syntactic, etc.) of linguistic variants, such as the Great Vowel Shift in English in the 14-16th century (Wolfe, 1972), other sound change in *Wu* dialect of Chinese (Shen, 1997), or lexical borrowing (Cheng, 1987). *Linguistic diffusion* (henceforth "diffusion") can be viewed as the shift in proportions of linguistic variants used by a population over time (Nakamura et al., 2007). Studying the manners in which diffusion occurs helps understand human cognitive capacities for language and socio-cultural constraints on language evolution (Croft, 2000; Labov, 2001).

Theories of diffusion usually assume an innovator-learner framework, discussing who mainly innovate or introduce preference for certain types of variants and who mainly learn variants in linguistic interactions (Mufwene, 2008) or examining factors that can affect individuals' choices of variants or languages (Labov, 2001; Nettle, 1999). Besides the small-scale, empirical approach in sociolinguistics (Croft, 2000; Fisiak, 1995; Labov, 2001), mathematical and behavioral simulations have been recently adopted to study the effect of linguistic, individual learning, and socio-cultural factors on language evolution. By quantifying contact patterns and social prestige, mathematical models help predict the outcome of language competition (e.g., Abram & Strogatz, 2003; Minett & Wang, 2008); by simulating linguistic behaviors, behavioral models trace the conventionalization of form-meaning mappings (e.g., Steels, 1995) and linguistic regularities (e.g., Gong, 2011) via local interactions, and reveal the correlation between population size or social connections and individual memory load or diffusion success (e.g., Dall'Asta et al., 2006; Ke et al., 2008). However, these studies usually separate individual and social factors in diffusion. For example, in mathematical models, individual choice of languages is mainly determined by global factors such as linguistic prestige, disregarding social connections. In behavioral models, hearers mainly acquire and update linguistic knowledge. Studies that connect networks with learning factors (e.g., Dall'Asta et al., 2006) only examine simple networks such as lattice networks, and others that consider complex networks (e.g., Ke et al., 2008) lack a systematic analysis of the effect of structural features on diffusion.

During diffusion, speakers or hearers, or both, can innovate or introduce identical or different preferences for variants. For example, speakers tend to use easily produced variants (e.g., easily pronounced pronoun forms in Cantonese), and hearers may prefer easily perceived or salient variants (Labov, 1994; Shen, 1997). Combining speaker's and hearer's preferences with social constraints due to network structures can better understand the mutual influence of individual learning (e.g., who introduce the preference for variants) and social networks (e.g., structural factors restricting linguistic interactions among individuals) on diffusion. In this paper, we evaluate such influence based on a diffusion model and a number of typical network structures. In the rest of the paper, we describe the diffusion model and adopted networks (Sec. 2), show (Sec. 3) and discuss (Sec. 4) the results, and finally conclude (Sec. 5).

2. Pólya Urn Diffusion Model and Network Structures

The Pólya urn model was first designed to study contagion (Johnson & Kotz, 1977; Marshall & Olkin, 1993). In the original model, a Pólya urn is an urn containing red or green balls; at each timestep, a ball is randomly drawn from the urn, and returned to it together with some balls having the same or different color. This process is then iterated. Our diffusion model, inspired by this prototypical model, contains N agents (individuals), each denoted by an urn. An agent is initiated with V tokens, each having a feature x_i (all feature values form F) and belonging to a particular type (v_1, v_2, … v_v). At each timestep, an interaction takes place between two or more agents, where a token v_i is drawn randomly from an agent (*speaker*), and p_i (the prestige of v_i, all prestige values form P) tokens of the same type are added to the same or other agent(s) (*hearer(s)*). Such drawing and returning processes repeat themselves, causing the distribution of variant types in all agents to change over time. *Mutation* may occur if an added token has a different type from the drawn one.

From a linguistic perspective, token drawing corresponds to production, and token adding corresponds to perception and knowledge update. Each type of linguistic variants possesses a *feature value* (similar to F). One type of variants may have a higher *prestige value* (similar to P) than the other, thus being preferred by speakers or hearers. During interactions, mutation corresponds to *transmission error*. Fig. 1 shows three examples of the Pólya urn dynamics in this model. This stripped-down model simulates production, perception, and update of variants during linguistic interactions, introduces variant preference from speakers or hearers, and traces the diffusion of variants in the population based on the distribution of different types of variants.

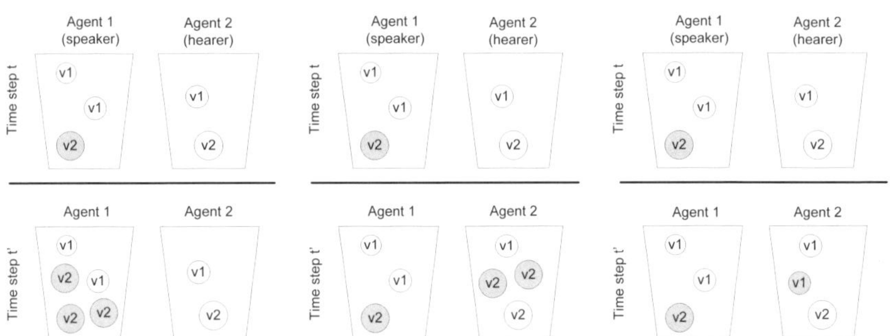

Figure 1. Pólya urn dynamics (N=2, V=2, F={1, 2}, P={1, 2}). Left: with speaker's preference: at time t, the speaker selects a token of v_2 to produce, and adds two tokens of v_2 to its own urn, which form the state at time t'; Middle: with hearer's preference, the hearer adds two v_2 to its own urn; Right: with hearer's preference and mutation, when the hearer adds two v_2, one is mutated to v_1.

The model uses social networks to define connections among agents, treating agents as nodes and connections as edges. It considers 6 types of representative networks: fully-connected network, star network, scale-free network, small-world network, two-dimensional (2D) lattice, and ring. Table 1 lists the average degree, clustering coefficient and average shortest path length of these networks. It is shown that: from ring to 2D lattice, average degree increases; from 2D lattice to small-world network or scale-free network, average shortest path length drops due to 'short-cuts' in small-world network or 'hubs' (nodes having many connections with others) in scale-free network; from 2D lattice to scale-free network, and then, to star network, level of centrality increases; more and more nodes tend to connect to some popular node(s).

Table 1. Network characteristics: values are calculated based on 100 nodes. A scale-free network is formed by preferential attachment, with average degree around 4; a small-world network is formed by rewiring from a 2D lattice, with the reviewing rate as 0.1. Numbers within brackets are standard deviations of values in scale-free and small-world networks. *Average degree*: average number of edges per node; *clustering coefficient*: probability for *neighbors* (directly connected nodes) of a node to be neighbors themselves; and *average shortest path length*: average smallest number of edges, via which any two nodes in the network can connect to each other.

Network	Average degree	Clustering coefficient	Shortest path length
Fully-connected	99	1.0	1
Star	1.98	0.0	1.98
Scale-free	3.94 (4e-14)	0.14 (0.038)	3.01 (0.071)
Small-world	4	0.17 (0.031)	3.79 (0.086)
2D lattice	4	0.5	12.88
Ring	2	0.0	25.25

For the sake of simplicity, in the following simulations, we set N=100, V=2, F={1,2}, P={1,2}, 5000 (50 interactions per agent) pair-wise interactions (only agents that are directly connected can interact, each agent in a connection can be either speaker or hearer, and each connection in a network has an equal chance to be chosen for interaction), and exclude mutation. Among the two types of variants, Type 2 is preferred, either by speakers (speaker's preference) or by hearers (hearer's preference). In a simulation, we measure $proportion(v_i,t)$ as the proportion of v_i in the population and $prop(t)$ ($=max\{proportion(v_i,t)\}$) as the proportion of the majority type, at 50 sampling points evenly distributed among 5000 interactions. In each type of network, we conduct 100 runs with speaker's preference and 100 with hearer's preference.

3. Simulation Results and Statistical Analysis

We conduct a 2-way analysis of covariance (ANCOVA) (dependent variable: *prop(t)* over 100 simulations; fixed factors: speaker's/hearer's preference and networks; covariate: 50 sampling points). Using ANCOVA, instead of ANOVA at a particular sampling point, is to neutralize the influence of the number of interactions. This analysis shows significant main effects of networks ($F(5, 61187) = 1111.425$, $p < .001$, $\eta_p^2 = .083$) and speaker/hearer's preference ($F(1, 61187) = 6905.606$, $p < .001$, $\eta_p^2 = .101$) on *prop(t)*. These effects are shown in Fig. 2, the left panel of which shows the marginal mean *prop(t)* with speaker's (solid line) and hearer's (dashed line) preference in different types of network (calculated as the mean value over all *prop(t)* at every sampling points) and the right panel shows the marginal mean *prop(t)* among networks (calculated as the mean value over all *prop(t)* in simulations with speaker's preference and with hearer's preference). Apart from these, the number of interactions has a significant effect ($F(1, 61187) = 108285.542$, $p < .001$, $\eta_p^2 = .639$).

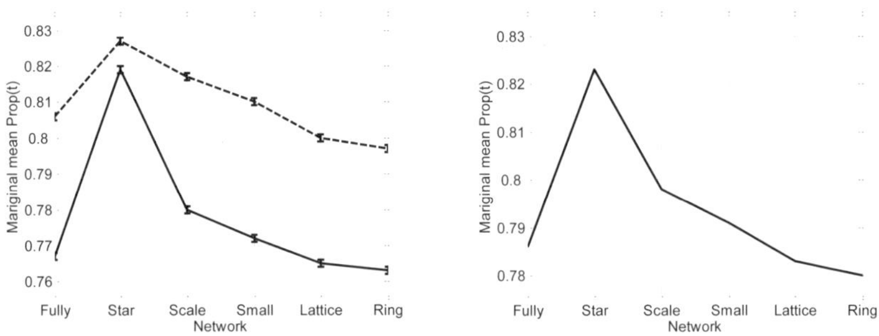

Figure 2. Simulation results. Left: marginal mean *prop(t)* with speaker's (solid line) and hearer's (dashed line) preferences in different networks. Right: marginal mean *prop(t)* in different networks.

In these simulations, due to its higher prestige value, Type 2 variants gradually become the majority type and diffuse in the population, indicated by high *prop(t)*. Meanwhile, speaker's and hearer's preferences show different diffusion efficiencies. This is evident in fully-connected network, which resembles the case of random interaction and excludes network influence. In this network, hearer's preference leads to a higher degree of diffusion than speaker's preference. Similar tendencies can be found in other networks. Furthermore, degrees of diffusion in different networks are different; star network has the highest *prop(t)* (the highest degree of diffusion), then, scale-free network, small-world network, lattice, and finally, ring.

4. Discussions

During one interaction, the preference introduced by a speaker or by a hearer has the same effect on the distribution of variants in these two contacting agents, as shown in Fig. 1. However, in a situation of multiple agents and iterated interactions, these two types of preference start to show different effects.

Speaker's preference is *self-centered*, disregarding other agents. For example, if an agent has a majority of Type 1 variants, when it interacts as the speaker with another agent whose majority variant type is Type 2, it still has a higher chance of choosing a token of Type 1 and increasing Type 1's proportion by adding tokens of the same type. In contrast, hearer's preference is *other-centered*, allowing the hearer's variant distribution to be adjusted by other agents. For example, if an agent has a majority of Type 1 variants, when it interacts as the hearer with another agent whose majority variant type is Type 2, it will have a higher chance of adding some Type 2 tokens, which will gradually adjust its variant distribution to become similar to others'. After iterated interactions, a uniform majority variant type in all agents can be achieved. Therefore, given the same number of interactions, hearer's preference for certain type of variants is more efficient for diffusion than speaker's preference, as shown by the significantly higher *prop(t)* with hearer's preference than that with speaker's preference in Fig. 2. Considering one-speaker-multiple-hearer interactions in real societies, the effect of hearer's preference will be further improved.

Due to the clear prestige advantage of Type 2 over Type 1, the value difference of *prop(t)* in these two preference conditions is not high, but the statistical analysis confirms that they are significantly different. This indicates that in real case diffusion studies we need to separate these two types of preference and pay attention to their possible different effects on diffusion, especially in a multi-agent human society.

The effect of networks on degree of diffusion can be ascribed to structural features of networks. The first candidate feature is *average degree*. Seen from Table 1, average degree is 2 in ring, 4 in 2D lattice. But the marginal mean values of *prop(t)* in these two networks are not significantly different (a post-hoc T-test of the marginal *prop(t)* does not show a significant difference, $t(198) = -0.759$, $p = 0.449$). However, in one-speaker-multiple-hearer interactions as in real societies, the effect of average degree becomes explicit (the same T-test shows a significant difference, $t(198) = -9.338$, $p < 0.001$). In addition, the similar results in ring and 2D lattice but different results in 2D lattice and scale-free or small-world networks indicate that there must be other structural features that are taking effect. And average degree alone fails to explain why star network, having the lowest average degree (1.98), has the highest *prop(t)*.

The second candidate is *level of centrality*. Star network has an extremely centralized structure; there is a hub connecting all the other nodes and participating in all interactions. With speaker's preference, the hub has many chances to update its variant distribution; with hearer's preference, any update of variant distribution can be quickly spread via the hub to others. Besides star network, scale-free network, due to preferential attachment, also has several nodes that connect many others, but the level of centrality in scale-free network is less than that of star network. Accordingly, its *prop(t)* is significantly smaller ($t(198) = -5.194$, $p < 0.001$). Lacking centralized structures in other types of networks causes their *prop(t)* to be much smaller than that in star or scale-free network. Level of centrality also explains why small-world network and 2D lattice, having identical average degree, end up having significantly different *prop(t)*($t(198) = 3.538$, $p < 0.001$). Small-world network is created via rewiring from 2D lattice. Such rewiring causes some nodes to have more edges than others, and these nodes will play a similar role as hubs to increase *prop(t)*. However, this way of introducing hubs is less efficient than preferential attachment, so *prop(t)* in small-world network is significantly smaller than that in scale-free network ($t(198) = -3.878$, $p < 0.001$).

Finally, *average shortest path length* reveals a combined effect of average degree and level of centrality; if a network has a high average degree and/or a high level of centrality, any two nodes in it can be connected via a small number of edges. Since star network has much lower average shortest path length (1.98), it has much higher *prop(t)*, and then scale-free network (3.01), small-world network (3.79), and 2D lattice (12.88). Since ring has the highest average shortest path length (25.25), its *prop(t)* is the lowest.

5. Conclusions and Future Work

This study discusses the effects of speaker's and hearer's preferences for certain types of variants and those of network structures on diffusion of linguistic variants in a population of individuals. The distinction of speaker's and hearer's preferences and the discovery of their different effects on diffusion extend the previous work that focuses more on hearer's effect on language change or diffusion. Identification of the effect of level of centrality on diffusion enriches the discussion of socio-cultural factors relevant for language evolution. Finally, this study can trigger some promising future work, such as examining the diffusion with contradictory speaker's and hearer's preferences or analyzing the effect of preference introduced by crucial nodes (e.g., hubs) in networks, especially in one-speaker-multiple-hearer interactions.

Acknowledgements

Gong is supported by the Society of Scholars in the University of Hong Kong. Tamariz is supported by the UK AHRC Grant AH/F017677/1.

References

Abram, D. M., & Strogatz, S. H. (2003). Modeling the dynamics of language death. *Nature*, 424, 900.

Cheng, R. L. (1987). Borrowing and internal development in lexical change. *Journal of Chinese Linguistics*, 15, 105-131.

Croft, W. (2000). *Explaining language change: An evolutionary approach*. Harlow, UK: Longman.

Dall'Asta, L., Baronchelli, A., Barrat, A., & Loreto, V. (2006). Non-equilibrium dynamics of language games on complex networks. *Physics Review E*, 74, 036105.

Fisiak, J. (Ed.) (1995). *Linguistic change under contact conditions*. New York: M. de Gruyter.

Gong, T. (2011). Simulating the coevolution of compositionality and word order regularity. *Interaction Studies*, 12(1): 63–106.

Hruschka, D. J. et al. (2009). Building social cognitive models of language change. *TRENDS in Cognitive Science*, 13, 464-469.

Johnson, N. L., & Kotz, S. (1977). *Urn models and their applications*. New York: Wiley.

Ke, J-Y., Gong, T., & Wang, W. S-Y. (2008). Language change and social networks. *Communications in Computational Physics*, 3, 935-949.

Labov, W. (2001). *Principles of linguistic change: Social factors*. Oxford, UK: Blackwell.

Marshall, A. W., & Olkin, I. (1993). Bivariate life distributions from Pólya urn model for contagion. *Journal of Applied Probability*, 30, 497-508.

Minett, J. W., & Wang, W. S-Y. (2008). Modelling endangered languages: The effects of bilingualism and social structure. *Lingua*, 118, 19-45.

Mufwene, S. S. (2008). What do creoles and pidgins tell us about the evolution of language? In S. S. Mufwene (Ed.), *Language evolution: Contact, competition and change* (pp. 272-297). London: Continuum.

Nakamura, M., Hashimoto, T., & Tojo, S. (2007). Language change among 'memoryless learners' simulated in language dynamics equations. In C. Lyon, C. L. Nehaniv, & A. Cangelosi (Eds.), *Emergence of communication and language* (pp. 237-252). London: Springer.

Nettle, D. (1999). Using social impact theory to simulate language change. *Lingua*, 108, 95-117.

Shen, Z-W. (1997). *Exploring the dynamic aspect of sound change*. Berkeley: University of California Press.

Steels, L. (1995). A self-organizing spatial vocabulary. *Artificial Life*, 2, 319-332.

Wolfe, P. M. (1972). *Linguistic change and the Great Vowel Shift in English*. Berkeley: University of California Press.

ONTOGENY OF TWO COMMUNICATIVE TOOLS: DISTANCE ENCODING & MULTIMODALITY IN DEICTIC POINTING

CHLOE GONSETH, ANNE VILAIN, & CORIANDRE VILAIN
GIPSA-Lab, Speech & Cognition Department, Grenoble University
Grenoble, 38000, France

The aim of this paper is to experimentally study the development of speech/gesture relationship within language. The participants, both adults and children, had to designate a target placed at two different distances. They had to perform a deictic gesture accompanied by a deictic word, or to use either of the two modalities independently. Using one vs two pointing modalities allowed us to specify the interaction between the two systems as a useful cooperation, in terms of communicative efficiency. Furthermore, articulatory cues in the vocal modality and kinematic cues in the gestural modality encode the target's distance, and that in a different way in adults as compared with children. The huge variability found in children indicates that they are learning to control the communicative tools they have.

1. Introduction

This study aims at questioning the functional relationship between speech and gesture in the linguistic communication of children and adults, and focusses on the process of spatial deixis. This process, allowing us to attract our interlocutor's attention, is most of the time performed in a multimodal way, as it can be realized both via the vocal and the gestural system, using various pointing gestures. These deictic gestures are universal across cultures; they occupy a particular function in adult language, being ubiquitous in everyday interactions and often accompanied by a deictic word such as "here" or "that" (Kendon, 2004). Data suggest that deictic pointing might be one of the most basic elements of referential communication, and maybe one of the precursors of the phylogenetic development of human language (Arbib, 2005).

In this study dealing with deixis, we investigate (i) the interaction between the vocal and manual systems as a possible cooperation, and (ii) the distance encoding in both vocal and manual pointing as a particular deictic, and therefore communicative function. The distance of a designated object with respect to the speaker and the listener is a spatial feature that we believe can be encoded both through the kinematic properties of manual pointing gestures and through the lexical and phonetic properties of the deictic terms that are used (see Bonfiglioli et al., 2009, for interaction between lexical encoding of distance and kinematic properties of pointing gestures). Deictic terms encoding distance can be either proximal (e.g. "here") or distal (e.g. "there"). Typological studies evidence a specific relationship between the encoded distance and the phonological features of the appropriate deictic term. Diessel (1999) notably demonstrated that proximal forms of deictics tend to contain more close vowels than distal forms. Close vowels, contrary to open vowels, are produced with the tongue positioned high in the mouth and with a consequently high jaw position. This is taken as a sound symbolism phenomenon, that is a consistent link beween phonetics and semantics. Our hypothesis is that this typological tendency might be explained by a very basic motor behaviour: speakers tend to open their mouth more when they designate distant objects than when they designate close objects.

In a former work on adult language (Gonseth et al., 2011), we showed that the distance of the target (close vs distant) and the modalities used to designate this target (*speech* vs *speech+gesture*) influenced either acoustical values or articulatory gestures. These findings suggest that distance can be encoded in vocal pointing and that vocal and manual systems cooperate within the particular deictic function. Such a crucial interaction between speech, gesture, and language in adults evidently calls for further studies during the development of linguistic communication. Deictic pointing is indeed crucial when it comes to language ontogenesis. The canonical index finger pointing is the first tool used by children to designate what surrounds them (Kita, 2003). Its use is consistently correlated with important landmarks in the development of verbal production and perception competencies (Özçalışkan & Goldin-Meadow, 2005) and related to gains in language development and future communicative abilities (Butcher & Goldin-Meadow, 2000). Speech/gesture interaction then appears to be a critical factor in the inception of communicative development.

For these reasons, we investigated speech/gesture cooperation and distance encoding in the use of multimodal communication by children, as compared to adults. Though gestures are extremely present in both adult and child communication, their use depends on the speaker's expertise. Children use the gestural modality as an introduction to the linguistic system, whereas gestures have more complex pragmatic functions in adults (e.g. to emphasize a specific discourse element). We then expect a different cognitive processing, resulting in a different spatial coordination between speech and gesture in children as compared with adults, and an evolution throughout the first years of linguistic development. Distance encoding, as a more subtle strategy, is expected to be controled later. The present investigation is thus meant to elaborate a developmental schedule of multimodal linguistic pointing.

2. Method

The objective of this study is to replicate the findings of our previous experiment (Gonseth et al. 2011), and to collect new data in 6 to 12 year old children, in order to characterize the evolution of the correlates of distance encoding in both modalities. Are the distance encoding and the speech/gesture cooperation intrinsic features of language use (i.e. observed in both children and adults) or efficient communicative strategies learnt by skilled speakers (i.e. not observed in children, or much more variable than in adult speakers)?

2.1. *Partipants*

Twenty-seven French-speaking adults (ages 18-36 years) participated in the study. Besides, we recorded six French-speaking children (ages 7-12 years, see table 1) as a pilot child sample. All participants were voluntary and naive as to the purpose of the study.

Table 1. Age of each child.

Participant	P1	P2	P3	P4	P5	P6
Age (years)	8	11	11	7	12	8

2.2. *Procedure*

The participants are in a soundproof room in front of two light-emitting diodes (LED), placed at 140 (D1) and 425 cm (D2). Both LEDs are out of arm's reach, but D1 is considerably closer than D2. They are aligned with respect to the subjects' eyes, so that the angle of the arm can not be used to disambiguate which target is pointed at, and so that there has to be a specific gesture for distance encoding. As a reply to the experimenter's question "C'est où?" ("Where is it?"), participants have to designate the turned-on LED, according to three conditions (participants presented 20 trials per condition):

1. *Speech*: name the turned-on LED using the deictic word "là"/"there", embedded in a carrier sentence (i.e. preceded by "c'est" / "it is").
2. *Gesture*: point at the target with an index finger pointing.
3. *Speech+gesture*: simultaneously name and point at the target.

We thus test a cooperation between speech and gesture: vocal and manual pointing are expected to be reinforced in unimodal conditions (*speech* or *gesture*) as compared to the bimodal condition (*speech+gesture*).

3. Recordings & measurements

3.1. *Articulatory and manual data*

Oro-facial and index movements were recorded with the motion capture system Optotrak. Three reference emitters were placed on the forehead, two emitters on the lips, and one emitter on the index. Lip opening was thus measured (lower-lip vertical position minus upper-lip vertical position, in mm), as well as the total duration and the holding duration (s) of the index finger pointing.

3.2. *Acoustical data*

Acoustical features of the vowels were recorded in order to get additional information on articulatory data. Oral productions were recorded via a microphone AKG C1000S. We isolated the vowel in the deictic word "là" ([a]) and measured the first formant (F1, in Hz) in the middle of the vowel.
What we are investigating is the intra-category phonetic variation according to the distance of the target, that is: refering to our previous results, [a] in "là" is expected to be more open when "là" designates a distant target.

4. Results

Failed trials were excluded from the analysis. The median values of acoustical, articulatory, and manual data were used for the statistical analysis, with a significance level fixed at $p < 0.05$, and two fixed factors: (1) three conditions C (*speech*, *gesture*, *speech+gesture*); (2) two distances D (140; 425 cm).
For adults, a repeated-measures analysis of the variance was conducted; for children, an analysis of the variance was conducted for each participant.

4.1. *Articulatory and acoustical data*

4.1.1. *Effect of distance and condition on lip opening*

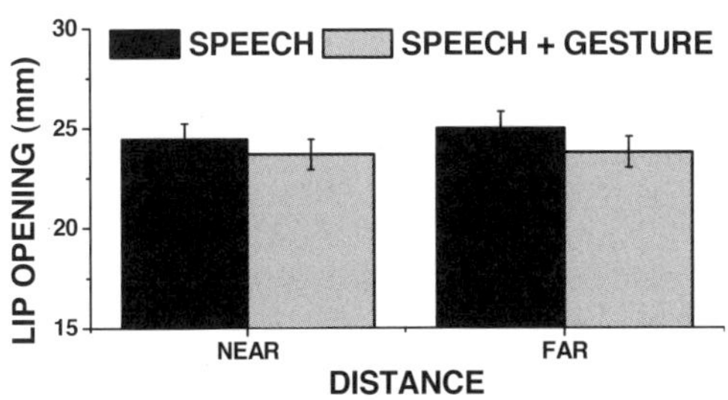

Figure 1. Lip opening values as a function of the condition and the distance for the adults.

Figure 1 illustrates lip opening variations as a function of both distance and condition in adults. Lip opening is influenced by the condition. It is indeed larger in the *speech* condition than in the *speech+gesture* condition ($F(1, 24)=17.06$, $p<0.05$). Furthermore, we find a significant effect of the distance ($F(1, 24)=8.87$, $p<0.05$). Regardless of the condition, lip opening is larger for farther distance.

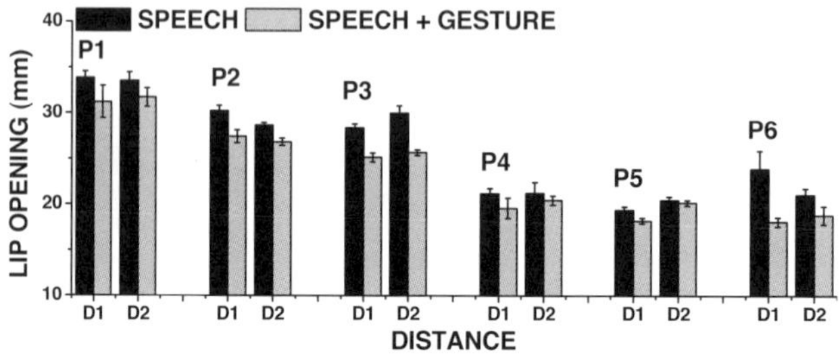

Figure 2. Lip opening values as a function of the condition and the distance for six children.

Figure 2 concerns lip opening variations for six children. For P1 and P4, lip opening does not vary as a function of the distance nor of the condition (P1 D: $F(1, 30)=0.28$, $p=0.60$, ns; C: $F(1,30)=1.99$, $p=0.17$, ns; P4: D: $F(1, 35)=1.17$, $p=0.29$, ns; C: $F(1, 35)=2.41$, $p=0.13$, ns). P2 and P6 show a significant effect of the condition (P2 D: $F(1, 35)=0.99$, $p=0.32$, ns; C: $F(1,35)=13.42$, $p<0.05$; P6 D: $F(1, 21)=1.51$, $p=0.23$, ns; C: $F(1, 21)=5.96$, $p<0.05$), whereas P5 shows a significant effet of the distance (D: $F(1, 32)=8.15$, $p<0.05$; C: $F(1,32)=1.59$, $p=0.21$, ns). Finally, both distance and condition affect the lip opening for P3 (D: $F(1, 35)=4.09$, $p=0.05$; C: $F(1,35)=39.54$, $p<0.05$).

4.1.2. *Effects of distance and condition on F1 values*

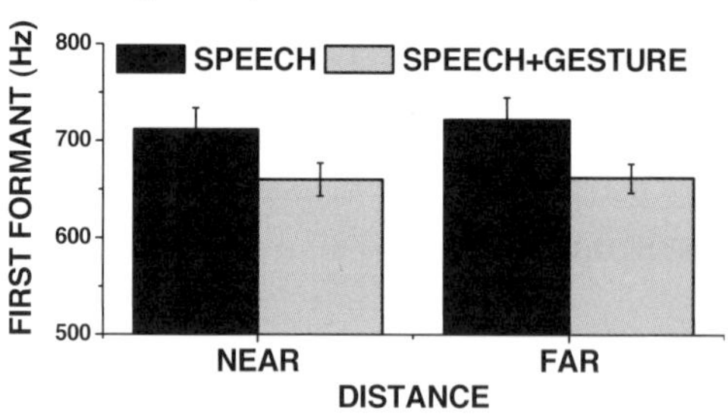

Figure 3. F1 values as a function of the condition and the distance for the adults.

Figure 3 illustrates F1 variations as a function of both distance and condition in adults. A significant effect of the condition is observed ($F(1, 26)=16.67$, $p<0.05$)

but no significant effect of the distance (F(1, 26)=0.84, p=0.36, ns). F1 values are higher in unimodal condition (*speech*) than in bimodal condition (*speech+gesture*) but do not vary as a function of the target's distance.

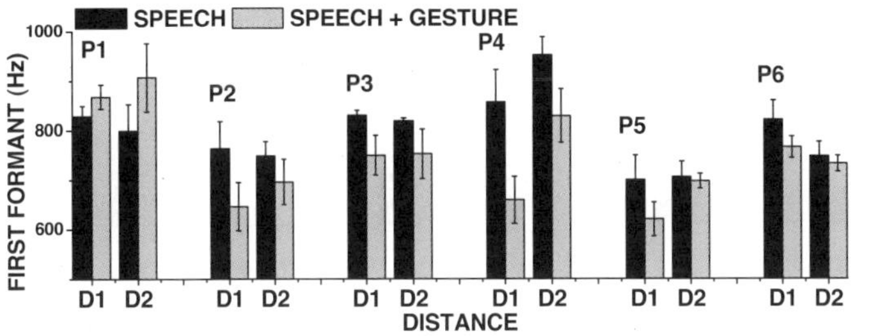

Figure 4. F1 values as a function of the condition and the distance for six children.

Figure 4 concerns F1 variations for six children. Four different patterns are found. Neither the condition nor the distance affect F1 values for P1 (C: F(1, 35)=1.81, p=0.19, ns; D: F(1, 35)=0.45, p=0.50, ns) and P6 (C: F(1, 18)=1.53, p=0.23, ns; D: F(1, 18)=1.80, p=0.19, ns). P2 and P3 show a significant effect of the condition (P2 C: F(1, 35)=8.02, p<0.05; D: F(1,35)=0.45, p=0.51, ns. P3 C: F(1,35)=12.69, p<0.05; D: F(1, 35)=0.17, p=0.68, ns). P5 presents a significant effect of the distance (D: F(1,36)=7.19, p<0.05; C: F(1,36)=0.20, p=0.66, ns). Finally, P4 shows a significant effect of both distance and condition (D: F(1, 37)=3.84, p=0.05; C: F(1, 37)=9.27, p<0.05).

4.2. *Kinematic encoding of the distance*

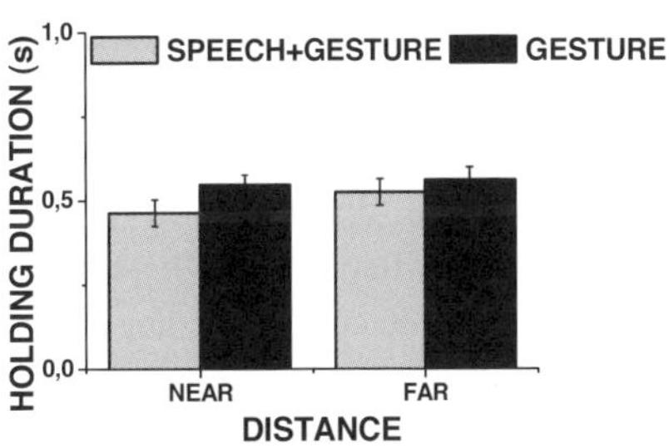

Figure 5. Holding duration as a function of the distance and the condition for the adults.

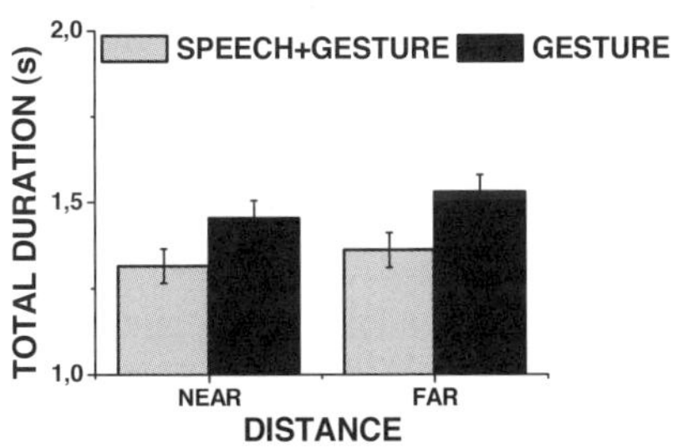

Figure 6. Total duration as a function of the distance and the condition for the adults.

Figures 5 and 6 illustrate the effect of both distance and condition on gesture durations in adults. We found a significant effect of both distance and condition (HD: D: F(1, 24)=19.84, p<0.05; C: F(1, 24)=32.60, p<0.05; TD: D: F(1,

24)=7.09, p<0.05; C: F(1, 24)=49.47). Adults perform longer manual pointing to designate distant objects and in unimodal condition.

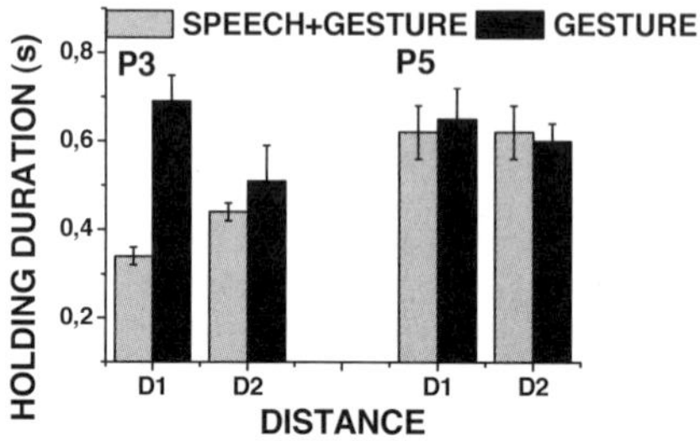

Figure 7. Holding duration as a function of the distance and the condition for two children.

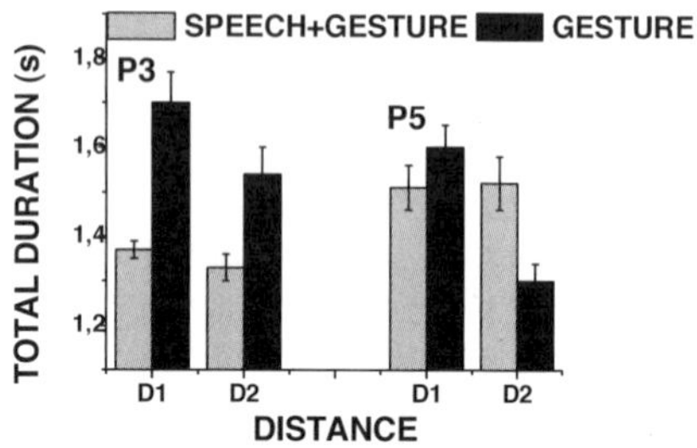

Figure 8. Total duration as a function of the distance and the condition for two children.

Figures 7 and 8 concern gesture durations for two children. Data for four participants are missing due to a technical problem. P3 presents an effect of the condition (HD: F(1, 37)=11.55, p=0.05; TD: F(1, 37)=25.71, p=0.05), but no effect of the distance (TD: F(1, 37)=0.001, p=0.97, ns; HD: F(1, 37)=0.24, p=0.63, ns), whereas no significant effects were found for P5 (C: HD: F(1, 38)=3e-04, p=,0.98 ns; TD: F(1, 38)=4e-04, p=0.98, ns; D: HD: F(1, 38)=0.23, p=0.63, ns; TD: F(1, 38)=0.95, p=0.33, ns).

5. Discussion & conclusion

Our data are, in coherence with our previous study, in favour of a specific distance encoding in both vocal and manual pointing. In adults, articulatory properties of the vocal gesture encode the distance information (i.e. lip opening, which increases with the distance of the target). This articulatory encoding suggests that the tendency of languages worldwide to associate close vowels with proximal deictics and open vowels with distal deictics could originate from a very basic motor correlate. The distance effect is observed here inside vocalic categories, discarding then the lexical origin of the distance encoding in language. For the adult group, gesture durations also depend on the target's distance: the index finger pointing lasts longer when directed to a distant object. Only two children out of six show F1 and/or lip opening increases as a function of the distance. This suggests that the distance encoding is not an intrinsic feature of language use but an efficient communicative strategy, which develops gradually during childhood.

Our study also attests the cooperation between the vocal and manual systems. They are used in a complementary way for the implementation of the linguistic function of deixis. The information is distributed on the two systems. We indeed observed in adults a significant effect of the mono- vs bimodality of the task on F1 values, lip opening values, and kinematic properties of the manual gesture. Moreover, this effect is significant for four out of six children on one or more parameters. It means that when participants cannot perform any manual pointing, they compensate with a reinforced vocal pointing, and reciprocally. This cooperation is mutual, since the manual pointing also depends on the presence or absence of the vocal pointing. Our hypothesis is that this cooperation might be a very basic feature of language communication, as it is more developped in children than distance encoding, the latter being a more elaborate communicative strategy, depending on more mature pragmatic skills. Further analyses are in progress to precisely determine different developmental profiles. However the large variability found in children indicates that an acquisition process is occuring, leading to the full mastery of these communicative tools.

References

Arbib, M. A. (2005). From Monkey-like Action Recognition to Human Language: An Evolutionary Framework for Neurolinguistics, *Behavioral and Brain Sciences,* 28: 105-167.

Bonfiglioli, C., Finocchiaro, C., Gesierich, B., & Rositani, F. (2009). A kinematic approach to the conceptual representations of this and that, *Cognition,* 111: 270-274.

Butcher, C., & Goldin-Meadow, Susan (2000). Gesture and the transition from one- to two-word speech: When hand and mouth come together. In D. McNeill (Ed.), *Language and gesture* (pp. 235-257). New York: Cambridge University Press.

Diessel, H. (1999). *Demonstratives: Form, Function, and Grammaticalization*. John Benjamins, Amsterdam.

Gonseth, C., Vilain, A., & Vilain, C. (2011). Deictic pointing: How do speech and gesture cooperate to encode distance information. Submitted.

Kendon, A. (2004). *Gesture: Visible Action as Utterance*. Cambridge University Press, Cambridge.

Kita, S. (Ed) (2003). *Pointing, Where Language, Culture, and Cognition Meet*. Psychology Press.

Özçalışkan, S. & Goldin-Meadow, S. (2005). Gesture is at the cutting edge of early language development, *Cognition*, 96(3), B101-B113.

SPEECH DEVELOPMENT IN PREVIOUSLY APHONIC CHILDREN AFTER AIRWAY RECONSTRUCTION RECAPITULATES EVOLUTION OF SPOKEN LANGUAGE

CAROLINE N GREEN

Kresge Hearing Research Institute, University of Michigan, 1301 Catherine Street, Ann Arbor, MI 48109, USA

LYNN E DRIVER

Division of Speech and Language Pathology, University of Michigan, 1500 E Med Center Drive, Ann Arbor, MI 48104, USA

LAUREN A BOHM & GLENN E GREEN

Department of Otolaryngology – Head and Neck Surgery, University of Michigan, 1500 E Med Center Drive, Ann Arbor, MI 48104, USA

Seven previously aphonic children underwent airway reconstruction enabling them to obtain phonation for the first time between the ages of 13 and 34 months. Prior to surgical intervention, children had normal language exposure but expressive language was severely limited due to an inability to phonate. Spoken language development was accelerated, but still occurred step-wise with the following distinct periods after reconstruction: (1) Exclusively vegetative functions of the larynx; (2) Voluntary control over vegetative laryngeal functions; (3) Babbling; (4) Simple words; (5) Speech. These findings suggest that control of laryngeal function is a prerequisite for speech development and can develop independently of language skills. A similar pattern for the evolutionary development of speech is proposed.

1.1. *Aphonic Children.*

When children are born prematurely, lung underdevelopment may necessitate endotracheal intubation. Prior to the removal of the endotracheal tube, some children will develop exuberant scar tissue below the vocal cords, necessitating a tracheostomy. For a rare subset of children, the scarring is so severe that no air can pass between the vocal cords. These children are unable to phonate precluding speech and markedly limiting expressive communication to gestures, oral clicking, and lip smacking. Nevertheless these children develop normal receptive language skills including age appropriate vocabularies and the ability to understand complex speech constructs.

Development of surgical techniques has made it possible to resect the scar tissue below the vocal cords, restoring an opening between the trachea and the larynx. This affords the children with the ability to phonate. In children who had normal language development prior to the development of scarring (e.g. as a result of a motor vehicle accident or house fire), reconstruction of the airway usually resulted in immediate return of normal speech. In contrast, the pattern of speech development in previously aphonic reconstructed (PAR) children was distinctly different and proceeded in a stepwise fashion.

2. Methods.

After obtaining approval from our institutional review board, the medical records of seven PAR children were identified and reviewed. These records were supplemented with formal speech-language pathology evaluation, clinical observations and a standardized telephone survey supplemented by parental documentation (see Bohm et al., 2010). Previous research by Oller et al. (2001) has demonstrated that parental reporting is a highly reliable method of differentiating canonical babbling from other infant vocalizations.

All PAR children had undergone airway reconstruction via a cricotracheal resection with hilar release as previously described by Taylor et al. (2010). In brief, a right posterolateral thoracotomy is used to divide the pulmonary ligaments and pericardium with mobilization of the mainstem bronchi carina and trachea. A suprahyoid release was performed. The trachea was separated from the esophagus and dissected into the thorax in continuity with the exposure obtained from the thoracic approach. The trachea was then divided with the scarred portion of the trachea and the tracheostomy removed. Patients were intubated and sedated in the pediatric intensive care unit for one week. Subsequently, the patients were extubated and placed in a modified Minerva brace to prevent neck hyperextension.

3. Results.

All seven PAR children had acquired high-grade subglottic scarring from prolonged endotracheal intubation. Reasons for intubation included prematurity

(5 children), retroperitoneal tumor (1 child), and congenital heart defect (1 child). Regardless of the indication and age of patient, prolonged intubation can result in scarring. However, scarring is generally more problematic in children due to their smaller larynges. All children underwent tracheostomy between -8 weeks and +8 weeks of age when corrected for prematurity. All children remained aphonic for the entire period prior to reconstruction. Other than expressive language, development was normal in all PAR children after age-correction for prematurity.

The mean age at reconstruction ranged from 13-34 months (with a mean of 23.6 months) when corrected for prematurity. All children were successfully decannulated, and no cases of laryngeal paralysis were noted.

3.1. *Nonverbal communications prior to reconstruction.*

Prior to reconstruction, no subjects had spoken language. Five of the PAR children had learned manual signs (3, 5, 15, 35, and 75 signs) and all but one used nonsign gestures such as pointing. Four PAR children used tongue clicking. Three used lip smacking. One had no communication skills prior to reconstruction. The rate of subsequent speech acquisition after reconstruction was independent of the amount of sign language the children had preoperatively (r= -.46).

3.2. *Exclusively vegetative laryngeal functions.*

PAR children had vegetative (involuntary) functions of the larynx noted immediately after extubation. These vegetative functions included full vocal cord abduction with breathing, cough with aspiration, crying and laughing. The full array of vegetative laryngeal sounds occurred within the first weeks after reconstruction. The children were often startled by their crying and laughing and would try, initially unsuccessfully, to recreate the sounds.

3.3. *Voluntary control over vegetative laryngeal functions.*

Vegetative control of the larynx (the voluntary ability to cough, cry or laugh) occurred in all subjects between 2 and 4 weeks after surgery with a mean of 3.1 weeks. With vegetative control of the larynx, the vegetative sounds could be produced on demand by all PAR children. In contrast to normal language development, a period of cooing did not occur in PAR children.

3.4. *Babbling.*

All PAR children had a distinct phase of babbling. Postsurgical canonical babbling began between 2 and 12 weeks after reconstruction with a mean of 6.8 weeks. The transition period from voluntary control of laryngeal function to babbling ranged from less than a week to 8 weeks. The age at onset of babbling was a corrected age of 25.3 months (15.5-34.5 months). In normal children, babbling occurs between six and ten months, with a peak at seven months as demonstrated by Oller & Eilers (1988).

The babbling of PAR children had the features of infant babbling. The babbling was rhythmic and repetitive with a consistent periodic pattern of production. The babbled phonetic units were clearly recognizable to both the PAR children and their parents but could not be initially utilized in words.

3.5. *First spoken word.*

The transition from babbling to first spoken word was often rapid, lasting less than a week in four subjects. Additional words were rapidly added for most children. The longest period of babbling without any words was 8 weeks.

3.6. *Final speech outcomes.*

All children now communicate with full sentences and have several hundred word vocabularies. The PAR children demonstrated increasing sophistication in their use of phonemes. As the children discovered how to make new sounds, they were incorporated into the language repertoire. Typically developing children gradually develop the ability to make more complex sounds, a process that will last into grade school. Among the PAR children, the longest period of time to attain age-appropriate language was just under two years.

4. Discussion.

Prior to reconstruction, PAR children had normal language exposure, normal cognitive ability and normal receptive language capability. Some of these children used signs, while others were dependent upon crude gestures for communication. Similarly, great apes are capable of flexible gestural communication (see Tomasello, 2008) and complex comprehension of spoken speech (see Savage-Rumbaugh, E.S. et al., 1993).

We propose that the development of oral language after airway reconstruction recapitulates the evolutionary development of spoken language.

4.1. *Comparison with nonhuman primates.*

As noted by Tomasello (2008), the great apes do not have referentially specific calls. Most of their calls are expressions of emotions rather than directed vocalizations. The calls may only be modified slightly in rate or form for different quantities of food, for example. The calls are similar whether raised with the same species, cross-raised with a species with a different call, or raised in isolation.

Similarly, PAR children initially have no control over vegetative laryngeal function having emotional vocalizations only. And when control over the vegetative laryngeal function is eventually developed, the produced sounds can only be slightly modified in rate or form. However, PAR children will play with these sounds, requiring up to eight weeks to develop ways of coordinating consonants with the laryngeal noise, at which point canonical babbling becomes the predominant acoustic output. For some PAR children, the transition between voluntary laryngeal control and babbling was the longest stage in the process of developing full speech.

Ellowson et al. (1998) noted that infant pygmy marmosets have vocalizations that have features similar to human babbling including highly repetitious, rhythmic vocalizations that occur without referent and resemble a subset of adult speech. In contradistinction, the babbling of PAR children appears to represent the novel modification of vegetative laryngeal sounds. Although the babbling of PAR children did not initially have meaning, once coordination of laryngeal and oral function had been achieved, the newly developed skills were rapidly used to create words that already existed in the children's receptive repertoire. Interestingly, neither the pygmy marmosets nor PAR children had a cooing period that preceded babbling.

4.2. *Pattern for the development of spoken language.*

PAR children despite having normal language exposure and cognitive function developed speech in a distinct stepwise fashion. Even though PAR children have age-appropriate cognitive skills, motor skills, manual gestures and receptive language, their pattern of spoken language development is similar to but accelerated in comparison to infants (see Vihman, 1996). This same pattern is proposed as the pattern for the evolutionary development of spoken language.

Table 1. Proposed pattern for the evolutionary development of spoken language.

Vocalization pattern	*Examples*
Nonverbal	Nonverbal communications
Involuntary Vegetative	Unintentional vocalizations
Voluntary Vegetative	Intentional vocalizations
Babbling	Novel intentional vocalizations
Simple Words	Specific meanings applied to novel vocalizations
Spoken Language	Complex language

We have shown that PAR children progressively are able to take advantage of increasing laryngeal control to communicate verbally. Interestingly and unexpectedly, the rate of progression through the stages and subsequent acquisition of simple words and spoken language occurred independently of the number of signs that had been learned prior to surgery. This finding suggests that vocalizations and language develop independently and can be acquired separately. But it is through progressively sophisticated control of laryngeal function that humans gain access to spoken language, from birth or after airway reconstruction.

References

Bohm, L.A., Nelson, M.E., Driver, L.E. & Green, G.E. (2010). Babbling, vegetative function and language development after cricotracheal resection in aphonic children. *The Laryngoscope*, 120, 2494-2497.

Elowson, A.M., Snowdon C.T. & Lazaro-Perea C. (1998). 'Babbling' and social context in infant monkeys: parallels to human infants. *Trends in Cognitive Sciences*, 2, 31-37.

Oller, D.K. & Eilers, R.E. (1988). The role of audition in infant babbling. *Child Development* 59, 441-449.

Oller, D.K., Eilers, R.E. & Basinger D. (2001). Intuitive identification of infant vocal sounds by parents. *Developmental Science* 4, 49-60.

Savage-Rumbaugh, E.S., Murphy, J., Sevcik, R.A., Brakke, K.E., Williams, S.L. & Rumbaugh D.M. (1993). Language comprehension in ape and child. *Monographs of the Society for Research in Child Development* 233:58:3-4, 1993

Taylor, J.C., Collar, R.M., Wilson, K.F., Ohye R.G. & Green, G.E. Cricotracheal resection with hilar release for pediatric airway stenosis. (2010) *Archives of Otolaryngology – Head and Neck Surgery*, 135, 256-259.

Tomasello, M. (2008). *Origins of Human Communication*. Cambridge, MA: The MIT Press.

Vihman, M.M. (1996). *Phonologic Development*. Cambridge, MA: Blackwell Publishers.

SYNTAX EVOLVED GRADUALLY

JAMES R HURFORD

Language Evolution and Computation Research Unit, School of Philosophy, Psychology and Language Sciences, University of Edinburgh, Edinburgh EH8 9AD, UK.

Syntax started by putting words together in the smallest ways, and moved on to slightly bigger ways. It is reasonable to think of a 'one-word stage' followed by a 'two-word stage', the first manifestation of productive combination. After that, the pace accelerated, so there is less sense in talking about a 'three-word stage', and little reason to talk of a 'four-word stage', as if these exact numbers played a formal role in the evolving language capacities. The language capacity has been constrained throughout its evolution by quantitative limits on processing. Social norms also affect the typical length and complexity of sentences. Where adults habitually speak in short simple sentences, children will grow up speaking similarly. The earliest (pre-)humans would have had more limited processing capacity than modern humans. This would have constrained their utterances, and their children would have tended to observe the same rough quantitative limits. Over hundreds of generations the capacity increased, by co-evolutionary mechanisms linking competence with performance. There are shades of protolanguage.

The title gives the message. The gradual continuity view contrasts with that typical of linguists close to Chomsky. For example, Berwick (1997) writes 'There is no possibility of an "intermediate" syntax between a non-combinatorial syntax and full natural language syntax – one either has Merge in all its generative glory, or one has effectively no combinatorial syntax at all, but rather whatever one sees in the case of agrammatic aphasics: alternative cognitive strategies for assigning thematic roles to word strings'. Outside linguistics, mathematical approaches in quite diverse fields find the term 'semicombinatorial' useful, for example in musical theory, metalogic, chemical physics, and molecular biology. These fields have found some value in conceiving of degrees of combinatoriality. Back in linguistics, it would be reasonable to see the various levels of the Formal Language Hierarchy as defining successive degrees of combinatoriality. First Order Markov languages require less combinatorial power than State Chain languages, which in turn require less combinatorial power than Phrase Structure languages.

Indeed such a scale of combinatorial power motivated the experiments comparing tamarins with humans, discussed by Fitch and Hauser (2004). Again outside linguistics, there is a large literature based on the possibility of different degrees of combinatorial complexity. I am concerned with quantitatively expressed degrees of combinatoriality. A combinatorial system with an upper bound of N on the size of its productions or the length of its derivations has less combinatorial power than one of the same type with an upper bound greater than N. In computer science, **bounded combinatorial** systems or procedures work within finite limits. Humans are physically real computing systems too. From an evolutionary point of view, it is sensible to hypothesize that humans have progressively evolved greater combinatorial powers. This is more plausible than a tale of an evolutionary jump, such as Berwick envisages, to the infinite products of 'Merge in all its generative glory'. Hence I envisage that the sentence-forming word-combining powers of humans started small, and evolved to be more extensive.

Bickerton's idea of protolanguage presupposes a clear distinction between the lexicon of a language and its syntactic system. Protolanguage reflects a hypothetical stage in language before 'syntax evolved'. In some publications, e.g. (Bickerton, 1998) it was proposed that syntax arrived by 'catastrophic evolution' in 'a single step from protolanguage'. More recently, Construction Grammar proposes that there is not a firm distinction between lexical items and grammatical constructions. What a modern language learner acquires is a set of constructions. Some of the acquired constructions have no internal morphosyntactic structure or variables in them – these are words. And some of the learned constructions are very general with many slots filled by variables – these are grammatical constructions in the traditional sense. There is a **syntax-lexicon continuum**. Given this continuum, the Bickertonian idea of protolanguage as a discrete stage with lexicon but no syntax loses its bite, and the possibility opens up of a more continuous, less catastrophic, account of language evolution. There was no phase-shift, like the boiling or freezing points of water, between stringing a few words together and more complex syntax. The protolanguage idea can still be useful as describing a stage in which all linguistic knowledge was in terms of specific lexical items, containing no variables at all, i.e. there was no knowledge of constructions other than words. So in this hypothetical, yet plausible, stage of language evolution, there were no big constructions, only (proto-)words, with specific phonological shapes and specific meanings (which could be simple or complex).

Language acquisition is a promising guide to language evolution. There is no absolute necessity for embryonic development to recapitulate the evolution of a species, but it often does. In the case of learned behaviour, we have no precedents, no fossils of the sequences in which earlier animals learned. Some conclusions can be drawn from parallels between brain growth in the species and in infants. 'Limited recapitulation, however, does characterize human neural maturation. Specifically, the neocortical association areas are late to mature and have demonstrated the greatest phylogenetic expansion. This parallel provides a basis for attempts to unravel the evolution of language phylogeny by examining its ontogeny.' (Gibson, 1996).

In the case of bodies of acquired knowledge, they have an inherent structure dictating the sequence in which they are acquired. At a gross level, this kind of 'structural' recapitulationism is true. The simpler theorems of Euclidean geometry are a basis for proofs of more complex theorems. Words must be acquired before sentences can be assembled by putting words together. It is not clear, however, that there is a logical necessity for a learning system to master three-word sentences only after it has mastered some two-word sentences. A number of studies of artificial learning systems conclude that gradually relaxing a limit on the complexity of input data facilitates, or even enables, learning of a whole complex system. Elman (1993) describes experiments which show that acquisition of a small but naturalistic context-free language is significantly facilitated by arranging the acquisition device (a recurrent neural net) in such a way that its 'working memory' is small at the outset of learning, and grows incrementally during the learning process. Goldowsky and Newport (1993) come to a similar conclusion in an unrelated study of learning facilitated by working in small increments. Because the evolution of language involved successive episodes of learning by each generation, the same logic applies to phylogeny as is shown by these studies applying to ontogeny. The same property in the structure of a complex system such as a language that makes it necessary to learn it incrementally from small beginnings also entails that it can only grow by successive acts of learning incrementally from small beginnings. Of course, no whole language system was in place for our ancestors to learn from, but the logic applicable to learning from given exemplars also applies to the evolutionary growth of a system by innovations that are to be learned by each generation. The innovations must make small increments to the complexity of the system.

There is one crucial difference between language evolution and language development. Modern children have caregivers and/or peers to learn from. Our ancestors had to make it up for themselves – they had no models. This difference could account for the slowness of the evolutionary process. It also introduces the possibility of exceptions to phylogeny/ontogeny parallelism. Here is an analogy. In the Industrial Revolution and its aftermath, in early-industrialized countries, trains historically preceded airplanes. Let's say this order of invention was necessary. But jump forward to the settlement of Alaska in the 20th century, after planes had been invented. Now there are towns in Alaska accessible only by air, and not by train. Planes came first to these towns, and trains will never come. Because of learning (about flight), it was possible for the later development to leapfrog over a stage which had been necessary when the evolution was moved on by innovative invention, not by learning from examples. Here is a linguistic parallel. The child inventors of Nicaraguan Sign Language (ISN) are the closest we have to people who have created a new language without learning it from any external source. We can compare their three- and four-word utterances with those of children acquiring language normally. One difference stands out. In normal language acquisition, children begin earlier to use grammatical morphemes and inflections. By contrast, three- and four-word utterances in the first cohort of ISN signers consisted only of content words. Examples are MAN PUSH WOMAN FALL (Senghas, 2000) and MAN CUP GIVE WOMAN RECEIVE (Senghas et al. 1997). This is a difference in degree. Normal children do use 'telegraphic' all-content-word utterances, such as *man clean car* and *goat try eat lid* without grammatical markers. But ISN signers in the first stages did not invent any grammatical morphemes at all. So child language development in languages with grammatical morphemes and inflections cannot be taken as a reliable model for the original creation of languages. Children who use grammatical morphemes, even in short utterances, have learned them from older speakers.

We have good general descriptions of the stages that modern children go through in acquiring syntax. It takes a child about 10 years. Let's say it would have taken our ancestors somewhere between 2 million and 50,000 years to evolve from no capacity for learned symbols or syntax to the modern capacity. Therefore, applying recapitulation, one aspect of building an evolutionary story is to stretch the timescale of the modern developmental stages by a factor of between 200,000 and 5,000. We can imagine reconstructing periods of apparently slow language growth, like the child's first year, and some explosions, like the syntax explosion seen after about age 2 in modern children. If you film a bomb exploding in ultra-slow motion, it is seen to be a gradual process. In that light, stretched over perhaps 2 million years, or even as little as 50,000 years, and with exponential growth later in the period, the evolution of the modern syntactic capacity seems less amazing. This is especially true given the parallel evolution of complex cultures among humans. It is not hard to imagine a succession of small culturally produced innovations in a language accumulating over such a period, accompanied by some gradual growth in memory and processing speed, paralleling what we see in children.

There are shades of protolanguage. Protolanguage has been envisaged as a discrete intermediate stage between no language at all and full human language. Thus conceived, protolanguage has been a fruitful focus for discussion. It has mostly been accepted as a reasonable, even necessary, stage in the evolution of language, simply characterized as a stage when there was a lexicon but no syntax. In a protolanguage, the 'words' could be uttered in sequence, but not in any regular order, and with no markers of grammatical structure. As Bickerton points out, even nowadays, we can see parallels with this hypothetical protolanguage type in the language of human toddlers (e.g. *Mommy sock, red me eat*), the attempts at English of Genie (e.g. *applesauce buy store*), and the utterances of a language-trained chimpanzee, Nim (e.g. *hug Nim hug*). The utterances of severely affected agrammatic aphasics can also look like protolanguage, e.g. . . . *Hahnemann Hospital . . . uh, uh, I . . . uh uh wife, Rosa . . . uh . . . take . . . uh . . . love . . . ladies . . . uh Ocean uh Hospital and transfer Hahnemann Hospital ambulance*. This simple protolanguage idea needs to be modified and seen not as a discrete uniform stage, but as having the possibility within it of gradual continuous growth towards syntactic organization.

Within the set of examples typically lumped together as protolanguage, there are differences in degree of organization, so that even within a 'protolanguage stage' some gradual growth along a continuum can be hypothesized. One should make a distinction between human productions like *red me eat* and *applesauce buy store* and Nim's productions such as *hug Nim hug*. The former may be protosentences, while the latter is just a string of words. Further, one should not classify all productions by trained apes homogeneously as 'protolanguage'. Some ape utterances, e.g. Kanzi's, are closer to sentencehood than some others, e.g. Nim's. The crudest form of sequential stringing together of words is dictated by a principle such as 'Say first what is most urgent to convey, then what is next uppermost in your mind, and so on'. Such an ordering of symbols is seen in a sequence of lexigrams used by Panzee, a chimpanzee, to direct a human to the location of some hidden kiwi fruit. While pointing, she signalled *hide, stick, hide, stick, stick, stick, hide, kiwi, kiwi* (Menzel, 2005). The first objective was to tell the human that something was hidden, hence *hide*; the second objective was to get the human to use a stick to poke about for the hidden object; then as the human homed in on the target, she told him what it was – kiwi fruit. There is no reason to think of Panzee's utterance as anything more than a disjointed monologue, perhaps guided along by the sequence of events she was responding to. The many repetitions are not like anything systematically seen in human sentences. Such repetitions are also characteristic of many of Nim's productions.

Contrast Panzee's utterance with Tervoort's (1968) example *You me downtown movie fun*. This was an utterance signed by a deaf student asking a girl out for a date. The deaf students and their teachers that Tervoort studied had not developed a full sign language, such as ASL or BSL, as far as can be seen. There is an important difference between the chimpanzee's *hide, stick, hide, stick, stick, stick, hide, kiwi, kiwi* and the human *You me downtown movie fun*. At some point in the evolution of language, discourse began to be chopped up into **sentence-sized units**. These units have an internal coherence distinguishing them from any kind of looser discourse-level organization. At its simplest this coherence is marked by pauses at the boundaries of the units. (Birdsong is organized into repertoires of discrete songs, intriguingly roughly human sentence-sized in physical duration, but without the propositional content, of course.) If there was any discrete step around the hypothetical protolanguage era, it was the introduction of this kind of hierarchical packaging of discourse into units longer than the elementary notes or words, and shorter than a whole discourse. Also, in *You me downtown movie fun* the apparently obligatory grouping of *you me* together shows the beginning of phrase-sized subunits within sentence-sized units. This point is implicit in discussions of examples such as *Mommy sock, red me eat,* and *applesauce buy store*, all produced by humans. The elements in these utterances are not ordered conventionally, but they are cited by their sources as if seen as packages, perhaps pronounced in a single intonation tune and bounded by pauses. But Nim's *hug Nim hug*, often mentioned on the same page as an example of protolanguage, is not necessarily of the same kind. It is repetitive and observers have given the impression that his utterances were not packaged into chunks with clear boundaries. Genie's *applesauce buy store* is in no way good English. But some of her other utterances show signs that she has acquired English word order; examples such as *Want milk, Mike paint* and *Big elephant*. These examples show a little more acquired syntactic organization. The example that Bickerton (1990) gives from Hawaiian Pidgin *Ifu laik meiki, mo beta make time, mani no can hapai* clearly has some syntactic structure, with a conditional clause introduced by *If*, and the last four words constituting a clause with a subject *mani* first, and an auxiliary verb *can* preceding a main verb *hapai*; this utterance is clearly more grammatically structured than the other examples. I therefore prefer not to count it as an example from a protolanguage; this speaker of Hawaiian Pidgin was already a long way towards a full Creole.

At least one fundamental feature of the relation between syntax and semantics, namely **compositionality**, is already rudimentarily present in purely asyntactic protolanguage. The principle of compositionality is that **The meaning of an expression is a function of the meanings of its constituent parts and the way they are put together**. In the purely pragmatic mode, with no grammatical rules or conventions for putting words together (beyond mere concatenation), there is already a simple systematic relationship between the meaning of a whole string and the meanings of its constituent words. For example, the meaning of *Mommy sock* is something to do with Mommy **and** something to do with a sock. The meaning of the whole is any proposition that a hearer can extrapolate from shared background knowledge and contextual clues, provided that this proposition is somehow about Mommy and a sock. The meaning of *Daddy car* is not the same as the meaning of *Mommy sock*, exactly because of differences among the meanings of *Mommy, Daddy, sock* and *car*.

References

Berwick, R. C. (1997). Syntax facit saltum: Computation and the genotype and phenotype of language. *Journal of Neurolinguistics 10(2-3)*, 231–249.

Bickerton, D. (1998). Catastrophic evolution: the case for a single step from protolanguage to full human language. In J. R. Hurford, M. Studdert-Kennedy, and C. Knight (Eds.), *Approaches to the Evolution of Language: Social and Cognitive Bases*, pp. 341–358. Cambridge: Cambridge University Press.

Elman, J. (1993). Learning and development in neural networks: The importance of starting small. *Cognition 48*, 71–99.

Fitch, W. T. and M. D. Hauser (2004). Computational constraints on syntactic processing in a nonhuman primate. *Science 303*, 377–380.

Gibson, K. R. (1996). The ontogeny and evolution of the brain, cognition, and language. In A. Lock and C. R. Peters (Eds.), *Handbook of Human Symbolic Evolution*, pp. 407–431. Oxford: Oxford University Press.

Goldowsky, B. N. and E. J. Newport (1993). Modeling the effects of processing limitations on the acquisition of morphology: the less is more hypothesis. In E. Clark (Ed.), *Proceedings of the 24th Annual Child Language Research Forum*, pp. 124–138. Stanford, CA: CSLI.

Menzel, C. (2005). Progress in the study of chimpanzee recall and episodic memory. In H. S. Terrace and J. Metcalfe (Eds.), *The Missing Link in Cognition: Origins of Self-Reflective Consciousness*, pp. 188–224. Oxford: Oxford University Press.

Senghas, A. (2000). The development of early spatial morphology in Nicaraguan Sign Language. In S. C. Howell, S. A. Fish, and T. Keith-Lucas (Eds.), *Proceedings of the Boston University Conference on Language Development, 24*, pp. 696–707. Boston: Cascadilla Press.

Senghas, A., M. E. V. Coppola, E. L. Newport, and T. Supalla (1997). Argument structure in Nicaraguan Sign Language: The emergence of grammatical devices. In E. Hughes, M. Hughes, and A. Greenhill (Eds.), *Proceedings of the Boston University Conference on Language Development, 21*, pp. 550–561. Boston: Cascadilla Press.

Tervoort, B. T. (1968). You me downtown movie fun? *Lingua 21*, 455–465.

THE CASE FOR NEANDERTHAL LANGUAGE—HOW STRONG IS IT?

SVERKER JOHANSSON
School of Education and Communication, University of Jönköping, Box 1026, Jönköping, SE-551 11, Sweden
lsj@hlk.hj.se

Did Neanderthals have language? This issue has been debated back and forth for decades, without resolution. But in recent years new evidence has become available. New fossils and archaeological finds cast light on relevant Neanderthal anatomy and behaviour. New DNA evidence, both fossil and modern, provides clues both to the relationship between Neanderthals and *Homo sapiens*, and to the genetics of language. In this paper, I review and evaluate the available evidence. My conclusion is that the preponderance of the evidence supports the presence of some form of language in Neanderthals.

1. Introduction

That modern humans have language and speech, and that our remote ancestors did not, are two incontrovertible facts. But there is no consensus on when the transition from non-language to language took place, nor any consensus on which species of human ancestors the first language users belonged to. Some authors regard language as the exclusive province of *Homo sapiens*, whereas others argue that at least proto-language in some form can be found in some earlier species. Neanderthals have a key position in this debate, being a late major side branch in human evolution, with human-like capacities in many other respects, notably a brain at least as large as ours.

All modern human populations have language, obviously. Given that language has at least some biological substrate (if not necessarily an innate grammar) this implies that the most recent common ancestor of all modern humans had language, and had all the biological prerequisites for language. This common ancestor lived at least 100,000 years ago (Johansson, 2011). This 100,000-year limit brings us back to a time when Neanderthals and *Homo sapiens* were living side by side, with similar material culture, and quite possibly encountering each other in the Middle East. Did only one of them have language, or both?

We will look here at what evidence from fossil anatomy, from DNA, and from archaeology can, and cannot, say about Neanderthal language. Language *per se* is not visible in either of these, so the evidence invoked is necessarily indirect, and requires bridging theories (Botha, 2008). A similar earlier review can be found in Schepartz (1993), and a fuller discussion of related issues in Johansson (2005).

2. Fossil anatomy

Our habitual use of speech is reflected in certain aspects of our anatomy that can be studied in fossils. Speech adaptations can potentially be found in our speech organs, hearing organs, brain, and in the neural connections between these organs.

Speech organs. The shape of the human vocal tract, notably the lowering of the larynx already in infancy, is very likely a speech adaptation, even though some other mammals, such as big cats, also possess a lowered larynx, and others dynamically lower the larynx (Fitch, 2009). Speech would not be impossible with an ape vocal tract, but it would be less expressive, with fewer vowels available (Lieberman, 2008; Boer & Fitch, 2010). The vocal tract itself is all soft tissue and does not fossilize, but its shape is connected with the shape of the surrounding bones, the skull base and the hyoid. Already *Homo erectus* had a near-modern skull base (Baba et al., 2003), but other factors than vocal tract configuration, notably brain size and face size (Bastir et al., 2010), strongly affect skull base shape, so the significance of this is unclear (Fitch, 2000). Hyoid bones are very rare as fossils, as they are not attached to the rest of the skeleton, but one Neanderthal hyoid has been found (Arensburg et al., 1989), as well as two hyoids from likely Neanderthal ancestors (Martínez et al., 2008), all very similar to the hyoid of modern *Homo sapiens*, leading to the conclusion that Neanderthals had a vocal tract adequate for speech (Houghton, 1993; Boë et al., 2007; Granat et al., 2007), but see also Lieberman (2007) and Fitch (2009). The hyoid of *Australopithecus afarensis*, on the other hand, is more chimpanzee-like in its morphology (Alemseged et al., 2006), and the vocal tract that Granat et al. (2007) reconstruct for *Australopithecus* is basically apelike.

Hearing organs. Some fine-tuning appears to have taken place during human evolution to optimize speech perception, notably our improved perception of sounds in the 2-4 kHz range. The sensitivity of ape ears has a minimum in this range, but human ears do not, mainly due to minor changes in the ear ossicles (Martínez et al., 2004). This difference is very likely an adaptation to speech perception, as key features of some speech sounds are in this region. The adaptation interpretation is strengthened by the discovery that a middle-ear structural gene has been the subject of strong natural selection in the human lineage (Olson & Varki, 2004). These changes in the ossicles were present already in likely Neanderthal ancestors (Martínez et al., 2004). Ear ossicles have also been found both from Neanderthals and from early *Homo sapiens*, likewise with no meaningful differences from modern humans (Quam & Rak, 2008).

Brain. The general size and shape of the brain, and the gross anatomy of the brain surface, can be inferred from well-preserved fossil skulls (Bruner, 2004). Neanderthal brains are as large as modern humans, but distinct in shape, lower and wider, whereas *H sapiens* skulls are larger in the parietal area (Bruner, 2008). Frontal widening around Broca's area is shared between Neanderthals and *H sapi-*

ens, going back to 2 Mya (Bruner, 2007), which adds some support for Neanderthal language. But other apes have brain structures with the same gross anatomy as both Broca and Wernicke (Gannon, Holloway, Broadfield, & Braun, 1998; Cantalupo & Hopkins, 2001), so the support is not strong.

Lateralization of the brain could have been informative, but there is no clearcut increase in lateralization of the brain in human evolution — ape brains are not symmetric (Balzeau & Gilissen, 2010) — and fossils are rarely undamaged and undistorted enough to be useful in this respect. But when tools become common, handedness can be inferred from asymmetries in the knapping process, the use-wear damage on tools, and also in tooth wear patterns (Uomini, 2009; Frayer, Fiore, Lalueza-Fox, Radovcic, & Bondioli, 2010), which may provide circumstantial evidence of lateralization, and possibly language (Steele & Uomini, 2009). Evidence for a human handedness pattern is clear among Neanderthals and their predecessors in Europe, as far back as 500,000 years ago (Frayer et al., 2010), and some indications go back as far as 1 million years ago (Uomini, 2009).

Neural connections. Where nerves pass through bone, a hole is left that can be seen in well-preserved fossils, providing a rough estimate of the size of the nerve that passed through them. A thicker nerve means more neurons, and presumably improved sensitivity and control. The hypoglossal canal, leading to the tongue, has been invoked in this context (Kay, Cartmill, & Balow, 1998), but broader comparative samples have shown that it is not useful as an indicator of speech (DeGusta, Gilbert, & Turner, 1999; Jungers, Pokempner, Kay, & Cartmill, 2003). A better case can be made for the nerves to the thorax, presumably for breathing control (Fitch, 2009). Both modern humans and Neanderthals have wide canals here, whereas *Homo ergaster* had the narrow canals typical of other apes (MacLarnon & Hewitt, 2004), indicating that the canals expanded somewhere between 0.5 and 1.5 million years ago.

In conclusion, the fossil anatomical evidence indicates that at least some apparent speech adaptations were present in Neanderthals. As the speech optimization, with its accompanying costs, would not occur without strong selective pressure for complex vocalizations, presumably verbal communication, this implies that Neanderthals already possessed non-trivial speech. No single one of the anatomical indications is compelling on its own, but their consilience strengthens the case for some form of Neanderthal speech.

3. Genes

Early genetic evidence from fossil mitochondrial DNA in Neanderthals clearly supported their separateness from *Homo sapiens*, and indicated that the last common ancestor lived at least 400,000 years ago (Krings, Geisert, Schmitz, Krainitzki, & Pääbo, 1999; Beerli & Edwards, 2002; Caramelli et al., 2003; Hodgson & Disotell, 2008; Endicott, Ho, & Stringer, 2010), though the limited number of individuals tested makes it impossible to exclude a modest level of admixture.

The fossil evidence points in the same direction, with the earliest modern humans in Europe more resembling Africans than Neanderthals (Tyrrell & Chamberlain, 1998), though archaic features in some fossils may be interpreted as evidence of hybridization (Rougier et al., 2007; Trinkaus, 2007).

A draft sequence of the full Neanderthal genome was presented recently (Green et al., 2010), in which substantial similarities were found between the Neanderthal sequence and modern Eurasians. Green et al. (2010) interpret this as strong evidence of gene flow from Neanderthals into the common ancestor of modern Eurasians, around 100,000 years ago, but caution is in order as it is extremely difficult to exclude contamination with modern human DNA during excavation and processing of the fossils (Lalueza-Fox, 2009). Wall and Kim (2007) found evidence of both severe contamination and other problems in earlier work by Green et al. (2006). Firm conclusions should await replication.

FOXP2. When mutations in the gene FOXP2 were associated with specific language impairment (Lai, Fisher, Hurst, Vargha-Khadem, & Monaco, 2001), and it was shown that the gene had changed along the human lineage (Enard et al., 2002), it was heralded as a "language gene". But intensive research has revealed a more complex story, with FOXP2 controlling synaptic plasticity in the basal ganglia (Lieberman, 2009) rather than language *per se*, and playing a role in vocalizations and vocal learning in a wide variety of species (Li, Wang, Rossiter, Jones, & Zhang, 2007; Haesler et al., 2004). Nevertheless, the changes in FOXP2 in the human lineage quite likely are connected with some aspects of language, even if the connection is not as direct as early reports claimed. Relevant for the issue of Neanderthal language is that the derived human form of FOXP2 is found also in fossil Neanderthal DNA (Krause et al., 2007,), but see also Benítez-Burraco, Longa, Lorenzo, and Uriagereka (2008) and Coop, Bullaughey, Luca, and Przeworski (2008). Likewise, the selective sweep driving the human form of FOXP2 to fixation may have taken place more than a million years ago (Diller & Cann, 2009), well before the split between *Homo sapiens* and Neanderthals.

4. Archaeology

Language use in itself is not archaeologically visible, but other forms of symbol use may be, and may be used as indicators that some level of semiotic abilities has been reached. Invoking ancient art, including pigments and personal ornaments, as indicators that the artists were capable of symbolic thought, or even as an indicator that language had evolved, is fairly common (Mellars, 1998; Henshilwood & Dubreuil, 2009). The precise connection between e.g. the decorative use of ochre and shell beads, and specific forms of language is, however, not worked out in detail, and not well supported (Botha, 2008).

The archaeological record has frequently been invoked as support for the late, sudden appearance of language in *Homo sapiens*, due to the perception of a technological and creative revolution around 40,000–50,000 years ago (e.g. Binford

(1989), Klein (1999), Li and Hombert (2002)). However, the appearance of a sudden dramatic ‘cultural revolution’ around 40,000 years ago, has turned out to be largely an illusion. The modern toolkit developed gradually over the course of more than 200,000 years (McBrearty & Brooks, 2000; Van Peer et al., 2003). Some aspects, such as blade technology, go back as far as 500,000 years (Johnson & McBrearty, 2010). Discoveries of works of abstract art (Henshilwood et al., 2002; Texier et al., 2010), pigment use (Henshilwood, d’Errico, & Watts, 2009; Watts, 2009), and personal ornaments (Bouzouggar et al., 2007; d’Errico & Vanhaeren, 2009), all substantially older than 40,000 years, add further support to the long timescale of McBrearty and Brooks (2000).

There was indeed a substantial and rapid increase in the *frequency* of symbolic behaviour in the Early Upper Paleolithic, but that increase may well be caused by demographic factors (Zilhão, 2007; Cartmill, 2010) rather than any cognitive changes. Similarly, ecological and energetic factors, rather than cognitive differences, may explain the sparsity of the Neanderthal artistic record, as evidenced by some undeniably modern human populations (e.g. Tasmanians) leaving archaeological records resembling those created by Middle Paleolithic Neanderthals (Roebroeks & Verpoorte, 2009).

Objects of the same type that are interpreted as evidence of symbolic behavior when found in a *sapiens* context, have also been found associated with Neanderthals in Europe (Langley, Clarkson, & Ulm, 2008; d’Errico, 2008; Watts, 2009; Zilhão, 2007) as well as objects that can reasonably be interpreted as art (d’Errico et al., 2003; Wynn & Coolidge, 2004). Whether Neanderthals may have copied such modernities from encroaching *Homo sapiens* (Mellars, 2005) or developed them independently (d’Errico, 2003) has been debated, but at least the painted shells of Zilhão et al. (2010) predate by a fair margin the arrival of *Homo sapiens*. There is also some evidence of ceremonial burial of Neanderthals (d’Errico et al., 2009). While these Neanderthal finds are simpler and less frequent than the ornaments and figurative art of later *Homo sapiens*, they nevertheless demonstrate some symbolic capacity in Neanderthals. And given that symbolic capacities are a prerequisite for language, and may be interpreted as indicative of the presence of language, this adds support to the case for Neanderthal language.

5. Conclusions

Both fossil evidence of speech adaptations in Neanderthals or earlier hominins, and archaeological indications of symbolic behaviour, support the presence of some form of language in Neanderthals. Note, however, that the anatomical evidence concerns proxies for *speech*, whereas the archaeological evidence concerns proxies for *language*. These are not synonymous. Language need not have started in a spoken modality; sign language may have been the original language (e.g. Corballis (2002)).

It remains a controversial issue whether the Neanderthals actually were a separate lineage, or just a subspecies of *Homo sapiens*, and whether there was any significant admixture when modern humans replaced Neanderthals in Europe (Herrera, Somarelli, Lowery, & Herrera, 2009). But a modest amount of admixture near the time of Neanderthal extinction would not materially affect the argument here, as both the speech adaptations and some of the "symbolic" archaeology predates the proposed time frame for admixture, and likely predates even the common ancestor of Neanderthals and *Homo sapiens*.

There is no real evidence indicating just how complex language Neanderthals may have had. A fair case can be made for it being complex enough to require fine-grained vocal distinctions, but reviewing possible protolanguages (Jackendoff, 1999; Johansson, 2005; Stade, 2009; Bickerton, 2009) is beyond the scope of this paper.

References

Alemseged, Z., Spoor, F., Kimbel, W. H., Bobe, R., Geraads, D., Reed, D., & Wynn, J. G. (2006). A juvenile early hominin skeleton from Dikika, Ethiopia. *Nature*, *443*(7109), 296–301.

Arensburg, B., Tillier, A., Vandermeersch, B., Duday, H., Schepartz, L., & Rak, Y. (1989). A middle palaeolithic human hyoid bone. *Nature*, *338*(6218), 758-60.

Baba, H., Aziz, F., Kaifu, Y., Suwa, G., Kono, R. T., & Jacob, T. (2003). Homo erectus Calvarium from the Pleistocene of Java. *Science*, *299*(5611), 1384–1388.

Balzeau, A., & Gilissen, E. (2010). Endocranial shape asymmetries in pan paniscus, pan troglodytes and gorilla gorilla assessed via skull based landmark analysis. *J Hum Evo 59:54-69.*

Bastir, M., Rosas, A., Stringer, C., Cuétara, J. M., Kruszynski, R., Weber, G. W., Ross, C. F., & Ravosa, M. J. (2010). Effects of brain and facial size on basicranial form in human and primate evolution. *J Hum Evo 58:424-431.*

Beerli, P., & Edwards, S. V. (2002). When did neanderthals and modern humans diverge? *Evolutionary Anthropology, Suppl 1:60-63.*

Benítez-Burraco, A., Longa, V. M., Lorenzo, G., & Uriagereka, J. (2008). Also sprach neanderthalis or did she? *Biolinguistics 2.2-3.225-232.*

Bickerton, D. (2009). *Adam's tongue.* Hill & Wang.

Binford, L. R. (1989). Isolating the transition to cultural adaptations: An organizational approach. In E. Trinkaus (Ed.), *The emergence of modern humans: Biocultural adaptations in the Later Pleistocene* (p. 18-41). Cambridge: Cambridge University Press.

Boë, L.-J., Heim, J.-L., Honda, K., Maeda, S., Badin, P., & Abry, C. (2007). The vocal tract of newborn humans and Neanderthals: Acoustic capabilities and consequences for the debate on the origin of language. A reply to Lieberman (2007a). *Journal of Phonetics*, *35*(4), 564–581.

Boer, B. de, & Fitch, W. T. (2010). Computer models of vocal tract evolution: an overview and critique. *Adaptive Behavior 18:36-47.*

Botha, R. (2008). Prehistoric shell beads as a window on language evolution. *Language & Communication 28:197-212.*

Bouzouggar et al. (2007). 82,000-year-old shell beads from North Africa and implications for the origins of modern human behavior. *Proceedings of the National Academy of Sciences*, *104*(24), 9964–9969.

Bruner, E. (2004). Geometric morphometrics and paleoneurology: brain shape evolution in the genus homo. *J Hum Evo 47:279-303.*

Bruner, E. (2007). Cranial shape and size variation in human evolution: structural and functional perspectives. *Childs Nerv Syst 23:1357-1365.*

Bruner, E. (2008). Comparing endocranial form and shape differences in modern humans and neandertals: a geometric approach. *PaleoAnthropology 2008:93-106.*

Cantalupo, C., & Hopkins, W. D. (2001). Asymmetric broca's area in great apes. *Nature 414:505.*

Caramelli, D., Lalueza-Fox, C., Vernesi, C., Lari, M., Casoli, A., Mallegni, F., Chiarelli, B., Dupanloup, I., Bertranpetit, J., Barbujani, G., & Bertorelle, G. (2003). Evidence for a genetic discontinuity between neandertals and 24,000-year-old anatomically modern europeans. *Proceedings of the National Academy of Sciences*, *100*(11), 6593-6597.

Cartmill, M. (2010). The human (r)evolution(s). *Evolutionary Anthropology 19:89-91.*

Coop, G., Bullaughey, K., Luca, F., & Przeworski, M. (2008). The timing of selection at the human foxp2 gene. *Molecular Biology and Evolution*, *25*(7), 1257-1259.

Corballis, M. C. (2002). *From hand to mouth: the origins of language.* Princeton: Princeton University Press.

DeGusta, D., Gilbert, W. H., & Turner, S. P. (1999). Hypoglossal canal size and hominid speech. *Proceedings of the National Academy of Sciences, 96*(4), 1800-1804.
d'Errico, F. (2003). The invisible frontier. a multiple species model for the origin of behavioral modernity. *Evolutionary Anthropology 12:188-202.*
d'Errico, F. (2008). The archaeology of language origins. In A. D. M. Smith, K. Smith, & R. Ferrer i Cancho (Eds.), *Evolution of language - evolang7* (p. 413-414). Singapore: World Scientific Publishing.
d'Errico, F., Henshilwood, C., Lawson, G., Vanhaeren, M., Tillier, A.-M., Soressi, M., Bresson, F., Maureille, B., Nowell, A., Lakarra, J., Backwell, L., & Julien, M. (2003). Archaeological evidence for the emergence of language, symbolism, and music — an alternative multidisciplinary perspective. *J World Prehistory 17:1-70.*
d'Errico, F., & Vanhaeren, M. (2009). Earliest personal ornaments and their significance for the origin of language debate. In R. Botha & C. Knight (Eds.), *The cradle of language* (p. 16-40). Oxford University Press.
d'Errico, F., Vanhaeren, M., Henshilwood, C., Lawson, G., Maureille, B., Gambier, D., Tillier, A.-M., Soressi, M., & Niekerk, K. van. (2009). From the origin of language to the diversification of languages: what can archaeology and palaeoanthropology say? In F. d'Errico & J.-M. Hombert (Eds.), *Becoming eloquent: Advances in the emergence of language, human cognition, and modern cultures* (p. 13-68). Amsterdam: Benjamins.
Diller, K. C., & Cann, R. L. (2009). Evidence against a genetic-based revolution in language 50,000 years ago. In R. Botha & C. Knight (Eds.), *The cradle of language* (p. 135-149). Oxford University Press.
Enard, W., Przeworski, M., Fisher, S. E., Lai, C. S., Wiebe, V., Kitano, T., Monaco, A. P., & Paabo, S. (2002). Molecular evolution of FOXP2, a gene involved in speech and language. *Nature, 418*(6900), 869–872.
Endicott, Ho, & Stringer. (2010). Using genetic evidence to evaluate four palaeoanthropological hypotheses for the timing of neanderthal and modern human origins. *J Hum Evo 59:87-95.*
Fitch, W. T. (2000). The evolution of speech: a comparative review. *Trends Cogn Sci 4:258-267.*
Fitch, W. T. (2009). Fossil cues to the evolution of speech. In R. Botha & C. Knight (Eds.), *The cradle of language* (p. 112-134). Oxford University Press.
Frayer, D. W., Fiore, I., Lalueza-Fox, C., Radovcic, J., & Bondioli, L. (2010). Right handed neandertals: Vindija and beyond. *J Anthropological Sci 88:113-127.*
Gannon, P. J., Holloway, R. L., Broadfield, D. C., & Braun, A. R. (1998). Asymmetry of chimpanzee planum temporale: humanlike pattern of wernicke's brain language area homolog. *Science 279:220-222.*
Granat, J., Boë, L.-J., Badin, P., Pochic, D., Heim, J.-L., Peyre, E., & Benoit, R. (2007). Predictions of the ability of reconstituted vocal tracts of fossils to produce speech. *Presented at International Congress of Phonetic Sciences 2007, Saarbrücken, Germany.*
Green, R. E., Krause, J., Ptak, S. E., Briggs, A. W., Ronan, M. T., Simons, J. F., Du, L., Egholm, M., Rothberg, J. M., Paunovic, M., & Paabo, S. (2006). Analysis of one million base pairs of Neanderthal DNA. *Nature, 444*(7117), 330–336.
Green et al. (2010). A draft sequence of the neandertal genome. *Science, 328*(5979), 710-722.
Haesler, S., Wada, K., Nshdejan, A., Morrisey, E. E., Lints, T., Jarvis, E. D., & Scharff, C. (2004). Foxp2 expression in avian vocal learners and non-learners. *The Journal of Neuroscience, 24*(13), 3164-3175.
Henshilwood, d'Errico, & Watts. (2009). Engraved ochres from the middle stone age levels at blombos cave, south africa. *J Hum Evo 57:27-47.*
Henshilwood, C. S., d'Errico, F., Yates, R., Jacobs, Z., Tribolo, C., Duller, G. A. T., Mercier, N., Sealy, J. C., Valladas, H., Watts, I., & Wintle, A. G. (2002). Emergence of modern human behavior: Middle stone age engravings from south africa. *Science, 295*(5558), 1278-1280.
Henshilwood, C. S., & Dubreuil, B. (2009). Reading the artifacts: gleaning language skills from the middle stone age in southern africa. In R. Botha & C. Knight (Eds.), *The cradle of language* (p. 41-61). Oxford University Press.
Herrera, K. J., Somarelli, J. A., Lowery, R. K., & Herrera, R. J. (2009). To what extent did neanderthals and modern humans interact? *Biological Reviews of the Cambridge Philosophical Society, 84*(2), 245–257.
Hodgson, J. A., & Disotell, T. R. (2008). No evidence of a neanderthal contribution to modern human diversity. *Genome Biology 9:206.*
Houghton, P. (1993). Neandertal supralaryngeal vocal tract. *Am J Phys Anthro 90:139-146.*
Jackendoff, R. (1999). Possible stages in the evolution of the language capacity. *Trends Cogn Sci 3:272-279.*
Johansson, S. (2005). *Origins of language — constraints on hypotheses.* Amsterdam: Benjamins.
Johansson, S. (2011). Constraining the time when language evolved. *Linguistic and Philosophical Investigations 10:45-59.*
Johnson, C. R., & McBrearty, S. (2010). 500,000 year old blades from the kapthurin formation, kenya. *J Hum Evo 58:193-200.*
Jungers, W. L., Pokempner, A. A., Kay, R. F., & Cartmill, M. (2003). Hypoglossal canal size in living hominoids and the evolution of human speech. *Human Biology 75:473-484.*
Kay, Cartmill, & Balow. (1998). The hypoglossal canal and the origin of human vocal behavior. *Proc Nat Acad Sci 95:5417-5419.*
Klein, R. G. (1999). *The human career: human biological and cultural origins.* Chicago: University of Chicago

Press.

Krause, J., Lalueza-Fox, C., Orlando, L., Enard, W., Green, R. E. E., Burbano, H. A. A., Hublin, J.-J. J., Hänni, C., Fortea, J., Rasilla, M. de la, Bertranpetit, J., Rosas, A., & Pääbo, S. (2007). The Derived FOXP2 Variant of Modern Humans Was Shared with Neandertals. *Current Biology 17:1908-1912.*

Krings, M., Geisert, H., Schmitz, R. W., Krainitzki, H., & Pääbo, S. (1999). Dna sequence of the mitochondrial hypervariable region ii from the neandertal type specimen. *Proceedings of the National Academy of Sciences, 96*(10), 5581-5585.

Lai, C., Fisher, S., Hurst, J., Vargha-Khadem, F., & Monaco, A. (2001). A forkhead-domain gene is mutated in a severe speech and language disorder. *Nature, 413*(6855), 519–523.

Lalueza-Fox, C. (2009). The neanderthal genome project and beyond. *Contributions to Science 5:169-175.*

Langley, Clarkson, & Ulm. (2008). Behavioral complexity in eurasian neanderthal populations: a chronological examination of the archaeological evidence. *Cambridge Arch J 18:289-307.*

Li, C. N., & Hombert, J.-M. (2002). On the evolutionary origin of language. In M. I. Stamenov & V. Gallese (Eds.), *Mirror neurons and the evolution of brain and language* (p. 175-206). Amsterdam: Benjamins.

Li, G., Wang, J., Rossiter, S. J., Jones, G., & Zhang, S. (2007). Accelerated FoxP2 evolution in echolocating bats. *PLoS ONE, 2*(9), e900.

Lieberman, P. (2007). Current views on neanderthal speech capabilities: a reply to boe et al. (2002). *J Phonetics 35:552-563.*

Lieberman, P. (2008). Old-time linguistic theories. *Cortex 44:218-226.*

Lieberman, P. (2009). Foxp2 and human cognition. *Cell 137:800-802.*

MacLarnon, A., & Hewitt, G. (2004). Increased breathing control: another factor in the evolution of language. *Evo Anthro 13:181-197.*

Martínez, I., Arsuaga, J. L., Quam, R., Carretero, J. M., Gracia, A., & Rodríguez, L. (2008). Human hyoid bones from the middle pleistocene site of the sima de los huesos (sierra de atapuerca, spain). *J Hum Evo 54:118-124.*

Martínez, I., Rosa, M., Arsuaga, J. L., Jarabo, P., Quam, R., Lorenzo, C., Gracia, A., Carretero, J. M., Castro, B. J. M. de, & Carbonell, E. (2004). Auditory capacities in Middle Pleistocene humans from the Sierra de Atapuerca in Spain. *Proceedings of the National Academy of Sciences, 101*(27), 9976–9981.

McBrearty, S., & Brooks, A. (2000). The revolution that wasn't: a new interpretation of the origin of modern human behavior. *J Hum Evo 39:453-563.*

Mellars, P. (1998). Neanderthals, modern humans and the archaeological evidence for language. In N. G. Jablonski & L. C. Aiello (Eds.), *The origin and diversification of language.* San Francisco: Calif. Acad. Sci.

Mellars, P. (2005). The impossible coincidence. a single-species model for the origins of modern human behavior in europe. *Evo Anthro 14:12-27.*

Olson, M. V., & Varki, A. (2004). The chimpanzee genome — a bittersweet celebration. *Science 305:191-192.*

Quam, R., & Rak, Y. (2008). Auditory ossicles from southwest asian mousterian sites. *J Hum Evo 54:414-433.*

Roebroeks, W., & Verpoorte, A. (2009). A "language-free" explanation for differences between the european middle and upper paleolithic record. In R. Botha & C. Knight (Eds.), *The cradle of language* (p. 150-166). Oxford University Press.

Rougier et al. (2007). Peştera cu Oase 2 and the cranial morphology of early modern Europeans. *Proceedings of the National Academy of Sciences, 104*(4), 1165–1170.

Schepartz, L. A. (1993). Language and modern human origins. *Yearbook of Physical Anthropology 36:91-126.*

Stade, C. (2009). Abrupt vs. gradual evolution of language: the case for semilanguage. *MA Thesis, UCL.*

Steele, J., & Uomini, N. (2009). Can the archaeology of manual specialization tell us anything about language evolution? a survey of the state of play. *Cambridge Arch J 19:97-110.*

Texier et al. (2010). A Howiesons Poort tradition of engraving ostrich eggshell containers dated to 60,000 years ago at Diepkloof Rock Shelter, South Africa. *Proceedings of the National Academy of Sciences, 107*(14), 6180–6185.

Trinkaus, E. (2007). European early modern humans and the fate of the neandertals. *Proc Nat Acad Sci 104:7367-7372.*

Tyrrell, A. J., & Chamberlain, A. T. (1998). Non-metric trait evidence for modern human affinities and the distinctiveness of neanderthals. *J Hum Evo 34:549-554.*

Uomini, N. T. (2009). The prehistory of handedness: archaeological data and comparative ethology. *J Hum Evo 57:411-419.*

Van Peer et al. (2003). The early to middle stone age transition and the emergence of modern human behaviour at site 8-b-11, sai island, sudan. *J Hum Evo 45:187-193.*

Wall, J. D., & Kim, S. K. (2007). Inconsistencies in neanderthal genomic dna sequences. *PLoS Genetics 3:e175.*

Watts, I. (2009). Red ochre, body painting, and language: interpreting the blombos ochre. In R. Botha & C. Knight (Eds.), *The cradle of language* (p. 62-92). Oxford University Press.

Wynn, T., & Coolidge, F. L. (2004). The expert neandertal mind. *J Hum Evo 46:467-487.*

Zilhão et al. (2010). Symbolic use of marine shells and mineral pigments by iberian neandertals. *Proceedings of the National Academy of Sciences 107 (3) 1023-1028.*

Zilhão, J. (2007). The emergence of ornaments and art: An archaeological perspective on the origins of "behavioral modernity". *J Archaeol Res 15:1-54.*

MEANINGS OF TOUCHING OBJECT PARTS IN POINTING

HARUMI KOBAYASHI
Division of Information design system, Tokyo Denki University, Hatoyama Hiki-gun, Saitama, 350-0394, Japan

TETSUYA YASUDA
Division of Information design system, Tokyo Denki University, Hatoyama Hiki-gun, Saitama, 350-0394, Japan

This study investigated the effect of adults' referential pointing actions in teaching novel part names of unfamiliar objects. The participants were 2-year-olds, 4-year-olds and adults. In Experiment 1, we examined the effect of simple pointing either with touching the object part or without touching it. In Experiment 2, we examined the effect of pointing with circular motion. The results were that if the object part was made salient by adequate referential actions with touching the object part or pointing with the forefinger's circular motion, young children and adults can learn novel part names of unfamiliar objects. Children's sensitivity to adults' part-oriented referential actions develops between ages 2 and 4.

1. Introduction

Pointing is a uniquely human gesture to convey referential intentions to others and used to teach children various things including language. One way in which children learn names of objects is through ostensive definition, that is, when an adult points to an object while uttering a word, the child makes an inference about what the word refers to. However, ostensive definition is essentially ambiguous in making inferences of word meanings. To solve this ambiguity problem, Markman (1989) stated that young children employ some constraints that regulate the relation between words and concepts of object categories. One example is the "whole object assumption", whereby children assume that a word refers to a whole object, rather than to any property or to any part of the object.

However, in actual word learning situations, speakers seem to know what kind of gestures are appropriate to make any part of an object more salient for others as Zukow (1990) pointed out. In particular, caregivers tend to use multiple referential actions to teach part names of objects. In our previous studies (SRCD, 2007), we found that mothers of 4-year-old children use a variety of referential actions when they were asked to teach part names of familiar and unfamiliar objects. Most mothers simultaneously touched an object part when they taught its part name. For example, when they were asked to teach "knock button" of a ball-point pen, they acted, or pointed at, or tapped the knock button with touching the part saying "(a) knock button" or other part name (e.g., "a part to push"). Almost no mothers pointed at the part with some distance, nor simply held or showed the whole object to the child without doing any referential actions on the object part. We (under preparation) asked a separate group of mothers of 4-year-olds to teach whole object names using the same experimental material. What we found was that mothers tended to simply hold or showed the whole object and the frequency of doing specific part-oriented actions was far lower than that of the part teaching situation. Thus, mothers seem to use appropriate gestures to teach part names.

This study examines the effect of adults' referential actions in children's leaning part names. Our idea is that if the child focuses on part of the object rather than the whole object through observation of the adult's referential actions, the child may be able to learn part names of even unfamiliar objects. We examined the effects of three types of referential actions, functional action, simple pointing, and rhythmic pointing with either touching the object part or not to explore whether these actions help young children focus on object parts and learn part names.

In the literature of word learning, learning part names has been more discussed in the use of linguistic cues rather than nonlinguistic cues (Markman & Wachtel, 1988; Saylor, Baldwin, & Sabbagh, 2002). Markman and Wachtel (1988) showed that children learned part names only when they could use knowledge about a whole object name and by applying the whole object assumption and mutual exclusivity, that is, an object category has only one object label. Saylor, Baldwin, & Sabbagh (2002) demonstrated that if an object is presented and its whole-name and one of its part names are juxtaposed, children can learn the part name of the object. However, whether children can learn part names using nonlinguistic cues, the results are mixed. Examined nonlinguistic cues were general direction of pointing (Mervis, Golinkoff, & Bertrand, 1994), facial expression (Moll, Koring, Carpenter, & Tomasello, 2006), tracing the contour of an object part (Hansen & Markman, 2009), and functional actions (Kobayashi, 1998).

Kobayashi (1998) examined whether Japanese 2-year-olds could learn novel part names of unfamiliar objects when an adult handled object parts in addition to pointing to and naming them. In one experiment, she presented an standard stimulus (a novel inverted U-shaped bolt with a nut), pointed to and named the part ('nut'), and handled the part by turning it around the bolt. In the test phase, she presented a nut [‘part choice’] or an inverted U-shaped bolt without a nut [‘whole choice’] (the U-shaped bolt without a nut had a similar overall shape to the standard object) and asked children, which they thought was the 'nut'. Another standard stimulus was a novel plate hanger with two springs. The 2-year-olds chose an isolated ‘part’ [a nut] that they had observed an adult manipulate, as the referent for the newly acquired part name. However, they chose the whole object [a U-shaped bolt without a nut] when they had not observed the adult manipulating the part. These results suggested that two-year-old children use pragmatic information garnered from adult actions upon object parts to learn part names. When an adult points towards and acts upon a specific part, young children may better understand the part to which the adult's ostensive definition applies. Because simple pointing does not clearly promote part identification, children may focus on the whole object.

The present study further examines the effect of referential action cues in learning part names. While there are many possible styles of pointing towards objects and parts, this study focuses on the effect of pointing and touching a critical part of an object. Two- and four-year-olds were selected as participants because the results of Kobayashi (1998), Saylor and Savage (2004), and pilot studies in our laboratory suggest that a developmental change in learning part names occurs between these ages: Two-year-olds are able to learn part names but their ability appears to be fragile, whereas 4-year-olds seem to be better able to learn part names. Experiment 1 examines the effect of pointing on the object part, either with touching or without touching. In a pointing without touching condition, an experimenter pointed at a critical object part from a distance of seven centimeters. This distance was chosen because it allows young children to successfully observe the relationship between the pointing finger and an object and a paper plate upon which the object was placed. If the distance was too small, young children might not easily distinguish between pointing with touching and pointing without touching. In Experiment 2, we used touch-pointing with circular motion instead of simple touch-pointing. In this circular motion touch-pointing, the experimenter pointed at the referent part with forefinger’s circular motion (0.5 cm diameter). Kobayashi (1998) showed that 2-year-olds recognized the experimenter’s action to move the referent part of an object and associated the part with given part label. If 2-year-olds are sensitive to an adult’s actions, they may recognize the circular motion of her forefinger and notice referential intentions.

2. Experimental 1

2.1. *Method*

Participants were 15 Japanese 2-year-olds, 14 4-year-olds from two preschools in Yokohama Area and Saitama Area in Japan, and 14 undergraduate university students in Japan.

The stimuli consisted of four sets of unfamiliar objects. Among these four object sets, two sets were exactly the same as the ones used in Kobayashi's (1998) study and we added two new sets, pump set, and clip set. In one set, the standard object was a u-shaped bolt with a nut. The test items in the first test phase (an isolated part task) were a nut (part choice) and a u-shaped bolt without a nut (whole choice). The test items for the second test phase (a transfer task) were an I-shaped bolt with a nut (part choice) and a U-shaped bolt without a nut (whole choice). The parts in each set had distinctive shapes. The shapes of the whole choice items were similar to the standard objects except that they did not contain the critical parts.

The condition consisted of two types, a touch-pointing and a no-touch-pointing. In the touch-pointing condition in the nut set, the experimenter first placed the standard object, a u-shaped bolt with a nut, on a white paper plate. She 'touch-pointed' the nut part and said in Japanese: "This is natto." ("Kore wa natto desu.") twice. Following the training phase, the isolated part test began. The experimenter presented two test items which were placed on a separate paper plates. She then asked the child, "On which plate do you find natto?" ("Docchi no osara ni natto ga aru kana?") After the isolated part test, a transfer test began. The experimenter presented two transfer test items in the same manner and asked: "On which plate do you find natto?" ("Docchi no osara ni natto ga aru kana? ") In the other sets, the procedure was identical with that of the nut set.

In the no-touch-pointing condition, the procedure was the same with the touch-pointing condition except that the experimenter pointed at the referent part of the object with distance of 7 cm. Thus, in this condition, the experimenter did not touch the object part at all in teaching the part name.

Japanese is a classifier language that does not have count/mass syntax as in English. The test question "On which plate do you find natto?" was chosen for both the isolated part test and the transfer test because this question does not imply any part/whole interpretation. ("Which is natto?" may exclude the possibility that natto is the part of an object.) The order of presentation of the four stimulus sets was counterbalanced across the children. The part items were presented on the left in one half of all test trials (2 trials) and on the right in the other half of all test trials (2 trials).

University students were randomly assigned to one of the four conditions that were identical to those used in the experiment conducted with 2- and 4-year-olds. The same materials and procedure were used except that the adult participants were instructed to imagine that the novel part names were words in a foreign language.

2.2. *Results and discussion*

Each child received one point when the child chose a part choice. Each child had two scores: an isolated part score and a transfer score. Each score was calculated based on performance in four trials. The data range of the score was 0 – 4. Figure 1 shows the part response scores in each condition. 0 cm's distance means the finger touched the object. 7 cm's distance means the finger did not touched and kept 7 cm distance from the object.

Age (2-year-olds, 4-year-olds, adults) × Point (touch-point, no-touch-point) × Object (isolated, transfer) 3-WAY ANOVA was computed using part response score as a dependent measure. Age and Point were between groups variable, and Object was a within group variable. There were significant main effects of age, $F(2,42)= 8.228$, $p<.005$., and point, $F(1,42)=19.652$, $p<.001$. There was also a significant interaction effect of age × point, $F(2, 42)=3.279$, $p<.05$. However, object effect was not significant, $F(1,42)=1.107$, $p>.1$. Other interaction effects were not significant either.

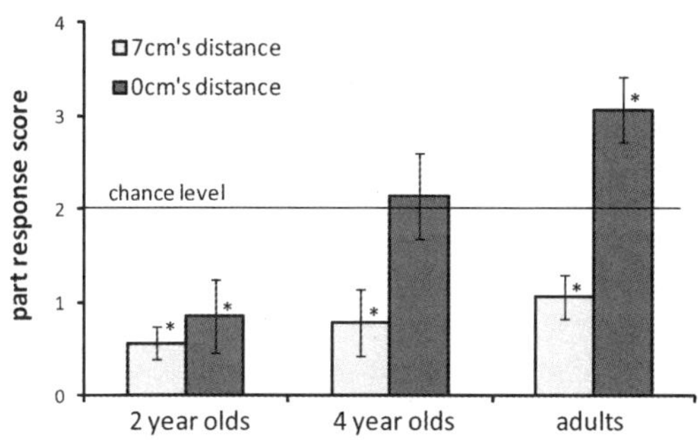

Figure 1. Part response score of each pointing in each age in experiment 1

Notes. * means the difference from chance level was significant ($p<.05$).

To explore the significant interaction effect age × point, simple main effects of age within each point type was computed. The age differences found in the touching condition were significant, $F(2,42)=10.932$, $p<.001$. Ryan's method was used to compare means of different age groups in the touch-pointing condition. All significant contrasts at significant level .05 are reported. In touch-pointing condition, 4-year-olds (M=2.143, SE=0.459) made more part responses than 2-year-olds (M=0.857, SE=0.389). Adults (M=3.071, SE=0.352) made more part responses than 2-year-olds and 4-yearolds. The difference between 4-year-olds and adults was not significant. However, in the no-touch-pointing condition, there was no significant difference of part response among 2-year-olds, 4-year-olds, and adults, $F(2,42)=0.575$, $p>.1$.

These results indicate that 1) When the critical part was NOT TOUCH-POINTED, all age groups chose whole choice. There was no age-related difference. 2) When the critical part was TOUCH-POINTED, 2-year-olds did not choose part choices, but adults chose part choices. 3) 4-year-olds' performance was in the middle of these age groups when the critical part was touched. Their performance was not different from chance level, but it was more than 2-year-olds and less than adults. 4) There was no difference between the isolated object condition and the transfer object condition in the performance of all age groups.

Why 2-year-olds did not choose part choice in touch-point condition? One possible reason is that 2-year-olds did not recognize the occurrence of the experimenters' forefinger touching the object part. In touch-point, the finger only briefly touched the referent part of an object. This movement might have been too subtle for 2-year-olds to recognize. They simply noticed that an object was pointed at and so they interpreted that the whole object was pointed and referred in the both conditions. Another possible reason is that they recognized the experimenter touched the object part, but they did not think the touch-pointing action meant that the touched part was referred. The touch-pointing action was not assumed to be a part specifying referential action. In order to examine these two hypotheses, we conducted Experiment 2.

3. Experimental 2

In Experiment 2, we used circular motion touch-pointing instead of simple touch-pointing. In this circular motion touch-pointing, the experimenter pointed at the referent part with forefinger's circular movement that was done with 0.5 cm diameter above the center of the object part.

3.1. *Method*

Participants were 15 Japanese 2-year-olds, 17 4-year-olds from two preschools in Tokyo Area and Saitama Area in Japan, and 17 undergraduate university students in Japan.

The children of each sex were randomly assigned to one of two conditions: Circular motion gesture with touching the part (0 cm distance) and circular motion gesture without touching the part (7 cm distance). The procedure was identical to that of Experiment 1 except that circular motion was added to pointing action.

3.2. *Results and discussion*

The scoring procure was identical with that of Experiment 1. Each child received one point when the child chose a part choice. Each child had two scores: an isolated part score and a transfer score. Each score was calculated based on performance in four trials. The data range of the score was 0 - 4.

Age (2-year-olds, 4-year-olds, adults) × Point (circular motion with 0 cm distance, circular motion with 7 cm distance) × Object (isolated, transfer) 3-WAY ANOVA was computed using part response score as a dependent measure. Age and Point were between groups variable, and Object was a within group variable. There was a significant main effect of point, $F(2,43)= 92.414$, $p<.001$. There was also a significant interaction effect of age × point, $F(2, 43)=6.935$, $p<.005$. However, age effect was not significant, $F(2,43)=0.505$, $p>.1$. Object effect was again not significant, $F(1,43)=3.633$, $p>.05$. Other interaction effects were not significant either. Figure 3 shows the part response score in each age and in each condition.

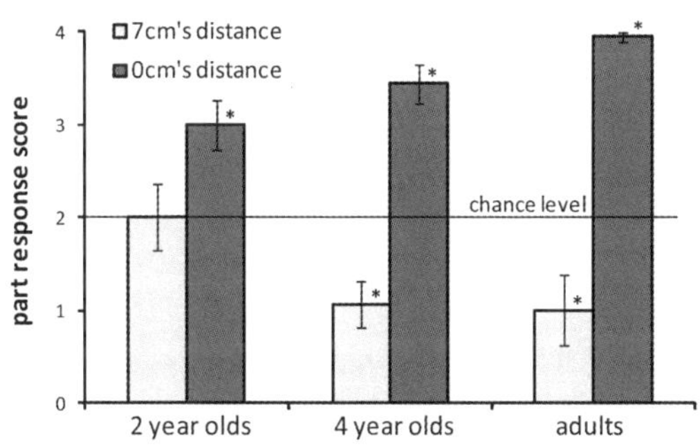

Figure 2. Part response score of each pointing in each age in experiment 2

Notes. * means the difference from chance level was significant ($p<.05$).

To explore the significant interaction effect age × point, simple main effects of age within each point type was computed. The age differences found in the circular motion with 7 cm distance condition were significant, $F(2,47)=4.347$, $p<.05$). Ryan's method was used to compare means of different age groups in the circular motion with 7 cm distance condition. All significant contrasts at significant level .05 are reported. Two-year-olds (M=2.000, SE=0.459) made more part responses than 4-year-olds (M=1.062, SE=0.258). Two-year-olds made more part responses than Adult (M=1.000, SE=0.378). The difference between 4-year-olds and adults was not significant.

These results indicate that 1) when the critical part was TOUCH-POINTED with circular motion, participants of all age groups chose part choices. 2) When the critical part was NOT TOUCH-POINTED with circular motion, 4-year-olds and adult did not choose part choices, whereas 2-year-olds responded randomly.

4. Conclusion

The results were that touching the object part was effective and the ability to recognize and use this touching-the-part information developed with age. 4-year-olds associated the part name to the touched part when object parts were pointed with touching and 4-year-olds' response patterns were similar to adult patterns. Two-year-olds were unable to learn part names if the object part was pointed with touching, but DID learn part names if the part was touch-pointed with circular motion. On the contrary, if the object part were not touched, all age groups including adults tended to associate the given label to the whole object. The study indicates that if the object part was made salient by adequate referential actions with touching the object part, young children and adults can learn novel part names of unfamiliar objects. Children's sensitivity to adults' part-oriented referential actions develops between ages 2 and 4.

Acknowledgements

This work was supported in part by Japan Grant-in-Aid for Scientific Research (C) KAKENHI (20500241).

Selected References

Kobayashi, H. (1998). How 2-year-old children learn novel part names of unfamiliar objects. Cognition 68, B41-51.

Markman, E. M. & Wachtel, G. A. (1988). Children's use of mutual exclusivity to constrain the meanings of words. Cognitive Psychology, 20, 120-157.

Moll, H., Koring, C., Carpenter, M., & Tomasello, M. (2006). Infants determine others' focus of attention by pragmatics and exclusion. Journal of Cognition and Development, 7(3), 411-430.

Zukow, P.G. (1990). Socio-perceptual bases for the emergence of language: an alternative to innatist approaches. Developmental Psychobiology, 23. 705-726.

THE EVOLUTION OF MORPHOLOGY AND THE DIVERSITY OF GRAMMATICAL SYSTEMS

ANJA LATROUITE

Department of Language & Information, Heinrich Heine Universität Düsseldorf, Universitätsstraße 1
40225 Düsseldorf, Germany

This paper addresses the question as to what the place of morphology in contrast to syntax in the evolution of language is. Based on recent research on morphology in sign languages and in polysynthetic languages, the point is made that morphology is more than 'word syntax' or 'lexicalized traces of phonology' and, thus, more than the result of an interaction between computational syntax and articulatory pressures. The view is supported that morphology is an important independent computational tool of language and that there is reason to believe that it may have developed independently of syntax. This obviously has a bearing on whether or not polysynthetic languages are viewed as an over-the-top development that arrived at a late point in time or not.

1. Introduction

One of the big challenges for linguists working on the evolution of language is the great grammatical diversity we find and the question as to how it developed. While some languages seem to rely entirely on morphological means to the point that utterances only consist of one single highly complex word (polysynthetic languages) with at times unclear morpheme boundaries, other languages exhibit only very little morphological complexity and rely primarily on word order, i.e. syntax (isolating languages). Interestingly this enormous difference in computational diversity does not seem to have sparked a lively discussion when it comes to the question as to how language evolved. At the forefront of much of the recent linguistic research is the question ,Why and how did syntax evolve?' (e.g. Bickerton 2007). The question as to why and how morphology evolved has come up (Carstairs-McCarthy 2005, 2010, Wunderlich 2008) as well, but is less often touched upon. This seems to be the case, because morphology is either viewed as (i) ,lexicalized traces of phonology', in the sense that bound morphemes and morphological phenomena in general are viewed as resulting from phonological processes or as (ii) ,word syntax' with many parallels to sentence syntax (à la 'today's morphology is yesterday's syntax'), often including fundamental criticism on the concept of ‚word' (cf. Haspelmath 2011), especially in polysynthetic languages. Oftentimes we find a mixture of the two views, given that morphology is regarded as a double-interface domain, divided into morphophonology on the one hand and morphosyntax on the other. Linguists with a special interest in syntax tend to focus on the latter aspects. In this view, morphology and syntax are equally good reflexes of the development of the computational part of language, so basically answering the question with respect to the development of syntax is viewed as answering some, if not most, of the questions regarding the development of morphology. However, there is reason to believe that the computational aspects of morphology differ quite significantly from those of syntax and represent an autonomous and distinct domain. Linguists with a special interest in phonology, like Carstairs-McCarthy (2005, 2010) argue that morphology developed independently of syntax once the symbolic character of sounds had evolved, although elements had to co-occur frequently in a certain order to fuse. One of the central ideas Carstairs-McCarthy (2010) puts forward is that much of morphology developed in response to two conflicting pressures: (i) the articulatory-phonological apparatus which encouraged the development of synonyms (due to the fact that words and string of words may be pronounced differently with higher or lower speech production rates), and (ii) the innate expectancy that different sounds/symbols should mean different things (synonymy-avoidance expectancy). In terms of the evolution of language the development of bound morphemes and, as such the development of greater morphological complexity, is then mainly the result of rapid or otherwise modified speech leading to (i) different sound qualities to which new meanings were attributed and (ii) the reduction of certain words that were fused to other elements, i.e. to affix formation. Obviously, a frequently recurring word order is taken for granted in this case so that the autonomous development of morphology is not that evident. Carstairs-McCarthy's approach goes very well with classic theories of grammaticalization (e.g. Hopper & Traugott 1983) concerned with the development of bound morphemes, and adds on top an explanation of allomorphy, which is seen as a remnant of allophonic variation that is no longer transparent to the speaker.

However, while Carstairs-McCarthy's theory works very well for the development of inflection (affixation and certain kinds of stem alternation), it does not seem to provide a straight-forward explanation for derivational morphology, especially as found in languages with templatic morphology or pervasive recursive reduplication that clearly cannot be viewed as derived from formerly independent lexical units being fused (cf. Wunderlich 2008). Similarly this approach does not seem to explain the development of polysynthetic languages or rich morphology languages that exhibit considerable variability with respect to affix order, like Tagalog (Schachter & Otanes 1972), Chichewa (Hyman 2003), Mapuche (Smeets 1989), Dakar Wolof (Buell et al. 2008) or Chintang (Bickel et al. 20007). As Ryan (2010) shows variability is oftentimes not explainable on phonological or syntacto-semantic grounds, but follows rules specific to the realm of morphology. Similarly, non-segmental morphological markers like tone or stress signaling conversion are not easily deducible from a hypothesized interaction of syntax and articulatory pressures as the source of morphology. Research on sign languages (Goldin-Meadow et al. 2007, Senghas et al. 2010) and the evolution of modulatory morphology seems to point to a similar direction. It could be shown that newly emerging sign languages develop non-concatenative morphology and reduplication early on within two generations. Aronoff (2005) argues that this is a consequence of the medium and can hardly be argued to show anything universal about language or language evolution given that non-concatenative morphology is not pervasively found and hardly a good candidate for a first step in the evolution of language. However, regardless of the fact that morphological computation may take a different form in sign languages, the fast development in those languages, that are probably a much better test case for newly emerging languages than most spoken creole languages, should be taken seriously.

As already pointed out by Jackendoff (2009) for composition, which he argues to be the coelacanth of grammar, the computational system of morphology differs significantly from syntax. This becomes also evident in the pervasive polyfunctionality of morphologically bound material, which is rather the norm than the exception (cf. Wunderlich 2007). In some cases affixes even get to mark mutually exclusive concepts (e.g. diminutive and augmentative) or unrelated concepts (e.g. causative and iterative), showing that morphology may simply signal the deviation from some kind of (language-specific) default concept, following a logic unknown to syntactic computation.

As pointed out by Van Valin (p.c,) the contrast between head-marking and dependent-marking languages is also relevant to the point made her. The usual dependent-marking as basic view claims that independent pronouns were phonologically reduced to clitics, which then fused with the verb. But this is problematic in two regards: firstly, the prevalence of zero as a marker for 3 person raises the question of how a zero pronominal underwent this process, and secondly branching direction predicts that in left-branching languages the argument markers should be prefixes and in right branching languages suffixes, but this is not the case (cf. Van Valin in press).

All this shows that if one delves deeper into morphological phenomena and goes beyond the kind of morphology regularly found in languages in which syntax plays a major role, the question ‚How did morphology evolve?' requires furthermore answers to the questions (i) 'What kind of morphological variety is out there?' and (ii) ‚What kind of morphology evolved independently of syntax in spoken languages and independently of articulatory phonology (in the gestural languages, but not only there)?' The question as to the precise nature of morphological computation is all the more important as the greatest diversity between languages is found in the complex realm of morphology, not in the realm of syntax. The enormous wealth and diversity within morphology compared to the relative low syntactic diversity we find may already be considered one good reason why morphology must have developed independently of syntax and very early in the history of language evolution.

2. Language evolution and polysynthetic languages

The answer to the question whether morphology evolved independently of syntax has a direct bearing on the classification of polysynthetic languages as exhibiting either ‚early' or ‚late' language structures in the evolution of language. Wunderlich (2008) points out that rich morphology languages tend to be found in hunter-gatherer communities (so-called 'old language' communities like the Khoi, Andamanese etc.), i.e. comparatively small communities where people share the same background and the frequency of recurrent communication situations helps the memorization of complex forms. Processing of memorized forms is fast and efficient and superior to the processing of single units that need to be combined compositionally, which is one distinct advantage of this kind of morphology. While morphologically complex languages are hard to learn for adults, language acquisition studies have shown that first language learners of polysynthetic languages exhibit no difficulty in acquiring morphologically highly complex languages, even if they contain 400 affixes, plenty of allomorphs, morphophonemic fusion and no clear-cut distinction between inflection and derivation (Fortescue 1984, Mithun 1989). By the age of two and half children, much like in Kirby's (2002) much less complex computer simulation, have analyzed their holophrastic language in a way that they have filtered out predicates, pronominal elements, object referring elements and around three dozen affixes, proving the point that homo sapiens is born with highly developed analytical skills regarding paradigmatic patterns and that there must be indeed an innate expectancy in infants that different sounds should mean different things. The difficulty adults experience in learning complex morphological systems could actually serve as second advantage for a community that wants to keep outsiders, rivals and/or potential enemies at a distance and in the dark about personal plans.

Ever since Brinton (1888), there has been the idea that (spoken) language may have first evolved as (holophrastic) cries and calls (e.g. Wray 2000, Arbib 2005, Dowman 2007) with complex meaning, which gradually got analyzed as containing distinctive meaning segments. The opposing view is that language started out with very simple referential utterances and a simple structure and then gradually went from a pidgin-like string of words to a complex computational system (cf. Bickerton 2007, Carstairs-McCarthy 2005). Is one claim as convincing as the other and are both equally well-suited to explain the evolution of morphology or the diversity of grammatical systems? (Note that the two views are not incompatible. There is good reason to believe that the first utterances may have consisted of both, holophrastic calls and simple referential utterances. However, if one has to choose, which one provides a more plausible story with respect to the existence of the two language types, one with a semi-holophrastic structure and one with an isolating structure?

Assuming the first hypothesis, one would have to conclude with Brinton (1888) and Dowman (2007) that the first languages were holophrastic or at least semi-holophrastic, exhibiting a number of synonymous utterances that got fractionized over time into recurring bits that were attributed meaning. As exemplified in Kirby (2002) or Oudeyer (2005) this scenario is plausible and can be reconstructed by computer-linguists. The idea would then be that the beginning the segmentation in these languages did not develop very far, e.g. not in a way that a variety of distinct clear-cut word classes evolved. In this view, the structure of polysynthetic languages like Tinné, Greenlandic or Mohawk would then be representative for the first languages.

The contrary position is taken by Fortescue (1992) and others who suggest that polysynthetic languages are at the end of a developmental process (from single words to clustering of words to fusion of these clustered words) and have reached a point of no return which is why they stopped participating in structural language changes that are characterized by a back and forth swing between synthetic and analytic; they stayed stable and polysynthetic. Interestingly, Fortescue (2002, 2008) also stresses how very ancient many polysynthetic languages are (something which seems to be true of morphologically complex languages in general. He adds that more often than not no lexical sources of derivational affixes can be found in these languages and that, even if these languages do not become analytic, many are on their way to less polysynthesis (e.g. a reduction of their affix number), not the other way around. In this view polysynthetic languages are the result of a rather unnatural ‚over the top drift' into a bizarre direction.

Note that while there are very good reasons to motivate why language communities that grow and interact with other language communities abandon rich intricate morphological systems little by little, as of yet there is not theory that can explain why a language should develop a rich intricate fusional system and move to a holophrastic one. Obviously this is one more reason that should make one think that the development of the computational domain of morphology preceded the development of the computational domain of syntax, all the more as much of morphology serves to categorize, mark and combine concepts and classes of concepts and also deviations from concepts as noted earlier.

If this reasoning is on the right track, then morphology deserves to take a bigger place in the research on the evolution of language than it currently does.

References

Arbib, M. A. (2005). From monkey-like action recognition to human language: An evolutionary framework for neurolinguistics. *Behavioral and Brain Sciences*, 28(2):105--124.

Aronoff, Mark, Irit Meir and Wendy Sandler (2005). The paradox of sign language morphology. *Language* 81.2, 301-344.

Bickel, Balthasar, Goma Banjade, Martin Gaenszle, Elena Lieven, Netra Prasad Paudyal, Ichchha Purna Rai, Manoj Rai, Novel Kishore Rai, and Sabine Stoll. 2007. Free prefix-ordering in Chintang. *Language* 83.43{73.

Bickerton, D. (2007): Language evolution: A brief guide for linguists. *Lingua*, 117(3):510-526.

Brinton, D. (1888): The Language of Palaeolithic Man. *Proceedings of the American Philosophical Society*, Vol 25, No. 128.

Buell, Leston, Mariame Sy, and Harold Torrence. 2008. The syntax of Mirror Principle violations in Wolof. Handout from the 2008 International Morphology Meeting, Vienna, February 2008.

Carstairs-McCarthy, A. (2005). The Evolutionary Origin of Morphology. In Maggie Tallerman (ed), *Language Origins: Perspectives on Evolution*. OUP.

Carstairs-McCarthy, A. (2010). *The Evolution of Morphology*. Oxford University Press.

Fortescue, M. (2002). The rise and fall of polysynthesis in the Eskimo-Aleut family. In N Evans & H Sasse (eds), *Problems of polysynthesis* , *Studia typologica,* 4 :257-275. Akademie Verlag GmbH, Berlin,.

Fortescue, MD (2008): The typological position and theoretical status of polysynthesis, *Tidsskrift for Sprogforskning*, 5:1-27.

Goldin-Meadow et al. (2007). How children make language out of gesture: Morphological structure in gesture systems developed by American and Chinese deaf children. *Cognitive Psychology*, 2007, 55:87-135.

Haspelmath, M. (2011) The indeterminacy of word segmentation and the nature of morphology and syntax. *Folia Linguistica* 45: 31-80.

Hopper, T. &Traugott E. (1993). *Grammaticalization*. Cambridge, England: Cambridge University Press

Hyman, Larry. 2003. Suffix ordering in Bantu: A morphocentric approach. *Yearbook of Morphology* 2002.245-281.

Jackendoff, R. (2009): Compounding in the Parallel Architecture and Conceptual Semantics, in R. Lieber, *The Oxford Handbook of Compounding,* Oxford University Press,

Klein, Wolfgang, and Clive Perdue (1997): The Basic Variety (or: Couldn't natural languages be much simpler?), *Second Language Research* 13, 301-347.

Kirby, S. (2002) Learning, bottlenecks, and the evolution of recursive syntax. In Ted Briscoe, (ed), *Linguistic Evolution through Language Acquisition: Formal and Computational Models*. Cambridge University Press.

Oudeyer P.Y. (2005) From holistic to concrete speech sounds. In Maggie Tallerman (ed*), Language Origins: Perspectives on Evolution*. OUP.

Ryan, K. (2010). Variable Affix Order: Grammar and Learning. *Language* 86, 4: 758-791.

Senghas, A. et al. (2010) The evolution of segmentation and sequencing: Evidence from homesign and Nicaraguan Sign Language. In Evolang 8, *The Proceedings of the Eighth International Conference on the Evolution of Language*.

Schachter, Paul, and Fe Otanes. (1972). Tagalog reference grammar. Berkeley, California: University of California Press.

Van Valin Jr., R. D. (in press). Head-marking languages and linguistic theory. In B. Bickel, L. A. Grenoble, D. A. Peterson, & A. Timberlake (Eds.), *What's where why? Language typology and historical contingency*. A festschrift to honor Johanna Nichols. Amsterdam: Benjamins.

Wray, A. (2000) Holistic utterances in protolanguage: the link from primates to humans. In Knight, C., Studdert-Kennedy, M. & Hurford, J. *The Evolutionary Emergence of Language: Social function and the origins of linguistic form*. New York: Cambridge University Press, 285-302.

Wunderlich, D. (2007). *Is the optimal affix polyfunctional*? Talk given at the Morphology Meeting 2007 in Leipzig.

Wunderlich, D. (2008) Spekulationen über den Anfang von Sprache. *Zeitschrift für Sprachwissenschaft* 27: 229-265.

WHAT'S THE SCOPE OF THE NAMING GAME? CONSTRAINTS ON SEMANTIC CATEGORIZATION

ANDY LÜCKING and ALEXANDER MEHLER

Goethe-Universität Frankfurt am Main, Text-Technology Group

Abstract

The *Naming Game* (NG) has become a vivid research paradigm for simulation studies on language evolution and the establishment of naming conventions. Recently, NGs were used for reconstructing the creation of linguistic categories, most notably for color terms. We recap the functional principle of NGs and the latter Categorization Games (CGs) and evaluate them in the light of semantic data of linguistic categorization outside the domain of colors. This comparison reveals two specifics of the CG paradigm: Firstly, the emerging categories draw basically on the predefined topology of the learning domain. Secondly, the kind of categories that can be learnt in CGs is bound to context-independent intersective categories. This suggests that the NG and the CG focus on a special aspect of natural language categorization, which disregards context-sensitive categories used in a non-compositional manner.

1. Motivation

The paradigmatic model of the evolution of natural language semantics is the *Categorization Game* (CG). We believe that the CG is a powerful account for the constitution of categories within agents, which is of great importance for linguistics and cognitive sciences. In this paper, we take a *semantic perspective* on the relation between the elements in the agents' lexica and the things these agents talk about, that happen to be colors. Taking a semantic stance, however, color predicates (i.e. the elements of the agents' lexica) are examples of but one out of various *kinds* of semantic predicates. To be more concrete, they are extensional and intersective. Since the majority of linguistic predicates is of a different kind, this suggests a *semantic* restriction of the CG. Since we talk about predicates of a different semantic *kind* (not of other predicates of the same kind), adding more simulation parameters or syntactic combination rules will probably not suffice to provide a semantic extension of the CG.

Our semantic assessment is based on the "semantic range" of categorization as documented in pertaining publications. We do not want to blame either quoted or not quoted authors. We think that the success of the CG even strengthens the need for a critical assessments not only of its current achievements (documented by a growing number of publications), but also of its possible shortcomings. It is this latter aspect that we want to bring up for discussion.

2. Introduction

The *Naming Game* (NG) has been used in order to simulate, model, reconstruct or predict different linguistic phenomena. We distinguish the following three variants:

- *Conventions.* The focus here is on how naming conventions evolve without explicit agreement between language users. Agents, modeled as word-object "mapping systems", converge onto the same mappings between words and objects. Note that although both sets involved are called "words" and "objects", the NG is independent of the kind or provenance of the elements to be conventionally associated.

- *Language Evolution.* The focus here is on how the members of a population come to develop a shared vocabulary (a "language") and how this language changes within the same generation (intra-generational change) or over various generations of agents (inter-generational change).

- *Categorization.* Recently, the NG has been played in a variant called *Categorization Game* (CG) that deals with perceptual categories. Perceptual categories are modeled as cognitive units that emerge in perceptible environments (Puglisi, Baronchelli, & Loreto, 2008). CGs enable the study of how linguistic categories emerge out of an interaction of perception and communication.

Despite the success of the NG in all these areas, we believe that its focus on a special class of predicates hinders it from being an encompassing model of predication. We shed light on this class of predicates mainly by example of the *Categorization Game* (CG). This is done as follows: in its simplest case (Section 3), the NG is shown to deal with words in the role of individual constants, so that it disregards predicates. CGs are capable of accounting for monadic categories, that is, properties in logics. However, in a stepwise argument we show (1) that CGs cannot readily go beyond properties (Section 4.1); (2) that CGs model context-independent categories (Section 4.2); and (3) that CGs are bound to intersective compositionality (Section 5). The class of categories of context-independent intersective properties is not representative for the majority of categories. Since the NG focuses on this *subset of natural language categories*, it appears to be a model of a special case of linguistic categorization rather than of the rule.

3. On the Core of the Naming Game Paradigm

The key ingredients of a *Naming Game* (NG) are a set of strings $\mathcal{W} = \{w_1, \ldots, w_m\}$ – henceforth called *words* – and a set of objects $\mathcal{O} = \{o_1, \ldots, o_n\}$, that is, the *meanings* of the words. A standard assumption that underlies the NG is that objects can be any kind of entities as, for example, concrete objects, relations, or situations (Baronchelli, Felici, Loreto, Caglioti, & Steels, 2006, p. 3). The strings can be sequences drawn from a finite alphabet (Steels & McIntyre, 1999) or terminal symbols that are output by a grammar (Hashimoto, 1997). A third ingredient is the set of agents $\mathcal{A} = \{a_1, \ldots, a_o\}$ whose elements are defined as subsets of $\mathcal{W} \times \mathcal{O}$ and whose projection onto the set of words is called *agent lexicon* $L(a_i)$, $a_i \in \mathcal{A}$. In the simplest case, agents are just functions from words to objects – cf. (Steels, 1995), where "A language $L = W \times M$ is a set of one-to-one mappings between words and meanings." See Baronchelli et al. (2006) for the interaction scheme by which a single round of the NG is played.

The ingredients of NGs have been enhanced in various ways. One variation is to account for frequencies of word-object mappings, another one is to take polysemy, homonymy (Steels & McIntyre, 1999) or synonymy (Baronchelli, Loreto, & Steels, 2008) into acount.

In any event, the *semantic* core of the NG can be captured by the following *Kernel Function of the Naming Game* (KFNG):

KFNG: Kernel Function of the Naming Game Agents $a \in \mathcal{A}$ correspond to *interpretation functions* $I_a : \mathcal{W} \to \mathcal{O}$ such that $\forall w \in L(a)$: $I_a(w) \in \mathcal{O}$. That is, for any agent, each word has exactly one meaning that equals a single object of the domain of objects. Seen from a logical point this is tantamount to individual constants (Gamut, 1991a, p. 65). Thus the semantic kind of the words that agents learn in a NG is that of *individual constants*.

The notion of individual constants is far too restricted when it comes to learning *predicates* that denote n-place relations. Look, for example, at the learning of a color term like *red*. If such a predicate would be treated as a proper name, it would be impossible to express that one object has a different shade of red than another or that different objects are equally red. It would even be impossible to predicate *of* an object that it is red at all. This is obviously not the way *red* is used in a natural language. Instead, a word like *red* is required to be a *predicate*, that is, to be a kind of expression that takes an argument, i.e., to be of arity 1 – in contrast to its treatment as an individual constant, that is, a function of arity 0. This approach fails to account for the application of predicates (of whatever arity > 1) onto individuals, that is, for the description of situations or events (Chierchia & McConnell-Ginet, 2000, p. 59). See, however, the claim of

Baronchelli et al. (2006, p. 3) according to which objects in a NG can be of a wide range of ontological provenance including individuals, properties, relations, situations and events. Our analysis of *red* suggests instead that words denoting properties are of a different *semantic* kind than names of individuals and therefore have to be modeled in a different way (Frege, 1891) – likewise for relations, situations and events. One may argue that this means to misunderstand the assumption of Baronchelli et al. (2006) who treat relations as complex objects of which words are predicated as properties. However, such an approach would neglect the basic semantic difference between names and predicates.

This does not mean, however, that it would be impossible to build CGs of more levels of predication. Seemingly, what is lacking on that account is a kind of abstraction that leads to relation-valued interpretation functions $I_a(w) \subseteq \mathcal{O}^n$. that in the case of polysemous predicates of arity $n = 1$ become set-valued. Under this regime, a word $w \in \mathcal{W}$ can be treated semantically as a predicate of a certain arity that can be applied to its arguments.

The next section discusses CGs as a variant of the NG that are based on set-valued interpretation functions in order to study the formation of color categories. We show that this variant is still restricted to a subset of predicates.

4. The Semantic Scope of the Categorization Game

CGs are usually played within the domain of colors. The object domain is made up of a continuum of wavelengths – mapped onto the interval of real numbers $[0, 1)$ – that is partitioned by agents into perceptual categories. The color domain is used to show how discrete linguistic categories emerge out of an interaction of perception and communication (Puglisi et al., 2008, p. 7936, p. 7939); see also (Steels & Belpaeme, 2005; Baronchelli et al., 2006). For the rules of the CG see Puglisi et al. (2008, Supporting Material).

A CG, like any language game, "requires discrimination and interpretation as well as production and parsing." (Steels, 2005, p. 220). A CG also involves category learning, since this is the goal of the game. All in all, three semantic ingredients are given in a single round of a CG:

1. *Predication.* Agents transmit words in order to communicate about the objects presented in a CG round. They also use pointing gestures to single out objects (Puglisi et al., 2008).

2. *First Order Categorization, or Discrimination.* Agents categorize objects according to their categorization scheme currently in force: a given object is *discriminated* by means of a perceptual category

(Steels, 1996; Puglisi et al., 2008), that is, by a judgement of the sort $o \in [\![C]\!]$.

3. *Second Order Categorization, or Learning* relates to the extension of categories, that is, the composition of $[\![C]\!]$ as a set. We deal with the kinds of categories that can be learnt in a CG in Section 5.

Since perceptual categories are defined as sets of objects, it follows that word meanings are exclusively modeled as sets of objects. Thus, CGs ground in an *extensional semantics.* Furthermore, predication and first-order categorization are intertwined in a Tarskian manner (Tarski, 1935): a predication can be true or false, depending on whether the object in question is an element of the category tied to the predicate in use. The functional principle of the CG can now be summarized as follows:

KFCG: Kernel Function of the Categorization Game Agents $a \in \mathcal{A}$ are interpretation functions $I_a \colon \mathcal{W} \mapsto \wp(\mathcal{O})$ such that

- $\forall w \in L(a) : I_a(w) \subseteq \mathcal{O}$. Initially, $I_a(w) = \mathcal{O}$.[a]

The interpretation function of the CG captures predication by the following Tarski-style semantic rule:

- an object o falls into a's perceptual category c denoted by w_c iff $o \in I_a(w_c)$.

In what follows, we hint at two restrictions of this model of perceptual categories: CGs are limited to properties (Section 4.1) and to context-independent categories (Section 4.2).

4.1. *Topology-related Restrictions*

Perceptual categories are supposed to be *non-overlapping* and *contiguous* subintervals of $[0, 1]$ – see, for example, Puglisi et al. (2008). These assumptions have three implications:

1. The notion of non-overlapping categories contrasts with the notion of prototypes (Rosch, 1978). In order to circumvent this contrast, one needs to account for fuzzy categories that can overlap.

2. Categories are never made up of non-adjacent subintervals. Actually, there are perceptual categories that are constituted in a discontinuous way. In the case of colors think of dyschromatopsia, where the non-contiguous intervals of red and green are grouped into one category.

[a]This approach implements a Platonic prior knowledge of agents about the color space as it predetermines the identity of the category domain. Further, the initial condition $I(w) = \mathcal{O}$ is related to a second-order predicate *color* as in *blue is the color of the sky.*

3. Categories are limited to sets of objects, that is, to properties. Thus, n-place relations like *between*, *give* or *preceding*, that require to be sets (of n-tuples) from $\wp(\mathcal{O}^n)$, $n > 1$, cannot be captured readily.

In the next subsection we argue that the properties that are learnable by CGs belong to the class of context-independent properties.

4.2. *Gradable Properties*

Prima facie, the CG fits perfectly to the domain of gradable properties like sizes (Steels, 1996, p. 338). As a result of size-related CGs, size intervals are segmented by agents into perceptual categories as the meanings of words like, say, "small", "large" and "giant". Any object that is an element of the partition denoted by *small* is classified as being of small size, *irrespective of its other properties*. However, in natural languages things are categorized as small or big in relation to a *tertium comparationis* – cf. Aristotle's discussion of the category of *quantity* (Aristoteles, 1998). Instead of being independently given sets of objects, size categories are *subsets* of their comparison class, i.e., they are *subsective* (Chierchia & McConnell-Ginet, 2000, p. 465). This suggests that CGs model properties, which in the latter sense are context-independent. Since CGs deal with single quality dimensions (Gärdenfors, 2000), this restriction might be justified, but to the cost of limiting the semantic scope of the game to a certain class of categories. A compositional approach, however, should allow for cross-categorization. Accordingly, we finally look at a compositional variant of the CG and show that it is bound to intersective predicates.

5. Compositionality

A compositional extension of the CG has been devised by Vogt (2005). Here, learning takes place in a 4-dimensional color-shape space, the *conceptual space* **rgbs**, where the color partition is modeled as a 3-dimensional **rgb** space. Each dimension of the conceptual space is partitioned into categories according to a number of categorical features playing the role of prototypes (Vogt, 2005, p. 214). A category is modeled as a 4-dimensional vector where each slot represents a certain quality dimension. An agent categorizes an object according to its "private ontology $\mathcal{O}_a$" (Vogt, 2005, p. 214) "by taking for each [object] feature $f_{i,j}$ the categorical feature $c_i \in \mathcal{O}_a$ nearest to $f_{i,j}$, and then combining each dimension to form the category $\mathbf{c}_j = (c_1, \ldots, c_n)$." (Vogt, 2005, p. 215). That is, partitions of the object space $\mathcal{O}_a$ are derived from partitions of the underlying spaces of quality dimensions whose partitions are independent of each other. Let us denote such a feature-related partition by $S(c_i)$ where c_i, $i \in \{1, \ldots, n\}$, is a prototypical feature. Now, if an object o is of category c_i we can write $o \in S(c_i)$ by analogy to one-dimensional CGs. Further, a statement of this sort is independent of any other statement $o \in S(c_k)$ for which $k \in \{1, \ldots, n\} \setminus \{i\}$. An object o belongs to $\mathbf{c}_j$ iff $o \in S(c_1) \wedge \ldots \wedge o \in S(c_n)$ iff $o \in S(c_1) \cap \ldots \cap S(c_n)$. Thus, this compositional extension of the CG is an *intersective* one (Chierchia & McConnell-Ginet, 2000, p. 459). It cannot deal with subsective predicates like (1) size terms as, for example, in *giant midget*, (2) with non-predicational predicates (e.g., *alleged*, *former*) (Chierchia & McConnell-Ginet, 2000, p. 459), and (3) with predicates that include semantic calibration (as necessary, e.g., for dealing with combinations like *stone lion* or *toy airplane* (Kamp & Partee, 1995)). This suggests that the kind of categories learnable by the KFCG is limited.

6. Conclusion

A compound predication like x *is a* P Q has to be modeled by creating a new complex predicate PQ instead of just building the conjunction $P \wedge Q$ (Gamut, 1991b, pp. 77f). The potential to enter into the formation of a new predicate is not possible, however, if the categories denoted by P and Q are fixed in terms of sets of objects. The enhancement necessary for dealing with the relational character of categories is to incorporate a mediating level between $\mathcal{O}$ and $\mathcal{W}$ – that is, to introduce *intensionality*. The need to distinguish three semiotic levels, viz. object, concept and symbol as connected in a semiotic triad, has already been advocated by Steels (2008, p. 224). Furthermore, in order to account for symbolic representations, one has to provide some modeling means for "how the expression of different meanings can be combined to create compositional representations" (Steels, 2008, p. 232). Accordingly, Steels and colleagues (Steels & De Beule, 2006a, 2006b) implement a grammar formalism, called *Fluid Construction Grammar* (FCG), capable of *representing* compositional constructions of (presumably) all kinds.However, as Steels (2008, p. 227, p. 237) notes, using prefabricated meaning representations does not answer the question about the evolution of categorization and categories. Thus, there is a missing link between compositional representations on the one hand and the genesis of the represented categories on the other hand. Thanks to the CG, this link is given for extensional, intersective categories like color categories. However, even in the domain of perceptual categories, so runs our argument, there is a range of semantic kinds of categories that seem to be outside the scope of current simulations.

References

Aristoteles. (1998). *Kategorien, Hermeneutik.* Hamburg: Meiner. (Translated by Hans Günter Zekl)

Baronchelli, A., Felici, M., Loreto, V., Caglioti, E., & Steels, L. (2006). Sharp transition towards shared vocabularies in multi-agent systems. *Journal of Statistical Mechanics: Theory and Experiment*, *2006*(06), P06014.

Baronchelli, A., Loreto, V., & Steels, L. (2008). In-depth analysis of the naming game dynamics: the homogeneous mixing case. *International Journal of Modern Physics C*, *19*(5), 785–812.

Chierchia, G., & McConnell-Ginet, S. (2000). *Meaning and grammar – an introduction to semantics* (2 ed.). Cambridge: MIT Press.

Frege, G. (1891). *Funktion und Begriff.* Reprinted in ? (?, p. 2–22).

Gamut, L. T. F. (1991a). *Logic, language, and meaning* (Vol. 1: Introduction to Logic). Chicago: The University of Chicago Press.

Gamut, L. T. F. (1991b). *Logic, language, and meaning* (Vol. 2: Intensional Logic and Logical Grammar). Chicago: The University of Chicago Press.

Gärdenfors, P. (2000). *Conceptual spaces.* Cambridge, MA: MIT Press.

Hashimoto, T. (1997). Usage-based structuralization of relationships between words. In P. Husbands & I. Harvey (Eds.), *Proceedings of the fourth european conference on artificial life* (pp. 483–492). MIT Press.

Kamp, H., & Partee, B. (1995). Prototype theory and compositionality. *Cognition*, *57*(2), 129–191.

Puglisi, A., Baronchelli, A., & Loreto, V. (2008). Cultural route to the emergence of linguistic categories. *PNAS*, *105*(23), 7936–7940.

Rosch, E. (1978). Principles of categorization. In E. Rosch & B. B. Lloyd (Eds.), *Cognition and categorization* (p. 27-48). Hillsdale, N. J.: Erlbaum.

Steels, L. (1995). A self-organizing spatial vocabulary. *Artificial Life*, *2*, 319–332.

Steels, L. (1996). Perceptually grounded meaning creation. In *Proceedings of the second international conference on multiagent systems* (pp. 338–344). Kyoto.

Steels, L. (2005). The emergence and evolution of linguistic structure: from lexical to grammatical communication systems. *Connection Science*, *17*(3–4), 213–230.

Steels, L. (2008). The symbol grounding problem has been solved. So what's next? In M. de Vega, A. M. Glenberg, & A. C. Graesser (Eds.), *Symbols, embodiment and meaning* (pp. 223–244). Oxford, NY: Oxford University Press.

Steels, L., & Belpaeme, T. (2005). Coordinating perceptually grounded categories through language: A case study for colour. *Behavioral and Brain Sciences*, *28*(4), 469–529. (Target article with open peer commentary)

Steels, L., & De Beule, J. (2006a). A (very) brief introduction to Fluid Construction Grammar. In *Proceedings of the 3rd workshop on scalable natural language understanding* (pp. 73–80). New York City.

Steels, L., & De Beule, J. (2006b). Unify and merge in Fluid Construction Grammar. In P. Vogt, Y. Sugita, E. Tuci, & C. Nehaniv (Eds.), *Symbol grounding and beyond: Proceedings of the third international workshop on the emergence and evolution of linguistic communication* (pp. 197–223). Rome, Italy.

Steels, L., & McIntyre, A. (1999). Spatially distributed naming games. *Advances in Complex Systems*, *1*(4), 301–323.

Tarski, A. (1935). Der Wahrheitsbegriff in den formalisierten Sprachen. *Studia Philosophica*, *1*, 261–405.

Vogt, P. (2005). The emergence of compositional structures in perceptually grounded language games. *Artificial Intelligence*, *167*(1–2), 206–242. (Connecting Language to the World)

THE ORIGINS OF LINGUISTIC PREDICATE/ARGUMENT STRUCTURE

ERKKI LUUK

Anglistik III, Heinrich-Heine-University, Düsseldorf, Geb. 23.21.01.66, Universitätsstr. 1, 40225 Düsseldorf, Germany

The paper shows the necessity to distinguish between four different predicate/argument structures – the perceptual, the logical, the linguistic and the conceptual – and posits their logical and temporal (albeit not necessarily evolutionarily linked) sequence: perceptual → conceptual → linguistic → logical. The substance of the linguistic predicate/argument structure and its possible relations to each of these other structures are discussed.

1. Introduction[1]

Predicate/argument (P/A) structure is a natural way of encoding modification, operation and relation (objects been modified by their properties, variables being operated on, elements being related with oneself or each other). A less formal and general (but still a valid) statement would be that P/A structure is a natural way of encoding **events** – objects/properties caught in actions/changes. Prototypically, nouns (N) denote objects/properties and verbs (V) denote actions/changes. There is a general agreement that argument and predicate are the syntactic/propositional functions of N and V, resp. (e.g. Broschart, 1997; Croft, 2005; Ramat, 1999; Sasse, 1993).

2. Perceptual P/A structure

The logical P/A distinction is well known (and we get to explaining the linguistic P/A structure below) but according to Hurford (2003b, 2003c), a P/A distinction is also hardwired in the brain, with distinct neural pathways for the perceptual P and A processing. As the claim is about higher mammals, this perceptual P/A structure is clearly distinct from the P/A structures in logic and language (as non-human species lack language – not to speak of mathematical

[1] Abbreviations: A argument, CCLI cultural constraints on linguistic interpretation, N noun, NL natural language, NP noun phrase, P predicate, S sentence, V verb, XP noun phrase or determiner phrase (depending on the theory).

logic, which is dependendent on the linguistic P/A structure). There is also a fundamental logical difference between linguistic (e.g. CAME(man)) and the corresponding perceptual (MAN(x) & CAME(x)) P/A formulas. We will return to this below.

3. Logical and linguistic P/A structures

Hurford (2003b, 2003c) has also formulated what he calls the 'Aristotle problem': in natural language, the same kind of term can fill both the argument and the predicate slot (e.g. *a man died* and *Plato is a man*), whereas in first (and second) order logics the same terms cannot be arguments and predicates.

Of course, there is a way around this problem in these logics – namely analyzing *a man* always as a predicate: e.g. ∃x (MAN(x) & DIED(x)) and MAN(plato), resp. (cf. Gazdar, Klein, Pullum, & Sag, 1985; Montague, 2002 [1973]; Pollard & Sag, 1994). However, besides complicating the semantics of *a man died*, the analysis contradicts our basic intuition of these two sentence being (roughly) of the same complexity. Another problem is the lack of semantic distinction between *man* and *be a man* (cf. Partee, 2002). It would be more natural to use higher-order logic here, e.g. DIED(A(man)) and A(MAN(plato)). Then, man and MAN would be, resp., an argument and a predicate of different orders, and the Aristotle problem would be solved without resorting to any "unnatural" semantics. At the same time, various logic-specific consideration (e.g. incompleteness) might prevent us from using logics of higher than first order altogether.

All this shows that if we want to describe an (or perhaps even the most) exact, parsimonious and natural way of P/A parsing of NL, referring to it as first, second or higher-order (or even worse, mathematical) logic is insufficient. For describing the P/A system of natural language, these logical P/A systems may be both too limited in some aspect and redundant in some other. For example, by barring predicates and arguments of different orders, first and second order logics may be too restrictive, while by allowing quantifiers (∃) and an explicit use of variables (x), all logics may be redundant for this particular task[2]. The problem of natural P/A parsing of NL is usually not even recognized, much less solved, which is the principal reason why one should, at this point at least, keep the linguistic and logical P/A systems strictly apart.

---

[2] The idea that connectives, quantifiers and variables might not belong to the semantic representation of NL is not new (cf. Lakoff & Ross, 1976; Purdy, 1991; Seuren, 2010).

4. Linguistic P/A structure: a universal

In Luuk (2009a, 2009b), I have tried to describe linguistic P/A system in some detail. As predicted by the consensus among linguists on P and A being the syntactic functions of V and N, resp. (see section 1), it was possible to establish N-A and V-P correspondences – nouns are linguistic arguments and verbs are linguistic predicates, while the set of linguistic arguments and predicates is not restricted to nouns and verbs. Technically, my solution to the Aristotle problem is the second of those mentioned above: a proper subset of higher-order logic, with multiple levels of linguistic arguments and predicates but without connectives and quantifiers. The exact structure of the logic of NL was irrelevant – what mattered was an optimal (the most exact, parsimonious and universal) description of the P/A system of NL. The Ps and As were defined in terms of NL entities (e.g. word classes and constructions), while their relations were described as various constructions and rules. As the system had to be universal, it was illustrated with numerous examples from different languages.

Although one cannot provide an evidence that all natural languages have Ps and As, this can be inferred from the inconceivability of an alternative (and indirectly also from the fact that all theories that explain both syntax and sentential semantics subsume P/A structure at some level or another). Modern language syntax is based on the principle that linguistic predicates take arguments that are differentiated by analytic (adpositions, word order) and/or synthetic (morphological) case markers. Thus, all languages that have adpositions or morphological case have linguistic P/A structure by definition. I am not aware of a modern language that would lack both. The universality of linguistic P/A structure also explains the universality of the sentence / noun phrase (S/NP) or, in a reformulated version, the S/XP distinction (the claims made by Carstairs-McCarthy (1999) and Hurford (2007), resp.). S is commonly defined through grammatical predicate (linguistic predicate). Thus, there can be no S before there is linguistic predicate, and there can be no linguistic predicate before there is linguistic P/A distinction (as predicate applies to an argument which is provided beforehand). Thus, the universality of S/XP reduces to the universality of linguistic P/A.

5. The evolution of linguistic P/A structure

Unless the whole complexity of natural language was there from the beginning, complex linguistic structures must have evolved from simpler ones. The same applies to linguistic P/A system. Several authors have suggested that nouns and verbs (i.e. primary linguistic arguments and predicates – Luuk, 2009a, 2009b) emerge at the earliest stages of language evolution (Heine & Kuteva, 2002, 2007; Hurford, 2003a; Newmeyer, 2003). Thus we have reasons to believe that linguistic P/A structure is both functionally and evolutionarily among the most fundamental ones in language.

5.1. *Are linguistic P/A structure and grammar interdependent?*

The fact that all human languages have linguistic P/A structure and grammar might point to an equivalence relation between the two. Being one of the most fundamental syntactic structures, linguistic P/A system implies syntax (Luuk, 2009a, 2009b). Oddly, however, it is possible to imagine syntax (and grammar) without linguistic P/A structure. It is simply not known whether the first grammar rule stipulated linguistic P/A structure. Thus the interdependence between NL grammar and linguistic P/A structure remains merely a possibility.

Word order is the simplest grammatical device (Heine & Kuteva, 2002; Johansson, 2006). The first word order constraint **automatically** results in two grammatically distinct categories for words[3]. Theoretically, a word order rule would suffice for linguistic P/A distinction. However, we do not know whether the first grammatical categories were word types (like *man go*) or just semantic roles (like *man forest* interpreted as 'a man go to the forest'). Owing to a greater transparency of interpretation and a greater potential for combinations, distinct word types would be the more plausible alternative. But distinct semantic roles would be a syntactically simpler, i.e. the more parsimonious alternative. Thus, linguistic A and P would be perhaps the most obvious but not the only candidates for the first grammatical categories. Other authors have proposed that the first grammatical distinction was N/V (Heine & Kuteva, 2002; Hurford, 2003a; Newmeyer, 2003), i.e. linguistic P/A.

5.2. *Conceptual P/A structure (the event structure)*

Obviously, linguistic P/A structure must reflect on the conceptual level, as it requires the ability to conceptualize the corresponding functions. As linguistic P/A structure is functionally motivated by, e.g., our ability to talk about events (i.e. objects/properties caught in actions/changes), it is plausible that the underlying ability to conceptualize events in the above-defined sense (which relies on a conceptual P/A structure) predates linguistic P/A structure, i.e. P/A

[3] Unless the constraint is phonological (e.g. that the word beginning with a vowel comes first) or lexical (e.g. that the word standing for the concept 'tree' comes first). Both of these possibilites seem remote at best.

marking in language. This conjecture is supported by the fact that linguistic P/A structure is useless without the ability to conceptualize the functions of linguistic predicate and argument but the ability to conceptualize events is useful even in the absence of language (e.g. in behavioral planning, which increases the individual's fitness). A capacity to conceptualize events could be both possible and adaptive to a non-linguistic species. Quite obviously, this raises the question whether there are extant non-human species possessing it. Some recent findings on, e.g., non-human mental time travel (Correia, Dickinson, & Clayton, 2007; Osvath, 2009; but see Suddendorf & Corballis, 2010), seem to suggest that there might be.

5.3. *Protolanguage subsumes conceptual P/A structure*

Protolanguage lacks syntax by definition (Bickerton, 1990; Jackendoff & Pinker, 2005). Yet, as the event structure (something happens, somebody does something etc.) is a natural and ubiquitious correlate of human conceptualization, events were most likely expressed in protolanguage as well. The alternative – the assumption that the event structure was brought about by language – is implausible for the following reasons: 1. What was there to communicate in protolanguage if not real or imaginary events from past, present or future? 2. If, on the other hand, events were conveyed and conceptualized in protolanguage not by the event structure, it is difficult to imagine a way for this. Worse, there would be no continuity between protolanguage and language (at least not in fundamental meaning-conveying structures). 3. As language depends on the event structure (but not vice versa), the event structure either antedated language or the two arose simultaneously. As compared to the normal course of evolution (with the functionally necessary core components evolving before their dependents – Budd, 2006), the latter possibility would be next to miraculous.

How were events expressed in protolanguage? As protolanguage is either holophrastic or arbitrarily concatenated language, and the holophrastic hypothesis (Wray, 1998) seems to be ruled out (Bickerton, 2003; Johansson, 2008; Tallerman, 2007), the obvious way would be single-word utterances and free concatenation (e.g. *field wolf*, *wolf field* etc.). How was interpretation constrained? Whereas language=grammar+lexicon, for protolanguage the respective formula is protolanguage=CCLI+lexicon. Cultural constraints on linguistic interpretation (CCLI) are the pragmatic, logical and ontological constraints that are not imposed on linguistic expression grammatically or lexically but are necessary to narrow down its interpretation. CCLI maintain an expectancy horizon as to what counts as an 'event' in a given culture – a complex of features such as salience, possibility, feasibility, familiarity, unexpectedness, emotionality (Dessalles, 2008) etc., which help to guide the interpretation, while together providing a culturally unique relevance criterion.

6. Conclusion

It might be worthwhile to summarize some claims made in this paper. 1. Nouns are linguistic arguments and verbs are linguistic predicates but the set of linguistic arguments and predicates is not restricted to nouns and verbs. 2. Linguistic P/A structure is both functionally and evolutionarily one of the most fundamental types in language. 3. Linguistic P/A structure is universal in modern languages. 4. The universality of S/XP can be reduced to the universality of linguistic P/A. 5. Linguistic P/A distinction is a plausible but not the only candidate for the first grammar rule.

If Hurford's (2003b, 2003c) intuitition and analysis in positing the perceptual P/A were correct, we have four different P/A structures in the following logical and temporal sequence: perceptual → conceptual → linguistic → logical. Observe that this does neither entail nor preclude that all these structures are evolutionarily linked. More specifically, the existence of an (intuititively appealing) evolutionary link between perceptual and conceptual P/A structures is unclear. Conceptual P/A structure is isomorphic to the linguistic one (see section 5.2), which means that it cannot be isomorphous with the perceptual P/A structure (as linguistic and perceptual P/A structures are non-isomorphic – see section 2). Of course, the non-isomorphism alone is insufficient to rule out the possibility of mapping perceptual P/A structure onto conceptual structure in a way that could (eventually) yield conceptual P/A structure. In whatever way conceptual P/A structure emerged, it was projected onto language as linguistic P/A structure at an early stage of language evolution.

Acknowledgements

This work was supported by the target-financed theme No. 0180078s08, the European Regional Development Fund through the Estonian Center of Excellence in Computer Science, EXCS, and the Alexander von Humboldt Foundation.

References

Bickerton, D. (1990). *Language and Species.* Chicago: University of Chicago Press.

Bickerton, D. (2003). Symbol and structure: a comprehensive framework for language evolution. In M. H. Christiansen, & S. Kirby (Eds.), *Language Evolution: The States of the Art* (pp. 77-93). Oxford: Oxford University Press.

Broschart, J. (1997). Why Tongan does it differently: categorial distinctions in a language without nouns and verbs. *Linguistic Typology*, *1*(2), 123-166.

Budd, G. E. (2006). On the origin and evolution of major morphological characters. *Biological Reviews of the Cambridge Philosophical Society*, *81*(4), 609-628.

Carstairs-McCarthy, A. (1999). *The Origins of Complex Language: An Inquiry into the Evolutionary Beginnings of Sentences, Syllables, and Truth*. Oxford: Oxford University Press.

Correia, S. P., Dickinson, A., & Clayton, N. S. (2007). Western scrub-jays anticipate future needs independently of their current motivational state. *Current Biology*, *17*(10), 856-861.

Croft, W. (2005). Word classes, parts of speech, and syntactic argumentation. *Linguistic Typology*, *40*(3), 431-441.

Dessalles, J.-L. (2008). From metonymy to syntax in the communication of events. *Interaction Studies*, *9*(1), 51-65.

Gazdar, G., Klein, E., Pullum, G. K., & Sag, I. (1985). *Generalized phrase structure grammar*. Oxford, UK: B. Blackwell.

Heine, B., & Kuteva, T. (2002). On the evolution of grammatical forms. In A. Wray (Ed.), *The Transition to Language* (pp. 376-397). Oxford: Oxford University Press.

Heine, B., & Kuteva, T. (2007). *The genesis of grammar: a reconstruction*. New York: Oxford University Press.

Hurford, J. R. (2003a). The language mosaic and its evolution. In M. H. Christiansen, & S. Kirby (Eds.), *Language Evolution: The States of the Art* (pp. 38-57). Oxford: Oxford University Press.

Hurford, J. R. (2003b). The neural basis of predicate-argument structure. *Behavioral and Brain Sciences*, *26*(3), 261-283; Discussion 283-316.

Hurford, J. R. (2003c). Ventral/dorsal, predicate/argument: the transformation from perception to meaning. *Behavioral and Brain Sciences*, *26*(3), 301-311.

Hurford, J. R. (2007). The origin of noun phrases: reference, truth, and communication. *Lingua*, *117*(3), 527-542.

Jackendoff, R., & Pinker, S. (2005). The nature of the language faculty and its implications for evolution of language (Reply to Fitch, Hauser, and Chomsky). *Cognition*, *97*(2), 211-225.

Johansson, S. (2006). Working backwards from modern language to proto-grammar. In A. Cangelosi, A. D. M. Smith, & K. Smith (Eds.), *The Evolution of Language: Proceedings of the 6th International Conference on the Evolution of Language (EVOLANG6)* (pp. 160-167). Singapore: World Scientific.

Johansson, S. (2008). Seeking compositionality in holistic proto-language without substructure: Do counter-examples overwhelm the fractionation process? In A. D. M. Smith, K. Smith, & R. Ferrer-i-Cancho (Eds.), *The Evolution of Language: Proceedings of the 7th International Conference (EVOLANG7)* (pp. 171-178). Singapore: World Scientific.

Lakoff, G., & Ross, J. R. (1976). Is deep structure necessary? In J. D. McCawley (Ed.), *Syntax and Semantics: Notes from the Linguistic Underground* (Vol. 7, pp. 159-164). New York etc.: Academic Press.

Luuk, E. (2009a). The noun/verb and predicate/argument structures. *Lingua*, *119*(11), 1707-1727.

Luuk, E. (2009b). *The noun/verb and predicate/argument structures*. Dissertationes Linguisticae Universitatis Tartuensis (Vol. 12). Tartu: Tartu University Press.

Montague, R. (2002 [1973]). The proper treatment of quantification in ordinary English. In P. Portner, & B. H. Partee (Eds.), *Formal Semantics: The Essential Readings* (pp. 17-34). Oxford: Blackwell.

Newmeyer, F. J. (2003). What can the field of linguistics tell us about the evolution of language? In M. H. Christiansen, & S. Kirby (Eds.), *Language Evolution: The States of the Art* (pp. 58-76). Oxford: Oxford University Press.

Osvath, M. (2009). Spontaneous planning for future stone throwing by a male chimpanzee. *Current Biology*, *19*(5), R190-R191.

Partee, B. H. (2002). Noun phrase interpretation and type-shifting principles. In P. Portner, & B. H. Partee (Eds.), *Formal Semantics: The Essential Readings*. Chicago: Blackwell Publishing.

Pollard, C., & Sag, I. (1994). *Head-Driven Phrase Structure Grammar*. Stanford: Center for the Study of Language and Information.

Purdy, W. C. (1991). A logic for natural language. *Notre Dame Journal of Formal Logic*, *32*, 409-425.

Ramat, P. (1999). Linguistic categories and linguists'categorizations. *Linguistics*, *37*(1), 157–180.

Sasse, H.-J. (1993). Syntactic categories and subcategories. In J. Jacobs, A. von Stechow, W. Sternefeld, & T. Vennemann (Eds.), *Syntax: an international handbook* (pp. 646–686). Berlin: Mouton de Gruyter.

Seuren, P. A. M. (2010). *The Logic of Language*. Oxford: Oxford University Press.

Suddendorf, T., & Corballis, M. C. (2010). Behavioural evidence for mental time travel in nonhuman animals. *Behavioural Brain Research*, *215*, 292-298.

Tallerman, M. (2007). Did our ancestors speak a holistic protolanguage? *Lingua*, *117*, 579-604.

Wray, A. (1998). Protolanguage as a holistic system for social interaction. *Language and Communication*, *18*(1), 47-67.

THE VOICE OF THINGS: THE REVOLUTION OF HUMAN LANGUAGE AND ITS ORIGIN FROM SOUND IMITATION

GIUSEPPE MAIORANO

Euromedia Italia srl, via Lupatelli 56, 00165, Rome, Italia

The true primeval origin of human language is regarded as a key-issue both in historical linguistics and in overall scientific research. An increasing interest is registered in recent times about this topic, and different, even conflicting proposals are presently on the ground. Which are the main difficulties about achieving a convincing ultimate solution? Aren't we late about the understanding of how, why and when human speech emerged, especially if we consider that more than 150 years have passed since the 'Darwinian Revolution' took place? But probably the solution is very near and, actually, it has been already proposed with parallel, although different, formulas which can be today fruitfully revised and emended. Among the classic 'glossogenetic' theories, the less welcomed 'onomatopoeic' and 'sound-symbolic' proposals are mainly considered here. Nevertheless, these theories, for which sounds for themselves give rise by imitation to analogous meaningful oral sounds, are taken here as the only acceptable proposals for the origin of human oral language - although first anticipated and then paralleled by gestural communicative behaviour and acts. Examples of such proposals are the works by F.W. Farrar, Field-Marshal Montgomery's grandfather: 'Origins of Language' and 'Chapters on Language', which go back to 1860 and 1865 respectively.

However, it seems necessary to simplify the whole question and reconsider it from the beginning. In fact, major misunderstandings and biases still exist which need to be cleared, namely:

- misuse of terms related to communication, language, speech, natural languages, and similarly to iconicity, onomatopoeia, sound-symbolism, whose employment indeed seems sometimes abused;

- shift of meaning and overlapping between the notions of 'origin' and 'evolution' of human language, possibly with misleading consequences for the whole argumentation process and its results;

- lack of proper 'time and space' location when dealing with the origin of human language in prehistoric ages and consequent loss of references to the coeval climatic conditions, basic human needs, health risks, group dimensions, hunting rules, technology level;

- asymmetrical evaluation of experimental results from apes, birds and other animals tests in relationship with their reduced communication faculties and speech capabilities, compared with the current human highly developed linguistic infrastructures, which are often overestimated when dealing with language origin;

- highly reduced and misunderstood role of the imitative/iconic sources in the foundation of the primitive human language and formation of the first words in prehistoric ages, when the situation was very far from the advanced mature state of natural languages, when sound imitation and human auditory/vocal channel began to replace gradually the pre-existing visual/gestural channel as the main human communication tool;

- agreed unavailability of the primitive phonemes and morphemes, due to the absence of material evidences and a huge time gap; truly, first human speech and later natural languages lost large part of their original features and underwent progressive sound, meaning and structure changes, meanwhile the natural sounds/noises have remained almost unchanged in time.

In the second part, the main research purposes are discussed:

- origin of human language from natural and man-made sound imitation, based on sound-meaning correlations, paralleled by a 'mapping' of the sensorial inputs from the environment and by the existence of a large archive of sounds, built-up in the human brain;

- comparison between language and writing, as to their origin and evolution, from the imitative beginnings to later less iconic forms (ideograms, cuneiform writing etc.) up to abstract alphabetic symbols, which still retain residual iconic traces;

- analysis of natural sounds, man-made noises, animal cries, and processing of linguistic data from different subjects; examples of archaic sound-meaning pairings like Lt. aqua, water, whose 'water-sound' root /kw/ acts as the first 'equality' or 'equivalence' mark.

As to the misuse of terms, this attitude can be referred, for instance, to 'language' in its wide sense of 'communication', and viceversa, but mainly to 'language', meaning both 'broad communication' and just only 'vocal communication' at the same time; that is, often in the beginning of a text dealing with the emergence of human language, this very term 'language' may indicate essentially human capacity of verbal communication, but in the following parts, the same term tends to stand for primates or animals intentional communicating acts among conspecifics.

Similarly, some confusion can be observed between 'onomatopoeia' and 'sound-synbolism', or other similar but not synonymous terms. In this instance, onomatopoeia is, ethimologically, the 'word-making' or creation of words from the imitation of environmental, animal and man-made sounds and noises, obviously referred to their respective sources, in a way that sounds and noises are transformed – I'd say 'translated' - into verbal linguistic items. Definitely, onomatopeia cannot replace or be replaced by the concept of sound-symbolism, meaning the latter a linguistic phenomenon or tendency by which single sounds – both vowels, consonants and their combinations - convey meanings or suggest sensorial experiences to the listeners or readers, such as smoothness, brightness, smallness. Onomatopeia can be taken as an extreme instance of sound-symbolism, but in order to admit sound-symbolism as a linguistic phenomenon, it is necessary that a human oral language be highly developed and be able to carry sensorial 'synaesthetic' charges.

Misleading effects are also provoked by similar slips from the search of the true language origins to that of the progressive evolution of an existing proto-language, to the analysis of the basic features, main advantages, language acquisition, speech disorders. This attitude can be motivated by the fact that, after some general statements, the 'glossogenetic' topic shows so complex to cope with, that the main intention is almost abandoned.

The questions of human language origin and its further evolution cannot be absorbed or compressed into each other. One of the main biases is the fact that most features of the imagined proto-language are searched within our historical spoken languages, and viceversa: an ingenuous belief we ought to avoid.

Another rather urgent question is the widespread tendency to space and time indefiniteness as to geography, environment, climate, life conditions before 50.000 BC, before the crucial maturity phase, when oral language began to show its efficacy by displaying such a power as to alter the biological and ecological balance on earth within few thousand years. Beyond the clear traces of abstract thinking and applied arts, the strongest evidence is the end of a rival species, Homo Neandertalensis, which, although well adapted to climatic conditions of the last ice age, could not withstand the expansion of modern Homo Sapiens, equipped with the most powerful endowment: oral language. Any possible evidence of Neandertals linguistic abilities or abstract thinking didn't have enough time to reach useful results.

Stone technology, food and water supply, hunting techniques, environmental risks, personal security, are among the main factors which have constrained the existence of modern Homo Sapiens before 50.000 BC, but especially hunting practices, group organization and camp location have been always critical elements in everyday life. Possibly, animal cries imitation has been a constant training which may have contributed both to improve sound imitation capabilities and to refine body parts in the speech anatomy of modern Homo Sapiens.

Inappropriate time and space location of linguistic phenomena can be highly misleading. Such coordinates could also be similarly lost when comparing communication abilities in animals, like apes and birds, with the highly developed human vocal and mental capabilities, which have evolved during thousands of years, matched the 'writing' revolutionary phase and reached the new complex and fast ICT current standards. Results from tests, obtained with animal species more readily apt to human language learning, are sometimes evaluated with too hard criticism in relationship with the less developed communication infrastructures – both physical and mental – of all tested animals, which are thus subject to huge evolutionary steps within relatively short times. Actually, these linguistically trained beings show unexpected linguistic capacity and potential, even if they could not develp physical, mental and cultural features, like modern humans.

But a widespread mistake is assigning a minimal or even null 'glossogenetic' role to 'imitative', 'expressive', 'nursery' and other similar forms – almost unanimously traced in most existing languages and largely accepted as a structural feature of human language. Also here, the usual comparison between the law percentage of such forms in modern languages and the unknown situation in the primitive vocabulary of human proto-language, is arbitrary and misleading. On the contrary, if we consider carefully some old or new linguistic 'roots' and 'global etymologies', they show a prevailing structural principle of the most ancient linguistic formations, based upon the imitative reproduction of human, animal and natural noises. One of these ancestral forms is related to the 'water-sound' and will be better discussed ahead. Clearly, the original function of the imitative principle, as one can see in the primitive 'embryonic phase', is very powerful and rather crucial when compared with later or currently weak – although still productive – linguistic role. Paradoxically, in the ongoing debate about the 'global etymologies' and their hypothetical worldwide validity in establishing the existence of a unique human proto-language, such forms are considered 'by definition' useless as indicators of linguistic genetic kinship. Why do we need to leave them out? Aren't actually these largely spread expressive and imitative formations what we are just looking for? What is particularly interesting in the said imitative glottogenetic theory, is the fact that most archetypal oral units should derive from coeval environmental, animal and man-made sounds, which basically do not differ from current natural sounds and from noises produced by traditional human working activities. As a consequence, such noises could be possibly reproduced, recorded and analyzed thanks to modern appropriate instruments and to suitable 'experimental archaeology' research projects. Therefore, the commonly accepted idea of the unavailability of evidences from the original speech and its archaic phonemes and morphemes, could be partially overcome and, despite the huge time gap, a series of features of the human proto-language be reconstructed.

The sound-based language origin theories – either imitative, iconic, onomatopoeic, sund-symbolic – are ancient and well known and do not need further explanation here, the aim of the present work being basically an attempt to free the theory from common biases.

Sound imitation – probably enhanced by paleolithic hunting practices – is based on easily available sound-meaning correspondences, chosen from a large archive of sounds and noises built up in the human brain with synaesthetic links to other specialized areas and communication channels. It is a simple straight idea which doesn't require too many explanatory steps and adaptations from one communication channel to the other, and the shift is minimal: the shortest in terms of 'transition' model. Obviously, the 'visual' and 'gestural' channel and practices have preceded and then paralleled the oral channel, and then became secondary and supplementary but still helpful for communication purposes, especially for deaf and dumb people.

The emergence of verbal human language from sound imitation can thus be explained with a long progressive biological pre-adaptation and further evolution within a hypothetical series of phases, the last one being the mature oral communication strategy whichc employed clearly perceivable linguistic units, supported by the first basic syntactic rules and devices.

Such a long process, implying a slow biological evolution and refinement in Homo Sapiens speech organs – which, anyway, all had originally different functions – is not far from the so called 'exaptation', and somehow it resembles later human technical achievements, like the 'wheel' used for transportation purposes: one of the most important mechanical inventions of all times, dating back to the half of the 4th millennium BC. But, indeed, its earliest known use, depicted on clay tablets, has been as a potter's wheel, employed in horizontal position, some hundreds years earlier. Later on, it acquired the upright position and changed its funtion, although the potter's wheel rimained still in use.

The glottogenetic topic has been dealt with by a number of authors since ancient times, but here we like to quote a particular 19th century scholar, contemporary with Charles Darwin: Rev. Frederic William Farrar, Field-Marshal Montgomery's grandfather. In his work 'Chapters on Language' (Farrar 1865) he states:

"...no connection is so easy and obvious, so self-suggesting and so absolutely satisfactory, as the acceptation of a sound to represent a sound" (p.23), "...if we examine the vocabulary of almost any savage nation for this purpose, what are. we certain to discover? That almost every name for an animal is a striking and obvious onomatopeia" (p.24).

The analogy between language and writing has been already proposed by several authors, but it is worth to underline here that the relatively recent achievement of writing can be traced back to the Upper-Paleolithic visual representations, obtained with different types of techniques on various kinds of surfaces, where such drawings and paintings shaw already communicative and maybe true linguistic intentions. They could be assumed as the first evidences of local 'epic cycles' or even small 'encyclopaedias' produced in distant world areas after the emergence of oral language. The 'abstraction' process, spanning from iconic pictorial beginnings to later more conventional codified signs (ideograms, logograms, hieroglyphs, cuneiform writing) and ahead, to syllabic and alphabetic systems, is very similar and show a trajectory from natural to abstract and, only apparently, artificial/conventional items, both in language and writing. But just like many current words, apparently non-iconic, some alphabetic signs still keep a part of their imitative iconic beginnings, like the very first letter of the alphabet 'A', the Greek 'Alpha' and Phoenician 'Aleph': both the visual – a reversed codified image of an ox-head - and even the acoustic features - imitative 'lap-sound' - are still perceptible.

The primitive visual channel of the old gestural communication system and the later auditory-vocal channel of the human language matched into a new refined tool, 'writing', once again related to the traditional powerful 'optical' endowment.

The main research program is based on recording, analyzing and comparing basic natural sounds from environment and atmospheric phenomena, animal cries, man-made noises – including rough materials transformation activities, body reactions to extreme temperatures, strong emotions, interjections. It entails collecting and processing linguistic data from subjects, differing in sex, age, mother-tongue, as in the research work on linguistic categorization of sounds by C. Lehmann (Lehmann 2003) and M. Magnus's unpublished 'Dictionary of English Sound'.

Tests with young kids gave interesting results, when dealing with rough materials, such as wood and stone. They show sensibility to the sounding of different types/sizes of timber, to tones, timbres and notes which can be compared with sound-meaning pairings in the range of /t/ and /d/ dental plosives with following vowels. As to English language /ta/, /te/, /ti/, /to/, /ty/ are easily related to a long series of iconic - or semi-iconic, i.e. compound - terms indicating basically wood hand tools or contact actions: tact, take, tack, technique, test, tick, tip, timber, timbre, touch, token, top, tool, type, and similar terms with prefixed 'IE mobile /s/'. The evolutionary trend is towards meanings of wooden fences, boundaries, limits: Etr. tular, Lt. Tiberis or Thybris, O.E. Thule, etc. and from these terms also: Lt. Hiberia, Lt. Hibernia, Gk. Hybris, or 'arrogance' - meaning accordingly Lt. superbia, that is 'overstepping' or 'passing the limits' – and finally the adverb/ preposition 'over', Gk. hyper, Lt. super, probably from PIE *uper.

An important ancestral sound-meaning pairing has been detected in terms related to Lt. aqua, water, one of Ruhlen's most widespread global etymologies (cf. Ruhlen's Global Etymologies, Bengtson & Ruhlen 1994) tied to the concepts of 'aquatic','liquid', 'fluid', 'cooking', whose 'water-sound' root /kw/ has been proposed as the first worldwide 'equality' or 'equivalence' mark, acquiring later a variety of grammatical functions, such as WH- interrogative and relative pronouns, conjuntions, etc. due to the apparent physical property of water: a constantly flat even horizontal surface.

References

Bengtson, J. D. & Ruhlen, M. (1994). Global Etymologies. In M. Ruhlen, *On the Origin of Languages: Studies in Linguistic Taxonomy* (pp. 277-366). Stanford: Stanford University Press

Farrar, F.W. (1865). *Chapters on Language,* London: Longmans, Green & Co.

Lehmann, C. (2003). *On the linguistic categorization of sounds.* Erfurt: University of Erfurt

EMPIRICAL APPROACHES TO RECURSION

MAURICIO MARTINS [1,2]
W. TECUMSEH FITCH [1]

[1]*Department of Cognitive Biology, University of Vienna, Althanstrasse 14, Wien, 1090, Austria*

[2]*Language Research Laboratory, Lisbon Faculty of Medicine, Av. Professor Egas Moniz, Lisboa, 1649-028, Portugal*

Although recursion has been hypothesized to be a necessary capacity for the evolution of language, the multiplicity of definitions being used has undermined the broader interpretation of empirical results. One of the major problems that stems from this multiplicity is the difficulty in drawing boundaries between recursion, hierarchical embedding and iteration. Here we propose a framework where recursion is defined as "the ability to represent different hierarchical levels with the same set of rules". This definition enables the prediction of specific behavioral traits such as the ability to generate new levels of embedding beyond those specified *a priori* (whether in the algorithm or in the input). Under this framework, we present new methods to assess the ability to represent embedded iteration and recursion in the visuo-spatial domain. Our results suggest that, in comparison with iteration, recursion is more strongly associated with verbal working memory and less associated with general visual resources (such as matrix reasoning and spatial working memory). Implications regarding language evolution are discussed.

1. Introduction

Recursion is one of the most controversially discussed terms in the cognitive sciences. Although it has been hypothesized as a human-unique trait and a as a necessary capacity for the evolution of language (Hauser et al., 2002), the multiplicity of definitions being used (Chomsky, 2010, Odifreddi, 1999, Hofstadter, 2008) has undermined the broader interpretation of empirical results. One of the major problems that stems from this multiplicity is the difficulty in drawing boundaries between recursion and similar processes such as hierarchical embedding and iteration (Hulst, 2010).

Although there has been a proliferation of literature arguing for and against the claim of recursion as uniquely human (Fitch et al., 2005, Pinker and Jackendoff, 2005), the debate remains unresolved. Some empirical paradigms have been considered relevant to address the topic (Fitch and Hauser, 2004, Abe and Watanabe, 2011) but since they fail to capture the distinction between recursion and hierarchical embedding, over-interpreting the results may be misleading (Bloomfield et al., 2011).

Given that brain computations are opaque to observers (until behavioral correlates have been found), definitions focused on algorithmic properties (such as "a recursive function is one that calls itself") may not be entirely relevant for empirical research. On the other hand, isolated analyses of signals (such as vocalizations, social interactions etc.) may be misleading since not all structures that can modeled using recursion are produced by recursive processes, neither are these structural properties necessarily perceived by observers.

To overcome these difficulties, we propose that only a definition focused on representational abilities such as "the ability to represent self-similarity across hierarchical levels" enables the prediction of recursion-specific behavioral traits: if a subject is able to represent different hierarchical levels with the same set of rules, then he may be able to generalize and generate new levels of embedding beyond those specified *a priori* (whether in the algorithm or in the input).

2. A new framework

The first challenge of investigating recursion is to build a framework that clearly distinguishes iteration from embedded iteration and recursion. Iterative processes involve the repetition of an operation a given number of times. These processes may or may not generate hierarchical structures and may or not create dependency relationships between different elements.

Hierarchical structures involve the embedding of constituents inside other constituents (i.e. the generation of dependency relationships between them). If the embedding involves constituents of the same category it is called recursive embedding (in the strict sense), otherwise it's called non-recursive. Iteration, hierarchical embedding and recursion are not mutually exclusive. Nevertheless it is possible to segregate the cognitive abilities that are necessary to represent the kind of information that they encode (Fig.1).

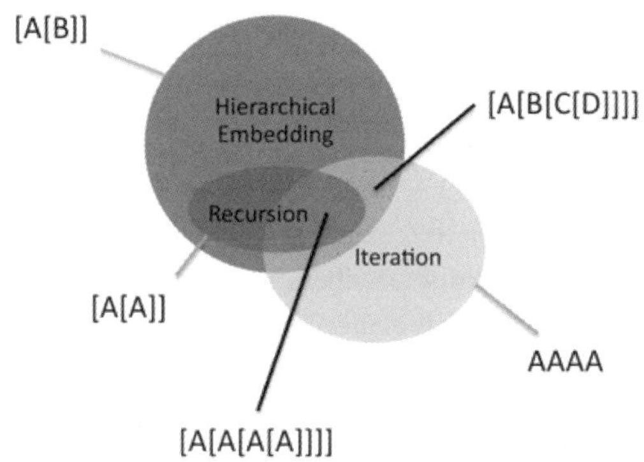

Figure 1. Examples of structures produced by iteration, hierarchical embedding and recursion and by the combination of these processes.

Consider the following process:

(1) Add the element ALPHABET(n) to the structure x(n) until n=3. Each cycle add 1 to n.

x(0) = A → x(1) = AB → x(2) = ABC → x(3) = ABCD

In these kind of iterative processes, each step is a separate act that can exist independently from the others (Kinsella, 2010). Such processes can create infinite sequences by unlimited concatenation (Lieberman, 2010) but cannot encode dependency relationships nor create new hierarchical levels (Pinker and Jackendoff, 2005). The encoding of dependencies requires the representation of rules that allow embedding, i.e. the representation that some constituents are contained within other constituents, structurally of functionally.

Consider the next example,

(2) Implement one of the following rules {Embed B on A; Embed C on B. Embed D on C}. Repeat the cycle 3 times:

x(0) = [A] → x(1) = [A[B]] → x(2) = [A[B[C]]] → x(3) = [A[B[C[D]]]]

For a given observer, the shape of the output in both examples, *(1)* and *(2)*, could be similar: *'ABCD'*. However, if the observer is able to represent rules of embedding, he has the possibility to interpret the positional attributes of the string *'ABCD'* as containing information about dependency relationships (e.g. "Right elements will be dependent over left elements"). This perceptual choice requires access to semantic information and will be influenced by biases that can be innate, cultural or contextual.

Another interesting issue relates to the limits of hierarchical processing with non-recursive embedding rules. For example, in the process *(2)* each hierarchical level is represented individually. In these circumstances, we can embed an infinite number of new constituents within the same hierarchical level (Lieberman, 2010), but we cannot create new hierarchical levels unless they are specified *a priori* (either as explicit rules in the algorithm, 'the grammar', or acquired *via* the input). Recursion overcomes this limitation. For example:

(3) Embed a member of the ALPHABET set in another member of the ALPHABET set

x(0) = [A] → x(1) = [A[B]] → x(2) = [A[B[C]]] → x(3) = [A[B[C[D]]]]

If a rule like *(3)* is used then all elements of ALPHABET (ALPHA) can be represented as having the same properties. Hence, the structure [A[B[C[D]]]] can be perceived as equivalent to [ALPHA[ALPHA[ALPHA[ALPHA]]]]. Within this framework, new hierarchical levels can be represented and generated without new rules being specified, as in the structure [A[B[C[D[E]]]]].

Using recursive rules to represent hierarchical structures may be advantageous in terms of flexibility. Although non-recursive rules may suffice to represent simple hierarchies, this method can become impractical for large and highly complex hierarchies (Koike and Yoshihara, 1993).

In spite of these processing advantages of recursion, it is not clear to what extent they are relevant empirically, given that it may be difficult to distinguish between an algorithm with a large set of rules and one that uses recursion (Verhagen, 2010). For this reason, in our opinion, the key "functionalist-cognitive accomplishment", as Harder (2010) puts it, "is the ability to take one incremental step beyond the given". This means that the key empirical test for recursion is the ability to represent dependency relationships that were not previously defined, or to represent information within hierarchical levels not previously 'available'. What this ability presupposes is the knowledge (or expectation) that all nodes within a hierarchy can behave similarly and can display the same properties relatively to the way they interact with the nodes 'above' and 'below'. This allows, for example, that we embed a noun phrase inside a noun phrase already embedded in a noun phrase ([$NP_{(n-1)}$[NP[$NP_{(n+1)}$]]]).

In summary, different cognitive processes may be identified by specific behavior signatures: a) Iteration can be detected by the ability to represent repetition of constituents; b) Hierarchical embedding by the ability to represent dependency relationships between constituents; c) Recursive embedding by the ability to represent new hierarchical levels beyond the given.

3. A new method

Under this framework, we developed a task to assess the ability to represent visuo-spatial hierarchies as recursive structures; and to apply these representations in the production of new levels of embedding. This method, called Visual Recursion Task (VRT), is based on the properties of geometrical self-similar fractals, which can be generated by applying recursive embedding rules a given number of iterations.

In a typical VRT stimulus, subjects are exposed to the first three iterations of a fractal structure generation. Then, they are asked to choose, from two possible alternatives, which corresponds to the 'correct' answer (fig.2; correct in this sense means the 4th iteration of the generating process).

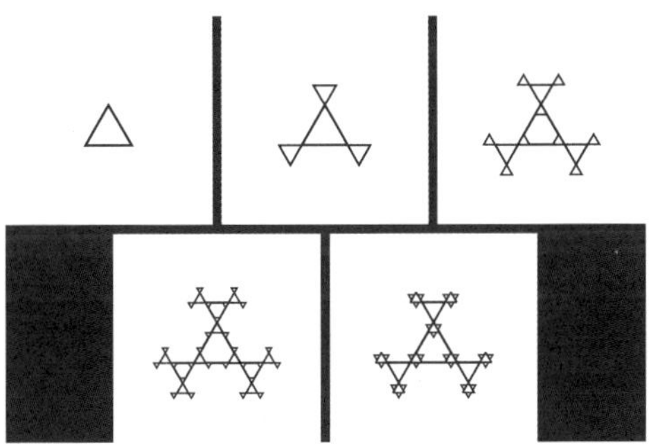

Figure 2. Example of VRT stimulus. The first three iterations are presented on the top row and the possible choices in the lower row.

In theory, in order to correctly generalize a particular recursive rule to further iterations, subjects have to: 1) Acquire categorical knowledge about constituents (square, triangles etc.), 2) Recognize that constituents are structured hierarchically (with dominance and subordination relationships); 3) Recognize that constituents at different hierarchical levels display similar behaviors (e.g. 'each triangle has smaller triangles at its vertices') and 4) Apply the abstracted rule one level beyond the given.

To distinguish between recursion and embedded iteration, a non-recursive control task (EIT) was also developed. In this task, iterative processes produce embeddings of constituents within a fixed hierarchical level, without generating new levels (Fig.3). The 'possible choice images' were paired within and between tasks (VRT and EIT) regarding number, size and shape of constituents.

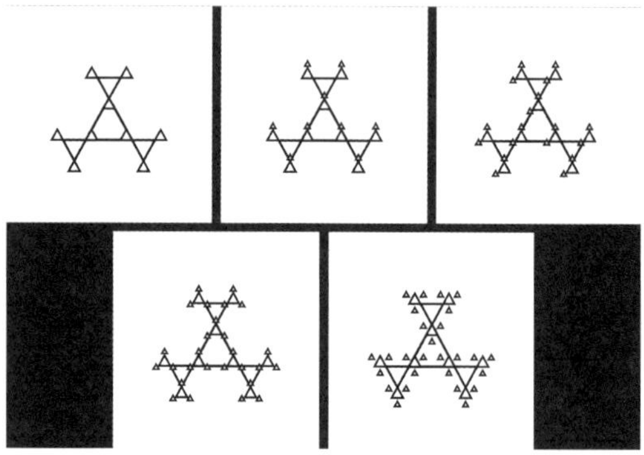

Figure 3. Example of a stimulus from the Embedded Iteration Task (EIT).

After validating the tasks, we tested different populations, together with some well-standardized cognitive measures (WASI Matrix reasoning and Vocabulary, Digit span and CANTAB Spatial Span). We found that:

1) The percentage of correct responses was lower in VRT than in EIT (87% vs. 92%; wilcoxon signed ranks, z = -2.995, p = 0.003) and the response time was longer (18sec vs. 16sec; z = -1.995, p = 0.046);

2) VRT accuracy was better predicted by verbal working memory (r= .413, p=0.023) than by spatial working memory (r= .342, p=0.135). The opposite pattern was found in EIT (spatial WM: r = .581, p= .005; verbal WM: r = .267, p= .153).

3) Principal component analysis (determinant = 0.007; Kaiser-Meyer-Olkin = .65; Bartlett's test of sphericity: χ^2 (36) = 84.5, $p < .001$) suggests that visual recursion relies on two orthogonal systems of processing: One related to visual iteration processing, matrix reasoning, spatial working memory and spatial short term memory (33% of the variance); and another related to the processing of serialized information such as counting, the manipulation of digits in working memory, and vocabulary (21% of the variance).

4. Discussion

Taken together, our results seem to indicate that: 1) visual hierarchical processing and visual recursion dissociate to some extent; and 2) visual recursion seems to correlate more strongly with either verbal resources OR with a general ability to process serial information.

These results are relevant to the previous discussion because in a language-independent domain, such as the visuo-spatial, it seems that the ability to build recursive representations recruits resources related to verbal or serial processing. Furthermore, given that abstract representations must be built for both hierarchical and recursive processing, it is interesting to note that the recursive modality relates more strongly with non-visual cognitive abilities. This may reflect the fact that recursive hierarchies are more regular (Helm et al., 1992), hence can be better represented by compressed abstract rules. Once these rules are used to encode information across hierarchical levels, this might reduce the memory load necessary to represent (visually) each constituent individually (Alvarez, 2011).

If these conclusions hold, the next empirical question is whether verbal or serial processing resources are a necessary condition for recursive representations or whether they are recruited when available, given that they enhance reasoning in general (Carruthers, 2002). New studies are underway to assess if humans can perform above chance in VRT, under conditions of verbal and motor masking. If so, this would support the hypothesis that recursion was available before the faculty of language, but could have been nevertheless recruited and perhaps improved by it.

Acknowledgements

We wish to thank Paolo Baldi for his insightful comments and suggestions. This research was supported by the Fundação para a Ciência e a Tecnologia grant SFRH/BD/64206/2009 and by the ERC advanced grant SOMACCA project number 230604.

References

Abe, K. & Watanabe, D. (2011). Songbirds possess the spontaneous ability to discriminate syntactic rules. *Nature Neuroscience,* 14**,** 1067-1074.

Alvarez, G. A. (2011). Representing multiple objects as an ensemble enhances visual cognition. *Trends in Cognitive Sciences,* 15**,** 122-131.

Bloomfied, T. C., Gentner, T. Q. & Margoliash, D. (2011). What birds have to say about language. *Nature Neuroscience,* 14, 947-948.
Carruthers, P. (2002). The cognitive functions of language. *Behavior and Brain Sciences,* 25, 657-74.
Chomsky, N. (2010). Some simple evo devo theses: how true might they be for language? *In:* Larson, R. K., Déprez, V. M. & Yamakido, H. (eds.) *The evolution of human language.* New York: Cambridge University Press.
Fitch, W. T., Hauser, M. & Chomsky, N. (2005). The evolution of the language faculty: Clarifications and implications. *Cognition,* 97, 179-210.
Fitch, W. T. & Hauser, M. D. (2004). Computational Constraints on Syntactic Processing in a Nonhuman Primate. *Science,* 303, 377-280.
Harder, P. (2010). Over the top - recursion as a functional option. *In:* Hulst, H. V. D. (ed.) *Recursion and Human Language.* Berlin/New York: de Gruyter Mouton.
Hauser, M. D., Chomsky, N. & Fitch, W. T. (2002). The Faculty of Language: What Is It, Who Has It, and How Did It Evolve? *Science,* 298, 1569-1579.
Helm, P. V. D., Van Lier, R. J. & Leeuwenberg, E. J. (1992). Serial pattern complexity: irregularity and hierarchy. *Perception,* 21, 517-544.
Hofstadter, D. R. (2008). *I Am a Strange Loop*, Basic Books.
Hulst, H. V. D. (2010). Re Recursion. *In:* Hulst, H. V. D. (ed.) *Recursion and Human Language.* de Gruyter Mouton.
Kinsella, A. (2010). Was recursion the key step in the evolution of the human language faculty? *In:* Hulst, H. V. D. (ed.) *Recursion and Human Language.* Berlin/New York: de Gruyter Mouton.
Koike, H. & Yoshihara, H. (1993). Fractal approaches for visualization of huge hiearchies. Proceedings of the 1993 IEEE Symposium on Visual Languages, pp.55-60.
Lieberman, P. (2010). The creative capacity of language, in what manner is it unique, and who had it? *In:* Larson, R. K., Déprez, V. M. & Yamakido, H. (eds.) *The evolution of human language.* New York: Cambridge University Press.
Odifreddi, P. G. (1999). *Classical recursion theory*, Elsevier.
Pinker, S. & Jackendoff, R. (2005). The faculty of language: what's special about it? *Cognition,* 95, 201-236.
Verhagen, A. (2010). What do you think is the proper place of recursion? Conceptual and empirical issues. *In:* Hulst, H. V. D. (ed.) *Recursion and Human Language.* de Gruyter Mouton.

OUTGROUP: THE STUDY OF CHIMPANZEES TO KNOW THE HUMAN MIND

TETSURO MATSUZAWA
Primate Research Institute, Kyoto University
Inuyama, Aichi 484-8506, Japan

1. Outgroup: the rational of studying chimpanzee mind for understanding human mind

I have been studying chimpanzees both in Japan and in Africa. My research partner is a female chimpanzee named Ai. Ai-project started as a sort of ape-language study in 1976, and still continues in terms of Comparative Cognitive Science (Matsuzawa, 2001; 2003; Matsuzawa *et al.*, 2006). In parallel to my laboratory work, I have visited Africa for the past 26 years to study wild chimpanzees in their natural habitat. There is a group of chimpanzees in the forest of Bossou, Guinea, West Africa (Matsuzawa *et al*, 2011).

I have visited wild bonobos, another species of the same genus of chimpanzees, in the Congo Basin in Ex-Zaire, Central Africa (Fig. 1).

Figure 1. Mother-infant bonobos in Wamba, Ex-Zaire, Central Africa.

I have also visited wild mountain gorillas in the Virunga volcano in Rwanda, East Africa (Fig 2).

Figure 2. Mother-infant gorillas in Virunga volcano, Rwanda, East Africa.

I have been studying wild orangutans since 1999 in the northern part of Borneo and the Peninsula in Malaysia, South-East Asia (Fig 3).

Figure 3. Mother-infant orangutans in BJ island, Malaysia, South-East Asia.

As you may know, human is a species labeled *Homo sapiens*. Many people still hold the naïve human-animal dichotomy. However, it is completely wrong. Human is a member of animal kingdom. Human is a member of mammals. Among the mammals, human belongs to the order called Primates, and the family called Hominoid. The family Hominoid consists of 4 genera, humans, chimpanzees (and bonobos), gorillas, and orangutans.

The idea of "Outgroup" may help you to understand the rational why you have to study the chimpanzees, gorillas, and orangutans to know the human nature, including the evolutionary origins of human language. Outgroup can be defined as "the ones who are not in the target group". Suppose that you are interested in the country Japan, it is good for you to go to the foreign countries. Suppose that you are interested in the nature of Japanese people, you must know that of the foreigners. Suppose that you are interested in the normal and standard development of human children, it is very important to have the deep understanding of the developmental disorders or autistic syndromes. In the same way, to know the human mind, it is very important to know the evolutionary neighbors, that means, chimpanzees, bonobos, gorillas, and orangutans.

The hominoid family is featured by having no tails: we have no tails, so do the chimpanzees, bonobos, gorillas and orangutans. Japanese language has only one word "*saru*" that reminds us of Japanese monkeys. In English, however, there is a clear distinction between "monkeys" that have tails and "apes" that have no tails at all. Thus, humans and the the great apes belong to the same family Hominoid that should be pitted against the group of monkeys.

Human body is an evolutionary product, so does the human mind. The body can be reconstructed from the fossil record such as skulls, bones, and teeth. However, the mind and the brain could not remain in the fossil record. Therefore, to know the evolutionary history of human mind, I have compared the mind of humans with that of the great apes, especially the chimpanzees.

2. Chimpanzees as an Outgroup: the education by master-apprenticeship

In the beginning of 21st century, scientists succeeded to read the whole genome of humans, about 3 billion base pairs of DNA. Following the human genome, the chimpanzee genome was also clarified. The result was amazing: 98.8% of genome was the same between humans and chimpanzees. There was only 1.2% difference between the two. We shared the latest common ancestor about 5 million years ago.

Chimpanzee is so like us. The life span of chimpanzee is about 50 years. Female chimpanzee gives a birth once every 5 years on the average. The gestation period is about 280 days in humans and 235 days in chimpanzees. Human baby weighs about 3 kg at the birth while chimpanzee baby is a little less than 2 kg. The brain volume triples during the development from the newborn to the adult in both humans and chimpanzees. Thus, the chimpanzees have to learn a lot of things during the course of development just like us (Sakai *et al*, 2011).

The chimpanzees of Bossou, for example, use a pair of stones as hammer and anvil to crack open oil-palm nuts. The hard hit breaks the hard-shell of the nut to get the edible kernel inside. This is a cultural tradition unique to Bossou community. From one generation to the next, chimpanzees have to learn what to eat and how to use the tools. It takes about 4 years for the young chimpanzees to acquire the skill of stone tool (Lonsdorf *et al*, 2010; Matsuzawa *et al*, 2001).

Fig.4 Chimpanzees at Bossou use a pior of stones for nut-cracking.

It is interesting to see the acquiring process. The chimpanzee way of learning is called Education by master-apprenticeship. Mother shows the good model but never teaches the child. The child has the strong motivation to make the copy of the mother's behavior. In return, the mother is highly tolerant to the child, never scolding nor neglecting. The intimate and affectionate mother-infant tie provides the basis of the long-term observation learning right after the birth.

3. Chimpanzees as an Outgroup: Good in eidetic memory but not good in symbolic representation

What is the difference between humans and chimpanzees? There are, of course, a lot of similarity and differences between the two species (see the recent topics, Ludwig *et al,* 2011, Martin & Matsuzawa, 2011). Our recent study succeeded to show the unique capability of chimpanzees. The chimpanzees, especially young ones, have an extraordinary memory capability, that might be called eidetic memory. They can remember the Arabic numerals at a glance.

Suppose that the numerals 1 through 9 appeared on the computer monitor screen for a brief duration such as 0.1 sec. You may be able to see that the numerals were on the screen, but you can't remember the numerals and the exact positions in such a brief duration. However, the chimpanzees can do it.

This is the first evidence that the chimpanzees can be better than humans in a cognitive task (Inoue & Matsuzawa, 2007; Matsuzawa, 2009).

Fig. 5. Chimpanzee Ayumu is doing the masking task of 9 numerals. When you touch the numeral 1 then the other numerals turn to be masking rectangles. The three young chimpanzees are good at remembering the numerals and the location at a glance (Matsuzawa, 2009).

In contrast, humans can imagine the things not in front of them. Human can associate the events, objects, color and so forth to the corresponding symbols. That means the language capability. For example, the word "red" does not have any physical similarity to the color red. However, when we see the word "red" we can easily remind of the color red. The word "bell" reminds us of the sound of the bell. The association of the symbol and the corresponding things is everywhere in human language but very difficult for chimpanzees (Matsuzawa, 2009; Matsuzawa, 2011).

In sum, the chimpanzees are living in the world of the here and now. They are very good at grasping what is present. However, they are not good at imaging the things that is absent. They seem to be not worried about their future, even tomorrow (Miyabe-Nishiwaki *et al.*, 2010). In contrast, the humans have the power of imagination. Starting from what we see and what we hear, we can easily imagine the world that is not really in front of us. We can think about the past a long time before the birth. We can think about the future after the death. The power of imagination sometimes makes us worried about our own future. We easily become in anxiety and turn to be depressive. However, the same power of imagination makes us hope to the future. Hope, that is the uniquely human nature.

4. Green Corridor Project: Conservation efforts in the wild

At the last, let me take this opportunity to introduce the current situation of wild chimpanzees. Chimpanzees distribute in the tropical rain forests and the surrounding areas near the equator in Africa. The number of chimpanzees was estimated to be about 1 million 100 years ago. It is now about 200,000. There are three major reasons why the population was quickly decreased.

The first reason is the deforestation. Local people cut down the trees for the slash and burn agriculture and the commercial logging. The second one is the poaching. There are some people who shoot the chimpanzees to eat. The meat of the wild animals is called "bush meat". There is a bush meat trade in which the dried meat is brought to the cities to be sold in the market. The third is the contagious disease. All kind of disease can be transmitted bilaterally between humans and chimpanzees. The deforestation, poaching, and contagious disease, all is originating from human activity.

We have to look for the way of peacefully co-existing with chimpanzees and other animals in the forests. The effort is called wildlife conservation. Bossou community, only 12 members at the moment, is isolated by the savanna and cultivated fields. To the east about 5 km away, there is Nimba mountains, the World Natural Heritage site designated by UNESCO. There must be about several hundred chimpanzees there (Matsuzawa *et al*, 2011).

We have been promoting the green corridor project. This is a project of planting trees to make a corridor between Bossou and Nimba, connecting the two isolated habitats. We made the tree nursery and planted about 10,000 young trees in the savanna every year in the past decade. However, it is not an easy task: we have got the bush fires twice. The planted trees had gone. Japanese proverb says "Fall seven times, get up eight". The continuous effort will transform the savanna into the fresh green forests someday in the future.

Acknowledgements

This study was financially supported by the MEXT grants 20002001 and HOPE project of KUPRI. I appreciate the collaboration my colleagues in Japan and in Africa. I also appreciate Dr. Dora Biro for her comments and editing English.

References

Inoue, S., & Matsuzawa, T. (2007) Working memory of numerals in chimpanzees. *Current Biology*, *17*, R1004-R1005.

Lonsdorf, E., Ross, SR., & Matsuzawa (2010) *The mind of the chimpanzee: Ecological and experimental perspectives.* Chicago, IL: University of Chicago Press.

Ludwig, V., Adachi, I., & Matsuzawa, T. (2011) Visuoauditory mappings between high luminance and high pitch are shared by chimpanzees (*Pan troglodytes*) and humans. PNAS, Published online, doi: 10.1073/pnas.1112605108

Martin, C., & Matsuzawa, T. (2011) Chimpanzees' use of conspecific cues in matching-to-sample tasks: public information use in a fully automated testing environment. *Animal Cognition, 14*, 893-902.

Matsuzawa, T. (2001). *Primate origins of human cognition and behaviour.* Tokyo: Springer.

Matsuzawa, T. (2009). Symbolic representation of number in chimpanzees. Current opinion in Neurobiology, *19*, 92-98.

Matsuzawa, T., Biro, D., Tatyana, H., Inoue-Nakamura, N., Tonooka, R., & Yamakoshi, G. (2001). Emergence of culture in wild chimpanzees: Education by master-apprenticeship. In: T. Matsuzawa (Eds.), *Primate origins of human cognition and behavio*, (pp. 557-574). New York: NY, Springer-Verlag doi: 10.1007/978-4-431-09423-4

Matsuzawa, T., Tomonaga, M., & Tanaka, M. (2006). *Cognitive development in chimpanzees.* Tokyo: Springer.

Matsuzawa, T., Humle, T., & Sugiyama, Y. (2011). *The chimpanzees at Bossou and Nimba.* Tokyo: Spriner.

Miyabe-Nishiwaki, T., Kaneko, A., Nishiwaki, K., Watanabe, A., Watanabe, S., Maeda, N., Kumazaki, K., Morimoto, M., Hirokawa, R., Suzuki, J., Ito, Y., Hayashi, M., Tanaka, M., Tomonaga, M., & Matsuzawa, T. (2010). Tetraparesis resembling acute transverse myelitis in a captive chimpanzee (*Pan troglodytes*): long-term care and recovery. *Journal of Medical Primatology*, *39*, 336-346.

Sakai, T., Mikami, A., Tomonaga, M., Matsui, M., Suzuki, J., Hamada, Y., Tanaka, M., Miyabe-Nishiwaki, T., Makishima, H., Nakatsukasa, M., & Matsuzawa, T. (2011) Differential prefrontal white matter development in chimpanzees and humans. *Current Biology, 21*, 1397-1402.

A MODULATION-DEMODULATION MODEL FOR SPEECH COMMUNICATION AND ITS EMERGENCE

NOBUAKI MINEMATSU

Graduate School of Info. Sci. and Tech., The University of Tokyo, Japan,
mine@gavo.t.u-tokyo.ac.jp

Perceptual invariance against large acoustic variability in speech has been a long-discussed question in speech science and engineering (Perkell & Klatt, 2002), and it is still an open question (Newman, 2008; Furui, 2009). Recently, we proposed a candidate answer based on mathematically-guaranteed relational invariance (Minematsu et al., 2010; Qiao & Minematsu, 2010). Here, transform-invariant features, f-divergences, are extracted from the speech dynamics in an utterance to form an invariant topological shape which characterizes and represents the linguistic message conveyed in that utterance. In this paper, this representation is interpreted from a viewpoint of telecommunications, linguistics, and evolutionary anthropology. Speech production is often regarded as a process of modulating the baseline timbre of a speaker's voice by manipulating the vocal organs, i.e., spectrum modulation. Then, extraction of the linguistic message from an utterance can be viewed as a process of spectrum *de*modulation. This modulation-demodulation model of speech communication has a strong link to known morphological and cognitive differences between humans and apes.

1. Introduction

Many speech sounds can be represented as standing waves in a vocal tube and their acoustic properties depend on the shape and length of the tube. The process of producing vowel sounds is very similar to that of producing sounds with a wind instrument. A vocal tube can be regarded as an instrument and, by changing its shape dynamically, sounds of different timbre such as [ɑːɛːiːɔːuː] can be generated.

The length and shape of the vocal tube varies among speakers. This is why voice quality differs among them and one can identify a speaker by hearing his voice. Figure 1 shows the tallest adult and the shortest adult in the world. There must be a very large gap in voice quality between the two, but they were able to communicate orally with no trouble the first time they saw each other. Human speech communication is very robust to acoustic variability caused by speaker differences. This is a good example of invariance and variability in speech processes.

In telecommunications, a message is transmitted to receivers by changing one parameter of a carrier wave in relation to that message. A sinusoidal wave is often used as carrier. This transmission scheme is called modulation and in (Wikipedia, 2011) it is explained by using the performance of a musician as a metaphor.

Figure 1. The tallest and shortest adults

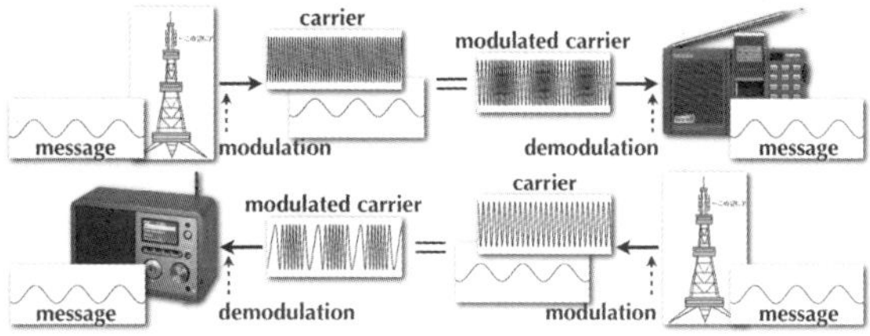

Figure 2. Frequency modulation and demodulation

> *A musician modulates the tone from a musical instrument by varying its volume, timing and pitch. The three key parameters of a carrier sine wave are its amplitude ("volume"), its phase ("timing") and its frequency ("pitch"), all of which can be modified in accordance with a content signal to obtain the modulated carrier.*

We can say that a melody contour is a pitch-modulated (frequency-modulated) version of a carrier wave, where the carrier corresponds to the baseline pitch.

We speak using our instruments, i.e., vocal organs, by varying not only the above parameters, but also the most important parameter, called the timbre or spectrum envelope. From this viewpoint, it can be said that an utterance is generated by spectrum modulation (Scott, 2007). The default shape and length of a vocal tube determines speaker-dependent voice quality and, by changing the shape or modulating the spectrum envelope, an utterance is produced and transmitted.

In a large number of previous studies in automatic speech recognition (ASR), to bridge a gap between the ASR performance and the performance of human speech recognition (HSR), much attention was paid to the dynamic aspects of utterances, and many dynamic features were proposed (Greenberg & Kingsbury, 1997; Hermansky & Morgan, 1994; Furui, 1981; Ostendorf et al., 1996). Although these studies proposed new features for ASR, if one views speech production as spectrum modulation, he may point out that these proposals did not provide a good answer to a very fundamental question of ASR and HSR: "what is the algorithm for spectrum *de*modulation?"

In telecommunications, a transmitted message is received via demodulation. In (Wikipedia, 2011), demodulation is explained as a process of extracting the original message intact from a modulated carrier wave. In any form of modulation, AM, PM, or FM, methods exist that can be used to analytically extract the message component exclusively by removing the carrier component from a modulated carrier. Figure 2 illustrates the processes of transmitting and receiving a message via FM. The process of spectrum *de*modulation, which in this case refers to speech recognition, should therefore be realized by a mathematical algorithm that extracts the linguistic message exclusively by removing the speaker-dependent voice quality, i.e., removing speaker identity, from an utterance.

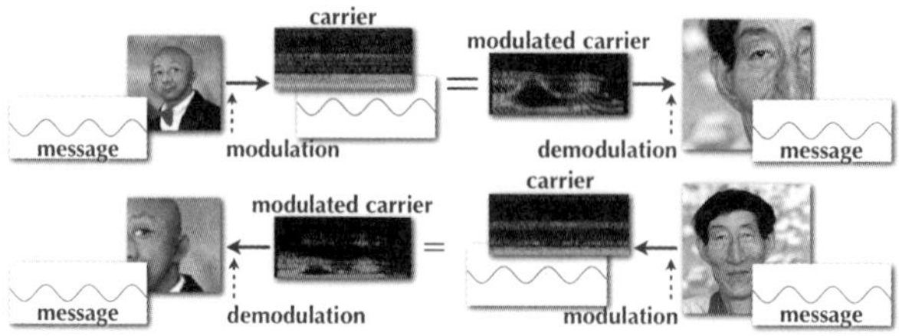

Figure 3. Spectrum modulation and demodulation with a message

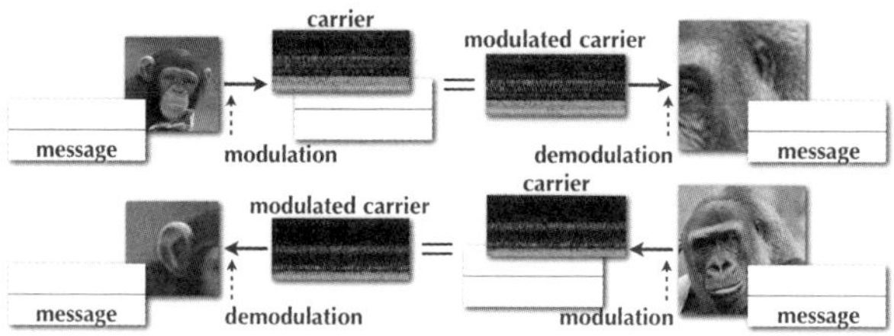

Figure 4. Spectrum modulation and demodulation with no message

This paper demonstrates that our proposal (Minematsu et al., 2010; Qiao & Minematsu, 2010) is a good candidate answer to the above question and that this answer is valid within the contexts of linguistics and evolutionary anthropology. Although this paper provides no new experimental results, we believe that it will provide a novel explanation of speech communication and its emergence.

2. Morphological and cognitive differences between humans and apes

2.1. *Morphological differences between humans and apes*

The proposed model regards a tongue as flexible modulator of the spectrum envelope. Here we discuss the morphological differences of the vocal organs between humans and apes (chimpanzees). Unlike humans, apes have two semi-independent tracts, one from the nose to the lung for breathing and the other from the mouth to the stomach for eating (Hayama, 1999). Apes can breathe and eat simultaneously but humans cannot. As a consequence, it seems reasonably difficult for apes to send an air flow directly from the lung to the vocal cavity. Further, apes have a much less flexible tongue (Takemoto, 2008). As a result, spectrum modulation is difficult. Why did humans gain this ability? One anthropological hypothesis that has been proposed is bipedal walking (Hayama, 1999), because of which the larynx dropped and the two tracts happened to develop an intersection.

Figure 3 illustrates the modulation-demodulation model of human speech communication. The two speakers have vocal tubes of different shape and length, and therefore their default voice timbre (carrier) is different. By dynamically manipulating the topology of the vocal tube, the timbre is modulated and a message is transmitted as a modulation pattern. Since receivers can efficiently demodulate an incoming modulated carrier, different body sizes do not cause problems.

Figure 4 depicts hypothetical voice communication between a small ape and a large ape for the purpose of illustrating our model. Like humans, they have their own unique voice timbre but unlike humans, it is reasonably difficult to embed messages in the voices via spectrum modulation. It is well-known that an ape can deliver some primitive messages to others using specialized calls. Our model does not deny their primitive vocal communication capabilities but assumes that their capabilities cannot be extended to a higher level of vocal communication, where thousands of different words are used and transmitted.

We have explained that a good and flexible timbre modulator is found only in humans' unique vocal tract morphology, but our model also claims that a good *de*modulator exists only in the human organs of hearing.

2.2. *Cognitive differences between humans and animals*

As explained in Section 1, a musical melody can be regarded as an FM version of a carrier wave. If we apply two different carriers to the same musical content, the result will be a melody and its transposition. From the two pieces, humans can extract the same musical content easily and this extraction is referred to as demodulation. But apes cannot perceive the equivalence between a melody and its transposed version (Hauser et al., 2003). It is difficult for apes to demodulate FM carriers. What about spectrum demodulation? Can they do this or not?

Human infants acquire spoken language via vocal imitation of the utterances of their parents. But they do not impersonate their parents. Their vocal imitation is not acoustic imitation. Vocal imitation is a trait that is rarely found in animals and humans are the only primates that exhibit it. We can find only a few other species that do, such as birds, dolphins and whales (Okanoya, 2008). But there exists a critical difference between the vocal imitation of humans and that of animals. Basically speaking, animals' imitation is acoustic (Okanoya, 2008). By interpreting this fact based on our model, we can say that animals imitate a modulated carrier, i.e., incoming signals themselves, not the message embedded in the carrier. It seems that animals also have difficulty in performing spectrum demodulation.

Which acoustic aspects of parents' utterances do infants imitate and which aspects do they ignore? One may assume that infants decompose the utterances into sequences of phonemes (text-like representation) and they realize each phoneme acoustically with their mouths. It seems however, that researchers of infant studies do not accept this assumption because infants do not have good phonemic awareness (Kato, 2003; Shaywitz, 2005). No infant acquires spoken language by reading text. In that case, what are they imitating? According to (Kato, 2003; Shaywitz, 2005; Hayakawa, 2006; Lieberman, 1980), infants are thought to extract holistic and speaker-independent speech patterns, called speech Gestalts, and

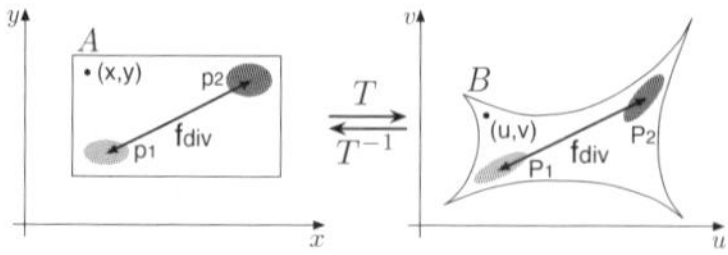

Figure 5. Transform-invariance of f-divergence

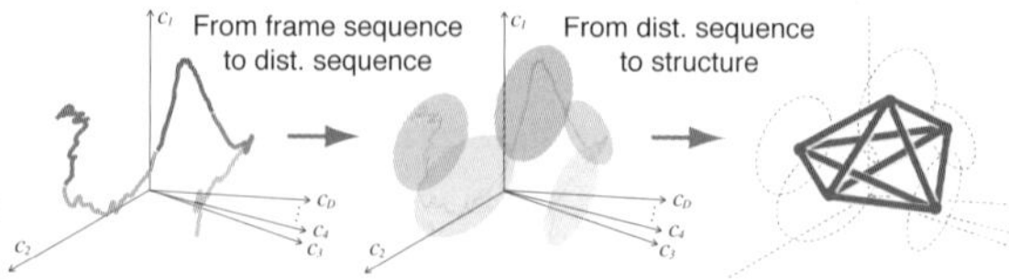

Figure 6. Transform-invariant shape of an utterance

they realize the patterns acoustically using their mouths. As far as we know, however, no researcher has proposed a physical definition for speech patterns that has the potential to lead to an algorithm of spectrum demodulation.

3. Implementation of the spectrum demodulation algorithm

3.1. *Removal of the speaker-dependent voice timbre*

Demodulation removes the carrier information and leaves the message intact. In (Minematsu et al., 2010; Qiao & Minematsu, 2010), we implemented this process on a computer using transform-invariant features. Speaker difference is often characterized as a transformation from one speaker's voice space to another's. This indicates that if one can represent an utterance using only transform-invariant features, that representation will contain no speaker-dependent features.

In (Qiao & Minematsu, 2010), we proved that f-divergence[a] is invariant with any kind of invertible and differentiable transform (sufficiency) and that the features invariant with any kind of transform have to be a function of f-divergence (necessity). Figure 5 illustrates the invariance of f-divergence and any speech event has to be characterized not as point but as distribution in a feature space.

3.2. *Computational implementation of speech Gestalts*

By representing an utterance only with f-divergence, we can obtain the speaker-independent speech pattern, i.e., the speech Gestalt. Figure 6 shows the extraction procedure. A speech trajectory in a feature space is converted into a sequence of distributions. Between every distribution pair, the f-divergence is calculated to form a distance matrix, which can specify a unique geometrical shape. This matrix is the mathematical expression for the speech Gestalt.

We have already applied this holistic representation to speech recognition (Minematsu et al., 2010; Qiao & Minematsu, 2010), pronunciation assessment (Suzuki et al., 2009) and dialect-based speaker clustering (Ma et al., 2009). If readers are interested in how effective the proposed holistic representation is at removing speaker identity from speech acoustics and extract the linguistic content exclusively, please refer to the above papers. Under the proposed method, two

[a] $f_{div}(p_1, p_2) \equiv \oint p_2(\boldsymbol{x}) g\left(\frac{p_1(\boldsymbol{x})}{p_2(\boldsymbol{x})}\right) d\boldsymbol{x} = f_{div}(T(p_1), T(p_2))$. Please refer to Figure 5.

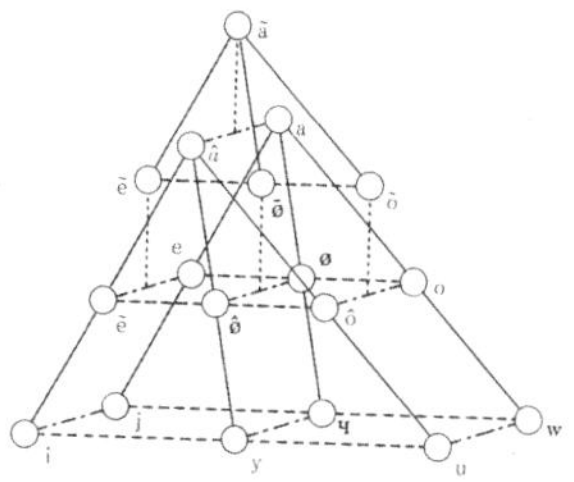

Figure 7. Jakobson's invariant system

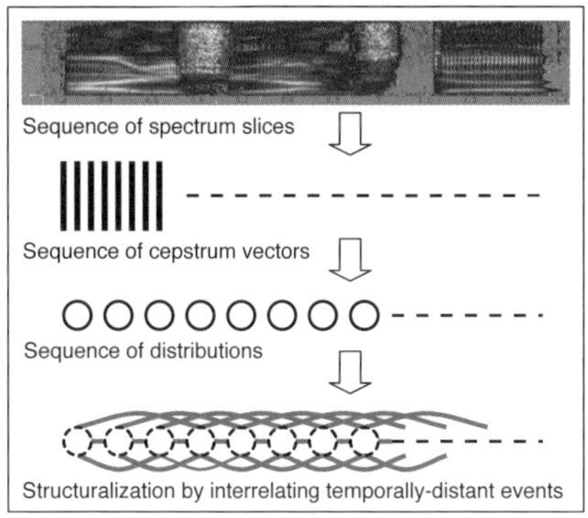

Figure 8. Extraction of a speech Gestalt

simulated utterances of the same message generated by the tallest man and the shortest man appear identical. Explicit model adaptation or feature normalization which are essential for the conventional ASR framework is not needed.

4. Discussion and conclusions

Similar claims are found in classical linguistics (Jakobson & Waugh, 1987; Ladefoged & Broadbent, 1957) and a recent study of speech science (Plummer et al., 2010). Figure 7 shows Jakobson's system of French vowels and semi-vowels and he wrote "we have to put aside the accidental properties of individual sounds and substitute a general expression that is the common denominator of these variables." In these studies however, no algorithm was proposed to remove the speaker-dependent features to extract an embedded message[b]. Further, speaker-independence (invariance) was not proved mathematically in a conclusive fashion.

Figure 8 shows the procedure of extracting a speaker-invariant pattern again. This figure and Figure 6 explain the same procedure from different viewpoints. A feature vector in Figure 8 corresponds to a point in the feature space in Figure 6. Clearly shown in Figure 8, invariant features exist as speech contrasts, which include not only local contrasts but also long-distant contrasts. As is well-known, all the textbooks on acoustic phonetics explain formant frequencies or spectrum envelopes as acoustic correlates with phonemes, i.e., linguistic messages. But it is also well-known that these features are strongly speaker-dependent. Our modulation-demodulation model claims that a linguistic message is transmitted mainly by speech contrasts, not just by local speech features observed at each time index. In Section 2.2, we explained apes' inability to perform demodulation, but apes can identify individuals very accurately by hearing the voices of the individuals. Considering these facts, for apes, formant frequencies and spectrum

[b]It should be noted that the method proposed in this paper aims not at normalizing speaker differences but at removing speaker identity from speech acoustics. As spectrum smoothing can remove pitch information from speech, our method can remove speaker information from speech.

envelopes are acoustic correlates with individuals and different acoustic features indicate different information (individuals). We speculate that it is through the acquisition of demodulation abilities that humans became able to extract the same message consistently from acoustically different sound streams. We argue that this invariant information is what we call language today.

In Section 2.2, we focused on the difference in vocal imitation between animals and humans. Although the following description may be out of the scope of this paper, we also found that in some cases acoustic imitation does become the default strategy for humans. Examples can be found in severely impaired autistics (Willey et al., 1999) and, in this case, the normal acquisition of speech communication often becomes difficult. Prof. Grandin, a professor of animal sciences, who is herself autistic, described the similarity in information processing between animals and autistics (Grandin et al., 2004). Autistics tend to memorize the details of input stimuli. An autistic boy wrote that he could understand what his mother was saying but that it was difficult for him to understand others (Higashida et al., 2005). He may not have a normal capability for demodulation.

In this paper, a modulation-demodulation model of speech communication is proposed to explain humans' capability for robust communication. This model however, claims nothing regarding the emergence of the syntactic structure of language, and it claims nothing either regarding why invariant speech patterns, which are merely topological patterns found in air particle vibrations around listeners' ears, can have very strong links with memory, i.e., what is stored as a topological pattern or cell assembly in the neural circuits of the listeners. But we believe that the ability to perform spectrum modulation and demodulation is at least a required condition for the emergence and development of spoken language.

References

Furui, S. (1981). Comparison of speaker recognition methods using statistical features and dynamic features. *IEEE Trans. ASSP*, *29*(3), 342-350.

Furui, S. (2009). Generalization problem in asr acoustic model training and adaptation. *Proc. IEEE Workshop on Automatic Speech Recognition and Understanding*.

Grandin, T., et al.. (2004). *Animals in translation.* Scribner.

Greenberg, S., & Kingsbury, B. (1997). The modulation spectrogram: in pursuit of an invariant representation of speech. *Proc. ICASSP*, 1647-1650.

Hauser, M. D., et al.. (2003). The evolution of the music faculty: a comparative perspective. *Nature neurosciences*, *6*, 663-668.

Hayakawa, M. (2006). Language acquisition and matherese. *Language*, *35*(9), 62-67.

Hayama, S. (1999). *The birth of human beings.* PHP Shinsho.

Hermansky, H., & Morgan, N. (1994). Rasta processing of speech. *IEEE Trans. SAP*, *2*(4), 578-589.

Higashida, N., et al.. (2005). *Messages to all my colleagues living on the planet.* Escor Pub.

Jakobson, R., & Waugh, L. R. (1987). *The sound shape of language.* Mouton De Gruyter.

Kato, M. (2003). Phonological development and its disorders. *J. Communication Disorders*, *20*(2), 84-85.

Ladefoged, P., & Broadbent, D. (1957). Information conveyed by vowels. *J. Acoust. Soc. Am.*, *29*, 98-104.

Lieberman, P. (1980). On the development of vowel production in young children. In G. H. Yeni-Komshian, J. F. Kavanagh, & C. A. Ferguson (Eds.), *Child phonology vol.1.* Academic Press.

Ma, X., et al.. (2009). Dialect-based speaker classification of chinese using structural representation of pronunciation. *Proc. Speech and Computer (SPECOM)*, 350-355.

Minematsu, N., et al.. (2010). Speech structure and its application to robust speech processing. *Journal of New Generation Computing*, *28*(3), 299-319.

Newman, R. S. (2008). The level of detail in infants' word learning. *Current directions in psychological science*, *17*(3), 229-232.

Okanoya, K. (2008). Birdsongs and human language: common evolutionary mechanisms. *Proc. Spring Meet. Acoust. Soc. Jpn.*, *1-17-5*, 1555-1556.

Ostendorf, M., et al.. (1996). From hmms to segment models: a unified view of stochastic modeling for speech recognition. *IEEE Trans. on SAP*, *4*(5), 360-378.

Perkell, J. S., & Klatt, D. H. (2002). *Invariance and variability in speech processes.* Lawrence Erlbaum Associates, Inc.

Plummer, A. R., et al.. (2010). Learning speaker normalization using semisupervised manifold alignment. *Proc. INTERSPEECH*, 2918-2921.

Qiao, Y., & Minematsu, N. (2010). A study on invariance of f-divergence and its application to speech recognition. *IEEE Trans. Signal Processing*, *58*(7), 3884-3890.

Scott, S. K. (2007). The neural basis of speech perception – a view from functional imaging. *Proc. INTERSPEECH*, 10-13.

Shaywitz, S. E. (2005). *Overcoming dyslexia.* Random House.

Suzuki, M., et al.. (2009). Sub-structure-based estimation of pronunciation proficiency and classification of learners. *Proc. IEEE Workshop on Automatic Speech Recognition and Understanding (ASRU)*, 574-579.

Takemoto, H. (2008). Morphological analyses and 3d modeling of the tongue musculature of the chimpanzee. *American Journal of Primatology*, *70*(10), 966-975.

Wikipedia. (2011). http://en.wikipedia.org/wiki/Modulation.

Willey, L. H., et al.. (1999). *Pretending to be normal: living with asperger's syndrome.* Jessica Kingsley Publishers.

SIGNALING CONVENTIONS: WHO LEARNS WHAT WHERE AND WHEN IN A SOCIAL NETWORK?

ROLAND MÜHLENBERND

Seminar für Sprachwissenschaft, University of Tübingen
roland.muehlenbernd@uni-tuebingen.de

MICHAEL FRANKE

Institute for Logic, Language and Information, Universiteit van Amsterdam
m.franke@uva.nl

Lewis (1969) invented signaling games to show that meaning convention can arise simply from regularities in communicative behavior. This paper contributes to the question how the formation of signaling conventions depends on the social structure of a population. Our results not only show that different language conventions can coexist, but also where to expect uniformity and language contact. We found that place and time of convention formation can be traced well to particular clusters of high/low values of suitable notions from formal network theory. Against prior expectations, we found that agent rationality is less important than network role in deciding how and when an agent adopts a convention.

1. Introduction

Lewisean signaling games have become a standard model for the pragmatic evolution of semantic meaning (cf. Steels, 1997; Nowak & Krakauer, 1999; Skyrms, 2010). In order to understand the applicability and conceptual adequacy of signaling game models, the most important theoretical question that needs to be addressed is under which circumstances stable signaling conventions can arise. Following a general trend in evolutionary game theory, recent studies have started to probe into the simplifying assumption underlying classical evolutionary dynamics that populations of agents are homogeneous, i.e., barring of social structure. Dispensing with this artificial assumption, Zollman (2005), for instance, has demonstrated for a so-called imitate-the-best dynamic how coexistent language conventions can evolve if the population of language users is arranged on a lattice. Wagner (2009) studied the same dynamic on so-called β-graphs (defined below) which exhibit more realistic small-world properties, namely a high clustering coefficient, paired with a low characteristic path length (Watts & Strogatz, 1998). Wagner's simulations showed that (i) the higher the clustering coefficients the larger the fractions of players that acquire a unique signaling convention, and

(ii) the lower the characteristic path length the smaller the number of connected regions of agents that use the same signaling convention.

This paper probes deeper into the relation between social structure and language evolution in order to further our knowledge of synthetic evolutionary processes in structured populations and thereby to pave the way for a more thorough understanding of the sociological factors of linguistic variability. While previous related work has focused on studying which *global* network structures are especially conducive to innovation and its spread (Ke, Gong, & Wang, 2008; Fagyal, Swarup, Escobar, Gasser, & Lakkaraju, 2010), the present paper investigates more closely the *local* network properties associated with (regions of) agents that have successfully learned a language or not. In distinction to previous studies, we also focus not on imitation, but on usage-based learning dynamics from evolutionary game theory. To study the effect of agent rationality on language evolutions, we considered best-response dynamics and reinforcement learning.

Our most striking results, in a nutshell, were these. Firstly, we found that languages form preferentially on locally highly connected subgraphs; borders between languages fall preferentially on regions "in between" highly connected subregions. Secondly, conventionalization depended crucially on local network properties, while the learning dynamics and the amount of agent rationality had hardly any noticeable effect. Thirdly, we compared the local properties of agents who had learned a language with those who had not, and of those who lived at the borders of language regions with those who lived in the interior. To characterize the differences we found, we made a distinction between *family men* and *globetrotters*, which we characterized by relative values of suitable clusters of properties from formal network theory. We found that learners and interior agents tend to be family men with tight local connections, while non-learners and border agents tend to be globetrotters with wide-ranging global connections. Finally, we found evidence that the first ones to adopt and stabilize a convention were family men.

2. Signaling games & learning dynamics

A signaling game is a game played between a sender S and a receiver R. Initially, nature selects a state $t \in T$ with prior probability $\Pr(t) \in \Delta(T)$, which S observes, but R doesn't. S then selects a message $m \in M$, and R responds with a choice of action $a \in A$. For each round of play, players receive utilities depending on (in the cheap-talk case we consider here) the actual state t and the response action a. We will here be concerned only with a simple variant of this game, which we call *Lewis game*: there are only two states that are equiprobable, two messages and two actions that correspond one-to-one with the states, indicated by the same index. Players share an interest in successful communication, expressed by utility function $\mathrm{U}(t_{\mathrm{i}}, a_{\mathrm{j}}) = 1$ if $i = j$ and 0 otherwise.

Although messages are initially meaningless in this game, meaningfulness arises from regularities in behavior. Behavior is defined in terms of strategies.

A *behavioral sender strategy* is a function $\sigma : T \to \Delta(M)$, and a *behavioral receiver strategy* is a function $\rho : M \to \Delta(A)$. A behavioral strategy can be interpreted as a single agent's probabilistic choice or as a population average. For a Lewis game, exactly two isomorphic strategy profiles constitute evolutionary stable states (Huttegger, 2007). In these, strategies are pure (i.e., action choices have probabilities 1 or 0) and messages associate states and actions uniquely, like so:

$$L_1: \quad \begin{array}{l} t_1 \longrightarrow m_1 \longrightarrow a_1 \\[1em] t_2 \longrightarrow m_2 \longrightarrow a_2 \end{array} \qquad\qquad L_2: \quad \begin{array}{ccccc} t_1 & & m_1 & & a_1 \\ & \times & & \times & \\ t_2 & & m_2 & & a_2 \end{array}$$

Classical evolutionary game theory assumes a homogenous population of agents and studies evolutionary processes on the aggregate population level. In this paper we focus instead on more fine-grained agent-based evolutionary dynamics. Agents repeatedly play a Lewis game with those agents they are connected with in their social network, and adapt their behavioral strategies based on learning from previous interactions. We consider two kinds of *learning dynamics* that differ with respect to how rational the learning agents are assumed to be: more rational best-response dynamics (BR) and less rational reinforcement learning (RL).

Best-response dynamics. The idea of BR-dynamics is simple: agents remember the past plays that they have been engaged in and derive from their memory a belief about their opponents' behavior; it is to that belief that they play a *rational* best response. We assume here that agents form a belief about the collective behavior of all of their neighbors, not keeping track of each agent separately. More concretely, a given agent's belief about his neighborhood's receiver (sender) behavior $B_r(a|m)$ ($B_s(t|m)$) is just a behavioral receiver (sender) strategy derived by keeping track of *all* of the agent's past interactions. The sender's expected utility for sending m in state t is $EU_s(m|t) = \sum_{a \in A} B_r(a|m) \times U(t,a)$. Accordingly, the receiver's expected utility is $EU_r(a|m) = \sum_{t \in T} B_s(t|m) \times U(t,a)$. A *best response* is an action choice that maximizes expected utility. This gives rise to the following *response rules for BR-dynamics*:

$$\sigma(m|t) = \begin{cases} \frac{1}{|\arg\max_m EU_s(m|t)|} & \text{if } t \in \arg\max_m EU_s(m|t) \\ 0 & \text{else} \end{cases} \tag{1}$$

$$\rho(a|m) = \begin{cases} \frac{1}{|\arg\max_a EU_r(a|m)|} & \text{if } a \in \arg\max_a EU_r(a|m) \\ 0 & \text{else} \end{cases} \tag{2}$$

Reinforcement learning with limited memory. RL can be captured by a simple model based on urns, also known as *Pólya urns* (cf. Roth & Erev, 1995; Skyrms, 2010). An urn models a behavioral strategy, in the sense that the probability of making a particular decision is proportional to the number of balls in the urn that correspond to that action choice. By adding or removing balls from an urn after each encounter, an agent's behavior is gradually adjusted. For signaling games, the sender has an urn Ω_t for each state $t \in T$, which contains balls for different messages $m \in M$. The number of balls of type m in urn Ω_t designated with $m(\Omega_t)$, the overall number of balls in urn Ω_t with $|\Omega_t|$. If the sender is faced with a state t she draws a ball from urn Ω_t and sends message m, if the ball is of type m. The same holds *mutatis mutandis* for the receiver. The resulting *response rules for RL-dynamics* are:

$$\sigma(m|t) = \frac{m(\Omega_t)}{|\Omega_t|} \quad (3) \qquad \rho(a|m) = \frac{a(\Omega_m)}{|\Omega_m|} \quad (4)$$

The learning dynamics are realized by changing the urn content dependent on the communicative success. In detail: if communication via t, m and a is successful, the number of balls in urn Ω_t is increased by $\alpha \in \mathbb{N}$ balls of type m and reduced by $\gamma \in \mathbb{N}$ balls of type $m' \neq m$. Similarly, for the receiver. In this way successful communicative behavior is more probable to reappear in subsequent rounds. In our experiments, all urns were initially filled with 100 balls and we set $\alpha = 10$ and $\gamma = 4$. From previous work (Mühlenbernd, to appear) we knew that in order to match the plasticity of different learning dynamics, we should consider BR-learners with *unbounded* memory but RL-learners with *bounded* memory. For that reason, an RL-learners' urns only reflected the impact of the last 300 interactions (irrespective of role) that the agent was engaged in. With an initially empty memory, BR-agents initially played entirely at random, just like their RL-cousins.

3. Network games: design and basic notions

We modeled a structured population as a β-graph. A β-graph is obtained by first considering a ring of nodes where each node is connected to its k nearest neighbors and subsequently, for each node, rewiring its k/2 left neighbors to a random vertex n with probability β (Watts & Strogatz, 1998). For our analysis, we created 10 such β-graphs with 300 nodes, $k = 6$ and $\beta \in \{.08, .09, .1\}$. These parameter choices ensured the small-worldliness of our networks that we had to keep small for obtaining enough data points at manageable computation costs. For each network, we ran 20 trials each with either only BR- or only RL-agents. Agents played the standard Lewis game. Communication happened randomly between neighbors on the network, and each agent's behavior was updated separately after each round of communication the agent was involved in. We recorded strategies of agents in suitably chosen regular intervals. Each trial ran until at least 90% of agents had acquired a language, or each network connection had been used 3000 times in either direction. The latter was to ensure a compromise between a short running time and sufficient time for learning, but also because we were interested in the results of learning after a realistic time-span, not in limit behavior.

Our main goal was to investigate the relationship between meaning evolution and social network structure. The theoretical challenge here lies in adequately characterizing local network roles in terms of formal notions of network connectivity, which can never be crisp, but must necessarily be of a probabilistic nature. For our present purposes, however, a rather straightforward cross-classification based on whether an agent is globally and/or locally well-connected turned out to have high explanatory value. Using suggestive terminology, we will be mainly concerned with two types of agents, *family men* and *globetrotters*. The former have tight local connections, with less global connections; the latter show the opposite pattern plus a high degree of connectivity.

In order to capture these notions more adequately, we look at suitable notions from social network theory (Jackson, 2008): *betweenness centrality* (BC), *closeness centrality* (CC), *degree centrality* (DC), *individual clustering* (CL) and *eccentricity* (EX).[a] High values for BC and CC, as well as low values of EX, characterize agents that are globally at a central position in the network. So, for a measure of *global connectedness* we looked at relative values of these properties. On the other hand, a high value for CL should be considered a measure for the agent's *local connectedness*. A high value for DC depicts a high degree of connectivity. Family men and globetrotters are thus characterized as follows:

	BC	CC	DC	EX	CL
family man	low	low	-	high	high
globetrotter	high	high	high	low	low

4. Results

Language regions. In order to determine which local network properties best characterize where, on average, learning would be most likely successful, we looked at what we will call *language regions*. A language region is a maximal subset of agents that have acquired the same language that forms a connected subgraph. Despite the different learning dynamics, our data confirmed Wagner's (2009) results that in small world networks like ours the number of language regions is small while the size of language regions is relatively big. Most of the time, two big language regions formed, one for each signaling convention. BR-dynamics, due to its slightly higher flexibility, was prone to produce a little more regional variability. On top of that, we also found that each connected language region of a given type had always a higher *average clustering* and *transitivity* value[b] than the expected average value for a connected subgraph with the same size n (= number of nodes), as depicted in Figure 1. We may conclude from this that local cliquishness supports the evolution of a local language.

[a]For the definition of BC, CC, DC and CL we refer to (Jackson, 2008), chapter 2. EX of a node v is the maximum distance from v to all other nodes in the graph.

[b]Given the (sub)-graph G: average clustering depicts the average CL value over all nodes in G and transitivity depicts the fraction of all possible triangles in G that are in fact in G.

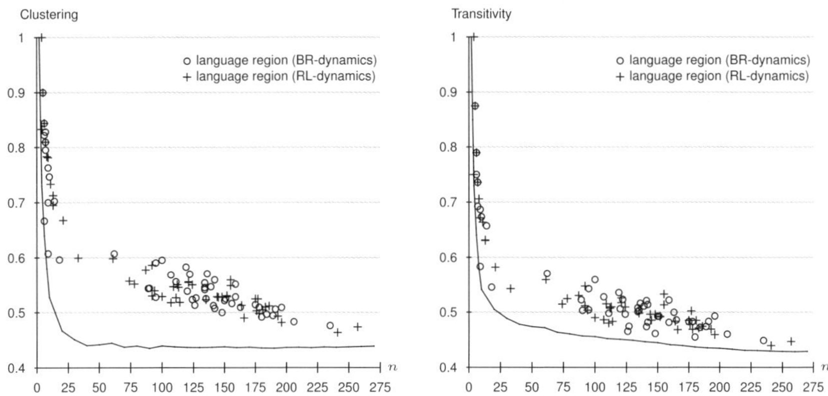

Figure 1. Comparing observed clustering and transitivity of language regions with expected values from randomly chosen connected subgraphs (solid lines, subgraph size along the x-axis).

Learners and border agents. Based on their learning success and network position, we classified agents into (i) *learners* vs. *non-learners* and (ii) *border agents* vs. *interior agents*. A learner is an agent who, by the end of a simulation run, has acquired the same signaling convention in both her sender and receiver role (for RL-agents this meant getting close enough to the pure strategy in question). Interior agents have only neighbors who learned the same language as they themselves, while border agents are agents whose neighborhood is not uniformly behaving in the same way that they do.

Our results were by and large the same for both learning dynamics: learners tend to be family men, border agents tend to be globetrotters (see Figure 2). Intuitively speaking, this means that in order to successfully learn a language in a social network an agent would have to be well embedded in a dense *local* structure. Globally well-connected agents, on the other hand, have difficulties learning a language in a heterogeneous network, because they might be torn between different locally firmly established conventions. (Naturally, the difference between interior and border agents also showed in the time course of learning: interior agents acquired their language significantly faster than border agents.)

Rationality. A certainly surprising result of our experiments was that the learning dynamics did not have much impact on the local network properties that characterize regional learning success. Phrased more strikingly, we could conclude that an agent's location in the network was more influential to his behavioral adaptation than his rationality. Still, there were, of course, notable differences between learning dynamics. The most obvious difference is that BR-learners settle into conventions much faster than RL-learners (see Figure 3).

	learn		non-learn	border		interior
			BR			
CL	0.452	$>$	0.427	0.404	$<$	0.488
CC	0.205	$<$	0.206	0.210	$>$	0.201
BC	0.013	$<$	0.014	0.017	$>$	0.010
DC	0.020	$\approx$	0.020	0.021	$>$	0.019
EX	7.699	$>$	7.672	7.584	$<$	7.786
			RL			
CL	0.453	$>$	0.423	0.405	$<$	0.488
CC	0.205	$<$	0.207	0.210	$>$	0.201
BC	0.013	$<$	0.015	0.017	$>$	0.009
DC	0.020	$\approx$	0.020	0.021	$>$	0.019
EX	7.700	$>$	7.653	7.573	$<$	7.800

Figure 2. Average local network properties of leaners vs. non-learners, and of border vs. interior agents by different learning dynamics. Symbols $<$, $>$, $\approx$ indicate whether differences in means are considered significant by a t-Test.

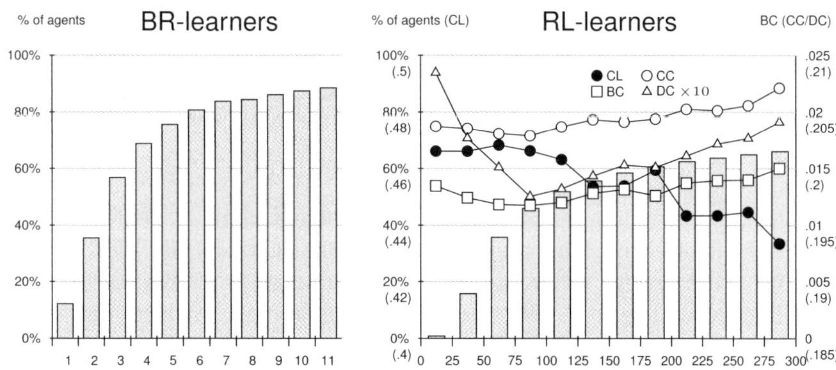

Figure 3. Temporal development of the proportion of agents having settled into their final language for both dynamics. The right picture also plots the average values for CL, BC, CC and DC for those RL-learners who have settled into their final language during the specified interval of rounds.

Founding fathers and stabilizers. The slower RL-dynamics moreover showed a very interesting connection between the temporal development of meaning formation and network structure (see Figure 3 on the right): there seem to be three phases of conventionalization which affect different network roles. In phase 1 (ca. 0-50) the first agents to adopt a convention, called *founding fathers*, have a much higher degree of connectivity (DC) as the agents of phase 2 (ca. 50-100), called *stabilizers*, who stabilize the language region around founding fathers. By comparing both groups, stabilizers are classical family men, whereas founding fathers are high-connected family men with more global influence. The last agents to adopt a convention, (after ca. 100 rounds) show more and more the mark of globetrotters. This suggests the interpretation that a convention is usually sparked by influential family men, while it takes a locally well-connected set of *real* family men to fix a meaning convention, so that it can also affect the globetrotters.

Conclusion. Our results showed that in small-world networks (realized by β-graphs) multiple language regions emerged and stabilized in each simulation run. Whereby the rationality of agents modeled by the appropriate learning dynamics influences the speed of learning, it rarely affects where conventions emerge and stabilize. We were able to show that instead global and local network properties have a deep impact on the particular realization of language regions.

References

Fagyal, Z., Swarup, S., Escobar, A. M., Gasser, L., & Lakkaraju, K. (2010). Centers and peripheries: Network roles in language change. *Lingua*, *120*, 2061–2079.

Huttegger, S. M. (2007). Evolution and the explanation of meaning. *Philosophy of Science*, *74*, 1–27.

Jackson, M. O. (2008). *Social and economic networks.* Princeton: Princeton University Press.

Ke, J., Gong, T., & Wang, W. S.-Y. (2008). Language change and social networks. *Communications in Computational Physics*, *3*(4), 935–949.

Lewis, D. (1969). *Convention.* Cambridge: Harvard University Press.

Mühlenbernd, R. (to appear). Learning with neighbours. *Synthese*, 1-23. (10.1007/s11229-011-9980-y)

Nowak, M. A., & Krakauer, D. (1999). The evolution of language. *PNAS*, *96*(14), 8028–8033.

Roth, A., & Erev, I. (1995). Learning in extensive-form games: experimental data and simple dynamic models in the intermediate term. *Games and Economic Behaviour*, *8*, 164–212.

Skyrms, B. (2010). *Signals: Evolution, learning & information.* Oxford: Oxford University Press.

Steels, L. (1997). The synthetic modeling of language origins. *Evolution of Communication*, *1*, 1–34.

Wagner, E. (2009). Communication and structured correlation. *Erkenntnis*, *71*, 377–393.

Watts, D. J., & Strogatz, S. H. (1998). Collective dynamics of small-world networks. *Nature*, *393*, 440–442.

Zollman, K. J. S. (2005). Talking to neighbors: The evolution of regional meaning. *Philosophy of Science*, *72*(1), 69–85.

HOMININ COOPERATION AND LANGUAGE EVOLUTION

ALBERT F. H. NACCACHE

Archaeology Department, Lebanese University, (ret.)
Beirut, Lebanon

The emergence of the specifically human life history stages of Childhood, Adolescence, and Postreproductive Lifespan must have affected hominin communities at the social, cognitive and communicative levels. Here we explore and try to identify what were the effects of the emergence of each new human life history stage on the social structures of hominin communities, then what were some of the effects of the new social structures on hominin distributed cognition, and, finally, what could these changes have meant for the evolution of the human linguistic communication system.

1. Introduction: Life History Stages and Language Evolution

The human life history cycle is markedly different from that of our closest relatives, the Great Apes. The latter comprises only three stages, Infant, Juvenile and Adult, while the human cycle is characterized by the addition of three derived stages, two of which, Childhood and Adolescence are evolutionary novelties unique to humans, and the third, Postreproductive Lifespan, is shared with big-bodied, big-brained and long-lived elephants, dolphins and whales, but not Great Apes (Hawkes and Paine, 2006). The human-specific life history stages emerged during the last two million years, the same evolutionary time frame of the emergence and accretion of the human linguistic communication system. However, research about the links between these two uniquely human developments has as yet barely scratched the subject's surface.

The first systematic effort to link human life history stages specifically to language evolution (Locke & Bogin, 2006) has not convinced in its particulars, and its account of the relationship between children and care-givers has been perceived as confused (Tallerman, 2008), while the "cooperative breeding hypothesis," a sustained effort to apply life history considerations to human evolution (Burkart, Hrdy & van Schaik, 2009; Hrdy, 2009), has as yet only presented hints about its potential implications for language evolution, hints which have, however, been favorably appraised (Knight & Power, 2010).

My purpose here is to explore the interplay of the evolution of human life history cycle with that of language. To do so, I will look at the social, cognitive and communicative implications on hominin societies of the emergence of Childhood, Postreproductive Lifespan and Adolescence. What were the effects of the emergence of each stage on the social structures of hominin communities? What were the main effects of the new social structures on hominin distributed cognition? And, finally, what might these changes have meant for language evolution? In view of the novelty of the multiple correlations attempted, only the briefest outline of answers will be presented.

2. Childhood

The human life history concept of Childhood refers to the age between weaning and permanent dentition, when the weaned infant is dependent on allomaternal care for survival and not yet a juvenile able to fend for herself (Hawkes & Paine, 2006; Bogin, 2009). There is a wide agreement that the "first shift in life history towards modern condition" was underway by 1.8 Mya (Foley & Gamble, 2009, p. 3270), and that "the life history of *H. erectus* included either a childhood stage for the first time or at least a significantly expanded childhood" (Nowell, 2010, p. S124; see also Gibbons, 2008).

By then, the body plan of *H. erectus* had been reorganized to something very similar to that of modern humans, with brain size in the 900 cc range, and nearly modern ratio of sexual dimorphism in size. These hominins were becoming proficient lithic tools manufacturers, displaying conscious planning (Stout, 2011), and were starting to climb up the predator's ladder. The generally accepted basis for approximating their social behavior is today's chimpanzee (Foley & Gamble, 2009, 3268). Chimpanzees have rich social relationships; adults occasionally play with infants and even adopt orphans, but relationships between adults and juveniles and/or infants are limited, and adults do not play with juveniles. Shared attention among chimpanzees takes place "horizontally," within groups whose members are of the same age, for instance when playing or patrolling. Still, this limited shared attention already sustains simple group-specific culturally transmitted behaviors, like the 42 identified so far.

By 1.8 Mya, the shift of hominin society away from competition and toward increased cooperation and sociality was such that cooperative breeding could sustain Childhood. At its incipience the childhood stage probably lasted for only a few months. However, for even such a short childhood to have been possible meant that *H. erectus* alloparents, adults helped by juveniles, must have engaged in systemic sustained collaborative interactions of association, exchange, shared attention and intention with children of the community other than their own. The gradual increase in the complexity of social relationships brought about by alloparenting led to a qualitative change in the deep social structure linking community members, and this by providing an inter-generational, 'vertical' link across age and sex subgroups (Hinde, 1976). This is the first of the few key additions to social structure from below, at the level of "families and descent groups," that distinguishes human from chimpanzee communities (Foley & Gamble, 2009, p. 3277). This pattern is taken for granted by us today, but its emergence revolutionized hominin communities.

To see how this "revolution" changed the basal hominin collective memory, we look at it in the distributed mind and/or cognition perspective (Johnson, 2001; Barrett & Henzi, 2005; Dunbar, Gamble & Gowlett, 2010). Collective memory is analyzed at three constitutive levels, the individual, the group and the cultural (Wang, 2008). At the individual level, we know that *H. erectus* brain size kept increasing, and so did, presumably, individual memory. At the group level, the new deep social layer that *H. erectus* society had acquired must have spread the distribution of collective memory among more of the group's individual constituents. And, given the cooperative cultural context generated by alloparents interacting with children, the scope of the potential content of a group's collective memory would have included a wider range of shared attention, intention and knowledge linked to the collective group behavior, be it for the construction of social reality or for interfacing with the environment. Thanks to the spread of shared attention and intention over most of the community members, hominin communities could develop, for the first time, "collective intentionality," the "glue of human culture," a shared intentional state that "may embrace any number of individuals, drawing them together into a loose unit of commonly held desires and plans" (Plotkin, 2011, p. 458). Collective intentionality "is not simply the sum of individual intentionalities making up a group and it is not reducible to them. It is the property of human social groups essential for the construction of social reality," and together with language, "one of the things that makes us human" (p. 458).

Collective intentionality is also intricately linked to language. The intimate sharing of attention between alloparents and children required a communication channel. If the basal hominin intentional communication system was still at the chimpanzee grade it would have had two modalities, fixed vocal displays and flexible gestural signals. The rich production of vocal displays is rigidly controlled, because they are "tightly tied to emotions," while "gestures are individually learned, intentionally and flexibly produced communicative signals" (Tomasello, 2008). Gestural signals could have provided the conduit for checking, following and directing attention required by alloparenting, and this because of the flexibility of their deployment and because they are ideally suited to implement pointing and other simple shared predications required to achieve child-adult-world triangulation, an essential building block of language (Bogdan, 2009). As illustrated by Bow, a 5 year old chimpanzee who initiated spontaneous gestural comments on topics of her own choice and expressed her own preferences (Katz, 2009), communication would have been bilateral. Gestures repeatedly used across generations by children who became alloparents would be integrated in the collective memory of the community.

With this system going, and since alloparents would not be compelled like chimpanzee mothers to keep the child in sight, the need of alloparents and children for communicating would have exerted a pressure to engage in the less proximity-constrained vocal displays. But, however good at imitation, the children would have been anatomically unable to fully reproduce the full-throated pant-hoots, grunts, barks and screams of the adults. Furthermore, the imitated utterances would not necessarily refer to the same emotional situations as those implied by the adult ones. We have in this the seeds of displacement and productivity, which, added to interchangeability, arbitrariness, specialization and cultural transmission already present in the basal hominin communication system, left the new "pre-language" hominin communication system just short of duality of patterning to display all of Hockett's "design features" of language.

3. Postreproductive Lifespan. Seniors

Menopause happens at the same age in chimpanzees and humans, and most probably the same holds for andropause, the age-related decrease of male testosterone levels. It is the hominin slower rate of somatic aging that increased the lifespan of *H. erectus* of both genders to an estimated 60 years (Bogin, 2009). I refer to the new social subgroup of hominin adults endowed with 10-plus vigorous postreproductive years (Gibbons, 2008) as "Seniors."

Cooperative breeding required intimate participation of males in hominin communities, increasing the probability that senior males would stay with their communities like senior females, and not become solitaries like their elephant and whale counterparts. The unprecedented pattern of interactions of seniors of both sexes with infants, children, juveniles and adults meant that a second major deep social structure had been added to *H. erectus* communities.

The effects of this new social structure on the community's memory would have been both simple and compound. The mere presence of seniors, with their great storehouses of accumulated knowledge, would have increased the collective memory of their groups, as happens to elephants' groups through their matriarchs (Penissi, 2001). Compound effects would be linked to the fact that now the community memory overlapped over three generations. First, due to the conservative nature of the seniors' memory, the collective memory would remain stable for longer periods. Secondly, there would be an increase in the total carrying capacity of the group collective memory because it would now be actively, consciously carried by a greater number of individuals. Furthermore, a regularly maintained and reproduced three-generation memory overlap would have made possible the expansion of the domain of shared predication, adding to child rearing and social grooming concerns those technological and social shared community activities that simple predication could carry. The resulting expansion in collective memory supported by increased shared understanding and communication might be what allowed hominin community to express and develop "mechanisms such as music, performance, language and codes of conduct employing second-order, social, emotions" (Gamble, Gowlett & Dunbar, 2011, p. 125). This can be timed with the increase in lithic variation displayed in the "Early Acheulean" (Stout, 2011) or "mode2B (Acheulean biface technology with enhanced symmetry)" (Foley & Gamble, 2009).

At first, the pre-language communication system achieved at the previous stage could have carried this enlarged collective memory. Nearly 50 years ago, Hockett and Ascher theorized that the shift from such a pre-language to full language happened when the pre-morphemes of pre-language began "to be listened to and identified not in terms of their acoustic gestalts but in terms of smaller features of sound that occurred in them in varying arrangements...," and "(w)ith this change, pre-morphemes became true morphemes, the features of sound involved became phonological components, and pre-language had become true language" (1964, p. 144), that is, a linguistic communication system exhibiting all the "design features" of language, including duality of patterning. Hockett and Ascher surmised that this shift had been the result of "a brilliantly successful 'mutation'" (p. 144). We would now surmise that this shift, positively selected for through culture, happened when the trend towards larger brains and neocortical connectivity crossed a threshold and the hominin brain had acquired the sensory powers needed to identify morphemes, as well as the ability to control their production (Lamb, 1998). The *terminus ante-quem* for the completion of this process would arguably be around 400,000 years ago, the present dating of both the emergence of "mode 3" (Foley & Gamble, 2009), and the acceleration in the accumulation rate of variations (Stout, 2011).

4. Adolescence

"Adolescence includes the years of postpubertal growth (approximately ages 10–18 years for girls and ages 12–21 years for boys, including the adolescent growth spurt)" (Bogin, 2009, p. 568). While the fundamental Darwinian-type selection behind Childhood was arguably decreased birth intervals, and Post-reproductive Lifespan was a byproduct of improved growth and development (Bogin, 2009), the selective pressure for Adolescence could only exist in a developed cultural environment, given that the primary function of the delayed growth spurt is to extend the length of the period of intense socialization. Adolescence is thus probably linked to early anatomically modern humans.

Adolescence is the period of peak inter-individual sociality: within the adolescents' peer-group; between adolescents and juveniles or children, as "babysitters" and supplementary food providers; or between adolescents and adults and/or seniors, as apprentices drawn in the formation of the apprenticeship bond. This is reflected in dramatic changes in behavior related to social cognition that happen in adolescence, paralleled by functional changes in the "social brain" structures responsible for the performance of social cognitive tasks (Blakemore, 2009). With the addition of adolescence, human society had acquired its last deep social structure related to life history stages.

We know the qualitative effect adolescence has on memory through the "reminiscence bump," the period of marked increase in memories of events formed during the transition from adolescence into adulthood, which is essential to the elaboration of social identity, at both the individual and collective levels (Wang, 2008). Adolescence is also linked to an increase in verbal fluency and pragmatic social cognitive abilities such as gossip, argumentation and verbal duels (Del Giudice, Angeleri, & Manera 2009). Also, adolescence is the period during which the drive to knowledge peaks, together with creativity and willingness to expend diligent efforts to learn through copying. All these characteristics of adolescence surely contributed to the elaboration of the social coordination aspect of language, through mechanisms begging further study.

But we can already infer a fundamental development in the nature of language acquisition and transmission directly related to adolescence. Before adolescence took roots in human society, language was acquired in a purely 'Vygotskian' epigenetic social immersion process of shared attention, which was the only source of anticipatory speaker-listener coupling, the prerequisite for shared understanding. And therefore the shared understanding was common to the whole group, and language was undifferentiated, non-specialized. In traditional hunter-gatherer societies, initiation is a socio-cultural ritual systematically linked to the community-sanctioned end of adolescence. When initiation started playing that role in *H. sapiens* societies, the community knowledge, and the words that carry it, became differentiated, with specialized knowledge domains accessible only to initiates. Investing words with knowledge and entwining them with rituals had the further advantage of increasing the stability of the community memory over longer stretches of time. The ratcheting effect of culture acquired greater traction, and the community knowledge could start to accumulate at accelerating rates.

5. Conclusion

From then on, Biological Evolution played no further role in Language Evolution, whose accretion was driven by purely socio-cultural mechanisms. The accumulation and maintenance of specialized and ecologically-relevant community knowledge is arguably what enabled the global expansion of *H. sapiens* across all ecological zones and landmasses of Earth. It is a common assumption that community knowledge was at first carried by storytellers. It is easy to imagine some community members becoming storytellers after having kept on perfecting their verbal ability over a long life while accumulating a large collection of representations of the physical, social and mental environments of their "People." The stories they collected and transmitted helped their People learn how to inhabit their world. In time, in the few favorable environments where settlements could be established, the dense cooperative networks of urban dwellers effected a quantum development: language *seen*, not *heard.* And exosomatic language tools accrued exponentially: writing, printing, internet ...

Hopefully, these glimpses at what the emergence of the specific human life history stages could have meant for the emergence and accretion of language will have indicated the potential fruitfulness of this avenue of research.

References

Barrett, L., & Henzi, P. (2005). The social nature of primate cognition, *Proc. R. Soc. B., 272*, 1865-1875.

Blakemore, S. J. (2008). The social brain in adolescence, *Nature Review, Neuroscience, 9*, 267-277.

Bogdan, R. J. (2009). *Predicative Minds. The Social Ontogeny of Propositional Thinking.* Cambridge, Mass. The MIT Press.

Bogin, B. (2009). Childhood, Adolescence, and Longevity: A Multilevel Model of the Evolution of Reserve Capacity in Human Life History, *American Journal of Human Biology, 21*, 567-577.

Burkart, J. M., Hrdy, S. B. & van Schaik, C. P. (2009). Cooperative Breeding and Human Cognitive Evolution," *Evolutionary Anthropology*, *18*, 175-186.

Del Giudice, M., Angeleri, R. & Manera, V. (2009). The juvenile transition: A developmental switch point in human life history, *Dev. Rev., 29*, 1-31.

Dunbar, R., Gamble, C. & Gowlett, J. (2010). *Social Brain, Distributed Mind.* Oxford. Oxford University Press.

Foley, R. & Gamble, C. (2009). The ecology of social transitions in human evolution, *Phil. Trans. R. Soc. B*, *364*, 3267-3279.

Gamble, C., Gowlett, J., & Dunbar, R. (2011). The Social Brain and the Shape of the Palaeolithic, *Cambridge Archaeological Journal*, *21(1)*, 115-125.

Gibbons, A. (2008). The Birth of Childhood, *Science*, *322*, 1040-1403.

Hawkes, K. & Paine, R. R. (2006). *The evolution of human life history*. Santa Fe. School of American Research Press.

Hockett, C. F., & Ascher, R. (1964). The Human Revolution, *Current Anthropology, 5(3)*, 135-168.

Johnson, C. M. (2001). Distributed primate cognition: a review, *Animal Cognition*, *4*, 167-183.

Katz, A. (2009). Communicative behavior of a five-year-old chimpanzee on the verge of a linguistic breakthrough, *www.lacus.org/volumes/34*

Knight, C. & Power, C. (2010). Cooperative Breeding Models: Implications for the Evolution of Language, *Evolang8*.

Lamb, S. M. (1998). *Pathways of the Brain. The Neurocognitive Basis of Language*. John Benjamins.

Locke, J & Bogin, B. (2006). Language and life history: A new perspective on the development and evolution of human language, *BBS*, *29*, 259-325.

Nowell, A. (2010). Working Memory and the Speed of Life, *Current Anthropology, 31*, S1, 121-133.

Plotkin, H. (2011). Human nature, cultural diversity and evolutionary theory, *Phil. Trans. R. Soc. B*, *366*, 454-463.

Pennisi, E. (2001). Elephant Matriarchs Tell Friend From Foe, *Science, 292*, 417-419

Stout, D. (2011). Stone toolmaking and the evolution of human culture and cognition, *Phil. Trans. R. Soc. B.*, *366*, 1050-1059.

Tallerman, M. (2008). Kin Selection and Linguistic Complexity, *Evolang7*

Tomasello, M. (2008). *Origins of Human Communication*. Cambridge, Mass. MIT Press.

Wang, Q. (2008). On the cultural constitution of collective memory, *Memory*, *16(3)*, 305-317.

MORPHING SOCIAL COMMUNICATION NETWORKS FROM CHIMPANZEE TO HUMAN TYPE

SARA A. NAJEM
Physics Department, McGill University, 3600, Montreal, H3A 2T8, Canada

JIHAD R. TOUMA
Physics Department, American University of Beirut, Beirut, Lebanon

ALBERT F. H. NACCACHE
Archaeology Department, Lebanese University, (ret.) Beirut, Lebanon

We present here a network model designed to check if the simple addition of structure through the diversification of social actors could progressively morph the random social communication networks of early *Homo* to the small-world communication networks of late Paleolithic hunter-gatherers (Naccache, 2012). The analysis of the network model confirmed the possibility of the transition, and in addition provided us with new insights in both the processes of network construction and of language evolution.

1. Introduction : Language and Communication Networks

Consider: Chimpanzees do not possess language and their social networks are random, while humans possess language and their social networks are of the small-world type. This situation, only recently apparent, presents a heuristic challenge at the intersection of Network Analysis and Language Evolution.

All networks had been assumed to be homologous since social networks started to be studied nearly a century ago (Boccaletti, Latora, Moreno, Chavez & Hwang, 2006). It is only in the last decade that progress in the theoretical studies of network structure revealed that networks could be assigned to four main kinds according to their connectivity properties: regular, random, scale-free and small-world (Watts & Strogatz, 1998; Barabási & Albert, 1999; Strogatz, 2001; Newman, 2003; Barabási, 2009). And it now appears that the chimpanzee social communication networks are of the random type (Lehman & Boesch, 2009; Clark, 2010), while human social networks have been found to be of the small-world type, and this both on theoretical grounds (Newman & Park, 2003; see also

Quillinan, Smith & Kirby 2010; Lusseau, Barrett & Henzi, 2011) and through ethnological studies of hunter-gatherers communities (Hamilton, Milne, Walker, Burger & Brown, 2007; Henrich & Broesch, 2011).

The scenario of language evolution that one of us is concurrently presenting at this conference (Naccache, 2012) lends itself very naturally to modeling, since it shares with Social Network Analysis a grounding in Hinde's conceptual framework of social relationships (Hinde, 1976; Brent, Lehmann & Ramos-Fernández, 2011). We therefore wondered if we could gain some new insights by translating this scenario in terms of networking dynamics. We report here on results which provide an affirmative answer to this exploratory query, and quite unexpectedly offer new insights into network construction.

2. Network Construction

Naccache's scenario (2012) proposes that the evolution of social communication networks from a basal hominin configuration, akin to that of the present-day chimpanzees, to those of hunter-gatherers happened through the successive diversification of the Great Apes life history stages of Infancy, Juveniles and Adults through the addition of the human specific life history stages of Childhood, Postreproductive Lifespan (Seniors) and Adolescence, and finally of Storytellers, a category which has only a social basis. Each diversification, apart from that of Seniors, preserves the demographics of its precedent stage, while adding one new actor with new connectivity properties.

The task at this early stage was to construct a model based on these evolving connectivity rules. All the metrics used to construct the model networks are presented in tables in the Appendices. The data used in Demographics (Table 4) and Geographical Ranges (Table 5) are simplified extrapolations from the literature. The connectivity percentages for the actors of the five stages of the scenario are presented in Table 1 to 3. These percentages stand for the probability that an individual from one category would intentionally, interactively and regularly communicate with another individual. The numbers used here are educated guesses inferred from the ethological and ethnological literature. However, tweaking these numbers in the models has shown that they are at least coherent among themselves and relatively robust, i.e., the models are not much affected by minor changes as long as the distributional proportions are roughly maintained.

It should be noted that range as we defined it here is a composite measure, reflecting a physical ability as well as knowledge and memory that allow an individual to range over a given ecological zone. This ambiguity is acceptable in the context of the present proof-of-concept exploration. The same context accounts for limiting the modeling to two groups in contact. Initial modeling with up to 5 groups showed that once a critical number of individuals is reached, here 100, the simulations are not influenced by further number increase.

2.1. *Matrices and Visualization*

Links between members (nodes) of a population of size N are encoded in an $N \times N$ connection matrix (with N between 25 and 50). The entry at (i, j) in the connection matrix sets the number of links from node i to node j. At most one link is allowed between any two nodes, resulting in matrices of zeroes and ones. Networks and associated matrices are constructed using Matlab©; then imported to Gephi (Gephi.org ©) for visualization on a flat, featureless terrain. A sample of a hundred networks is generated for statistical analysis at each stage.

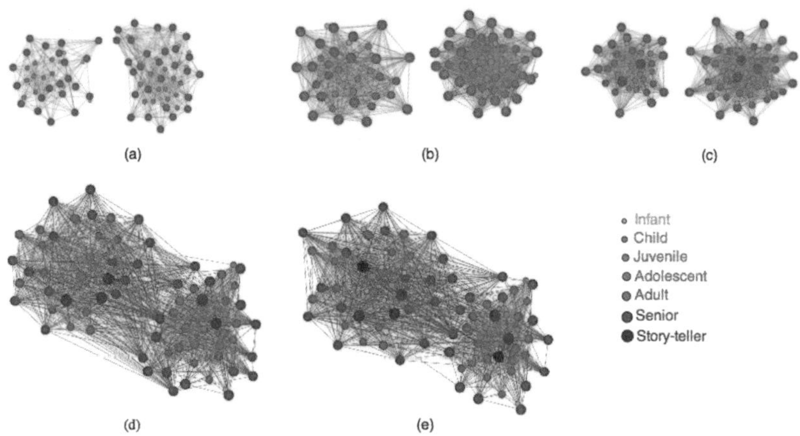

Figure 1.

3. Network Characterization

Networks are characterized by their Clustering Coefficient, C, Average Path Length, l, and Node Degree, k (Newman, 2003). C measures transitivity in a network. Three nodes form a triangle if they are all connected, a triplet if one of the links is missing. C at a given node is defined to be proportional to the ratio of the number of triangles to the number of triplets. l is a measure of the efficiency of communication in a network. It is proportional to the average of the shortest paths connecting all pairs in the population. k measures the number of links at a given node, while p_j is the distribution of node degrees over the network. Together, C, l, k and p_j determine the type of a network. Small-world networks display C similar to regular networks, but have a much lower l, while p_j is binomial in random networks, but right-skewed in small-world, whereas it follows a power law in scale-free networks.

Furthermore, as a proxy for information flow, we measured the variation of Entropy in our model (Suzuki, Buck & Tyak, 2005). Entropy is a measure of the unpredictability of an event. Predictable events do not contribute to our knowledge, while unlikely and/or less probable events do. In the present case, the probability of the occurrence of an event stands for the probability of a link formation. Improbable links increase the overall unpredictability of the network and therefore its entropy, while definite links have zero entropy.

4. Network Analysis

The main results of our analysis are summarized in Fig. 2 and 3. The discontinuity in Fig. 2(a) reflects the fact that prior to stage 4, the two groups in our network are disconnected, and l is calculated separately for each group. We note a sharp decrease with childhood at stage 2 followed by a smaller drop to stage 3. By stage 4, l can be globally defined. Its large value at stage 4 reflects local (short) links between the groups introduced by adolescents. The addition of storytellers brought about a small but significant drop in l. Fig. 2(b) shows a steep increase in C with the emergence of childhood in stage 2, followed by relatively small and non-significant variations. Entropy, not shown here, exhibited a continuous increase with stages, the sharpest of which happens at the stage 5.

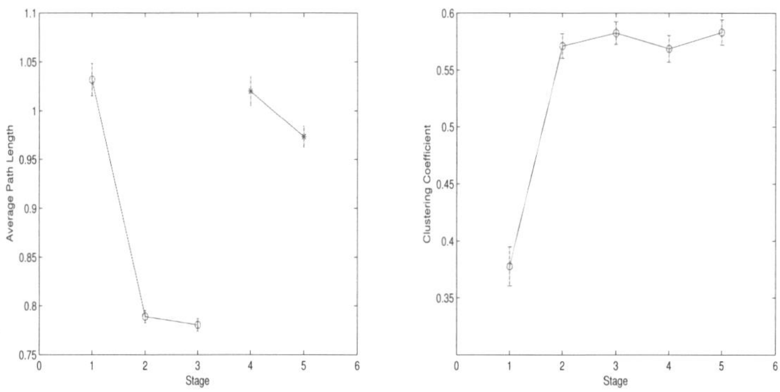

(a) (b)

Figure 2.

Our starting point was the overlaying of a collection of three random subnetworks representing Infants, Juveniles and Adults. At each subsequent stage, one of these subnetworks was split in two. This network growth process is distinct from the formal rewiring procedure introduced by Watts and Strogatz (1998), therefrom WS, or the preferential attachment prescription of Barabási and Albert (1999). To check the significance of the value of C and l of our network construction we mapped them onto those of WS. Mapping relied on the following steps. A graph of fixed size N is distinguished by (C, l) depending exclusively on the choice of (k, α). As we specify k, and allow α to span the interval [0,1], we generate all network types which are now set apart by their values on the

$C(k, \alpha)$ and $l(k, \alpha)$ curves. Each of our steps is characterized by (C_s, l_s) for a given average degree k_s and standard deviation σ. Those are then located on appropriate $C(k, \alpha)$, $l(k, \alpha)$ of the WS construction. By simultaneously changing $k \in [k_s - \sigma, k_s + \sigma]$ and α, we ran an exhaustive check to ascertain the pair (k, α) that yields (C, l) comparable to (C_s, l_s). To determine the network type of our stages 4 and 5 we then compared their C_s and l_s with those of a random and regular graphs respectively with same N, and k, as determined by the mapping. The high C and low l at stages 4 and 5 put the associated networks in the

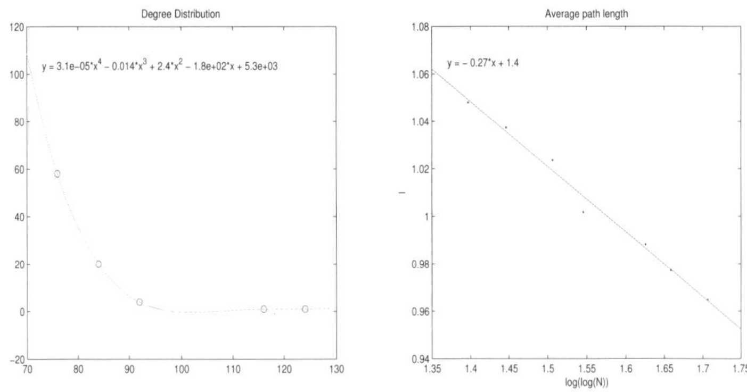

(a) (b)

Figure 3.

small-world/scale-free category. Further tests on the scaling of l with network size were run to differentiate between the two types. l for stage 4 networks showed a $log(log(N))$ dependence on size (Fig. 3(b)). This, together with the power law behavior in the tail of their degree distribution (Fig. 3(a)), identifies stage 4 networks as scale-free. On the other hand, l of stage 5 networks showed a $log(N)$ variation with size, which along with their location on the WS sequence, unambiguously identified them as small-scale networks.

A quite unexpected, but very interesting result is that by successively differentiating actors (node categories), we reproduced the WS family of rewired networks, albeit through a new, alternative route to the sequence identified by WS construction spanning from regular to random networks.

5. Conclusions and future research

In conclusion, this little toy model of the evolution of social communication network has shown us that it is possible to morph in 4 steps the social structure of chimpanzee social networks into a social configuration formally congruent with that attested today for hunter-gatherers communities.

More importantly, it highlighted the importance of Childhood in the process, that is the importance of the transition from chimpanzee atomism and aggression to cooperatively breeding social groups. The Childhood stage of our model started the process of morphing the random chimpanzee-grade network into small-world type. It is the basis upon which linguistic communication, a cooperative behavior, could develop.

Finally, it strongly suggests that life history (biological) factors are not enough by themselves to drive the process, and that socio-cultural factors must have played a decisive role at at least two stages. First, something like socially uninhibited adolescents is needed to overcome the lack of inter-groups social communication, a feat not achieved by chimpanzee groups who practice philopatry and female dispersals. Simply moving young adult females from one group to another remains a "socially silent structure" (Chapais, 2011), and does not allow intergroup socialization or communication. Secondly, to attain the full characteristics of small-world networks, a purely social and cultural step is needed, here provided by the storytellers, who play the role of communication hubs.

This scenario of how hominin societies achieved the release from the constraint of proximity that distinguishes them from chimpanzee society (Foley & Gamble, 2009) is defensible and does the job assigned to it, but there might be other scenarios that would achieve the same result.

Now that this toy model is debugged, our next project is to use it to explore more realistic intergroup interactions, that is, to probe for the criteria that sets the limits of the active human social networks at 150 members and of the megaband at 500 (Grove, 2010, 407).

6. Appendices (see sec. 2. Network Construction)

Table 1. Stage 1

	Infants (0-7yrs)	Juveniles (7-18yrs)	Adults $\supset$ (18-45yrs)	Mothers$_j$ (18-45yrs)
Infants$_i$	0	0	0	δ_{ij}
Juveniles	0	0.9	0	0
Adults	0	0	0.3	0.3
Mothers$_j$	δ_{ij}	0	0.3	0.3

$\delta_{ij} = 1$ if $i = j$ and 0 otherwise.

Table 2. Stage 2

	Infants$_i$ (0-3yrs)	Children (3-7yrs)	Juveniles (7-18yrs)	Adults $\supset$ (18-45yrs)	Mothers$_j$ (18-45yrs)
Infants$_i$	0	0.5	0	0.1	δ_{ij}
Children	0.5	0.9	0.4	0.2	1
Juveniles	0	0.4	0.9	0.3	1
Adults	0.1	0.2	0.3	0.4	0.4
Mothers$_j$	δ_{ij}	1	1	0.4	0.4

Table 3. Stages 3, 4 and 5.

	Infants$_i$ (0-3yrs)	Children (3-7yrs)	Juveniles (7-12yrs)	Adolescents (12-18yrs)	Adults $\supset$ (18-45yrs)	Mothers$_j$ (18-45yrs)	Seniors (45-70yrs)	Storytellers (45-70yrs)
Infants$_i$	0	0.5	0	0	0.1	δ_{ij}	0.1	0.1
Children	0.5	0.9	0.4	0.5	0.2	1	0.5	0.8
Juveniles	0	0.4	0.9	0.2	0.3	1	0.2	0.8
Adolescents	0	0.5	0.2	0.9	0.5	0.5	0.2	0.8
Adults	0.1	0.2	0.3	0.5	0.4	0.4	0.3	0.8
Mothers$_j$	δ_{ij}	1	1	0.5	0.4	0.4	0.3	0.8
Seniors	0.1	0.5	0.2	0.2	0.3	0.3	0.2	0.8
Storytellers	0.1	0.8	0.8	0.8	0.8	0.8	0.8	0.8

Table 4. Demographics

	Stage 1	Stage 2	Stage 3	Stage 4	Stage 5
Infants	20%	10%	10%	10%	10%
Children	0%	10%	10%	10%	10%
Juveniles	30%	30%	30%	15%	15%
Adolescents	0%	0%	0%	15%	15%
Adults	50%	50%	40%	40%	40%
Seniors	0%	0%	10%	10%	8%
Storytellers	0%	0%	0%	0	2 %

Table 5. Geographical Ranges

	Stage 1	Stage 2	Stage 3	Stage 4	Stage 5
Infants	10 km	10 km	10 km	10 km	10 km
Children	–	6-8 km	6-8 km	6-8 km	6-8 km
Juveniles	8 km	8 km	8 km	8 km	8 km
Adolescents	–	–	–	16 km	16 km
Adults	12 km	12 km	12 km	12 km	12 km
Seniors	–	–	5-6 km	5-6 km	5-6 km
Storytellers	–	–	–	–	5-6 km

References

Barabási, A-L. and Albert, R (1999). Emergence of Scaling in Random Networks. *Science, 286*, 509-512 .

Barabási, A-L. (2009). Scale-Free Networks: A Decade and Beyond. *Science, 325*, 412-413 .

Boccaletti, S., Latora, V., Moreno, Y., Chavez, M. and Hwang, D.-U. (2006).Complex networks: Structure and dynamics, *Physics Reports, 424*, 175 308.

Brent, L., Lehmann, J. and Ramos-Fernández, G. (2011). Social Network Analysis in the Study of Nonhuman Primates: A Historical Perspective. *American Journal of Primatology ,73*, 720-730.

Chapais, B. (2011). The Deep Social Structure of Humankind, *Science, 331*, 1276-1277.

Clark, F. E. (2010). Space to Choose: Network Analysis of Social Preferences in a Captive Chimpanzee Community, and Implications for Management. *American Journal of Primatology, 71*, 1-10.

Foley, R. and Gamble, C. (2009). The ecology of social transitions in human evolution, *Phil. Trans. R. Soc. B*, 364, 3267-3279.

Grove, M. (2010). The Archaeology of Group Size, in Dunbar, R., Gamble, C. & Gowlett, J., *Social Brain, Distributed Mind* (pp. 391-411) Oxford: Oxford University Press.

Hamilton, M. J., Milne, B. T., Walker, R. S., Burger, O. and Brown, J. H. (2007). The complex structure of hunter-gatherer social networks, *Proc. R. Soc. B, 274*, 2195-2203.

Henrich, J. and Broesch, J. (2011). On the nature of cultural transmission networks: evidence from Fijian villages for adaptive learning biases. *Phil. Trans. R. Soc. B, 366*, 1139-1148.

Hinde, R. A. (1976). Interactions, Relationships and Social Structure, *Man, ns,11/1*, 1-17.

Lehmann J. and Boesch C. (2009). Sociality of the dispersing sex: the nature of social bonds in West African female chimpanzees, *Animal Behaviour 77* 377387.

Lusseau, D., Barrett, L. and Henzi, S. (2011). Formalising the multidimensional nature of social networks. *<arXiv:1101.3735v1>* [physics.soc-ph]

Naccache, A. F. (2012). Hominin cooperation and language evolution, *Evolang9.*

Newman, M. E. J. (2003). The structure and function of complex networks. *SIAM Review, 45*, 167-256.

Newman, M. E. J. and Park, J. (2003). Why social networks are different from other types of networks, *Physical Review, E, 68*, 036122.

Quillinan, J., Kirby, S. & Smith, K. (2010). Co-evolution of language and social network structure through cultural transmission. *Evolang8.*

Strogatz, S. H. (2001). Exploring complex networks, *Nature, 410*, 268-275.

Suzuki, R., Buck J. R. and Tyack, P. L. (2006). Information entropy of humpback whale songs. *J. Acoust. Soc. Am, 119 (3)*,1849-1866.

Watts, D. and Strogatz, S. H. (1998). Collective dynamics of 'small-world' networks, *Nature 393*, 440-442.

GESTURE AND THE ORIGINS OF LANGUAGE

DILLON NIEDERHUT

Department of Anthropology, University of California at Berkeley, 232 Kroeber Hall Berkeley, 94720-3710, United States of America

Manual gestures have been argued to be an evolutionary precursor to fully linguistic, vocal language in the genus *Homo*. It is possible that, in these particular historical scenarios, the bimodal nature of human utterance and the heterogeneous nature of both spoken language and visuospatial gesture have not been considered. Evidence from functional imaging studies suggests that codified signs are processed by a shared, modality-independent cortical network that is not activated by iconic gestures, pointing, or other forms of utterance. We conclude that the neurological evidence does not speak in favor of a gesture-first origin of human language.

1. Introduction

Many accounts concerning the evolution of language have focused on gesture as a precursor to spoken language. This is an attractive hypothesis because any two humans can quickly establish a basic system of communication using pointing and pantomime (Tomasello 2006) even when they do not speak the same language, and because humans are not the only primates to employ gesture as a means of communication, which has been observed in chimpanzees, mandrills, and capuchins (Laidre 2011; Perry 2011). In other words, gesture came first, but how that relates to the evolution of language remains an open question, especially since the kinds of gesture used spontaneously produced by non-human primates are not necessarily the same as those hypothesized to have led to signed systems of communication (Cartmill, Beilock, & Goldin-Meadow 2012).

For the purposes of this paper, we are concerned with scenarios that posit a causal link between early gesture and the evolution of fully codified communication. Gentilucci and Corballis (2006) argue that language began with iconic gestures, which were understood via fronto-parietal mirror neuron activity in the listener (see Rizzolatti & Sinigaglia 2010). This transitioned into gestures performed by the mouth and throat, after which they became vocal. Tomasello (2006) puts forth a similar argument, where spoken language began as pantomime gestures that became codified via a “drift toward the arbitrary”. Armstrong and Wilcox likewise posit a beginning for language in iconic gesture, except now it becomes codified via a process of ritualization within each individual (2007).

However, as Kendon (2010) notes, there are no human cultures besides those of the congenitally deaf which forgo spoken language and communicate only via gesture. This is not what we should expect if spoken language is a relatively recent development built upon a ubiquitous and successful visuomanual communication system (e.g. writing is a recent development based on speech and some cultures are not literate). Furthermore, all spoken languages in practice use gestures concomitantly with their vocalization, and not one instead of the other. As research groups in the gesture community have established, both gesture and speech have variants that cover linguistic and non-linguistic forms of communication (see McNeill 1992 on Kendon's Continuum, Duncan 2003 on Bolinger). If spoken language was built on top of the codified part of a gesture system, we would not expect spoken language to include counterparts to all of the non-linguistic gestural forms.

2. Defining Gesture

For the purpose of this discussion, we will consider gesture as a motor behavior perceived in the visuospatial domain that can be understood to convey an idea and is "deliberately expressive" (Kendon 2004). This is intended to include McNeill's definition of co-speech gesture along with emblems and pointing (2005). As researchers of gesture have been careful to articulate, one of its most important features is diversity.

When we say 'conveys an idea', we mean that gesture serves as a small but effective prompt to elicit a concept, whether in the mind of the gesturer or an observer. A recent meta-analysis examining benefits of bimodal utterance showed that gesture appears to strongly aid an observer's understanding of a visual or motoric concept (Hostetter 2011). This effect was increased when the gesture was related to information not available in the auditory modality). Likewise, Krauss has shown that gesture can serve as an aid for the gesturer (2001). Gestures are observed in signers, where they also convey non-redundant information (Liddell & Metzger 1998), even though the modality is the same.

However, we cannot say that gesture is a phenomenon subservient to speech or sign production, as it is also used to manage cognitive resources. Speakers can use hand and arm movements to "offload" concepts about spatial relations from working memory, allowing for greater resources to spent on other tasks (for review, see Goldin-Meadow & Wagner 2005). They have also documented instances of gesture-speech mismatches, in which the gestures performed while explaining how the solution to a problem appear to demonstrate the correct understanding of that problem, yet do not match the spoken explanation.

We have said that gestures convey concepts, but the content is not necessarily distinct from speech. Batons or beats, in which the speaker moves a hand or arm in a rhythmic fashion, do not necessarily convey a separate meaning in utterance. However, as McNeill points out, they can change the pragmatic meaning of vocal utterance (1992).

Note that each of the purposes we have attributed to visuospatial gestures can also be provided by vocalizations. We can use the auditory modality to offload cognitive resources, e.g. reciting a phone number. It can also be used to add non-redundant information to gestures, such as describing landmarks when giving directions. Thus, gestures appear to serve the same purposes as vocal utterance. To further this argument, let us consider several different forms of gesture and how they are matched in the vocal modality.

An EMBLEM, or quotable gesture, is a conventionalized sign that stands for a word, or phrase. Common examples include the American *okay* sign, nodding, and shrugging the shoulders. Researchers have long recognized that emblems are culturally codified in a manner similar to spoken language (beginning with David Efron in the 70s, see Kendon 2004).

An ICONIC gesture is one that indicates a referent by resemblance. Icons appear to be more common in gesture than in spoken language, perhaps because the visuospatial modality is more amenable to iconic representations (Sweetser 2008). In spoken language, iconicity is present as onomatopoeia, but may also include phrase ordering among other things.

POINTING is a deictic gesture which indicates a particular object, group, or location, especially to distinguish them from other objects, groups, or locations. In the vocal modality, this can be accomplished with the use of demonstrative pronouns.

INTERACTIONAL GESTURES manage discourse by moderating the interaction between two or more people. Examples include the fingers together palm forward gesture which indicates that one would like the other person to stop or wait. In spoken language, the course of an interaction can be managed with words (e.g. *stop* or *excuse me*), as well as non-linguistic vocalizations such as the extraneous *uh* or *um*.

BEATS or BATONS are rhythmic arm movements. This is accomplished in the vocal modality by fluctuations in amplitude and rate of phoneme production. Prosody is also capable of changing the pragmatic interpretation of an utterance. Goodwin documents an aphasic patient who is able to request that his wife tell a story using only the words *yes*, *no*, and *and* (1995).

In conclusion, the diversity of both function and form in vocal and visuomanual utterance appear to be matched one-to-one. In other words, gesture is not only iconicity and pantomime; neither is vocalization only codified signs. They appear to covary with respect to their purpose, form, and linguistic content.

3. Language and the Brain

While evidence for localization of function in the nervous system extend back at least to the ancient Romans (Finger 2000), the first arguments for localization of language began with Paul Broca (1861). Since then, production and comprehension of codified language has been broadly localized to two areas, referred to as BROCA'S AREA and WERNICKE'S AREA (see Lecours, Lhermitte, & Bryans 1983 for review), with other areas that become active dependent on context. Broca's area, located in the posterior inferior frontal gyrus, appears to be critical for understanding and producing grammatically correct speech. Wernicke's area, which includes the posterior superior temporal gyrus and in some accounts the supramarginal and angular gyri as well, has been implicated in understanding and producing words (for a more recent example, see Sahin, Pinker, Cash, Schomer, & Halgren 2009).

Given that gesture uses different muscle groups and is perceived in a different sensory modality than vocalization, gesture will necessarily involve different cortical motor and sensory regions for production and comprehension. There have been some arguments that, because patients with Broca's aphasia also experience difficulty gesturing, Broca's area must be the center for some sort of generalized language function; however, research has shown that trauma tends to impair gesture along with speech production because motor areas for hand and arm movements are located next to motor areas for mouth movements in the frontal lobe and not because they rely on the same network (Papagno, Sala, & Basso 1993). That is, if Broca's aphasiacs have difficulty gesturing, it is because they have difficulty moving their arms and hands to do anything (apraxia). More recent work has shown that non-verbal semantic processing (and not the ability to produce fluent speech) is predictive of the ability to gesture (Hogrefe, Ziegler, Weidinger, & Goldenberg 2011), and furthermore that individuals with difficulty speaking tend to gesture more than their vocalizing counterparts as a means of compensation (Gullberg, de Bot, & Volterra 2008).

Generally speaking, gesture recruits a mirror neuron system based on visuomotor experience. This system includes the lateral occipitotemporal (OT), posterior superior temporal sulcus (STS), and anterior intraparietal sulcus (aIP), which have been reported in other studies to be associated with the analysis of motion, biological motion and representation of intention/goals, respectively (Allison, Puce, & McCarthy 2000; Hamilton & Grafton 2006; Klaes, Westendorff, Chakrabarti, & Gail 2011). Individuals with autism spectrum disorder show anatomical abnormalities in these areas (Zilbovicius, Meresse, Chabane, Brunelle, Samson, & Boddaert 2006), which is consistent with them being necessary for understanding the goals and states of others. Different studies have shown that gesture variably recruits the STS bilaterally along with the left aIP (Hubbard, Wilson, Callan, & Dapretto 2009), the left posterior STS along with the angular gyrus (in Wernicke's area) and the premotor area

(Skipper, Goldin-Meadow, Nusbaum, & Small 2009), and both the STS and lateral OT in both hemispheres (Dick, Goldin-Meadow, Hasson, Skipper, & Small 2009).

It will be important to bear in mind that the following results are based on intraindividual subtractive fMRI studies where the participants were usually viewing (i.e. not producing) gestures. These kinds of studies can be subject to rough localization due to summed individual variability, and conflicting findings depending on the baseline condition used in subtraction. Thus, these results do not reveal whole networks, and comparisons across studies should be read with some skepticism. We will discuss most of the gesture types listed above.

Emblems have been shown to recruit the left posterior inferior frontal gyrus, in hearing subjects (Lindenberg, Uhlig, Scherfeld, Schlaug, & Seitz 2011). In deaf subjects emblematic gestures recruit classic perisylvian language areas in native ASL signers. The authors concluded that emblems are not notably different from ASL signs in their cortical representation (Husain, Patkin, Thai-Van, Braun, & Horowitz 2009).

Iconic gestures appear to activate the bilateral STS, and the left STS (Holle, Obleser, Rueschemeyer, & Gunter 2010). Another study has shown activation in Wernicke's area along with supplementary motor areas, but the authors' definition of an iconic gesture differs from the previous paper (Green et al. 2009). It is not entirely clear what this represents beyond analysis of biological motion, but classic language areas are either not active, or are recruited less strongly than in emblems or signing.

Pointing has been shown to activate the left aIP and left lateral OT (Pierno et al. 2009), which may represent following a line to a target. Another study reported activation in right posterior STS and right medial prefrontal cortex (de Langavant et al. 2011). A study on eye-pointing reported activity bilaterally in the STS and aIP, suggesting that pointing with the eyes and hands share a processing path in humans (Hadjikhani, Hoge, Snyder, & Gelder 2008).

Beats have been shown to mediate the auditory response to language via activation in the left planum temporale, which is adjacent to the primary auditory area, supporting the argument that they serve as visual prosodic modifiers (Hubbard, Wilson, Callan, & Dapretto 2009). This is corroborated by a study showing the effect of visual stimuli on music perception (Schulz & Lipscomb 2007).

What we have seen in these functional imagining data is different forms of gesture using different cortical networks, but also that some of the vocal-manual form pairs share systems. Emblems, which are codified like linguistic speech and signs, are neurally represented like them. Iconic gestures, which are not codified but are still governed by social convention (Kendon 2004) do not recruit the classic language areas to the same extent as emblems. Non-codified gestures, such as pointing and beats use processing paths that may be shared with vocal forms of deixis and prosody.

4. Conclusions

Both gesture and speech are communication systems which can express culturally codified signs, icons, and prosody. Both gesture and speech share cortical systems that are appropriate for the form of utterance they analyze, and appear to diverge only in modality specific systems. If the ability to produce spoken, codified language was built on top of iconic gesture or pantomime, we would expect that vocalizations and gesture would not be constitutively co-expressed and that vocal utterance would be restricted to codified forms. Furthermore, the anatomically and functionally distinct systems used by these forms are more consistent with pre-existing neurological functions that were exapted for the broad purpose of communication regardless of modality, and not a single system that incrementally added specialized iconic and linguistic areas.

Acknowledgements

The author thanks the anonymous reviewers for their insightful comments. This paper is based in part on work supported by the National Science Foundation, grant # DGE 1106400.

References

Alibali M, Kita S. (2010). Gesture highlights perceptually present information for speakers. *Gesture 10*, 3-28.

Allison T, Puce A, McCarthy G. (2000). Social perception from visual cues: role of the STS region. *Trends in Cognitive Science 4*, 267-278.

Armstrong D & Wilcox S. (2007). *The Gestural Origin of Language*. New York: Oxford University Press.

Broca P. (1861). Loss of speech, chronic softening and partial destruction of the anterior left lobe of the brain. *Bulletin de la Société Anthropologique 2*, 235-238.

Cartmill E, Beilock S, Goldin-Meadow S. (2012). A word in the hand: action, gesture, and mental representation in humans and non-human primates. *Philosophical Transactions of the Royal Society B 367*, 129-143.

De Langavant L, Remy P, Trinkler I, McIntyre J, Dupoux E, Berthoz A, Bachoud-Lévi. (2011). Behavioral and neural correlates of communication via pointing. *PLoS ONE 6*, e17719.

Dick A, Goldin-Meadow S, Hasson U, Skipper J, Small S. (2009). Co-speech influence neural activity in brain regions associated with processing semantic information. *Human Brain Mapping 30*, 3509-3526.

Duncan S. (2003). Gesture in language: issues for sign language research. In Emmorey K (Ed). *Perspectives on Classifier Constructions in Sign Language*. Mahwah: Lawrence Erlbaum Associates.

Finger S. (2000). *Minds Behind the Brain: A history of the pioneers and their discoveries*. New York: Oxford University Press.

Gentilucci M, Corballis M. (2006). From manual gesture to speech: A gradual transition. *Neuroscience and Biobehavioral Reviews 30*, 2006.

Goldin-Meadow S, Wagner S. (2005). How our hands help us learn. *Trends in Cognitive Sciences 9*, 234-241.

Goodwin C. (1995). Co-constructing meaning in conversations with an aphasic man. *Research on language and social interaction 28*, 233-260.

Green A, Straube B, Weis S, Jansen A, Willmes K, Konrad K, Kircher T. (2009). Neural integration of iconic and unrelated coverbal gestures: a functional MRI study. *Human Brain Mapping 30*, 3309-3324.

Gullberg M, de Bot K, Volterra V. (2008). Gestures and some key issues in the study of language development. *Gesture 8*, 149-179.

Hadjikhani N, Hoge R, Snyder J, Gelder B. (2008). Pointing with the eyes: The role of gaze in communicating danger. *Brain and Cognition 68*, 1-8.

Hamilton A, Grafton S. (2006). Goal representation in human anterior intraparietal sulcus. *Journal of Neuroscience 26*, 1133-1137.

Hogrefe K, Ziegler W, Weidinger N, Goldenberg G. (2011). Non-verbal communication in severe aphasia: Influence of aphasia, apraxia, or semantic processing? *Cortex*, epub ahead of print.

Holle H, Obleser J, Rueschemeyer S, Gunter T. (2010) Integration of iconic gestures and speech in left superior temporal areas boosts speech comprehension under adverse listening conditions. *NeuroImage 49*, 875-884.

Hostetter A. (2011). When do gestures communicate? A meta-analysis. *Psychological Bulletin 137*, 297-315.

Hubbard A, Wilson S, Callan D, Dapretto M. (2009). Giving speech a hand: Gesture modulates activity in auditory cortex during speech perception. *Human Brain Mapping 30*, 1028-1037.

Husain F, Patkin D, Thai-Van H, Braun A, Horwitz B. (2009). Distinguishing the processing of gestures from signs in deaf individuals: an fMRI study. *Brain Research 1276* 140-150.

Kendon A. (2004). *Gesture: Visible action as utterance*. New York: Cambridge University Press.

Kendon A. (2010). Language's matrix. *Gesture 9*, 355-372.

Klaes C, Westendorff S, Chakrabarti S, Gail A. (2011). Choosing goals, not rules: deciding among rule-based action plans. *Neuron 70*, 536-548.

Krauss R. (2001). Why do we gesture when we speak? *Current Directions in Psychological Science 7*, 54-59.

Laidre M. (2011). Meaningful gesture in monkeys? Investigating whether mandrills create social culture. *PLoS ONE 6*, e14610.

Lecours A, Lhermitte F, Bryans B. (1983). *Aphasiology*. East Sussex: Baillière Tindall.

Liddell S, Metzger M. (1998). Gesture in sign language discourse. *Journal of Pragmatics 30*, 657-697.

Lindenberg R, Uhlig M, Scherfeld D, Schlaug G, Seitz R. (2011). Communication with emblematic gestures: Shared and distinct neural correlates of expression and reception. *Human Brain Mapping*, epub ahead of print.

McNeill D. (1992). *Hand and Mind: What gestures reveal about thought.* Chicago: University of Chicago Press.

McNeill D. (2005). *Gesture & Thought*. Chicago: University of Chicago Press.

Papagno C, Sala S, Basso A. (1993). Ideomotor apraxia without aphasia and aphasia without apraxia: the anatomical support for a double dissociation. *Journal of Neurology and Psychiatry 56*, 286-289.

Perry S. (2011). Social traditions and social learning in capuchin monkeys (Cebus). *Philosophical Transactions of the Royal Society B 366*, 988-996.

Pierno A, Tubaldi F, Turella L, Grossi P, Barachino L, Gallo P, Castiello U. (2009). Neurofunctional modulation of brain regions by the observation of pointing and grasping actions. *Cerebral Cortex 19*, 367-374.

Rizzolatti G, Sinigaglia C. (2010). The functional role of the parieto-frontal mirror circuit: interpretations and misinterpretations. *Nature Reviews Neuroscience 11*, 264-274.

Sahin N, Pinker S, Cash S, Schomer D, Halgren E. (2009). Sequential processing of lexical, grammatical, and phonological information within Broca's area. *Science 326*, 445-449.

Schutz M, Lipscomb S. (2007). Hearing gestures, seeing music: Vision influences perceived tone duration. *Perception 36,* 888 – 897.

Skipper J, Goldin-Meadow S, Nusbaum H, Small S. (2009). Gestures orchestrate brain networks for language understanding. *Current Biology 19*, 661-667.

Sweetser E. (2008). What does it mean to compare language and gesture? Modalities and contrasts. In Guo J, Lieven E, Budwig N, Ervin-Tripp S, Nakamura K, Ozcaliskan S (Eds). *Crosslinguistic Approaches to the Psychology of Language: Studies in the Tradition of Dan Isaac Slobin.* New York: Psychology Press.

Tomasello M. (2006). *Origins of Human Communication.* Cambridge: MIT Press.

Zilbovicius M, Meresse I, Chabane N, Brunelle F, Samson Y, Boddaert N. (2006). Autism, the superior temporal sulcus and social perception. *Trends in Neuroscience 29*, 359-366.

AMBIGUITY RESOLUTION AND EVOLUTION OF WORD ORDER

MIEKO OGURA
Linguistics Laboratory, Tsurumi University
Yokohama, 230-8501, Japan

WILLIAM S-Y. WANG
Department of Electronic Engineering, The Chinese University of Hong Kong
Hong Kong, China

We examine the lexical and syntactic ambiguities from an evolutionary perspective of sequential and combinatorial relationships in the prefrontal brain and the evolution of word order as resolution of these ambiguities. We find that there is temporal ambiguity after the verb in SVO sentences, which causes the activation of the inferior frontal gyrus, while there is no activation in SOV sentences. This implicates the earliest human language evolved the SOV word order. We then demonstrate that the postnominal relative clause evolved from the paratactic clause with a non-relativized shared NP. Embedding took place by pulling the head noun to a position before the relative clause to avoid perceptual ambiguity arising from center-embedding which demands too much of our short-term memory. This also produced the word order change from OV to VO. Language evolves procedures to avoid lexical and syntactic ambiguities. It is not specifically lexical or syntactic, but a general cognitive tendency to attempt to resolve ambiguity, or to avoid the burden on working memory in the left inferior frontal gyrus.

1. Introduction

Deacon (1992, 1997) states that evidence reviewed from animal lesion studies suggests that the lateral prefrontal region contains areas that are of critical importance for certain classes of learning abilities, i.e., the sequential relationships or conditional relationships. The specialized roles in attentional and intentional functions of the ventral prefrontal areas came to be used for language processing because they were predisposed to perform the particular combinatorial and sequencing calculations necessary to acquire certain symbols with complex sets of conditional relationships. He considers that a significant role of the combinatorial processes in language reflects a general property of symbolic communication. The process of acquiring a new symbol requires not only that one learns the association between the symbol and its concept but also one learns its association with other symbols.

The more complicated the combinatorial relationships, the more prefrontal systems are taxed. The mnemonic and attentional threshold tends to prevent the particular sets of combinatorial and sequencing calculations. In the present study, we examine the lexical and syntactic ambiguities from an evolutionary perspective of sequential and combinatorial relationships in the prefrontal brain and the evolution of word order as resolution of these ambiguities.

2. Lexical Ambiguity Resolution and the Evolution of SOV Word Order

2.1. *Neural Bases of Ambiguity Resolution in Polysemous Words*

Relatively few neuroimaging experiments have yet addressed the neural substrates of lexical ambiguity resolution. Recently Zempleni et al. (2007) examine the neural substrates of homophone comprehension using event-related functional MRI. In this section we investigate the neural bases of the ambiguity resolution in polysemous words using near-infrared spectroscopy (NIRS).

In the current paradigm, the polysemous verb "break" was presented in English SVO and SV sentences. We chose "break", which is the most polysemous verb in WordNet (version 2.0, Cognitive Science Laboratory, University of Princeton, 2003). WordNet lists 59 meanings of "break" from the highest-frequency meaning, and we chose the meaning from the top 20 meanings, where both transitive and intransitive meanings were included. Our prediction was that there is temporary ambiguity of the meaning of the verb in SVO sentences, and this ambiguity is resolved by the following context, i.e., the object. To confirm our prediction, we conducted the experiments in Japanese SOV and SV sentences. Our prediction was that in these constructions the contexts that precede the verb specify the meaning of the verb, and there is no temporary ambiguity of the verb. We chose the verbs "kowasu"(transitive), "kowareru"(intransitive), "yaburu" (transitive), "yabureru" (intransitive) which have the same concept with the English verb "break".

The sentences were presented auditorily to the subjects. The subjects were instructed to comprehend the sentences silently. All the sentences were within 6s in length. The interval between the sentences was 25s to allow the hemodynamic response to return to the baseline before initiating the following trial. The first experiment presented the 5 English SVO sentences (*He broke the glass plate; He broke the alarm clock!; He broke my radio!; He broke the law; Three inmates broke jail*) and 5 SV sentences (*The figurine broke; The clouds broke; The coffee maker broke; The ranks broke; The surf broke*) randomly to the 6 native English speakers. The second experiment presented the 5 Japanese SOV sentences (*Kare wa* [He] *tegami wo* [letter] *yabutta* [tore]; *Kare wa* [He] *madogarasu wo* [windowpane] *yabutta* [broke]; *Sensou wa* [war] *heiwa wo* [peace] *yabutta* [broke]; *Anata wa* [You] *yakusoku wo* [promise] *yabutta* [broke]; *Shuujin ga* [Convict] *rou wo* [jail] *yabutta*[broke]) and 5 SV sentences (*Kono nuno wa* [This cloth] *sugu yaburerudarou* [will tear easily]; *Garasu wa* [Glass] *yabureyasui* [breaks easily]; *Wahei koushou wa* [Peace talks] *yabureta* [broke]; *Kanojyo wa kekkon ni* [Her marriage] *yabureta* [has failed]; *Madogalass wa* [Windowpane] konagona ni kowareta [broke into pieces]) randomly to the 6 native Japanese speakers. The changes in hemoglobin (Hb) concentrations and their oxygenation levels in the bilateral frontal areas were recorded using NIRS systems (ETG-7000; Hitachi, Tokyo, Japan). 3 lines of 11 probes were fitted on the bilateral frontal lobe. There were 52 channels in the optical path of the brain between the nearest pairs of emission and detection probes.

Figure 1 shows the average value of the oxy-Hb changes of the 6 subjects at the 52 channels in the frontal lobe, which correspond to the 52 rectangles, for the English SVO sentences in solid lines, and that for the Japanese SOV sentences in broken lines. The figure shows the time course of the oxy-Hb changes between the range of 0.10 and -0.10 mM mm at each of the 52 channels, when we face the subjects wearing the probe pads. Thus the left hemisphere appears on the right and the right hemisphere on the left. The parietal region appears on the top and the anterior region at the bottom. The subjects were asked to look at the fixation cross in the center of the paper on the desk to be in the controlled state of rest. This was the baseline for the oxy-Hb changes, and the horizontal line of the 0 mM mm is the baseline. The two vertical lines at each of the 52 channels show the period of 6s when the sentence was presented. The average of the subjects' Hb responses to the stimuli is shown during this period and the interval of 25s before the following stimulus.

In Figure 1 we find that the left frontal lobe, especially the inferior frontal gyrus, including Broca's area, which is marked in a solid circle, is activated in English SVO sentences, as compared with Japanese SOV sentences with no activation of the left inferior frontal gyrus. In English SVO sentences, there is temporal ambiguity after the verb "break". Multiple word meanings are accessed initially and kept active until a choice can be made among the alternatives by the context, i.e., the object (Zempleni et al. 2007). Then, during disambiguation by the context, the left inferior frontal gyrus shows the activation maximum.

In Japanese SOV sentences, the context is given before the verb and there is no temporary ambiguity of the verb, hence no activation of the left inferior frontal lobe. There is activation of the left precentral gyrus of the frontal lobe, which is marked in a broken circle, whose efferent neurons contact motor neurons and control muscle contractions (primary motor cortex).

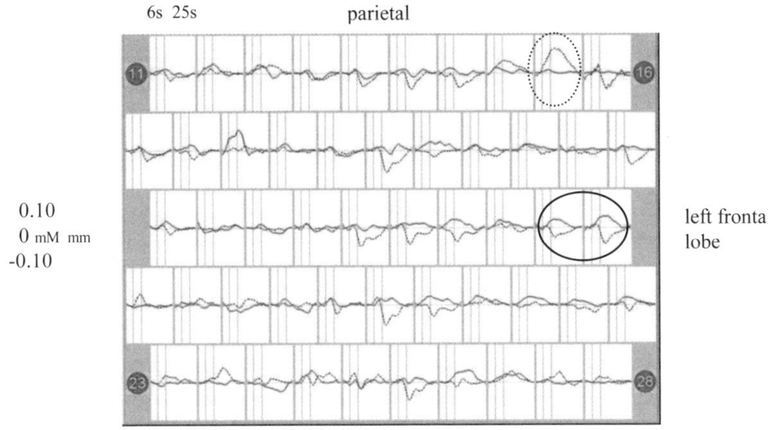

Figure 1: The oxy-Hb changes at the 52 channels in the frontal lobe for the English SVO and Japanese SOV sentences

Figure 2 shows the average value of the oxy-Hb changes of the 6 subjects for the SV sentences in English in solid line, and for that in Japanese in broken line. In Japanese there is no activation of the left frontal lobe except the left precentral gyrus, which is marked in a broken circle, as in the SOV sentences. However in English, there is activation in the left inferior frontal lobe, which is marked in a solid circle, contrary to our prediction, and in the right hemisphere, which is marked in a broken circle. Even though the context is given before the verb and there is no temporary ambiguity of the verb, multiple word meanings are accessed in the left inferior frontal lobe. As for the activation of the right hemisphere, Faust & Chiarello (1998) investigate hemispheric differences in the use of context during ambiguity resolution. They suggest that right hemisphere may maintain all the meanings, which might be useful when revision of the selected interpretation is necessary. In English SV sentences where the object does not appear after the verb, the revision occurs to the meaning of verb specified by the subject. Hence there is activation of the right hemisphere.

2.2. *Evolution of SOV Word Order*

We find that the presence of the context profoundly influences the comprehension of semantically ambiguous polysemous words. In SOV sentence,

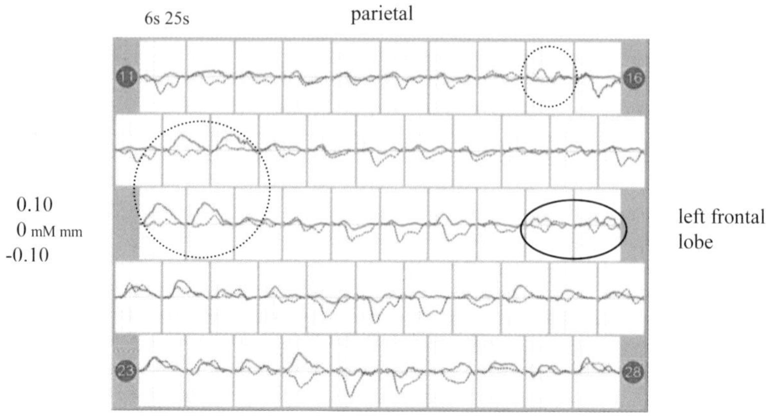

Figure 2: The oxy-Hb changes at the 52 channels in the frontal lobe for the English SV and Japanese SV sentences

the preceding biasing context specifies the meaning of the verb. Hence there is no ambiguity of the verb. However, in SVO sentence, there is temporal ambiguity of the meaning of the verb. The left inferior frontal gyrus, mostly Broca's area, has been suggested to subserve a general mechanism for selecting among competing semantic representations. From a wider perspective, selection between competing representations may call on some aspect of working memory (Stowe, et al. 2005, Zempleni et al. 2007).

We assume that language evolves avoiding or minimizing ambiguity. We therefore speculate that the earliest human language had SOV word order, where there is no temporal ambiguity of the verb. The SOV word order evolved avoiding the temporal ambiguity of the verb, more generally, avoiding the workload on mnemonic processing of symbolic combinations in the left inferior frontal gyrus. Goldin-Meadow et al. (2008) consider that actor-patient-action order may reflect a natural sequencing for representing events. Entities are cognitively more basic and less relational than actions, which might lead participants to highlight entities involved in an action before focusing on the action itself, thus situating actor and patient before action. They suggest that, initially, a developing language co-ops the actor-patient-action order used in nonverbal representations and uses it as a default pattern, thus displaying SOV order, which may have the virtue of semantic clarity.

Newmeyer (2000) claims that the earliest human language had rigid SOV order. He considers that protolanguage had thematic structure, and the thematic role of syntactic positions is revealed more directly in SOV language than SVO languages. Our experiments show the neural bases of Newmeyer's argument.

3. Syntactic Ambiguity Resolution and the Evolution of Word Order from SOV to SVO

3.1. *Center-embedding and the Relative Clause*

Kuno (1974) attempts to explain the Greenberg's universals due to limitations on the human perceptual mechanisms. For example, OV languages have relative clauses preceding their head noun, while in VO languages relative clauses are postnominal. He links this fact to the perceptual difficulties created by center-embedding. He conjectures that center-embedding demands too much of our short-term memory; center-embeddings are difficult to process because constituents cannot be completed immediately, forcing the language processor to keep lexical material in memory until it can be discharged. We assume that languages tend to evolve procedures to avoid or minimize center-embedding. In this section we show that the interaction between the evolution of postnominal relative clause and perceptual ambiguity arising from center-embedding caused the change from SOV to SVO.

3.2. *Evolution of the Postnominal Relative Clause and the SVO Word Order*

The emergence of linear adjacency of modifiers might well be the underpinning of hierarchical arrangement of words into phrase structures (Jackendoff 1999). We assume that the same mechanism operates in the clause combining. The juxtaposed paratactic clauses develop into higher-order hypotactic clauses and further subordinate clauses or, in its extreme form, embedding, by hierarchical arrangement. Recursion, or embedding recursion, is the product of a diachronic process of hierarchical arrangement of paratactic clauses. [1]

The relative clause in English started out essentially as a paratactic clause as shown in (1). [2] Here the shared NP is replaced with an anaphoric demonstrative pronoun, and the presence of a coordinating conjunction marks it not as a relative pronoun but as an anaphoric demonstrative pronoun.

(1) Eac þis land wæs swiþe afylled mid munecan.
Also this land was exceedingly filled with monkes
7 þa leofodan heora lif æfter scs Benedictus regule. (1086)

---

[1] Hauser, Chomsky & Fitch (2002) submit that a distinction should be made between the faculty of language in the broad sense (FLB) and in the narrow sense (FLN). They hypothesize that FLN only includes recursion and is the only uniquely human component of the faculty of language. But recursion appears in a wide range of human behaviors, and it is shared with other human cognitive domains and possibly other species.

[2] The example is from A-manuscript in C. Plummer (ed.), *Two of the Saxon Chronicles Parallel*, 1892.

& they lived their lives after St Benedict's rule

'This land too was filled with monks living their lives after the rule of St Benedict.'

Then the anaphoric personal or demonstrative pronoun was placed at the beginning of the second clause as shown in (2).[3] This is the paratactic stage of adjunction in a relative clause.

(2) 7 <u>ealles</u> benæmde *þes he on Englalande hæfde* (1102/10-1)

& all seized that he in England had

'and seized all that he had in England.'

This paratactic adjunctive relative clause was embedded as a dependent clause immediately after its nominal head as shown in (3). In the OV structure, it could not take place by moving the relative clause back after the head noun inside the main sentence since this produces numerous, perceptually problematic center-embedded structures. Instead, the head noun was pulled to a position before the relative clause. This also produced the word order change from OV to VO. Our discussions based on the Old English data can be extended to the evolution of the postnominal relative clause and the word order change from OV to VO in general (Ogura 2001, 2003).

(3) 7 sceawode <u>þet madmehus 7 þa gersuman</u> *þe his fæder ær gegaderode*: (108[7]/167-8)

& inspected the jewell-house & the treasures which his father formerly gathered

'and inspected the treasury and the riches which his father had accumulated.'

A number of PET and fMRI studies have found activation in the left inferior frontal gyrus during the processing of complex or syntactically ambiguous sentences (Stowe et al. 2005). Left inferior frontal gyrus has a general role related to working memory or storage of information. This function supports syntactic processing as well as lexical processing (see section 2), and may indeed not even be specifically linguistic.

4. Conclusion

We have shown that there is temporal ambiguity after the verb in SVO sentences, which causes the activation of the inferior frontal gyrus, while there is no activation in SOV sentences. This implicates the earliest human language evolved the SOV word order. Then we have demonstrated that the postnominal relative clause evolved from the paratactic clause with a non-relativized shared NP. Embedding took place by pulling the head noun to a position before the relative clause to avoid perceptual ambiguity arising from center-embedding. This also produced the word order change from OV to VO.

---

[3] The examples in (2) and (3) are from C. Clark (ed.), *The Peterborough Chronicle 1070-1154*, 1957. The heads are underlined, and the relative clauses are italicized.

Language evolves procedures to avoid lexical and syntactic ambiguities. It is not specifically lexical or syntactic, but a general cognitive tendency to attempt to resolve ambiguity, or to avoid the burden on working memory in the left inferior frontal gyrus.

Acknowledgements

This work is supported by the grants from the Human Frontier Science Program and the Ministry of Education, Culture, Sports, Science and Technology of Japan.

References

Deacon, T. W. (1992). "Brain-language Coevolution". In J. Hawkins & M. Gell-Mann (ed.), *The Evolution of Human Languages* (pp.49-83). Redwood City, Ca.: Addison-Wesley.

Deacon, T. W. (1997). *The Symbolic Speacies: The Co-evolution of Language and the Brain*. New York/London: W. W. Norton.

Faust, M. & Chiarello, C. (1998). "Sentence Context and Lexical Ambiguity Resolution by the Two Hemispheres". *Neuropsychologia,* 36, 827-835.

Goldin-Meadow, S., So, W.C., Özyürek, A., & Mylander, C. (2008). "The Natural Order of Events: How Speakers of Different Languages Represent Events Nonverbally". *PNAS,* 105, 9163-9168.

Hauser, M. D., Chomsky, N., & Fitch, W. T. (2002). "The Faculty of Language: What Is It, Who Has It, and How Did It Evolve?" *Science,* 298, 1569-1579.

Jackendoff, R. (1999). "Possible Stages in the Evolution of the Language Capacity". *Trends in Cognitive Science,* 3/7, 272-279.

Kuno, S. (1974). "The Position of Relative Clauses and Conjunctions", *Linguistic Inquiry,* 4,117-136.

Newmeyer, F. J. (2000). "On the Reconstruction of 'Proto-World' Word Order". In C. Knight, M. Studdert-Kennedy & J. R. Hurford (Eds.), *The Evolutionary Emergence of Language* (pp.372-388). Cambridge: Cambridge University Press.

Ogura, M. (2001). "Perceptual Factors and Word Order Change in English". *Folia Linguistica Historica,* XXII, 233-253.

Ogura, M. (2003). "Evolution of Word Order". *Folia Linguistica Historica,* XXV, 21-39.

Stowe, L. A., Haverkort, M. & Zwarts, F. (2005). "Rethinking the Neurological Basis of Language". *Lingua,* 115, 997-1042.

Zempleni, M-Z, Renken, R., Hoeks, J.C.J., Hoogduin, J. M., & Stowe, L. A. (2007). "Semantic Ambiguity Processing in Sentence context: Evidence from Event-Eelated fMRI". *NeuroImage,* 34, 1270-1279.

WHEN RECURSION COLLAPSES: EVIDENCE FROM DISCOURSE INTERACTION

TOSHIO OHORI

Language & Information Sciences, University of Tokyo, 3-8-1 Komaba, Meguro-ku Tokyo, 153-8902, Japan

This study examines subordinate structures in grammar by adopting the framework developed by Heine & Kuteva (2007). It will be shown that while subordinate structures, which are taken to be quintessential instances of recursion in language, develop out of the combination of simple structures via well-understood process of grammaticalization, they also undergo further development and subordinate clauses may stand out by themselves without being connected to the main clause. The implication of this fact is that subordinate structures are rather fluid in natural and situated language interaction, and that we might need to take a different outlook on the nature of recursion taking advantage of the recent development of the study of discourse interaction.

1. Introduction

The notion of recursion has been one of the key issues in the discussion on the origin and evolution of human language (Hauser, Chomsky, & Fitch 2002). Its evolutionary trajectory was described by Heine & Kuteva (2007) adopting the model of grammaticalization theory. They claim that the recursive structure in grammar, namely complex NP (noun phrase) and subordination, developed out of simpler structures via conceptually-motivated expansion of the source construction in "pre-grammar" (e.g. by re-categorizing a propositional event as an object), drawing upon documented records of linguistic history.

This study is an attempt at a further application of grammaticalization theory to the problem of language evolution, with special attention to the *collapse*, rather than the rise, of the subordination structure in grammar. It will be shown that in the real-world conversational discourse, subordinate clauses often stand out by themselves without being accompanied by the main clause, and that the grammatical markers for subordination take on rather different pragmatic functions for conversational management. This phenomenon was discussed by Ohori (1995, 2001) under the name of "suspended clauses" and by Evans (2007) under the name of "insubordination" (also cf. Progovac et al. 2006 for a general discussion of "nonsententials"). While Heine & Kuteva (2007) give a cursory mention of loss of recursion, it is limited to the attrition of NP structure, and hence the present study is expected to shed new light on the nature of recursive structure in grammar.

2. Data & Method

There are two sources of data. One is cross-linguistic, i.e. data from a variety of languages of the world, with the purport to demonstrate that the phenomena under investigation should best be understood as a general tendency of human languages. Another source of data is the audio-visual recording of conversational discourse interaction. There are totally 19 recordings of conversation, each lasting 10-15 minutes. Conversation participants were all undergraduate university students whose native language was Japanese. The recording was conducted in Tokyo in June 2005. Due to space limitation, however, only selected portions from the corpus will be reproduced below as representative examples.

3. Analysis: Suspended Clause Constructions (SCCs)

3.1. *Cross-linguistic data*

Schematically, the development of SCCs (i.e. collapse of subordination structure) can be represented in the following way:

(1) sub[Clause1]-marker + main[Clause2] : subordination structure
 > sub[Clause1]-marker : suspended structure

The relative position of the "marker" for subordination may vary depending on languages. Examples are provided below from English (2)-(3), German (4), Kham (Tibeto-Burman) (5), Tauya (Papuan) (6), and Kayardild (Tangkic, Australia) (7). [1]

(2) **If** only you could finish this in time!
(3) I don't mind, **though**.

---

[1] Abbreviations are as follows: 1, 2, 3=person, COBL=complementizing oblique, COMP=complementizer, ERG=ergative, GEN=genitive, IMM=immediate, IND=indicative, LOC=locative, NMZ=nominalizer, NOM=nominative, OBJ=object, P=patient, PFV=perfective, PL-plural, PRED=predicate, PRT=particle, Q=question, S=subject, SG=singular, STAT=stative, SUB=subordinator, TOP=topic

(4) **Daß** (mir) niemand den Saal verlaßt!
'Nobody should leave the room' (Panther & Thornberg, 2003)

(5) la:-ye sahmolo basma-rə o-ra-səih-**wo**
leopard-ERG three mountain.goat-PL 3S-3P-kill-NMZ:PFV
'the leopard killed three mountain-goats' (Watters, 2007)

(6) ya bramani yate-e-na-**ʔa**
1SG (name) go-1/2-SUB-IND
'I only went to Brahman (with no particular consequence or in vain)' (Macdonald, 1988)

(7) mala-**ntha** bala-**thurrka** kamarr-**urrk**
sea-COBL hit-IMM.COBL rock-IMM.OBJ.COBL
'(Let's leave here,) because the sea is hitting the rocks now' (Evans, 2007)

(4) is an instance of complementation structure, where *daß* is usually glossed 'that'. In (5) the form *-wo* is a nominalizer, translatable as '(the fact) that', which is another commonly found strategy for encoding subordination. For (6), the subordination marker may be glossed 'while/though' in context. For (7), each constituent of the clause bears a special marker COBL, all of which indicate that the clause is formally subordinate. Further examples can be found if we expand our database.

3.2. *Conversational Data*

Typologically, Japanese is head-final, agglutinative (suffixing), pro-drop, and clause-chaining language. In canonical cases, the main clause follows the subordinate clause. (8), (9), and (10) are instances of adversative-adverbial, causal-adverbial, and complementation structures occurring as SCC respectively.

(8) Iya, are-wa otona? n, otona, wakai otona da na. aa nanka
No that-TOP adult hm adult young adult PRED PRT ah well
moo kawaikatta-**noni**. Nige-ta nige-ta nige-ta.
oh cute.PAST-NONI run-PAST run-PAST run-PAST
'No, that was adult, yea, adult, young adult. Ah, well, oh (it) was cute-**though**. (It) ran and ran and ran' [#608-4]

(9) B: Soo, ryoo. Ryoo-na no.
right dorm dorm-PRED PRT
'Yeah, dorm. (It's) dorm'
A: Hoo.
really

'Really'

B: Beddo-toka, tsukue-toka, kuroozetto-tte saisho-kara acchi-no
bed-etc desk-etc closet-TOP start-from there-GEN
ryoo-mono-ga hait-teru-**kara**.
dorm-thing-NOM put.in-STAT-REASON
'Things like bed, desk, and closet--from the start the dorm's things are already installed-**because**' [#610-2]

(10) B: Soo, imada Rooson-de.
right as.yet Lawson-LOC
'Right, at Lawson'

C: Naze mazu Rooson-ka-tte-iu,
why at.all Lawson-Q-COMP-say

A: Honsoo-si-teiru-**to-iu**.
running.around-do-STAT-COMP-say
'(He) is running around-**that**.'

C: soko-kara
there-from
'Why at Lawson, in the first place, (please start) from there' [#606-1]

Here again, there is a "collapse" of subordination in both adverbial and complementation structures. SCCs typically occur at transition-relevant points in conversation (i.e. when an interlocutor finishes his/her turn) with non-continuing intonation contour, and the next speaker immediately takes the floor without any lengthy negotiation of turn-taking. Put differently, both the speaker and the hearer tacitly share the understanding that the apparently subordinate-marked clause are in fact independent linguistic construct and can be readily put to use as such in discourse with special pragmatic functions. For example, both (8) and (9) have a strong effect of urging the hearer to have sympathy for the speaker, an effect quite natural in a situated and "glooming"-like discourse interaction. (10) has an effect of distancing and thereby representing the situation being talked about as a kind of reenactment.

3.3. ***Summary***

The above sketch shows that the instances of subordinate clauses occurring as independent sentences are found in a wide variety of languages. An important point to note in this connection is that "normal", i.e. subordinate uses and "suspended/insubordinate" uses coexist within a same language, with functional stratifications.

4. Discussion

The above survey of the SCCs expands the scenario of grammaticalization drawn by Heine & Kuteva (2007) by detailing the fate of subordinate structure once established through either the expansion or integration of simpler structures. In the history of documented languages, this sort of rise and fall of a particular grammatical structure is quite commonly found, and indeed we can envisage a cycle of grammaticalization for the subordinate structure, namely:

(11) Sentence1 + Sentence2 (juxtaposition of simple sentences)
  > sub[Clause1]-marker + main[Clause2] (subordination)
  > sub[Clause1]-marker (suspended clause)
  > Sentence (simple sentence)

How long does a grammar take to develop SCCs? There is so far no conclusive evidence, but one study based on documented historical records reports that the span for the Japanese causal-adverbial marker *kara* to develop a suspended use was about a few centuries (Higashiizumi, 2006). Put in an evolutionary perspective, this is a matter of blinking. Thus one possible consequence of the facts reported in the above section is that, however speculative, all through the history of human languages, the rise and fall of subordination (and of recursion, by implication) has been a recurrent phenomenon. Stretching this idea a bit further, one might speculate that, contrary to the "mainstream" conception about recursion, it is a fairly fluid phenomenon, at least if we look at individual grammatical constructions.

One factor motivating the flexible use of subordinate structures might be a communicative one. People share both attention and intention in discourse interaction, and this sharing of communicative goal could lead to an ad-hoc but situated "bricolage" of a grammatical structure, though a detailed examination of the pragmatic functions of SCCs is obviously in order.

5. Conclusion

This study has shown that, while the conception of recursion itself may remain an important core feature of the human language, its grammatical realization can be rather fluid, oftentimes conditioned by discourse-interactional features. At the same time, studying language "in the wild" by closely examining situated conversation may turn out to be a fruitful direction of research in the pursuit to understand the evolution of human language.

Acknowledgements

The present study was partly supported by the Grant-in-Aid for Scientific Research (C) #22520392, Japan Society for the Promotion of Science.

References

Evans, N. (2007). Insubordination and its uses. In I. Nikolaeva (Ed.) *Finiteness: Theoretical and empirical foundations*. (pp. 366-431) Oxford: Oxford University Press.

Hauser, M. D., Chomsky, N. & Fitch, W. T. (2002). The faculty of language: what is it, who has it, and how did it evolve? *Science, 298,* 1569-1579.

Heine, B., & Kuteva, T. (2007). *The genesis of grammar: A reconstruction*. Oxford: Oxford University Press.

Higashiizumi, Y. (2006). *From a subordinate clause to an independent clause: A history of English BECAUSE-clause and Japanese KARA-clause*. Tokyo: Hituzi Syobo.

Macdonald, L. (1988). Subordination in Tauya. In J. Haiman and S.A. Thompson (Eds.), *Clause combining in grammar and discourse*. (pp. 227-246) Amsterdam: John Benjamins.

Ohori, T. (1995). Remarks on suspended clauses: a contribution to Japanese phraseology. In M. Shibatani & S.A. Thompson (Eds.), *Essays on semantics and pragmatics*. (pp. 201-218) Amsterdam: John Benjamins.

Ohori, T. (2000). Framing effect in Japanese non-final clauses: toward an optimal grammar-pragmatics interface. *Berkeley Linguistic Society*, 23, 471-480.

Panther, K-U., & Thornburg, L. (2003). Metonymies as natural inference and activation schemas: the case of dependent clauses as independent speech acts. In K-U. Panther & L. Thornburg (Eds.), *Metonymy and pragmatic inference*. (pp. 126-147) Amsterdam: John Benjamins.

Progovac, L., Paesani, K., Casielles, E., & Barton, E. (Eds.) (2006). *The syntax of nonsententials: Multidisciplinary perspectives*. Amsterdam: John Benjamins.

Watters, J. (2007). *A grammar of Kham*. Cambridge: Cambridge University Press.

COGNITIVE CONSTRUAL, MENTAL SPACES AND THE EVOLUTION OF LANGUAGE AND COGNITION

MICHAEL PLEYER

Department of English Literature and Linguistics, Ruprecht-Karls-Universität Heidelberg, Kettengasse 12, Heidelberg, D-69117, Germany

In this paper I argue that there is a wealth of relevant theorizing in the field of Cognitive Linguistics that can make important contributions to the study of the evolution of language and cognition. Theoretical explications of the conceptual, interactive, symbolic and perspectival dimension of language in Cognitive Linguistics, especially in the domain of cognitive construal operations, are highly relevant for evolutionary accounts of language. Specifically, I propose that the Mental Spaces and Conceptual Integration framework, popularly known as "blending theory", is very well suited to model the representational system that had to evolve in the human lineage in order to make possible the interactive and dynamic process of meaning construction fundamental to linguistic interaction.

1. Introduction

As Ray Jackendoff (2010) notes, "your theory of language evolution depends on your theory of language." Cognitive Linguistics (CL) (e.g. Cuyckens & Geeraerts 2007; Evans & Green 2006) sees language as an integral part of cognition. Language, in this view, is intimately connected to other cognitive domains and intricately tied up with the human conceptual system. From a language evolution perspective, then, it is this tight integration of language and cognition that needs to be explicated and accounted for in evolutionary terms.

More specifically, on the side of the speaker, in CL language is seen as expressing conceptualizations that are based on speakers' situated and embodied experience with the world around them as well as with other social agents. On the side of the hearer, linguistic constructions serve as prompts for the dynamic construction of a mental representation "in particular contexts with particular cultural models and cognitive resources" (Fauconnier 2004: 658). Language is thus fundamentally *conceptual*, *symbolic* and *interactive* in nature. These then, are other aspects that from a CL-point of view have to be elucidated in any account of the evolution of language and cognition.

One of the most important notions in CL, however, is that of *construal*. It is thus central that this notion be grounded in an evolutionary account of the linguistic system. In CL, language is seen as construing the world in a specific way and thus embodying a particular perspective on the world (Geeraerts 2006: 4). Through and with language we establish and mentally construct specific *perspectives on topics*, that is, specific ways in which events and objects are portrayed, understood and viewed.

This means that from the point of view of CL it is the *perspectival* nature of language and its social and cognitive foundations that are of the highest interest in discussing how language evolved as a system that is tightly integrated with human cognition. In this paper I set out to elaborate on this aspect and spell out in more detail what kinds of evidence and theorizing are relevant in answering the question of the evolution of language and cognition from the point of view of CL.

I will first discuss the notion of construal in CL in more detail, before turning to the importance of perspective-taking in the evolution of language and cognition. I will then argue that the Cognitive-Linguistic theory of Mental Spaces and Conceptual Integration (Fauconnier 2004; Fauconnier & Turner 2002), popularly known as 'blending theory,' is ideally suited to model the kind of representational apparatus that had to evolve in order to support the interactive and dynamic discursive meaning construction fundamental to linguistic interaction (Oakley & Hougaard 2008).

2. Construal in Cognitive Linguistics

In terms of cognitive construal, in a linguistic utterance a conceptualizer invites his or her interlocutor to attend jointly to an object of conceptualization in a specific way. This 'specific way' refers to the particular aspect of a conceptualized situation that is highlighted and that attention is directed to in the construal (Verhagen 2007: 60). On the side of the speaker, then, the way that language is used to express conceptualizations can be spelled out more precisely: Most crucially, perspectival linguistic utterances are employed to organize conceptual content with respect to a particular vantage point and *perspective*. On the side of the listener, they serve as prompts for the allocation of *attention* to a particular aspect of the cognitive representation evoked in the listener (Talmy 2007).

Within any language there is a significant flexibility in terms of alternative representations and construals, enabling speakers to alternate between these and actively use the perspectival potential inherent in language. In other words, language incorporates an extensive and elaborate system by which degrees of *salience* are assigned to parts of an expression, its reference or its context (Talmy 2007).

Saying that language is *perspectival*, then, captures the fact that it contains a structured inventory of linguistic constructions which can be employed as a means for different kinds of construal operations when talking about a particular situation (Verhagen 2007: 49).

The evolution of this inventory is sure to be a matter of cultural evolution within a given language (Hurford 2012). But what is crucial is that on a general level, linguistic construal operations are instantiations of basic cognitive capacities for cognitive construal, such as the capacities to selectively assign prominence to certain aspects of a conceptualization, to develop a shared point of view and to take different perspectives on the same topic. As stressed in the introduction, it is especially the perspectival nature of language and the cognitive machinery supporting it that is fundamental to an evolutionary account of language.

3. Perspective-Taking and the Evolution of Language and Cognition

A number of current accounts have stressed the importance of the socio-cognitive dimension of human interaction in accounting for the origins and evolution of human language. In particular, they have stressed the importance of a capacity for perspective-taking (e.g. Dubreuil 2008; Tomasello 2008). For example, the work of Michael Tomasello and colleagues in the areas of developmental psychology, language acquisition and comparative psychology has demonstrated that infants' and young children's cognitive and linguistic development depends crucially on their ability to jointly engage in and attend to shared goals, plans and intentions in cooperative collaborative activites within a joint attentional frame and a shared frame of reference (Tomasello 2008).

Most importantly, together with these *socio-cognitive capacities*, infants and young children also show unique *social motivations* for sharing psychological states and collaborating in joint activities with others as well as for aligning themselves with them and in a sense being like them. This is called *shared intentionality* by Tomasello and colleagues (Carpenter 2011). Thus from very early on infants and young children display an emerging ability as well as motivation to *take*, *set*, and *share perspectives* (Moll & Tomaello 2007).

Conversely, this shared intentionality infrastructure that serves as the foundation of human interaction and linguistic development seems not to be present in the other great apes to the same degree (Rosati et al. 2010). For example, they tend not to produce and understand declarative pointing as well as joint engagement characterized by a shared perspective.

Human infants, on the other hand, show evidence that they quite readily understand and use pointing as a way to share a perspective on a topic from 12 months of age onwards. What is more, from 14 months of age they seem to show some sensitivity to the adult's perspective when interpreting a pointing gesture (Moll & Tomasello 2007; Tomasello 2008). The same sensitivity for the adult's perspective can be observed in their early word learning from 18 months of age on. It is also a crucial foundation of children's meaning acquisition (Tomasello 2003). Lastly, the ability to take and express different perspectives on the same referent seems to emerge early in children's third year of life (E. Clark 1997).

Taken together, these data indicate that perspective-taking in cognition and the shared intentionality infrastructure can be seen as precursors of, and important foundations for, the acquisition of linguistic construal operations, perspective-taking in language and language acquisition more generally.

This, then, also lends support to the assumption that the emergence of shared intentionality and perspective-taking might have played a crucial role in hominid evolution and the evolution of language.

However, the exact nature and structure of perspective-taking skills in language and cognition remain far from clear. During hominid evolution, social agents must have become able to represent topics, i.e. what an interaction is 'about' or the 'question under discussion' (Roberts 2004) in a way that they understood them to be socially shared and common ground between speaker and hearer (H. Clark 1996). They also must have developed the ability to represent the fact that they have a specific perspective on a topic that might differ from other viewpoints, but that these perspectives can also be shared. But what these representations might look like and how they could be modeled is a question that is rarely addressed in enough detail in the literature on the topic (Tomasello 2008; Dubreuil 2008).

It is in addressing this problem that CL can go beyond simply specifying which kinds of linguistic capacities should be grounded in an evolutionary account. As CL has developed an elaborate theoretical apparatus for the description of mental processes of perspectival meaning construal it lends itself to modeling the structure of the conceptual representations involved in linguistic interaction (Evans & Green 2006; Oakley & Hougaard 2008; Verhagen 2007).

Specifically, I argue that the framework of Mental Spaces and Conceptual Integration (hereafter MSCI) can be used to model meaning construction as a dynamic, interactive phenomenon. In addition, this model is ideally suited to capture the *conceptual*, *symbolic*, *interactive*, and *perspectival* nature of language (and cognition) in a unified representational format. The MSCI-framework, then, presents a promising candidate for a model of what kind of representational system had to evolve in the human lineage to make language possible (Fauconnier & Turner 2002).

4. The Mental Spaces and Conceptual Integration Framework

Mental spaces are defined as small conceptual packets that are dynamically constructed 'online' in linguistic interaction and other cognitive activities. They contain multiple conceptual elements and are structured by linguistic and contextual information, as well as by stable conceptual knowledge representations stored in long-term memory, such as cognitive models and frames.

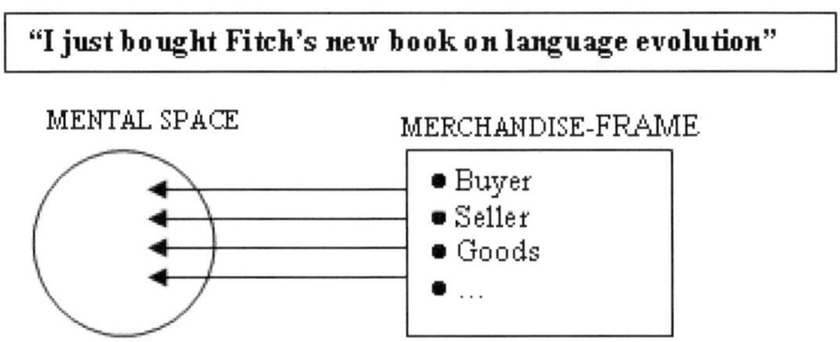

Figure 1. A mental space structured by the merchandise frame (e.g. Fauconnier & Turner 2002).

As discourse and thought unfold multiple different mental spaces are dynamically set up, interconnected and modified. Information from multiple mental spaces can be conceptually integrated into complex networks that serve as models very well suited for explicating the cognitive representations involved in linguistic interaction.

What is most important for the question of how the phenomenon of perspective in language and cognition can be modelled in MSCI is that mental spaces within a conceptual integration network can be assigned different statuses. For example, a mental space can be classified as a hypothetical space, a counterfactual space, a belief space, and so on. Even more interestingly for current purposes, the analytical tools of *Viewpoint Space*, *Base Space*, *Focus Space* and *Event Space* are specifically aimed at capturing the perspectival dimension of cognitive and linguistic construal and allow the location of events and situations relative to a viewpoint (Evans & Green 2006; Polzenhagen 2008).

The *Viewpoint Space* can be described as the perspective from which an event or situation is construed and evaluated. As discourse progresses, the viewpoint within a conceptual integration network can shift. The *Base Space* denotes the speaker's reality space and initialising viewpoint or perspective. The *Focus Space* is the space that is currently under construction, is most active, and on which the current orientation of the speaker lies. In temporal settings, the *Event Space* can be described as the temporal space in which the event encoded in a construal takes place (Polzenhagen 2008).

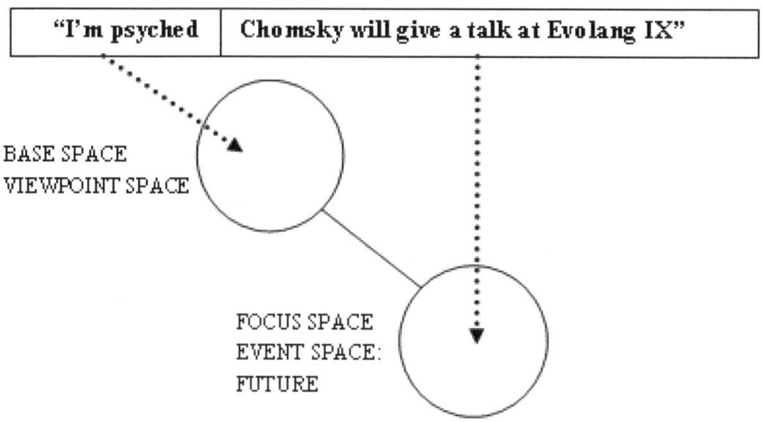

Figure 2. MSCI-model of the sentence "I'm psyched Chomsky will give a talk at Evolang IX," corresponding to the conceptualization expressed by the speaker and triggered in the hearer, respectively.

As discourse unfolds Viewpoint and Focus Space can be shifted and new mental spaces can be added and related to each other. In addition to shifts in Viewpoint and Focus Space, mental spaces can also be assigned a new status. For example, in an ongoing discourse a mental space can be re-evaluated as a belief space ("I'm psyched Chomsky will give a talk at Evolang IX – At least I think he'll give one"), or a counterfactual space ("If Chomsky had given a talk at Evolang IX I would've been psyched").

Through these shifts within the same conceptual integration network, i.e. the same network of interconnected mental spaces containing conceptual information, and additions to these networks, MSCI can capture what is one of the most important aspects of the evolution of language and cognition from the point of view of CL and other theories of language evolution. It offers a promising explication of the representational mechanism underlying discourse management and linguistic interaction which allows social agents to take, set, share, and negotiate *different perspectives on the same topic.*

5. Conclusion

To conclude, the MSCI serves as an ideal model for the kind of representational system that needed to evolve to support language. Mental Spaces and Conceptual Integration networks can provide the abstract mental structure that enables shifting of focus, viewpoint, and perspective more generally and allows us to differentially direct and allocate our attention to various parts of a conceptualization (Fauconnier 2004: 662). Thus, theories of cognitive construal and explications of the conceptual, symbolic, interactive and perspectival dimensions of language in CL have much to offer language evolution research.

A further integration of MSCI and research and theorizing on the evolution of language and cognition therefore seems to be a very fruitful area for future research. In addition, a continued dialogue between CL and language evolution research appears to be a highly worthwhile enterprise with promises of cross-fertilisation and progress for both disciplines.

Acknowledgements

I wish to thank Sonja Kleinke, Klaus-Peter Konerding and Frank Polzenhagen for helpful discussions of the notions elaborated on here. I am also grateful to Monika Pleyer, Martin Zettersten and three anonymous reviewers for their comments on a draft of this paper.

References

Carpenter, M. (2011). Social Cognition and Social Motivation in Infancy. In U. Goswami (Ed.). *The Wiley-Blackwell Handbook of Childhood Cognitive Development* (pp. 106-128). 2nd Edition. Malden, MA: Blackwell.

Clark, E. V. (1997): Conceptual Perspective and Lexical Choice in Acquisition. *Cognition,* 64,1-37.

Clark, H. H. (1996). *Using Language*. Cambridge: Cambridge University Press.

Dubreuil, Benoît (2008). What do Modern Behaviors in Homo Sapiens Imply for the Evolution of Language? In A. D. M. Smith, K. Smith, and R. Ferrer i Cancho (Eds.). *The Evolution of Language. Proceedings of the 7th International Conference* (pp. 99-106). Singapore: World Scientific.

Evans, V., & Green, M. (2006). *Cognitive Linguistics: An Introduction.* Edinburgh: Edinburgh University Press.

Fauconnier, G. (2004). Pragmatics and Cognitive Linguistics. In: L. R. Horn and G. Ward (Ed.). *Handbook of Pragmatics* (pp. 657-674). Malden, MA: Blackwell.

Fauconnier, G. & Turner, M. (2002). *The Way We Think: Conceptual Blending and the Mind's Hidden Complexities*. New York: Basic Books.

Geeraerts, D. (2006). Introduction: A Rough Guide to Cognitive Linguistics. In D. Geeraerts (Ed.). *Cognitive Linguistics: Basic Readings* (pp. 1-28). Berlin: de Gruyter.

Geeraerts, D., & Cuyckens, H. (Eds.) (2007). *The Oxford Handbook of Cognitive Linguistics*. Oxford: Oxford University Press.

Hurford, J.R. (2012): *The Origins of Grammar: Language in the Light of Evolution II*. Oxford. Oxford University Press.

Jackendoff, R. (2010). Your Theory of Language Evolution Depends on Your Theory of Language. In R. Larson, V. Déprez and H. Yamakido (Eds.). The *Evolution of Human Language: Biolinguistic Perspectives* (pp. 63-72). Cambridge: Cambridge University.

Moll, H. & Tomasello, M. (2007). Co-Operation and Human Cognition: The Vygotskian Intelligence Hypothesis. *Philosophical Transactions of the Royal Society,* 362,639-648

Oakley, T. &, Hougaard, A. (Eds.) (2008). *Mental Spaces in Discourse and Interaction*. Amsterdam/Philadelphia: John Benjamins.

Polzenhagen, F. (2008). The So-Called Tense-Aspect System of the English Verb: A Cognitive-Functional View. In H.-G. Wolf, L. Peter and F. Polzenhagen (Eds.). *Focus on English: Linguistic Structure, Language Variation and Discursive Use. Studies in Honor of Peter Lucko* (pp. 219-246). Leipzig: Leipziger Universitätverlag.

Roberts, C. (2004). Context in Dynamic Interpretation. In L. R. Horn and G. Ward (eds.) *Handbook of Pragmatics* (pp. 197-220). Malden, MA: Blackwell.

Rosati, A. G., Santos, L.R., and Hare, B. (2010). Primate Social Cognition: Thirty Years After Premack and Woodruff. In M. L. Platt and A. A. Ghazanfar (Eds.). *Primate Neuroethology* (pp. 117-143). Oxford: Oxford University Press.

Talmy, L. (2007). Attention Phenomena. In H. Cuyckens and D. Geeraerts (Eds.). *The Oxford Handbook of Cognitive Linguistics* (pp. 264-293). Oxford: Oxford University Press.

Tomasello, M. (2003). *Constructing a Language: A Usage-Based Theory of Language Acquisition.* Cambridge, MA: Harvard University Press.

Tomasello, M. (2008). *The Origins of Human Communication*. Cambridge, MA; London, England: MIT Press.

Verhagen, A. (2007). Construal and Perspectivization. In D. Geeraerts and H. Cuyckens (Eds.). *The Oxford Handbook of Cognitive Linguistics* (pp. 48-81). Oxford: Oxford University Press.

SPATIAL DYNAMICS OF LANGUAGE

ARCHISHMAN RAJU
St. Stephen's College, Delhi University,
University Enclave,
New Delhi, 110007, India
archishmanraju@hotmail.com

We propose a new model for studying the evolutionary dynamics of infinite populations in space. This is combined with the model of Nowak et al. to study the evolution of language. It is clear that if grammatical coherence is to be combined with co-existence, then language variation across space needs to be studied. We first study only the change in language user populations, ignoring the evolution of languages themselves. We study the stability of boundaries in some simple cases, and also show how the presence of a barrier can be modeled. Finally, we show results of numerical simulations of the model and allow extinction and emergence of languages. We find that languages can co-exist and form stable boundaries.

1. Introduction

The interest in models of language dynamics has been increasing over the past few years. Several models have come up in recent times attempting to describe the evolutionary behavior of languages (Vogt, 2009). In particular, there has been a lot of study on the influence of various geographical features on the Abrams-Strogatz model (Abrams & Strogatz, 2003) (Schulze & Stauffer, 2006) (Patriarca & Heinsalu, 2009) (Kandler, 2009). We here propose a model to study the influence of space on the model proposed by Nowak et al. (Nowak, Komarova, & Niyogi, 2001) Whereas work of this kind has been done before (Lee, Collier, Stabler, & Taylor, 2005) (Chio & Chio, 2006), it is almost always done with finite populations and/or stochastic computer simulations. We propose a way of retaining the simplicity of the infinite population model and combining it with spatial dynamics.

Spatial dynamics has long been known to promote co-existence, with numerous applications in the evolution of cooperation (Nowak, Bonhoeffer, & May, 1994) (Roca, Cuesta, & Sanchez, 2009). There are two major models for spatial dynamics. One is the cellular automaton model, which looks at individuals located at lattice sites who interact in some neighborhood, with no possibility of migration (Lindgren & Nordahl, 1994). The other is the ecological population dynamics model (Skellam, 1991), which has also recently been applied to game theoretic modeling (Wakano, Nowak, & Hauert, 2009). Our model can be looked upon as a continuum limit of the first model applied to the evolution of language.

A key feature of languages is their great diversity. Variation across space is one of the simplest explanations of this diversity. In particular, we are interested in studying if a purely deterministic algorithm, with random initial conditions, can give rise to boundaries between different languages.

2. Model

We briefly describe the model of Nowak et al. Consider a finite search space of grammars/languages, which we assume to be equivalent, $(L_1, L_2, ..., L_n)$. Let the pairwise relation between each of the languages, denoting their similarity, be given by a matrix $[a_{ij}]$. Let x_i denote the relative frequency of speakers of language L_i where $\sum_{i=1}^{n} x_i = 1$. At each stage there is a payoff, given by $F(i,j) = (a_{ij} + a_{ji})/2$ and the fitness f_i is given by $\sum_{j=1}^{n} F(i,j)x_j$. As parents teach their children, there is a probability of learning some other language given by the matrix $[q_{ij}]$. The dynamics is then given by

$$\dot{x_i} = \sum_{j=1}^{n} f_j q_{ji} x_j - \phi x_i, \tag{1}$$

where ϕ is the average fitness, given by

$$\phi = \sum_{j=1}^{n} f_j x_j. \tag{2}$$

We now propose to include space into the equation. Let S be the area of some region, and X be the total population in the region. Let $x = \frac{X}{S}$ be a uniform population density which is chosen, without loss of generality, to be 1. $x_i(\boldsymbol{r})$ is now the population density speaking language L_i where $\boldsymbol{r}$ is the position vector. The first assumption implies $\sum_{i=1}^{n} x_i(\boldsymbol{r}) = 1$. The total population density is always constant and there can only be individual variations in population densities of languages across space.

Now, $P(\boldsymbol{r}, \boldsymbol{r}')$ is a function which gives the probability of interaction as a function of $\boldsymbol{r}$ and $\boldsymbol{r}'$ where $\boldsymbol{r}'$ is the current position. We then propose the following modified fitness function

$$f_i(\boldsymbol{r}') = \int_S \sum_{j=1}^{n} F(i,j) x_j(\boldsymbol{r}) P(\boldsymbol{r}, \boldsymbol{r}') dS. \tag{3}$$

The integration is assumed to be over two dimensional space. The equation for language dynamics then is

$$\dot{x_i}(\boldsymbol{r}') = \sum_{j=1}^{n} f_j(\boldsymbol{r}') q_{ji} x_j(\boldsymbol{r}') - \phi x_i(\boldsymbol{r}'). \tag{4}$$

3. Computer Simulations

We simulate the above as follows. We consider a flat square spatial grid. The boundaries are *not* periodic. The total population at each grid point is held constant. We assume that the population at each grid point can interact within a certain percentage of the total area. There is no interaction beyond that area. We consider a probability of interaction that decreases linearly with distance. We also use the Moore neighborhood so that diagonal neighbors are assumed to be at the same distance as side neighbors. Let r, c stand for row and column and let r', c' represent the current row and column. Let $d_r = |r - r'|$, $d_c = |c - c'|$. Then, in terms of grid points, the equation we are solving is

$$\dot{x}_i(r', c') = \sum_{j=1}^{n} x_j(r', c') f_j(r', c') q_{ji} - \phi x_i(r', c'), \tag{5}$$

where

$$f_i(r', c') = \sum_{r,c} \sum_{j=1}^{n} x_j F(i, j) P(d_r, d_c) \tag{6}$$

and

$$P(d_r, d_c) = (1 - \max(d_r, d_c)/s), d1, d2 \leq T, \tag{7}$$

$$P(d_r, d_c) = 0, d1, d2 > T, \tag{8}$$

where T is some number. T is equal to $0.2\sqrt{N}$ where N is the number of grid points. Our $[a_{ij}]$ matrix is as follows. $a_{ij} = a_{ji}$ and a_{ii} is always 1. For any language, a_{ij} is 0.2 for one other randomly chosen language and 0.005 otherwise. The $[q_{ij}]$ matrix is decided by a memoryless learning algorithm with the number of sentences, $w = 20$. We show simulation results in Figure 1. Different languages dominate in different areas leading to boundaries between languages (which we will call language boundaries to differentiate them from the boundaries of our grid). They boundary conditions are not crucial for the formation of language boundaries as Figure 2 shows. The system, however, reaches an equilibrium. We now propose a way to make the process dynamic by including the fact that the languages themselves evolve.

We first run the simulation and determine the time scale in which the system settles to an equilibrium. We also note the equilibrium proportions of languages and set a certain threshold t by hand based on these proportions. Then after a certain amount of time, which corresponds to the time scale, we do the following. If $x_i(\boldsymbol{r}) < t$ is true everywhere, then we first set $x_i = 0$ everywhere. Then we reset the $[a_{ij}]$ matrix and introduce a small amount of x_i (slightly greater than t) at a square about a randomly chosen grid point. We appropriately rescale the other populations so that $\sum_{i=1}^{n} x_i(\boldsymbol{r}) = 1$. We use two algorithms for resetting the a_{ij} matrix. The first chooses a_{ij} randomly from the range $[0, 0.5]$. The other sets

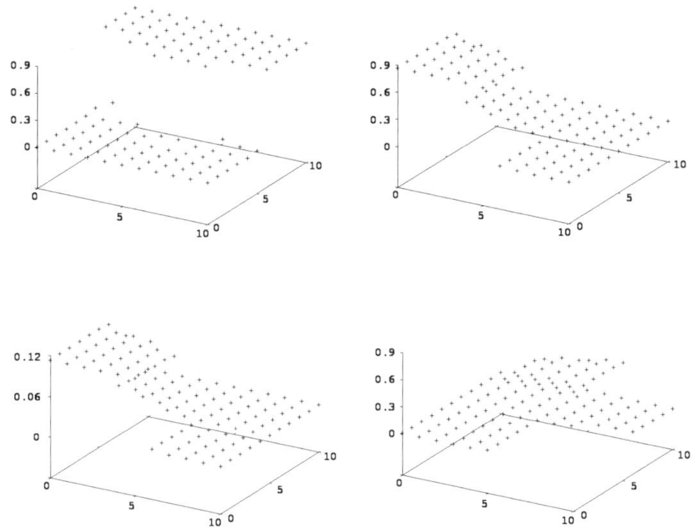

Figure 1. The simulation had 121 grid points and 6 languages. For each language i, a_{ii} is is always 1. Each language i is close to one other randomly chosen language k so that $a_{ik} = 0.2$ and $a_{ij} = 0.005$ for all other languages j. The number of sentences $w = 20$. Three languages become dominant and occupy different areas. In each area, the language close to the dominant language occupies a significant share of the population. The graphs are a plot of the population density of four of these languages with space. The scale shows which language is dominant and which language merely occupies a share of the population.

$a_{ij} = 0.5\mu_j$ where μ_j denotes the average of x_j about the square. This assures that the new languages are more likely to be related to languages already present in the area.

Both algorithms lead to different though interesting results. In the following, a language i is said to be 'related' to language j dominant in some area S if the coefficient a_{ij} is high enough for the language i to go above the threshold t in S. In the non-random algorithm, each one of the initially extinct languages become related to a dominant language and consequently go above the threshold in a certain area. The system then reaches an equilibrium. In the random algorithm, usually one gets a solution with one language dominant over the whole grid. Each language goes above the threshold on every grid point by becoming related to the dominant language. The process is not completely deterministic in both cases because the grid point where the language emerges is always chosen randomly. Hence, the process can lead to very different results. One such typical process for the random algorithm is shown in Figure 3.

As a last point, we note that it is very easy to model natural boundaries or

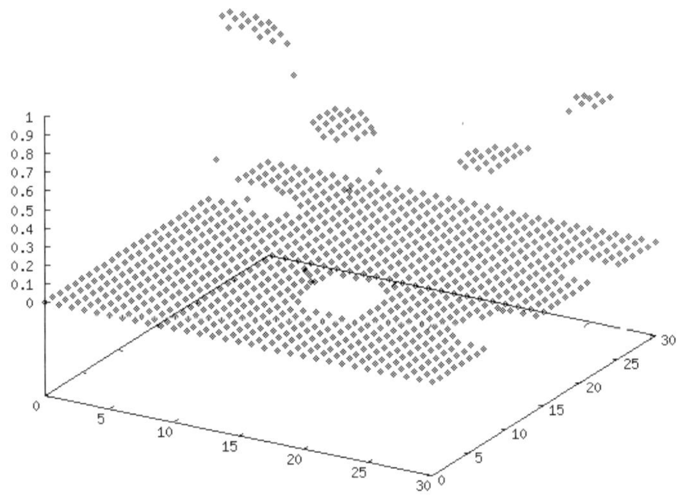

Figure 2. The simulation had 961 grid points and 20 languages. For each language i, $a_{ii} = 1$ and $a_{ij} = 0.005$ otherwise. The number of sentences $w = 50$. Clusters of the same language form at different parts. This shows that the boundary conditions are not crucial for the formation of language boundaries. The graph is a plot of the population density of one of these languages with space. The other languages either occupy different areas or have gone extinct.

geographical barriers in this model by abruptly cutting of the probability of interaction either way along a certain curve. If the algorithm is random or the initial conditions are different, this will usually lead to language boundaries corresponding with this geographical barrier.

4. Analysis

We would like to show some analytical results in simplified settings in this section. We work in one dimension for convenience. First we discuss stability of the boundaries. Let us for the moment work with the case where for every language i, $q_{ii} = 1$ and $q_{ij} = 0, \forall j \neq i$. The equation without space then comes under a well studied class of equations called the replicator equation (Hofbauer & Sigmund, 1998). Imagine a situation with two languages L_1, L_2, which vary with one coordinate s which can take values in the range $[0, 1]$. Let L_1 have a population density of 1 in the region $[0, X)$ and L_2 have a population density 1 in the region $[X, 1]$. We are concerned with the conditions for emergence of L_1 at X.

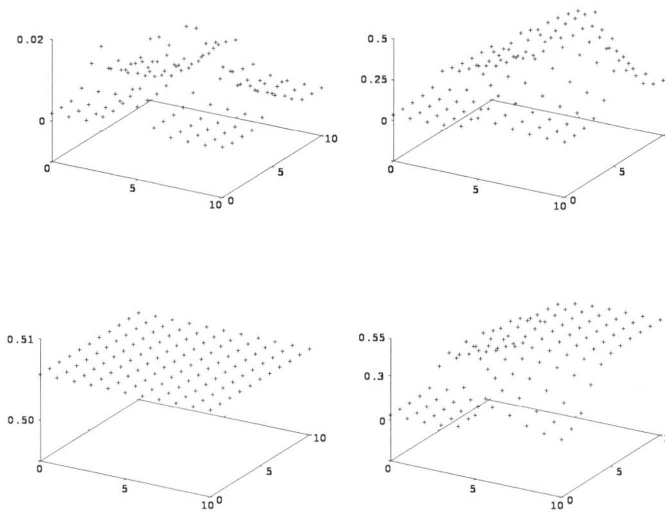

Figure 3. The simulation had 121 grid points and 6 languages. Initially for each language i, a_{ii} is is always 1 and $a_{ij} = 0.005$ otherwise. The number of sentences, $w = 20$. After a certain time, 5 units, the contents of the a_{ij} matrices of the extinct languages are decided using the random algorithm. The graphs are a plot of the population density of one of the languages with space at different times. Starting from top-left and going clockwise, we see an extinct language slowly coming up at the boundaries of other dominant languages before taking over the whole population. The plots are at time 5, 25, 40, 90 units respectively.

Let $a_{12} = a_{21} = a$ where a is in the range $[0, 1)$. Let $P(s)$ give the probability of interaction with neighbourhood points at point X. For emergence of L_1, we want the fitness of L_1 to be greater than that of L_2 which gives

$$\int_0^X P(s)ds + a\int_X^1 P(s)ds > a\int_0^X P(s)ds + \int_X^1 P(s)ds, \tag{9}$$

which simplifies to

$$\int_0^X P(s)ds > \int_X^1 P(s)ds. \tag{10}$$

Hence, the condition is independent of a. It can be shown for a linearly decreasing distribution with $P(X) = 1, P(0) = 0, P(1) = 0$, the condition simplifies to $X > 0.5$. Hence the boundaries are unstable in this specific case because any deviation from $X = 0.5$ will lead to one language dominating. To get co-existence, it is necessary that the interactions are local. If $P(s)$ goes to 0 after some small s then the fitness of the two will be equal and the boundaries will be stable. The interactions in our computer simulation are local.

Finally we would like to see the conditions for emergence of a new language. Based on observations from our simulations, we note that a new language can emerge at the boundaries of languages which are not related if it is related to all of them. We would like to make this more precise. Imagine two languages which are not related to each other ($a = 0$) and suppose they form stable boundaries at $s = X$. The interactions are local. Now we introduce a small amount of population of some L_3 at $s = X'$ and let us assume $a_{31} = a_{32} = a$. Let $P'(s)$ give the probability of interaction at point X'. The condition for emergence of L_3 over L_1 is then

$$a \int_0^1 P'(s)ds > \int_0^X P'(s)ds, \tag{11}$$

$$a > \frac{\int_0^X P'(s)ds}{\int_0^1 P'(s)ds}. \tag{12}$$

Clearly if $X' < X$, and the interactions are local and go to 0 before $s = X$, then $\int_0^1 P'(s)ds = \int_0^X P'(s)ds$. This leads to $a > 1$ which means the new language can never emerge. The best chances for the new language to emerge then are at the boundaries. If $X' = X$, then if the situation is symmetrical we get $a > 0.5$. This shows how a new language might emerge. A small amount of mutation or diffusion however is necessary for the emergence of the new language at other points in space.

The above derivation was under the assumption that L_1 and L_2 themselves are not related. We showed that as long as the a_{ij} matrix is symmetric, the stability of the boundaries of L_1 and L_2 does not depend on how they are related to each other (in the absence of other languages). However, if they are related, similarity can help protect against invasion by other languages. Therefore, language boundaries are more more stable if the two languages are related.

5. Conclusions

We have suggested a new model for studying evolutionary dynamics with space which is similar to a continuum limit of the cellular automaton model. We applied this model to the model for evolution of language of Nowak et al. and find through simulations that it can lead to co-existence of different languages. We also suggested a way of allowing the languages themselves to evolve and investigated simplified settings analytically. We find that similar languages can co-exist and form stable boundaries.

Acknowledgements

I am grateful to Dr. S. Krishna, Dr. M. Venkadesan, E. J. Philips and A. Mukherjee for discussions. I acknowledge support from a KVPY fellowship.

References

Abrams, D. M., & Strogatz, S. H. (2003). Linguistics: Modelling the dynamics of language death. *Nature*, *424*(6951), 900.

Chio, C. D., & Chio, P. D. (2006). Simulation model for the evolution of language with spatial topology. In *Evolution of language, 6th international conference (evolang6).*

Hofbauer, J., & Sigmund, K. (1998). *Evolutionary games and population dynamics.* Cambridge University Press.

Kandler, A. (2009). Demography and language competition. *Human Biology*, *81*(2-3), 181-210.

Lee, Y., Collier, T. C., Stabler, E. P., & Taylor, C. E. (2005). The role of population structure in language evolution. In *10th international symposium on artifical life and robotics.*

Lindgren, K., & Nordahl, M. G. (1994). Evolutionary dynamics of spatial games. *Physica D: Nonlinear Phenomena*, *75*(1-3), 292-309.

Nowak, M. A., Bonhoeffer, S., & May, R. M. (1994). Spatial games and the maintenance of cooperation. *Proceedings of the National Academy of Sciences of the United States of America*, *91*(11), 4877-4881.

Nowak, M. A., Komarova, N. L., & Niyogi, P. (2001). The evolutionary dynamics of grammar acquisition. *Journal of Theoretical Biology*, *209*(1), 43-59.

Patriarca, M., & Heinsalu, E. (2009). Influence of geography on language competition. *Physica A: Statistical Mechanics and Its Applications*, *388*(2-3), 174-186.

Roca, C. P., Cuesta, J. A., & Sanchez, A. (2009). Effect of spatial structure on the evolution of cooperation. *Physical Review E*, *80*(4).

Schulze, C., & Stauffer, D. (2006). Recent developments in computer simulations of language competition. *Computing in Science and Engineering*, *8*(3), 60-67.

Skellam, J. G. (1991). Random dispersal in theoretical populations. *Bulletin of Mathematical Biology*, *53*(1-2).

Vogt, P. (2009). Modeling interactions between language evolution and demography. *Human Biology*, *81*(2-3), 235-258.

Wakano, J. Y., Nowak, M. A., & Hauert, C. (2009). Spatial dynamics of ecological public goods. *Proceedings of the National Academy of Sciences*, *106*(19), 7910-7914.

ARE WEB SEARCH QUERIES AN EVOLVING PROTOLANGUAGE?

RISHIRAJ SAHA ROY
Indian Institute of Technology Kharagpur
Kharagpur, 721302, India
rishiraj@cse.iitkgp.ernet.in

MONOJIT CHOUDHURY and KALIKA BALI
Microsoft Research India
Bangalore, 560025, India
{monojitc, kalikab}@microsoft.com

Searching information on the World Wide Web by issuing queries to commercial search engines is one of the most common activities engaged in by almost every Web user. Web search queries have a unique structure, which is more complex than just a bag-of-words, yet simpler than a natural language. This structure has been evolving over the past decade which is an artefact of the way search engines are evolving and aggressively using feedback from past users to serve current and future users better. In this paper, we argue that queries can be considered as an evolving protolanguage from functional, structural and dynamical points of view. Therefore, Web search logs, a perfectly preserved and rich dataset, can probably reveal several interesting facts about the evolution of protolanguage.

1. Introduction

Web users communicate their information need to a search engine through *queries*. The fact that search engines do not really "understand" or "process" *Natural Languages* (NLs) drives average Web users to specify their queries in a language that has a structure far simpler than NL, but perhaps more complex than the commonly assumed bag-of-words model. In fact, Web search queries define a new and fast evolving language of its own, whose dynamics is governed by the behavior of the search engine towards the user and that of the user towards the engine. With a small number of highly popular terms and a large number of rarer terms, search queries possess properties strikingly similar to NL, yet have several unique features (Spink et al., 2001; Saha Roy et al., 2011) – they define a language on their own.

The objective of this paper is to present and carefully scrutinize the proposition that "Web search queries can be considered as an evolving *protolanguage*." While a couple of past researchers (Guichard, 2002; Dessalles, 2006) have cursorily mentioned this idea, there has been no detailed analysis, at least from the perspective of language evolution, of the structure of queries and the nature of interactions between users and search engines that have led to this structure. Queries are mostly formulated as short and ad hoc strings of words with little or no grammatical structure. They exhibit properties such as a relaxed word order, absence of long range dependencies and relatively few inflections, that have also been suggested as features of a protolanguage. Therefore, studying queries and their evolution can perhaps help us understand the various facets of language and protolanguage evolution. This might be especially useful in light of the fact that historical data and large-scale controlled experiments are major bottlenecks in language evolution research.

At the very outset we want to note that there is a fundamental difference between evolution of human language and that of queries: while human language is used for communication between two human beings (presumably) having very similar cognitive capabilities, queries are used as the means of communication between a human user and a search engine, which are incomparable not only in terms of their cognitive capabilities, but also in their biological and cultural history of language use. This asymmetry between the communicating agents in the context of queries can raise serious doubts about the basic proposition presented in this paper. However, we believe that there is an alternative and perhaps a more realistic interpretation of this communicative behavior, which is to assume that ultimately queries are actions of the users on a shared environment represented by the search engine. While the users might believe that they are communicating their information need to the search engine through their queries (which of course is true), the search engine behaves pretty much like a blackboard and its response is dependent completely on the action-response of other users in the past. This is especially true for modern commercial search engines which extensively rely on user queries, URL clicks and explicit feedbacks on relevance of documents for learning and improvement of the search models. Thus, we can visualize this situation as an indirect communication between two human users mediated through a shared environment (or channel) which is the search engine. It is a well-known fact that the channel (such as the structure of our articulatory and perceptual devices) has a profound effect on the structure and dynamics of the evolving language.

In the next three sections, we present analogies between queries and (proto-)languages from functional, structural and dynamical perspectives. In the last section, we present a synthesis of the salient ideas emerging from these three orthogonal perspectives on queries that point to the strong parallels between Web search queries and existing notions of protolanguage.

2. Functional Aspects of Web Search Queries

Web search queries are small fragments of texts (symbols) that are used to communicate the information need of an individual to a search engine. In this regard, the basic function of queries is similar to that of languages, which is transmission of information. Hockett (1960) proposed thirteen design features of a communication system. NLs possess all these features and in this section we see that a large number of these features are present in queries as well. Some of these features, such as **semanticity**, **arbitrariness**, **discreteness** and **duality of patterning**, are exhibited in queries by virtue of the fact that the building blocks of queries are, after all, words – which are also the basic units of NL. However, with respect to some of the other features, NL and queries are analogous in their structure and function. We discuss the other design features here.

Vocal-auditory channel: All spoken human language is produced using the vocal tract and auditory channel. While the role of vocal-auditory channel is currently irrelevant for queries, they are produced and perceived by writing (typing) and reading of text.

Broadcast transmission and directional reception: Human language can be heard if it is within the range of another person's auditory channel. Additionally, a listener, who shares the same time and space of the speaker, has the ability to determine the source of a sound by binaural direction finding. In the case of Web search, queries issued by a user are recorded in the search engine log files. The engine uses these logs to generate *query completions* for another user. This way, a query can be potentially broadcast to millions of new users. A new user can *choose* to be receptive of these completions (similar to signals) by enabling this specific feature on their search engine.

Rapid fading: Waveforms of spoken language dissipate over time and do not persist. A hearer can only receive specific auditory information at the time it is spoken. This feature is related to the modality of language, and as queries are mainly textual, they are therefore less ephemeral than spoken language.

Interchangeability: A person has the ability to both speak and hear the same signal. Anything that a person is able to hear, s/he has the ability to reproduce through spoken language. Similarly, users have the ability to understand and reformulate somebody else's query. If a person has seen a query, s/he can also use that query.

Total feedback: Speakers have the ability to hear themselves speak. Through this, they are able to monitor their speech production and internalize what they are producing through language. A user also knows what query s/he has issued, monitors it and internalizes its use.

Specialization: Human language sounds are specialized for communication, that is, humans speak mainly to transmit information. Query words too are specialized for specific information needs of the user.

Displacement: NL has the ability to refer to things in space and time and communicate about things that are currently not present. Queries also allow the users to seek information about past and future events or objects.

Productivity: NL allows for the creation of new and unique meanings of utterances from previously existing utterances and sounds. Likewise, a pre-existing set of words (around 1.2 million in our dataset sampled through Bing Australia[a]) can be combined to formulate unseen queries.

Traditional transmission: Human language is not completely innate and acquisition depends in part on the learning of a language. Users can learn how to formulate queries from search experts, engine guidelines, books (Ray et al., 1998), engine feedback and mimicking other users.

Thus, from a purely functional perspective, Web search queries are very similar to NL.

3. Structural Aspects of Web Search Queries

We analyzed around 16.7 million Web search queries collected through Bing Australia in the year 2008–'09 to understand query structure. The average length of a query in this dataset was found to be 4 words, which is much higher than the earlier reported average of 2.21 words per query (Jansen et al., 2000). Short queries (one or two words) constitute 18.96% of the queries and are mostly named entities and dictionary entries. Long queries, which have nine or more words and comprise only 3.23% of all queries in our dataset, are generally grammatically correct natural language sentences, computer generated error messages and song lyrics.

Traditionally, queries were assumed to be an unordered set of keywords, commonly referred to as the bag-of-words model. While this might still be the case for short (< 4 words) and a significant portion of medium length (between 4 and 8 words) queries, the latter often exhibit more complex structure than a bag-of-words model, but not as complex as NL. For example, the query *gprs config nokia n96 telstra australia* is clearly not semantically equivalent to *telstra gprs n96 config nokia australia*. This is largely due to the presence of multiword expressions (MWEs) and conceptual units within such queries. Medium length queries are on the rise today owing to the vast improvements in the performance of search engines on such queries.

Although a random permutation of the words within a query does not necessarily lead us to a query which is semantically equivalent, it turns out that queries can almost always be segmented into contiguous chunks of words such that all permutations of these segments represent semantically equivalent queries. Recent research has established the usefulness of query segmentation and the presence of a structure in queries using a variety of Web resources to accomplish the task (Hagen et al., 2011). Segments can be considered to be broadly of two types – *heads*, representing the core information need, and *modifiers*, indicating specific intent of the user (Saha Roy et al., 2011). The semantics of queries depend largely on the interaction and dependencies between heads and modifiers. For example, in the query *compare internet explorer and mozilla firefox*, *internet explorer* and *mozilla*

[a]http://www.bing.com/?cc=au

firefox represent heads, while *compare* and *and* appear as modifiers. More complex dependency models have also been proposed for queries (Bendersky et al., 2009).

There have not been many studies to understand the unique linguistic structure of queries. Barr et. al. (2008) showed that 70% of all words in queries are nouns, followed by adjectives (7.1%) and prepositions (3.7%). In a recent study, Saha Roy et al. (2011) have shown that word co-occurrence networks constructed from query logs reveal interesting similarities and differences between queries and NL. Like NL, a two-regime degree distribution in word or segment co-occurrence networks of queries reveals the existence of a small kernel and a very large periphery. But unlike NL, where a large fraction of sentences are formed only using the kernel words, most queries consist of units (words/segments) both from the kernel and the periphery. Word co-occurrence networks for NL have small average shortest path (the small world effect) which, it has been argued, facilitates fast word access in the mind. The analysis of query networks thus shows that queries do not exactly behave like languages at a cognitive level, but share sufficient similarities to rule out the possibility of them lacking any linguistic structure. Hence, they might be considered similar to a protolanguage evolving between humans.

There is no concrete empirical evidence for the existence of protolanguage, though "the hypothesis of a protolanguage helps to bridge the otherwise threatening evolutionary gap between a wholly alingual state and the full possession of language" (Bickerton, 1995). There have been several speculations and suggestions on the structural aspects of a protolanguage. Wray (1998) and Smith (2006) suggest that protolanguages have short sequences of symbols strung into ad hoc sentences, a feature characteristic of queries, in that the average query is significantly shorter than the average natural language sentence. Dessalles (2006) suggests that there is no consistent ordering of the symbols in a protolanguage, nor are there inflections or long range dependencies. Queries fit in well with this hypothesis too. Wray (1998) and Dessalles (2006) further suggest that protolanguage has a simple or no grammar, which is true for queries. Wray (1998) also suggests that there are a limited number of referential symbols in a protolanguage, which is not true for queries. This claim, however, has been contested by Smith (2006). We note that for queries there is already an agreed-upon huge vocabulary that consists of words that we have readily borrowed from NL. Words specific to the query language or new interpretations of existing symbols (if any) are few (e.g., *wiki*, which generally indicates that the source of the result pages should be *Wikipedia*).

4. Dynamics of Web Search Queries

Search engines are *complex adaptive systems* that are able to communicate with humans and evolve at two levels – algorithms and models. Search engines have come a long way since the first generation search systems (McBryan, 1994). Even though search engine companies rarely publish parts of their internal algorithms, the huge volume of Web IR literature over the last decade is an indication enough that search algorithms have evolved. Algorithmic evolution for search engines include more sophisticated machine learning algorithms for ranking and use of a higher number of features for retrieval. These changes are analogous to agents undergoing anatomical modifications over several years – like the unique structure of the vocal tract and the descended position of the larynx in humans (Hauser et al., 2002).

Evolution of the model, on the other hand, is information that the search system learns from user interactions and uses to present better results in the future. Models are learnt by the search engine through constant user feedback and preferences gathered during the course of Web searches. More and more Web data is crawled to make better document models. More query logs are used to build better query analysis models. Query log analysis can be used to study individual search behavior, query duplications, user sessions and query correlations (Silverstein et al., 1999). Clickthrough data (Joachims, 2002; Xue et al., 2004) and pseudo-relevance feedback (Yu et al., 2003) are also used by search engines to enrich their models of relevance.

This evolution of models is similar to the cultural transmission of language. Adaptation of the search engine is a population-level phenomenon, where individual users are agnostic to the fact that their interactions with the search engines indeed affect the response of the search engine for other users and vice versa. Cultural transmission for the language of queries can be considered from two aspects: Experts teaching novices how to search, and new users learning search tips and tricks from the collective knowledge of the Web, or relevant books (Ray et al., 1998) – like traditional language transmission. An individual's competence in language is derived from data which is itself a consequence of the linguistic competence of other individuals (Smith et al., 2003). Modern theories of cultural evolution recognize that cultural traditions are socially transmitted from person to person between and within generations (Steele et al., 2010). Individual click data or search engine use affect the engine as a whole. Users unknowingly affect the response of the engine towards other users, effectively transmitting information of some kind through the engine.

Incorporation of user feedback has tremendously improved the performance and perception of the popular commercial search engines. While the algorithmic components of a search engine rarely make any attempt to understand NL or complex queries, search engines can intelligently process very complex queries just by learning from past user behavior. This gives an average user the impression that the search engine is indeed getting smarter, and consequently they are motivated to formulate more complex queries. This results in a population level snowball effect leading to increase in the structural complexity of the queries.

5. Discussions and Conclusions

In this research, we have highlighted some similarities that Web search queries are observed to share with an evolving protolanguage, giving evidence from three different aspects. First, the function and some of the basic features of queries are similar to that of NL. Second, the structure of the queries are in between that of a random bag-of-words and a full-fledged NL form. Nevertheless, this structure seems to be evolving in complexity. Third, the evolutionary dynamics of queries is analogous to models of cultural evolution for language. Although this evolution is actually an outcome of the interactions between the users via the search engine, it seems as though the search engine is itself evolving in this process.

In conclusion, we would like to draw the attention of the language evolution research community to Web search queries, which can provide an immensely potent source of data for understanding the structure and dynamics of protolanguage and NL evolution. Nevertheless, one must also keep in mind the fact that after all, queries are issued by agents, and search engines are designed by engineers who already have a very complex linguistic communication system in place to express their ideas. This will surely bias the evolution of queries in certain directions which may or may not reflect the true evolution of a protolanguage.

Acknowledgments

The first author would like to thank Microsoft Corporation and Microsoft Research India for his Microsoft Research India PhD Fellowship Award, which supported this work.

References

Barr, C., Jones, R., & Regelson, M. (2008). The linguistic structure of english web-search queries. In *Proceedings of the conference on empirical methods in natural language processing* (pp. 1021–1030). Stroudsburg, PA, USA: Association for Computational Linguistics.

Bendersky, M., Croft, W. B., & Smith, D. A. (2009). Two-stage query segmentation for information retrieval. In *Proceedings of the 32nd international acm sigir conference on research and development in information retrieval* (pp. 810–811). New York, NY, USA: ACM.

Bickerton, D. (1995). *Language and human behavior.* University College London Press.

Dessalles, J.-L. (2006). Du protolangage au langage : modèle d'une transition. *Marges linguistiques*, *11*, 142–152.

Guichard, E. (2002). *L'internet : mesures des appropriations d'une technique intellectuelle.* These, Ecole des hautes études en sciences sociales.

Hagen, M., Potthast, M., Stein, B., & Bräutigam, C. (2011). Query segmentation revisited. In *Proceedings of the 20th international conference on world wide web* (pp. 97–106). New York, NY, USA: ACM.

Hauser, M. D., Chomsky, N., & Fitch, W. T. (2002). The faculty of language: What is it, who has it, and how did it evolve? *Science*, *298*(5598), 1569-1579.

Hockett, C. F. (1960). The origin of speech. *Scientific American*, *203*, 88-96.

Jansen, B. J., Spink, A., & Saracevic, T. (2000). Real life, real users, and real needs: a study and analysis of user queries on the web. *Information Processing and Management*, *36*(2), 207 - 227.

Joachims, T. (2002). Optimizing search engines using clickthrough data. In *Proceedings of the eighth acm sigkdd international conference on knowledge discovery and data mining* (pp. 133–142). New York, NY, USA: ACM.

McBryan, O. A. (1994). Genvl and wwww: Tools for taming the web. In *Proceedings of the first international world wide web conference* (pp. 79–90).

Ray, E. J., Ray, D. S., & Seltzer, R. (1998). *Altavista search revolution.* Osborne Publishing.

Saha Roy, R., Ganguly, N., Choudhury, M., & Singh, N. K. (2011). Complex network analysis reveals kernel-periphery structure in web search queries. In *Proceedings of the 2nd international acm sigir workshop on query representation and understanding* (pp. 5–8). New York, NY, USA: ACM.

Silverstein, C., Henzinger, M. R., Marais, H., & Moricz, M. (1999). Analysis of a very large web search engine query log. *SIGIR Forum*, *33*(1), 6-12.

Smith, K. (2006). The protolanguage debate: bridging the gap? In *Proceedings of the 6th international conference on the evolution of language* (p. 315-322).

Smith, K., Brighton, H., & Kirby, S. (2003). Complex systems in language evolution: The cultural emergence of compositional structure. *Advances in Complex Systems (ACS)*, *6*(04), 537-558.

Spink, A., Wolfram, D., Jansen, M. B. J., & Saracevic, T. (2001). Searching the web: the public and their queries. *J. Am. Soc. Inf. Sci. Technol.*, *52*, 226–234.

Steele, J., Jordan, P., & Cochrane, E. (2010). Evolutionary approaches to cultural and linguistic diversity. *Philos Trans R Soc Lond B Biol Sci*, *365*(1559), 3781-3785.

Wray, A. (1998). Protolanguage as a holistic system for social interaction. *Language and Communication*, *18*(1), 47-67.

Xue, G. R., Zeng, H. J., Chen, Z., Yu, Y., Ma, W. Y., Xi, W., & Fan, W. (2004). Optimizing web search using web click-through data. In *Cikm 2004* (pp. 118–126). New York, NY, USA: ACM.

Yu, S., Cai, D., Wen, J. rong, & Ma, W. ying. (2003). Improving pseudo-relevance feedback in web information retrieval using web page segmentation. In *Intl. world wide web conf. (www)* (pp. 11–18).

LANGUAGE CHANGE IN SOCIALLY STRUCTURED POPULATIONS

RUTH SCHULZ, MATTHEW WHITTINGTON, AND JANET WILES

School of ITEE, The University of Queensland, St Lucia 4072, Australia

Language contact is a significant external social factor that impacts on the change in natural languages over time. In some circumstances this corresponds to language competition, in which individuals in a population choose one language over another based on their social interactions. We investigated the dynamics of language change in two initially separate populations of agents that were then mixed with levels of influence determined by the social classes of the two populations, with 16 different combinations tested. As expected, the study found that how the communities interact with each other impacts on the communal language developed. However, it was also found that the acquisition of new words was substantial even with limited interaction between populations and low levels of influence, and that comprehension could be well established across language groups even when production of words from the other language group was low.

1. Introduction

Language changes over time as individuals learn from their peers and from previous generations. All natural languages change, through drift, dialect interference, and foreign interference (Thomason & Kaufman, 1988). Language change may be influenced by external sociolinguistic and internal psycholinguistic factors (Aitchison, 1991). When populations are isolated, languages undergo independent evolution, leading to the formation of dissimilar languages. When populations interact, language contact is an external factor that frequently results in language change, often through the borrowing of words (Thomason, 2001). In situations where a community has no shared language a pidgin may emerge, taking elements from the existing languages of individuals in the community (Aitchison, 1991). Social factors affect the extent of language change in a contact situation, with more prestigious languages less likely to change than less prestigious ones (McMahon, 1994).

Competition between languages has been studied using parameterized models speaking one of two possible languages (Abrams & Strogatz, 2003), with extensions allowing bilingualism (Castello, et al., 2008) and considering population densities (Patriarca & Leppänen, 2004). Simple models of language competition predict that two languages cannot co-exist stably, with one eventually driven to extinction (Abrams & Strogatz, 2003; Castello, et al., 2008). Other models represent languages as bit-strings, allowing individuals to learn aspects of languages and enabling language elements to remain even when the species that used the language is driven to extinction (Kosmidis, Halley, & Argyrakis, 2005). The degree of contact between multiple populations affects the convergence of a communal language (Gong, Minett, & Wang, 2008).

Another type of model for investigating language evolution is agent-based modeling, including language games (Steels, 1995) and iterated learning (Kirby & Hurford, 2002). Agent-based models allow populations of agents to develop shared lexicons with meaningful referents and enable investigations into changes in meaning and word use over time. The variability of agent interactions and the asymmetry of some social structures are best modeled with agents, rather than by modeling field effects. Our previous work on language change demonstrated that a range of factors influence how language changes over generations of agents, including the period of individual language learning, concept formation methods, and the social interactions (Schulz, Wyeth, & Wiles, 2010).

Social interactions between agents have been specified by the social networks of individuals, comparing regular, small world, and community structured networks (Castello, et al., 2008), finding different times to extinction for languages in competition. Another model of differential social interactions implemented a theory of influence based on popularity, derived from social impact theory (Nettle, 1999). Measures of popularity have been used to weight the influence of an individual on others' language updates and to determine the probability of an individual participating in an interaction (Gong, 2010). Popularity was found to impact on the speed of categorization and whether new words would spread through a population.

In this paper, we introduce a new component into models of influence, in which we deliberately separate influence from frequency in the language learning processes. We chose to implement an agent-based model of language with two populations of agents, and to study the impact of differential social interactions on the lexicons of agents in the populations. This project extends our earlier work on the Lingodroid project (Schulz, Wyeth, & Wiles, 2011) by introducing a social-class structure to the agent interactions. The Lingodroids are agents that explore a spatial environment and interact socially to construct shared lexicons for spatial concepts. The use of populations of agents with spatial representations results in evolved languages in which lexicons and semantics can be compared in detail between language learners, enabling analyses which would not be possible for more abstract methods for representing languages.

2. Methods

Agents were designed to interact socially to form concepts and lexicons for place names (called *toponyms*), distances, and directions (Schulz, Glover, Milford, Wyeth, & Wiles, 2011; Schulz, Wyeth, et al., 2011). A grid world was used to provide a simple spatial environment for the agents to move and interact in.

2.1. *Agent Interactions*

The agents interacted through three types of conversations. Through *where-are-we* conversations, agents created a shared lexicon for toponyms to describe locations in the world. Using the toponym lexicon, agents then created a shared lexicon for distances through *how-far* conversations and for directions through *what-direction* conversations. In a conversation:

1. Two agents were randomly chosen from the population of agents, one as the speaker and the other as the hearer;
2. Topic selection occurred, with different methods used:
   a. In a *where-are-we* conversation, the speaker was placed in one of the grid squares, the hearer was placed close by in one of the grid squares within a 2 square neighbourhood of the speaker's location, and the hearer requested that the speaker name the current location;
   b. In a *how-far* conversation, the hearer randomly chose two toponyms from its lexicon (possibly the same word) and requested that the speaker name the distance between the specified toponyms;
   c. In a *what-direction* conversation, the hearer randomly chose two different toponyms from its lexicon and requested that the speaker name the direction from 'North' to the first of the specified toponyms when located at the second toponym;
3. The speaker produced an utterance to describe the topic;
4. Both agents updated their lexicons.
5. Failure: The interaction ended in failure if the speaker did not understand the toponyms specified in a *how-far* or *what-direction* conversation, or if the speaker did not have or invent a word to describe the topic.

If the hearer did not know the word used by the speaker, the word was added to its lexicon. The process of updating lexicons depended on the agents' classes and the interaction type (see the next section for details).

2.2. *Lexicon Construction*

Agents stored the associations between words and component parts of concepts, called *concept elements*, in three distributed lexicon tables (Schulz, Wyeth, et al., 2011), one each for toponyms, distances, and directions. The concept elements for toponyms were grid squares. Concept elements for distances and directions were created as the agents experienced new distances and directions in *how-far* and *what-direction* interactions. The association, a_{ij}, between a concept element, i, and a word, j, was updated as follows:

$$a_{ij} \leftarrow a_{ij} + q \tag{1}$$

where q was the influence determined by the classes of the speaker and the current agent. When the classes of the speaker and the current agent were the same (including when the speaker was the current agent), q was equal to 1. When the classes of the speaker and the current agent were different, q was equal to the influence associated with the speaker's class by the current agent, a value between 0 and 1. For a mixed population with two classes, a single value was specified for each class, with $q1$ determining the influence class 2 has on class 1, and $q2$ determining the influence class 1 has on class 2.

In each interaction, the speaker produced an utterance to name the concept element, i, by calculating the confidence value, h_{ij}, for each word, j, as follows:

$$h_{ij} = \sum_{k=1}^{X} \frac{a_{kj}(D - d_{ki})}{D} \Big/ \sum_{m=1}^{N} c_{mj} \tag{2}$$

where a_{kj} was the stored association between the concept element, k, and the word, j; d_{ki} was the distance between the concept elements k and i; c_{mj} was the count of the number of times the word, j, had been used together with the concept element, m; X was the number of concept elements within a neighborhood D, of concept element i; and N was the total number of concept elements. Words were invented with probability, p, as follows:

$$p = \begin{cases} 0.05 & \text{if } \mathrm{h}_{\mathrm{ij}} = 0 \\ k \exp(-h_{ij} / ((1 - h_{ij})T) & \text{otherwise} \end{cases} \tag{3}$$

where k=1, h_{ij} was the confidence value of the concept element-word pair, and T was the temperature, setting the word invention rate.

The key difference from previous Lingodroid studies was that associations between words and concepts were separated from word-use frequency to allow influence to differentially affect confidence values.

2.3. *Performance Measures*

Two performance measures were used to analyze the resulting lexicons: production coherence and comprehension coherence. Production coherence was calculated per lexicon over a set of concept elements: the squares of the grid for toponyms, every 0.5 squares for distances, and every 10° for angles. Production coherence was scaled between 0 and 100%, with higher values indicating that the robots produced similar words for similar concept elements (for details, see Schulz, Wyeth, et al., 2011). Comprehension coherence for a word was calculated as the average distance between the location, distance, or direction chosen by each agent in the population for that word. The comprehension coherence of a lexicon was the average comprehension coherence of all words in the lexicon. Comprehension coherence for locations and distances was measured in squares (meters), and for directions in degrees, with lower values indicating that words in the lexicon were interpreted similarly across the population.

3. Study Design

Initially, two separate populations of eight agents negotiated toponym, distance, and direction lexicons through 28,000 interactions of each type (*where-are-we*, *how-far*, and *what-direction*). The two populations were then combined, with one population set to class 1 and the second set to class 2. The combined population further negotiated their lexicons through 2000 interactions of each type. The agents used a neighborhood size of two squares (meters) for locations and distances and 30° for directions; the size of the grid world was 15 squares by 15 squares; and the word invention temperature was 0.02. Each population was assigned one of four possible social classes, which affected the lexical updating processes of its own and the other population. The study formed a 4x4 design with the influence values *q1* and *q2* set to 0, 1/3, 2/3, or 1. Each of the sixteen conditions produced one shared language. The resulting languages were analyzed for diversity and coherence in production and comprehension.

4. Results

The initial lexicons of the agents contained 44 and 62 toponyms (with production and comprehension coherences of 73.7% and 1.61m, and 67.8% and 1.56m), 8 and 10 distance words (78.7% and 0.31m, and 68.9% and 0.62m) and five and four direction words (95.2% and 58.0°, and 80.0% and 45.3°). The final lexicon sizes were either the same as the initial values, when the influence of the other class was equal to 0, or had increased to 71–102 toponyms, 17–19 distance words, and 9 direction words. Words acquired from the other class were not well established, as indicated by lower coherence values (see Figure 2) and by the agents' lexicons (see Figure 1).

As expected, production coherence within each class decreased as the influence of the other class increased for all three lexicons (as q increased from 0 to 1, toponym coherence decreased from 70.8% to 40.7%, distance coherence decreased from 72.4% to 50.4%, and direction coherence decreased from 87.0% to 66.1%). However, there was no correlation between comprehension coherence and influence. For toponyms, within-class coherence remained between 1.59m and 1.63m, and between-class coherence varied between 2.40m and 2.63m, with similar results obtained for distances and directions. The interaction between influence and the resulting lexicons can be clearly seen in the toponyms chosen, and the distance and direction templates used to choose words (see Figure 1).

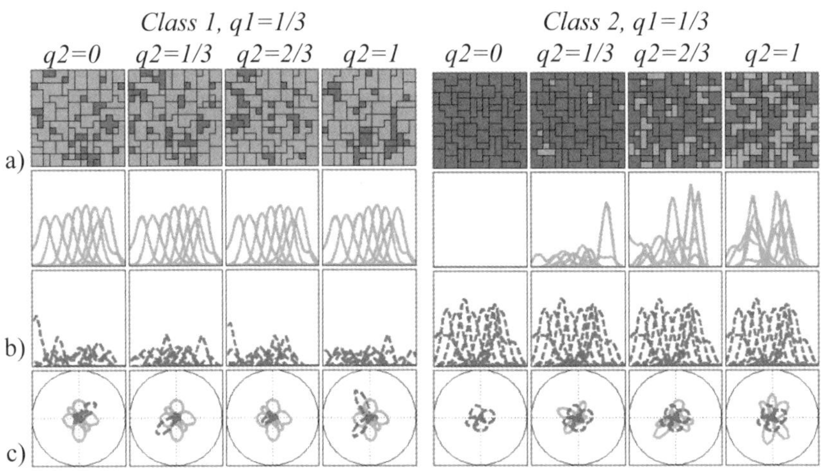

Figure 1 Lexicons for $q1$=1/3 and $q2$=0, 1/3, 2/3, and 1. Each column shows the lexicons of a single agent at the end of the mixed interactions. The color of each word indicates the original class that used the word, with light blue for class 1 and dashed red for class 2. a) In the toponym lexicons, boundaries between toponyms are indicated with black lines. Across all $q2$ values, the class 1 agent has used some class 2 toponyms, depending on the specific interactions of the agent. As the influence of class 1 increased from $q2$=0 to $q2$=1 the number of class 1 toponyms used by the class 2 agent increased. b) Distance templates show the confidence for each word from 0 to 1 (y-axis) over distances from 0m to 20m (x-axis), separated into class 1 words (top row) and class 2 words (bottom row). For the class 2 agent, as $q2$ increased, the templates for class 2 words remained similar to the initial templates and the confidence in class 1 words increased. c) Direction templates show the confidence of each word from 0° to 360°, with 'North' pointing towards the top of the page. The circle corresponds to a confidence value of 1. The interplay between class 1 and class 2 words can be seen at all levels of influence. If a word from the other class corresponded to a concept that was not confidently associated with a word, then this word gained popularity in both classes.

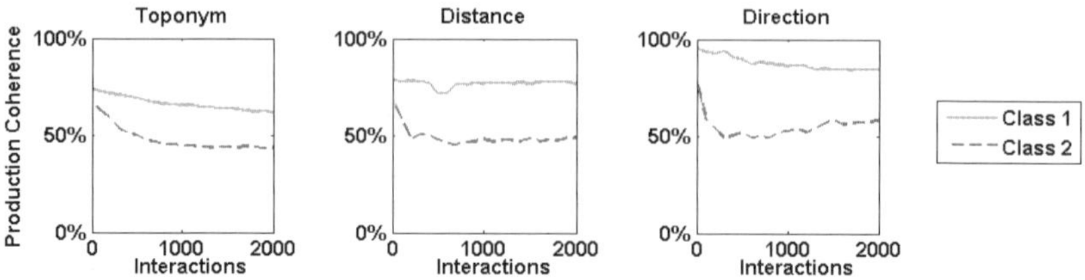

Figure 2 Production coherence for the toponym (left), distance (middle), and direction (right) lexicons for both classes throughout the mixed interactions for $q1=1/3$ and $q2=1$. Production coherence for class 2 decreased for all lexicons as many of the class 1 words were used by class 2 agents (from 67.8% to 43.8% for toponyms, from 59.4% to 48.7% for distances, and from 80.6% to 58.3% for directions). For class 1, production coherence was more stable (from 73.7% to 61.7% for toponyms, from 93.7% to 84.1% for distances, and from 74.4% to 77.0% for directions), as the words chosen by class 1 agents predominantly remained the same.

5. Discussion

The study presented in this paper has shown that differential social interactions impact on the communal language developed by two initially separate populations of agents, in particular how quickly words are acquired and how well established they become. While words are acquired quickly with both low and high influence, high influence allows words to become well established in the population sooner. These results are consistent with the findings from previous studies on language competition, in which communal languages develop (Gong, et al., 2008) or one language is driven to extinction but has contributed words to the remaining language (Kosmidis, et al., 2005). However, the results also show that the acquisition of new words can be substantial with small numbers of interactions and small amounts of influence. In particular, while agents may not choose to use the words of another class, comprehension may be well established.

Language contact and competition have a significant impact on changes in natural languages (Thomason & Kaufman, 1988). Situations in which language contact occurs include different social classes, trade, invasion, and a multicultural society. The spatial language change model presented in this paper has shown that brief contacts between populations with low influence may result in individuals acquiring significant numbers of words.

Our model of language learning incorporating social status intentionally separated influence from word frequency. We have proposed one mechanism to achieve this separation, with interesting consequences for word production and comprehension. The methodology could be extended from influence between groups to social structure within a group. Further research could determine whether this mechanism is necessary or sufficient, and the extent to which the model corresponds to the influence that human social structures have on vocabulary learning in multilingual situations.

References

Abrams, D. M., & Strogatz, S. H. (2003). Linguistics: Modelling the dynamics of language death. *Nature, 424*, 900.

Aitchison, J. (1991). *Language change: progress or decay?* (2nd ed.). Cambridge: Cambridge University Press.

Castello, X., Eguiluz, V. M., Miguel, M. S., Loureiro-Porto, L., Toivonen, R., Saramaki, J., et al. (2008). Modelling language competition: Bilingualism and complex social networks. In A. D. M. Smith, K. Smith & R. Ferrer i Cancho (Eds.), *The Evolution of Language: Evolang 7* (pp. 59-66). Singapore: World Scientific Publishing.

Gong, T. (2010). The effect of social popularities on linguistic categorization. In A. D. M. Smith, M. Schouwstra, B. De Boer & K. Smith (Eds.), *The Evolution of Language: Evolang 8* (pp. 160-167). Singapore: World Scientific Publishing.

Gong, T., Minett, J. W., & Wang, W. S. Y. (2008). Exploring social structure effect on language evolution based on a computational model. *Connection Science, 20*(2-3), 135-153.

Kirby, S., & Hurford, J. R. (2002). The emergence of linguistic structure: an overview of the iterated learning model. In A. Cangelosi & D. Parisi (Eds.), *Simulating the Evolution of Language* (pp. 121-148). London: Springer Verlag.

Kosmidis, K., Halley, J. M., & Argyrakis, P. (2005). Language evolution and population dynamics in a system of two interacting species. *Physica A: Statistical Mechanics and its Applications, 353*, 595-612.

McMahon, A. M. S. (1994). *Understanding language change*. Cambridge: Cambridge University Press.

Nettle, D. (1999). Using Social Impact Theory to simulate language change. *Lingua, 108*(2-3), 95-117.

Patriarca, M., & Leppänen, T. (2004). Modeling language competition. *Physica A: Statistical Mechanics and its Applications, 338*(1-2), 296-299.

Schulz, R., Glover, A., Milford, M., Wyeth, G., & Wiles, J. (2011). *Lingodroids: Studies in Spatial Cognition and Language*. Paper presented at The International Conference on Robotics and Automation.

Schulz, R., Wyeth, G., & Wiles, J. (2010). Language change across generations for robots using cognitive maps *Artificial Life XII*. Odense, Denmark.

Schulz, R., Wyeth, G., & Wiles, J. (2011). Lingodroids: Socially grounding place names in privately grounded cognitive maps. *Adaptive Behavior, 19*(6), 409-424.

Steels, L. (1995). A self-organizing spatial vocabulary. *Artificial Life, 2*(3), 319-332.

Thomason, S. G. (2001). *Language contact*. Edinburgh: Edinburgh University Press.

Thomason, S. G., & Kaufman, T. (1988). *Language contact, creolization, and genetic linguistics*. Berkeley: University of California Press.

LANGUAGE LATERALIZATION, CATEGORICAL PERCEPTION AND LANGUAGE EVOLUTION

LAN SHUAI

Department of Chinese, Translation and Linguistics, City University of Hong Kong
83 Tat Chee Avenue, Kowloon, Hong Kong

TAO GONG

Department of Linguistics, University of Hong Kong, Pokfulam Road, Hong Kong

In relation to language evolution, we discuss the relationship between the structural asymmetry of two brain hemispheres and the functional lateralization of categorical perception in speech processing. We propose that since the structure of the left hemisphere allows perceiving fast changing acoustic cues and categorizing phonemes, speech and language processing that involves phonological processing should be left lateralized. Meanwhile, a high degree of hemispheric lateralization could enhance the power of perceiving a large amount of speech sounds and facilitate language emergence, which may also cause a left lateralization of language and speech processing.

1. Introduction

Speech and language are unique functions of human beings (Hauser et al., 2002). Not only the cognitive functions, such as syntactic processing, reading, writing, and so on, which belong to the language faculty and are absent in other species, but many other presumably special aspects of language processing also exist solely or at least to the greatest extent in human beings. These aspects include *categorical perception* (CP, the nonlinear response to an equal acoustic distance of the frequency features during the perceptual tasks of phoneme identification and discrimination, Liberman et al., 1957) of speech sounds and *lateralization* (hemispheric asymmetry) of cognitive functions. Although these two aspects have been discussed extensively in studies of speech and language, how they correlate with language evolution has not been clarified. In this paper, we propose that the greatest hemispheric asymmetry in the human brain enables a strong CP effect, which causes a left lateralization of speech and language processing, during the emergence and evolution of language. The following sections illustrate respectively the structural lateralization, the functional lateralization of speech and language, CP, and their connections with language evolution.

2. Structural Lateralization

Given that the two hemispheres look similar at a first glance, the functional asymmetry of them seems intriguing: Why speech and language functions are left lateralized, whereas musical, spatial, emotional functions, and so on, are right lateralized? In fact, a close scrutinizing reveals a significant difference between the two hemispheres.

In the human brain, volumes of gray and white matters are different in the two hemispheres. Especially for the temporal lobe, which is crucial for speech processing, the language-related regions in the left hemisphere have a significantly greater volume of gray and white matters than the right homologue regions (Geschwind & Levitsky, 1968). This asymmetry can be ascribed to the number difference of cells (Rosen et al., 1993) and cytoarchitectural difference in the two hemispheres (Galaburda et al., 1978). It is known that the size of the pyramidal cells in cortex layer III is larger in the left hemisphere than in the right (Hutsler & Gazzaniga, 1996). Such larger cells tend to have thicker or more heavily branched axons, and these axons in the left hemisphere are more heavily myelinated compared to the right homologue regions (Anderson et al., 1999). These could be the reasons for the greater volumes of gray and white matters in the left temporal regions than in the right (Zatorre et al., 2002).

White matter forms long-distance, cortico-cortical connections, and its volume is also greater in the left arcuate fasciculus than in the right homologue region (Parker et al., 2005). This may indicate a faster speed of information transition between the frontal and temporal regions within the left hemisphere, compared to the right hemisphere. Such structural asymmetry may also be an underlying factor causing the left lateralization of language functions (Barrick, 2007). Speech sounds are processed in the temporal lobe; the primary auditory cortex (PAC) is involved in perceiving speech, and the Wernicke's area is involved in speech comprehension. A stronger and faster connection between the temporal lobe and the frontal lobe, where the decision is made (Binder et al., 2000), may allow the left hemisphere to do faster perception.

3. Speech Sounds and Functional Lateralization

Given the structural asymmetry between the left and right hemispheres, the two hemispheres are appropriate for processing different acoustic stimuli, thus leading to a general functional lateralization in specific domains. For example, the structural asymmetry could be the reason for the left hemispheric advantage in processing the fast changing acoustic cues and the right hemispheric advantage in processing the slow varying and fine-grained pitch changes. Since speech contains abundant fast changing acoustic properties, whereas music melody is full of nuance frequency variations, a left lateralization of speech and a right lateralization of music domain are reasonable (Zatorre et al., 2002).

In perceiving speech sounds, we not only passively receive signals, but also analyze and interpret their meanings. This requires recognizing the minimal distinguishable sound patterns—phoneme. In neuroimaging studies, a strictly controlled procedure has been used to locate the brain regions in charge of phoneme perception, and the superior temporal sulcus (STS) is found to be one such region (Möttönen et al., 2006). Interestingly, this region overlaps with the region of CP (Liebenthal et al., 2005). This overlap is not accidental. CP makes perception and discrimination of phonemes more robustly and reliably, because it avoids small acoustic changes around phoneme prototypes from altering the perceptual results (note that the CP here concerns phonemes with fast changing acoustic properties, instead of fine-grained spectral analysis as in the perception of human voice. As shown in previous work (e.g., Belin et al, 2000; Belin & Zatorre, 2003), the perception of human voice induces a right hemisphere dominance, opposite to CP processing. The lateralization pattern of conspecific vocalization processing (Gil-da-Costa & Hauser, 2006; Petkov et al., 2008) is also accordant with that of humans).

CP can be viewed not only as an advantage to make distinctions across phoneme boundaries, but also as a gross and rough discrimination of fast frequency changes happening in a short duration. Due to innate psychophysical factors (Eimas, et al., 1971) or after a long-term training (Hayes-Harb, 2007), a good discriminability exists between phoneme prototypes. Small acoustic changes around these prototypes are hardly detectable and assimilated to the prototypes to form gross categories. Sounds with slow frequency changes do have the least CP (see Section 4), but this does not mean that there are no prototypes of these types of phonemes or people cannot distinguish them well. On the contrary, the features of these sounds have long durations in the frequency domain, which correspond to slow frequency changes in the temporal domain, so it is much easier to distinguish acoustically the variations even around the prototypes of these sounds. Such a good discriminability around phoneme prototypes diminishes CP, but does not affect the perception of phoneme prototypes. Therefore, even there is no clear boundaries between phonemes with slow frequency changes, people will not confuse them.

From this perspective, CP is not a special or marvelous phenomenon in speech perception; it is just *a trade-off between the granularity in the frequency domain and the rate of frequency changes in the temporal domain.* CP can be viewed as a "side effect" of the fast changing acoustic properties; as mentioned above, the left hemisphere is specialized in perceiving sounds with fast frequency changes (Jamison et al., 2006), so it is not surprising that CP is left lateralized (Liebenthal et al., 2005). Zatorre et al. (2002) propose that the left lateralized speech perception is due to both the structural difference between the left and right hemispheres and the relative preference for the fast or slow frequency changes with gross or nuance frequency granularity of the two hemispheres. In addition to this, we want to emphasize that the degrees of CP and lateralization are highly correlated, as shown in the next section based on the evidence of processing different types of phonemes.

4. CP and Lateralization of Consonants, Vowels and Tones

Lateralization of various types of phonemes is highly correlated with the degree of CP. It was first reported that stop-consonants have a strong CP (Liberman et al., 1957), and in both dichotic listening and neuroimaging experiments, stop-consonants and VOT (voice onset time) show a strong left lateralization effect (Poeppel, 2003). As for isolated steady-state vowels and level tone categories, which do not have frequency changes, no CP effects are found (Repp, 1979; Francis et al., 2003). CP becomes explicit only when steady-state vowels or level tones are presented with context. According to this, we treat the degree of CP of steady-state vowels and level tones as the lowest among these conditions. Apart from level tones, CP is also found between contour and level tone categories (Wang, 1976; Francis et al., 2003), since contour tones contain faster frequency changes than level tones. In general, tones are bilaterally processed, but a recent ERP study found a greater degree of left lateralization of Cantonese contour tones, compared to level tones (Shuai et al.). All these reveal a trend of the degrees of left lateralization and CP of these types of phoneme: stop-consonants or VOT > contour tones > steady-state vowels or level tones.

It has been verified that the degree of left lateralization correlates with the rate of frequency change (Jamison et al., 2006). If CP corresponds to the rate of frequency change, CP should also correlate with left lateralization. As discussed before, there is a trade-off effect between the fine-grained discriminability in the frequency domain and the rate of frequency changes in the temporal domain: the faster the frequency changes, the rougher the discrimination results are. And CP is a consequence of a less accurate discrimination of sounds, especially around phoneme prototypes, when there is a faster frequency change in these sounds. Stop-consonants and VOT have the strongest and clearest CP. They have a short duration (less than 100 ms), and their frequency changes lie in a broad band. Contour and level tone categories can also be discriminated based on frequency change, though these changes are longer at the syllable duration (greater than 200 ms) and in a narrow frequency band, and the rate of frequency changes of contour tones is much less than that of stop-consonants. Moreover, CP of contour and level tones is not as strong as that of stop-consonants or VOT, and the least categorically perceived types are steady-state vowels and level tones, which do not have any frequency changes in either a broad or a narrow band.

All these reveal a close relation between CP and lateralization. Considering that the faster the frequency changes, the greater the left lateralized the phoneme is, it is reasonable that the degree of CP correlates with left lateralization.

5. Evolution and Speech Perception

In this section, we examine CP and lateralization in nonhuman animals and propose that the evolution of structural lateralization and functional specialization regarding different frequency changes enable and help language emergence.

Other animals have structural lateralization, which is manifested in the gray and white matter volumes (Buxhoeveden et al., 2000) and long-term white matter volume along the lateral sulcus (Rilling et al., 2008). But the degree of lateralization in these animals is not as high as that in humans. In addition, although other primates or rodents can perceive certain pairs of phonemes categorically, their performance is not as stable as humans' (Thompson, 2000). Furthermore, the sharpness of CP is consistent with the degree of lateralization in both humans and other animals; the greater the asymmetry between the two hemispheres, the acuter the CP.

So far, there is no direct comparison in different species regarding the correlation between CP and structural lateralization, and there is no direct comparison in humans between CP of different types of phonemes and functional lateralization. These are promising directions to pursue regarding language emergence. Based on the available results, we can observe that a stronger CP relates to not only a greater structural lateralization between human and other animals, but also a greater functional left lateralization with respect to various types of phonemes.

Considering that CP correlates with structural and functional lateralization and CP is a trade-off in discriminating sounds with different degrees of frequency changes, we propose that a strong structural lateralization could enhance the ability of discriminating both fast and slow frequency changes, and CP could improve the stability of perceiving phonemes with fast changing acoustic properties. Apart from fast changing acoustic cues, the fine-grained discriminability of slow changing acoustic cues is also preserved. These two functions are respectively lateralized in the left and right hemispheres, and such functional lateralization greatly enriches the types of sounds that we can discriminate.

There is evidence that patients having difficulties in language function, such as developmental dyslexia, have low degrees of lateralization (Habib, 2000). They also have a less sharp boundary in the CP test of stop-consonants compared to normal subjects (Vandermosten, 2010). This evidence not only supports the relationship between CP and lateralization, but also links these phenomena with language functions. Probably due to a less degree of structural lateralization caused by an abnormal brain development, the perception of fast or slow changing sounds and CP are less specialized in the left and right hemispheres, thus leading to a less sharp CP and a delay of the development of phonological awareness and other language functions, such as reading and writing, because all these functions require a phonological processing.

Based on the evolutionary trait, lateralization and CP are highly correlated. The abnormal lateralization and less acute CP performance of developmental dyslexic patients show that the development of language functions is based on a good CP ability and an appropriate brain asymmetry.

6. Conclusion

This paper presents a novel view that links lateralization with CP. We propose that the structural lateralization increases the types of sounds that people can discriminate, and that CP corresponds to the functional lateralization of fast and slow changing sounds, both of which boost the emergence of speech and language functions.

Acknowledgements

This work is supported by the Society of Scholars in the Humanities in the University of Hong Kong.

References

Anderson, B., Southern, B. D., & Powers, R. E. (1999). Anatomic asymmetries of the posterior superior temporal lobes: a postmortem study. *Neuropsychiatry, Neuropsychology, and Behavioral Neurology*, 12, 247-254.

Barrick, T. R., Lawes, I. N. Mackay, C. E., & Clark, C. A. (2007). White matter pathway asymmetry underlies functional lateralization. *Cerebral Cortex*, 17, 591-598.

Belin, P., Zatorre, R. J. Lafaille, P., Ahad, P., Pike, B. (2000). Voice-selective areas in human auditory cortex. *Nature, 403*, 309-312.

Belin, P., Zatorre, R. J. (2003). Adaptation to speaker's voice in right anterior temporal lobe. *Neuroreport, 14*, 2105-2109.

Binder, J. R., Liebentral, E., Possing, E. T., Medler, D. A., & Ward, B. D. (2004). Neural correlates of sensory and decision processes in auditory object identification. *Nature Neuroscience*, 7, 295-301.

Buxhoeveden, D., & Casanova, M. (2000). Comparative lateralisation patterns in the language area of human, chimpanzee, and rhesus monkey brains. *Laterality*, 5, 315-330.

Eimas, P. D., Siqueland, E. R., Jusczyk, P. W., & Vigorito, J. (1971). Speech perception in infants. *Science,* 171, 303-306.

Francis, A. L., Ciocca, V., & Ng, B. K. C. (2003). On the (non)categorical perception of lexical tones. *Perception & Psychophysics*, 65(7), 1029-1044.

Galaburda, A. M., Sanides, F., & Geschwind, N. (1978). Human brain: Cytoarchitectonic left-right asymmetries in the temporal speech region. *Archives of Neurology*, 35, 812-817.

Geschwind, N., & Levitsky, W. (1968). Human brain: Left-right asymmetries in temporal speech region. *Science*, 161,186-187.

Gil-da-Costa, R., & Hauser, M. D. (2006). Vervet monkeys and humans show brain asymmetries for processing conspecific vocalizations, but with opposite patterns of laterality. *Proceedings of the Royal Society B-Biological Sciences, 273*, 2313-2318.

Habib, M. (2000). The neurological basis of developmental dyslexia: an overview and working hypothesis. *Brain*, 123(12), 2373-2399.

Hauser, M., Chomsky, N., & Fitch, W. T. (2002). The Language Faculty: What is it, who has it, and how did it evolve? *Science*, 298, 1569-1579.

Hayes-Harb, R. (2007). Lexical and statistical evidence in the acquisition of second language phonemes. *Second Language Research*, 23(1), 65-94.

Hutsler, J., & Gazzaniga, M. (1996). Acetylcholinesterase staining in human auditory and language cortices: regional variation of structural features. *Cerebral Cortex*, 6, 260-270.

Jamison, H. L., Watkins, K. E., Bishop, D. V. M., & Matthews, P. M. (2006). Hemispheric specialization for processing auditory nonspeech stimuli. *Cerebral Cortex*, 16, 1266-1275.

Liberman, A. M., Harris, K. S., Hoffman, H., & B. Griffith. (1957). The discrimination of speech sounds within and across phoneme boundaries. *Journal of Experimental Psychology*, 54, 358-368.

Liebenthal, E., Binder, J. R., Spitzer, S. M., Possing, E. T., & Medler, D. A. (2005). Neural substrates of phonemic perception. *Cerebral Cortex*, 15, 1621-1631.

Möttönen, R., Calvert, G. A., Jääskeläinen, I. P., Matthews, P. M., Thesen, T., Tuomainen, J., & Sams, M. (2006). Perceiving identical sounds as speech or non-speech modulates activity in the left posterior superior temporal sulcus. *Neuroimage*, 30(2), 563-569.

Parker, G. J. M., Luzzi, S., Alexander, D. C., Wheeler-Kingshott, C. A. M., Ciccarelli, O., & Lambon Ralph, M. A. (2005). A Lateralization of ventral and dorsal auditory-language pathways in the human brain. *Neuroimage*, 24, 656-666.

Petkov, C. I., Kayser, C., Steudel, T., Whittingstall, K., Augath, M., & Logothetis, N. K. (2008). A voice region in the monkey brain. *Nature Neuroscience, 11,* 367–374.

Poeppel, D. (2003). The analysis of speech in different temporal integration windows: cerebral lateralization as 'asymmetric sampling in time'. *Speech Communication*, 41, 245-255.

Repp, B. H. (1979). Categories and context in the perception of isolated steady-state vowels. *Journal of Experimental Psychology: Human Perception and Performance*, 5(1), 129-145.

Rilling, J. K., Glasser, M. F., Preuss, T. M., Ma, X., Zhao, T., Hu, X., & Behrens, T. E. J. (2008). The evolution of the arcuate fasciculus revealed with comparative DTI. *Nature Neuroscience*, 11, 426-428.

Rosen, G. D., Sherman, G. F., & Galaburda, A. M., (1993). Neuronal subtypes and anatomic asymmetry: changes in neuronal number and cell-packing density. *Neuroscience*, 56, 833-839.

Shuai, L., Ho, J. P-K., Gong, T., & Wang, W. S-Y. On the existence of contour feature of lexical tones. In preparation.

Thompson, R. (2000). Categorical perception and conceptual judgment by nonhuman primates: the paleological monkey and the analogical ape. *Cognitive Science*, 24(3), 363-396.

Vandermosten, M., Boets, B., Luts, H., Poelmans, H., Golestani, N., Wouters, J., & Ghesquière P. (2010). Adults with dyslexia are impaired in categorizing speech and nonspeech sounds on the basis of temporal cues. *Proceedings of the National Academy of Sciences*, 107(23), 10389-10394.

Wang, W. S.-Y. (1976). Language change. In S. R. Harnad, H. D. Steklis, & J. Lancaster (Eds.), *Origins and evolution of language and speech* (pp. 61-72). New York: New York Academy of Sciences.

Zatorre, R. J., Belin, P., & Penhune, V. B. (2002). Structure and function of auditory cortex: music and speech. *Trends in Cognitive Sciences*, 6, 37-46.

POTENTIAL STAGES IN THE CULTURAL EVOLUTION OF SPATIAL LANGUAGE

MICHAEL SPRANGER

Sony CSL Paris, 6, rue Amyot,
Paris, 75005, France
spranger@csl.sony.fr

This paper investigates the function and formation of spatial language involving landmarks. We argue for two points. First, landmarks have an important function in spatial language. Agents that can use different landmarks and express their choice perform better than agents who cannot. Second, the use of landmarks has a positive effect on evolving systems of spatial relations. Agents that have the cognitive ability for using landmarks and agents that can express their choice of landmark are more successful in building spatial relation systems than those without. Based on this evidence the paper hypothesizes potential stages in the evolution of spatial language. Communicative success and in combination with environmental conditions can be driving forces for agents to go from a stage without landmarks to systems that allow arbitrary objects to be used as landmarks.

1. Introduction

A primary function of spatial language is to locate objects in spatial environments. Here is an example of a *locative* phrase from German.

(1)	*der*	*Block*	*links*	*der*	*Kiste*
	the.NOM	block.NOM	left.PREP	the.GEN	box.GEN

'The block to the left of the box'.

This seemingly simple phrase conveys a particular way of conceptualizing reality by integrating a number of syntactic and semantic *strategies*. The phrase combines the *projective* spatial relation "links" (left) with a landmark – an inanimate object denoted by the phrase "der Kiste" (the box). The speaker choose to explicitly *mark* the landmark (not obligatory). The relationship between the spatial category and the landmark is conveyed using the German case system (obligatory).

The strategic choices manifest in such an utterance are culturally coordinated. The fact that inanimate objects can serve as landmarks for spatial relations is true for many languages but certainly not for all. Some languages restrict landmark use to only animate objects or only humans, or – even more radical – just to trees (Levinson, 2003). Moreover, the strategies for expressing conceptual choices – lexicon and grammar – differ across languages (Svorou, 1994).

The diversity of strategies is something that comes as no surprise to people studying spatial language across cultures (Levinson & Wilkins, 2006; Levinson, 2003). But many questions remain about the evolutionary mechanics of spatial language. Recently, a number of attempts are made at explaining the evolution of aspects of spatial language such as toponyms (Schulz et al., 2006), the role of perspective – "me" and "you" – (Steels & Loetzsch, 2008), the origins of conceptualizatian strategies (Spranger, 2011b) and grammar (Spranger et al., 2010). In this paper we focus on the role of landmarks including perspective but also inanimate objects. We follow standard methodology for evolutionary explanations (Tinbergen, 1963) applied to the cultural level (Steels, 2006).

2. Spatial Language Games

Figure 1. This figure shows the set-up for spatial language game experiments. The images left and right show the internal situation model as perceived by each robot.

We use *language games* to study the cultural origins of spatial language. Two robots from a population are interacting in a shared environment and are trying to draw each others attention to objects in the vicinity using language. The set-up is exemplarily shown in Figure 1. The environment consists of a number of blocks of equal size and color (circles), a box (rectangle) and the interlocutors (arrows). The vision system of each robot tracks objects in the vicinity and establishes a model of the environment consisting of blocks (circles) with real-valued distances and orientations of objects with respect to the body of the robot. The environment is open-ended. New blocks, boxes and robots are added or removed and their spatial configuration changed.

1. Each agent perceives the environment after both have established a joint attentional frame (Tomasello, 1995).

2. The speaker randomly selects an object from the situation model (further called the topic T). The speaker tries to find a discriminating spatial relation applied to a particular landmark or perspective for describing T. Subsequently, the speaker looks up the words he associates with the spatial relation and the landmark and produces an utterance.

3. The hearer looks up which relation is associated with the utterance and also tries to look up words for landmarks in memory. He examines the context to find out whether there is a unique object which satisfies the spatial relation with respect to the landmark. The hearer then points to this object.

4. The speaker checks whether the hearer points to T. If the hearer pointed correctly the game is a success and the speaker signals this outcome to the hearer. If the game is a failure, the speaker points to the topic T.

There is a lot to say about processing machinery necessary for making these games work. For this paper, we have developed techniques and operational models that allow agents to flexibly and autonomously conceptualize spatial reality and express these conceptualizations in situated interactions (Spranger, 2011a).

3. The Function of Landmarks in Spatial Language

We can use language games to quantify the function of landmarks in spatial language with respect to communicative success. For this we equip agents with different language and conceptualization strategies and measure their performance in multi-agent simulations. In all populations agents are using *projective* spatial relations equivalent to English "front", "back", "left" and "right". The relations are defined as a similarity functions which are computed from the difference in angles between an object and the prototypical angle of the category (Spranger, 2011a). We compare 5 populations.

egocentric (ego) Agents use a single spatial relation in each utterance which is always interpreted egocentric to each robot. For instance, if the speaker conceptualizes "left" to refer to an object, the hearer will interpret the relation from his perspective.

perspective, unmarked (pp, um) Agents use the perspective of themselves but also of the other robot (similar to Steels & Loetzsch, 2008). Upon hearing the term "left" the hearer retrieves the best possible interpretation taking into consideration his own and the other robot's perspective on the environment. Similarly, the speaker might use an utterance such as "left" but refer to a position left of the hearer rather than left of himself.

perspective, marked (pp, m) Agents are using different perspectives but also clearly marking which perspective was used. For example, the speaker might say "left you" to indicate spatial relation and perspective.

landmarks, unmarked (lm, um) This population can use perspective (robots) and allocentric landmarks (the box), in conceptualizing reality. They do not communicate which object was used.

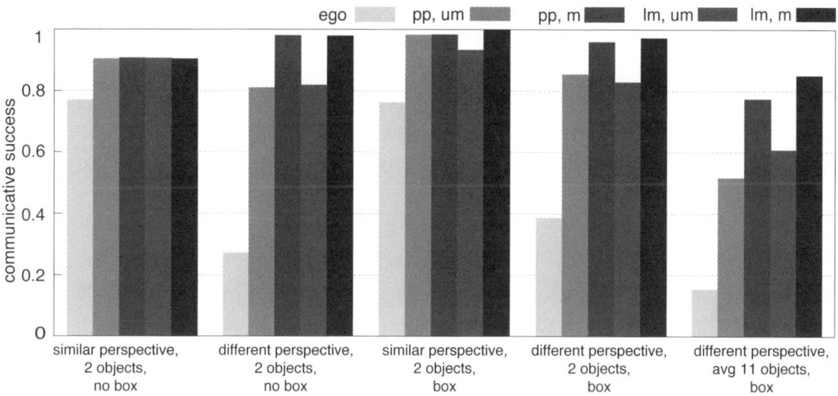

Figure 2. Results for populations of 10 agents tested in different experimental conditions. For each result agents interacted 2000 times. Every successful interaction counts with 1.0, otherwise with 0.0. These scores are averaged over all interactions.

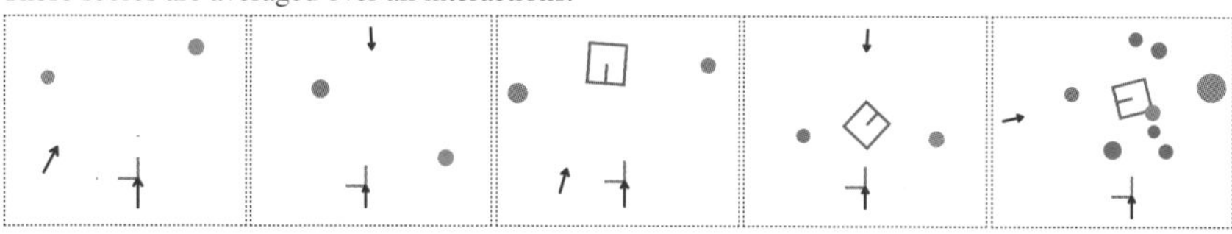

Figure 3. Examples of spatial scenes from each experimental condition ordered from left to rights as in Figure 2. Left, for instance, agents (black arrows) share a similar perspective on the spatial scenes, there are always 2 objects per scene (circles) and no box. To the right the most difficult condition is shown. Agents have differing perspectives, there are on average 11 objects and there is a box.

landmarks, marked (lm, m) Same population as *landmarks, unmarked*. But, agents express which landmark they use in all utterances.

Figure 2 shows communicative performance of each population in different experimental conditions. Each condition consists of many spatial situations, each of which include two robots and blocks whose positions change. But, the conditions differ in whether a box is present or the average number of objects and the typical perspective of robots (see Figure 3).

Clearly, the results show that agents capable of using different perspectives and landmarks perform better in communication than agents without. The effect increases the more objects are in each spatial context and the more the viewpoints of the interlocutors on the scene diverge. This is because agents which use different landmarks are much more flexible. They have more choice of relation-landmark pairs and often can choose one that fits best or better for discrimination. There are three important observations. First, if the environment is simple and agents have a similar perspective on the scene, it is sufficient to use egocentric interpretation of phrases. Second, the best strategy is to use any landmark possible (both robots and allocentric landmarks). Third, marking which landmark or perspective was used always outperforms the unmarked case in which agents use different landmarks but cannot express them.

The *unmarked* populations are interesting because they effectively show possible and maybe necessary intermediate evolutionary steps between a purely egocentric spatial language strategy and one that allows landmarks to be used and expressed. To develop a full-blown landmark systems, agents have to go through an unmarked stage where using a particular object as landmark is possible.

4. The Formation of Spatial Relation Systems and Landmarks

Previous work has shown how agents can culturally evolve lexical systems of spatial relations (Spranger, 2011a). Here, we apply these insights and study the effect of landmarks on such systems. We re-use the populations introduced in the previous section. All spatial relations (and terms) are removed from agents and instead they are provided with the following language change operators,

Invention Speakers invent new spatial terms and categories when they cannot discriminate a topic T from the context.

Adoption Upon hearing an unknown term the hearer uses the information from the speaker's pointing to learn not only the term but also the spatial relation the speaker might have used.

Alignment Invention and adoption happen in single interactions and it takes time for the new relations and terms to spread. Alignment operators orchestrate the gradual coordination of linguistic knowledge in the population. Agents continuously update their internal representations (Garrod & Doherty, 1994) by changing category representations, i.e. prototypical angles, over time and by rewarding and punishing categories and words based on success in interactions.

Figure 4 shows the dynamics of these operators over time. Agents start without spatial relations and spatial terms. Gradually they invent and align their linguistic repositories. At the same time the population becomes more successful in communication. Figure 5 compares different populations in a number of experimental conditions (same as used earlier). When agents do not have the means to use landmarks they fail in developing successful systems of spatial relations (if the environment is complex). Again the populations which can express the landmark they are using are outperforming agents which cannot. Agents which can use the full scope of landmarks (me/you/box) available in scenes outperform those which can only use perspective (me/you) which outperform those that can only use an egocentric strategy.

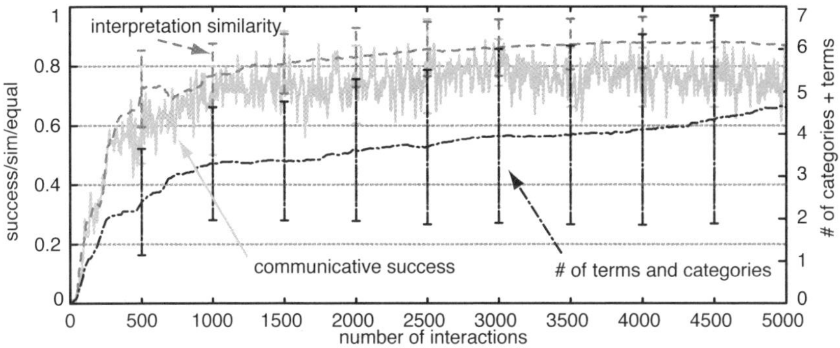

Figure 4. Dynamics of a population of 10 agents which develop a spatial category system (egocentric strategy) of 5 spatial relations in the *similar pp, 2 obj, no box* condition (5000 interactions, 8 trials). At the same time the spatial relations align across the population (see rise in *interpretation similarity*).

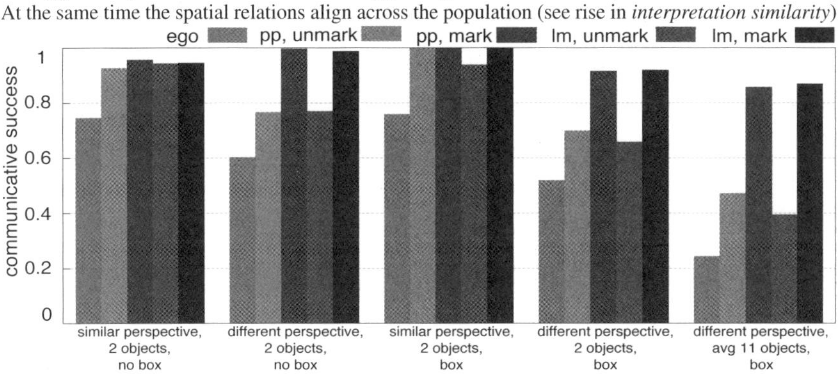

Figure 5. Comparison of different populations forming spatial relation systems (same experimental conditions as in Figure 2, 8 trials). Every population consists of 10 agents which first develop a spatial language system (5000 games) and then their communicative success is measured (2000 interactions).

Notice, how *landmark, unmarked* performs worse than the *perspective, unmarked*. The reason is that, upon hearing a new term agents have to adopt it using a particular landmark. This decision is essentially random, because agents were given no other means of deciding. The *landmark, unmarked* population has more landmarks to choose from. Therefore, agents are more likely to choose wrong. This makes clear that intermediary stages are necessary and that perspective strategies are suitable intermediaries.

Lastly, Figure 6 shows that agents can evolve a system of spatial relations while *at the same time* evolving a lexicon for expressing which landmark was used. The following is an example utterance one agent in such a population uttered

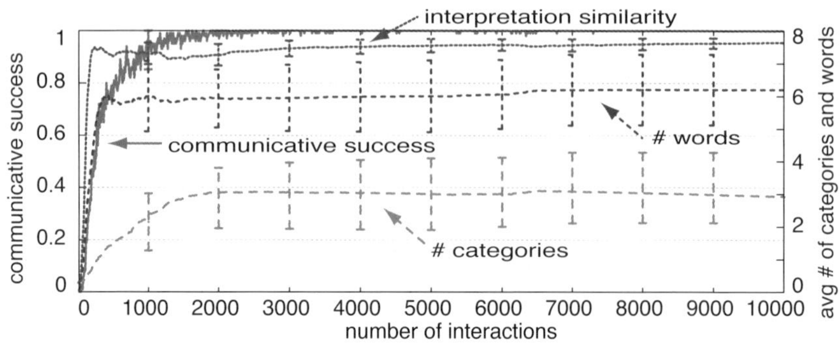

Figure 6. This population forms a system of projective spatial relations and words for marking perspective and landmarks. There are three the difference between the average number of words (*# constructions*) and the average number of spatial relations (*# categories*).

after 5000 interactions.The agent is using a category that he developed which behaves similarly to "left".

(2) *wutobe taketo*
box category-12
'to the left of the box'.

5. Discussion and Outlook

The experimental evidence presented in this paper suggests two important points. First, the function of landmarks in spatial language can be defined in terms of communicative success. Landmarks enable agents to communicate successfully about spatially distributed objects. Second, necessary stages for the evolution of spatial language such as unmarked conceptualization strategies are possible. It is obvious that before a landmark can be expressed or marked in language it must have a particular function in conceptualization. The question is whether such an initially unmarked case does lead to higher success so that the intermediate stage is sustainable. In the experiments, unmarked populations are performing better than the egocentric-only populations which shows that they are sustainable. Furthermore, marking of landmarks outperforms both the unmarked and the egocentric case. Judging from the results, perspective is another possible intermediary between egocentric systems and full landmark systems.

Communicative success is not the only area where use of landmarks can have positive effects. Steels and Loetzsch (2008), for instance, argue for the impact of perspective marking on cognitive effort which is the amount of processing required on the side of the hearer. The same argument also holds for the systems presented in this paper but it was omitted for space reasons.

Spatial language does not evolve in a vacuum. Rather the interaction of strategies described in this paper with other strategies such as toponyms, but also the interaction of different syntactic strategies (see Levinson & Wilkins, 2006 for an overview of different strategies) are important for understanding why particular strategies are present in one language but not in others. These are issues which certainly merit exploration and remain to be studied.

Acknowledgements

The author thanks Martin Loetzsch and Luc Steels for help in gathering the robotic data. Funding was provided by Sony CSL Paris and by the EU FP7 project Alear.

References

Garrod, S., & Doherty, G. (1994). Conversation, co-ordination and convention: an empirical investigation of how groups establish linguistic conventions. *Cognition*, *53*(3), 181–215.

Levinson, S. C. (2003). *Space in Language and Cognition: Explorations in Cognitive Diversity.* Cambridge University Press.

Levinson, S. C., & Wilkins, D. (2006). *Grammars of Space.* Cambridge University Press.

Schulz, R., Stockwell, P., Wakabayashi, M., & Wiles, J. (2006). Towards a spatial language for mobile robots. In *The evolution of language (evolang 6)* (pp. 291–298). World Scientific.

Spranger, M. (2011a). *The evolution of grounded spatial language.* Unpublished doctoral dissertation, Vrije Universiteit Brussels (VUB), Brussels, Belgium.

Spranger, M. (2011b). Recruitment, Selection and Alignment of Spatial Language Strategies. In *Advances in artificial life, ecal 2011.* MIT Press.

Spranger, M., Pauw, S., & Loetzsch, M. (2010). Open-ended semantics co-evolving with spatial language. In *The evolution of language (evolang 8)* (pp. 297–304). World Scientific.

Steels, L. (2006). How to do experiments in artificial language evolution and why. In *The evolution of language (evolang 6)* (pp. 323–332). World Scientific.

Steels, L., & Loetzsch, M. (2008). Perspective alignment in spatial language. In *Spatial language and dialogue* (pp. 70–88). Oxford University Press.

Svorou, S. (1994). *The grammar of space* (Vol. 25). John Benjamins.

Tinbergen, N. (1963). On aims and methods of ethology. *Zeitschrift für Tierpsychologie*, *20*(4), 410–433.

Tomasello, M. (1995). Joint attention as social cognition. In *Joint attention: Its origins and role in development.* Lawrence Erlbaum Associates.

VISUAL ARTIFICIAL GRAMMAR LEARNING: COMPARATIVE RESEARCH ON HUMANS AND BIRDS

NINA STOBBE
TECUMSEH W. FITCH

Department of Cognitive Biology, University of Vienna, Althanstrasse 14 Vienna, 1090, Austria

Artificial grammar learning (AGL) can be a useful tool for exploring rule learning strategies linked to pattern perception and pattern rule learning, a prerequisite for language acquisition. Most AGL studies reasonably make use of sequentially presented acoustic strings, resulting in stimuli that in their composition resemble human speech. To overcome possible working memory constraints imposed by sequential string presentation and to thus be able to directly compare performance of humans to other species with different memory capacities, we developed an AGL task in the visual domain. Presenting visual pattern elements simultaneously instead of sequentially minimizes the amount of required working memory. This approach allowed us to evaluate performance levels of two bird species, kea (Nestor notabilis) and pigeons (Columba livia), in direct comparison to human subjects. All avian and human subjects were able to learn pattern regularities without explicit instructions and generalised learned rules to novel stimuli. Detailed testing suggests that birds and humans did not always acquire the same pattern rule, and birds made use of alternative strategies to those defined by the experimenters.

1. Introduction

The capacity to learn and recognize complex regularities and generalize patterns that follow abstract rules is thought to be a prerequisite for the ability to acquire language in humans (e.g., Pinker, 1994). In earlier years, the mainstream position implied that language acquisition mechanisms are domain-specific and thus unique to humans (Chomsky, 1957). In the past decade, however, several studies indicated that more general pattern learning mechanisms are involved in early language learning (Kirkham et al. 2002; Christiansen & Chater, 2008). The general cognitive ability to extract regularities from patterns has been suggested to constitute a domain-general learning mechanism that evolved independent of linguistic functions and might thus be shared with non-human animals.

Comprehensive AGL experiments with humans demonstrate that even infants and children are able to rapidly learn abstract rules underlying presented patterns without any explicit instructions or feedback [e.g., Aslin et al., 1998; Gomez & Gerken, 1999; White et al. 2008). Based on the assumption that some of the learning mechanisms involved in AGL tasks might be shared with other animal species, several AGL studies have recently been carried out with different animal species (Fitch & Hauser, 2004; Toro & Trobalón, 2005; Gentner et al. 2006; Saffran et al., 2007; Van Heijnigen et al. 2009), suggesting that some non-human animals are also able to recognize regularities in stimulus sets and at least partly generalise these rules. These findings suggest that comparative studies on a variety of species can yield further insight into the basic cognitive and neural requirements for rule learning and abstraction.

Due to the fact that initial language learning in human infants is based on acoustic input, it is plausible that the majority of AGL studies in humans and nearly all AGL-studies in non-human animals have been carried out using acoustic stimuli. However, single elements of acoustic stimuli (e.g., single syllables) have to be presented sequentially, thus requiring the mental storage of elements to obtain the complete acoustic information of a stimulus. It has been suggested that this memory demand can constitute a considerable constraint in rule learning tasks. This finding might be particularly worth taking into account when performing comparative AGL experiments with humans and non-human animals since the short-term memory capacity of different species can differ significantly.

Aiming to expand the current knowledge on comparative rule learning abilities in humans and non-human animals, we designed a novel artificial grammar learning task. To overcome possible memory constraints, we presented visual stimuli in a simultaneous instead of a sequential manner. Additionally, we aimed to avoid any learning bias due to potential relevance of stimuli such as human speech syllables or bird vocalisations. The visual stimuli were created following abstract pattern rules, thus ruling out any influence of biological relevance of the stimuli, and were presented to humans as well as to two bird species, pigeons (*Columba livia*) and kea (*Nestor notabilis*).

The first aim of the present study was to find out whether all three species are able to discriminate between stimuli following different pattern rules. Secondly, we explored the generalisation abilities of humans and birds by testing them with novel stimuli that differed from the original stimuli in various visual features. If subjects did not simply memorize specific training stimuli, they were expected to correctly choose "grammatical" novel stimuli over "non-grammatical" ones, despite superficial visual differences from the original stimuli. We also assessed whether subjects can generalise the learned rule across stimulus size, i.e., if the number of constituting elements is increased while the underlying rule stays the same. Finally, the crucial test for abstraction of the experimenter-intended rule comprised stimuli that violated the underlying grammar rule by including either one additional element or one element less than the "grammatical" stimuli. Consequently, these "non-grammatical" stimuli were perceptually were similar to the "grammatical" stimuli and correct choice of the latter required understanding of the underlying rule. The results suggest that all bird subjects and some human subjects failed to learn the exact underlying grammatical rule without explicit instructions or cues, but readily learned alternative strategies to solve the generalization tasks at least to some extent.

2. Methods

Stimuli were made up of square tile-like elements. The single elements comprised 1 pixel black frames and internal complex geometrical patterns thereby constituting a visual analogue to the complex acoustic stimuli used in acoustic AGL studies. The patterns were created algorithmically, using Python (www.python.org) code implemented in Nodebox (www.nodebox.net). One category of elements (A) included rounded, continuous shapes generated as Bezier curves and colours from the blue/grey spectrum. The other category (B) contained small polygons in colours from the red/green spectrum bordered by straight lines and were clearly distinguishable from the A-elements. We created 12 elements of each category that were then assembled according to two different rules. Stimuli of the first grammar (hereafter referred to as $(AB)^n$) were made up of a string of AB units. In the stimuli of the second grammar (A^nB^n), a group of A-elements was followed by a group of B-elements. The number of A-elements matched the number of B-elements in all grammatical stimuli. The $(AB)^n$ grammar corresponds to a finite-state grammar (FSG), while the A^nB^n stimuli cannot be captured by a FSG and require a context-free (CF) or stronger grammar.

For the training phase, we created 240 stimuli of each grammar ensuring that each stimulus of one grammar had a corresponding stimulus with the same elements arranged according to the other grammar. To expose subjects to a variety of grammatical stimuli, half of the stimuli consisted of 4 elements (2 A and 2 B) and half of them consisted of 6 elements (3 A and 3 B). One particular element never appeared more than once in a stimulus, but specific A-elements were always paired with specific B-elements, forming constant bigrams (e.g., A1B1A2B2 or A1A2A3B1B2B3).

For the test phase, we first ran 4 different test types to assess the generalisation ability of our study species. Novel stimuli were created according to the same rules as the training stimuli (*generalisation test*). We also generated further stimuli that matched the patterns of the training stimuli, but differed in the included colours (*colour test*). To test whether orientation of the stimuli influences the ability of generalisation, we also created stimuli that were rotated by 90° clockwise (*rotation test*). Since training stimuli comprised fixed bigrams of A- and B-elements, we scrambled all elements so that there was no longer a specific relationship between the elements (e.g., A3B6A5B1; *scrambled test*) in order to test generalisation beyond correlated bigrams. For probing whether subjects are able to generalise the learned pattern rule beyond the n they had seen in training (i.e., arbitrary numbers of A- and B-elements), stimuli with 8 elements (4 A and 4 B) and 10 elements (5 A and 5 B) were created by adding either one or two additional pairs of elements (*Extensions*).

Finally, *Foil*-stimuli were generated by either adding one element to a grammatical stimulus or removing one element, which resulted in unequal numbers of A- and B-elements (A^nB^m). This was done for stimuli initially consisting of 2, 3 and 4 elements of each element type. Elements were removed or added either at the beginning of the stimulus or at the end leading to four different foil types per grammar type: $B(AB)^2$, $(AB)^2A$, $B(AB)^3$, $(AB)^3A$ and A^2B^3, A^3B^2, A^3B^4, A^4B^3, respectively.

For all species, subjects were divided in two groups for which either the $(AB)^n$ or the A^nB^n stimuli were the positive (rewarded) stimuli. Subjects were trained and tested in a two-alternative forced choice (2 AFC) procedure to discriminate between the stimuli of the two grammars by clicking/pecking on the correct stimulus on a touch screen. Each trial involved the simultaneous presentation of two stimuli in fixed positions on a black background on the computer screen. During training and for the first 5 experiments, choices of subjects were reinforced in all trials allowing a certain degree of learning during tests. However, in testing for generalisation to *Extensions* and *Foil*-stimuli, responses to probe-trials were not reinforced. In training and all experiments, the positive stimulus was presented simultaneously with the corresponding stimulus of the other grammar, i.e., a $(AB)^n$ stimulus was presented together with the corresponding A^nB^n stimulus. To avoid that the subjects base their decision purely on rejecting the obviously "non-grammatical" stimuli in the *Foil*-test, the *Foil*-stimuli were presented together with the corresponding positive stimulus.

3. Results

3.1. *Humans*

All 20 participants reached the training criterion of at least 70% first correct choices within a set of 30 training trials. In the following test trials, performance did not differ between the two groups trained on either $(AB)^n$ or A^nB^n (factor group: Wald Chi-Square 3.43, p=0.06). Performance in the generalisation tasks was at a very high level, subjects of both groups chose the correct stimulus in more than 90% of the 240 trials. Humans were also able to generalise the pattern rule to stimuli with extended numbers of tiles (n=4 and n=5) without any difficulties. However, when confronted with the foil stimuli with either an element added or taken away, performance significantly dropped (factor test: Wald Chi-Square 43.27, p>0.001). Only 6 out of 10 participants trained on $(AB)^n$ performed significantly above chance and 2 out 10 participants in the A^nB^n group did not pass the test scoring less than 70% correct first choices.

3.2. *Birds*

Both bird species successfully learned to discriminate between $(AB)^n$ and A^nB^n stimuli. While kea in both groups passed the training phase on average in 15 ± 1 sessions (mean ± SE; corresponding to 600 ± 40 trials), most pigeons took much longer to reach the learning criterion ($(AB)^n$ group: 85 ± 20 sessions; A^nB^n group: 53 ± 24 sessions). The type of test had a significant influence on performance in both kea and pigeons (Wald Chi Square 10253.66 and 2514.86, both $p<0.001$). When confronted with the first four generalisation tasks, level of performance was generally higher for kea than for pigeons (figure 1). All kea generalised the pattern rule to novel stimuli, novel colours, rotated and scrambled stimuli. Pigeons readily generalised to novel stimuli of the same type as the training stimuli, but many of the pigeons did not pass the significance level with the other three types of stimuli.

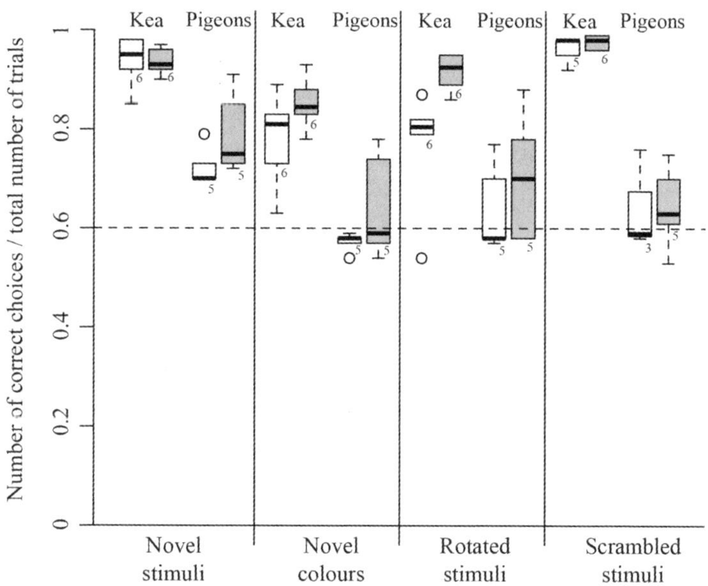

Figure 1: Performance of kea and pigeons in four different generalisation tasks. White symbols indicate subjects trained on $(AB)^n$ grammar, grey symbols indicate subjects trained on A^nB^n grammar. Numbers below boxplots specify sample size. The dashed line marks the level of significance (binomial test).

In the final tests, extending the stimuli to either 4 or 5 elements per tile type did not impair performance compared to the first generalisation task with novel stimuli in both bird species (both $p>0.45$). However, when birds had the choice between a correct stimulus and a foil stimulus (A^nB^m), members of both species chose randomly without any preference for either stimulus type.

4. Discussion

Training of both humans and two bird species in a 2 AFC resulted in successful discrimination of two types of visual stimuli, each arranged according to specific pattern rules. In humans and kea, subsequent transfer of the pattern rule to novel stimuli was successful when confronted with novel stimuli that followed the same rule and that either consisted of the same pattern elements arranged in different orders, included novel colours, were rotated around 90° counterclockwise or consisted of scrambled A- and B-elements (eliminating A/B-correspondences present in the training stimuli). The ability to transfer the general pattern discrimination to novel instances suggests that both species did not solely learn specific features of the training stimuli such as single elements, A/B bigrams or colour configuration, but acquired a more general pattern rule. Pigeons only performed highly above chance level in the first generalisation task and many of them showed difficulties in applying the pattern rule to novel stimuli with changed visual features, suggesting that they relied on more stimulus-specific features in the initial discrimination acquisition.

The results so far suggest that humans and kea were able to extract a pattern rule from the presented patterns without any explicit instructions, and to transfer this rule successfully to novel instances. However, subjects could have passed all of the tests so far by perceptually discriminating between stimuli consisting of alternating A´s and B´s versus clusters of A´s followed by clusters of B´s without matching the numbers of elements. Performance of pigeons in the previous discrimination tasks already suggested that they had learned a more general rule of categorising stimuli as "grammatical" "non-grammatical" (such as alternating versus clustered element types). However, kea of both groups also failed to reject foil stimuli, choosing between correct and foil stimuli in a random manner. Surprisingly, although performing in all previous tasks was near to ceiling level, even some of the human participants failed to correctly classify these foil stimuli as incorrect. We conclude that the subjects failing in the foil test acquired a pattern rule based on alternating versus block-consistent structure of A- and B-elements (i.e., they detected local dependencies), but ignored the total numbers of A´s and B´s.

In our study, subjects that failed to reject foil stimuli appear to have acquired alternative strategies that still allowed them to choose the correct stimulus well above chance level in the generalisation tasks that required transfer to novel stimuli. Given that the stimuli presented during training and first generalisation tests did not force the subjects to pay attention to the matching numbers of A´s and B´s, this feature was not always included in the acquired rule even in humans, and was never included by either bird species. Moreover, simultaneous presentation of "grammatical" and "non-grammatical" stimuli throughout the main parts of our study might have led subjects to base their decisions, and thus their acquired rule, mainly on the differences between the two stimulus classes. In general, many generalisation tests can be solved based on alternative strategies (e.g., clusters versus alternations of elements) that do not correspond to the experimenter-intended pattern rule. The use of alternative strategies is particularly to be expected when single elements do not possess any dependencies besides their position in the stimulus (Hochmann et al., 2008) or multiple generalisations are possible based on the initial stimuli (Gerken 2010). Alternative strategies can lead to above-chance performance in a variety of generalisation tasks, thus often leading to the false conclusion that subjects have in fact acquired the exact grammar structure intended by the experimenter (Zimmerer et al., 2010).

Our study represents the first attempt to study mechanisms of artificial grammar learning across three different species. The results suggest that all bird subjects and some human subjects failed to learn precisely the intended underlying grammatical rule without explicit instructions or cues, but readily developed alternative strategies to solve the generalisation tasks to a considerable extent.

Acknowledgements

This project was funded by the ERC Advanced Grant SOMACCA, project number 230604.

References

Aslin, R. N., Saffran, J. R. & Newport, E. L. (1998) Computation of conditional probability statistics by 8-mont-old infants. Psychol. Sci. 9, 321-324.

Chomsky, N. (1957). *Syntactic structures*. The Hague: Mouton.

Christiansen, M. H. & Chater, N. (2008). Language as shaped by the brain. *Behavioral and Brain Sciences, 31*, 536-53.

Fitch, T. W. & Hauser, M. D. 2004 Computational constraints on syntactic processing in a nonhuman primate. Science 303, 377-380.

Gentner, T. Q., Fenn, K. M., Margoliash, D. & Nusbaum, H. C. 2006 Recursive syntactic pattern learning by songbirds. Nature 440, 1204-1207.

Gerken, L. (2010) Infants use rational decision criteria for choosing among models of their input. Cognition 115, 362-366.

Gomez, R. L. & Gerken, L. (1999) Artificial grammar learning by 1-year-olds leads to specific and abstract knowledge. Cognition 70, 109-135.

Hochmann, J., Azadpour, M. & Mehler, J. (2008) Do humans really learn A^nB^n artificial grammars from exemplars? Cogn. Sci. 32, 1021-1036.

Kirkham, N. Z., Slemmer, J. A. & Johnson, S. P. (2002). Visual statistical learning in infancy: evidence for a domain general learning mechanism. *Cognition, 83*, B35-B42.

Pinker, S. (1994). *The language instinct*. New York: Morrow.

Toro, J. M. & Trobalón, J. B. 2005 Statistical computation over a speech stream in a rodent. Atten. Percept. Psychophys. 67, 867-875.

Van Heijningen, C. A. A., de Visser, J. Zuidema, W. & ten Cate, C. 2009 Simple rules can explain discrimination of putative recursive syntactic structures by a songbird species. Proc. Natl. Acad. Sci. U.S.A. 106, 20538-20543.

White, K. S., Peperkamp, S., Kirk, C. & Morgan, J. L. (2008) Rapid acquisition of phonological alternations by infants. Cognition 107, 238-265.
Zimmerer, V. C., Cowell, P. E. & Varley, R. A. (2010) Individual behavior in learning of an artificial grammar. Mem. Cogn. 39, 491-501.

SYNTAX OF MIND – SEMANTICS OF MIND

TWO FRAMEWORKS FOR COMPARATIVE APPROACHES TO THE EVOLUTION OF LANGUAGE AND MUSIC

XIAOXIA SUN

School of Foreign languages, Northeast Normal University, Renmin Road 5268 Changchun, 130024, Peoples Republic of China

UWE SEIFERT

Institute of Musicology, University of Cologne, Albertus-Magnus-Platz Cologne, 50923, Germany

It is argued that a comparative approach to language and music will be fruitful for a deeper understanding of the human mind in general and the evolution of language and music in particular. Two research programs, entitled "the Syntax of Mind" and "the Semantics of Mind" are identified, distinguished and briefly characterized. The Syntax of Mind framework focuses on recursion and starts from a syntactic perspective on language and music as inaugurated by Noam Chomsky and adapted e.g. by W. Tecumseh Fitch. Two approaches to recursion are distinguished: a) recursion in the context of the Chomsky hierarchy and b) recursion conceptualized as MERGE within the minimalist program. Michael A. Arbib's action-oriented Extended Mirror System Hypothesis of language evolution is discussed as, at present, the most promising program of a Semantics of Mind approach, which is in the spirit of cognitive linguistics, and is grounded in brain research via mirror mechanisms. For both programs their potentiality as a framework for a comparative evolutionary approach to music and language is briefly reflected on.

1. Introduction

Recently Anirudhh Patel (2008; cf. also Katz & Pesetsky to appear) proposed a comparative approach to music and language as a research paradigm. Our claim is that such a comparative approach will also be fruitful for evolutionary considerations to understand both higher neurocognitive functions as well as their mutual dependency concerning their functional architecture and possible neuronal implementations. Only recently biolinguistic and biomusicological research on the evolution of these functions has begun to influence each other (Botha & Knight 2009; Dehaene & Petit 2009; Botha 2009; Fitch 2010, Hauser

& McDermott 203; Rebuschat, Rohrmeier, Hawkins, & Cross 2012). Although up to now there has been no systematic exchange of ideas between these two research strands, to us, it seems that there are two main linguistic research programs suitable to function as conceptual frameworks for future comparative approaches to the music and the language faculty of the human mind/brain. One is more in the spirit of Chomskyan generative grammar and the minimalistic program. Such approaches focus on structural or syntactical aspects of language and music. Therefore, in comparing music and language phonology and syntax come to the fore (e. g. Hauser, Chomsky & Fitch 2002; Fitch 2010). We use "Syntax of Mind" as an umbrella term for such approaches to characterize this program. The other program is more in the spirit of cognitive linguistics. Music and language are to be explained in referring to general cognitive processes such as memory, attention, learning, and emotion/motivation. In linguistics, then, semantics, pragmatics, prosody, and discourse comprehension come to the fore. We term these approaches "Semantics of Mind". Michael Arbib's Extended Mirror System Hypothesis of language evolution based on mirror mechanisms to explain the gestural origin of the language-ready brain comes to mind (Arbib 2001, 2002, 2005, 2006, 2008, to appear). In the following, we briefly characterize both programs in relation to a comparative approach.

2. Syntax of Mind: Recursion in generative grammar and Minimalism

Current discussions of language within the Syntax of Mind framework focus on the role of recursion in connection with the idea of discrete infinity, meaning that an infinite set of objects (e.g. an infinite set of sentences) is generated by a finite set of rules, e.g. grammatical rules, from a finite set of objects, e.g. words and their syntactical categories. Although strongly related, two conceptualizations of recursion are to be distinguished in the Syntax of Mind approach: The first conceptualizes recursion within generative grammar and automata theory as a distinguishing property of rule systems characterizing descriptions of self-embedding structures in the Chomsky hierarchy. The second conceptualization is used in the minimalist program and captures recursion with the operation MERGE.

2.1. *Recursion: Generative grammar and cognitive neuroscience of language*

Discrete infinity, a key idea in generative grammar, Minimalism and language research, takes the finiteness of the human brain into account. Because of its finiteness the human brain is modeled as in the framework of automata theory most adequately as finite automaton (Chomsky 1963). But Chomsky "proved" that natural languages are more complex than regular grammars, which are formally equivalent to finite automata. His argument was that natural languages such as English include hierarchically nested self-embedding structures. Therefore, natural languages must be formalized at least as context-free grammars. For the argument it is assumed that there is no upper bound for self-embedding and that languages can be theoretically conceived of as infinite sets of sentences. Context-free grammars are formally equivalent to push-down automata and according to the Chomsky hierarchy push-down automata are computationally more powerful than finite automata. So, theoretically a system such as the human brain has to represent and process structures, which in principle are more complex than itself. Therefore, in the early days of generative grammar, Noam Chomsky introduced his well-known competence-performance distinction. Within the Chomskyan framework of natural language complexity, i. e. the Chomsky hierarchy, it is normally accepted that the processing of natural human languages involves at least processing of structures of phrase-structure grammar complexity, i. e. , processing of structures whose complexity is at least captured by context-free grammars (c.f. Petersson, Folia & Hagoort 2010 for a critical discussion of the Chomsky hierarchy within language research). Furthermore, it is assumed that long-distance dependencies need at least to be described by context-free grammars and non-human animals are unable to process such structures. At best non-human animals are only able to process structures of complexity of finite-state or regular grammars (Fitch & Hauser 2004 relate the idea of structural complexity of natural languages within automata theory to empirical research on the evolution of the language and music faculty; cf. Fitch 2010). There seems to be some evidence that only humans are able to learn such structures and that non-human primates cannot learn to process self-embedding recursive structures implicit in audio signals. (Conway & Christiansen 2001; Fitch & Hauser 2004). Angela Friederici and her group inspired by Hauser & Fitch (2004) examined humans with brain imaging using the artificial grammar learning as experimental design paradigm (e.g. Bahlmann, Schubotz, & Friederici 2008). The results showed that the frontal operculum of the primary premotor cortex is involved in the processing of sound sequences that do not contain self-embedding recursive structures. This area seems to be involved in the processing of rhythms and motor sequences and its task may be the prediction of the next element in a sequence. These are evolutionary old areas, still present in apes and monkeys today. Further fMRI studies using sequences containing self-embedding recursive structures revealed that instead of this part of the operculum, Broca's area is activated. Broca's area is unique to humans and not present in apes. For example, the semantics of calls is represented in Brodmann area 22 in apes (e.g., orang-utan) that corresponds to Wernicke's area involved in the representation of the semantics of language. But a specific area for syntactical processing of the call system, equivalent to complex articulated speech like Broca's area in humans, is missing.

2.2. *Recursion: Minimalism and the cognitive neuroscience of language*

In the minimalist program with the goal of principled explanation, the focus lies on MERGE as the key operation realizing recursion according to the language-faculty-in-a-narrow sense hypothesis (FLN hypothesis; Hauser, Chomsky, & Fitch 2002). Based on MERGE recently an Identity Thesis of Music and Language has been proposed (Katz & Pesetsky to appear). This thesis states that although at a "surface level" language and music appear distinct a careful analysis concerning the underlying computational operations such as MERGE reveals that these are identical. Therefore, music and language are identical. This seems to be in accordance with Noam Chomsky's view (personal communication June 2011) that under evolutionary considerations music like the natural number system is a derivative of FLN (but cf. Jackendoff to appear). At present empirical evidence is lacking on how MERGE might be implemented in the brain's neural architecture, and therefore, a fortiori, claims concerning the evolutionary role of MERGE must remain speculative. Hence, in the Syntax of Mind program, in a first step, highly theoretical terms such as MERGE, LEX or others need to be related to empirical research in cognitive neuroscience of language and music (cf. Grodzinsky & Friederici 2006 for an overview of such current efforts in the cognitive neuroscience of language).

3. Semantics of Mind: Mirror mechanisms and the evolution of language and music

As already mentioned, in the Semantics of Mind program, cognitive domains such as language and music are to be explained by more general neurocognitive processes such as memory and emotion. Mirror mechanisms are such processes and they have been applied to explain action and language processing as well as social cognition (Rizzolatti & Sinigaglia 2008). Michael Arbib's Extended Mirror System Hypothesis (EMSH) states a gestural origin of language based on mirror mechanisms and imitation. Up to now, the EMSH has not been discussed in the literature concerned with the evolution of music (e.g., Hauser & McDermott 2003, Justus & Hutsler 2005, McDermott & Hauser 2005; Rebuschat, Rohrmeier, Hawkins, & Cross 2012).

3.1. *The Extended Mirror System Hypothesis of language evolution*

The EMSH is in contrast with the traditional view that natural language evolved through social communication from call systems; it states that language syntax and denotational semantics evolved out of gestures, i.e. proto-signs, and the activities related to the brain's mirror mechanisms. Seven stages are hypothesized for language evolution (Arbib 2001, 2002, 2005, 2006). There are three pre-hominid stages S1, S2, and S3. Stages S4, S5, and S6 distinguish the hominid line from that of the great apes. The final stage S7 is claimed to result from cultural evolution. The stages are characterized as follows: S1: grasping; S2: a mirror system for grasping, shared with common ancestors of humans and monkey; S3: a "simple" imitation system, shared with common ancestors of humans and chimpanzee; S4: a "complex" imitation system; S5: a manual-based communication system (proto-sign) used in pantomime and manual communication; S6: speech (proto-speech), a vocal-based communication system exploiting the brain mechanisms that evolved to support proto-sign, an open-ended production and perception of sequences of vocal gestures, and emotional shading; S7: language, co-evolution of cognitive and linguistic complexity. Stages S6 and S7 are separate, but perhaps interleaved. EMSH postulates Stages S3 and S4, in which imitation is a key mechanism, to go beyond the "basic" mirror system from recognizing single actions to being able to copy compound actions. Especially S4, the development of a "complex" imitation system, seems to be central the transition from australopithecines to Homo. The "complex" imitation system at stage S4, which forms the "speech-like" areas of the early hominids, mediated orofacial and manuo-brachial communication, but not "speech", i.e. the call system. The combinatorial properties of language are inherent in the manuo-brachial system. Stage S5, i.e. proto-signs, would have been present in a rather limited form in Homo erectus and further development took place in connection with "cultural evolution". Stage S6 mediated the computational pathway between the call area located in the cingulate cortex and Broca's area to form speech and then language. How may "music" fit into the framework provided by the Extended Mirror-System Hypothesis? We speculate that "music" comes in at stages S4, S5 and S6 as sound structures used for a group's emotion regulation in communicative social interaction exploiting the phatic function (cf. Cross 2010) of these structures simultaneously. The details need to be specified and worked out in future research (cf. (Arbib to appear) for a first encounter of research on music, language, and the brain in the context of an action-oriented research paradigm). Broca's area and the premotor may serve as a starting points to relate mirror mechanisms in language, music and action from a point of view of cognitive neuroscience. Broca's region is traditionally known to be involved in syntactical language processing. It seems to have evolved in the process of human evolution out of the inferior parts of the premotor cortex. In Macaques this area is called F5 and it is supposed by some authors to be homologue to Broca's area. It has been shown by Stefan Koelsch (2011) that processing of musical syntax, i.e. sequences of musical events, seems to be supported by the network supporting language processing, especially Broca's area and its homotope in the right hemisphere. During music-syntactic processing in the left and right hemisphere, several areas in and near Brodmann area 44 (BA 44), such as the ventrolateral premotor cortex (vlPMC), the inferior fronto-lateral cortex (IFLC), the superior and inferior pars opercularis and the anterior superior temporal gyrus (aSTG) show activations. IFLC (BA 44) and vlPMC are involved in the analysis, recognition and prediction of sequential auditory information processing. Research results from cognitive neuroscience of music (Koelsch 2011) suggests that Broca's area, i. e., the pars opercularis of the inferior frontal gyrus (IFG) which corresponds to BA 44, is bilaterally involved in the processing of musical syntax. For Koelsch (2011) it seems likely that the (inferior) part of BA 44 is generally involved in hierarchical processing of syntactic information. Neuroscientific research indicates that this area is not only involved in music processing but also in processing of complex hierarchical structures, especially long-distance dependencies, in language and action sequences. In general Broca's area and some related areas seem to be involved in language processing, motor imitation and music perception. Furthermore, cognitive neuroscience research indicates the involvement of Broca's area in tool use. Besides other anatomical structures, the ventral premotor cortex (PMCv) seems to be involved in the syntactic processing of music, especially of those structures that are describable by finite state grammars. For language there seems to be some evidence that local relations and simpler structures are processed in PMCv.

4. Conclusion

We showed that there are two promising research programs for an integrative comparative approach to language and music evolution: Syntax and Semantics of Mind. In the Syntax of Mind program, the theoretical concept recursion is related to self-embedding language structures in automata theoretical terms of the Chomsky hierarchy. Via self-embedding structures recursion has been linked to empirical research in cognitive neuroscience and biology of language using the paradigm of artificial grammar learning, focusing on Broca's area and the premotor cortex taking evolutionary consideration into account. Recursion is investigated as MERGE in Minimalism but the neurocognitive reality of such concepts needs to be investigated further, especially in cognitive neuroscience of music, to support evolutionary considerations. The Semantics of Mind program, in addition to current cognitive neuroscience research on the involvement of Broca's area in action, language, and music processing, exploits the homology of F5 and Broca's area and mirror mechanisms to account for an evolutionary history of language and music. After reviewing the different research strands, to us, at present the Semantics of Mind program, in particular the action-oriented EMSH, seems to some extent more promising than the Syntax of Mind program because a) it encompasses the communicative and phatic function of language and music; b) it integrates emotional aspects which form an integral part in the understanding of the human mind; c) it is well grounded in brain and biological research; d) it grounds language and music in action, i.e. in motor theories of consciousness and the human brain's higher mental functions; e) it opens up to investigate the role of tool use in the evolutionary formation of higher neurocognitive functions in primates (e. g. Johnson-Frey 2004).

References

Arbib, M. A. (Ed.) (to appear). *Language, Music and the Brain: A Mysterious Relationship.* Cambridge, MA: The MIT Press.

Arbib, M. A. (ed.) (2006). *Action to language via the mirror neuron system.* Cambridge : Cambridge University Press

Arbib, M. A. (2005). From monkey-like action recognition to human language: An evolutionary framework for neurolinguistics. *Behavioral and Brain Sciences*, 28, 105–167.

Arbib, M. A. (2002). The mirror system, imitation, and the evolution of language. In K. Dautenhahn, & C. L. Nehaniv (Eds.), *Imitation in animals and artifacts.* (pp. 229–280). Cambridge, MA: The MIT Press.

Arbib, M. A. (2001). Co-evolution of human consciousness and language. In P. C. Marijuán (Ed.), *Cajal and consciousness: Scientific approaches to consciousness on the centennial of Ramón y Cajal's textura: Vol. 929. Annals of the new academy of sciences* (pp. 195-220). New York: New York Academy of Sciences.

Bahlmann, J., Schubotz, R. I., & Friederici, A. (2008). Artificial grammar processing engages Broca's area. *Neuroimage*, 42, 525–534.

Botha, R. (2009). On musilanguage/"Hmmmmm" as an evolutionary precursor to language. *Language & Communication*, 29, 61–76.

Botha, R., & Knight, C. (Eds.) (2009). *The Prehistory of Language.* Oxford University Press.

Chomsky, N. (1963). Formal properties of grammar. In R. D. Luce, & R. R. Bush, & E. Galanter (Eds.), *Handbook of Mathematical Psychology. Vol. II: Chapters 9-14* (pp. 323-418). New York: Wiley.

Conway, C. M., & Christiansen, M. H. (2001). Sequential learning in non-human primates. *Trends in Cognitive Sciences, 5(12)*, 539-546.

Cross, Ian (2010). The Evolutionary Basis of Meaning in Music: Some Neurological and Neuroscientific Implications. F. C. Rose (Ed.), *The Neurology of Music* (pp. 1–15). London: Imperial College Press.

Dehaene, S. & Petit, C. (Eds.) (2009). *Collège de France: Parole et musique – Aux origines du dialogue humain. Colloque annuel 2008.* Paris: Odile Jacob

Fitch, W. T. (2010). *The Evolution of Language*. Oxford: Oxford University Press.

Fitch, W. T., & Hauser, M. (2004). Computational constraints on syntactic processing in a non-human primate. *Science, 303*, 377-380.

Grodzinsky, Y. & Friederici, A. (2006). Neuroimaging of syntax and syntactic processing. *Current Opinion in Neurobiology*, 16, 240–246.

Hauser, M., & McDermott, J. (2003). The evolution of the music faculty: A comparative perspective. *Nature neuroscience*, *6(7)*, 663-668.

Hauser, M. D., Chomsky, N., & Fitch, W. T. (2002). The faculty of language: what is it, who has it, and how did it evolve? S*cience*, 298, 1569–1579.

Jackendoff, R. (to appear). What is the human language faculty? Two views. *Language;*http://ase.tufts.edu/cogstud/incbios/RayJackendoff/humanlanguage.pdf

Johnson–Frey, S. H. (2004). The neural bases of complex tool use in humans. *Trends in Cognitive Sciences*, 8, 71–78.

Justus, T., & Hutsler, J. J. (2005). Fundamental issues in the evolutionary psychology of music: Assessing innateness and domain specifity. *Music Perception*, *33(1)*, 1-27.

Katz, J., & Pesetsky, D. (to appear). The identity thesis for language and music. http://ling.auf.net/lingBuzz/000959

Koelsch, Stefan (2011). Towards a neural basis of music processing: a review and an updated model. *Frontiers in Psychology;* doi: 10.3389/fpsyg.2011.00110 .

McDermott, J., & Hauser, M. (2005). The origins of music: Innateness, uniqueness, and evolution. *Music Perception*, *33(1)*, 29-59.

Patel, A. D. (2008*). Language, Music, and the Brain*. Oxford: Oxford University Press.

Petersson, K. M., Folia, V., & Hagoort, P. (2010). What artificial grammar learning reveals about the neurobiology syntax. *Brain & Language;* advance online publication. doi:10.1016/j.bandl.2010.08.003.

Rebuschat, P.; Rohrmeier, M.; Hawkins, J.; Cross, I. (Eds.) (2012). *Language and Music as Cognitive Systems.* Oxford: Oxford University Press.

Rizzolatti, G., & Sinigaglia, C. (2008). *Mirrors in the Brain. How our Minds Share Actions and Emotions*. Oxford/New York: Oxford University Press.

DISPLACEMENT IN COMMUNICATION

KAORI TAMURA & TAKASHI HASHIMOTO
School of Knowledge Science
Japan Advanced Institute of Science and Technology (JAIST)
1-1, Asahidai, Nomi, Ishikawa, 923-1292, Japan
tamura@jaist.ac.jp, hash@jaist.ac.jp

Displacement, the ability to refer to things that are spatially and temporally remote, is one of the important features of human language. In order to clarify what is truly unique to human language, we consider displacement in the context of communication. Various situations involving displacement are classified and examined. It is suggested that displaced understanding, which is not based on direct experience is unique to human beings. An experimental framework to investigate the cognitive mechanism of displacement in communication is introduced. The result of a preliminary experiment leads to a hypothesis that feature extraction is one of the mechanisms that enables displacement in communication.

1. Introduction

Displacement, the ability to refer to things that are remote in space or time (or both) from where the talking goes on, is one of the features of human language (Hockett, 1960). By virtue of this characteristic, human beings can refer not only to presently existing things but also to past or future events and imaginary objects or states. By contrast, most symbolic communication in animals—for example in the alarm calls of vervet monkeys (Seyfarth et al., 1980)—refer to present stimuli, such as predators and cannot convey information on absent objects.

Displacement is a concept that defines this difference between human beings and animals, and the understanding of displacement is thought to contribute to the study of the origin and evolution of human language. On the other hand, the conventional definition of Hockett (1960) includes the waggle dance of honeybees (Frisch, 1967) as an example of displacement. Thus, given his perspective, it is not clear which aspect of displacement is unique to human beings. Here we attempt to understand displacement as something unique to human language by focusing on the displacement that takes place between a speaker and a listener. In order to achieve this objective, we propose an experimental setup and develop a hypothesis.

2. Displacement on the Listener Side and Displacement Not Based on Direct Experience

Displacement has been studied as "displaced reference" or "displaced speech" in the fields of cognitive and language development (Hurford, 2007; Liszkowski et al., 2009; Morford & Goldin-Meadow, 1997). Studies have focused on the ability in human speech to make reference to absent objects. However, it is difficult to distinguish the displacement that is said to occur in the waggle dance from that of human beings, as long as we focus only on displaced reference, displacement on the speaker's side.

Human language is usually used to communicate intentions and knowledge to others so that these may be held in common[1]. In this way, a listener can obtain a knowledge that only a speaker has. An understanding of the displaced references of the speaker requires a consideration of the displacement that takes place on the listener's side. In addition, we will need to examine displacement by considering the interaction of the speaker and the listener. Thus, we regard displacement on the listener's side as "displaced understanding," treating it in terms of communication that includes not only displaced reference but also displaced understanding.

Problematically, previous research also does not separate displacement issues from those of memory. For example, Liszkowski et al. (2009) investigate whether prelinguistic infants and chimpanzees are able to refer to absent objects by pointing gestures. They demonstrate that prelinguistic infants are capable of engaging in such pointing, while chimpanzees are scarcely able to do so. However, these researchers do not clearly indicate if this divergence in behavior with absent objects stems from a difference in memory or in displacement ability. If the latter, it appears that some ability associated with displacement exists separate from memory. To specify this distinction, we regard communication about absent objects based on what the speaker and/or listener have experienced in advance as "displacement based on memory."

3. The Classification of Displacement

In order to make the displacement unique to human beings clear, we classify displacement in communication. Based on the points raised above, we set two axes:

1. The distinction of the speaker and the listener
2. The distinction of displacement based on memory and that *not* based on direct experience

Table 1 shows the classification of displacement for the speaker and the listener according to two axes. The columns represent distinctions of three states: that where the referent presently exists (present), that were it does not presently exist

[1] Note that we do not argue that human language has evolved for communication.

but exists in memory (memorized), and that where it does not presently exist and is not present in memory (unexperienced).

Table 1. Classification of displacement in communication

	Speaker			*Listener*		
	present	memorized	unexperienced	present	memorized	unexperienced
1	○			○		
2		○		○		
3			○	○		
4	○				○	
5		○			○	
6			○		○	
7	○					○
8		○				○
9			○			○

Rows 3, 6, and 9 of Table 1 are the cases where the speaker refers to an object that he or she has not experienced before. They are similar to a situation where the speaker is producing a referent, and thus creativity is strongly present. We exclude these cases because they do not fit with the purpose of this inquiry, which focuses on displacement.

Row 1 in Table 1 is not a state with displacement, since the referents exist in the present for both the speaker and the listener. Row 2 is the state where the referent exists for the listener but not for the speaker, who knows it in advance. For example, consider a situation where the speaker and the listener are talking on the phone, and the speaker refer to a building that he or she has seen before and that the listener actually stands before. Displaced reference but not displaced understanding works here, since the listener can understand the speaker's reference based on the present object. Focusing only on displaced reference, we cannot distinguish 2 from 5 or 8 and cannot make a clarifying statement about displacement that is unique to human beings.

In addition, we should especially focus on the difference between rows 4 and 5 and rows 7 and 8 in Table 1. The latter two seem possible only when displacement is unique to human linguistic communication, while the former can also be seen in the symbolic communication of animals. The distinction between the rows 4 and 5 and rows 7 and 8 is explained below.

Row 4 of Table 1 is the state where the referent presently exists for the speaker but not for the listener, who understand the speaker's reference based on prior memory. This state corresponds to the alarm calls of the vervet monkey (Seyfarth et al., 1980). For example, a speaker monkey makes an alarm call that refers to a situation with a predator. Another individual who hears the alarm call can take a corresponding avoidance behavior to the specific predator based on memory before encountering the real predator. Although displaced reference does not work here, displaced understanding of the speaker's reference based on memory is present.

Row 5 of Table 1 is the state where the referent is not present for both the speaker and the listener. They refer to and understand the referent based on memories. This state is thought to correspond to the waggle dance of honeybees. When a speaker bee conveys information on the location of absent honey, displaced reference and displaced understanding based on memory seem to be present. The state covered by Row 5 has been regarded as an example of the conventional definition of displacement (Hockett, 1960). If we focus only on the speaker, these nonhuman communications are also included in the cases of displacement. However, the displacement of the waggle dance of honeybees can be clearly distinguished from the displacement that is unique to human communication.

Displacement that is unique to human linguistic communication is covered by rows 7 and 8 of Table 1. Row 7 is the state where the referent is present for the speaker, but not for the listener, who has not experienced it before. For example, in a phone conversation, the speaker talks about a building in front of him or her, and the listener has not seen or heard about the building. This case does not meet the conventional definition in that the displaced reference does not work here. The listener, however, understands to what the speaker refers, which is neither a present object nor a memory. This state is seen daily in human but not animal communication.

Row 8 of Table 1 is the state where the referent does not presently exist for both the speaker and the listener. Based on his or her memory, the speaker refers to an object that the listener has not seen or heard about. This state corresponds, for instance, to a situation in which the speaker talks about a building he or she has seen, and the listener has neither seen nor heard about it. Here both displaced reference based on memory and displaced understanding *not* based on direct experience are realized. This situation involves displacement unique to human beings.

Based the above observations, we claim that displaced understanding *not* based on direct experience is the key factor in realizing displacement unique to human beings. Furthermore, we think it is effective to consider the utterances of the speaker that make displaced understanding possible for the listener.

4. Experimental Framework to Investigate Displacement in Communication

To investigate displacement in communication and especially displaced understanding *not* based on direct experience, we construct an experimental framework. We aim at understanding the cognitive mechanisms of displacement unique to human beings by extracting those properties involved in communicative displacement.

Human beings use natural language as a medium for the realization of displacement so naturally and without any trouble. For this reason, natural language is not suitable to extract those properties and to analyze the mechanism of displacement. This makes us adopt an experimental approach that restricts the media for communication. An artificial symbol system is often used as a communication medium in such an approach (Scott-Phillips & Kirby, 2010); however, its range of expression is too tight to enable the speaker to engage in free displaced reference. We need to investigate how the speaker makes displaced understanding possible for the listener. Thus we think that the use of drawing as a symbolic mechanism is reasonable for our purpose. As drawing is not a common medium for communication, we expect that drawing requires some devices to achieve displacement and that we can analyze them.

Fay et al. (2003) use drawing as a medium in this experimental approach to communication. Their experiment assumes two roles, each corresponding to the speaker and the listener: a "director," who expresses assigned objects by drawing, and a "matcher," who identifies the references of director's drawings. Two subjects are paired, and they draw pictures of the same objects, exchanging the two roles in turn. Fay et al. (2003) confirm that the transition from icon to symbol in graphical expressions occurs through the interaction between subjects.

We examine displacement in communication with a focus on displaced understanding by redesigning the experiment of Fay et al. (2003). We modify it in two ways:

First, the drawing tasks given in their experiment are objects that both the speaker and the listener know in advance (e.g. Robert De Niro). These tasks correspond to the situation, that of Row 5 of Table 1, in which displacement is based on memory. We change these tasks to cover entities that the listener has not directly seen or heard.

Second, in Fay et al.'s experiment, subjects are asked to identify an object from finite choices. However, in giving the listener finite options, the condition that the entity referred to by the speaker should not be experienced beforehand by the listener is not fulfilled. For this reason, we let listeners freely indicate what the speaker intends, instead of preparing finite options.

In order to investigate how the speaker composes expressions that make displaced understanding possible for the listener, we observe the way in which the speaker devises his or her expressions so that the listener will deduce the entity. Therefore, we feed back the listener's answer to the speaker and let he or she redraw a picture to make the next answer close to the correct one.

Subjects communicate using electric drawing pads and computer displays in separate rooms and not through the usual communicative media, such as verbal exchange or eye contact. They can use only black lines for drawing. The use of linguistic characters, such as alphabet or kana, and the use of meaningful symbols, such as algebraic signs, is prohibited.

By virtue of these modifications, we can inquire into the cognitive mechanisms required for displacement in communication that are depicted in the Row 8 of Table 1.

5. Feature Extraction as a Cognitive Mechanism for Displacement

We conducted a preliminary experiment based on the framework proposed in the previous section. We observed that subjects made drawings in which two or more graphical expressions were combined for absent objects. Extracting a partial feature of each drawing permits the representation of a feature of an object. Figure 1 shows an example. A subject expressed the task “sour boot” by drawing pictures of “lemon” and “boot” in combination. In this example, the subject, who drew “lemon,” inferred that “boot” had the feature “sour,” the same possessed by “lemon.”

Figure 1. An example of drawing expressing the task “sour boot”

When a speaker relates what a listener has not directly experienced, he or she may express the features of the object by using another object that has the same features. We name this mechanism “feature extraction.” We hypothesize that “feature extraction” permits displacement in communication.

Along with this mechanism, subjects drew pictures that represent the experiences when we typically experience the features that a speaker is trying to convey. In the example of Figure 1, the subject tried to draw a picture of eating a lemon, when we typically feel sour. This kind of expressions is viewed as a way to make a listener realize the feature, based on what they have experienced.

However, these expressions also cause misunderstandings. Listeners tend to understand speakers’ drawings based on their own experiences. When a speaker tells what a listener has not experienced, this tendency hinders the understanding. As in the example above, the other subject who saw Figure 1 understood that the “lemon” is “sour”, but could not combine the feature “sour” with “boot.” In another example, although a subject expressed the task "bitter fire" by drawing a picture of eating fire, the other subject saw the picture as "burn injury."

In order to understand the speaker's expression, the listener needs to guess the feature that the speaker attempts to convey. The situations of rows 5 and 8 of Table 1 differ in that the listener in one remembers an object and in the other has not experienced it. For example, the situation of row 5 corresponds to the task "sour lemon," and that of row 8 corresponds to "sour boot." Turning to these, we can demonstrate the tendencies of human feature extraction and clarify one of the cognitive mechanisms enabling displaced understanding by the listener.

In addition to feature extraction, analogical inferences also seem to work as mechanisms that realize displacement, as well as feature extraction. We assume two types of analogical inferences; one is cognitive analogy and the other is linguistic analogy. Cognitive analogy is an analogical inference based on similarity. It arises when the listener understands the referent that he or she has not directly experienced through the comparison of it with an object that has similar features. This analogy is thought to be based on the cognitive common ground of the speaker and listener. Linguistic analogy is an analogical inference based on construction rules (Hashimoto, Nakatsuka and Konno, 2010). It combines the forms that represent objects and helps to express the referent by uniting objects that are hard to be combined from a cognitive viewpoint.

We hypothesize that these three mechanisms, feature extraction, cognitive analogy, and linguistic analogy, enable displacement in human communication.

6. Summary and Conclusion

We consider that in order to understand the characteristics of displacement unique to human beings, it is critical to consider displacement in the context of communication and not just displaced reference or speech. We examined the characteristics of displacement by classifying it according to two axes: the distinction of speaker and listener, and the distinction of displacement based on memory and *not* direct experience. From our findings, we claim that displaced understanding *not* based on direct experience is the key factor to realize the displacement unique to human beings. We introduce an experimental framework to study cognitive mechanisms that achieve displacement in communication. From this preliminary experiment, we propose the hypothesis that feature extraction operates as a mechanism that enables displacement in communication.

Acknowledgements

This work was supported by a Grant-in-Aid for Scientific Research on Innovative Areas, "The study on the neural dynamics for understanding communication in terms of complex hetero systems (No.4103)" (No.21120011), and a Grant-in-

Aid for Scientific Research (No.23300085) of The Ministry of Education, Culture, Sports, Science, and Technology, Japan

References

Fay, N., Garrod, S., Lee, J., Oberlander, J. (2003). Understanding interactive graphical communication. *Proceedings of the 25th Annual Conference of the Cognitive Science Society*, Boston, MA

Frisch, K. von. (1967). *The dance language and orientation of bees*. Cambridge, Mass.: The Harvard University Press.

Hashimoto, T., Nakatsuka, M., Konno, T. (2010). Linguistic analogy for creativity and the origin of language. *The Evolution of Language: Proceedings of the 8th International Conference (evolang8)*, Utrecht

Hockett, C. F. (1960). The origin of speech. *Scientific American*, 203, 3, 89-96.

Hurford, J.R. (2007). *The origin of meaning*. Oxford University Press, pp. 36-41

Liszkowski, U., Schafer, M., Carpenter, M., Tomasello, M. (2009). Prelinguistic infants, but not chimpanzees, communicate about absent entities. *Psychological Science*, 20, 5, 654-660.

Morford, I. P., Goldin-Meadow, S. (1997). From here and now to there and then : The development of displaced reference in homesign and English. *Child Development*, 68, 3, 420-435

Scott-Phillips, T. C., Kirby, S. (2010). Language evolution in the laboratory. *Trends in Cognitive Sciences*, 14, 9, 411-417

Seyfarth, R. M., Cheney, D. L., Marler P. (1980). Monkey responses to three different alarm calls: evidence of predator classification and semantic communication. *Science*, 210, 801-803

THE EMERGENCE OF MORPHOSYNTACTIC CASE SYSTEMS

REMI VAN TRIJP

Sony Computer Science Laboratory Paris, 6 Rue Amyot
Paris, 75005, France
remi@csl.sony.fr

Despite centuries of research, the origins of grammatical case are more mysterious than ever. This paper addresses some unanswered questions through language game experiments in which a multi-agent population self-organizes a morphosyntactic case system. The experiments show how the formal part of grammatical constructions may pressure such emergent systems to become more economical.

1. Introduction

Case has long been considered as a universal category, but the abundance of counter evidence from diachronic studies and linguistic typology has forced linguists to go back to the drawing board. Many scholars nowadays agree that case is constructed in some way (Croft, 2001), so any evolutionary account of case has to explain *why* and *how* a speech population may succeed in doing so.

The *why* question seems obvious at first glance: to mark *event structure* (i.e. the relations between events and their participants). However, not all languages have evolved a case system but instead exploit a different strategy for marking event structure, such as word order (English) or verbal marking (Swahili). There are also more radical languages such as Riau Indonesian (Gil, 2008) that hardly ever indicate 'who did what to whom' and leave it up to the listener to infer the correct meaning from the context. If event structure can be communicated successfully without overt marking, the *why* question already becomes less obvious. Consequently, a number of recent studies seek answers in innate biases and function-independent iterated learning (see for instance Moy, 2006), but none of these attempts have shown how a case system may evolve.

A different answer, suggested and demonstrated by Steels (2004), is that case is *culturally* selected for communication because it reduces the cognitive effort that a listener needs for interpretation. Building on these first experiments, earlier Evolang contributions have shown how a multi-agent population can self-organize a case system and repurpose it if it starts to decay (van Trijp, 2008, 2010). The case systems that evolved in this work exhibited a degree of polysemy and grammatical complexity that go well beyond the one-to-one mappings that are typically

Figure 1. In the experiments, agents play language games in which they describe real-world events to each other. In this scene, one puppet is moving towards another one.

found in experiments on artificial language evolution, as can be gleaned from the following examples where *-tux* marks the actor of an event and *-pav* and *-my* behave like locative case markers (illative and elative):

(1) *Boy -tux move-inside house -pav*
boy case-12 entered house case-5
'The boy entered the house.'

(2) *Jack -my go-away Jill -tux*
Jack case-10 walk away from Jill case-12
'Jill walked away from the boy.'

Despite promising results, a number of important issues remain. First, all case systems that evolved in these experiments were semantically much more coherent than the abstract case systems found in natural languages. For example, the nominative case in German marks the Patient of an event in passive constructions rather than the Agent as in active constructions. Secondly, while the experiments successfully operationalized the *language strategy* that allows speakers to establish a case system, it is still an open question how such a strategy itself originates through cultural evolution.

This paper tackles these two issues through language game experiments that explore a syntactic route to the development of case. Assuming that more 'economical' case systems have a selective advantage over costly ones (in the sense of required memory), the experiments show how the formal properties of an emergent system may cause a feedback loop that steers the linguistic behavior of language users in novel situations. This feedback loop is not caused by case-specific learning biases, but rather by general cognitive functions such as coercion.

2. Description Games

Case is explored by modelling situated dialogs (i.e. language games) in which case becomes relevant. Here, agents play *description games* with each other about real-world events (Steels, 2004) as depicted in Figure 1.

2.1. *Scenario of a Description Game*

Here is the scenario of the description game:

1. Assume a population N of agents and a world W consisting of a set of individual objects that participate in dynamic events (such as walking).
2. Each game, two agents are randomly selected from the population to act as the speaker and listener. Both agents observe the same scene and build a situation model (i.e. a factbase for their current experiences).
3. The speaker *conceptualizes* a meaning to express and *produces* an utterance for expressing that meaning.
4. The listener *parses* the utterance into a meaning and *interprets* it.
5. If the listener can interpret the meaning without conflicts with his situation model, he signals agreement and the game succeeds. If not, the game fails.

2.2. *Assumptions and Scaffolds*

The agents are no blank slates but start with some knowledge and capacities in order to focus on case. First, the agents are assumed to have joint attention and to build up the same situation model to exclude interferences from perceptual differences. Events are perceived through a camera (Steels, 2004). The agents are able to recognize 6 monovalent events (such as *appear*), 12 bivalent events (such as *grasp*) and 3 trivalent events (such as *give*). Each scene contains maximally 7 objects.

Events and objects are represented as a series of facts in the agent's situation model using a first order logic representation. A factbase for the scene in Figure 1 may look as follows: {∃ e, x, y: boy(x), girl(y), walk(e), walker(e, x), walk-destination(e, y)}, which includes an explicit representation of the participant roles 'walker' and 'walk-destination'. The meaning space contains 39 unique participant roles.

Each language game, the speaker conceptualizes a *participant frame*, which can be any combination of an event's participant roles. There are three possibilities in the current example: two frames only overtly express one participant (corresponding to *the boy is walking* and (someone) *is walking to the girl*) and one frame profiles the entire event (corresponding to *the boy is walking to the girl*). Meanings use the same logic representation but include variables (indicated by a question mark), which are bound to their referent in interpretation. The function of a case system is to mark which variables refer to the same object, as illustrated here for German (with the meanings in italics under the words):

(3)

Der Junge	ging		**zu dem** Mädchen.
boy(?x)	*walk(?ev)*		*girl(?y)*
?x = ?a └	*walker(?ev, ?a)*	*walk-destination(?ev, ?b)* ——	┘ *?y = ?b*

The agents, however, start without such a grammar and only know lexical constructions for events and objects. They would describe the scene in Figure 1 as *boy walk girl*, an associative utterance with free word order. Because no relations between events and participants are marked, the listener has to *infer* from the situation that the boy was the walker ($?x = ?a$) and that the girl was the destination ($?y = ?b$). Each inference is counted as one unit of *cognitive effort*.

3. Self-Organization of a Morphosyntactic Case System

Agents are equipped with a *language strategy* for inventing, adopting and aligning a case system. This section compares two morphosyntactic case strategies: an idiosyncratic strategy and a coercion strategy.

3.1. *Two Morphosyntactic Strategies for Case*

The innovation and adoption components of a strategy include *diagnostics* and *repairs* for detecting and solving problems during processing. The case strategies involve a particular configuration of the following diagnostic and repairs:

- *Diagnostic (both strategies)*: Detect whether cognitive effort is minimal during interpretation. If not, report a problem.
- *Repair 1 (both strategies)*: Invent (speaker) or adopt (listener) a new case.
- *Repair 2 (only coercion strategy)*: Try to reuse an existing case through coercion.

Innovation is speaker-based: the speaker always parses his own utterance to estimate its effect on the listener, and may detect a problem of cognitive effort for interpretion (*diagnostic 1*). If so, one solution for the problem for both the idiosyncratic and coercion strategy is to invent a new case (*Repair 1*). First, the agent makes an argument structure construction that assigns case to the proper participant (e.g. the boy). The agent also extends the verb's valence (which is initially empty) with the new case, stating for example that a 'walker' can be categorized as 'case-1'. Valence plays a crucial role during the build-up of the utterance structure in processing because it makes the utterance structure compatible with the argument structure construction, as illustrated in the left of Figure 2. The agent also invents a case marker, which serves as the surface form of the new case. Another solution, only accessible to agents equipped with the coercion strategy, is to *reuse* an existing case through coercion (*Repair 2*, the right in Figure 2). Coercion is a domain-independent operation that enables a grammatical construction to impose its constraints even if it violates the conventions of a language. A famous example is *Pat sneezed the napkin off the table* (Goldberg, 1995), in which the intransitive verb *sneeze* is coerced into a Caused-Motion frame. In the experiments, agents can coerce a case if it *discriminatory*, that is, if it cannot already be used for marking another role in the same event.

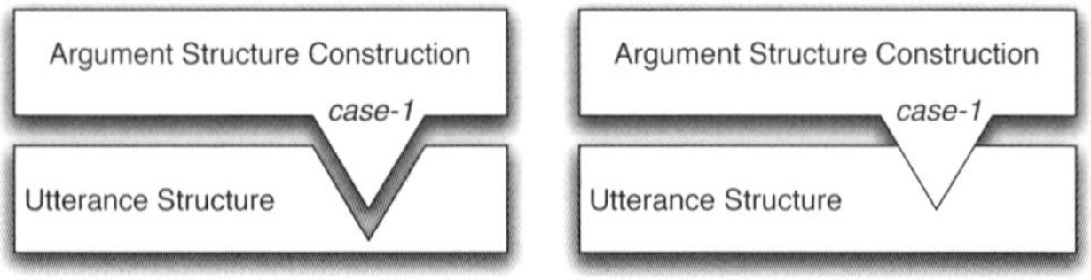

Figure 2. Left: routine processing of a case mapping. The utterance structure has been made compatible with a grammatical construction by the lexicon. Right: Despite a mismatch between the utterance structure and the grammatical construction, the construction can impose its structure through coercion.

Adopting a case is possible through the same diagnostic and repairs. The only difference is that the listener may observe an unknown case marker (*Repair 1*) that can be coupled to the problem of cognitive effort, or that he observes a known case marker in a new distribution (*Repair 2*). Technical details on processing and coercion can be found in Steels and van Trijp (2011).

Since variation is inevitable in a multi-agent population, the agents need a way to **align** their inventories with each other. Both strategies use a crude alignment strategy in which the listener always changes a verb's valence to be compatible with the last cases that the verb occurred with, thereby often overriding earlier, conflicting choices. The most frequent cases will thus be retained in the population, while the others are simply forgotten.

3.2. *Results for the Idiosyncratic Case Strategy*

Figure 3 shows the results for a population of 10 agents equipped with the idiosyncratic strategy. All values represent the mean of ten series of 10.000 language games; error bars indicate standard error. The X-axis shows the number of language games, the Y1-axis (left) shows variation and the running average of cognitive effort, and the Y2-axis (right) shows the number of cases.

The chart shows that the agents succeed in minimizing the **cognitive effort** they need for interpretation. Cognitive effort is calculated as a Simple Moving Average of the effort measured in the last 10 language games (see section 2.2). **Variation** measures whether all agents converge on the same meaning-to-form mappings. For example, if the most frequent case for a participant role is adopted by 40% of the population, variation for that meaning-to-form mapping is 60%. Population-wide variation averages over the individual variation scores. The chart shows that there is no variation in the beginning, as the agents all share the same lexical language. Variation then rises when the agents start inventing new cases and it reaches a maximum of about 50%, which means that only half of the agents have adopted the dominant cases in the population. However, variation then goes

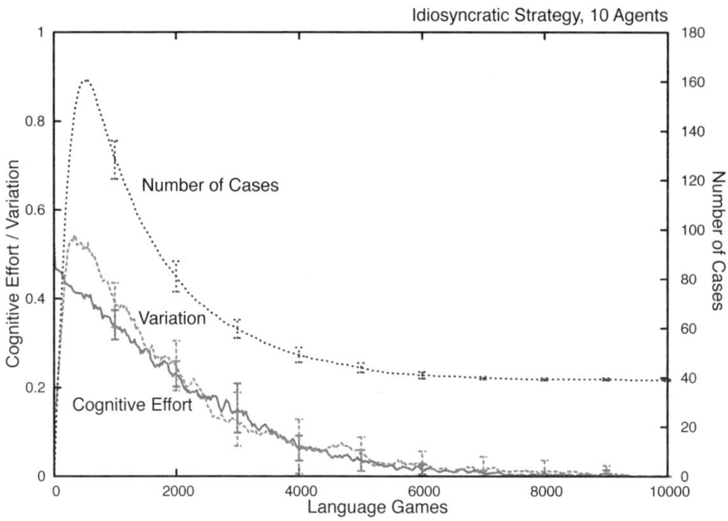

Figure 3. This chart shows that the agents with the idiosyncratic case strategy succeed in reducing the cognitive effort needed for interpretation (full line) as they develop a coherent case system. However, each case is verb-specific hence the emergent case system is not expressive.

down to a minimum, which means that the agents successfully align their inventories with each other. The **number of cases** shows the average amount of cases that are actively used in the population. At its maximum, the agents need to cope with 160 competing cases, but the alignment strategy allows them to converge to a shared set of 39 idiosyncratic cases for 39 participant roles. This one-to-one mapping however means that the emergent case system is not productive, and that the number of cases grows linearly if new event meanings need to be expressed.

3.3. *Results for the Coercion Case Strategy*

Figure 4 shows the same measures for a population that uses coercion. The agents succeed in reducing the cognitive effort they require to a minimum. Variation shows similar results as well, rising to 45% early on and then gradually sloping down to almost zero. A spectacular difference is however observed in the number of cases that circulate in the population: the maximum never exceeds 8 cases (so not all agents innovated) and the final systems count 4 to 7 cases. The 'redundancy' of more than 3 markers is due to the effect of frequency on conventionalization. In comparison, case systems in natural languages vary between two (e.g. Mapudungun) and more than twenty cases (e.g. Hungarian; Iggesen, 2005).

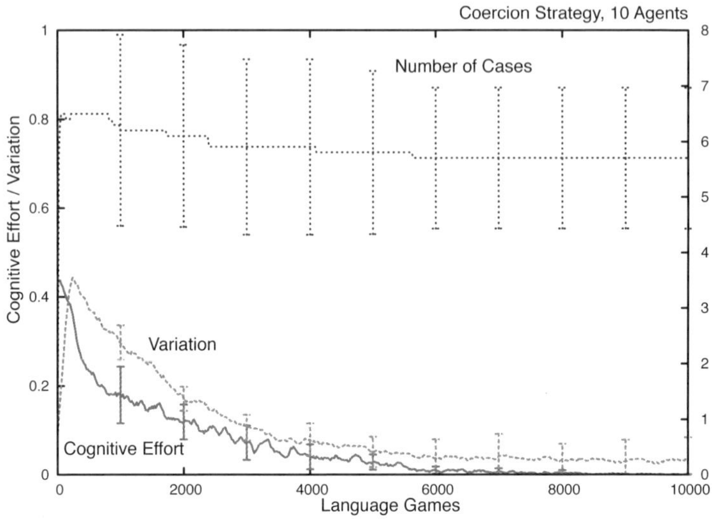

Figure 4. When exploiting coercion, the agents drastically reduce the number of cases in their case system while at the same time minimizing cognitive effort.

Coercion thus allows the agents to develop a more economical case system in terms of inventory size, which also entails that the system is more expressive than the idiosyncratic one. However, whereas case markers in natural languages are often semantically motivated, the cases developed here are entirely arbitrary: a case that marks an agent-like participant in one event may be reused for marking location in another event. Without any clear system that motivates *how* the agents can expand their case system, they constantly introduce conflicting solutions.

4. Discussion and Conclusion

This paper addressed two of the shortcomings of earlier work on the evolution of case. First, whereas previous studies focused solely on semantics, this paper explored a syntactic route in order to reveal which formal pressures may steer an emergent case system towards a more economical paradigm. Secondly, by operationalizing those formal pressures through the general cognitive function of coercion rather than a domain-specific learning bias, the experiments take a promising step towards explaining how a population can develop a case *strategy* from scratch.

However, the results also show mismatches with case systems found in natural languages. Innovation in such systems are not random, but functionally motivated, whereas the mappings between meaning and form in the experiments are entirely arbitrary. The results therefore reveal that theories that predict that case systems evolve to become more economical and learnable (e.g. Tallerman, 2008) only tell part of the story: case also evolves in a way that language users can maximize their chances of being immediately understood when they need to expand their system to accommodate for novel situations. Future research therefore needs to show how the semantic and syntactic routes to the origins of case can intersect to explain how functionally motivated, yet abstract case systems may evolve.

Acknowledgements

The work reported in this paper was carried out at Sony CSL Paris. I would like to thank my colleagues at the VUB AI-Lab of the University of Brussels and at Sony CSL Paris and Luc Steels (director of both labs) for all their feedback.

References

Croft, W. (2001). *Radical construction grammar: Syntactic theory in typological perspective.* Oxford: OUP.

Gil, D. (2008). How much grammar does it take to sail a boat. In G. Sampson, D. Gil, & P. Trudgill (Eds.), *Language complexity as an evolving variable.* Oxford: Oxford University Press.

Goldberg, A. (1995). *A construction grammar approach to argument structure.* Chicago: Chicago UP.

Iggesen, O. A. (2005). Number of cases. In M. Haspelmath, M. S. Dryer, D. Gil, & B. Comrie (Eds.), *The world atlas of language structures* (pp. 202–205). Oxford: OUP.

Moy, J. (2006). *Word order and case in models of simulated language evolution.* Unpublished doctoral dissertation, University of York, York.

Steels, L. (2004). Constructivist development of grounded construction grammars. In W. Daelemans (Ed.), *Proceedings 42nd annual meeting of the association for computational linguistics* (pp. 9–19). Barcelona.

Steels, L., & van Trijp, R. (2011). How to make construction grammars fluid and robust. In L. Steels (Ed.), *Design patterns in Fluid Construction Grammar.* Amsterdam: John Benjamins.

Tallerman, M. (2008). Case-marking systems evolve to be easy to learn and process. *BBS*, *31*, 534–535.

van Trijp, R. (2008). The emergence of semantic roles in Fluid Construction Grammar. In A. D. Smith, K. Smith, & R. Ferrer i Cancho (Eds.), *The evolution of language. proceedings of the 7th international conference (evolang 7)* (pp. 346–353). Singapore: World Scientific Press.

van Trijp, R. (2010). Strategy competition in the evolution of pronouns: A case-study of Spanish leísmo, laísmo and loísmo. In A. Smith, M. Schouwstra, B. de Boer, & K. Smith (Eds.), *The evolution of language (evolang 8)* (pp. 336–343). Singapore: World Scientific Press.

HOLISTIC OR SYNTHETIC PROTOLANGUAGE: EVIDENCE FROM ITERATED LEARNING OF WHISTLED SIGNALS

TESSA VERHOEF & BART DE BOER

ACLC, University of Amsterdam, Spuistraat 210,
Amsterdam, 1012 VT, Netherlands
t.verhoef@uva.nl, b.g.deboer@uva.nl

SIMON KIRBY

Language Evolution and Computation Research Unit,
School of Philosophy, Psychology and Language Sciences, University of Edinburgh
Edinburgh EH8 9AD, UK
simon@ling.ed.ac.uk

Many arguments have been proposed in favor of and against the idea of protolanguage as a set of holistic utterances that were later segmented into words. This paper presents data from a human iterated learning experiment which corroborates arguments in favor of holistic protolanguage and forms a counterexample to some of the arguments that were proposed against it. This experiment involves iterated learning and recall of a set of (initially) holistic whistles produced with a slide whistle. Over generations, the whistle sets become easier to learn and discrete, combinatorial structure emerges.

1. Introduction

Did human protolanguage consist of holistic utterances that were segmented into words (Wray, 1998; Arbib, 2005) or did it start with simple words that were combined into more complex structures (Bickerton, 1990; Tallerman, 2007)? Both positions are plausible from a comparative perspective: although all human languages use complex combinatorial structure, most primate communication systems do not. In such systems one call corresponds to one meaning, and calls do not have discernible internal structure. At the most, varying intensity of the calls corresponds to varying intensity of the message (Slocombe & Zuberbühler, 2006). These are hallmarks of a holistic system. However, examples have also been observed of systems where combinations of calls appear to have different meanings than the individual calls in isolation (Zuberbühler, 2002). This may indicate a more synthetic system.

Arguing against holistic protolanguage, Tallerman (2007) points out why holistic protolanguage would be unlikely to lead to compositional syntax. First of all, holistic protolanguage would by definition be irregular. In addition, if it is learned, it is expected to change rapidly over generations, just as modern language does. Tallerman therefore argues that this would not provide a sufficiently stable target for analysis into components. In response to this argument, it has been pointed out that learners often overgeneralize and that inconsistencies in the input do not necessarily prevent the discovery of regularities (K. Smith, 2008; Fitch, 2010). This argument is backed up by computer simulations showing that regularization does indeed happen in cultural transmission (Kirby, Smith, & Brighton, 2004), as well as by cultural learning experiments with humans that show emergence of compositional structure from initially holistic sets of utterances (Kirby, Cornish, & Smith, 2008).

Tallerman's (2007) response to these arguments and to the computational models is that they already assume that there are building blocks – the target words are built up out of a set of discrete segments. She assumes that the task of segmenting signals into relevant elements is impossible if there are no predefined segments, because in that case even the tiniest distinctions between signals should be considered potentially significant. She therefore does not find demonstrations that rely on pre-existing segments convincing.

Here we present experimental results that address the above-mentioned concerns. The data were obtained from a human iterated learning experiment (based on Kirby et al., 2008) intended to investigate the emergence of combinatorial structure in sets of continuous signals. The experiment starts with sets of *continuous* signals that have no regularities. After they have been transmitted over a number of experimental generations, it turns out that human overgeneralization causes the sets of signals to become regularized. Also, the system becomes more constrained and predictable which allows learners to focus on relevant signal variations (Verhoef, Kirby, & Padden, 2011).

2. Cultural transmission of an artificial whistled language

The experiment described below involved learning and recall of twelve distinct whistle sounds that were produced with a slide whistle (see figure 1). The reason for using the slide whistle was to minimize the influence of pre-existing knowledge of speech and phonology. Four parallel diffusion chains were created of ten generations (40 subjects participated in total) in which each participant was exposed to either the recall output of the previous participant in the same chain or the initial whistle set. The initial set was the same in all four chains and these

Figure 1. A slide whistle.

whistles were selected from a database which was created in a pilot study. They were chosen to be holistic and not to exhibit combinatorial structure (more details are reported in Verhoef et al. (2011)). The whistles were not connected to any referent because the goal was to simulate the emergence of 'bare phonology' (Fitch, 2010) and we wanted to control for possible influences of semantics such as iconicity or compositionality.

2.1. *Qualitative observations*

Remembering twelve distinct whistles after limited exposure is not easy and participants usually do not recall all of them. In their productions, they overgeneralize the structure that appears present to them and this results in an introduction of mirrored, combined or repeated versions of existing whistles. The signals consequently share more and more elements, yielding increased combinatorial structure. Recall accuracy also increases, indicating that the more structured sets are more easily remembered.

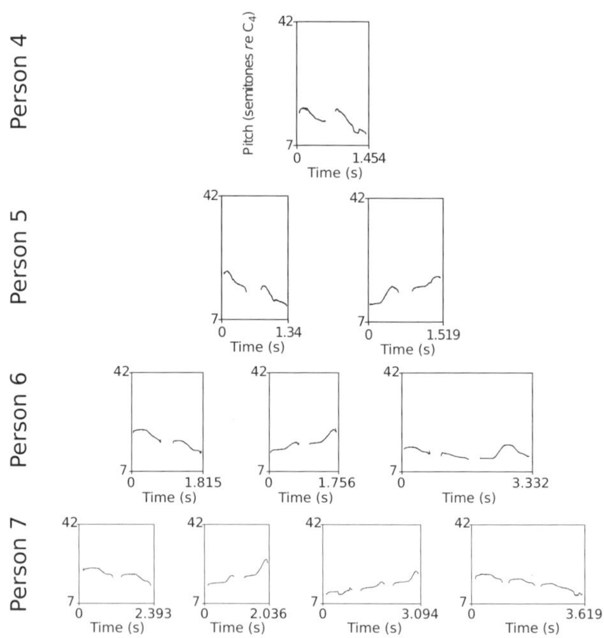

Figure 2. An example of cumulative mirroring, repetition and borrowing. Person 5 mirrors the whistle from the previous set, then person six borrows one of the two in a new whistle and finally this new whistle becomes generalized to fit the pattern of the original two, but repeated. This predictable system is stable towards the end of the chain. The whistles are plotted as pitch tracks.

An example of such cumulative increase of structure over generations is shown in figure 2. In this example combined mirroring, repetition and borrowing results in a predictable system that is stable and persists after its innovation. In the productions of person four there is not yet another whistle that resembles the one shown here with 'two slides down', but in generation five a mirrored version of this whistle appears. Then, in generation six one of these is borrowed and combined into a new whistle. This one may have been interpreted by person seven as having meant to be a repetition of the 'slide down' element present in the original two, because suddenly a 'three slides down' version appears as well as a mirrored 'three slides up' version which fills a gap in this regular system.

Figure 3 shows a fragment of a whistle set that emerged in one of the chains in generation ten. This set exhibits a set of basic building blocks (short level tones and down-up slides) that are systematically reused and combined. Qualitatively, basic elements and systematic recombination can be observed in all four emerged sets of whistles.

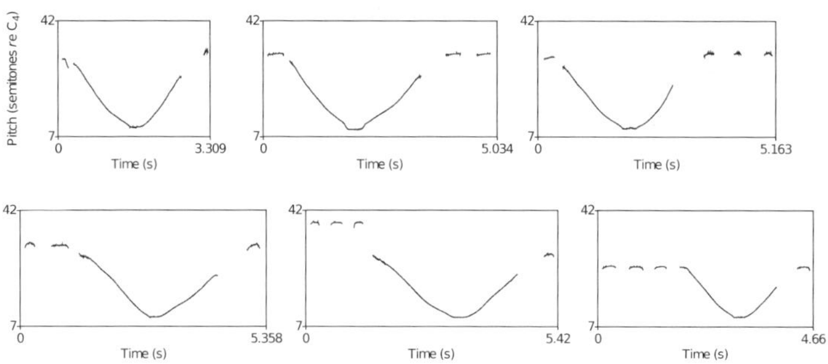

Figure 3. Fragment of the whistles plotted as pitch tracks in the last set of a chain. Basic elements can be identified that are systematically recombined.

2.2. *Quantitative measurements*

In order to quantify these observations, the recall errors of all participants were measured as well as the entropy (Shannon, 1948) of the whistle sets at each generation.

To determine the recall error we measured the distance between two whistles using Derivative Dynamic Time Warping (Keogh & Pazzani, 2001) on the whistle's plunger movement trajectories. Then, the recall error for a participant was measured by comparing the whistles of this person's learned input and recalled output. This was done by pairing the whistles of the two sets in all possible ways, then computing the distance between the paired signals and taking the lowest sum of distances, which belongs to the most optimal pairing. Figure 4 shows this measure for the four chains, with the generations on the horizontal axis. A significant cumulative decrease in recall error was measured using Page's (1963) trend test (L=1318, m=4, n=10, p<0.05), implying an increase of learnability and reproducibility of the whistle sets.

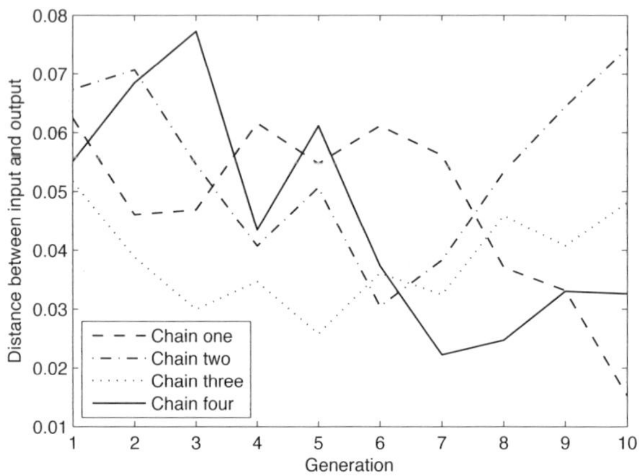

Figure 4. Recall error on the whistle sets over generations for all four chains, demonstrating that the signalling system evolves through cultural transmission to be more learnable.

To compute the entropy, the whistles were divided into segments, taking silences within a whistle as segment boundaries. Then, using all segments that occur in the set of twelve whistles, hierarchical clustering was used to group together those segments that were so similar that they could be considered the same category or building block. Clustering continued until there was no pair of segments left with a distance smaller than 0.08, using the distance measure described above. Equation (1) from Shannon (1948) was then used to compute entropy, where p_i is the probability of occurrence of building block i.

$$H = -\sum p_i \log p_i \tag{1}$$

Figure 5 shows this measure for the four chains, with the generations again on the horizontal axis and 0 referring to the initial set. A significant cumulative decrease in entropy (L=1853, m=4, n=11, p<0.001) was measured and this implies an increase of structure and predictability as well as more efficient coding and compressibility.

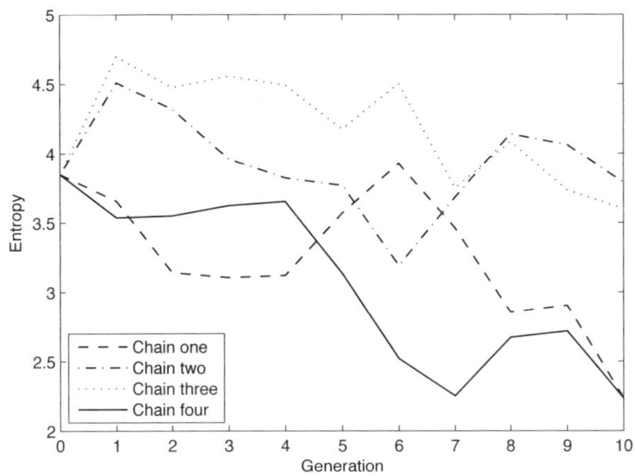

Figure 5. Entropy of the whistle sets over generations for all four chains.

3. Discussion

The results show that modern human learners quickly generate structure in initially structureless (holistic) sets of continuous signals. Because the initial set is too difficult to learn precisely, learners tend to overgeneralize the structure they (think they) observe. This introduces reuse of a small set of building blocks and increases the learnability of the set of signals. This is in line with the observations of iterated learning of sets of utterances that consisted of discrete symbols (Kirby et al., 2008). Interestingly, the sets of signals were so small that it is unlikely that the emergence of the combinatorial structure was due to any pressure to keep the signals distinct, as was originally proposed by Hockett (1960) and analyzed by Nowak, Krakauer, and Dress (1999) and Zuidema and de Boer (2009). It appears that the emergence of combinatorial structure in the experiment is rather due to properties of the way humans learn and generalize signals.

The results address Tallerman's (2007) objections against the possibility of a holistic protolanguage. Apparently, modern humans have no problems finding (apparent) structure in holistic, continuous utterances. Of course, the utterances in the experiment had no meaning associated with them, so the question of whether regularities in the signals will be associated with regularities in the meaning is not directly addressed. However, the experiments show that participants introduce combinatorial structure very rapidly. Thus, continuous, holistic signals can transform into signals built up out of discrete segments, independent of meaning. Subsequently, as Kirby et al. (2008) have shown, signals built up of discrete elements with an associated meaning (but without a systematic form-meaning mapping) can transform into systems with a systematic form-meaning mapping.

As for the argument about rapid change: rapid change does happen in the experiments, but it leads to structure and better learnability. This is an example of how repeated application of a learning system with limitations creates a linguistic system that is learnable (Zuidema, 2003). Therefore the argument that the changeability of a culturally transmitted holistic system would prevent emergence of structure is not supported by empirical evidence from modern human behavior.

Of course, these observations do not necessarily generalize to ancestral hominins, who may have had very different cognitive adaptations. However, as K. Smith (2008) has pointed out, research with cotton-top tamarins (Hauser, Newport, & Aslin, 2001) has shown that at least some non-human primates already have simple abilities for segmenting streams of speech. It is therefore possible that the ability to find regularities in speech is much older than the split between humans and the other apes, and that the crucial innovation was in the ability to reproduce and generalize learned signals. However, given a pre-existing ability to analyze, we can expect that re-use of regularities could have been possible at the earliest stages of protolanguage.

Although our findings refute arguments against holistic protolanguage, we are not necessarily arguing for an extended holistic protolanguage phase. It appears that such a system would perhaps not be stable for many consecutive generations, because combinatorial structure at the signal level would emerge rapidly. We also do not exclude the possibility that the holophrases were concatenated into larger constructs simultaneously, following a synthetic scenario. In fact, it would be possible to have aspects of both holistic and synthetic protolanguage in one system: holistic phrases break up into smaller units, while at the same time words could be combined into short utterances. As A. Smith (2008) suggested, there is no fundamental contradiction between these two points of view.

At our present state of knowledge, these ideas are still speculative and preliminary. However, we hope to have shown that iterated learning experiments can throw empirical light on the debate between holistic and synthetic protolanguage – a debate which for a long time has been mostly philosophical. Our study is just the first step in a possible series of more refined experiments.

Acknowledgements

We thank Carol Padden, Alex del Giudice, Jelle Zuidema and Wendy Sandler for helpful suggestions and discussions.

References

Arbib, M. (2005). From monkey-like action recognition to human language: An evolutionary framework for neurolinguistics. *Behavioral and brain sciences*, *28*(2), 105–124.

Bickerton, D. (1990). *Language and species.* The University of Chicago Press.

Fitch, W. (2010). *The evolution of language.* Cambridge University Press.

Hauser, M., Newport, E., & Aslin, R. (2001). Segmentation of the speech stream in a non-human primate: statistical learning in cotton-top tamarins. *Cognition, 78*(3), B53-B64.

Hockett, C. (1960). The origin of speech. *Scientific American, 203*, 88–96.

Keogh, E. J., & Pazzani, M. J. (2001). Derivative dynamic time warping. In *First SIAM International Conference on Data Mining (sdm2001)* (pp. 1–11).

Kirby, S., Cornish, H., & Smith, K. (2008). Cumulative cultural evolution in the laboratory: An experimental approach to the origins of structure in human language. *Proceedings of the National Academy of Sciences, 105*(31), 10681–10686.

Kirby, S., Smith, K., & Brighton, H. (2004). From UG to universals: Linguistic adaptation through iterated learning. *Studies in Language, 28*(3), 587–607.

Nowak, M., Krakauer, D., & Dress, A. (1999). An error limit for the evolution of language. *Proceedings of the Royal Society of London, 266*, 2131–2136.

Page, E. B. (1963). Ordered hypotheses for multiple treatments: A significance test for linear ranks. *Journal of the American Statistical Association, 58*(301), 216–230.

Shannon, C. E. (1948). A mathematical theory of communication. *Bell System Technical Journal, 27*, 379–423, 623–656.

Slocombe, K. E., & Zuberbühler, K. (2006). Food-associated calls in chimpanzees: responses to food types or food preferences? *Animal Behaviour, 72*(5), 989-999.

Smith, A. (2008). Protolanguage reconstructed. *Interaction Studies, 9*(1), 99–115.

Smith, K. (2008). Is a holistic protolanguage a plausible precursor to language? *Interaction Studies, 9*(1), 1–17.

Tallerman, M. (2007). Did our ancestors speak a holistic protolanguage? *Lingua, 117*(3), 579–604.

Verhoef, T., Kirby, S., & Padden, C. (2011). Cultural emergence of combinatorial structure in an artificial whistled language. In *Proceedings of the 33rd Annual Conference of the Cognitive Science Society* (pp. 483–488). Cognitive Science Society.

Wray, A. (1998). Protolanguage as a holistic system for social interaction. *Language and Communication, 18*(1), 47–67.

Zuberbühler, K. (2002). A syntactic rule in forest monkey communication. *Animal Behaviour, 63*(2), 293–299.

Zuidema, W. (2003). How the poverty of the stimulus solves the poverty of the stimulus. In S. Becker, S. Thrun, & K. Obermayer (Eds.), *Advances in Neural Information Processing Systems 15* (pp. 51–58). Cambridge, MA: MIT Press.

Zuidema, W., & de Boer, B. (2009). The evolution of combinatorial phonology. *Journal of Phonetics, 37*(2), 125–144.

THE INFORMATION RATE OF MODERN SPEECH AND ITS IMPLICATIONS FOR LANGUAGE EVOLUTION

JOHN VILLASENOR, YUXING HAN, DANIEL WEN, ESTHER GONZALEZ AND JIANWEN CHEN

Electrical Engineering Department, University of California, Los Angeles
Los Angeles, CA 90095 USA

JIANGTAO WEN

Department of Computer Science and Technology
Tsinghua University, Beijing, 10084, China

We present a method based on the discipline of information theory applied to analysis of phonemes to quantitatively assess the rate at which information is conveyed in modern speech. Our results suggest that the information rates in modern speech lie in the range between several dozen and about 100 bits per second, and indicate the presence of a nuanced set of tradeoffs between efficiency and redundancy among different modern languages. We believe that the framework described here provides a potentially valuable tool to help address questions regarding the extent to which evolutionary increases in language sophistication were also accompanied by increases in communication efficiency.

1. Introduction

While it is obvious that spoken language conveys information, it is much less obvious how to rigorously quantify how much information is conveyed on a per syllable, per phoneme, or per unit time basis. Why, for example, in order of magnitude terms, does saying the equivalent of "The tiger is charging!" take much closer to 1 second than to 0.01 or 100 seconds in modern languages? The answer clearly relates to the amount of time it takes to vocalize the appropriate string of phonemes. But beneath that simple answer lie much more complex questions regarding why it takes that long, how to mathematically quantify the rate of information transfer in speech, the extent to which that rate has at least some element of universality across modern languages, and the resulting implications for language evolution.

Measurement of the information contained in the strings of phonemes that comprise speech involves much more than simply counting the length of the strings. As is well established in the discipline of information theory, the entropy that constitutes a measure of the underlying amount information in a communications signal (Cover & Thomas, 2006) relates to not only to the size of the "alphabet" – i.e. the set of symbols that can be concatenated in order to produce a message – but also to the frequencies of occurrence of the different symbols in the alphabet and to the statistical correlations among them. Given that speech is the result of many hundreds of thousands of years of evolutionary development and that producing it involves costs in time and energy, it has clearly benefited from various optimizations to make it an efficient way to convey information (Zipf, 1949). Speech also contains significant amounts of redundancy, which involves the sacrifice of efficiency in order to provide robustness in noisy environments.

An important set of questions relates to the quantitative efficiency of modern speech and the extent to which, due to historical, cultural, and other factors, there are differences among the information rates and in the efficiency/redundancy tradeoffs across modern languages. Perhaps most importantly from the standpoint of understanding the role of communication efficiency in language evolution, it is of great interest to examine whether, despite these differences, the rate at which information is conveyed in modern languages falls within a reasonably bounded range of values, indicating that this range, therefore, is a fundamental characteristic of modern human speech. In the present paper we provide a framework to quantitatively assess the communications efficiency of modern speech, apply this framework to a large data set from American English, Mandarin Chinese, and Castilian Spanish, and discuss the results and their implications with respect to language evolution.

2. Measuring Speech Entropy

In the field of information theory, entropy is a measure, usually expressed using units of binary "bits" (i.e., ones and zeros), of the information content contained in the symbols used to convey a message. Information theory has been vital to the design of many modern digital information processing technologies such as JPEG, Wi-Fi, and mobile phone networks. Entropy measures are averages that can be used to compute the expected information content of strings of symbols. Thus, to the extent that the entropy of written English is approximately 1.25 bits per character as reported by Cover and King (1978), a string of 1000 English characters can be expected, on average, to contain the equivalent of about 1250 bits of information.

The measurement of entropy involves the identification and analysis of how the symbols in an alphabet are used to construct messages. If an alphabet contains N different symbols, with the ith symbol occurring with probability p_i where $0 \leq i \leq N-1$, then the first-order entropy of the information source measured in bits per symbol is $H_1 = -\Sigma_{i=[0,\ N-1]}\ p_i \log_2 p_i$ bits of information (Shannon, 1948). Higher order entropy measurements embody information about conditional probabilities in the symbol stream. For example, the second order entropy H_2 provides a measure of the average information per symbol given knowledge of the immediately preceding symbol.

In the present paper, we measure the entropy – or in other words, the number of bits of information – associated with phonemes. Despite the extensive application of information theory in other domains, there has been very little research aimed at applying it to spoken language at the phoneme level (a notable exception is a study of Russian described by Yaglom and Yaglom (1983)).[1] The total number of phonemes across all known languages is relatively modest, and phonemes have been extensively researched and classified, including through the International Phonetic Alphabet (IPA) developed under the auspices of the International Phonetic Association and updated most recently in 2005 (International Phonetic Association, 1999 and 2005). A phoneme-based approach has the advantage not only of directly using the constituent building blocks of speech, but also of normalizing across speed variations among different speakers within the same language. In the present study, in addition to measuring the information per phoneme, we measure the average number of phonemes per syllable and combine this with the phoneme entropy results to obtain the average number of bits of information per syllable.

3. Methods and Results

The study was performed on spoken dialog that was transcribed into written form. Spoken dialog was used instead of source materials that were inherently written in nature to avoid data integrity problems due to the differences between word choices, phrasing, etc. in spoken versus written language. A data set of spoken American English containing 215,535 phonemes (corresponding to 65,735 syllables) was used. For spoken Mandarin Chinese the data contained 279,087 phonemes (corresponding to 99,647 syllables). For spoken Castilian Spanish the size of the data set was 222,493 phonemes (containing 112,896

[1] In contrast with the relative dearth of information theoretic treatments of human speech, there have been many papers discussing the application of information theory to animal communication. See, for example, McCowan, Hanswer, and Doyle (1999).

syllables). The average number of phonemes per syllable in this data set is 3.28 for American English, 2.80 for Mandarin, and 1.97 for Spanish.

The data were converted into a representation using the phonemes for each language in accordance with the alphabet in the IPA as applied to each language. Within each language, overall phoneme counts were then aggregated across the entire data set to get a probability of occurrence for each phoneme; these probabilities in turn were used to compute the first order entropy. The first-order entropy furnishes a measure of the average amount of information conveyed by each phoneme. The probabilities of phoneme pairs were also computed and used to obtain the second order entropy, which is a measure of the average amount of information in each phoneme given knowledge of the previous phoneme. This is an important metric given the strong probabilistic relationships between temporally adjacent phonemes in speech. The results of the entropy analysis are presented in Table 1.

Table 1. Entropy results, measured in number of bits of information

	American English	*Mandarin Chinese*	*Castilian Spanish*
1st order entropy per phoneme	4.76 ± .03	4.36 ± .03 (5.07 ± .03 with tones)	3.96 ± .03
1st order entropy per syllable	15.61 ± .11	12.21 ± .07 (14.21 ± .07 w/tones)	7.80 ± .05
2nd order entropy per phoneme	3.04 ± .10	1.84 ± .07 (2.55 ± .07 with tones)	3.04 ± .08
2nd order entropy per syllable	9.96 ± .32	5.16 ± .19 (7.16 ± .19 with tones)	6.00 ± .16

The ranges in Table 1 correspond to 95% confidence intervals for the first order entropy, and to bounds on the 95% confidence intervals for the second order entropy. Results are given both in terms of phonemes and syllables. The syllabic measure is important because syllables are a more consistent baseline to associate with the time duration of a particular segment of speech. Thus, while the analysis in terms of phonemes allows computation of the information content in terms of the basic phonemic alphabet used for speech, conversion to entropy on a per syllable basis provides a measure that, when combined with data regarding the syllable rate, enables computation of the information rate of speech measured in bits per second.

Table 1 also explicitly considers the contribution to entropy of tones in Mandarin Chinese, which uses the extra dimension of pitch variation associated with each syllable to convey meaning, providing extra information in a manner not present in English or Spanish. A choice among four tones conveys two extra bits of information per syllable for Mandarin Chinese, or, equivalently, 0.71 bits of extra information on a per phoneme basis.

The lower relative first order and second order syllable entropies for Spanish may be due at least in part to the fact that Spanish (as well as the other Latin-derived languages) has a much richer grammar than either English or Chinese in terms of inflection in relation to verb conjugations for different persons, tenses and moods. These more complex verb forms increase robustness at the cost of efficiency, thus lowering the information per syllable.[2]

It is also instructive to combine the results in Table 1 with syllable rate data recently published by Pellegrino, Coupé, and Marsico (2011),[3] who measured English, Mandarin, and Spanish speech rates at an average of 6.19, 5.18, and 7.82 syllables per second respectively.[4] Multiplying these numbers by the first order entropies in Table 1 gives average English, Mandarin, and Spanish information rates of 97, 74, and 61 bits per second respectively. For the second order entropies in Table 1, the corresponding information rates are 62, 37, and 47 bits per second. In giving these results, it is important to emphasize that within the above ranges, faster is not necessarily better. Communication is a tradeoff between efficiency and redundancy: both are important, and different languages may use this tradeoff differently.

4. Application to Language Evolution

Three languages is of course far too small a sample to draw any definitive general conclusions about modern speech, but the results are suggestive of some common ranges. For example, for all three languages studied the first order entropy results lie within a range between 3.9 and 4.8 bits per phoneme. It is

---

[2] Grammar involves coherence across structures that can be dozens of phonemes in length. Lower order entropy measurements do not directly capture correlations across these distances. However, grammar that is designed to deliver robustness at the cost of efficiency may indirectly influence low-order entropy results due to energy minimization: while longer phrases would generally require more energy to produce, this increase can be offset through corresponding adjustments to phoneme probabilities and correlations over very short time scales. The results of these adjustments could potentially be visible in low order entropy measurements.

[3].Pellegrino et al. (2011) also reported what they termed "syllabic information density," though using a very different approach based on the comparative syllable count of sequences assumed to have equivalent semantic content across different languages. Interestingly, there are some broad similarities in the information density results between that study and the syllable entropy results in the present paper, in particular with respect to the lower information per syllable for Spanish.

[4] There is significant variation in syllabic rates given in the literature. For example, for English, while Pellegrino et al. (2011) reported a mean of 6.19 syllables per second, Robb et al. (2004) reported between 4 and 5 syllables per second.

also noteworthy that for a fourth language, Russian, the first order phoneme entropy has been reported at 4.77 (Yaglom & Yaglom, 1983). The second order phoneme entropies are lower as required given the presence of inter-phoneme correlations, but they, too, suggest the existence of an approximate common range, in this case from about 2.5 to somewhat over 3 bits per phoneme. There is more variation in the information rates in bits per second, but even then, in approximate terms, the results lie within a reasonably bounded range.

If we posit that there is some universality to the information rates across modern languages, what does this mean in terms of language evolution? As researchers including Aiello (1998), Aiello and Dean (1990), and Duchin (1990) have noted, humans have unique vocal tract structures and articulation capabilities that are directly responsible for the ability to generate the range of phonemes present in speech. The importance in the evolution of language of assembling sequences of symbols such as phonemes is well recognized. For example, Jackendoff (1999) has advocated an incremental view of language evolution, an approach that he describes as a middle ground between the innate view advocated by Chomsky (1975) and one that emphasizes the role of evolution (Donald, 1999). In Jackendoff's proposed steps, the concatenation of symbols is a critical milestone on the way to a protolanguage; as he notes, "concatenating symbols opens up many opportunities for enhancing expressive power and precision." (Jackendoff, 1999:275).

While there is a large body of literature devoted to the evolutionary growth of language sophistication, information theoretic studies that examine concatenations of symbols such as phonemes can contribute to understanding a closely related issue that has received far less attention: how speech efficiency, which is a direct function of the amount of information per phoneme and the rate at which phonemes are produced, may have developed over evolutionary time scales.

The evolutionary imperatives associated with language development clearly played a role. The question of why it takes closer to 1 second than to 0.01 or 100 seconds to say "The tiger is charging!" can therefore be answered in part by considering the time spans associated with reaction and movement. If it takes several seconds to hear a warning of approaching danger, understand it, and start to flee, whether it takes 0.01 or 1 second to utter the warning makes little overall difference. There would have been a distinct absence of selective pressure to reduce the time to utter warnings down to 0.01 seconds, since that is far shorter than the time needed to process and react to the information. On the other hand, a system of spoken language requiring 100 seconds to convey the warning would clearly be inadequate.

Thus, there is an evolutionarily determined range of information rates within which speech is neither too slow nor unnecessarily fast, and there is nothing at all accidental about the fact that speech conveys information at time scales consistent with human perception and movement. However, within that viable range, the question of where a specific modern language falls, or fell, is less related to evolution and is instead the likely result of cultural, historical, and other factors. Those factors are probably responsible for at least some of the differences in information rates observed in this study.

So how did humans come to communicate at the specific range of information rates characterizing modern speech? There are many possibilities. One possibility is that physical agility and speed, neurological and vocal tract structural characteristics, and linguistic systems have all evolved roughly in tandem in a mutually consistent manner. It is also possible that the physiological characteristics that enable speech production, having evolved to essentially their modern state, then remained relatively static as communication rate improved. In addition, there may have been some evolutionary pressures to increase redundancy, leading to slower and therefore less efficient (though presumably increasingly sophisticated) vocal communication.

The above entropy-based measurements provide quantitative support for the existence of a specific range of information transfer rates in modern speech and an indication of how those rates differ across languages. In that respect, these measurements can therefore play an important role in quantifying how language conveys information. But, they do not tell the whole story. In the future, it may be of interest to combine the methods described in this paper for measuring absolute information rates with approaches designed to capture the correlations and meaning not only across neighboring phonemes but also across longer linguistic structures.

5. Conclusions

Given the critical role of grammar, semantics, pragmatics, and many other factors in conveying information through spoken language, to suggest that phoneme or syllable entropy alone is sufficient to fully characterize language efficiency would be a gross oversimplification. However, we believe that the results presented here can constitute an important piece of the overall puzzle, as they directly consider the underlying information associated with the use of the phonemic alphabet that is the foundation of speech. Our results suggest that modern speech conveys information at rates ranging from several dozen to about 100 bits per second, and also indicates the presence of significant inter-language variations. This, in turn, has important implications with respect to language evolution, in particular to questions relating to when and how the information transfer rates of modern speech developed, whether the amount of inter-language variation observed today may have changed as language evolved, and the possibility that speech information rate and/or redundancy may still be evolving.

References

Aiello, L. C. (1998). The foundations of human language. In N. G. Jablonski and L. C. Aiello (Eds.), *The Origin and Diversification of Language.* San Francisco: California Academy of Sciences.

Aiello, L. C. & C. Dean. (1990). *An introduction to human evolutionary anatomy.* London, UK: Academic Press.

Chomsky, N. (1975) *Reflections on Language*. New York, NY: Pantheon.

Cover, T. M. & Thomas, J.A. (2006). *Elements of Information Theory, 2nd Ed.* Hoboken, NJ: John Wiley & Sons.

Cover, T. M. & King, R. C. (1978) A convergent gambling estimate of the entropy of English. *IEEE Trans. Information Theory,* (24)4, 413-421.

Donald, M. (1999). Preconditions for the evolution of protolanguages. In M. C. Corballis and S. E. G. Lea (Eds.), *The Descent of Mind* (pp. 138-154). Oxford: Oxford University Press.

Duchin, L. E. (1990). The evolution of articulate speech: Comparative anatomy of the oral cavity in Pan and Homo. *Jnl. of Human Evolution*, 19, 687-698.

International Phonetic Association. (1999). *The Handbook of the International Phonetic Association.* Cambridge: Cambridge University Press.

International Phonetic Association. (2005). Reproduction of the International Phonetic Alphabet. http://www.langsci.ucl.ac.uk/ipa/fullchart.html.

Jackendoff, R. (1999). Possible stages in the evolution of the language capacity. *Trends in Cognitive Sciences,* 3(7), 272-279.

McCowan, B., Hanswer, S. F., & Doyle, L. R. (1999) Quantitative tools for comparing animal communication systems: information theory applied to bottlenose dolphin whistle repertoires. *Animal Behaviour*, 57, 409-419.

Pellegrino, F., Coupé, C., & Marsico, E. (2011) A cross-language perspective on speech information rate. *Language*, 87, 539-558.

Robb, M. P., MacLagan, M. A., & Chen, Y. (2004) Speaking rates of American and New Zealand varieties of English. *Clin. Ling. & Phonetics*, 18, 1-15.

Shannon, C. E. (1948). A mathematical theory of communication. *Bell System Technical Journal,* 27, 379-423, 623-656.

Yaglom, A. M. & Yaglom, I, M. (1983). *Probability and Information*. Boston: D. Reidel.

Zipf, G. K. (1949). *Human Behavior and the Principle of Least Effort.* Cambridge: Addison-Wesley Press.

ROBUSTNESS AS A DESIGN FEATURE OF SPEECH COMMUNICATION

BODO WINTER

Dept. of Cognitive and Information Sciences, University of California, Merced, 5200 North Lake Rd., Merced, CA, 95343, USA

MORTEN H. CHRISTIANSEN

Department of Psychology, Cornell University, Ithaca, NY, 14853, USA
Santa Fe Institute, 1399 Hyde Park Rd., Santa Fe, NM, 87501, USA

As a communication system, human language is incredibly robust. In this paper, we identify some of the mechanisms that make speech communication robust in the face of noise and variation. We argue that many phenomena that are usually studied for their own sake (speech adaptation, accommodation, distributed redundancy) work together in order to increase the robustness of speech. Robustness can thus be used as a unifying concept for a seemingly disparate collection of experimental data. We outline the implications of robustness for the study of language evolution, and we discuss how both biological and cultural evolution may have played a role in making language robust. Taking the robustness of language into account makes it clear that not only do linguistic systems evolve with respect to functional considerations, but also with respect to how those functions can be maintained in the light of a multitude of perturbations.

1. Introduction

Robustness is the property of a system that enables it to cope with noise and interference; it is what allows a system to maintain its function despite internal and external perturbations. The concept has received a lot of attention in complexity science and biology (for a review, see Kitano, 2004), but it has received considerably less attention in language research – despite the fact that language obviously seems to have some degree of robustness, otherwise we wouldn't be able to talk in a variety of acoustic environments and with varying degrees of environmental noise. Moreover, linguistic communication even works despite a large amount of variation: each and every utterance is different along some dimension. Speakers differ with respect to sex, age, dialect, personality and many other characteristics that affect speech patterns (inter-speaker variation), and utterances differ from one another because of motor variability (intra-speaker variation). The presence of robustness raises key questions for language evolution research: what are the specific properties that make it possible for us to communicate in the face of noise and variation, and how did these evolve?

Looking at speech communication in particular, it is possible to uncover how many different parts of language work together to safeguard the communication process against perturbations. However, rather than there being a hotchpotch of different unconnected properties that increase robustness, we argue that the different properties can be characterized as a small set of **robustness-enhancing features** over which generalizations can be made:

1. Speech adaptation and motor equivalence
2. Speech accommodation
3. Distributed redundancy

This list is not meant to be exhaustive. For now, we focus on the robustness of the speech signal, but note that there are additional robustness enhancers at other levels of linguistic description, e.g., there is considerable redundancy in morphosyntax (bipartite morphemes, participant roles that are encoded simultaneously through word order and case, etc.). Moreover, we focus on the perspective of speech production, as others have already explored the robustness of speech perception (e.g., Diehl, 2011). In the following, we discuss the theoretical and empirical support for each of the three robustness-enhancing features in turn.

2. Speech adaptation

In this paper, we use the term "adaptation" not in its evolutionary sense, but to describe the observation that language users are able to rapidly adapt to the onset of environmental noise (e.g., Grynpas et al., 2011). Similarly, speakers are able to react appropriately to temporary or long-term mechanical speech impediments (e.g., Tremblay et al., 2003; Bressman, 2006). Speech adaptation is a feedback mechanism that detects changes in the acoustic output of one's own speech and quickly alters speech production in order to arrive at a more intelligible output.

Experimental evidence for speech adaptation comes from auditory feedback studies, where speakers that produce speech are played back a synthetically altered version of their own speech (e.g., shift in pitch). With this paradigm, it was shown that people are able to adapt to changes in loudness (e.g., Lane &

Tranel, 1971), fundamental frequency (Jones & Munhall, 2000) and formant frequencies (Tremblay et al., 2003). Speech adaptation acts both short-term in a rapid and automatic fashion, as well as on a long-term basis, and it also works with feedback from the sensorimotor system (Tremblay et al., 2003). The potential power of speech adaptation as a robustness enhancer is shown by the fact that intelligibility is assured even despite such extreme impediments as tongue splits (Bressman, 2006).

Speech adaptation is closely linked to the notion of motor equivalence, the idea that there are multiple ways in which to produce acoustic outputs that have identical linguistic effects on the listener. This idea comes from early experiments where participants were still able to produce intelligible speech despite mechanical interference due to speech adaptation (e.g., Folkins & Abbs, 1975). One perspective on this data is that speech sounds tend to be within so-called "quantal" regions (Stevens, 1979)—that is, regions within the articulatory apparatus that allow a high degree of motor variation while keeping the amount of acoustic variation at a minimum. Having speech patterns within these quantal regions not only assures robustness against external perturbations, but also against the inherent degree of variability in speech movements (gestures will almost always miss a given articulatory target region to a certain degree).

The evolutionary significance of speech adaptation is two-fold. First, given that adaptation only works if there is some degree of motor equivalence, it becomes important to explain how speech sounds came to exhibit this property. We hypothesize that there may be evolutionary pressures in cultural language evolution towards higher degrees of motor equivalence. Speech sounds which are in articulatory regions that do not afford a lot of variation will tend to be more acoustically variable – and this inevitably leads to higher degrees of misperception. Sounds that are often misperceived are unstable in diachronic terms, and will either disappear or develop towards a pattern that is less prone to misperception (Blevins, 2004). Preliminary support for such a process can be gleaned from simulations which show that sound systems develop towards perceptually more distinct regions (e.g., de Boer, 2001), however, we are currently unaware of computational simulations that specifically address the role of motor equivalence.

Second, the fact that people are able to perform adaptation rapidly, automatically and non-consciously suggests that there may also be a biological component to this ability, thus opening the possibility for biological evolution having played a role (e.g., speakers who were better at speech adaption may have had a selective advantage). Alternatively, the speech adaptation mechanism might be a spandrel, e.g., the ability to perform adaptation might be a simple outgrowth from our general capacity to imitate, which may be a prerequisite for language (e.g., Donald, 2005). Intriguingly, speech adaptation seems to have corollaries in other species. House finches, for example, perform rapid real-time frequency shifts of their songs in response to urban noise (Bermúdez-Cuamatzin et al., 2011). The presence of behavioral adaptation mechanisms in other species may allow us to address its possible connection to imitation, as well as whether it is a spandrel or a biological adaptation.

3. Speech accommodation

Whereas speech adaptation is a response to changes in one's own speech patterns, accommodation refers to changes with respect to the speech patterns of others. People can either increase or decrease similarity of their speech patterns (convergence and divergence, respectively), however, speech convergence seems to be much more common than divergence (e.g., Giles & Coupland, 1991: 66).

The major theory that seeks to explain accommodation behavior, Communication Accommodation Theory (CAT, e.g., Giles & Coupland, 1991), grounds speech convergence in the common desire to decrease social distance with our interlocutors. While this is very much *one* likely source of speech convergence behavior, other evidence indicates that speech convergence cannot be a solely social phenomenon; e.g., speakers rapidly converge to recordings of nonwords (e.g., Goldinger, 1998), individual syllables presented out of context (Nielsen, 2005), and to computerized agents even if they do not feel sympathetic to those agents (Staum Casasanto et al., 2010). Thus, we suggest, from an evolutionary perspective, that speech convergence also serves to increase robustness. By having a mechanism through which we can increase the similarity of the communicative code over repeated interactions, we can deal with the diversity of different speakers.

Just like speech adaptation, accommodation is a rapid, automatic and often non-conscious process. Hence, the question arises whether speech accommodation simply follows from having the (biological) ability to imitate, or whether there is a specific biological adaptation towards being better at accommodating. Again, there are important and interesting corollaries in other species, which possibly allow testing these views: both birds (e.g., Mammen & Nowicki, 1981) and non-human primates (Lemasson & Hausberger, 2004) exhibit evidence for the convergence of communicative codes.

4. Distributed redundancy

Many researchers have argued that language has some degree of redundancy (e.g., Pinker & Jackendoff, 2005). In speech, redundancy is ubiquitous. For example, stress is simultaneously cued by pitch, loudness, duration and spectral slope. Utterance endings are cued by a loss of energy, a reduction in pitch, final lengthening and sometimes a following pause. Word boundaries are cued by (depending on the language) transition probabilities, phonotactics, stress, word-final lengthening, word-final phonological processes and sometimes a following pause. Evidence that this **cue layering** actually increases robustness comes from cut-off studies (e.g., Cho, 1996), where listeners have fewer cues available and then use the other cues, or from noise overlay studies (e.g., Xu et al., 2005).

Many of these cues arise epiphenomenally because of simple biomechanical or physical reasons. For example, the fact that pitch is increased after aspirated as opposed to non-aspirated stops has to do with the higher amount of glottal airflow which then leads to a faster glottal vibration. Due to the increased flow, the glottis cannot help but to vibrate faster after aspirated stops and thus, this additional cue comes "for free". Whether a correlate in speech production is then actually used as a cue depends on the perceiver, but as Moreton (2004: 13) says, "correlates of a contrast are typically cues to that contrast."

However, redundancy in and by itself is not enough to facilitate language use; the redundancy also needs to be **distributed** in the temporal domain. Very loud broadband noise would be able to selectively interfere with all phonetic cues at a given point in time, but if the information is spread out over the signal, misperception at a particular point in time can be dealt with by retrieving the information later. This kind of temporal distribution is ubiquitous in phonetic systems, e.g., Cho (1996) showed that Korean listeners are able to decide whether Korean stops are tensed, lax or aspirated purely based on voice quality differences in the following vowel. Xu and colleagues (2005) showed that people are able to locate the position of sentential focus even well after the focused constituent because of cues that follow the constituent (called "post-focus compression").

The sound systems of the world's languages seem to exhibit distributed redundancies to a great extent. We take this as an indication that there potentially are selective pressures towards languages being more redundant. These pressures could manifest themselves through cultural language evolution. This view is in line with recent trends in phonology, where different researchers have started to focus on the evolution of sound patterns through perceptual and articulatory constraints. Accordingly, Blevins (2004) argues that the sound patterns that are most frequently observed in the languages of the world are those that are easy to produce and easy to perceive. Part of what makes a phoneme or a contrast easy to perceive is determined by the amount of redundancy and by the spread of this redundancy. The idea that language as a system converges on higher degrees of redundancy leads to the testable predictions for linguistic typology: the most frequent sound patterns of the world should also be the most redundant ones.

5. Conclusions

Our list of robustness enhancers is meant to be a first step towards thinking about robustness as a general property of speech communication—a property that likely extends to other areas of language as well. Because the enhancing features that we identified are present (to some degree) in *all* languages, we hypothesize that robustness may be a **design feature** of language and thus of similar importance to the evolution of language as arbitrariness and duality of patterning (cf. Hockett, 1960). Moreover, the concept of robustness provides a unifying perspective on a seemingly diverse set of descriptive and experimental data, ranging from the speech production studies that demonstrate redundancy to experiments on adaptation and accommodation.

If robustness is an important feature of language, the question naturally arises as to what its origin may be. As outlined in the sections above, both cultural evolution and biological evolution may have played a role. Speech adaptation and speech convergence via accommodation seem to derive from the biology of the speakers of a language. However, this leaves unresolved whether there were specific adaptations towards these skills, or whether these capabilities simply follow from our more general capability to imitate and therefore may be a reflection of prior biological abilities. One avenue into investigating the biological nature of these capabilities is by looking at other species (which sometimes show signs of adaptation and accommodation), another is by conducting individual differences studies (see, e.g., Misyak & Christiansen, in press). For example, the view that speech accommodation is a spandrel that follows from our imitation capacity makes the prediction that people who are better at implicitly imitating (also with respect to non-linguistic behaviors) should more readily perform speech convergence when talking to others.

With respect to motor equivalence, functional redundancy and its temporal distribution, we suggest that cultural evolution may be the predominant factor that produces these robustness-enhancing features. From the simple assumption that speakers tend to stick with those patterns that are most easily perceived, and best received in face of perturbations, it follows that speech systems should evolve in the direction of more "quantal" regions of the speech apparatus and towards more distributed redundancy.

We conclude by noting that the evolutionary hypothesis we have forwarded in this paper has primarily relied on reinterpretations of existing results in the speech literature. However, our notion of robustness also allows us to derive new testable hypotheses. For example, convergence of speech patterns between interlocutors should be stronger in noisy environments. Or, if participants are asked to interact with one another using an artificial language, then we would expect that across multiple experimental generations, they would show a tendency towards using forms with higher degrees of redundancy and more temporally distributed cues. Hence, thinking about language from the perspective of robustness and making robustness a topic for further investigation may prove very fruitful for future research into the evolution of language.

References

Bermúdez-Cuamatzin, E., Ríos-Chelén, A. A., Gil, D., & Garcia, C. M. (2011). Experimental evidence for real-time song frequency shift in response to urban noise in a passerine bird. *Biology Letters*, 7, 36-38.

Blevins, J. (2004). *Evolutionary phonology: The emergence of sound patterns*. Cambridge: Cambridge University Press.

Bressmann, T. (2006). Speech adaptation to a self-inflicted cosmetic tongue split: Perceptual and ultrasonographic analysis. *Clinical Linguistics & Phonetics*, 20, 205-210.

Staum Casasanto, L., Jasmin, K., & Casasanto, D. (2010). Virtually accommodating: Speech rate accommodation to a virtual interlocutor. In S. Ohlsson & R. Catrambone (Eds.), *Proceedings of the 32nd Annual Conference of the Cognitive Science Society* (pp. 127-132). Austin: Cognitive Science Society.

Cho, T. (1996). Vowel correlates to consonant phonation: an acoustic-perceptual study of Korean obstruents. M.A. thesis, University of Texas at Arlington.

Diehl, R. L. (2011). On the robustness of speech perception. *International Congress of Phonetic Science*, Hong Kong.

Donald, M. (2005). Imitation and mimesis. In S. Hurley & N. Chater (Eds.), *Perspectives on Imitation: From Neuroscience to Social Science, Volume 2: Imitation, Human Development, and Culture* (pp. 282-300). Cambridge, MA: MIT Press.

Folkins, J. W., & Abbs, J.H. (1975). Lip and jaw motor control during speech: Responses to resistive loading of the jaw. *Journal of Speech and Hearing Research*, 18, 207-220.

Goldinger, S. D. (1998). Echoes of echoes? An episodic theory of lexical access. *Psychological Review*, 1052, 251-279.

Giles, H. (1973). Accent mobility: a model and some data. *Anthropological Linguistics*, 15, 87-109.

Giles, H., & Coupland, N. (1991). *Language: Contexts and consequences*. Pacific Grove: Brooks/Cole.

Grynpas, J., Baker, R., & Hazan, V. (2011). Clear speech strategies and speech perception in adverse listening conditions. *International Congress of Phonetic Science*, Hong Kong.

Hockett, C. (1960). The origin of speech. *Scientific American*, 203, 88-111.

Jones, J. A., & Munhall, K. G. (2000). Perceptual calibration of F0 production: Evidence from feedback perturbation. *Journal of the Acoustical Society of America*, 108, 1246–1251.

Kitano, H. (2004). Biological Robustness. *Nature*, 5, 826-837.

Lane, H. L., & Tranel, B. W. (1971). The Lombard sign and the role of hearing in speech. *Journal of Speech Language and Hearing Science*, 14, 677-709.

Lemasson, A., & Hausberger, M. (2004). Patterns of vocal sharing and social dynamics in a captive group of Campbell's monkeys (Cercopithecus campbelli campbelli). *Journal of Comparative Psychology*, 118, 347-359.

Mammen, D. L., & Nowicki, S. (1981). Individual differences and within-flock convergence in chickadee calls. *Behavioral Ecology and Sociobiology*, 9, 179-186.

Misyak, J. B., & Christiansen, M. H. (in press). Statistical learning and language: An individual differences study. *Language Learning.*

Moreton, E. (2004). Realization of the English postvocalic [voice] contrast in F1 and F2. *Journal of Phonetics*, 32, 1-33.

Nielsen, K. (2005). Specificity and generalizability of spontaneous phonetic imitation. *Proceedings of the 9th International Conference on Spoken Language Processing*, Pittsburgh, USA.

Pardo, J. S. (2006). On phonetic convergence during conversational interaction. *Journal of the Acoustical Society of America*, 19, 2382-2392.

Pinker, S., & Jackendoff, R. (2005). The faculty of language: what's special about it? *Cognition*, 95, 201-236.

Stevens, K. N. (1989). On the quantal nature of speech. *Journal of Phonetics*, 17, 3-45.

Tremblay, S., Shiller, D. M., & Ostry, D. J. (2003). Somatosensory basis of speech production. *Nature*, 423, 866-869.

Xu, Y., Xu, C.X., & Sun, X. (2004). On the temporal domain of focus. *Speech Prosody,* Nara, Japan, *81-84.*

THE COOPERATIVE NATURE OF CONVERSATION. EVIDENCE FROM CONVERSATIONAL EXCHANGES

PRZEMYSŁAW ŻYWICZYŃSKI & SŁAWOMIR WACEWICZ

Department of English, Nicolaus Copernicus University, Fosa Staromiejska 3
Toruń, 87-100, Poland

The cooperative dimension of human linguistic communication has been gaining increasing recognition as a central problem in the evolution of language. Our paper documents the phenomenon of cooperative norms in conversation, with evidence gained through the application of the tools of Conversational Analysis (CA) to a corpus of spoken conversational exchanges. The backdrop to our discussion is the concept of planbox escalation, a 'default' exclusively goal-oriented strategy, which we relate to the notion of *Pan economicus* from comparative psychology. We focus on the way conversational exchanges, especially what we call economic exchanges, diverge from the predictions of this model, thus pointing to the existence of cooperative norms.

1. Introduction

The cooperative dimension of language has been appreciated in linguistics and philosophy at least since H. P. Grice (1975). However, as is well known, cooperation in general is not evolutionarily stable and constitutes an exception to the rule rather than the natural default state. Consequently, when viewed from the evolutionary perspective, the cooperative nature of human linguistic communication constitutes an important problem and an explanatory target.

In theory, cooperation is not normally expected to evolve because Darwinian agents act to maximize (inclusive) fitness, and under ordinary circumstances the alternative strategy, i.e. defection, leads to greater fitness gains. This prediction is consistent with research on our closest relatives, chimpanzees, who prototypically behave as self-interested agents maximising their immediate payoffs (hence the term *Pan economicus*, cf. Jensen et al. 2007). Although recent studies point to important exceptions from this pattern (e.g. unrewarded instrumental helping, Warneken & Tomasello 2006), we take it to be a safe general conclusion that the behaviour of unenculturated apes usually approximates the *economicus* stance, which contrasts starkly with human natural other-regarding proclivities.

In our paper, we do not intend to offer speculation on the origin of cooperation in hominins (creatures whose phylogenetic distance from *H. sapiens* is smaller than from the genus *Pan*). Rather, we:

(1) provide evidence for the other-regarding[1], i.e. highly cooperative, character of (a subset of) conversational exchanges, thus documenting empirically an important difference between human communication and the predictions of the default 'selfish' model of communication; the data come from the analysis of spoken exchanges studied with the methods of Conversational Analysis (e.g. Sacks & Schegloff 1973, Sacks 1992, Davidson 1984, Pomeranz 1984);

(2) on the theoretical side, we connect our findings to a broader model by Tomasello (2008); while this can be seen as a post-factum fit, an advantage of our findings is that they have been reached independently of this model.

2. Goals and planboxes

An interesting perspective on the problem of cooperation is afforded by a study of conflicts and conflict resolutions in conversational exchanges. In discourse and text linguistics, linguistic communication – and prototypically conversation – is often understood in terms of goals that conversants seek to accomplish by means of a communicative act (see e.g. Widdowson 1975, de Beaugrande & Dressler 1981, Krzeszowski 1997). A common approach to goal-orientedness in discursive interaction, particularly in textual and computational theories of communication, is based on the idea of problem solving first proposed by Newell and Simon (1972) and developed by de Beaugrande and Dressler (1981). Accordingly, a problem is defined as a pair of states – the initial state and the goal state – "whose connecting pathway is subject to failure (not being traversed)" (de Beaugrande & Dressler 1981: 37); the problem is solved when the pathway leading from the initial state to the goal state is found. In the case of verbal communication, connectivity between the initial and the goal states is established by *discursive pathways*, that is, discourse constitutes a means of traversing the path from the starting point to the goal. Problem solving is closely related to planning, the process by which participants evaluate possible pathways in terms of their utility in forwarding the goal state and, on the basis of such evaluations, opt for the pathway which appears to be the most expedient. In short, planning consists in choosing the most expedient discursive strategy.

De Beaugrande and Dressler explain what discursive strategies are by using

---

[1] An other-regarding act does not imply psychological or genetic altruism, and could still be reanalyzed as 'selfish' in the sense of increasing the agent's own fitness when a broader spectrum of costs and benefits is considered.

the notion of a *planbox* introduced by Schank and Abelson. "Planbox" is "a particular method of achieving a goalstate" (Meehan 1975: 82). Furthermore, de Beaugrande and Dressler propose that planboxes should be arranged with regard to the degree of escalation they involve – from the least violent to the most violent. Thus, escalation is seen as a consequence of blocking away the goal state. Consider the following example (de Beaugrande & Dressler 1981: 170):

John wanted Bill's bicycle. He walked over to Bill and asked him if he would give it to him. Bill refused. Then John told Bill he would give him five dollars for it, but Bill would not agree. John told Bill he would break his arm if he didn't let him have it. Bill let John have the bicycle.

In the above example of planbox escalation, John's sole concern is with his goal of getting Bill's bicycle – in the face of Bill's refusal, the logic of John's actions depends on the economic criterion of calculating the amount of resources he is prepared to expend in following this goal against benefits accrued by accomplishing it. It is very important to observe that the underlying rationale of pure cost/benefit analysis legitimises the model of planbox escalation as a default model of communicative interaction: firstly, it is naturally sound from the point of view of evolutionary stability, and secondly, it is actually reflected in the *economicus* ethos of non-human apes mentioned above.

3. Conversational exchanges

While it is intuitively obvious that human communication does not follow simple planbox escalation, it is interesting to show empirically the actual deviations from the predictions of the planbox model. In doing so, we base upon the results from an earlier study into patterns of value assignment in conversation exchanges (Żywiczyński 2010). The data, comprised of 81 naturally occurring spoken interactions, came from conversational corpora of contemporary English.[2] Following the tradition of Conversation Analysis (CA), the basic analytical unit of conversation was identified as an *adjacency pair*, that is, a pair of functionally related turns at talking, such as question-answer, greeting-greeting, or offer-acceptance (Sacks 1992). Conversational turns differ in *preference organisation*: turns with preferential organisation are structurally simple and delivered without hesitation, while dispreferentially organised turns are structurally complex and usually incorporate delays, prefaces, accounts, or declination components.

[2] See Żywiczyński (2010) for details.

Żywiczyński (2010) found a strong correlation between dispreference phenomena and the presence of blockages to conversants' goals, which henceforth will be referred to as *interactional clashes*. Further, the corpus study uncovered two basic classes of adjacency pairs – one class, typified by invitations, offers, requests, and questions, is related to transfer of goods, services, and information; the other class, represented by assessments and self-deprecations, concerns aligning interactants' view on a particular aspect of reality. We will respectively designate adjacencies belonging to these two classes as *economic* and *phatic* exchanges.

4. Phatic exchanges

Pomerantz (1984) notes that conversants routinely coordinate their views on a particular aspect of reality since agreement between them appears to facilitate other discursive activities. Expectedly then, phatic exchanges show a strong orientation towards preferred scenarios, with preferred turns often taking form of enhanced and upgraded agreements in the case of assessments and disagreements in the case of self-deprecations:

[1] Turn 1 A: It's a beautiful day out, isn't it? ((ASSESSMENT))
Turn 2 B: Yeh it's just gorgeous ((PREFERRED: HYPERBOLIC AGREEMENT))
(Pomerantz 1984: 62)

In interactional terms, it can be said that participants of phatic exchanges are particularly eager to acknowledge the clash-free status of their interactions. The corpus material indicated that clash-holding assessments and self-deprecations are relatively rare and when they occur, interactants take strong measures to cushion the effect of clashes. For example, respondents' disagreement is often communicated by means of either silence or non-enthusiastic agreement, such as weakened agreement, token agreement, or downgraded agreement, which gives initiators the freedom to interpret it as a move confirming their prior assessment (preferential interpretation) or as challenging it (dispreferential interpretation):

[2] Turn 1 A: She's a fox!
Turn 2 B: She's a pretty girl ((WEAKEND AGREEMENT)) (Pomerantz 1984: 68)

Generally, interactants engaged in both assessment and self-deprecation sequences are focused on upholding the clash-free status of discourse. On the one hand, this tendency is demonstrated by enthusiastic agreements to prior assessments and forceful disagreements to prior self-deprecations in clash-free discourses (interaction [1]) and on the other by the avoidance of open disagreements to prior assessments and open confirmations of prior self-deprecations in clash-holding discourses (interaction [2]). In the latter case, interactants modify their opinions and even resign from them with a view to averting a crisis created by global clashes. Such a strong orientation of phatic exchanges towards the state of interactional balance indicates that the primary concern of the conversants is collaborative face-maintenance, rather than the pursuit of own instrumental goals via planbox escalation.

5. Economic exchanges

In economic exchanges, transfer of goods, services, etc. can proceed in two opposite directions: either from the initiator of an exchange towards the respondent, as is the case in invitations and offers, where the invitee or the 'offeree' is the intended beneficiary of the transfer; or from the respondent towards the initiator, for examples in requests and questions, where it is the requester or the questioner who is the intended beneficiary of the transfer. Thus, the directionally of transfer leads to the sub-classification of economic adjacencies into *other-benefiting exchanges* (e.g. invitations and offers) and *self-benefiting exchanges* (e.g. requests and questions). Given the above characterisation, interactional clashes arising during other-benefiting exchanges should be seen as blocking the initiator's extra-discursive goal of effecting economic transfer towards the respondent, whereas in self-benefiting exchanges clashes block the initiator's extra-discursive goal to receive economic transfer from the respondent:

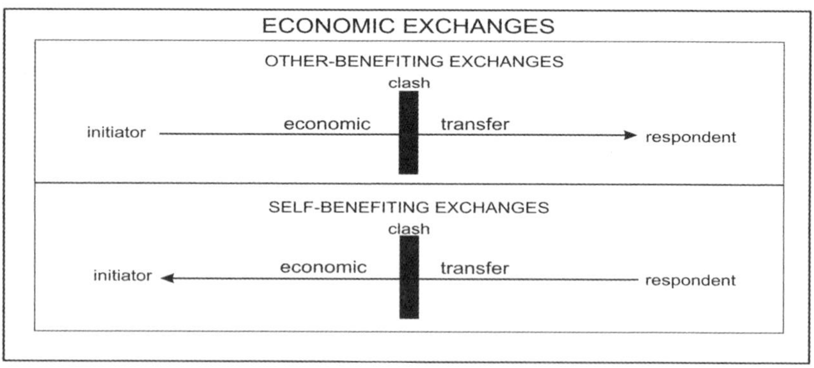

Figure 1. The representation of the economic dimension of discourse in other-benefiting exchanges (above) and self-benefiting exchanges (below)

It turned out that economic organisation has consequences for the interactional structure of exchanges. Namely, when a dispreferred scenario is instigated in other-benefiting exchanges, a reparatory action, i.e. an action undertaken with a view to resolving an interactional clash, is usually started by the initiator (i.e. inviter or offerer), who proposes a modified or an altered version of an original invitation or request, as illustrated below:

[3] Turn 1 A: Uh: would it be alright if we came in a little early <invitation>
Turn 2 B: (0.2) <absence of response at the completion point interpreted by A as rejection <implicative>
Turn 3 A: Would that upset //you? <the initiator's subsequent version of invitation>
Turn 4 B: I: don't think so (Davidson 1984: 115)

On the other hand, repairs in self-benefiting sequences are usually introduced by respondents. For example in request exchanges, respondents' most common tactic is to grant an altered version of an original request, or alternatively to delay the granting of a request, as in [4], Turn 2:

[4] Turn 1 A: Will you read me this story
Turn 2 B: Well after I've washed the dishes I'll read you that story (.) yes

Hence, it can be argued that economic exchanges have an other-regarding character in the sense that initiative for reparatory steps following a clash is taken by the source rather than the target of transfer of goods. To reiterate, in other-benefiting exchanges, where the objective is to bring benefit to the respondent (i.e. intended beneficiary of an exchange), reparatory initiative is taken by the initiator with the aim of effecting some form of economic transfer to the respondent (such is, for example, the role of modified invitations or offers put forward by the inviter or offerer); in self-benefiting exchanges, where the objective is to bring benefit to the initiator (i.e. intended beneficiary of an exchange), reparatory initiative is taken by the respondent with the aim of effecting some form of economic transfer to the initiator (for example, by suggesting altered versions of original requests). Thus, conversants typically initiate reparatory action that is economically costly to themselves but beneficial to their conversational partners. This finding in particular stands in direct opposition to the predictions of the planbox model, in which the strategy of short-term utility maximisation would necessarily lead to opting for the opposite pattern.

6. Conclusions

In our view, the study of interactional processes demonstrates the inadequacy of teleological accounts of conversational interaction, thus documenting the qualitative difference of human communication. Rather than adhering to individualistic agendas, as predicted by the planbox escalation model, discourse participants help each other in accomplishing their respective extra-discursive goals and, in doing so, are prepared to resign from their own economic gains (in economic exchanges) or withhold personal opinions (in phatic exchanges) – as illustrated by the analysis of dispreferred sequences in the preceding sections. These phenomena point to the existence of a normative element which receives priority to the pursuit of individualistic goals: adherence to the norm acts to override the order of participants' short-term extra-linguistic payoffs. In the most general terms, this normative element is expressed as interactants' commitment to cooperate in forwarding each other's extra-discursive goals and – in the event that the pursuit of these goals is blocked – as a commitment to collaboratively solve the emergent interactional crisis.

While an ultra-cooperative character of human communication in general is not controversial, its evolutionary emergence remains a puzzle. Probably the most comprehensive account has been developed by Tomasello (1999, 2008, 2011). Specifically an attempt can be made to explain the emergence of conversational cooperativeness with reference to the evolution of indirect reciprocity based on reputational mechanisms, as envisaged by Tomasello. Seen in this light, our study of cooperative aspects of conversational exchanges both gains support from, and gives ground to, the investigation into the origins of the "cooperative infrastructure of human collaboration and communication" (Tomasello 2008: 201). Undoubtedly, a deeper evolutionary understanding of cooperative norms in conversation requires further research, especially into their universality and acquisition, pointing to the need for cross-cultural and developmental studies.

Acknowledgements

This research was supported by grant 3704/B/H03/2011/40 from the Polish National Science Centre.

References

Beaugrande, R. de & Dressler, W. (1981). *Introduction to Text Linguistics*. Harlow: Longman.

Davidson, J. (1984). Subsequent Versions of Invitations, Offers, Requests, and Proposals Dealing with Potential or Actual Rejection. In: J. M. Atkinson & J. Heritage (Eds.), *Structures of Social Action: Studies in Conversation Analysis* (pp. 102-128). London: Macmillan.

Grice, H. P. ([1975] 1999). Logic and Conversation. In: A. Jaworski & N. Coupland (Eds.), *The Discourse Reader* (pp. 66-77). London: Routledge.

Jensen, K., Call, J., and Tomasello, M. (2007). Chimpanzees Are Rational Maximizers in an Ultimatum Game. *Science, 318*, 107-109.

Krzeszowski, T. P. (1997). *Angels and Devils in Hell: Elements of Axiology in Semantics*. Warsaw: Energeia.

Meehan, J. (1975). Using Planning Structures to Generate Stories. *American Journal of Computational Linguistics*, 33, 78-94.

Newell, A. & Simon, H. (1972). *Human Problem Solving*. Englewood Cliffs: Prentice Hall.

Pomerantz, A. 1984. Agreeing and Disagreeing with Assessments: Some Features of Preferred and Dispreferred Turn Shapes. In: J. M. Atkinson & J. Heritage (Eds.), *Structures of Social Action: Studies in Conversation Analysis* (pp. 57-101). London: Macmillan.

Sacks, H. 1992. *Lectures on Conversations. Volumes I and II*. Oxford: Blackwell.

Sacks, H. & Schegloff, E. (1973). Opening up Closings. *Semiotica*, 7(4), 289-327.

Schank, R. & Abelson, R. (1977). *Scripts, Plans, Goals, and Understanding*. Hillsdale: Erlbaum.

Tomasello, M. (1999). *The Cultural Origins of Human Cognition*. Cambridge, Massachusetts: Harvard University Press.

Tomasello, M. (2008). *Origins of Human Communication*. Cambridge, Massachusetts: The MIT Press.

Tomasello, M. (2011). *Why We Cooperate*. Cambridge, Massachusetts: The MIT Press.

Warneken, F. & Tomasello, M. (2006). Altruistic Helping in Human Infants and Young Chimpanzees. *Science, 311*, 1301–1303.

Widdowson, H. (1975). *Stylistics and the Teaching of Literature*. London: Longman.

Żywiczyński, P. (2010). *The Axiology of Spoken Interaction*. An Essay on the Organisation of Conversational Behaviour. Toruń: Wydawnictwo UMK.

Abstracts

POSTNATAL ACQUIREMENT OF THE ABILITY TO DISCRIMINATE CULTURLY SHARED SONG SYNTAX IN SONGBIRDS

KENTARO ABE

Graduate School of Biostudies, Kyoto University, Yoshidakonoe, Sakyo-ku, Kyoto, Kyoto 606-8501, JAPAN

PRESTO, Japan Science and Technology Agency, Saitama, JAPAN

Revealing how human brain process vocal languages are one of the ultimate goals in the field of neuroscience. Since the vocal communication of some avian species have many similar aspects to the human speech, songbirds have been studied as an animal model to analyze the neuronal mechanisms of how human utter and comprehend vocal signals. Nonetheless, birdsongs and human languages have several major differences; thus what aspect of human languages we can reveal by studying songbirds has been debated. One of such major differences among human and avian vocal communication have been considered whether or not the sequential orderings of the elements, such as words or syllables, contain biologically meaningful information. The songs of avian species are often considered to be uttered in order to proclaim the territory or to attract mates. In this context, their song has been considered to have meaning as a whole song, and the sequential orderings of the syllables in it do not have much information. In accordance to this view, evidence that songbirds vary the sequential structure in a particular one song to change the meanings of the vocal signals is currently limiting. The lack of semantical aspects in their vocal sequences is a salient difference to the human languages, in which words or phrases are well ordered according to the grammatical rules to contain specific meanings in the sentences.

Some species of passerine birds sing songs with variable syllable sequence. By analyzing the spontaneous behavioral reaction in one of such songbird species, the Bengalese finch (*Lonchura striata* var. *domestica*), we analyzed whether the ordering of the syllables in their natural songs contains any biologically meaningful information. By performing artificial modification of syllable sequences in the natural conspecific songs, we analyzed whether they can discriminate the difference and cause difference in their behavioral reactions (Abe and Watanabe, 2011). We found that both the male and female Bengalese finches could distinguish even a subtle modification of syllable sequences in the song, although the phonological features of each syllables were identical. Notably, however, not all of the syllable sequence modifications could be distinguished, and the modifications that could be discriminated and those that could not were shared among the individuals, indicating the existence of a specific rule in the sequential orderings of syllables in their songs, shared within the social community.

How do the Bengalese finches develop the ability to discriminate the syntactical aspects in auditory information? One possibility is that the species specific syntactic rules are encoded genetically, and birds possess the innate ability to discriminate the songs that breaks such rules. The other possibility is that the knowledge to discriminate sequential rules in their songs is acquired postnatally. By restricting the variation of the songs that the birds have been exposed, we revealed that the Bengalese finch postnatally acquires the knowledge to discriminate the sequence modified songs through the exposure to various songs of their conspecifics.

Our results suggest that the sequential organization of syllables in birdsongs convey some intraspecific meaningful information at least sufficient to cause behavioral difference, although we are still ignorant to what kind of meaning they are conveying. These findings suggest the possibility that birdsong might have some aspects of semantic components in their syllable sequences, and thus offer a comparative animal model to further examine aspects of the biological basis of the complex information processing involved in language comprehension.

References

Abe, K., & Watanabe, D. (2011). Songbirds possess the spontaneous ability to discriminate syntactic rules. *Nature Neuroscience, 14-8*, 1067-74.

A SIMPLE INTEGRATED FRAMEWORK FOR INVESTIGATING GENETIC AND CULTURAL EVOLUTION OF LANGUAGE

TSUBASA AZUMAGAKITO, REIJI SUZUKI, TAKAYA ARITA

Graduate School of Information Science, Nagoya University
Furo-cho, Chikusa-ku, Nagoya, 464-8601, Japan
azumagakito@alife.cs.is.nagoya-u.ac.jp

Two areas concerning language evolution have received increasing interest in recent years: the genetic evolution of the language faculty and the cultural evolution of language. However, these study areas are somewhat separate, and there is a need to integrate these efforts and explore the relevant gene-culture coevolutionary interactions (Mesoudi et al., 2011). The relationship between genes and language is extremely complex; therefore, there is much controversial discussion on various aspects, including the role of learning (Suzuki & Arita, 2008). Fundamentally, several researchers argue that cultural evolution has little influence on the genetic evolution of language although, various results have shown that genetic biases are essential for a proper understanding of language evolution (Fitch, 2011). For example, Chater et al. (2009) have shown, by using a computational model, that there are strong restrictions on the conditions under which the Baldwin effect can embed arbitrary linguistic constraints and the effect only emerges when language provides a stable target for natural selection.

This paper proposes an integrated computational framework for investigating possible scenarios of genetic and cultural evolution of language. Specifically, we would like to demonstrate cultural evolution to investigate phylogenetic dynamics of language and, at the same time, genetic evolution of phenotypic plasticity to investigate the Baldwin effect in language evolution, while keeping the framework as simple as possible. The main idea is to express the linguistic space in the polar coordinate system and gradually move the individuals and languages using genetic and cultural evolutionary dynamics in the space. In the model, the linguistic space is expressed in the polar coordinate system as shown in Fig. 1. Each language is represented as a point, and its radius and angle correspond to its expressiveness that makes a benefit of successful information sharing, and numerical defined structural feature, respectively. Each agent is also represented as a point and a fan-shaped field surrounding the point. This field corresponds to the set of languages that the focal agent can acquire for information sharing with other agents. The location of the point, the agent's *innate language*, and the size of the field, its *linguistic plasticity*, are determined by real-valued genotypes of each agent. Agents and languages coevolve according to the genetic and cultural evolutionary dynamics: *to survive, agents must talk with many others by using expressive languages and have lower linguistic plasticity cost* and *languages must move towards the center of their users, and divide, merge or go extinct according to the distribution of their users.*

The following is a typical coevolutionary scenario we observed: In early stages of evolution, a wide variety of languages appeared, similar to the Cambrian explosion, through division processes based on the language use by agents with different innate languages (Fig. 1). Then, the population of agents split into some dominant clusters due to the benefit of information sharing with many agents, which subsequently brought about the emergence of dominant clusters of languages. Finally, the population converged to a unique language. This may reflect a domination process of minor languages by major languages. We also found that the parameters dealing with the linguistic plasticity strongly affect the speed of coevolution and the final expression ability of the dominant language.

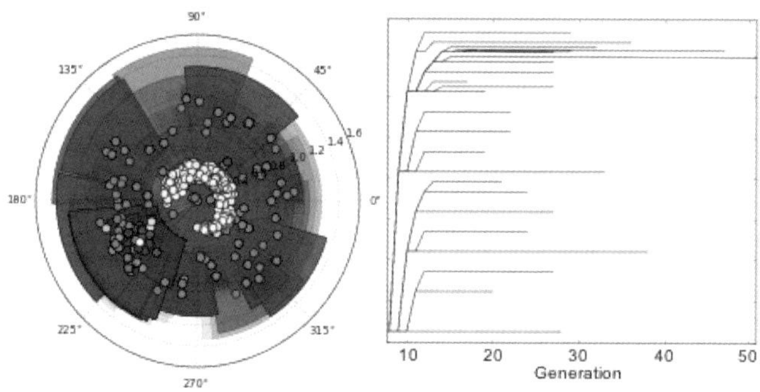

Figure 1. The left figure shows a coordinate distribution of languages and agents at an early stage of evolution. The agents and the languages are expressed by gray and white circles, respectively. The fan-shaped fields surrounding agents represent their linguistic plasticity. The right figure shows a generated phylogenetic tree of a language.

References

Chater, N., Reali, F., & Christiansen, M. H. (2009). Restriction on biological adaptation in language evolution. *Proceedings of the National Academy of Sciences*, *106*, 1015–1020.

Fitch, W. T. (2011). Genes, language, cognition, and culture: Towards productive inquiry. *Human Biology*, *83*(2), 323–329.

Mesoudi, A., Mcelligott, A. G., & Adger, D. (2011). Introduction: Integrating genetic and cultural evolutionary approaches to language. *Human Biology*, *83*(2), 141–151.

Suzuki, R., & Arita, T. (2008). How learning can guide evolution of communication. *Proceedings of Artificial Life XI*, 608–615.

AN ADAPTATIONIST APPROACH TO THE AUDIENCE DESIGN HYPOTHESIS

RACHAEL BAILES
Language Evolution and Computation Research Unit, School of Philosophy, Psychology & Language Sciences
The University of Edinburgh
r.l.bailes-2@sms.ed.ac.uk

One way of analysing current theoretical accounts within linguistics and human behaviour is to evaluate their accordance with evolutionary theory (Kinsella, 2009; Scott-Phillips, 2010). I will extend this approach to evaluate current psycholinguistic models concerning the constraint of common ground on comprehension, an area of current debate in the experimental literature. As pointed out by Tooby & Cosmides (1990), psycholinguists must not only consider the processing costs of processing mechanisms, but also consider a functional evolutionary explanation. I will consider the mechanisms of common ground comprehension as adaptations to the task of communication and suggest that an adaptationist psycholinguistics can better differentiate between accounts.

Every time interlocutors use language, they are tasked with coordinating with one another in order to converge upon meanings successfully. Speakers cooperatively adapt their speech in line with their assumptions about listeners (Krauss & Fussell, 1991). The hypothesis explored in the presented study is the audience design hypothesis, which posits that speakers and listeners maintain a model of the knowledge they share with their interlocutor. This shared knowledge, known as common ground, provides a domain of copresent information in which all utterances can be successfully interpreted, and comprises physical copresence, linguistic copresence and community membership (Clark & Murphy, 1982). The audience design hypothesis posits that common ground determines the production and comprehension of utterances from the earliest point of processing; as such, it fully constrains comprehension (Hanna et al., 2003; Brown-Schmidt, 2009). In contrast to this view is the perspective adjustment model (Barr & Keysar, 2006). According to this view, interlocutors do not distinguish between private and shared information in the processing of utterances and employ an egocentric mechanism. This may be followed by an optional adjustment stage, which corrects for violations of common ground (cf. Kronmüller & Barr, 2007). These rivaling accounts are a topic of extensive debate in current psycholinguistics.

I will present an adaptationist evaluation of the psycholinguistic models outlined above. While the perspective adjustment model assesses the processing costs of common ground comprehension, it does not outline a mechanism that is well-designed for solving the functional task of communication and as such does not lend itself to an adaptationist account. I will show that, in order for a cognitive account of comprehension to bear a functional evolutionary explanation, it must be fully constrained by common ground. As such, the audience design hypothesis is most compatible with an evolutionary framework.

References

Barr, D. & Keysar, B. (2006). Perspective taking and the coordination of meaning in language use. In Traxler, M. J. & Gernsbacher, M. A. (Eds.), *Handbook of Psycholinguistics*, 2nd Edition, (pp . 901-938) New York: Academic Press.

Brown-Schmidt, S. (2009). Partner-specific interpretation of maintained referential precedents during interactive dialog. *Journal of Memory and Language 61*, 171-190.

Clark & Murphy. (1982). Audience design in meaning and reference. In J.F. Le Ny, & W. Kintsch (Eds), *Language and comprehension* (pp. 287-299). Amsterdam: North-Holland.

Hanna, J.E., Tanenhaus, M.K. & Trueswell, J.C. (2003). The effects of common ground and perspective on domains of referential interpretation. *Journal of Memory and Language 49*, 43-61.

Kinsella, A.R. (2009) *Language evolution and syntactic theory.* Cambridge: Cambridge University Press.

Krauss, R.M. & Fussell, S.R. (1991). Perspective-taking in communication: Representations of others' knowledge in reference. *Social Cognition, 9(1),* 2-24.

Kronmüller, E. & Barr, D. (2007). Perspective-free pragmatics: Broken precedents and the recovery-from-preemption hypothesis. *Journal of Memory and Language 56*, 436-455.

Scott-Phillips, T.C. (2010). The evolution of relevance. *Cognitive Science 34 (4), 583-560.,*

Tooby, J. & Cosmides, L. (1990). Toward an adaptationist psycholinguistics, *Behavioural and Brain Sciences*, 760-761.

THE EXPONENT OF ZIPF'S LAW IN LANGUAGE ONTOGENY

JAUME BAIXERIES, RAMON FERRER-I-CANCHO

Complexity and Quantitative Linguistics Lab, LARCA Research Group / TALP Research Center, Departament de Llenguatges i Sistemes Informàtics, Universitat Politècnica de Catalunya, Campus Nord, Edifici Omega, Jordi Girona Salgado 1-3. Barcelona, 08034, Catalonia (Spain)

jbaixer@lsi.upc.edu, rferrericancho@lsi.upc.edu

BRITA ELVEVÅG

Psychiatry Research Group, Department of Clinical Medicine, University of Tromsø & Norwegian Centre for Integrated Care and Telemedicine (NST), University Hospital of North Norway, UNN-Åsgård, 9291 Tromsø, Norway.

brita@elvevaag.net

Word frequencies follow Zipf's law, namely the probability of the r-most frequent word is approximately $p(r) \sim r^{-\alpha}$, where α is the exponent of the law (Zipf, 1949). The relevance and the utility of this law has been debated for several decades (Miller & Chomsky, 1963; Suzuki, Tyack, & Buck, 2005; McCowan, Doyle, Jenkins, & Hanser, 2005; Manin, 2008). Proponents of the position that Zipf's law does not capture any deep property of language have argued that one can simply reproduce this law by typing at random on a keyboard (Miller & Chomsky, 1963; Suzuki et al., 2005). However, the viability of random typing reproducing the law has been reviewed in depth (Ferrer-i-Cancho & Elvevåg, 2009; Ferrer-i-Cancho & Gavaldà, 2009) and parameters that could adequately fit actual word frequencies from a statistically rigorous perspective are not forthcoming (Ferrer-i-Cancho & Elvevåg, 2009). A further argument against the utility of Zipf's law, namely that the law carries no information about the complexity of a communication system (Suzuki et al., 2005) will be empirically evaluated here. We contend that if this idea is viable, the exponent α should not depend on the complexity of the communication system. This is a central issue for the evolution of language from an ontogenetic and phylogenetic perspective: various theoretical models (Nowak, Plotkin, & Jansen, 2000; Corominas-Murtra, Valverde, & Solé, 2009) assume that α remains constant with a value of 1 as the complexity of the communication system increases.

The evolution of α as a function of age in children over the period where multi-word sentences develop (around 1-3 years) was analysed employing transcripts from the Childes database (MacWhinney, 2000). Four languages were considered:

English, Dutch, German and Swedish. The two major findings were: (a) α tends to be negatively correlated with age and (b) this negative correlation is relatively rare in the adults interacting with these children. The idea that α does not change as a communication system evolves or develops to a higher complexity (Nowak et al., 2000; Corominas-Murtra et al., 2009; Suzuki et al., 2005) needs to be re-examined. Indeed, α may help establish the actual complexity of a communication system.

Acknowledgements

This work was supported by the grant *Iniciació i reincorporació a la recerca* from the Universitat Politècnica de Catalunya (JB, GM & RFC), the grant BASMATI (TIN2011-27479-C04-03) from the Spanish Ministry of Science and Innovation, SMSI (JB, GM & RFC), the grant OpenMT-2 (TIN2009-14675-C03) from the SMSI (RFC) and the Northern Norwegian Regional Health Authority, *Helse Nord RHF* (BE).

References

Corominas-Murtra, B., Valverde, S. V., & Solé, R. (2009). The ontogeny of scale-free syntax networks: phase transitions in early language acquisition. *Advances in Complex Systems*, *12*(3), 371392.

Ferrer-i-Cancho, R., & Elvevåg, B. (2009). Random texts do not exhibit the real Zipf's-law-like rank distribution. *PLoS ONE*, *5*(4), e9411.

Ferrer-i-Cancho, R., & Gavaldà, R. (2009). The frequency spectrum of finite samples from the intermittent silence process. *Journal of the American Association for Information Science and Technology*, *60*(4), 837-843.

MacWhinney, B. (2000). *The CHILDES project: tools for analyzing talk.* Mahwah, NJ: Lawrence Erlbaum Associates.

Manin, D.-Y. (2008). Zipf's law and avoidance of excessive synonymy. *Cognitive Science*, *32*(7), 1075-1098.

McCowan, B., Doyle, L. R., Jenkins, J. M., & Hanser, S. F. (2005). The appropriate use of Zipf's law in animal communication studies. *Anim. Behav.*, *69*, F1-F7.

Miller, G. A., & Chomsky, N. (1963). Finitary models of language users. In R. D. Luce, R. Bush, & E. Galanter (Eds.), *Handbook of mathematical psychology* (Vol. 2, p. 419-491). New York: Wiley.

Nowak, M. A., Plotkin, J. B., & Jansen, V. A. (2000). The evolution of syntactic communication. *Nature*, *404*, 495-498.

Suzuki, R., Tyack, P. L., & Buck, J. (2005). The use of Zipf's law in animal communication analysis. *Anim. Behav.*, *69*, 9-17.

Zipf, G. K. (1949). *Human behaviour and the principle of least effort.* Cambridge (MA), USA: Addison-Wesley.

RECONCILING THE DIVERSITY OF LANGUAGES WITH THE BIOLOGICAL UNIFORMITY OF THEIR SPEAKERS

ANDREA BARONCHELLI

Departament de Fisica i Enginyeria Nuclear, Univ. Politecnica de Catalunya, C. Nord B4, 08034 Barcelona, Spain
andrea.baronchelli@upc.edu

NICK CHATER

Warwick Business School
The University of Warwick, Coventry CV4 7AL, United Kingdom
Nick.Chater@wbs.ac.uk

ROMUALDO PASTOR-SATORRAS

Departament de Fisica i Enginyeria Nuclear, Univ. Politecnica de Catalunya, C. Nord B4, 08034 Barcelona, Spain
romualdo.pastor@upc.edu

MORTEN H. CHRISTIANSEN

Department of Psychology, Cornell University, Ithaca, NY 14853, USA
christiansen@cornell.edu

How can the contrast between the astonishing diversity of human languages and the relative rigidity of other animal communication systems be reconciled with the uniformity of their biological bases? Here we propose a possible new solution to this fundamental puzzle for evolutionary biology.

Natural communication systems differ widely across species in both complexity and form, ranging from the quorum-sensing chemical signals of bacteria, to the color displays of cuttlefish, the waggle dance of honeybees, and the alarm calls of vervet monkeys. Crucially, though, within a given species, each of these communication systems has very limited variability (Hauser, 1996). In contrast, diversity is characteristic of almost every aspect of human language, and is a consequence of divergent cultural evolution following human migration (Cavalli-Sforza & Feldman, 2003). Languages variously employ tones, clicks, or manual signs to signal differences in meaning; some languages lack the noun-verb distinction (e.g., Straits Salish), whereas others have a proliferation of fine-grained syntactic categories (e.g., Tzeltal); and some languages do without morphology (e.g., Mandarin), while others pack a whole sentence into a single word (e.g., Cayuga). This diversity makes human language unique among animal communications systems. Yet the biological basis for language, like other animal communication systems, is generally considered to be uniform across the species (Pinker, 1995).

In this talk, we present a series of simulations providing a rigorous computational implementation of a new theoretical perspective that reconciles the diversity of human language with the presumed uniformity of its biological basis. We model a population of individuals, and consider different scenarios for the interaction between their genes and the language they speak (Chater, Reali, & Christiansen, 2009). We then let the population split, and observe the consequences of the diverse parameter settings on the linguistic and genetic divergence of the new populations. In particular, we take into account different linguistic and genetic mutation rates, the possible influence on the genes on language, and both the cases of isolated and interacting populations. The results show that only adaptations for flexible learning combined with continual cultural evolution can reconcile the diversity of languages with the biological uniformity of their speakers.

Overall, our work suggests that humans have evolved a biological basis for keeping up with the cultural evolution of language, instead of a special-purpose linguistic system analogous to the visual system (Chomsky, 2005). In this picture, linguistic diversity arises from an evolved uniform genetic foundation for cultural linguistic evolution, additionally shaped by non-linguistic constraints deriving from a uniform biological basis of general perceptual, cognitive, and pragmatic abilities that predate the emergence language (Deacon, 1998; Christiansen & Chater, 2008).

References

Cavalli-Sforza, L., & Feldman, M. (2003). The application of molecular genetic approaches to the study of human evolution. *nature genetics*, *33*, 266–275.

Chater, N., Reali, F., & Christiansen, M.H. (2009). Restrictions on biological adaptation in language evolution. *Proceedings of the National Academy of Sciences*, *106*(4), 1015.

Chomsky, N. (2005). *Rules and representations.* Columbia Univ Pr.

Christiansen, M.H., & Chater, N. (2008). Language as shaped by the brain. *Behavioral and Brain Sciences*, *31*(05), 489–509.

Deacon, T. (1998). *The symbolic species: The co-evolution of language and the brain.* WW Norton & Company.

Hauser, M. (1996). *The evolution of communication.* MIT press, Cambridge, MA.

Pinker, S. (1995). *The language instinct.* HarperPerennial New York, NY.

HOMO COMBINANS

CEDRIC BOECKX
ICREA & Center for Theoretical Linguistics, Universitat Autonoma de Barcelona, Barcelona, Spain

In this talk I would like to pay attention to the process of lexicalization, which I argue is the key event in the evolution of the human language faculty (in the narrow sense of the term).

It is commonly assumed that the key evolutionary step that gave us our distinctness is cognitive in nature. Accordingly, the quest for 'humaniqueness' amounts to identifying the factor (or factors) that make(s) human cognition special. In the words of Hauser (2009)

[a]nimals share many of the building blocks that comprise human thought, but paradoxically, there is a great cognitive gap between humans and animals. By looking at key differences in cognitive abilities, [we hope to] find the elements of human cognition that are uniquely human. The challenge is to identify which systems animals and human share, which are unique, and how these systems interact and interface with one another.

The program can be seen as an extension of Hauser, Chomsky and Fitch (2002): from FLN to HCN (Human Cognition in the Narrow sense; that which is specific and unique to human cognition), or (building on Fodor 1975), LOTN (Language of Thought Narrow).

Hauser (2009) presents four evolved mechanisms of human thought that give us access to a wide range of information and the ability to find creative solutions to new problems based on access to this information:

1. the ability to combine and recombine different types of information and knowledge in order to gain new understanding;

2. to apply the same "rule" or solution to one problem to a different and new situation;
3. to create and easily understand symbolic representations of computation and sensory input; and
4. to detach modes of thought from raw sensory and perceptual input.

Details of formulation aside, Hauser's hypothesis is a very familiar one. The essence of Hauser's claim really goes back to the Descartes' fascination with human cognitive flexibility, its fluidity, its detachment from perception, and its unbounded character---in short, its creative character. This is what led the Cartesians to claim that Man has no instinct, by which they meant that Man's cognitive faculties rise above the here and now. This too was clear to Konrad Lorenz, who said that "man is a specialist in not being specialized."

To be sure, scientists have found that some animals think in ways that were once considered unique to humans. For example, some animals have episodic memory, or non-linguistic mathematical ability, or the capacity to navigate using landmarks. In sum, animals have a rich mental life, full of modules or what L. Spelke calls 'core knowledge systems.' What Man seems to have in addition is the ability to systematically transcend the boundaries of modular thought and engage in cross-modular concept formation.

I claim that this ability of building bridges across modules is directly related to language, specifically the ability to lexicalize concepts (uprooting them from their modules) and combine them freely via Merge (itself a very generic, set-formation operation, not specific to the language faculty). The emergence of lexical items was the sort of perfect storm that gave Man his niche. Once concepts are dissociated from their conceptual sources by means of a lexical envelope, the mind truly becomes algebraic, and stimulus-free.

The creation of the human lexicon, which, if I am correct, goes hand in hand with unbounded Merge, is what lies behind the creative aspect of our thought process. With language, creativity emerged, understood (as did Arthur Koestler) as "the sudden, interlocking of two previously unrelated skills or matrices of thought," an almost limitless capacity for imagination, metaphorical extension, etc.

One need not follow Hauser (2009) in positing four distinct mechanisms to account for humaniqueness. One key event (the emergence of this ability to lexicalize) suffices. Going back to Hauser's four ingredients for human specificity listed above, we can now claim that by means of lexical envelopes, humans are able to "detach modes of thought from raw sensory and perceptual input," and lexicalize at will ("create and easily understand symbolic representations of computation and sensory input"). Via Merge, humans have "the ability to combine and recombine different types of information and knowledge in order to gain new understanding, and apply the same "rule" or solution to one problem to a different and new situation."

With lexical items freely available and combinable ("Merge"), the human mind became capable of true swiss-army-knife style cognition. Before that the tools at the animal's disposal were exquisitely tuned to their tasks, but too isolated. Their effects could only be combined sequentially; they could not be seamlessly and smoothly integrated with one another. With language, the human mind developed into a key ring, where all keys (concepts) can be combined and available at once, thanks to the hole (edge property) that they all share.

'Words' gave Man a truly general language of thought, a *lingua franca*, where before there were only modular mutually incomprehensible dialects/(proto-) languages of thoughts. It significantly altered Man's conceptual structures---how humans think the world. By merging lexicalized concepts, Man was able to hold in mind concepts of concepts, representations of representations, and associations of associations. *Homo* became *Homo combinans*.

References

Fodor, J. A. (1975). *The language of thought*. Cambridge, MA: Harvard University Press.

Hauser, M. D. (2009). The possibility of impossible cultures. *Nature*, 460, 190-196.

Hauser, M. D., Chomsky, N. & Fitch, W. T. (2002). The faculty of language: What is it? Who has it? And How did it evolve? *Science*, 298, 1569-1579.

THE EFFECTS OF MODIFIED VARIABLES ON AN ITERATED LEARNING MODEL OF LINGUISTIC EVOLUTION BY CULTURAL TRANSMISSION

JON WILLIAM CARR

Language Evolution and Computation Research Unit, University of Edinburgh
Dugald Stewart Building, 3 Charles Street, Edinburgh, EH8 9AD, UK
j.w.carr@sms.ed.ac.uk

It has been suggested that human language emerged as a function of three adaptive processes: evolution by natural selection, individual learning, and cultural evolution (Kirby & Hurford, 2002). In this paradigm, biological evolution is intrinsically difficult to explore due to the ephemeral nature of language; however, the interface between learning and cultural evolution has been tested in a variety of mathematical, computational, and experimental models. These models demonstrate that systematic linguistic structure can arise from the transmission of language across multiple language users. Kirby, Cornish, and Smith (2008) introduced an experimental method for studying the cumulative effect that cultural transmission has on language, and their iterated learning model represented the first experiment on human participants to suggest that the cultural transmission of language leads cumulatively to the appearance of linguistic design without any explicit designer.

A new version of this experiment was conducted with a number of modified variables allowing us to test the resilience of the experimental paradigm. The modifications introduced to this version of the experiment were:

1. the addition of an auditory modality in the learning phase by means of a synthesized voice

2. a different set of meanings, which include shape, colour, and number

3. a larger syllabary from which the initial randomly-generated languages were concatenated

This version of the experiment also adopted a different approach to the inter-generational filtering strategy, which exposes each participant to learning material of equal size (14 items), which arguably promotes a more controlled experiment. Despite these modifications, the learnability of the artificial languages increased over the course of the experiment in a way that is strikingly similar to the results observed by Kirby et al. (2008). However, the emergence of compositional linguistic structure was less forthcoming. This presents a problem: if the languages evolve to become easier to learn, yet a strong degree of compositionality does not emerge, then there must exist at least one other mechanism by which the languages optimize their successful transmission.

The results suggest that this mechanism might lie in a different type of linguistic adaptation. Specifically, the size of the signal-space (i.e. the syllable structures employed by a language) tended to shrink over the course of the experiment, which appears to make the languages easier to learn. Although this in itself is interesting (demonstrating that languages can find novel and perhaps unexpected ways to circumvent a bottleneck), a consequence of the shrinking signal-space is that the probability of a chance alignment between signal and meaning becomes increasingly more likely to occur as the experiment progresses. It is therefore hypothesized that, by allowing the languages to evolve further, a level of compositional structure comparable with Kirby et al. (2008) might eventually emerge under this modified paradigm.

In addition to supporting the general findings of Kirby et al. (2008), these results highlight two important points. Firstly, the experimental outcome is sensitive to the experimental environment, and small changes in the variables can have complex and unexpected effects on the results. Secondly, a language whose signal-space is not optimized to transmission through a given bottleneck must firstly undergo phonological optimization (towards a stable syllabary) before it becomes conducive to the evolution of grammatical structure by means of fractionation.

References

Kirby, S., Cornish, H., & Smith, K. (2008). Cumulative cultural evolution in the laboratory: An experimental approach to the origins of structure in human language. *Proceedings of the National Academy of Sciences of the United States of America*, *105*(31), 10681—10686.

Kirby, S., & Hurford, J. R. (2002). The emergence of linguistic structure: An overview of the iterated learning model. In A. Cangelosi & D. Parisi (Eds.), *Simulating the evolution of language* (pp. 121—147). London: Springer Verlag.

IS PANTOMIME A LIKELY STAGE IN LANGUAGE EVOLUTION? EVIDENCE FROM HUMAN AND PRIMATE GESTURE

ERICA A CARTMILL & SUSAN GOLDIN-MEADOW

Department of Psychology, University of Chicago, 5848 S. University Ave. Chicago, 60615, USA

Gestural origin of language theories (e.g. Corballis, 2002; Armstrong & Wilcox, 2007) have garnered increasing interest, fueled by studies of great ape gestural communication and primate mirror neurons. Gesture, particularly pantomime, has been suggested as a key stage of hominid communication before the codification of a shared symbolic system (Arbib, 2005). Pantomime is an attractive candidate because it can be understood without a conventional system and allows sharing of novel or absent events through iconic representation. Arbib (2005) proposes that increased imitation abilities in the human lineage (driven by hierarchical processing of action sequences) provided the foundation for iconic representation of action through gesture. This became the beginnings of pantomime. His proposal leads one to ask: what are the challenges in developing a pantomime-based system, and how early could this stage occur? To this end, we discuss acquisition and use of iconicity in human and ape gesture and point out difficulties in developing an iconic system.

Iconic gesture is a powerful communicative and cognitive tool because it can represent objects and events outside of real-world acts. However, iconic gesture is a complex task even for modern humans, and involves a level of symbolic understanding beyond imitation. Pantomime-like gestures involving manipulation of imaginary objects are complex, and young children struggle with them (Overton & Jackson, 1973). Children do not use iconic gestures until near age three, well *after* they have acquired conventional gestures that rely on shared meanings. Furthermore, young children do not map iconic gestures to referents more quickly than conventional gestures, indicating that iconicity in gesture does not aid early stages of language learning (Namy et al., 2004). The relationship between language learning and language evolution must be addressed, but evidence from developmental studies indicates that understanding meaning through iconicity is not a straightforward or easy task.

There is also scant evidence that apes are able to use iconicity. Iconic gesture use has occasionally been reported in apes (Tanner & Byrne, 1996; Russon & Andrews, 2010), but these reports are atypical. Apes can use iconic pictures to find food, but only when the pictures are accompanied by conventional cues (Herrmann et al, 2008). Differences in the mirror neuron system provide a possible partial explanation for primates' limitations in the use of iconicity. The monkey mirror system does not respond to simulated actions on imaginary objects—just the sort of gestures that are central to pantomime (Rizzolatti & Craighero, 2004). In contrast, the human brain shows mirror-like properties during iconic gesture (Grezes et al., 2003). The way gesture is processed by the human mirror system may be necessary for developing iconic gesture. We conclude pantomime likely facilitated language evolution, but argue that it did not necessarily precede conventional gestures and that iconicity could not confer an advantage until the gesturers were very much like modern humans.

References

Arbib, M.A. (2005). From monkey-like action recognition to human language: An evolutionary framework for neurolinguistics. *Behavioral and Brain Sciences, 28*, 105–167.

Armstrong, D.F., & Wilcox, S. E. (2007). *The gestural origin of language*. Oxford: Oxford University Press.

Corballis, M.C. (2002). *From hand to mouth, the origins of language*. Princeton, New Jersey, Princeton University Press.

Grezes, J., Armony, J.L., Rowe, J., Passingham, R.E. (2003). Activations related to "mirror" and "canonical" neurons in the human brain: an fMRI study. *Neuroimage 18*, 928–937.

Herrmann, E., Melis, A.P., Tomasello, M. (2006). Apes' use of iconic cues in the object-choice task. *Animal Cognition, 9*, 118-130.

Namy, L., Cambell, A.L., Tomasello, M. (2004). The changing role of iconicity in non-verbal symbol learning: a u-shaped trajectory in the acquisition of arbitrary gestures. *Journal of Cognition and Development, 5*, 37-57.

Overton, W.F. & Jackson, J.P. (1973) The representation of imagined objects in action sequences: a developmental study. *Child Development*, *44*, 309-314.

Rizzolatti, G. & Craighero, L. 2004 The mirror-neuron system. *Annual Review of Neuroscience*, 27, 169–192.

Russon, A., & Andrews, K. (2011). Orangutan pantomime: Elaborating the message. *Biology Letters*, *7,* 627-630.

Tanner, J. E., & Byrne, R. W. (1996). Representation of action through iconic gesture in a captive lowland gorilla. *Current Anthropology, 37*, 162–173.

IS *AND* A FOSSIL?: COORDINATION AND THE ORIGIN OF COMPOSITIONALITY

WAYNE COWART
DANA MCDANIEL, KATHRYN H. THOMPSON, TATIANA ROMANCHISHINA
Department of Linguistics, University of Southern Maine
Portland, ME, 04104-9300, USA

Providing an account of the origin of compositionality is one of the central challenges in studies of the evolution of language. We review a possible way to approach this challenge that focuses on coordination, the apparently universal capacity of language users to link sequences of clauses or sequences of similar constituents, as in *Jo caught the ball and Fido barked* or *Fido chased the stick and the ball.* We consider the possibility that coordination in modern language is a linguistic 'fossil'. Applying criteria emerging from various recent proposals (Bickerton 1990, 2010; Jackendoff 2002; Fitch 2010), we conclude that there is indeed evidence for this view of modern coordination. If our account is on the right track, modern language is a hybrid system whose components (Merge and coordination) are logically more distinct than their relatively smooth integration in performance would suggest.

We review evidence from various sources that shows that speakers treat coordinates as though they are different data structures from those hierarchically generated by Merge. In particular we focus on recent experimental findings comparing agreement phenomena in coordinate and subordinate structures in English and Russian. These phenomena suggest that speakers apply substantively different cognitive functions to the two kinds of structure.

We present an account that traces the developmental path of coordination from a prelinguistic cognitive function to the protolanguage and into modern language.[1] An attractive evolutionary approach to accounting for coordination in modern language is to seek an antecedent function that would plausibly have

[1] Though the morphological manifestations of coordination exhibit interesting diachronic and cross-linguistic patterns, we are concerned here only with the origin of the conceptual-intentional function they invoke.

been among the cognitive resources available to pre-linguistic human ancestors. We propose that there is a potential precedent for the relevant function embedded within the Approximate Number System, a quantitative function that has been demonstrated in a wide range of species (including human infants and adults) and that figures in accounts of mathematical ability in modern humans (Dehaene 1997; Xu et al. 2005; Carey 2009). We suggest that an aggregating (set-making) function was exapted into the human communication system.

Our account explores the ways in which an aggregating mechanism of this sort might have played various roles in the development of a protolanguage. A particularly promising aspect of the proposal is its account of the emergence of lexical features, which Merge would later exploit. We derive the emergence of features from the cognitive logic of set-making (aggregation), which requires that the linguistic processing system track and distinguish both the characteristics that qualify an item for membership in a set and those that set it apart from other members of that set.

A protolanguage incorporating coordination could then provide necessary prerequisites for Merge. When Merge appeared, humans would already have a lexicon enriched with features, one suitable for the application of the new function. However, we suggest that humans would have continued to use coordinate structures along with those derived via Merge, eventually becoming adept at integrating the two into the seemingly unified structures that exist in modern language, with hierarchically complex conjuncts within coordinate phrases, and with coordinate phrases embedded within hierarchical structures.

References

Bickerton, D. (1990). *Language & species*. Chicago, University of Chicago Press.

Bickerton, D. (2010). On two incompatible theories of language evolution. *The evolution of human language: biolinguistic perspectives*. R. K. Larson, V. Déprez and H. Yamakido. New York, Cambridge University Press.

Carey, S. (2009). *The origin of concepts*. New York, Oxford.

Dehaene, S. (1997). *The number sense : how the mind creates mathematics*. New York, Oxford University Press.

Fitch, W. T. (2010). *The evolution of language*, New York.

Jackendoff, R. (2002). *Foundations of language : brain, meaning, grammar, evolution*, Oxford University Press.

Xu, F., E. S. Spelke, et al. (2005). "Number sense in human infants." *Developmental Science* 8(1): 88-101.

THE FIRST WORD WAS NOT A NOUN

CORY CUTHBERTSON
Flat 5, 12-14 Queen Victoria Street
Reading, RG1 1TG, United Kingdom

The first words to arise in human language could not be attributed a part-of-speech until the advent of a syntactic system with minimally two categories. Yet, different parts-of-speech have often been proposed as emerging first during language evolution, most commonly nouns (Smith, 1767; Aitchison, 1996; Li, 2002; Luuk, 2009), but also verbs (Diamond, 1959).

While definitions vary on what constitutes a part-of-speech, it is generally agreed that all languages contain them, though which categories and how they behave varies (Schachter, 1985). Sometimes they are defined by their semantic meaning (ex. nouns denote objects and verbs denote actions), but these definitions are based on tendencies only, and are no way to predict syntactic distribution. For instance the word *seem* is a verb, but not an action, and the word *nightmare* is a noun, but not an object. In some languages, such as Nuuchahnulth (Nootka), almost any stem can function as a noun, verb or adjective (Lander & Testelets, 2006), so the semantics of a word is no certain way to attribute its part-of-speech, and so syntacticians often look to a word's function in a sentence for its category (Evans and Green, 2006). If there was once a one-word stage of language, its semantics too would say nothing about a hypothetical syntactic distribution, and it would effectively be categoryless.

Adam Smith (1767) suggested nouns were the first to emerge, as language began with proper names. Diamond (1959) concluded verbs were the original part-of-speech, because while vocabularies have been increasing, the amount of verbs has stayed the same, suggesting their primacy. Aitchison (1996) suggests there may have been an initial nouns-only stage, as children learn nouns first, and it is more common to change nouns into verbs than vice versa. Li (2002) suggests nouns were the first to arise, as the most basic symbolic concept refers to a concrete object. Luuk (2009) offers 11 reasons in support of nouns being first to arise, which he concludes provides "overwhelming evidence" that they are more fundamental, and therefore predate verbs. However, Luuk's points only justify that verbs were unlikely to have existed at a stage before nouns, and they don't necessitate a stage where nouns existed solely by themselves.

In these studies offering a "first" part-of-speech, the researcher is either using a semantic definition of that category, or is defending the unlikeliness of other parts-of-speech as existing first. However, if an isolated word is not functioning with other words, it is category-less. As Tallerman and Hurford have noted, "one cannot talk of any distinct category until there is another category to contrast it with." (Heine and Kuteva 2007, p. 59) In a purely lexical system where syntax did not exist, nouns, verbs and adjectives did not either. The first part-of-speech would only have arisen in conjunction with another, when linguistic elements were first used in reference to each other and the first grammatical distinction was made.

References

Aitchison, J. (1996). *The seeds of speech: Language origin and evolution.* Cambridge: Cambridge University Press.

Evans, V., & Green, M. (2006). *Cognitive linguistics: An introduction.* Edinburgh: Edinburgh University Press.

Heine, B., & Kuteva, T. (2007). *The genesis of grammar: A reconstruction.* Oxford: Oxford University Press.

Lander, Y., & Testelets, Y. (2006). Nouniness and specificity: Circassian and Wakashan. Paper presented at the conference *Universals and Particulars in Parts-of-Speech Systems,* Amsterdam.

Li, C. N. (2002). Missing links, issues and hypotheses in the evolutionary origin of language. In T. Givon and B. F. Malle (Eds.), *The Evolution of Language out of Prelangauge* (pp. 83-106). Amsterdam: John Benjamins.

Luuk, E. (2009). The noun/verb and predicate/argument structures. *Lingua*, 119, 1707-1727.

Schachter, P. (1985). Parts-of-speech systems. In T. Shopen (Ed.) *Language typology and syntactic description* (pp. 3-61). Cambridge: Cambridge University Press.

Smith, A. (1767). *The theory of moral sentiments: To which is added a dissertation on the origin of languages* (3rd ed.). London.

ICONICITY IN STRUCTURED FORM AND MEANING SPACES

BART DE BOER

ACLC, University of Amsterdam, Spuistraat 210,
1012 VT Amsterdam, the Netherlands

1. Introduction

Experiments on the emergence of phonological structure show that humans exploit structure in the meaning space to create structure in their sets of signals (Verhoef *et al.*, 2011). This can be regarded as a confounding factor, as *iconicity* is generally considered to play a minor role in language. However, sound symbolism and onomatopoeia are well-documented. Moreover, in sign languages iconicity plays a more prominent role. But what exactly is iconicity? Formal models of language evolution tend to focus either on structure in the form space or structure in the meaning space, but not on the interaction between the two spaces. Zuidema and Westermann (2003) are an exception. They show that in robust signaling systems, meanings that are close together must be represented by forms that are close together. This defines a form of iconicity. The question then arises why and how complex signaling systems (language) loose iconicity.

2. Iconic form-meaning mappings

In order for meanings that are close together to have corresponding signals that are close together, the topology of the form space must correspond to the topology of the meaning space. In Zuidema and Westermann's (2003) model both form and meaning spaces are 1-dimensional. In nature, this occurs for example in chickadee alarm calls, were predator size is coded in the number of calls, fig 1A (Templeton *et al.*, 2005). Such a system is *open*, because forms that have never been observed can be understood and meanings that have never been encountered can be expressed. At the same time it is *holistic*, as the message does not consist of separable components. This is not limited to 1-dimensional form and meaning spaces: bee dance expresses 2-dimensional meanings (direction and distance) with 2-dimensional forms (waggle angle and duration, fig.

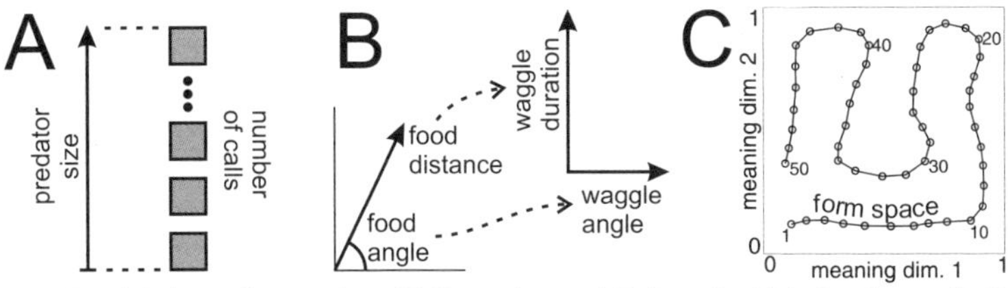

Figure 1: Panel A shows the mapping of 1-D meanings to 1-D forms in chickadee alarm calls. Panel B shows the mapping of 2-D meanings to 2-D forms in bee dance. Panel C shows a mapping of 2-D meanings to 1-D forms and the ensuing discretization of the meaning space: forms 1–10, for example may be used to indicate a low value along meaning dimension 2.

1B). Given that form spaces – especially acoustic ones – may be more limited than meaning spaces, it is useful to consider what happens when the form space has fewer dimensions than the meaning space. One solution is for the form space to fold to cover the meaning space as fully as possible. The output of a computer model (a Kohonen self organizing map) in fig. 1C shows that this results in *discretization* of the meaning space: most variation in the form space does not cause large changes in one of the meaning dimensions. However, in order to express a point in the meaning space, now a *pair* of forms is needed. Also, the discretization is *arbitrary*: there are many equivalent ways in which the 1-dimensional form space can cover the 2-dimensional meaning space.

3. Discussion

Because iconic form-meaning mappings are robust and open, they may have played a role in the early evolution of human language. The discretization of a meaning space of higher dimensionality than the available form space may provide a transition from a holistic to a combinatorial system. Because the discretization is arbitrary, conventions are then needed. This model provides a theoretical framework for understanding the transition from an iconic signaling system to an arbitrary, discretized and conventionalized one. Both the emergence of an iconic mapping and the transition to a discretized, conventional and possibly combinatorial system can be tested with experimental iterated learning.

References

Templeton, C. N., Greene, E., & Davis, K. (2005). Allometry of alarm calls: Black-capped chickadees encode information about predator size. *Science, 308*, 1934–1937.

Verhoef, T., de Boer, B., Del Giudice, A., Padden, C., & Kirby, S. (2011). Cultural evolution of combinatorial structure in ongoing artificial speech learning experiments. *CRL Technical Report UCSD, 23*(1), 3–11.

Zuidema, W., & Westermann, G. (2003). Evolution of an optimal lexicon under constraints from embodiment. *Artificial Life, 9*(4), 387–402.

NEITHER NATURE NOR NURTURE: COEVOLUTION, DEVOLUTION, AND UNIVERSALITY OF LANGUAGE

TERRENCE W. DEACON

The Department of Anthropology, University of California, Berkeley, Berkeley, California, USA

Why has the study of language origins seemed so nearly intractable? I think that part of the answer is that we persist in assuming it must have arisen only by the actions of natural selection (or mutational miracle) and/or cultural convention. This either/or dichotomy ignores a number of critical factors, even when it is assumed that both play a role. I argue that many of the most significant factors arise neither from nature nor nurture.

Two under-appreciated evolutionary processes (1 &2) and two largely ignored (3 & 4) sources of ubiquitous constraints need to be introduced to provide a complete understanding of the factors contributing to the human language capacity and the deep commonalities (near universals) shared by most languages.

1.Symbolic niche construction effects:

Language and brain co-evolved; i.e. language structures adapt (over thousands of years) to human neurological constraints and brains adapt (over hundreds of thousands of years) to the peculiar demands of symbolic communication. This means that human brains have become adapted to function well in a novel artificial symbolic niche rather than merely in a social-biological ecology.

2.Exaptation effects due to relaxed selection:

The recruitment of old brain structures to handle the new demands of language was made possible due to the relaxation of selection pressures, which allowed novel synergistic functional relationships to develop between brain structures that were previously functionally independent.

3.Semiotic constraints:

The development of symbolic communication brought with it a number of intrinsic semiotic constraints arising neither from nature nor from nurture that universally constrain (but don't determine) the functional classes of grammar and combinatorics of syntax. These account for the major functional categories of grammar, the combinatorial structure of predication, and the capacity for recursive structure.

4. Processing constraints:

These are mostly due to limitations on working memory. For the combinatorial power of symbolic communication to be utilized in real time a considerable fraction of the process of symbolic combinatorial search must be automated. This requires a high degree of regularization and simplification of the indexical and iconic operations that support symbolic reference. These operations, which must function deductively (i.e. without option) are embodied in the functional morphology and syntax of a language.

The list must also include three nature-nurture effects that are important influences leading to convergent linguistic evolution, though they are secondary in effect and more variable in their expression.

5. Innately evolved cognitive and mnemonic biases (e.g. highlighted in functional theories of grammar),

6. Discourse demands of the social functions of language (e.g. highlighted in systemic functional linguistics).

7. Cultural conventions of communication (e.g. specialized dialects and exceptional cases such as the Piraha language).

This talk will focus on the first four of these influences and especially 2 and 3, which have been almost entirely ignored in past and current theories of language origins. Ignoring these influences is responsible for much of the controversy and mystery that has surrounded the discussion of the distinctiveness of the human language adaptation and the remarkable parallelisms of language structure worldwide.

COMPARATIVE HISTOLOGICAL DATA BETWEEN THE VOCAL FOLDS OF HUMANS AND BONOBO

DIDIER DEMOLIN[1] AND SERGIO HASSID[2]

[1]*GIPSA-Lab, Université Stendhal Grenoble,* [2]*Department of O.R.L. and Head and Neck surgery, Hôpital Erasme, Université Libre de Bruxelles,*

Didier.Demolin@gipsa-lab.grenoble-inp.fr, Sergio.Hassid@erasme.ulb.ac.be
Université Stendhal, Domaine universitaire BP25, 38040 Grenoble Cedex 9, France,
Hôpital Erasme, Route de Lennik 808, 1070 Bruxelles, Belgique

Histological aspects of primate vocal folds are important for understanding differences vocal functions between species. It has been claimed that vocal folds are more tensed and that the thyro-arythenoïd muscle is stiffer for non-human primates. Hirano (1991) claimed that the arrangement of the tissues in the cover layer of the monkey is different in other mammals and adult mans and that the mucosa is stiffer than in humans or in dogs. One important fact from a comparative and evolutionary perspective is that Hirano's (1974, 1991) seminal description of vocal folds has not been extended yet to other non-human primates. Human vocal folds consist of a body layer (thyro-arytenoïd muscle) and a cover layer (epithelium and lamina propria). Inside the larynx, the fundamental role played by the crico-arythenoïd muscle has not been extended to non-human primates. No extensive investigation of the molecular and cellular structure of the non-human primate vocal folds has been done despite the importance of the subject (Schön Ybarra 1995). The arrangement of elastic and collagenous fibers immediately under the epithelium makes the mucosa stiffer in monkeys than in human or dog (Schön Ybarra 1995). The paper presents results of a study made on the vocal folds of an adult female Bonobo. Two types of staining (similar to Hirano's for humans) i.e. Hematoxyn-Eosin and Elastica Van Gieson have been made. Coronal slices were dissected at anterior, medial and posterior locations in the vocal folds. Results show that globally the structure of the vocal folds is identical between Bonobo and humans (Pseudo stratified ciliated epithelium of respiratory type). The ventricle is larger for Bonobo, likely due to their connection to the air sacks that do not exist for man. The false vocals folds are more prominent for Bonobo. Reinke's space and the elastic cone are bigger in Bonobo than in man. Malpighian metaplasy suggests that there was much contact between the vocal folds and between the true and false vocal folds of this adult Bonobo specimen. There are cilia on the upper part of the epithelium where there is little or no contact between the vocal folds and the false vocal folds (Figure 1). This is visible in the ventricular part in Figure 2. This last point is important since this could help to understand acoustic observations made during Bonobo vocalizations. This is particularly true for the contribution of the false vocal folds and the air sacs which contribute to their acoustic signature. This needs confirmation with data from other specimens but suggests however that a comparison of the histological structure of vocal folds between humans and Bonobo may shed light on differences in their vocalizations.

Key words: Histology, vocal folds, human, Bonobo

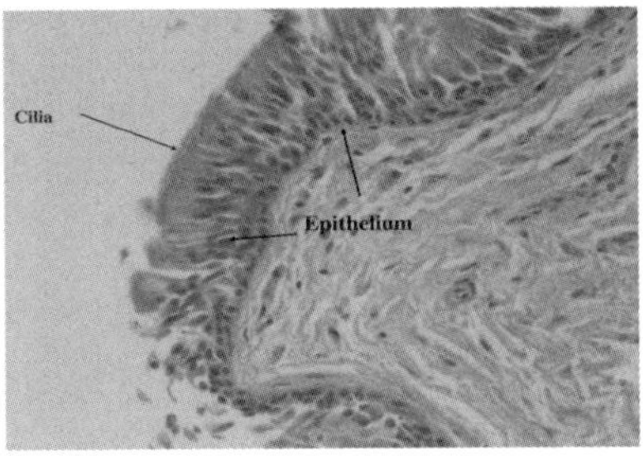

Figure 1

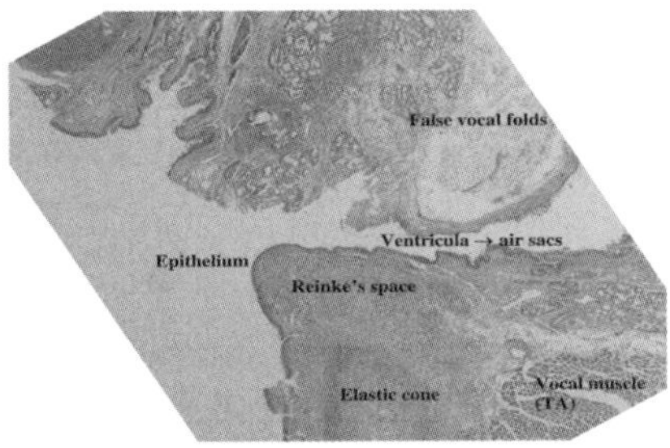

Figure 2

References

Hirano, M. (1974). Morphological structure of the vocal cord as vibrator and its variations, *Folia Phoniatrica* 26. 89-94.

Hirano, M. (1991). Phonosurgical anatomy of the larynx. In *Phonosurgery: Assessment and surgical Management of Voice Disorders.* C.N. Ford and D. Bess (eds.) Raven Press, New-York.

Schön Ybarra, M.A. (1995). A comparative approach to the non-human primate vocal tract: implications for sound production. In *Current topics in primate vocal communication.* E. Zimmerman, J.D. Newman & U. Jürgens (eds.). Plenum Press, New-York. 185-198.

ON SOME PARALLELS BETWEEN THE VOCAL APPARATUS AND MUSICAL INSTRUMENTS, AND THEIR CONSEQUENCES FOR THE EVOLUTION OF LANGUAGE AND MUSIC

JOSÉ ROBERTO DO CARMO JR.
Department of Linguistics, University of São Paulo, Av.Prof.Luciano Gualberto São Paulo, 05508-900, Brazil

In this paper we argue that (1) the vocal apparatus and musical instruments are both source-filter devices; (2) the way these devices work help us understand what phonological and melodic sound systems share and what they don't; (3) this comparative approach can shed light on the evolution of language and music. The Source-Filter Theory (Fant, 1960), asserts that the speech sounds result from two consecutive processes: a source produces an initial sound and a filter modifies it. Basically, when a human speaks the *vibration* of the vocal cords function as a glottal source of energy and the *displacement* of the organs of the mouth and throat function as the filter. The combined action of source and filter produces the two phonological macro-categories, consonants and vowels. With this mechanism, a human can produce thousands of syllables, which are the basic building blocks of speech. The English syllables inventory, for example, runs to something around 16,000 syllables (Barker, s.d.). Musical instruments can be seen as source-filter devices as well. The source-function can be performed by the strings of a guitar, the wooden bars of a xylophone, the reed of a clarinet, and so on, while the filter-function is performed by sound boxes and tubes in many different shapes and sizes, built from a whole array of different materials. However, musical instruments present a crucial difference in relation to the vocal apparatus: their filters are *permanently static.* One can pluck or bow the strings of a violin but one cannot change the shape of its body. This is true for any melodic instrument, even for those which apparently have a movable filter, like the jew's harp or the trombone, for example. As tones are the outcome of the source vibration, we have nothing but tones as the output of a musical instrument. In this order of ideas, the mobility of the filter seems to be the key factor distinguishing musical and linguistic sounds,
which are therefore organized in systems conversely oriented. In language – including the tone languages – the prosodic features (pitch, duration and

intensity) play a secondary, marginal role; in music, they play a primary role and in fact constitute the core of the system.

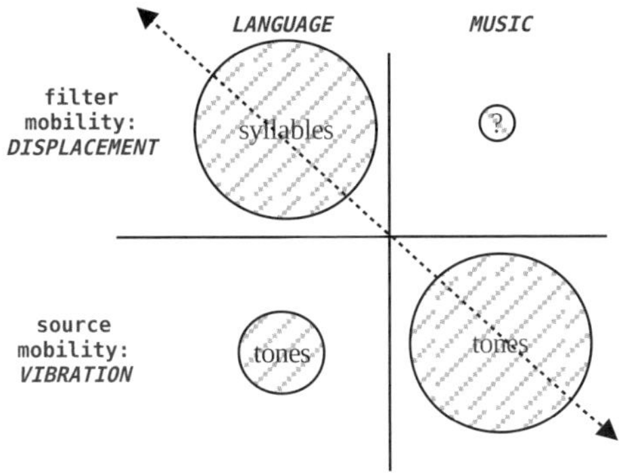

Fig. 1 The dashed line with arrows shows the divergence in the evolution of music and language.

We know that several anatomical changes in the vocal tract were decisive for the emergence of human language (de Boer, 2010). Crucially, the lowered larynx and the angle between mouth and pharynx created the room necessary for the improvement of tongue mobility, that is, the *filter mobility*. On the other hand, from the source-filter model perspective, what distinguishes a modern flute from its probably oldest ancestor (the disputed Divje Babe flute), or a modern string instrument from the ancient lyra is the range of tones they produce (Fig.1). As instruments evolve, their range increase. If we consider the three basic features of musical tones (pitch, duration and intensity), the current violin has a range of about 2,400 sounds and a piano has 4,488 sounds, within the same violin-like and piano-like timbres. This approach opens up new ways of thinking the parallels and oppositions between music and language (Brown, 2001). Despite being a crucial question to our understanding of the evolution of music and language, as far as we know no serious attempt has been made to explore this research pathway.

References

Barker, Chris (s.d.) *How many syllables in English*. <http://semarch.linguistics.fas.nyu.edu/barker/Syllables/index.txt>

Brown, S. (2001) “The 'Musilanguage' Model of Music Evolution”. In: *The Origins of Music* (pp.271-301). MIT Press.

de Boer, B.G. (2010) “Modelling vocal anatomy’s significant effect on speech”. *Journal of Evolutionary Psychology* 8(4) 351–366

Fant, G. (1960) *Acoustic Theory of Speech Production*. Mouton: The Hague.

TOPOGRAPHIC LEARNING AND THE ARBITRARY, CATEGORIAL LEXICON

T. MARK ELLISON
IO Institute of Linguistics & University of Western Australia
Perth, Australia
mark@iolinguistics.com

1. Introduction

Topographic mappings are relations that preserve distance or similarity between inputs and outputs. The topographicity of a relation R can be expressed by

$$T(R) = \sum_{(i_1,o_1),(i_2,o_2)\in R} s_I(i_1,i_2)s_O(o_1,o_2) \qquad (1)$$

where s_I and s_O are similarity measures on the input and output spaces respectively. A topographic learner is an agent that extrapolates the most topographic mapping compatible with the data they have seen and problem-specific conditions: formally, it maximises $T(R)$ over some free variables, inputs and/or outputs in one or more pairs in R. In unsupervised learning, the output values are free variables; in supervised learning some of them are not.

Topographic mappings and learners are neurologically plausible, as topographic mappings are found throughout vertebrate brains (Silver & Kastner, 2009). Neural topographic mappings in early stages of information processing develop unsupervised, but mappings linking cortical areas with separate (eg. sensory) inputs will engage in supervised learning.

The lexicon, relating meanings and forms, is a crucial mapping in the structure of any language, and it's processing has been linked with ventral neural pathways connecting frontal and dorsal language areas (Agosta et al., 2010). In the continuous spaces of conceptual experiences and possible enunciations, language acquirers construct finite contiguous semantic categories that the lexicon relates to arbitrary but equally categorial sets of possible expressions. It seems an unpromising target for modelling by topographic learners, as cross-linguistic studies show little large-scale topographic systematicity between forms and meanings (Shillcock, Kirby, McDonald, & Brew, 2001). However, supervised topographic learners construct arbitrary, categorial mappings when faced with uncorrelated input-output data (Ellison, 2011), and these mappings show little gross topographic structure.

In this paper, I show that a community of topographic learners, initialised with random input-output pairs, but doping the initialisation corpus for replacements with pairs generated from existing members, rapidly converges on a single mapping. Lexically, this means that uniform semantic categories and forms develop. Furthermore, although some of the data presented to the learners is conventional rather than random, the converged mapping is arbitrary, categorial and if at all topographic, only weakly and locally. So convergence preserves the important features of lexica.

2. Simulation

A community of simulated topographic learners, using topographic extrapolation (Ellison, 2011), were initialised each with random input-output pairings from continuous spaces. At each step, meaning-form pairs were generated by the community, a member was deleted, and a new member was created with 20% of its data community-generated, the remainder random. (The high proportion of random data reflects our exposure to a lot of language unrelated to our immediate environment.) Multiple runs of the simulation showed consistent and rapid convergence on a single mapping – with 500 data items, and 10 agents in the community, a 90% drop in mean square mapping differences occurred within 40 replacements. The resulting mappings were consistently both categorial and arbitrary, showing little global topographic structure.

3. Conclusion

Simulated topographic learners offer a neurofunctionally plausible approach to modelling cognitive mappings. Given random input from continuous spaces, they produce mappings that are categorial and arbitrary, key features the lexicon. Simulations with iterated learning produce rapid convergence of the lexicon, even with noisy stimuli, while maintaining categoriality and arbitrariness.

References

Agosta, F., Henry, R. G., Migliaccio, R., Neuhaus, J., Miller, B. L., Dronkers, N. F., Brambati, S. M., Filippi, M., Ogar, J. M., Wilson, S. M., & Gorno-Tempini, M. L. (2010). Language networks in semantic dementia. *Brain*, *133*(1), 286-299.

Ellison, T. M. (2011). Categorisation as topographic mapping between uncorrelated spaces. In D. Dowe (Ed.), *Solomonoff 85th memorial conference proceedings.* Springer Verlag.

Shillcock, R., Kirby, S., McDonald, S., & Brew, C. (2001). *Filled pauses and their status in the mental lexicon.*

Silver, M. A., & Kastner, S. (2009). Topographic maps in human frontal and parietal cortex. *Trends in Cognitive Sciences*, *13*(11), 488–495.

SOCIAL INTERACTION IS CRITICAL TO THE EVOLUTION OF HUMAN COMMUNICATION SYSTEMS (AND WHY)

NICOLAS FAY, BRADLEY WALKER, ALAN BAILEY

School of Psychology, University of Western Australia, 35 Stirling Highway Perth, WA 6009, Australia

We have argued that social interaction is critical to the evolution of human communication systems such as language (Fay, Garrod, Roberts, & Swoboda, 2010; Garrod, Fay, Lee, Oberlander, & MacLeod, 2007). The research reported here shows: (1) interaction, and not simple observation, is necessary to evolve effective (i.e., easy to interpret) and efficient (i.e., easy to produce) human communication systems; (2) two aspects of interaction (imitation and feedback) independently contribute to the evolution of these novel human communication systems.

To study how human communication systems arise and evolve we have developed a lab task that requires participants to create a communication system de novo. Participants communicate a set of recurring items (e.g., 'Arnold Schwarzenegger', 'Drama', 'Loud') to a partner by drawing on a shared electronic whiteboard. Like the game Pictionary© participants are prohibited from using conventional language (i.e., letters), forcing them to create a new communication system from scratch. Typically, participants play the game in pairs, alternating between drawing roles (communicating items from a pre-defined list of 16 items) and matching roles (identifying what is being drawn from the same list of items) from game to game. The game is played 6 times with the same item set used on each game (presented in a different random order). Thus, each player is the drawer on 3 games and the matcher on 3 games. Both participants can draw at any time (i.e., the matcher can annotate the drawings produced by their partner). Item selection (by the matcher) brings the current trial to an end and instigates the next trial. Feedback on communication success is not given.

Three things happen when participants play the game in interacting pairs: (1) their ability to identify the referent of the drawings improves from game 1 to 6,

(2) their drawings become simpler and more symbolic across games, and (3) their drawings become increasingly aligned with (or similar to) those produced by their partner. In other words, the communication systems become more effective, more efficient and more shared.

Expt. 1 compares two explanations of the above process, observational learning and interaction. All drawing activity by interacting pairs was recorded and an observer was yoked to each pair. The yoked observer believed s/he was actively taking part in the interaction, but s/he was not. On half the games they received drawings produced by a member of the interacting pair (and tried to pick out its referent), and on the other half they drew each item with the intention of communicating to their 'partner' (who never received their drawings). Compared to those actively involved in the interaction, identification accuracy, drawing refinement and drawing alignment was lower among yoked participants.

Expt. 2 examined what is important about social interaction. Two aspects of interaction were identified: imitation (i.e., copying your partner's drawings) and feedback (i.e., drawing annotation and item selection). Four conditions were created: no imitation, no feedback, no imitation & no feedback and unrestricted (i.e., imitation & feedback were permitted). When imitation and feedback were permitted identification accuracy improved: drawings became increasingly refined and aligned across games. Identification accuracy was unaffected by the removal of feedback, but prohibiting imitation reduced identification accuracy. Removing imitation had little effect on drawing refinement, but removing the opportunity for feedback meant that drawings were not refined across games (i.e., they remained structurally complex).

In conclusion, social interaction is crucial to the origin and evolution of effective, efficient and aligned human communication systems. Two aspects of interaction independently contribute to this process: imitation promotes effective communication systems and feedback promotes efficient communication systems. Thus, we propose that language evolved, and continues to evolve as a result of social coordination.

References

Fay, N., Garrod, S., Roberts, L., & Swoboda, N. (2010). The interactive evolution of human communication systems. *Cognitive Science, 34*(3), 351-386.

Garrod, S., Fay, N., Lee, J., Oberlander, J., & MacLeod, T. (2007). Foundations of Representation: Where Might Graphical Symbol Systems Come From? *Cognitive Science, 31*(6), 961-987.

SEARCHING FOR SUBSTANCE IN THE BALDWIN EFFECT: WHEN LEARNING CAUSALLY AFFECTS GENETIC ADAPTATION

VANESSA FERDINAND, SIMON KIRBY, KENNY SMITH
Language Evolution and Computation Research Unit
School of Philosophy, Psychology & Language Sciences
The University of Edinburgh

"The Baldwin Effect does not reliably refer either to a theory-neutral empirical phenomenon, or to a single hypothesis, or to an identifiable mechanism..." (Depew 2003, p.5).

The Baldwin Effect is a broadly defined concept in which some form of a phenotypic or learning search affects the rate or outcome of genetic evolution. This is a potentially important concept in language evolution, where cultural learning is a powerful force that could cut certain paths for genetic evolution to follow. However, long-standing underspecification as to the exact nature of this effect has produced disparate research and a general ambivalence toward the concept in our field.

Of the several incarnations of the Baldwin Effect in the language evolution literature, it is most informative to look at those that utilize computational models, because modeling forces one to be explicit about the mechanism. Here, we will explain the mechanisms behind two of the most influential computational models of the Baldwin Effect: Hinton & Nowlan (1987) and Chater, Reali & Christiansen (2009), and detail the necessary and sufficient conditions for obtaining the Baldwin Effect in both cases. In both of these models, each agent in a population possesses a genotype which determines their success at learning a target phenotype or language, and then they reproduce in accordance to their success. Over time, the alleles in the gene pool come to encode the features in the target and this is identified as an occurrence of the Baldwin Effect.
In a reimplementation of the Chater, Reali & Christiansen model, we demonstrate that this version of the Baldwin Effect still occurs when either

phenotypic plasticity, the learning search, or both are removed from the model, and we discuss the appropriateness of applying the concept of the Baldwin Effect to these cases. Furthermore, the Baldwin Effect in this model occurs fastest when there is neither a phenotypic nor learning search, and as phenotypic plasticity is increased, the Baldwin Effect degrades and inevitably disappears. This calls into question whether the Baldwin Effect is something that can occur in biological evolution, where the phenotype is a buffer that prevents selection from operating directly on genotypes.

We also expand upon Chater, Reali & Christiansen's coevolutionary model (Experiment 3), where the Baldwin Effect occurs while language is changing (due to random linguistic mutation), but only above a high threshold of direct influence of genes on the language. In our version, agents may transmit imperfectly learned languages to the next generation, where all learning errors are governed by an agent's genetic biases. This eliminates the genetic influence parameter by building it into the learning algorithm (so that it dynamically changes as the genes and language coevolve) and yields a slightly more naturalistic model of language change via cultural transmission. In this model, the Baldwin Effect also occurs while languages change, but for different levels of genetic influence than obtained in the original model. This case does not illustrate a conventional view of the Baldwin Effect where the learning search finds the target and then the genes follow suit and encode it, but rather an indirect, dynamical pathway in which the learning search causally affects the outcome of a genetic search, in a sense similar to niche construction.

References

Chater, N., Reali, F. & Christiansen, M. H. (2009). Restrictions on biological adaptation in language evolution. *Proceedings of the National Academy of Sciences*, *106*, 1015-1020.

Depew, D. J. (2003). Baldwin and his many effects. In B. H. Weber and D. J. Depew (Eds.), *Evolution and Learning* (pp. 3-31). Cambridge, MA: MIT Press.

Hinton, G. E. & Nowlan, S. J. (1987). How learning can guide evolution. *Complex Systems*, *1*, 495-502.

MOLECULAR WINDOWS INTO SPEECH AND LANGUAGE

SIMON E. FISHER
Max Planck Institute for Psycholinguistics, Wundtlaan 1, 6525 XD Nijmegen, The Netherlands

Genes that are implicated in neurodevelopmental disorders can provide novel insights into the neural bases and evolutionary origins of human spoken language. My colleagues and I previously discovered that people with mutations disrupting FOXP2 have problems mastering sequences of co-ordinated mouth movements needed for fluent speech, accompanied by expressive and receptive language impairments affecting spoken and written modalities. The FOXP2 gene encodes a type of regulatory protein which acts to switch on and off other genes. It is evolutionarily ancient, present in similar form in diverse vertebrate species, where it helps regulate the development and function of corresponding subpopulations of neurons. Analyses of molecular evolution in primates indicate that the FOXP2 protein sequence underwent accelerated change on the human lineage after splitting from the chimpanzee, indicating that its role(s) may have been modified in our ancestors. Nevertheless, it is emphasised that FOXP2 should not be viewed as the mythical "gene for speech" or "gene for language", but instead as one piece of a complex puzzle involving multiple factors. My talk will describe how FOXP2 can be used as a unique window into key neurogenetic pathways. To this end, researchers are exploiting a wide range of systems, from neuronal models, mutant mice and songbirds, to humans themselves. For example, using functional genomic screening of human neurons grown in the laboratory, my laboratory identified the CNTNAP2 gene (a member of the neurexin superfamily) as a downstream target directly regulated by FOXP2. Intriguingly, CNTNAP2 is itself associated with common language impairments, has been implicated in language delays of autistic children and may also affect linguistic abilities in the normal range of variation. High-throughput screening has enabled us to isolate many additional FOXP2 targets, including genetic networks involved in outgrowth of neurites from neurons, as well as in plasticity of synapses (connections between neurons). Moving to animal models of FOXP2 dysfunction, we have shown that point mutations implicated in human speech deficits yield impaired learning of motor skills in mutant mice. Electrophysiological recording suggests that this may be mediated by altered plasticity of Foxp2-expressing networks, particularly in corticostriatal circuits. Overall, this work demonstrates how we can begin to bridge gaps between molecules, neurons and the brain, helping us to build more sophisticated models of the relationships between genes, speech and language. Finally, the FOXP2 story shows how an appreciation of the language of genetics (what genes actually are and what they can and cannot do) is needed to constrain discussions regarding the genetics of language.

References

French CA, Jin X, Campbell TG, Gerfen E, Groszer M, Fisher SE, Costa RM. (2011). An aetiological Foxp2 mutation causes aberrant striatal activity and alters plasticity during skill learning. *Molcular Psychiatry*. DOI: 10.1038/mp.2011.105. [Epub ahead of print]

Vernes SC, Oliver PL, Spiteri E, Lockstone HE, Puliyadi R, Taylor JM, Ho J, Mombereau C, Brewer A, Lowy E, Nicod J, Groszer M, Baban D, Sahgal N, Cazier JB, Ragoussis J, Davies KE, Geschwind DH, Fisher SE.(2011). Foxp2 regulates gene networks implicated in neurite outgrowth in the developing brain. *PLoS Genetics*. 7(7), e1002145. Epub 2011 Jul 7.

Whitehouse AJ, Bishop DV, Ang QW, Pennell CE, Fisher SE. (2011). CNTNAP2 variants affect earlylanguage development in the general population. *Genes, Brain and Behavior*. 10(4), 451-456.

Fisher SE, Scharff C. (2009). FOXP2 as a molecular window into speech and language. *Trends in Genetics*. 25(4):166-177.

Vernes SC, Newbury DF, Abrahams BS, Winchester L, Nicod J, Groszer M, Alarcón M, Oliver PL, Davies KE, Geschwind DH, Monaco AP, Fisher SE. (2008). A functional genetic link between distinct developmental language disorders. *The New England Journal of Medicine*. 359(22), 2337-2345.

Groszer M, Keays DA, Deacon RM, de Bono JP, Prasad-Mulcare S, Gaub S, Baum MG, French CA, Nicod J, Coventry JA, Enard W, Fray M, Brown SD, Nolan PM, Pääbo S, Channon KM, Costa RM, Eilers J, Ehret G, Rawlins JN, Fisher SE. (2008). Impaired synaptic plasticity and motor learning in mice with a point mutation implicated in human speech deficits. *Current Biology*, 18(5), 354-362.

ME TO WE:
COOPERATION, CONFLICT, AND THE EVOLUTION OF LANGUAGE

JACOB G. FOSTER

Department of Sociology, University of Chicago, 1126 East 59th Street
Chicago, IL 60637, USA
jgfoster@uchicago.edu

Human language provides an honest, low-cost, and inexhaustible medium for communication. Explaining how such a system could evolve amongst individuals with conflicting interests remains a challenge. Scott-Phillips (2008), drawing on animal signaling theory, argues that reputation and punishment are the most plausible mechanisms for stabilizing honest, cooperative communication against defectors. But as Boyd and Richerson (2009) point out, these mechanisms can stabilize behaviors other than honesty. Therefore, while reputation and punishment can keep language honest once it arises, its origins must rely on other mechanisms.

The rise of language roughly coincided with the rise of cumulative culture and large-scale cooperation with unrelated conspecifics (Boyd & Richerson, 2009). While most work on the evolution of cooperation focuses on competition within groups as a barrier to cooperation, a flurry of recent work emphasizes competition *between* groups as a *catalyst* of cooperation. I propose that intergroup competition is also essential to the evolution of language. I first discuss the evidence that intergroup competition favors the evolution of intragroup cooperation. I then argue for similar positive feedbacks between conflict, cooperation, and language (a form of cooperation). Finally, I show that the sociology of violence supports strong selection for sophisticated capacities like abstract language.

Using a nested tug-of-war model of intergroup competition, Reeve and Hölldobler (2007) show that non-trivial levels of costly cooperation can arise by individual selection, even under limited relatedness. They also show that patchy resources promote cooperation. Cooperation, in turn, can make resources more patchy (through niche construction) and intergroup competition more intense, further increasing cooperation. Bowles (2009), considering archaeological and ethnographic data, argues that levels of intergroup violence in ancestral human populations (roughly 14% of all deaths) were high enough to select for costly altruistic behavior when it leads to success in intergroup conflict. Finally, Boyd and Richerson (2009) connect culture with cooperation, arguing that Middle Pleistocene environmental fluctuations selected for cumulative culture, which in turn created stable cultural differences on which cultural group selection for cooperation could act—most simply through intergroup competition.

Thus, ancestral intergroup competition provided strong selective pressure for intragroup cooperation, removing a key barrier to honest communication and the evolution of proto-language. As it evolved, language enhanced other emerging cooperative behaviors, e.g. coordinated foraging and combat, and accelerated cultural differentiation. Language also decreased the cost of altruistic punishment through the reporting of unseen events, further stabilizing both honest signaling and other forms of cooperation (Boyd, Gintis, Bowles, & Richerson, 2003).

Did language have a *direct* impact on intergroup competition? Ethnographic research suggests that ancestral intergroup violence consisted of long periods of attrition followed by the sudden defeat of one side (Boyd & Richerson, 2009). Recent work in the sociology of violence (Collins, 2009) reveals the same pattern, in which the sustained mobilization of material and emotional resources is key. The need to mobilize emotional resources may have played an essential role in later language evolution, selecting for the ability to use abstract and decontextualized language. Emotional resources are mobilized through appeals to group identity and demonizing narratives of difference and atrocity. Appeals to group identity require language: the "group" is an abstract concept, as is the network of social relations binding it. Atrocity narratives require abstract language (appealing to moral instincts) and decontextualized language (discussing distant events). Reports of enemy numbers or movements require decontextualized, abstract language, too. The ability to use such sophisticated language, even if costly, would have spread if it sufficiently improved group success in conflict. Indeed, language may have affected individual fitness more through improving group performance in intergroup violence than improving individual performance in the quotidian activities (like foraging or tool manufacture) on which theorists typically focus.

References

Bowles, S. (2009). Did warfare among ancestral hunter-gatherers affect the evolution of human social behavior? *Science*, *324*, 1293–1298.

Boyd, R., Gintis, H., Bowles, S., & Richerson, P. (2003). The evolution of altruistic punishment. *Proc. Natl. Acad. Sci. USA*, *100*, 3531–3535.

Boyd, R., & Richerson, P. (2009). Culture and the evolution of human cooperation. *Phil. Trans. Roy. Soc. B*, *364*, 3281–3288.

Collins, R. (2009). Micro and macro causes of violence. *Intl. J. of Conflict and Violence*, *3*, 9–22.

Reeve, H., & Hölldobler, B. (2007). The emergence of a superorganism through intergroup competition. *Proc. Natl. Acad. Sci. USA*, *104*, 9736–9740.

Scott-Phillips, T. (2008). On the correct application of animal signaling theory to human communication. In A. Smith, K. Smith, & R. F. i Cancho (Eds.), *The evolution of language* (pp. 275–282). London: World Scientific.

A SEARCH FOR METACOGNITION IN AVIANS

KAZUO FUJITA

Graduate School of Letters, Kyoto University, Yoshida-honmachi, Sakyo
Kyoto, 606-8501, Japan

1. Introduction

Previous studies suggest that some mammal species such as primates, cetaceans, and rodents may be metacognitive. However, positive results for metacognition are scarce in birds. Because of their completely different brain structure, avians provide a useful model for how this higher cognitive function is materialized. Here I report three experiments in search for metacognitive judgments in birds.

2. Experiment 1: Retrospective metacognition

This experiment tested whether birds were able to retrospectively monitor their confidence of a preceding discrimination (Nakamura, et al., 2011).

Pigeons and bantams chose between a "risk" icon and a "safe" icon immediately after they performed a visual search to peck at a target color among distracter colors on the touch-sensitive monitor. The "risk" icon resulted in a food reinforcement for correct visual search and a timeout for incorrect search. The "safe" icon nondifferentially resulted in either food or a conditional reward.

The birds chose the "safe" icon more often after incorrect visual search than after correct visual search. This differential use of "safe" and "risk" icons generalized to new visual searches with different colors or patterns, and in one pigeon, to a bar-length classification task. The results suggested that these birds may retrospectively monitor their confidence of a preceding perceptual decision.

3. Experiment 2: Concurrent metacognition

This experiment asked whether pigeons recognize their knowledge of ongoing serial response tasks (Iwasaki, et al., under revision).

Pigeons were asked whether they would request a hint for the ongoing three-item serial response task. Pecking at the hint icon resulted in flickering square around the next item to peck at.

Some of the pigeons tended to request a hint more often at earlier stages of learning each serial response task than at later stages. The results suggest that these birds may recognize their own knowledge of the sequence.

4. Experiment 3: Prospective metacognition

This experiment asked whether pigeons would prospectively judge their knowledge of the coming serial response task (Iwasaki & Fujita, in preparation).

Pigeons chose between the serial response task with a hint option or that without the hint option before they went into the serial task. The serial task to come was either well-trained or novel, which was signed by corresponding icons before starting the task choice.

Some pigeons tended to choose the hint-available trial for novel serial tasks more often than for well-trained tasks.

5. Discussion

We have found at least partially positive evidence in three different situations. Metacognitive judgments may not be beyond avians' capacity. More species of birds ought to be tested in the future.

Acknowledgements

This work was supported by the Grant-in-Aide for Scientific Research (S), No. 20220004, from Ministry of Education, Culture, Sport, Science and Technology (MEXT), Japan. The experiments were conducted in collaboration with N. Nakamura (Chiba University), S. Iwasaki, S. Watanabe, and T. Betsuyaku (Kyoto University).

References

Iwasaki, S., Watanabe, S., & Fujita, K. Do pigeons (*Columba livia*) seek information when they have insufficient knowledge? (under revision)

Nakamura, N., Watanabe, S., Betsuyaku, T., & Fujita, K. (2011). Do birds (pigeons and bantams) know how confident they are of their perceptual decisions? *Animal Cognition*, 14(1), 83–93.

SIMULATING THE COEVOLUTION OF LANGUAGE AND JOINT ATTENTION

TAO GONG

Department of Linguistics, University of Hong Kong, Pokfulam Road, Hong Kong

LAN SHUAI

*Department of Chinese, Translation and Linguistics, City University of Hong Kong
Tat Chee Avenue, Kowloon, Hong Kong*

Joint attention, as a set of socio-cognitive abilities to establish common ground in general communicative activities (Tomasello et al., 2005), is essential for social behaviors such as cooperation and language, yet the reason why humans, compared with nonhuman primates, possess an exclusively high level of joint attention remains unknown. Comparative evidence between humans and contemporary animals implies that a high level of joint attention is a human-unique prerequisite for communication and language (Tomasello, 2008), but such conclusions overlook the limitations of the comparative approach and fail to address questions such as whether the initial level of joint attention in humans must be high, and if not, what factors induce the level difference.

We propose *an evolutionary explanation* for the level difference of joint attention. We suggest that via exaptation, joint attention was adopted to comprehend linguistic utterances encoding simple, frequent events taking place in the immediate environment of conversations. Once it starts to assist linguistic comprehension, joint attention triggered the acquisition of preliminary linguistic knowledge. With its level being correlated with linguistic comprehension, according to *the socio-biological explanation* (Hurford, 1989), communicative success could help adjust the level of joint attention among language users. This scenario indicates that the initial level of joint attention in humans was not very high, and that the level difference could result from a *coevolution* (Thompson, 1994) with language. It also shows that during language origin comprehension underwent a transition from relying on nonlinguistic information to relying on linguistic information, which led to *displacement* (Hockett, 1960) in language.

Finally, it highlights the reverse role of language in general cognitive abilities and the importance of biological evolution and culture for language evolution.

We illustrate this scenario based on *the lexicon-syntax coevolution model* (Gong, 2011), where joint attention boils down to the availability of topics from non-linguistic information (*cues*), and the probability of acquiring correct topics (*reliability of cue*, *RC*) reflects the level of joint attention and is subject to change. The model incorporates *genetic transmission* of the level of joint attention and *cultural transmission* of language among individuals of the same or different generations. *Communicative success* (*CS*) affects the level of joint attention via *natural* and/or *cultural selection*. With natural selection, adults with higher CS have higher chances as parents to reproduce; otherwise, parents are chosen randomly. With cultural selection, adults with higher CS have higher chances as teachers to talk to offspring; otherwise, teachers are chosen randomly. In all the 4 sets involving different combinations of these selections, offspring copy parents' RC with occasional *mutation* (increase or decrease RC with a fixed amount). Simulation results show that: 1) with no selections, joint attention has to overcome a threshold to trigger a language with good CS, which indicates a correlation between joint attention and linguistic understandability; and 2) via mainly natural selection, CS can boost an initially-low level of joint attention, and get an initially-high level of joint attention *ratcheted* (Tomasello, 1999) at a relatively high level. This study offers a new perspective on the level difference of joint attention as well as other language-related abilities between humans and nonhuman species, and highlights the importance and inter-relation of biological evolution, individual learning, and cultural transmission.

References

Hockett, C. F. (1960). The origin of speech. *Scientific American*, 203, 88-96.

Hurford, J. R. (1989). Biological evolution of the Saussurean sign as a component of the Language Acquisition Device. *Lingua*, 77, 187-222.

Thompson, J. N. (1994). *The coevolutionary process*. Chicago, IL: University of Chicago Press.

Tomasello, M. (1999). *The cultural origins of human cognition*. Cambridge, MA: Harvard University Press.

Tomasello, M. (2008). *Origins of human communication*. Harvard: MIT Press.

Tomasello, M., Carpenter, M., Call, J., Behne, J., & Moll, H. (2005). Understanding and sharing intentions: The origins of cultural cognition. *Behavioral and Brain Sciences*, 28, 675-691.

Gong, T. (2011). Simulating the coevolution of compositionality and word order regularity. *Interaction Studies*, 12(1), 63-106.

NEUTRAL MODELS FOR LANGUAGE EVOLUTION

THOMAS L. GRIFFITHS
Department of Psychology, University of California, Berkeley,
3210 Tolman Hall MC 1650, Berkeley, CA 94720-1650, USA

Identifying the evolutionary forces that we need to appeal to in order to explain aspects of human languages requires having a clear understanding of the effects of those forces. Evolutionary biologists use *neutral models* to characterize how systems evolve in the absence of selection (e.g., Kimura, 1983). Neutral models are valuable as a means of obtaining insight into the effects of evolutionary forces other than selection – mutation and genetic drift – and as a null hypothesis that can be used when testing for the presence of selection.

In this talk, I will present several candidates for neutral models of language evolution. These models are defined by studying the effects of cultural transmission of information by Bayesian agents, using a paradigm based on the iterated learning model (Kirby, 2001; Griffiths & Kalish, 2007). Focusing on cultural transmission removes the most common form of selection appealed to in models of cultural evolution, which is the selection of who to learn from (e.g. Boyd & Richerson, 1985). Within this framework it is also possible to define models that are selectively neutral at the level of individual words or constructions, recreating and extending the classic Wright-Fisher model of genetic drift (Reali & Griffiths, 2010). I will summarize basic mathematical results concerning the predictions of these models and present evidence from laboratory experiments simulating cultural transmission with human participants that bears out these predictions.

I will use these neutral models to illustrate three points. First, we can explain a surprising range of phenomena without needing to appeal to forces analogous to selection, including cultural universals in color term systems (Xu, Dowman, & Griffiths, 2010), S-shaped curves in language change, power-law frequency distributions, and lexical replacement rates (Reali & Griffiths, 2010). Second, in cultural evolution, mutation is a far more interesting and powerful force than in biological evolution. Accounts of cultural evolution often borrow heavily from theories and models that have been developed for biological evolution, which emphasize the role of selection. In cultural evolution, the mechanisms of transmission are human learning and memory, which can play a significant role in evolutionary change. Finally, developing good neutral models has the potential to let us answer deep questions about ancient and modern languages, such as how much time needs to pass for a set of languages to lose the influence of a common ancestor (Rafferty, Griffiths, & Klein, 2009).

Acknowledgements

The work I will present was supported by grants SES-0631518, BCS-0704034 and IIS-1018733 from the United States National Science Foundation.

References

Boyd, R., & Richerson, P. J. (1985). *Culture and the evolutionary process.* Chicago, IL: University of Chicago Press.

Kimura, M. (1983). *The neutral theory of molecular evolution.* Cambridge: Cambridge University Press.

Griffiths, T. L., & Kalish, M. L. (2007). Language evolution by iterated learning with Bayesian agents. *Cognitive Science, 31,* 441-480.

Kirby, S. (2001). Spontaneous evolution of linguistic structure: An iterated learning model of the emergence of
regularity and irregularity. *IEEE Journal of Evolutionary Computation*, *5*, 102–110.

Rafferty, A., Griffiths, T. L., & Klein, D. (2009). Convergence bounds for language evolution by iterated learning. *Proceedings of the 31st Annual Conference of the Cognitive Science Society.*

Reali, F., & Griffiths, T. L. (2010). Words as alleles: Connecting language evolution with Bayesian learners to models of genetic drift. *Proceedings of the Royal Society, Series B, 277,* 429-436.

Xu, J., Griffiths, T. L., & Dowman, M. (2010). Replicating color term universals through human iterated learning. *Proceedings of the 32nd Annual Conference of the Cognitive Science Society.*

PALEOGENOMICS AND THE VOCAL AUDITORY CHANNEL IN ARCHAIC HUMANS

JOHN HAWKS

Department of Anthropology, University of Wisconsin-Madison, 1180 Observatory Drive Madison, 53593, USA

Language requires not only a detailed anatomical and neurological system of language production, but also a highly adapted system of reception. To listen, we must first hear. Considering the frequency and amplitude range of human speech, the necessity of perceiving a large number of distinct speakers, and the spatial distances covered by vocal communication in humans compared to other primates, it would seem likely that humans have distinctive auditory adaptations to language. Yet theories of language origins have made very little reference to the sense of hearing. For example, a review of 10 recent books about language origins finds none that even have ``hearing" listed in the index.

This blind spot is not defensible in terms of comparative biology. Although other primates also have sophisticated patterns of vocal communication, experimental evidence and evolutionary ecology both demonstrate that primates use portions of the vocal channel specialized to their physical environment, social group structure. Sympatric species use different portions of the sound spectrum and distinct call types. It has been known since the 1930's that humans and chimpanzees differ in their auditory receptivity across the sound spectrum. In particular, chimpanzees show poor hearing performance across the frequencies from 1000 to 8000 Hz relative to humans. These frequencies are important to differentiating human vowel sounds from each other.

Genes related to hearing in humans are relatively well characterized. Mutations in more than 100 different genes can give rise to Mendelian deafness, and these genes constitute several systems related to the normal development of the middle and inner ear. Some mutations induce syndromes that affect other epithelial or nervous tissues, others are hearing-specific. Together they allow us to scaffold the genetic network underlying normal hearing.

The genetics of hearing have evolved substantially in humans compared to other primates. Collectively, the network of genes related to hearing in gene ontology (GO) analyses show significant evidence of positive selection on the human lineage, in the time since our evolutionary divergence from chimpanzees.

Some of these genes, for example, alpha tectorin (*TECTA*), are among the strongest cases for positive selection across the genome. The functional consequences of these genetic changes are not known, but they support the hypothesis that the evolution of human communication required changes in the auditory apparatus.

The observation of selection on the human lineage does not by itself give us much information about the relationship between hearing evolution and language evolution. To address language evolution, it is important to tie the evolution of the auditory system that receives language to the vocal system and brain, which generate language.

Fossil and paleogenomic evidence now can address the timing of evolution in the human vocal-auditory channel. The fossil record is comparatively rich today compared to the situation ten years ago. Hyoid bones are known from four fossil hominins, including one from *Australopithecus* (Dikika, Ethiopia) and two from archaic *Homo* (Atapuerca, Spain, and Kebara, Israel). Substantial detail about the form of the ear canal and middle ear bones has also come to light. *Australopithecus* lacked humanlike vocal capacities, but had evolved some degree of specialization in the auditory system, while a humanlike vocal and auditory range had emerged by 600,000 years ago in early *Homo*.

Here, I describe the paleogenomic evidence for hearing in archaic humans. Low-coverage drafts of the complete genomes are available from three Neandertals from Vindija, Croatia, as well as one non-Neandertal archaic human from Denisova Cave in the Altai Mountains. Our work compares the coding sequence of genes related to hearing in humans to these archaic humans and to other hominoids. These comparisons make clear that nearly all of the amino acid-coding changes that occur in humans relative to other primates were present in these archaic humans. If hearing evolution was a consequence of selection associated with language, the evidence from paleogenomics is in accord with fossil evidence in placing most of this evolution early in our genus.

Additionally, the 1000 Genomes Project data allow us to find Neandertal and Denisova-derived haplotypes within modern populations. A large fraction of the genomes of Neandertals occur in at least some living humans. These are usually rare variations today, present in fewer than one percent of the world's population. However, they may contribute to human phenotypic variation. In the case of hearing, few possible amino acid differences between Neandertals and the typical human can be found. Every one of these appears to be present in at least one of the 1000 Genomes subjects, so that we cannot identify any fixed genetic basis for hearing variation between humans and Neandertals. This does not imply that they were identical to us, but does show that any recent evolution of hearing has left a substantial store of variability that encompasses these archaic people.

INFANTS' OWN-CRY PERCEPTION FOR LANGUAGE ACQUISITION

REIKO HOSHI-SHIBA[1, 2, 5], YULRI NONAKA[2], HIROMI NITO[1], AKEMI UTSUMI[3], KATSUMI MIZUNO[4], YOSHIHARU MUKAI[3], KAZUO OKANOYA[1, 2, 5]

[1]*Emotional Information Joint Research Laboratory, Brain Science Institute, RIKEN*
2-1 Hirosawa, Wako, Saitama 351-0198, Japan

[2]*JST-ERATO Okanoya Emotional Information Project*
2-1 Hirosawa, Wako, Saitama 351-0198, Japan

[3]*Department of Hygiene and Oral Health, Showa University*
1-5-8 Hatanodai, Shinagawa-ku, Tokyo 142-8555, Japan

[4]*Department of Pediatrics, Showa University*
1-5-8 Hatanodai, Shinagawa-ku, Tokyo 142-8555, Japan

[5]*Graduate School of Arts and Sciences, The University of Tokyo*
3-8-1 Komaba, Meguro-ku, Tokyo 153-8902, Japan

The aim of study

Infants can cry soon after birth. In the first year of life, they start speaking to imitate some of the words spoken by the people around them. This is due to the ability of vocal learning. For this ability, it is necessary that the aural-oral loop is constructed in their neural structure to control their vocalization by hearing their own voice. To control vocalization, it is important that infants perceive and recognize their own-cry especially. In this study, we analyzed the infants' own-cry perception by near infrared spectroscopy (NIRS) measurement.

Experimental procedure

Nine healthy infants at 1 months of age (MOA) participated in the experiments. We prepared four types of sound stimulation for 8 seconds: the infant's own-cry, the time-reversed their own-cry, pure tones with the envelope of their own-cry's waveform and other infants' cry. Each infant was presented the sound stimuli randomly for 5 times each, while the brain activity was measured by NIRS. The changes in concentration of oxygenated hemoglobin (oxy-Hb) and deoxy-Hb were calculated from NIRS data. We analyzed the oxy-Hb concentration changes evoked by presented sounds in both hemispheres using a paired t-test.

Results and Discussion

In 1 MOA infants, most significant increase in oxy-Hb concentration to their own-cry presentation was observed in the left hemisphere and right hemisphere. To the presentation of the time-reversed own-cry and other infants' cry, significant increase in oxy-Hb were also observed in both hemispheres. But the increase level was less than to own-cry. No significant increase in oxy-Hb concentration was observed to the presentation of pure tones with the envelope of their own-cry's waveform. Thus, infants' own-cry presentation caused the most significant increase in brain activity more than presented other sounds in their early days of life. The infants' "crying" behavior, which can attract the attention of caregivers, is considered one of the reasons of acquiring the ability to control human respiration, and therefore, the ability of vocal learning (Okanoya & Merker, 2007). This result suggests that infants' "crying" behavior and the perception of their own-cry may have an important function in vocal learning. Vocal learning ability is considered one of the pre-adaptation skills for language acquisition, so that infants' develop this ability is considered very important for language acquisition.

References

Okanoya, K., & Merker, B. (2007). Neural substrates for string-context mutual segmentation: A path to human language Emergence of Communication and Language (pp. 421-434). New York: Springer Verlag.

EVOLUTION OF SYMBOLIC COMMUNICATION IN THE PERCEPTUAL CROSSING EXPERIMENT

HIROYUKI IIZUKA[1] DAVIDE MAROCCO[2] HIDEYUKI ANDO[1]
TARO MAEDA[1]

[1] *Information Science and Technology, Osaka University, 2-1 Yamadaoka Suita, 565-0871, Japan*

[2] *Centre of Robotics and Neural Systems, University of Plymouth, Drake Circus, Plymouth PL4 8AA, United Kingdom*

A new line of research, which goes beyond spoken language and centres on communication in a broader sense, has been recently labelled experimental semiotics by Bruno Galantucci (2009). As Galantucci points out, the main difference between experimental semiotics and the pragmatics studies is twofold: (a) the theoretical focus shifts from spoken language to other forms of communication, e.g. graphical communication; and (b) the objective focuses on the emergence of new forms of communication, rather than studying the use of pre-existing forms of communication.

In order to investigate the emergence of communication and language with the experimental semiotics, there are some interesting studies where communication is established with different modalities (e.g. Galantucci, 2005). Usually, many of these experimental approaches use the external feedback by an experimenter. However, communication system must be closed in itself. Imagine a situation where there is no communication between two individuals. Only actions exist before the establishment of a communication system. It means that there is even no way to confirm if the embodied interactions required to communicate can be properly done since the process of confirmation must be achieved through communication itself. Only joint actions and sharing experiences are allowed, and communication must emerge and evolve out of those interactions.

Therefore, our aim of this paper is to present a human experiment that attempts to investigate how human communication establishes and evolves without any external feedbacks from mere physical interaction exploiting social agreement as a joint action between interactors.

In our experiment, a pair of subjects interact with each other through limited actions and perceptions. Subjects can move a single finger left or right along a rail fixed on a desk. The detected position of their finger on the rail is sent to a computer and the subjects share virtually the same environment (the same rail). A voice coil motor is attached to the subject's fingernail to transmit vibrations as tactile stimulations. The voice coil motor is activated when the subjects occupy the same position. They need to develop a communication system with these limited action and perception. The communication task is a collective categorisation where they are asked to judge whether or *not* the figure displayed on a monitor is *same* as the figure that the partner is watching. The three kinds of figures, i.e. sharp, square and circle, are used and no instructions about figures are given. 30 seconds in a trial are given to subjects to freely interact with each other to achieve the task.

In order to investigate the role of agreement as a joint action for the language evolution, two different conditions to answer for *same* or *different* are compared. One is staying together (vibration) for *same* and staying away for *different* at the end of trials. Another is that each subject writes down *same* or *different* on a paper. The former way requires agreement but not for the latter.

Our results show that it is possible to evolve the communication system without any external feedbacks and that agreement as a joint action plays an important role to evolve the communication system. We also found that it is easier to evolve the communication system by exploiting the agreements as joint actions compared with the condition without the agreement. Other findings are that the established communication system exploits the turn-taking structure in order to make information flows between the subjects in the non-directional environment and that an association is developed between behaviours and perceptive categories in order to effectively communicate what the subjects are watching.

References

Galantucci, B. (2005). An experimental study of the emergence of human communication systems. Cognitive Science, 29(5),737-767.

Galantucci, B. (2009). Experimental Semiotics: a new approach for studying communication as a form of joint action. Topics in Cognitive Science, 1(2), 393–410.

RECENT ARCHAEOLOGICAL EVIDENCE SUGGESTS MUCH EARLIER EMERGENCE OF HUMAN UG

MASAYUKI IKE-UCHI
Department of English, Tsuda College, Tokyo, JAPAN
ikeuchi@tsuda.ac.jp

The goal of this paper is to show that recent archaeological evidence suggests the possibility that human UG emerged much earlier than has so far been generally assumed, that is, at least 130,000 years ago.

It has usually been hypothesized that UG emerged some time before *Homo sapiens*'s Out of Africa migration, which is thought to have taken place roughly 50,000 years ago (e.g. Klein, 2008, Balter, 2011, etc.). This is the simplest hypothesis that easily and correctly explains the uniformity (e.g. the existence of recursion/Merge (Hauser et al., 2002)) of all current human languages.

First, according to Armitage et al. (2011) and Beyin (2011), archaeological assemblages from Jebel Faya, United Arab Emirates, suggest the presence of modern humans in eastern Arabia by about 125,000 years ago, even if one suspends judgment on Qafzeh and Skhul in the Levant (e.g. Shea, 2008).

Further evidence is concerned with the status of *Homo sapiens* in North and South Africa. The cultural and behavioral advancement of North African *H. sapiens* has recently been pointed out/summarized (d'Errico, 2009, Balter, 2011, etc.). And earlier groups of *H. sapiens* in South Africa were cognitively, technologically and culturally rather advanced (e.g. Marean et al., 2007, Marean, 2010) (but for a different view, see Klein (2008), etc.). These pieces of evidence imply that the emergence of UG might be further moved up, that is, to before the original group of anatomically modern humans in East Africa got separated and spread to North and South Africa (Klein, 2008).

Assuming that the above pieces of archaeological evidence are correct and that the null hypothesis introduced above is on the right track, they strongly suggest that UG emerged at least as early as 130,000-150,000 years ago, for the early Out of Africa event must have taken place some 130,000 years ago and expansion from East Africa to North and South Africa was even earlier. This suggestion would correctly explain why both European and Asian languages (and for that matter all human languages) have recursion/Merge as a common property, assuming that humans in East Africa who trekked into Jebel Faya through the southern route later reached (southern/southeastern) Asia and that those in North and East Africa arrived in Europe (and Asia) through the Nile corridor. Note that the complex multiple-dispersal Out of Africa scenario (Gunz, 2009, Gracea, 2010) is consistent with this hypothesis.

Notice also that the above hypothesis may require reinterpretation of a widely accepted assumption like the so-called "Great Leap Forward" 50,000 years ago. One possible reasonable interpretation is: A small mutation/rewiring in the brain of one *Homo sapiens* in East Africa took place as early as 130,000 years ago and yielded a language gene, as argued above. Then it took 60,000-80,000 years for this gene to spread through a significantly large number of people in Africa, which made "Great Leap Forward" possible.

References

Armitage, S. et al. (2011). The southern route "Out of Africa": Evidence for an early expansion of modern humans into Arabia. *Science*, *331*, 453-456.

Balter, M. (2011). Was North Africa the launch pad for modern human migrations? *Science*, *331*, 20-23.

Beyin, A. (2011). Upper Pleistocene human dispersals out of Africa: A review of the current state of the debate. *International Journal of Evolutionary Biology*, *Volume 2011*.

d'Errico, F. et al. (2009). Additional evidence on the use of personal ornaments in the Middle Paleolithic of North Africa. *PNAS*, *106*, 16051-16056.

Garcea, E. ed. (2010). *South-Eastern Mediterranean peoples between 130,000 and 10,000 years ago*. Oxford and Oakville: Oxbow Books.

Gunz, P. et al. (2009). Early modern human diversity suggests subdivided population structure and a complex Out-of-Africa scenario. *PNAS*, *106*, 6094-6098.

Hauser, M. et al. (2002). The faculty of language: What is it, who has it, and how did it evolve? *Science*, *298*, 1569-1579.

Klein, R. (2008). Out of Africa and the evolution of human behavior. *Evolutionary Anthropology*, *17*, 267-281.

Marean, C. (2010). When the sea saved humanity. *Scientific American*, *August*, 55-61.

Marean, C. et al. (2007). Early human use of marine resources and pigment in South Africa during the Middle Pleistocene. *Nature*, *449*, 905-909.

Shea, J. (2008). Transitions or turnovers? Climatically-forced extinctions of *Homo sapiens* and Neanderthals in the east Mediterranean Levant. *Quaternary Science Reviews*, *27*, 2253-2270.

SOUND SYMBOLISM HELPS INFANTS' WORD LEARNING

MUTSUMI IMAI, MICHIKO ASANO

Faculty of Environment and Information Studies, Keio University, 5322 Endo Fujisawa, Kanagawa, 252 0882, Japan

MICHIKO MIYAZAKI, HIROYUKI OKADA

Tamagawa University Brain Science Institute, 6-1-1, Tamagawa-gakuen Machida, Tokyo, 194-8610, Japan

HENNY YEUNG

The Institute for Neurosciences and Cognition, Paris Descartes University 45, rue des Saints-Pères, 75006 Paris, France

KEIICHI KITAJO

Rhythm-based brain comuptation unit, RIKEN Brain Science Institute, 2-1, Hirosawa Wako, Saitama, 351-0198 Japan

GUILLAUME THIERRY

ESRC Centre for Research on Bilingualism in Theory & Practice, Bangor University College Rd Bangor, Gwynedd LL57 2DG Wales, UK

SOTARO KITA

School of Psychology, University of Birmingham, Edgbaston Birmingham, B15 2TT, UK

Sound symbolism refers to a non-arbitrary relationship between linguistic sound and meaning. It has been suggested to play a facilitative role in verb learning, which occurs in a late stage of word learning in children (at three years or older; Imai et al., 2008). Outstanding questions are whether infants are sensitive to sound symbolism at or before the onset of word learning, and how the sensitivity influences the subsequent initial stage of word learning.

In two experiments, we demonstrated that (1) 11- to 12-month-old Japanese infants, who are not yet able to speak, are sensitive to sound symbolism and (2) sound symbolism facilitates novel word learning (object-word association) in 14-

month-old infants. In Study 1, we conducted an ERP study in which 11- to 12-month-old Japanese infants were presented with combinations of a visual shape and a linguistic auditory sound (i.e., a novel word). The shape-word combinations were either sound-symbolically matched or mismatched. Results showed that the ERPs to sound-symbolically mismatched stimuli were more negative going than those to sound-symbolically matched stimuli at around 300-600 ms after the auditory onset, which indicates that 11-month-old infants are sensitive to sound symbolic relationships. In Study 2, we conducted an object-word association task using a preferential looking paradigm. In a learning phase, 14-month-olds were familiarized with associations of objects with round or spiky shapes and auditory presented novel words, which were either sound symbolically matched or mismatched (between-participant factor). In the following test phase, infants heard the familiarized word and saw two objects, one of which was the correct "referent" of the word (i.e., the object had been associated with the presented word). When the infants were asked to look at the correct referent, those in the match condition preferentially looked at the correct referent right after the test objects were presented; however, infants in the mismatch condition looked at the correct and filler objects equally. This suggests that sound symbolism fostered object-word association, which is a first step for word learning, at 14-months of age.

Collectively, these results indicate that infants are sensitive to sound symbolic relationship between linguistic sound and concept at or prior to word learning (11-months), and then the sensitivity to sound symbolism facilitates object-word association (i.e., novel word learning). Some researchers suspected that language may have started as synesthesic neural integration between auditory and visual modalities and that infants are more sensitive to sound symbolism than adults because the primary sensory cortical areas are less specialized in infants (e.g., Maurer et al., 2006; Ramachandran & Hubbard, 2001). Sound symbolism may provide infants at the initial stage of word learning with referential insights for speech sounds.

References

Imai, M., Kita, S., Nagumo, M., & Okada, H. (2008). Sound symbolism facilitates early verb learning. *Cognition 109*, 54-65.

Maurer, D., Pathman, T., & Mondloch, C. J. (2006). The shape of boubas: Sound-shape correspondences in toddlers and adults. *Developmental Science, 9,* 316-322.

Ramachandran, V. S., & Hubbard, E. M. (2001). Synaesthesia - A window into perception, thought, and language. *Journal of Consciousness Studies, 8*, 3-34.

MALE GIBBONS CHANGE THE NOTE ORDER ACCORDING TO THE BEHAVIORAL SITUATIONS

YOICHI INOUE[1], WAIDI SINUN[2], SHIGETO YOSHIDA[3], KAZUO OKANOYA[4]

[1]The School of Arts and Sciences, the University of Tokyo, Tokyo, 153-8902, Japan; [2]Research and Development Division Yayasan Sabah Group, Yayasan Sabah Headquarters Complex Level 12, Menara Tun Mustapha, P. O. Box 11622, 88817 Kota Kinabalu, Sabah, Malaysia; [3]Emotional Information Joint Research Laboratory, RIKEN Brain Science Institute, Wako 351-0198, Japan; [4]JST, ERATO, Okanoya Emotional Information Project, Wako 351-0198, Japan, Emotional Information Joint Research Laboratory, RIKEN Brain Science Institute, Wako 351-0198, Japan, Department of Life Sciences, Graduate School of Arts and Sciences, the University of Tokyo, Tokyo, 153-8902, Japan

Gibbons sing songs with multiple elements (notes). Previous studies revealed that gibbon songs follow some syntactical rules, and that gibbons recognize the syntactical differences of songs. Mitani and Marler (1989) examined the phonological structure of wild male agile gibbon (*Hylobates agilis*) songs. They revealed that gibbon songs were produced by reference to a set of rules and the gibbons respond somewhat differently to normal and syntactically rearranged playback songs. Geissmann et al. (2005) investigated the note order of male Silvery gibbon (*Hylobates moloch*) songs. Based on changes in the proportion of note types, they classified male songs into two phases: introductory phase and main phase. In the main phase, they calculated first 4 or 5 successive note orders in 11 individuals, and found that male gibbons have individually-preferred note sequences which might follow certain syntactical rules. Clarke et al (2006) compared the acoustic structure of predator-induced duets with regular duets in white-handed gibbon (*Hylobates lar*). They found that the note order of predator-induced duets were different from that of normal duets, although the call note repertoires were identical. Moreover, these syntactic differences were meaningful to conspecifics, because the neighboring groups also sang the predator-induced duets in reply to the predator-induced duets of conspecifics.

We examined more details about gibbon song syntax. We have conducted field observations on the Mueller's gibbon (*Hylobates Muelleri*) at Danum Valley

Conservation Area in northern Borneo. We followed one gibbon group near the Borneo Rainforest Lodge (BRL) for one week in succession in August and December every year. We aimed to record the certain individual's vocal samples while collecting its behavioral data. By this approach, we tried to examine whether gibbons change the note order according to the behavioral situations. From 2001 to 2009, we successfully followed this group for a total of 100 days and recorded 68 male song episodes, which consists of about 8,000 song bouts. We classified the song episodes into 5 contexts: morning song, late morning song, song against playback, encounter song, and song within family (Fig.1). Male songs of Mueller's gibbon consist of "wa" and "oo" notes. We calculated transition probabilities of tree-consecutive-note by dividing frequencies of each transition by total occurrences of transition for each episode. For example, if note order was "wa oo wa oo wa", results were two "wa-oo-wa" transitions and one "oo-wa-oo" transition. Thus, the transition probabilities of the sequences were 0.66 and 0.33, respectively. We found that the observed transition probabilities were deviated from those expected from prevalence of each song note. In addition, the composition of transition patterns was different among behavioral situations. The result suggests that male gibbons might alter note order to create different messages, based on some underlying rules. As gibbon belongs to ape and phylogenitically-near human, this finding may provide insight into the evolution of human language.

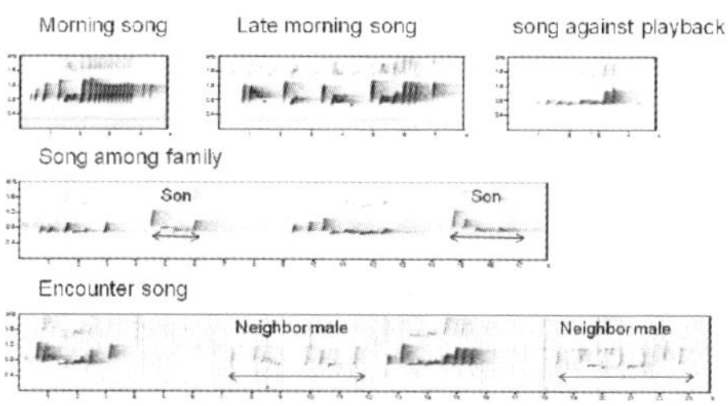

Figure 1. Examples of sonograms in 5 contexts.

References

Clarke, E., Reichard, U. & Zuberbühler, K. 2006: The syntax and meaning of wild gibbon songs. PLoS One, 1(1), e73.

Geissmann, T., Bohlen-Eyring, S. & Heuck, A. 2005: The male song of the Javan silvery gibbon (*Hylobates moloch*). Contributions to Zoology 74, 1-25.

Mitani, J. C. & P. Marler. 1989. A phonological analysis of male gibbon singing behavior. Behaviour 109, 5: 20-45.

TRIADIC NICHE CONSTRUCTION: A SCENARIO OF HUMAN BRAIN EVOLUTION REALIZING TOOL-USE AND LANGUAGE

ATSUSHI IRIKI

RIKEN Brain Science Institute,
Wako 351-0198, Japan

'Niche-construction' denotes an evolutionary process whereby the activities of organisms modify their habitat, to which in turn the organisms evolve to adapt, thus creating their own 'ecological niche' in the environment. This concept could be extended to include the 'cognitive niche' as a newly acquired class of cognitive capacity, and the 'neural niche' as a portion of neural tissue added through expansion of the brain.

In the course of human evolution and human history, our ancestors have created new habitats from modified hunter–gatherer environments to agricultural landscapes with villages, and then to modern civilized technological cities. The evolution of various new cognitive capacities, including those underwriting the manufacture and use of tools and the production and comprehension of languages, has enabled these ecological transformations. Such new cognitive capacities in turn are an outcome of the dramatic expansion of the human brain and of new functional brain areas. Humans have constructed a new 'niche' in each of these ecological, cognitive and neural domains.

The above three classes of niche have coevolutionary interdependencies. Such interactions might have accelerated hominin evolution, which seems remarkably rapid if it was simply the product of natural selection driven by exogenous environmental change. It is possible that ecological changes to habitats have occurred not as a cause of hominin cognitive evolution, but rather as a result of it, with consequent selection pressures acting on the neural basis of behavioural adaptations to the modified environment. New brain functions would constitute the basis for further innovation in cognitive functioning and thus further modifications to the ecological niche, providing a feedback loop for 'triadic niche constructions'.

Expansion (or increase in capacity) of organs as an adaptive response to ecological pressures seems to be a general biological and evolutionary tendency to make the phenotypic system robust—the brain will not be an exception. Multisensory integration and coordinate transformation for the control of reaching movements in the inhabited space is an essential function of the nervous system, for which evolution finally endowed primates with a well-developed parietal cortex. The shift of body-space structure associated with the emergence of hominin bipedalism may have further pushed this trend forward to give this area, and the extended opercular cortex, further resources. Such neural enhancement (construction of the neural niche) happened to enable the processing of abstract information, detached from actual physical constraint, by applying and re-using existing principles for spatial information processing to realize novel mental functions (construction of the cognitive niche)—ultimately leading to language. Purposeful manipulation of the body image in space, required for tool use, would have accelerated interactive links between the neural and cognitive niches—tool use requires transformation of various bodily and spatial coordinates, as well as logical and sequential relations of action components.

Tools represent materialized cognitive brain functions. They have been created one after another and incorporated into hominin habitats as constituent elements (construction of the ecological niche). A human-modified environment puts pressure on succeeding generations to adapt to it, perhaps by acquiring further resources for the relevant organs. Epigenetically induced plasticity (including developmental or learning mechanisms) would participate in such processes—and this is a subject for future biological investigations. In this way, extra genomic information could be transmitted between generations via mutual interactions among ecological, neural and cognitive domains of niches, which may have contributed to hominin evolutionary processes (that is, 'triadic niche construction'). This scenario would locate the human brain as part of an evolving holistic ecosystem.

Acknowledgements

This study was supported by the Funding Program for World-leading Innovative R&D on Science and Technology.

PHASE THEORY AND THE ROLE OF COGNITIVE CONSTRAINTS IN THE MAXIMAL EXPANSION OF SYNTACTIC TREES

ARITZ IRURTZUN
IKER-CNRS (UMR 5478), Campus de la Nive, Château-Neuf, 15 place Paul Bert, Bayonne, 64100, The Basque Country (France)

I discuss the relationship between syntactic phase theory and some general constraints in the cognitive domain. Particularly, I argue that the maximal expansion of a syntactic tree before phasal spell out (measured in the number of 'branches') corresponds roughly to Miller's (1956) 'magical number 7'.

1. 'Classical' phase theory

Initially, the phase-based theory of syntactic computation (*cf.* Uriagereka 1999, Chomsky 2000, 2001) was introduced to frame linguistic theory within a biolinguistic perspective; phase-based computations were thought of as a feature of optimal design, *i.e.* derivations working on phases are more economical than 'global' derivations, for the formers save memory load. Since then, there has been an important advancement on the analysis of syntactic phases and their correlates at the interfaces. Nowadays, it is widely accepted that alongside C and *v*, D and P are also phase heads (*cf., i.a.* Svenonious (2004)). Thus, phases constitute the core of the functional categories of the Principles & Parameters framework. Furthermore, the general assumption is that the arrangement of P(hase heads) and N(onphase heads) is necessarily P – N – P – N, something that has been nicely deduced from the mechanics of inheritance and featural cyclicity (*cf.* Richards 2007). However, while the original justification for phases was a psychological one, since then, the exploration of the psychological nature of syntactic phases has been brushed aside in favor of more language-internal and 'mechanistic' analyses like Richards' (2007). In this talk, I would like to reconcile both the original idea and the recent analyses of phasal architecture by proposing that the Phase Impenetrability Condition (PIC) encodes the general constraint proposed by Miller (1956).

2. Proposal

Authors like Hurford (2007) have suggested that the well-known short-term memory restriction might play a crucial role in language design: according to Hurford, the general and well established restriction on the maximal number of arguments that a predicate can take (roughly, 3-4) might not be a language-specific feature but it rather could derive from a more general constraint of our short-term memory: the 'Magical Number' 7 (plus or minus 2). I would like to extend this way of reasoning and apply it to the structure of syntactic phases proposed by Chomsky (2000, 2001). I will argue that the PIC of Chomsky (2001), also known as 'PIC_2', derives from having sent to interpretation (in PHON, SEM) a syntactic object that maximally expands up to the chunk limits proposed by Miller (1956) (roughly, of the range of 3 information bits). In this sense, the phasal structure building would not be a language-specific feature but the reflex of a more abstract feature of our cognition that is built in the language system just as in other areas of cognition (see, *e.g.*, Sears & Pylyshyn 2000).

Thus, the corollary of my proposal is that human language shows indeed features of 'economy', or 'optimality', like phase-based computations. However, I will argue that this is not due to the use of language as a communicative tool but rather to some more abstract and general principles of optimality of design (Chomsky's 'third factor' effects). Features like the ones that are being discovered in as diverse areas as plant phyllotaxis (*cf.* Green (1989), Webster & Goodwin (1996)), the structure of the cardiovascular system of vertebrates (*cf.* West, Brown & Enquist (1997)), or the patterns of wiring of the nervous system of nematodes (*cf.* Cherniak et al. (2004), Cherniak (2009)).

Acknowledgements

This research benefited from the help of the following projects: FFI2008-04789 (MICINN), GIC07/144-IT-210-07 (EJ), HiTeDi (UPV/EHU) and ISQI (ANR).

Selected references

Chomsky, N. (2001). Derivation by phase. In M. Kenstowicz (Ed.), *Ken Hale: A life in language* (pp. 1–52). Cambridge, MA.: MIT Press.
Hurford, J.R. (2007). *The Origings of Meaning: Language in the Light of Evolution*. Oxford: Oxford University Press.
Miller, G. A. (1956). "The magical number seven, plus or minus two". *Psychological Review* 63.2: 81–97.
Richards, M., (2007). On feature-inheritance: an argument from the Phase Impenetrability Condition. *Linguistic Inquiry, 38.3*: 563-572.
Sears, C.R. & Z. Pylyshyn. (2000). Multiple object tracking and attentional processing. Canadian Journal of Experimental Psychology 54.1: 1-14.

MODELLING THE EVOLUTION OF CREOLES

FREDRIK JANSSON[1], MIKAEL PARKVALL[2], PONTUS STRIMLING[1]
[1]Centre for the Study of Cultural Evolution, and
[2]Department of Linguistics,
Stockholm University, SE-106 91 Stockholm, Sweden

Creoles are languages that typically derive their vocabulary from an already existing language (often a Western European one), even though the native speakers of this language are often in the minority, but whose structure differs from it. Most creoles emerged in the wake of European overseas colonisation during the past couple of centuries, and are often associated with slavery.

The emergence of creole languages has received a great deal of scholarly attention. Are they (or rather, if one accepts a pidgin-to-creole evolutionary path, their pidgin ancestors) the result of imperfect second language acquisition? On the face of it, this is a compelling view, but it needs to make two specific assumptions: first, that one language is more prestigious than the others, and second, that lexicon, phonology and syntax evolve differently, something which makes the hypothesis difficult to test empirically. Some creolists (Baker 1990, 1995) rather picture a situation in which everyone involved (including masters as well as slaves) made efforts to communicate in whatever linguistic material was at hand. The goal would thus only have been successful communication, rather than the acquisition of an existing (prestigious) language.

To be able to test a complex dynamic such as this, we need a formal model that makes the predictions of the theory explicit, but little formalising and hypothesis testing has been done, and to fill this gap, we have developed a mathematical model of the evolution of creoles, partly related to models like *the Naming Game* (Steels 1996), but analytically tractable. In accordance with the view held by Baker and others, the model does not assume asymmetric motivation. Agents meet in pairwise interactions and try to communicate. Once they meet they update the frequency with which they use the language item (a word, a sound or a syntactical feature) they just heard. We have shown that in order for a common language to develop, it is required that agents learn more from each other when they use the same language item than when they do not.

Under the assumption of coordinated learning, we have tested the model on the evolution of Mauritian creole, the only creologenetic setting where we both can assume the creole to have emerged locally, rather than having been imported from elsewhere, and where we have highly detailed demographic data, from Baker & Corne (1982). With this data, for largely all learning rates, the model correctly predicted a vocabulary of an almost exclusively French origin.

For a structural or phonological feature, there are a finite number of parameter settings, and languages share traits, thus reinforcing one another. With joint forces, French is not the obvious output of the model for these features. We have used linguistic data from the *World Atlas of Language Structures* (Haspelmath et al. 2005), combined with the structural features of Grant & Baker (2007:24-7) and the *UCLA Phonological Segment Inventory Database*, for all eight languages represented in the population in the early history of Mauritius. In computer simulations, our model generated a language which is highly similar to Mauritian creole as we know it today, and indeed more so than any of the languages involved in its genesis. In contrast, motivational biases, such as prestige or a reduced willingness to learn after having been on the island for a while are worse at predicting the specific features of Mauritian Creole.

The model, together with mathematical analysis and simulations, thus gives insight into what are some possible and impossible processes underlying the development of a common language, and also gives predictions about which features it will contain. For our data, the model manages to provide correct predictions for lexicon, phonology and syntax with the same parameter settings, taking only demographic considerations, without specific assumptions such as a motivation or prestige bias.

References

Baker, P., & Corne, C. (1982). *Isle de France Creoles: Affinities and origins.* Ann Arbor: Karoma Publishers.

Baker, P. (1990). Off target? *J. of Pidgin and Creole Languages*, *5*, 107-119.

Baker, P. (1995). Motivation in creole genesis. In P. Baker (Ed.), *From Contact to Creole and beyond* (pp 3-15). London: University of Westminster Press.

Grant, A., & Baker, P. (2007). Comparative Creole typology and the search for the sources of Mauritian Creole features. In P. Baker and G. Fon Sing (Eds.), *The making of Mauritian Creole* (pp 197-216). London: Battlebridge Pub.

Haspelmath, M., Dryer, D., Gil, D., & Comrie B. (Eds.) (2005). *The World Atlas of Language Structures.* Oxford: Oxford University Press

Steels, L. (1996). A self-organizing spatial vocabulary. *Artificial Life*, *2*, 319-332.

INNATE TEMPLATE DIFFERENCE COULD INDUCE SIGNAL COMPLEXITY: A COMPARISON OF SONG FEATURES UNDER AUDITORY ISOLATION BETWEEN WILD AND DOMESTICATED FINCHES

HIROKO KAGAWA[1,3], KENTA SUZUKI[2,4], MIKI TAKAHASI[1], KAZUO OKANOYA[1,2,3]

1. Graduate School of Arts and Sciences, The University of Tokyo, Meguro, Tokyo, 153-8902, Japan 2. ERATO, Okanoya Emotional Information Project, Japan Science Technology Agency, Wako, Saitama, 351-0198, Japan 3. RIKEN Brain Science Institute, Wako, Saitama, 351-0198, Japan 4. Graduate School of Science and Engineering, Saitama University,Saitama, Saitama, 338-8570, Japan

Bird songs are acquired by vocal learning. Mechanism and evolution of birdsongs partly parallels those of human language. Songs of Bengalese finches, which are composed of complex sequence, have been studied as a key to understand evolution of signal complexity. Bengalese finches are domesticated from wild white-rumped munias. Songs of domesticated finches contain more tonal sounds and complex note-to note transition than those of wild strains (Okanoya, 2004). Takahasi & Okanoya (2010) found differences in learning property between the two strains using a cross-fostering paradigm. Wild finches imitated a conspecific tutor's song more precisely than domesticated finches do. However, domesticated finches imitated both tutor's songs roughly equally. The domesticated strain may produce their own songs based largely on innate template. Auditory isolation experiments enable us to examine the genetic contribution to song learning. We examined the songs of isolated and normal birds from both strains in order to compare characteristics of innate templates.

Isolated-birds were raised by only females from day 10 post-hutch to isolate from conspecifec songs. Then, they were housed alone in sound proof chamber from day 35. Normal birds were raised by their parents. We used six normal birds in each strain, seven isorated-birds in white rumped munias and six isorated-birds in Bengalse finches. We recorded songs at day 120, when normal leaning period is over. We analyzed 30 songs per individuals.

As a result of song comparison, we found song parameter differed between isolated wild and domesticated strains (Fig.1). Pitch structure in each song note of isolated white rumped munias had higher variance than those of isolated Bengalse finches (Fig. 1). In addition, variance of pitch differed between isolated and normal birds in white-rumped munias, but not Bengalese finches. Thus, the influence of acoustic isolation may differ between species. Pitch in the isolated white-rumped munias, but not in the isolated Bengalese finches, was variable and unstable, indicating that the extent of dependency on innate template could differ between the two strains.

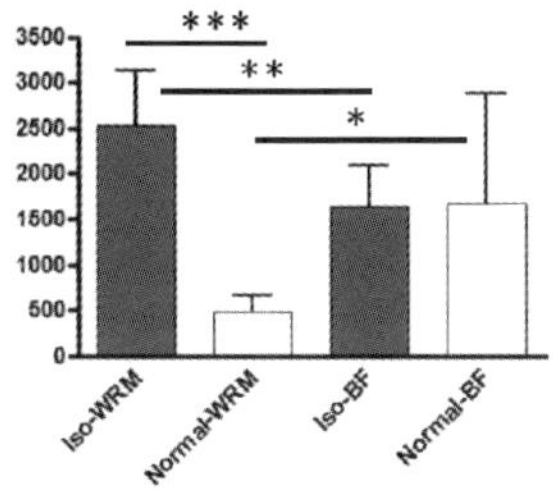

Figure 1. Variance pitch in song note differs between Begalese finches (BF) and white rumped munias (WRM). "Iso" indicates birds were raised in auditory isolation.

Song evolution from white rumped munias to Bengalse finches might be due to relaxed selection in the process of domestication (Deacon, 2010; Okanoya, 2004). Song-learning strategy of domestic strains could be more dependent on innate template than that of wild strains. In the wild, song features which increase individual fitness depend on environmental variables. Juvenile white-rumped munias could learn song features, which is adapted to local areas, from surrounding conspecifics. However the learning strategy may be altered in a domestic environment because relaxed natural selection could enlarge range of fitness in song feature. This change in relation to song learning might produce sequential song diversity in domestic strains. Our result gives new insights about evolution of learnable complex signal including human language.

References

Deacon, T. W. (2010). Colloquium paper: a role for relaxed selection in the evolution of the language capacity. *Proceedings of the National Academy of Sciences of the United States of America, 107* , 9000-9006.

Okanoya, K. (2004). Song syntax in Bengalese finches: proximate and ultimate analyses. *Advances in the Study of Behavior, 34,* 297-346.

Takahasi, M., & Okanoya, K. (2010). Song Learning in Wild and Domesticated Strains of White-Rumped Munia, Lonchura striata, Compared by Cross-Fostering Procedures: Domestication Increases Song Variability by Decreasing Strain-Specific Bias. *Ethology, 116*, 396-405.

THE ROLE OF STS IN MIMETIC-WORD PROCESSING: SOUND SYMBOLISM OR BIOLOGICAL MOTION?

JUNKO KANERO

Department of Psychology, Temple University, 1701 North 13th Street, Philadelphia, PA 19122, USA

MUTSUMI IMAI

Department of Environment and Information, Keio University at Shonan-Fujisawa, 5322 Endo, Fujisawa, Kanagawa, 252-8520, Japan

HIROYUKI OKADA & TETSUYA MATSUDA

Brain Science Institute, Tamagawa University, Machida, Tokyo, 194-8610, Japan

What is the origin of language? Supported by a growing acceptance of the notion of embodiment, it is quite natural to think the emergence of spoken language is deeply related to the human perception of the world. Some researchers claimed that sound symbolism might be the key to understanding the link between protolanguage and language (e.g. Ramachandran & Hubbard, 2001). Although the phenomenon of sound symbolism has been extensively studied, the neural representation of sound-symbolic words is yet to be revealed.

Arata et al. (2010) examined how Japanese sound-symbolic words are processed in the brain, using functional magnetic resonance imaging (fMRI). In their study, participants were presented short video clips depicting a person moving across the screen accompanied with sound-symbolic motion words (mimetic words) and non-sound-symbolic words (adverbs and verbs). Stronger activation was observed in the right posterior superior temporal sulcus (pSTS) for mimetic words in comparison to verbs and adverbs. Based on the prior finding that the right pSTS is also activated by nonlinguistic environmental sounds (Thierry et al., 2003), Arata and colleagues argued that the processing of these sounds and sound-symbolic words might involve a common mechanism.

However, the pSTS is also known to be related to several other cognitive functions, and it is somewhat difficult to draw an unambiguous interpretation that sound-symbolic words are processed as environmental sounds. For example, the pSTS activation has been observed in many studies on biological motion (e.g.

Grossman & Blake, 2002). Arata et al. (2010) used human motions as their stimuli, and the observed activation might simply reflect the enhanced activation caused by the paired presentation of biological motion and mimetic words.

In order to clarify the role of the pSTS for sound-symbolism processing, the present fMRI study tested whether the pSTS is activated during the processing of motion and mimetic word as well as of shape and mimetic word. The stimuli were animation clips of line drawings of various shapes with arms and legs, which moved across the screen (for the motion condition) or stayed still in the center of screen (for the shape condition). A mimetic word (*gitaigo* e.g. furafura) was presented after each animation clip, and participants rated the degree of sound-symbolic match between the motion/shape and mimetic word.

The fMRI data suggest that, during the presentation of mimetic words, the right pSTS was similarly activated in both types of trials (motion/motion). The activation was stronger when participants rated the motion/shape and mimetic word as well-matched. Thus, the participation of the right pSTS in sound-symbolic-word processing is not restricted to biological motion. In connection to the results by Thierry et al. (2003), the right pSTS activation suggests the possibility that sound-symbolic mimetic words have dual status, processed as linguistic sounds as well as environmental sounds.

Some researchers suspect that language may have started as spontaneous neural integration between auditory and visual modalities. The integration is purported to involve the temporo-parieto-occipital (TPO) junction area which is adjacent to the pSTS. This synesthesic integration across modalities may have led to oral (as well as bodily) gesture, whereby protolanguage was born (e.g., Ramachandran & Hubbard, 2001). The activation of the right pSTS observed in our study may be in harmony with this view.

This study is the first to examine the role of the right pSTS for the processing of sound symbolism in more than one domain. The findings of the study further indicate the possibility that sound symbolism served as the link between protolanguage and language, providing an important implication for the evolution of language.

References

Arata, M., Imai, M., Okuda, J., Okada, H. & Matsuda, T. (2010). Gesture in language: How sound symbolic words are processed in the brain. In S. Ohlsson & R. Catrambone (Eds.), *Proceedings of the 32nd Annual Meeting of the Cognitive Science Society* (pp. 1374-1379). Austin, TX: Cognitive Science Society.

Grossman, E. & Blake, R. (2002). Brain areas active during visual perception of biological motion. *Neuron*, 35, 1167-1176.

Ramachandran, V. S., & Hubbard, E. M. (2001). Synaesthesia - a window into perception, thought, and language. *Journal of Consciousness Studies*, 8, 3-34.

Thierry, G., Giraud, A. L., & Price, C. (2003). Hemispheric dissociation in access to the human semantic system. *Neuron*, 38, 499–506.

A PARSIMONIOUS REPRESENTATION WITH HIDDEN STATES FOR BIRDSONG SYNTAX: AN IMPLICATION TO HUMAN SYNTAX EVOLUTION

KENTARO KATAHIRA[1,2,3], KENTA SUZUKI[1,3,4], HIROKO KAGAWA[3,5], KAZUO OKANOYA[1,3,5], MASATO OKADA[1,2,3]

1. *ERATO, Okanoya Emotional Information Project, Japan Science Technology Agency, Wako, Saitama, 351-0198, Japan*
2. *Graduate School of Frontier Sciences, The University of Tokyo, Kashiwa, Chiba, 277-8561, Japan*
3. *RIKEN Brain Science Institute, Wako, Saitama, 351-0198, Japan*
4. *Graduate School of Science and Engineering, Saitama University, Saitama, Saitama, 338-8570, Japan*
5. *Graduate School of Arts and Sciences, The University of Tokyo, Meguro, Tokyo, 153-8902, Japan*

Birdsong has attracted attention as a biological model of human language. Among songbirds, the Bengalese finches (*Lonchura striata var. domestica*) are unique in that their songs are described by a finite state syntax, and thus provide an opportunity to investigate how complex syntactical rule emerges as an evolutionary process (Okanoya, 2004). To relate the findings from studying birdsongs to human language, it is crucial to characterize the statistical and syntactical properties of the sequencing rules in birdsongs. However, these properties of birdsongs have not yet been fully addressed.

In the present study, we first investigated the statistical properties of the songs of the Bengalese finches (Katahira et al., 2011). Based on manual-annotated song note labels, we showed that there were significant higher-order context dependencies in Bengalese finch songs, that is, which note appeared next depended on more than one previous note. We then investigated the statistical models for explaining the higher-order dependencies. To do this, we used the Bayesian inference method and a model selection technique. We applied hidden Markov models (HMMs) with various history dependencies to the acoustic features of Bengalese finch song and selected a suitable model based on the Bayesian model comparison, the predictive performance, and the degree of agreement with manual annotation. As a result, the first-order HMM, in which the present state depends only on the last state, was sufficient and suitable for describing and predicting the Bengalese finch songs. We found that this result is due to a many-to-one state mapping to song notes by which the first-order HMM can generate apparently complex sequences with higher-order dependencies (Katahira, Okanoya & Okada, 2007; also discussed in Jin & Kozhevnikov, 2011). These results imply that the songbird brain has parsimonious neural representation for generating apparently complex sequences.

In order to investigate how our findings can be related to evolutionary schema for the song syntax of Bengalese finch, we then applied our analytical method to the songs of the white-rumped munias (*Lonchura striata*), which are the wild ancestor of the Bengalese finch. The song of white-rumped munia was reported to be simple and show a high linearity compared to the Bengalese finch song (Honda & Okanoya, 1999). However, we found that the entropy of the hidden state transitions, which is a measure of randomness in sequences, did not significantly differ between the songs of these two species. This result suggests that, the syntactical complexity of Bengalese finch song emerged from the acquisition of the ability for the many-to-one mapping from hidden states to song notes, rather than the state transition itself. The present study provides an insight about how the apparently complex structure of the birdsong syntax can emerge by a simple mechanism.

References

Honda, E. & Okanoya, K. (1999). Acoustical and syntactical comparisons between songs of the white-backed munia (*Lonchura striata*) and its domesticated strain, the Bengalese finch (*Lonchura striata var. domestica*). *Zoological science*, *16*, 319-326.

Jin, D.Z., Kozhevnikov, A.A. (2011). A Compact Statistical Model of the Song Syntax in Bengalese Finch. *PLoS Computational Biology*, *7*, e1001108.

Katahira, K., Okanoya, K. & Okada, M. (2007). A neural network model for generating complex birdsong syntax. *Biological Cybernetics*, *97*, 441-448.

Katahira, K., Suzuki, K., Okanoya, K. & Okada, M. (2011). Complex sequencing rules of birdsong can be explained by simple hidden Markov processes. *PLoS ONE*, *6*, e24516.

Okanoya, K. (2004). The Bengalese finch: a window on the behavioral neurobiology of birdsong syntax, *Annals of the New York Academy of Sciences*, *1016*, 724-735.

EXPRESSION ANALYSIS OF LANGUAGE-RELATED GENES IN THE COMMON MARMOSET BRAIN

MASAKI KATO[1], KAZUO OKANOYA[2], TAKU KOIKE[1], SHIGERU WATANABE[3], ATSUSHI IRIKI[1]

[1]*Laboratory for Symbolic Cognitive Development, Brain Science Institute, RIKEN, 2-1 Hirosawa, Wako, 351-0198, Japan*

[2]*Laboratory for Biolinguistics, Brain Science Institute, RIKEN, 2-1 Hirosawa Wako, 351-0198, Japan*

[3]*Graduate school of Human relations, Keio University, 3-1-7 Mita Minato-ku, 108-0073, Japan*

Language is a characteristic tool in human communication, and hypotheses regarding the origin of language such as gestural communications and vocal communications have been proposed. The evolution of vocal control is thought to be important for the use of spoken language in humans. Therefore, we focused on the molecular basis of vocal communication. Vocal communication plays an important role in animal cognition and social interaction, and some animals have several distinct vocalizations, which can be context-dependent. The common marmoset (*Callithrix jacchus*), a New World monkey with many types of vocalizations (Pistorio et al., 2006), is a valuable primate species for studying the neural and neurochemical basis of higher-order cognitive and emotional functions.

The typical molecular biological approach towards understanding human language is linkage analysis of genetic disorders. Some candidate genes for the molecular basis of human language have been isolated by genetic analysis of patients with inherited language disorders. The FOXP2 gene, a member of the forkhead box (Fox) group of genes encoding transcription factors, is a candidate gene for inherited human speech deficiencies (Lai et al., 2001). Candidate genes for dyslexia such as ROBO1, DCDC2, and KIAA0319 have also been identified. Dyslexia is a developmental reading disability with a neurobiological basis, and sometimes subjects with dyslexia have specific language impairments (SLIs). The relationship between dyslexia and SLIs is controversial, and has not been established (Bishop & Snowling, 2004). To help understand the neural basis of language, it is important to analyze the expression of language-related genes in the non-human primate brain as a model for the human brain. Several FoxP2 transgenic animals have been generated (review by Enard, 2011). Disruption of Foxp2 in mice affects ultrasonic vocalization. Additionally, FoxP2 knockdown in the striatum of the zebra finch causes inaccurate song imitation and a reduction in spine density. Knock-in of the humanized Foxp2 in mice results in the increased length of dendrites in the cortex, striatum, and thalamus, while dyslexia-related genes (Robo1, Dcdc2, and Kiaa0319) play an important role in neuronal migration and axon growth during brain development (Galaburda et al., 2006).

In this study, we performed a comparative analysis of the FOXP2 and dyslexia-related gene expression patterns in the brain of the common marmoset. Our results showed that FOXP2 was expressed in the cortex, basal ganglia, and thalamus. These FOXP2 expression patterns were similar to those of other animals such as birds, mice, and humans (fetus), suggesting that FOXP2 expression patterns are conserved in the marmoset brain, as in birds, mice, and human. Moreover, almost all regions expressing FOXP2 overlapped with those expressing dyslexia-related genes. In particular, the expression patterns of these genes overlapped in the basal ganglia and the thalamus. These expression patterns may suggest that the overlapping regions are involved in vocal communication and that the overlap could explain why patients with dyslexia often have SLIs.

References

Bishop, D.V. & Snowling, M.J. (2004) Developmental dyslexia and specific language impairment: same or different? *Psychol Bull*, *130*, 858–886.

Enard W. (2011) FOXP2 and the role of cortico-basal ganglia circuits in speech and language evolution. *Curr Opin Neurobiol*, *21*, 415–424.

Galaburda, A.M., LoTurco, J., Ramus, F., Fitch, RH. & Rosen, GD. (2006) From genes to behavior in developmental dyslexia. *Nat Neurosci*, *10*, 1213–1217.

Lai, C.S., Fisher, S.E., Hurst, J.A., Vargha-Khadem, F. & Monaco, A.P. (2001) A forkhead-domain gene is mutated in a severe speech and language disorder. *Nature*, *413*, 519–523.

Pistorio, A.L., Vintch, B. & Wang, X. (2006) Acoustic analysis of vocal development in a New World primate, the common marmoset (*Callithrix jacchus*). *J Acoust Soc Am*, *120*, 1655–1670.

SONG MEMORY INCLUDING SEQUENTIAL INFORMATION IN MALE BENGALESE FINCHE'S AUDITORY AREA

YOKO KATO

Lab for Biolinguistics, Brain Science Institute, RIKEN, Hirosawa Wako, 351-0198, Japan

MASAKI KATO

Graduate school of Human relations, Keio University, Mita Tokyo, 108-8345, Japan

KAZUO OKANOYA

Lab for Biolinguistics, Brain Science Institute, RIKEN, Hirosawa Wako, 351-0198, Japan

Male Bengalese finches sing complex sequences in their courtship songs. They learn own songs during a developmental period by using auditory feedback. Auditory feedback is an essential ability for human languages therefore songbirds are an excellent model for understanding neural mechanisms of auditory/motor processing. During the learning period, birds compare own vocalization with the remembered auditory template. Bengalese finches have to memorize their song template by phonological information and sequential information. They would teach us how auditory areas process the two aspects of the songs and how the motor processing refers the auditory information.

In this study, we focused on the auditory processing of male's own songs. The question is whether auditory areas process male songs by phonological information only or including sequence. We used habituation-dishabituation method of neural activations in the auditory areas. Presentations of recorded songs elicit neural activities in the secondary auditory areas; the caudomedial nidopallium (NCM) and caudomedial mesopallium (CMM). These neural activities produce an immediate early gene ZENK in neurons. Though, we could use the ZENK expressions as a marker of neural activities in these areas. Mello et al. (1995) reported that repeated presentations of a same song decreased

ZENK expressions in the auditory areas. It reflected habituation of the auditory processing to the stimulus. After the habituation, subsequent new song presentations elicited a recovery of the full ZENK expressions that reflected dishabituation of the auditory processing.

By using this method, we presented the bird's own song repeatedly for initial 2.5h to induce the habituation. After the habituation period, we switched the stimuli to a shuffled sequence song for 30 minutes. The shuffled song was phonologically intact but sequentially different from the original song. We predicted that if the auditory areas discriminated the shuffled stimuli then recovered ZENK expressions would be detected. If auditory areas do not process the sequential information then the neural activities would decrease. To compare the ZENK expressions, we also used a continuous same song presentation and a new song presentation for control groups.

We detected the ZENK expression by *in situ* hybridization after the song presentations. ZENK expressions of the shuffled song were intermediate of the new song presentation and the same song presentation (Jonckheere-Terpstra trend test, CMM $p < 0.001$ ***, NCM $p < 0.05$ *). Our previous results using same method in female Bengalese finches revealed that the auditory areas couldn't distinguish sequential differences of stimulus (Kato et al. 2010). Contrary to the females, we found the male auditory areas were partially activated by the shuffled song.

Our result suggested that the male auditory areas process not only phonological information but also sequential information of their own songs. Previous understanding of auditory processing was that the areas focused on acoustical processing of songs and then, the sequential processing occurred in the downstream motor circuit. Our findings suggest that the sequential processing is prepared in the auditory areas. Therefore the motor processing might refer the auditory information to produce correct song sequences.

References

Mello, C., Nottebohm , F., & Clayton, D. (1995) Repeated exposure to one song leads to a rapid and persistent decline in an immediate early gene's response to that song in zebra finch telencephalon. *The Journal of Neuroscience*, 15: 6919-6925.

Kato, Y., Kato, M., Hasegawa, T., & Okanoya, K. (2010) Song memory in female birds: neuronal activation suggests phonological cording. *NeuroReport*, 21: 404-409.

PITCH INTERVALS IN RELATION TO THE ORIGIN OF LANGUAGE

AI KAWAKAMI[1,2] KIYOSHI FURUKAWA[1] KAZUO OKANOYA[2,3,4]

[1] *Graduate School of Fine art, Tokyo University of the Arts, 12-8 Ueno Koen, Taito-ku, Tokyo 110-8714, Japan*

[2] *Emotional Information Joint Research Laboratory, RIKEN BSI, 2-1 Hirosawa, Wako, Saitama 351-0198, Japan*

[3] *JST ERATO Okanoya Emotional Information Projects, 2-1 Hirosawa, Wako, Saitama 351-0198, Japan*

[4] *Graduate School of Arts and Sciences, Tokyo University, 3-8-1 Komaba, Meguro-ku, Tokyo 153-8902, Japan*

Purpose of study

A communicative system consisting of acoustic elements common to language and music has been suggested to be an evolutionary predecessor to language and music. It has been considered that language and music diverged from this common origin (Brown, 2000). One of the elements shared by language and music is considered to be an interval which would concern emotional communication common to language and music. Earlier research suggested that dissonant intervals communicated sadness in both speech and music (Curtis & Bharucha, 2010). However it remains unknown that how the interval was associated with the emotion that was actually evoked in people. In this study, we investigated the emotions (cognitive judgment of emotion and emotional experience) using the interval as an ancestor common to language and music.

Procedure

24 participants listened to various musical intervals and rated the intensity of two kinds of emotions using the two-dimensional evaluation; arousal (active / passive) and valence (pleasant / unpleasant). The perceived emotion meant a judgment on how the interval generally "should be felt", therefore, we used the instruction "How do ordinary people feel listening to this interval?" to measure it. We explained that "ordinary people" meant average Japanese. On the other hand, we used "How did you yourself feel listening to this interval?" for measuring the felt emotion. Six musical intervals consisted of a minor second interval, a perfect fifth interval, a major third interval, a major sixth interval, an augmented fourth interval, and an octave interval.

Results and Discussion

The ratings obtained for each dimension were analyzed separately. As a result, we found that the perceived emotion was significantly different from the felt emotion in dissonant intervals such as minor second interval and augmented fourth interval only for evaluative dimension (pleasant / unpleasant). Participants answered that ordinary people would feel more unpleasant than they actually experienced to listen to dissonant intervals. It is essential for human's language acquisition to gauge the emotion of collocutor. Therefore, we presume that participants estimated other's emotion larger than the emotion that they felt. At the same time, now that language has specific meanings, interval might not influence the induction of emotion.

References

Brown, S. (2000). The "musilanguage" model of musical evolution. In N. L. Wallin, B. Merker, and S. Brown (Eds.), *The origins of music* (pp. 271-300). Cambridge, MA: The MIT Press.

Curtis, M. E., & Bharucha, J. J. (2010). The minor third communicates sadness in speech, mirroring its use in music. *Emotion*, *10*, 335-348.

MINIMIZATION OF UNIVERSAL GRAMMAR, RELIANCE ON THIRD FACTOR PRINCIPLES, AND FEASIBILITY OF INQUIRY INTO EVOLUTIONARY ORIGINS

HISATSUGU KITAHARA

Institute of Cultural and Linguistic Studies, Keio University, 2-15-45 Mita, Minato-ku Tokyo, 108-8345, Japan

Adopting a "biolinguistic" perspective, Chomsky (2005) identifies "three factors that interact to determine (I-) languages attained: genetic endowment (topic of Universal Grammar), experience, and principles that are language- or even organism-independent." Since the early 90's, there has been a conceptual shift of focus in the study of generative grammar from the first factor (genetic endowment) to the third factor (language-independent principles). Chomsky (2007) highlights this shift with the following two opposing questions: "Throughout the modern history of generative grammar, the problem of determining the character of [I-language] has been approached 'from top down': How much must be attributed to UG to account for language acquisition? The [minimalist program] seeks to approach the problem 'from bottom up': How little can be attributed to UG while still accounting for the variety of I-languages attained, relying on third factor principles?" Under this "bottom up" approach, Chomsky (2008) notes: "Evidently, inquiry into evolutionary origins become more feasible the less special structure is attributed to UG."

In this paper, adopting the "bottom up" approach, I explore the possibility that UG provides no machinery beyond what is needed to satisfy the interface conditions, thereby contributing to the feasibility of inquiry into evolutionary origins. An obvious problem facing this approach, however, is the presence of cross-linguistic variation. For example, consider ordering relations: In English, a head-initial language, all heads precede their complements, while in Japanese, a head-final language, all heads follow their complements (see among others, Kuroda (1988)). Thus, a question arises: How can universal minimum machinery (provided by UG and constrained by third factor principles) capture such cross-linguistic variation (exhibited by I-languages attained)? In this paper, examining some specific UG machinery implemented for constructing structures and establishing relations, I suggest a new way of capturing the observed differences between these two languages.

The core assumption adopted in this paper is that Merge is the sole structure-building operation available to I-language. Merge is defined in the simplest form: Merge takes X and Y, forming {X, Y}, and it can apply freely as long as it confirms to third factor principles (such as the no-tampering condition and the inclusiveness condition). Given this much, first consider the relevant aspects of English derivations, e.g. *John criticized Mary*. In this derivation, Merge first takes V and Obj, forming {V, Obj}. The next step is to *externally* merge v* to {V, Obj}, forming {v*, {V, Obj}}. Finally, SUBJ is merged to {v*, {V, Obj}}, forming {Subj, {v*, {V, Obj}}}. Now consider the relevant aspects of Japanese derivations, e.g. *Taroo-ga Hanako-o hihansi-ta* (Taroo-Nom Hanako-Acc criticize-Past). Recall that Merge can apply freely as long as it confirms to third factor principles. Thus, in this derivation, unlike its English counterpart, I propose that Merge first takes two heads V and v*, forming {V, v*}. Then, OBJ is merged to {V, v*}, forming {Obj, {V, v*}}. The next step is to *internally* merge v* to {Obj, {V, v*}}, forming {v*, {Obj, {V, v*}}}. Finally, SUBJ is merged to {v*, {Obj, {V, v*}}}, forming {Subj, {v*, {Obj, {V, v*}}}}.

What is surprising is that, despite their different executions of Merge, these two derivations yield syntactic objects, arguably identical in the eyes of the conceptual-intentional systems. As for the sensorimotor systems, however, if verbal elements get pronounced at the position of v* in English, while at the position of V in Japanese, then the English derivation yields the surface order of Subj-v*+V-Obj, while the Japanese derivation yields the surface order of Subj-Obj-V+v*. Thus, given Merge, third factor principles, and verbal morphology, it follows that analytical languages such as English tend to be head-initial, while agglutinative languages such as Japanese lean toward head-final.

References

Chomsky, N. (2005). "Three Factors in Language Design," *Linguistic Inquiry* 36, 1-22.

Chomsky, N. (2007). Approaching UG from below. In *Interfaces + recursion = language?*, U. Sauerland and H.-M. Gärtner (eds.), 1-29. Berlin: Mouton de Gruyter.

Chomsky, N. (2008). "On Phases," *Foundational Issues in Linguistic Theory: Essays in Honor of Jean-Roger Vergnaud*, R. Freidin, C. P. Otero and M. L. Zubizarreta (eds.), 133-166, Cambridge: MIT Press.

Kuroda, S.-Y. (1988). "Whether we agree or not: A comparative syntax of English and Japanese," *Linguisticae Investigationes* 12, 1-47.

WHY LANGUAGE HAS STRUCTURE: NEW EVIDENCE FROM STUDYING CULTURAL EVOLUTION IN THE LAB AND WHAT IT MEANS FOR BIOLOGICAL EVOLUTION

SIMON KIRBY

Language Evolution & Computation Research Unit,
School of Philosophy, Psychology & Language Sciences
The University of Edinburgh
simon@ling.ed.ac.uk
@SimonKirby

Where do the characteristic design features of human language come from? In particular, how do we come to have a language that allows us to express novel utterances and have them reliably be understood? One answer is that this highly adaptive trait is simply an innately encoded feature of our biological endowment, tuned by natural selection under pressure for successful communication (e.g. Pinker & Bloom, 1990). In recent years, however, an alternative view has been set out that suggests language adapts not through a process of gradual biological evolution, but rather as a result of cultural evolution as it is transmitted in a population through repeated learning and use (e.g., Kirby, Dowman, & Griffiths, 2007). This process, known as *iterated learning*, can be studied in the lab by creating artificial languages and observing how they evolve as they are acquired and transmitted by experimental participants (Kirby, Cornish, & Smith, 2008).

In this talk, I will show that productive linguistic structure only emerges in these artificially evolving languages in certain specific conditions. These shed light on where the familiar design features of human language come from, and explain some emerging data from real languages in unusual circumstances. I conclude that language structure is an emergent compromise between being *compressible* and *expressive*, driven by pressures from learning and communication respectively.

These results have important implications for our understanding of the basic design features of human language (Hockett, 1960). I will argue that many of these design features arise inevitably as a result of two fundamental ones: *semanticity* and *traditional transmission*. The cognitive support for these two features represent the crucial biological pre-adaptations for language. At the end of the talk I will give a tentative suggestion for how and why these evolved, setting the stage for the inevitable emergence of structured language.

References

Hockett, C. F. (1960). The origin of speech. *Scientific American*, *203*, 88–96.

Kirby, S., Cornish, H., & Smith, K. (2008). Cumulative cultural evolution in the laboratory: an experimental approach to the origins of structure in human language. *Proceedings of the National Academy of Sciences*, *105(31)*, 10681–10686.

Kirby, S., Dowman, M., & Griffiths, T. (2007). Innateness and culture in the evolution of language. *Proceedings of the National Academy of Sciences*, *104(12)*, 5241–5245.

Pinker, S., & Bloom, P. (1990). Natural language and natural selection. *Behavioral and Brain Sciences*, *13*, 707–784.

HOW IS PRAGMATIC GROUNDING FORMED IN SYMBOLIC COMMUNICATION SYSTEMS?

TAKESHI KONNO, JUNYA MORITA, AND TAKASHI HASHIMOTO
School of Knowledge Science, JAIST,
1–1, Asahidai, Nomi, Ishikawa, 923–1292 Japan
{t-konno, j-morita, hash}@jaist.ac.jp

How does the human linguistic communication system evolve? In recent years, researchers have begun to investigate the cultural evolution of language using an experimental paradigm to understand the emergence of the human communication system (Scott-Phillips & Kirby, 2010). One of the central issues is how symbol systems emerge from common grounds such as conventional behavior. In his experiment, Galantucci (2005) observes that routine behavior conveyed implicit information. Scott-Phillips, Kirby, and Ritchie (2009) show that common ground is important in order to judge certain behavior as being communicative.

Among these findings, a critical issue is the expressing of informative intentions, a unique feature in human communication (Tomasello, 2003). Humans pragmatically ground their intentions. Even if we use the same symbols, we can communicate different meanings depending on the context. From this viewpoint, it is important to determine how pragmatic grounding is formed in symbolic communication systems.

To investigate how pragmatic grounding develops, Konno, Morita, and Hashimoto (2011) designed a game experiment on the basis of the game created by Galantucci (2005). In the revised experimental setting in which pragmatic grounding was clearly observed as a role division, message exchange and movement of location were restricted to once per round in order to make the connection among turn-taking, messages, and movement clearer than those in Galantucci's (2005) experiment. In the experiment, it is confirmed that the communication systems with effective symbol usage develop if the participants have implicit behavioral tendencies, such as the use of a small number of symbols, meeting at the usual place, and smooth turn-taking. However, the findings show that the implicit behavioral tendencies do not contribute to the division of roles using turn-taking. We continued to analyze how participants' intention of assuming roles was expressed in messages and turn-taking behaviors.

In our experiment, the dyads engaged in a coordination game. The game environment contained two agents and four intercommunicating rooms. At the beginning, the agents were randomly located in different rooms. Each player, who were unaware of the location of the other, aimed to bring her/his agent into the same room as the other. Each player could send symbolic messages, which were transmitted immediately to the other, by composing two figures whose meanings and usage were not predefined and shared between the participants. Thus, the players could manage turn-taking, that is, they could decide who would be the first/second sender. To play this game effectively, participants needed to divide the roles in communication. For example, one player sent a message indicating her/his current location and the other decided on a destination to where both agents could move. The players had to notice the necessity of the role division and express their intention to assume roles in messages and/or in turn-taking.

We confirmed that some participants realized the division of roles. They successfully communicated their intentions, for example, "willing to communicate the present location" and "willing to communicate the destination". The intentions of a message composing of the same symbols referring to a concrete location were interpreted correctly according to the context. This function was implemented by turn-taking as means.

Konno et al. (2011) showed that the implicit behavioral tendencies did not contribute to the division of roles using turn-taking. However, we found that the development of the same semantic and syntactic rules contributed to the realizing of the division of roles, namely, pragmatic grounding. We suggest that the participants take notice of others' intentions to indicate a present location and destination on the basis of the same mappings between concrete locations and symbols. Further qualitative exploration suggests that developing the same semantic and syntactic rules through integrating the individuals' partial rules is an effective method for realizing pragmatic grounding. When the participants made up all the rules individually, even if the rules of one side were understood by the other, they tended not to achieve pragmatic grounding.

References

Galantucci, B. (2005). An experimental study of the emergence of human communication systems. *Cognitive science*, *29*(5), 737–767.

Konno, T., Morita, J., & Hashimoto, T. (2011). Symbol communication systems integrate implicit information in coordination tasks. In *The 3rd international conference on cognitive neurodynamics.* Hokkaido, Japan.

Scott-Phillips, T., & Kirby, S. (2010). Language evolution in the laboratory. *Trends in Cognitive Sciences*, *14*(9), 411–417.

Scott-Phillips, T., Kirby, S., & Ritchie, G. (2009). Signalling signalhood and the emergence of communication. *Cognition*, *113*(2), 226–233.

Tomasello, M. (2003). *Constructing a language: A usage-based theory of language acquisition.* Harvard University Press, Cambridge.

THE EVOLUTION OF MORPHOLOGICAL AGREEMENT

RICHARD LITTAUER
Computational Linguistics, Universität des Saarlandes, Saarbrücken, 66041, Germany

Morphological agreement either arose late in the evolution of language (Heine & Kuteva, 2007) or, as an essential part of semantic neural mapping, was present in the earliest stages of protolanguage (Hurford, 2002, Casey and Kleunder, 1995). The main proposed reasons for its evolutionary origins stem from the functions of agreement: pro-drop, redundancy, as an aid in parsing, and syntactic marking, among others. Here, I seek to encourage discussion and examine the evidence surrounding the possibility that morphological agreement is more than detritus by bringing together the diverse uses for it that have not previously been considered simultaneously. I suggest that the ability to evolve agreement (as not all languages exhibit morphological agreement) occurred simultaneously with proto-syntax in protolanguage (Carstairs-McCarthy, 2010) basing my arguments on the functions mentioned above, as well as on the presence of varying complexity in morphological agreement, and the nature of modern pidgins and child language acquisition. I use the canonical agreement hierarchy, developed by Corbett (2006), to support this further by asserting that many of the principles suggested may reflect the first morphological functions, just as typological universals have traditionally been used to make implications about protolanguage. An example of a hierarchical feature that may be used to shed light on protolanguage might be, for instance, that verb and subject agreement is more common cross-linguistically than verb object agreement, especially in languages with free word order. Additionally, early language communities may have had different pressures on linguistic evolution and morphological complexity than modern languages, including differences in the amount of shared information (such as morpho-phonological phenomena) between small and larger ones. I argue that morphological agreement is an integral part of language evolution, and that the origin of agreement in protolanguage may not have followed the same paths (particularly language internally and as a process of grammaticalization) as modern agreement formation processes. By doing this I hope to call attention to the lack of study in this particular area, and to emphasize the possible importance of agreement in evolutionary theories of language, and to recommend further experimental and empirical avenues for research.

References

Carstairs-McCarthy, A. (2010). *The Evolution of Morphology*. Oxford, UK: Oxford University Press.

Casey, S., and Kluender, R. (1995). Evidence for intermediate forms in the evolution of language. In A. Dainora, R. Hemphill, B. Luka, B. Need, S. Pargman (Eds.), *Papers from the 31st Regional Meeting of the Chicago Linguistic Society*, Volume *i* The Main Session, (pp. 66–80). Chicago, IL: Chicago Linguistic Society.

Corbett, G. (2006). *Agreement*. Cambridge, UK: Cambridge University Press.

Heine, B., and Kuteva, T. (2007). The Genesis of Grammar. Oxford, UK: Oxford University Press.

Hurford, J.R. (2002). The Roles of Expression and Representation in Language Evolution. In A. Wray (Ed.) *The Transition to Language* (pp. 311–334). Oxford, UK: Oxford University Press.

RE-DATING THE LOSS OF LARYNGEAL AIR SACS IN *HOMO SAPIENS*

RICHARD LITTAUER
Computational Linguistics, Universität des Saarlandes, Saarbrücken, 66041, Germany

Laryngeal air sacs are a product of convergent evolution in many different species of primates, bats, and other mammals. Air sacs have been lost in *Homo sapiens*. This has been argued to have occurred before *Homo heidelbergensis*, due to a loss of the bulla in the hyoid bone from *Australopithecus afarensis* (Martinez, 2008), at a range of 500kya to 3.3mya. (de Boer, to appear). Possible reasons for the loss of laryngeal air sacs include infection, the ability to modify breathing patterns and reduce need for an anti-hyperventilating device (Hewitt et al, 2002), and the selection against air sacs as they are disadvantageous for subtle, timed, and distinct sounds. (de Boer, to appear). Further, it has been suggested that the loss goes against the significant correlation of air sac retention to evolutionary growth in body mass (Hewitt et al., 2002). I argue that the loss of air sacs may have occurred on the more recent side of the timeline, as the loss of the bulla in the hyoid does not exclude the possibility of airs sacs, as air sacs can herniate around surrounding tissue (Frey et al., 2007), and as the diachronic connection between the bulla and the air sacs is opaque. Further, the weight measurements of living species as a justification for the loss of air sacs despite a gain in body mass I argue to be unfounded given archaeological evidence, which suggests that the laryngeal air sacs may possibly have been lost only after size reduction in *Homo sapiens* from *Homo heidelbergensis*. I will flesh out these arguments, first presented in Littauer (to appear). Finally, I suggest two further possible pressures on laryngeal air sacs in Homo sapiens. First, the linguistic niche of hunting would have been better suited to higher frequency, directional calls as opposed to lower frequency, multidirectional calls, especially in a savannah-like environment. It is worth noting that the influence of the savannah on the evolution of the larynx has been explored before (Hombert, 2010). I argue here that the loss of air sacs might have then been advantageous, as lower frequencies produced by air sac vocalisations over bare ground have been shown to favour multidirectional over targeted utterances (Frey and Gebler, 2003). Secondly, the reuse of air stored in air sacs could have possibly been disadvantageous toward sustained, regular heavy breathing. In short, it is possible the loss of air sacs occurred on a more recent scale than previously considered.

References

Boer, B. de. (to appear). Air sacs and vocal fold vibration: Implications for evolution of speech.

Frey, R, & Gebler, A. (2003). The highly specialized vocal tract of the male Mongolian gazelle (Procapra gutturosa Pallas, 1777--Mammalia, Bovidae). *Journal of anatomy*, *203*(5), 451-71.

Frey, R., Gebler, A., Fritsch, G., Nygrén, K., & Weissengruber, G. E. (2007). Nordic rattle: the hoarse vocalization and the inflatable laryngeal air sac of reindeer (Rangifer tarandus). *Journal of Anatomy*, *210*(2), 131-159.

Hewitt, G., MacLarnon, A., & Jones, K. E. (2002). The functions of laryngeal air sacs in primates: a new hypothesis. *Folia primatologica international journal of primatology*, *73*(2-3), 70-94.

Hombert, J.-M. (2010). Ecological and sexual explanations for larynx lowering. In A.D.M. Smith, M. Schouwstra, B. de Boer, and K. Smith (Eds.), *The Evolution of Language (EVOLANG 8),* (pp. 421-422). Hackensack, NJ: World Scientific.

Littauer, R. (to appear). A Reanalysis of Anatomical Changes for Language.

Martínez, I., Arsuaga, J. L., Quam, R., Carretero, J. M., Gracia, a, & Rodríguez, L. (2008). Human hyoid bones from the middle Pleistocene site of the Sima de los Huesos (Sierra de Atapuerca, Spain). *Journal of human evolution*, *54*(1), 118-24.

ON THE ORIGIN OF THE HIERARCHY OF COLOR NAMES

VITTORIO LORETO
Physics Dept., Sapienza University of Rome,
Piazzale Aldo Moro 5, 00185 Roma, Italy and
Institute for Scientific Interchange (ISI), Viale Settimio Severo 65, 10133 Torino, Italy
vittorio.loreto@roma1.infn.it

ANIMESH MUKHERJEE
Institute for Scientific Interchange (ISI),
Viale Settimio Severo 65, 10133 Torino, Italy
animesh.mukherjee@isi.it

FRANCESCA TRIA
Institute for Scientific Interchange (ISI),
Viale Settimio Severo 65, 10133 Torino, Italy
tria@isi.it

One of the fundamental problems in cognitive science is how humans categorize the visible color spectrum (Berlin & Kay, 1969). The empirical evidence of the existence of universal or recurrent patterns in color naming across cultures is paralleled by the observation that color names begin to be used by individual cultures in a relatively fixed order (Berlin & Kay, 1969). The origin of this hierarchy is largely unexplained. Here we resort to multi-agents simulations (Puglisi, Baronchelli, & Loreto, 2008; Baronchelli, Gong, Puglisi, & Loreto, 2010), where a population of individuals, subject to a simple perceptual constraint shared by all humans, namely the human Just Noticeable Difference, categorizes and names colors through a purely cultural negotiation in the form of language games (Steels & Belpaeme, 2005; Puglisi et al., 2008). We found that if one ranks different regions of the visible spectrum according to the time needed for a population to reach consensus on a color name for each specific region, color spectrum regions get organized into a hierarchy with [*red*, (*magenta*)-*red*], [*violet*], [*green/yellow*], [*blue*], [*orange*] and [*cyan*] appearing in this order (see Fig. 1). The hierarchy observed in our modeling scheme features a very good quantitative agreement with the empirical observations of the World Color Survey (Berlin & Kay, 1969; Cook, Kay, & Regier, 2005; Baronchelli et al., 2010). Our results demonstrate a clear possible route to the emergence of hierarchical color categories, confirming that the theoretical modeling in this area has now attained the required maturity to make significant contributions to the ongoing debates concerning language universals (Roberson, Davies, & Davidoff, 2000; Evans & Levinson, 2009).

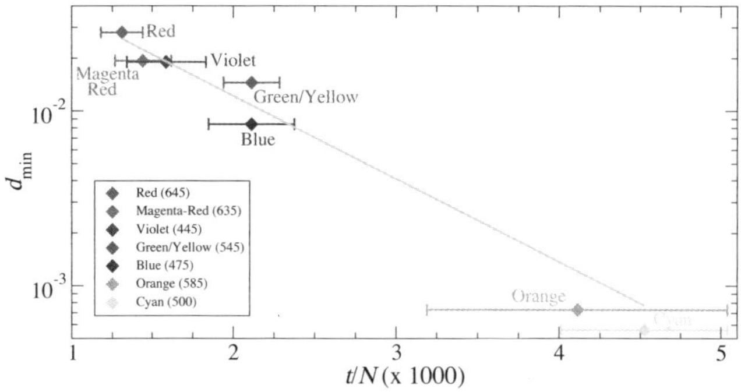

Figure 1. Time needed to reach consensus versus the value of Just Noticeable Difference, d_{min}, for different regions of the color space corresponding to the colors reported in the legend (the approximate wavelength (nm) associated with each colored data point is within parenthesis). Time is measured as number of games per agent (N is the population size). The gray line represents a fit of the data with an exponential function of the form $Ae^{-\alpha t}$.

References

Baronchelli, A., Gong, T., Puglisi, A., & Loreto, V. (2010). Modelling the emergence of universality in color naming patterns. *Proc. Natl. Acad. Sci. USA (PNAS)*, *107*, 2403-2407.

Berlin, B., & Kay, P. (1969). *Basic Color Terms.* Berkeley: University of California Press.

Cook, R., Kay, P., & Regier, T. (2005). The world color survey database: history and use. In H. Cohen & C. Lefebvre (Eds.), *Handbook of categorisation in the cognitive sciences.* (pp. 224–242). Amsterdam and London: Elsevier.

Evans, N., & Levinson, S. C. (2009). The myth of language universals: Language diversity and its importance for cognitive science. *Behavioral and Brain Sciences*, *32*(05), 429–448.

Puglisi, A., Baronchelli, A., & Loreto, V. (2008). Cultural route to the emergence of linguistic categories. *Proc. Natl. Acad. Sci. USA (PNAS)*, *105*(23), 7936.

Roberson, D., Davies, I., & Davidoff, J. (2000). Color categories are not universal: Replications and new evidence from a stone-age culture. *Journal of Experimental Psychology: General*, *129*(N/A), 369–398.

Steels, L., & Belpaeme, T. (2005). Coordinating perceptually grounded categories through language: A case study for colour. *Behavioral and Brain Sciences*, *28*(04), 469–489.

THE MEANING OF NONSENSE WORDS

GARY LUPYAN
University of Wisconsin-Madison,
Department of Psychology
Madison, WI USA

DANIEL CASASANTO
The New School for Social Research,
Department of Psychology
New York, NY USA

Can a nonsense word convey meaning? On traditional accounts of language, words are viewed as entries in a mental lexicon, (Jackendoff, 2002), and the answer is a clear 'no'. If word-meanings are contained in lexical entries, then nonsense words, lacking such entries are by definition meaningless. On an alternative view (Elman, 2004; Casasanto & Lupyan, 2011; Lupyan & Thompson-Schill, in press), the meaning of a word is the effect it has on the mind of the listener. Rather than *having* meanings, words are *cues* to meaning. A word is said to be meaningful insofar as its effect across individuals is measurably similar: An instruction to draw a "dog" will tend to produce drawings that are similar to each other and, artistic skill notwithstanding, can be reliably labeled by outside observers as examples of dogs. But what happens if instead of using a familiar word-cue like "dog" the cue is a novel word?

The words-as-cues account of word-meaning predicts that even nonsense words with no obvious relation to existing wordforms can have meaning if the phonology of the nonsense word happens to tap into the perceptual/semantic system in a way that is measurably similar across individuals. One example of this phenomenon has been investigated in the context of sound symbolism. For example, individuals consistently match nonsense words like "tukeetee" and "baluma" to sharp/angled and rounded shapes, respectively (Kohler, 1947; Kovic, Plunkett, & Westermann, 2010; Maurer, Pathman, & Mondloch, 2006).

In the present work we sought to determine if nonsense words which have been previously shown to be reliably correlated with particular shapes, and which have no reliable association with existing English words can nevertheless systematically affect the behavior of participants on an open-ended task. We began by replicating classic sound-symbolism findings (see Perniss, Thompson, & Vigliocco, 2010 for review) in a novel way: by presenting participants with a single image and asking them to choose the most appropriate word among 4 alternatives. The word "gogaa" was preferentially chosen for a rounded pattern and the word "tukeetee" for a zig-zag pattern. Systematic preferences were also shown for real words. The word "tukeetee" was chosen by 16/30 participants as the best match to "knife" $\chi(3)=13.2$, $p=.004$.

Next, we asked two groups of participants to draw what they think a knife called a "Tukeetee" (or "Teetay") in a foreign language looks like. The drawings (without names) were then rated on perceived sharpness by additional participants. We found a highly reliable difference in perceived sharpness: knives drawn in response to a *tukeetee* prompt were significantly sharper than those drawn in response to a *teetay* prompt, $F(1,11)=27.88$, $p<.0005$. In a followup study, we found that knives drawn to a "gogaa knife" prompt were reliably more rounded than knives drawn to tukeetee/teetay prompts.

Our results show that nonsense words can alter people's behavior in much the same ways as real words. Just as asking participants to draw a "curved knife" vs. a "straight knife" leads to systematically different representations and resultant drawings, systematic changes to behavior can be elicited using nonsense words. In effect, one can communicate using "nonsense" words, though in a limited way. The words we used here have been used previously in sound-symbolism studies; the generalizability of our results remains to be determined.

Arbitrary relationships between form and meaning can be viewed as a solution to the need to distinguish semantically similar concepts and a communication channel with limited iconic potential (Monaghan et al., in press). Importantly, despite lifelong experience with this largely arbitrary mappings of sounds to meanings, people readily use iconic properties as a cue to meaning. Although conclusions regarding the role of iconicity in language evolution remain speculative, our results highlight the surprising degree to which language processing makes use of iconic principles.

Casasanto, D., & Lupyan, G. (2011). Ad Hoc Cognition. Presented at the Annual Conference of the Cognitive Science Society, Boston, MA.

Elman, J. L. (2004). An alternative view of the mental lexicon. *Trends in Cognitive Sciences*, *8*(7), 301-306.

Jackendoff, R. S. (2002). *Foundations of language: Brain, meaning, grammar, and evolution*. Oxford, England: Oxford University Press.

Kohler, W. (1947). *Gestalt Psychology: An introduction to new concepts in modern psychology*. New York: Liveright Publishing Corporation.

Kovic, V., Plunkett, K., & Westermann, G. (2010). The shape of words in the brain. *Cognition*, *114*(1), 19-28.

Lupyan, G., & Thompson-Schill, S. L. (in press). The evocative power of words: Activation of concepts by verbal and nonverbal means. *Journal of Experimental Psychology-General.*

Maurer, D., Pathman, T., & Mondloch, C. J. (2006). The shape of boubas: sound-shape correspondences in toddlers and adults. *Developmental Science*, *9*(3), 316-322.

Perniss, P., Thompson, R. L., & Vigliocco, G. (2010). Iconicity as a General Property of Language: Evidence from Spoken and Signed Languages. *Frontiers in Psychology*, *1*.

NONHUMAN PRIMATES DO DECLARE! DECLARATIVES AS EVIDENCE FOR MENTAL TIME-TRAVEL IN APES

HEIDI LYN[a]
PATRICIA GREENFIELD[b]
SUE SAVAGE-RUMBAUGH[c]
KRISTEN GILLESPE-LYNCH[b]
WILLIAM D. HOPKINS[d]

a. Department of Psychology, University of Southern Mississippi, 730 E. Beach Blvd., Long Beach, MS 39560 USA

b. Department of Psychology and FPR-UCLA Center for Culture, Brain, and Development, University of California, Los Angeles CA 90095

c. Great Ape Trust of Iowa, Des Moines, IA 50320

d. Department of Psychology, Agnes Scott College, 141 E. College Ave, Decatur, GA, 30030 USA and Department of Psychobiology, Yerkes National Primate Research Center, Emory University, 954 Gatewood Rd. NE, Atlanta, GA 30329 USA

One hypothesis surrounding the evolution of language suggests that the key difference between humans and their nonhuman primate relatives is human cooperation, particularly as measured by the relative lack of declarative (strictly communicative) as opposed to imperative (request-driven) communication in apes (Tomasello, 2007). Indeed, one researcher has gone so far as to say that, ''Although some apes, especially those with extensive human contact, sometimes point imperatively for humans, *no apes point declaratively ever*'' (Tomasello, 2007 italics added by the authors).

Similarly, mental time travel - the ability to project oneself mentally into the future, to plan for specific events, or the past to remember specific occurrences has been much discussed in the literature (e.g. Suddendorf & Corballis, 1997). It has been argued that this ability also may be a uniquely human capability and may be an evolutionary discontinuity between humans and apes.

Here we present the use and comprehension of declaratives in language-competent apes (chimpanzees and bonobos who can use a symbolic keyboard and comprehend English at the level of a 2 ½ year old child) (Lyn, et al., 2011). Data comes from daily notes of symbol usage and also from object-choice tests.

In contrast to the preceding hypotheses, these apes both comprehended and used declaratives, including declarative points, in tests and in their own keyboard and gestural utterances. The apes used declaratives to name objects, to interact and negotiate, and to make comments about other individuals.

In addition, the apes also made comments about past and future events, suggesting an understanding of mental time-travel. The frequency of the apes' statements about the past was similar to those of two children in the one-word stage (X^2 residuals showed no genus differences), but the apes made more future statements than the children (all ape X^2 residuals > 2.0). For example:

Statements of intention: Kanzi touches the ICE symbol, then goes to small refrigerator, opens the door, scrapes ice from freezer and eats.

Past activity or action (immediate): I had been helping Panpanzee jump off the sloped platform in bdrm. One time she stayed up there for quite a while before working up the nerve to jump onto the table next to me. As she landed she lay on her tummy and touched the JUMP lexigram on the faceplate there. She appeared to be thinking about what she had just done.

If the apes were biologically incapable of declaratives or mental time travel, one could argue for a uniquely biological adaptation that drove the evolution of language in humans. However, because these abilities are shared with our nearest evolutionary relatives, a specific genetic adaptation for the appearance of these abilities is not indicated. However, human cultural interaction was required for the apes' most frequent understanding and use of declaratives, and the development of human socio-communicative interaction remains an important likely evolutionary adaptation of humankind.

Acknowledgements

Funding for this study was provided by NIH grants HD-56232 and HD-38105. Correspondence should be addressed to Heidi Lyn, heidi.lyn@usm.edu.

References

Lyn, H., Greenfield, P. M., Savage-Rumbaugh, S., Gillespie-Lynch, K., & Hopkins, W. D. (2011). Nonhuman primates do declare! A comparison of declarative symbol and gesture use in two children, two bonobos, and a chimpanzee. *Language and Communication, 31*, 63-74.

Suddendorf, T., Corballis, M.C., 1997. Mental time travel and the evolution of the human mind. *Genetic, Social, and General Psychology Monographs* 123, 133–167.

Tomasello, M. (2007). If They're So Good at Grammar, Then Why Don't They Talk? Hints From Apes' and Humans' Use of Gestures. *Language Learning and Development, 3*(2), 133-156.

BUILDING A LANGUAGE-COMPETENT SPECIES: CONTRIBUTIONS OF BRAIN AND ENVIRONMENT TO COGNITION AND COMMUNICATION IN APES AND MONKEYS

HEIDI LYN[a]
JAMIE L. RUSSELL[b]
JENNIFER SCHAEFFER[b]
PETER PIERRE[c]
ALLYSON J. BENNETT[c]
SCOTT FEARS[d]
ROGER WOODS[d]
WILLIAM D. HOPKINS[b,e]

a. Department of Psychology, University of Southern Mississippi, 730 E. Beach Blvd., Long Beach, MS 39560 USA

b. Department of Psychobiology, Yerkes National Primate Research Center, Emory University, 954 Gatewood Rd. NE, Atlanta, GA 30329 USA

c Wake Forest University School of Medicine, Winston-Salem, NC 27157, United States

d. University of California, Los Angeles (UCLA), Los Angeles, CA 90095, United States

g. Department of Psychology, Agnes Scott College, 141 E. College Ave, Decatur, GA, 30030 USA

One continuing evolutionary focus in psychology is the relative contributions of biology (nature) and environment (nurture) to communication and cognition. While extremely difficult to piece apart, we offer here lines of evidence that suggest specific contributions of each of these factors, specifically, language areas of the brain that show differences between monkeys, apes and humans, and communicative and cognitive abilities that are boosted by socio-communicative environments in apes.

1.1. *Brain*

Recent publications have shown that chimpanzees share with humans some brain asymmetries in language area analogs. Most specifically, the planum temporale in chimpanzees *(Pan troglodytes)* encompasses Wernicke's area, which is implicated in language and speech processing in humans and is also larger in chimpanzees on the left side of the brain. Here we present evidence that the same asymmetry is found in a small sample of bonobos *(Pan paniscus)* (Hopkins, Lyn, & Cantalupo, 2009). However, a much larger sample of 3 different monkey species (vervet monkeys *(Chlorocebus aethiops sabaeus)*, rhesus *(Macaca mulatta)* and bonnet *(Macaca radiata)* monkeys, do not show the left-side asymmetry in gray matter - suggesting that the biological adaptation of an asymmetric planum temporale occurred before humans split from *Pan* but after the split from monkeys (Lyn et al., 2011).

1.2. *Environment*

We recently showed that apes with enriched socio-communicative environments outperformed those with standard environments in an object-choice task. Here we tested chimpanzees and bonobos on a larger series of tasks to test their understanding of the physical world, tool use, social cognition, and communication (Russell, Lyn, Schaeffer, and Hopkins, in press). Results suggest that apes from an enriched environment outperformed the apes from standard environments on all tasks, but particularly on tasks that required communication. Evolutionarily, these findings may reinforce the idea that communication abilities in humans may be more socially supported than other cognitive processes.

Acknowledgements

Support for this study was provided by NIH grants NS-42867, HD-56232 and HD-60563 to W.D. Hopkins; NIH Roadmap for Biomedical Research, Grant U54, RR021813, to S. Fears and R. Woods; and NIH grants AA-11997, AA-13995 to A. J. Bennett and AA-013973 to M. Laudenslager.

References

Hopkins, W. D., Lyn, H., & Cantalupo, C. (2009). A preliminary study of volumetric and lateralized differences in the brains of chimpanzees *(Pan troglodytes)* and bonobos *(Pan paniscus). American Journal of Primatology, 71*, 1-10.

Lyn, H., Pierre, P. J., Bennett, A. J., Fears, S. C., Woods, R., & Hopkins, W. D. (2011). Planum temporale grey matter asymmetries in chimpanzees *(Pan troglodytes)*, vervet *(Chlorocebus aethiops sabaeus)*, rhesus *(Macaca mulatta)* and bonnet *(Macaca radiata)* monkeys. *Neuropsychologia*, *49,* 2004-2012.

Russell, J. L., Lyn, H., Schaeffer, J. A., & Hopkins, W. D. (in press). The role of socio-communicative rearing environments on the development of social and physical cognition in apes. *Developmental Science.*

DYNAMIC EXPRESSION OF CADHERINS CONTROLS VOCAL LEARNING

EIJI MATSUNAGA[1], KENTA SUZUKI[2], RYOKO NAKAGAWA[3], TOHRU KUROTANI[2], KAZUO OKANOYA[4]

[1]Lab for Symbolic Cognitive Development, RIKEN Brain Science Institute, Hirosawa 2-1 Wako, Saitama 351-0198, JAPAN; [2]JST, ERATO, Okanoya Emotional Information Project, Hirosawa 2-1 Wako, Saitama 351-0115, JAPAN, [3]Grad. Sch. of Biomedical Sciences, Hiroshima Univ., Kasumi 1-2-3, Hiroshima 734-8551, JAPAN, [4]Dep. of Life Sciences, Grad. Sch. of Arts and Sciences University of Tokyo, Komaba 3-8-1, Meguro, Tokyo 153-8902, JAPAN

Vocal learning is a fundamental human ability. Since songbirds learn their vocalization through imitation during their juvenile stage as well, they have been used as good model animals in the study of the neural basis of human verbal learning (Bolhuis et al., 2011). Numerous anatomical and physiological studies have shown that songbirds have a neural network called the 'song system' that is specialized for vocal learning and production. However, although there have been important discoveries (Fisher & Scharff, 2009), it still remains largely unknown what molecular mechanisms regulate the vocal learning and production of songbirds. To explore molecular mechanisms of avian vocal learning, we performed *in situ* hybridization screening and found that type-II cadherins show song nuclei-related expressions in Bengalese finches. Cadherins are cell adhesion molecules belonging to the cadherin superfamily that are expressed widely in a variety of tissues (Takeichi, 2007). Among them, type-II cadherins show neural circuit-related expressions. During the vocal learning process, birds first listen to the father's song (sensory learning stage), then practice singing by themselves (sensorimotor learning stage), and finally copy the father's song. Interestingly, we found that type-II cadherin expressions are switched in the robust nucleus of arcopallium (RA) from *cadherin-7* (*Cad7*)-positive to *cadherin-6B* (*Cad6B*)-positive during the phase from sensory to sensorimotor learning. Since the expression switching of cadherins was strongly related with vocal development, we hypothesized that this cadherin expression switching is involved in vocal learning and production. To address this possibility, next, we performed overexpression experiments of *Cad7* in the RA nucleus of juvenile or adult finches with a lentiviral vector system, and analyzed the effects on vocal production with various acoustic characteristics. Although GFP-overexpressing control birds showed no defects, overexpression of *Cad7* in the juvenile and the adult stages resulted in severe defects in vocal production. In both cases, harmonic sounds typically seen in the adult Bengalese finch songs were particularly affected. Furthermore, to investigate mechanisms regulating vocal production, we performed electrophysiological and morphological analysis of cadherin function in rat hippocampal cultured neurons. Cad6 increased but Cad7 decreased frequency of miniature excitatory postsynaptic current and the number of dendritic spines. Thus, cadherins may control vocal production, particularly harmonic sounds, probably by modulating neuronal morphology and activity of the RA nucleus. It appears that the switching of cadherin expressions from sensory to sensorimotor learning stage enhances vocal production ability to make various types of vocalization that is essential for sensorimotor learning in a trial and error manner. On the other hand, we found that cadherin knockout mice showed vocal production defects. It has been proposed that protocadherin is involved in human cerebral asymmetry and language (Williams et al., 2006). Thus, our results support the notions that some molecular mechanisms of vocal learning (e.g. FoxP2 and cadherin superfamily) are shared among various species from birds to humans.

References

Bolhuis, J.J., Okanoya, K. & Scharff, C. (2010) Twitter evolution: converging mechanisms in birdsong and human speech. *Nature Review Neuroscience 11*, 747-759.

Fisher, S.E. & Scharff, C. (2009) FOXP2 as a molecular window into speech and language. *Trends in Genetics 25*, 166-177.

Takeichi, M. (2007) The cadherin superfamily in neuronal connections and interactions. *Nature Review Neuroscience 8*, 11–20.

Williams, N.A., Close, J.P., Giouzeli, M. & Crow, T.J. (2006) Accelerated evolution of Protocadherin11XY; a candidate gene-pair for cerebral asymmetry and language. *Amer J Med Genet* 141B, 623-633.

SIMULATING THE EFFECTS OF CULTURAL COADAPTATION ON RATES OF ENDOGENOUS AND EXOGENOUS LANGUAGE CHANGE

LUKE MCCROHON
Graduate School of Information Science and Technology,
The University of Tokyo, Bunkyo-Ku, Tokyo, 113-0033, Japan
luke.mccrohon@gmail.com

1. Introduction

I have previously argued (McCrohon, 2011) that cultural evolution operating on languages will lead to the coadaptation of their parts, making those parts easier to learn/use in combination. Furthermore, I argued that in the case of lexical items, differences in the coadaptation potential of word classes may partially explain observed patterns of lexical diffusion (Haugen, 1950). My argument focused on the cultural selection pressures faced by newly borrowed words, and was based on the complexity hypothesis of evolutionary biology (Jain, Rivera, & Lake, 1999) which offers an explaination of analogous patterns of horizontal gene transfer between biological species (Rivera, Rain, Moore, & Lake, 1995).

In the current paper I build on my earlier work and suggest cultural coadaptation not only affects rates of contact induced exogenous change, but also influences rates of language internal endogenous change. To explore both these hypotheses, I develop an agent based simulation of lexical transmission featuring coadaptation that includes both endogenous and exogenous language change.

If, as I claim, coadaptation affects rates of language change, this has consequences for both the cultural evolution of languages and the biological evolution of the language faculty due to its coevolutionary interdependence. For example, Christiansen and Chater (2008) have argued that cultural change proceeds too quickly for genes to adapt to. But if, highly coadapted aspects of language prove resistant to change, they may provide stable targets for biological adaptation.

2. Computational Model

The simulation model is built from a population of probabilistic lexical learners whose learning probability is partially determined by the degree of similarity between their learning target and words already in their lexicon. This is intended to model analogical learning, a process whereby existing memories are used to enhance the learning of new information. This mechanism introduces a bias into the learning process which allows co-adaptation between lexical items.

When subjected to iterated learning, populations of these agents gradually evolve arbitrary linguistic conventions comparable to those seen in real languages. Agents are configured in such a way that even following the establishment of these conventions, a certain level of endogenous change will continue, meaning that conventions never became completely fixed. The agents were arranged differently as described in each of the simulations outlined below.

3. Simulations

The first simulation considered endogenous change in a single fully connected population of agents and was used to understand basic simulation behavior. Results largely conformed to my initial hypothesis, but did reveal the importance of a number of extra-linguistic parameters on simulation behaviour.

The second simulation allowed separate connected populations to co-adapt in isolation before bringing them into communicative contact where their rates of borrowing were observed. Various restriction were placed on the coadaptation process, and I will discuss those which proved interesting.

The third simulation investigated whether an observation made by Aikhenvald and Dixon (2006), that diffusion is more likely to occur between structurally similar languages, also applies to populations of my agents. A single population was allowed to co-adapt before being divided into sub-populations, which were then isolated from each other. Following various periods of isolation, sub-populations were brought back into contact, and the rates of diffusion were observed.

For each simulation, results will be presented and briefly discussed in relation to how well they match observed patterns of linguistic change. A possible physiological experiment on linguistic co-adaptation will also be briefly suggested.

References

Aikhenvald, A., & Dixon, R. (2006). *Grammars in contact: a cross-linguistic typology.* Oxford University Press.

Christiansen, M. H., & Chater, N. (2008). Language as shaped by the brain. *Behavioral and Brain Sciences*, *31*(5), 489-509.

Haugen, E. (1950). The analysis of linguistic borrowing. *Language*, *26*(2), 210-231.

Jain, R., Rivera, M. C., & Lake, J. A. (1999). Horizontal gene transfer among genomes: The complexity hypothesis. *Proceedings of the National Academy of Sciences*, *96*(7), 3801-3806.

McCrohon, L. (2011). The generalized complexity hypothesis and diffusion between culturally coadapted systems. In *Proceedings of the 23rd meeting of the human behavior and evolution society.* Montpellier, France.

Rivera, M. C., Rain, R., Moore, J. E., & Lake, J. A. (1995). Genomic evidence for two functionally distinct gene classes. *Proceedings of the National Academy of Sciences*, *95*(11), 6239-6244.

THE DROSOPHILA FOXP GENE IS REQUIRED FOR OPERANT SELF-LEARNING: IMPLICATIONS FOR THE EVOLUTION OF LANGUAGE

E. MENDOZA[1], J. COLOMB[2], J. RYBAK[3], H-J PFLÜGER[2], T. ZARS[4], C. SCHARFF[1], B. BREMBS[2]

[1] *Inst. Biol. – Behavioral Biology , Freie Universität Berlin, Berlin,14195, Germany*

[2] *Inst. Biol. – Neurobiology , Freie Universität Berlin, Berlin,14195, Germany*

[3] *Neuroethology, Max-Planck Institute for Chemical Ecology, Jena, 07745, Germany*

[4] *Biological Sciences, University of Missoury – Columbia, Columbia, MO 65211, USA*

The Forkhead Box P2 (FOXP2) transcription factor is the first gene discovered to be involved in the development of speech and language. Vocal learning has been classified as a form of operant learning (Skinner, 1957): first exploratory, highly variable actions are being initiated (i.e., babbling or subsong) and then sensory feedback shapes the initiation of future behaviour, reducing its variability (i.e., crystallised song, language). In what may appear at first to be a very superficial analogy, "mere homonyms, with at most a vague similarity of meaning" (Chomsky, 1959), operant self-learning in tethered flying *Drosophila* mimics these features of vocal learning: the animal first initiates highly variable, exploratory actions, then sensory feedback shapes the initiation of future behaviour, reducing its variability.

In the operant self-learning paradigm that we used (Wolf & Heisenberg, 1991; Brembs & Plendl, 2008; Brembs, 2011), the tethered fly's attempts to turn are measured by a torque meter and divided into two domains, roughly corresponding to 'left' and 'right' turns, respectively. Fixed in space in a featureless environment, the fly alternates between turning directions in a highly variable, random-like fashion (Maye et al., 2007). Making punishment by an infrared heat beam contingent on one set of manoeuvres (e.g., right turning attempts), leads to a reduction in the variability of the behaviour as the fly restricts its turning manoeuvres to the unpunished side (i.e., left turning attempts). This reduction outlasts the application of the heat beam after a given training period and the flies restrict their yaw torque to the previously unpunished side, even when the heat is permanently switched off. Importantly, this self-learning paradigm contains no external predictive cues. If such cues are added, the self-learning paradigm turns into a world-learning paradigm where the external cues are predominantly learned, instead of the fly's own behaviour (Brembs & Plendl, 2008).

The four different FoxP genes in vertebrates probably arose from serial duplications of a single ancestral FoxP gene after the separation from the invertebrate clades. The invertebrate FoxP orthologue corresponds most closely to the ancestral form of the gene at the base of the bilateria (Santos et al., 2011), thus lending itself to investigating the depth of the functional conservation among the members of the FoxP gene family. Mutant analysis and RNAi-mediated knockdown of the *Drosophila* orthologue, *dFoxP,* revealed its necessity for operant self-learning (including habit formation) but not for operant world-learning, in which no motor learning occurs. Furthermore, we were able to detect subtle alterations in the brain anatomy of FoxP^{3955} mutant flies, including a reduced volume of the optic glomeruli. We are currently in the process of determining whether this developmental *dFoxP* function is causally related to the learning deficit, or whether *dFoxP* activity is also required during learning.

Our results are consistent with the hypothesis that the FoxP-dependent component of language evolved from an ancestral operant self-learning mechanism. The homology between invertebrate FoxP and its descendant genes, together with the similarities between habit formation and birdsong crystallisation (Costa, 2011) leads us to postulate that habit formation in vertebrates may also be engaging this same mechanism. Our discovery traces one of the evolutionary roots of language back to the last common ancestor of vertebrates and invertebrates, the 'Urbilaterian', more than half a billion years before the first word was ever spoken, a remarkable exaptation.

References

Brembs B (2011) Spontaneous decisions and operant conditioning in fruit flies. *Behav. Proc.* 87:157-64.

Brembs B, Plendl W (2008) Double dissociation of PKC and AC manipulations on operant and classical learning in *Drosophila. Curr. Biol.* 18:1168-1171.

Chomsky N (1959) *Review of Skinner's Verbal Behavior.* Language 35:26-58.

Costa RM (2011) A selectionist account of de novo action learning. *Curr. Opin. Neurobiol.* 21:579-86.

Maye A, Hsieh C-H, Sugihara G, Brembs B (2007) Order in spontaneous behavior. *PLoS ONE* 2:e443.

Santos ME, Athanasiadis A, Leitão AB, DuPasquier L, Sucena E (2011) Alternative splicing and gene duplication in the evolution of the FoxP gene subfamily. *Mol. Biol. Evol.* 28:237-47.

Skinner BF (1957) *Verbal Behavior.* Copley Publishing Group.

Wolf R, Heisenberg M (1991) Basic organization of operant behavior as revealed in *Drosophila* flight orientation. J. *Comp. Physiol. A* 169:699-705.

THE EVOLUTION OF MISCOMMUNICATION

GREGORY J. MILLS

Psychology Dept., Stanford University, 450 Serra Mall, Stanford, CA 94305, USA
gjmills@stanford.edu

A common theme running through models of dialogue is how they contrast their accounts with the "communication-as-transfer-model" (Clark, 1997). This model idealizes the *perfect delivery* involving a hearer recovering exactly the same representation intended by the speaker. Deviations from representational parity are explained by "noise" in the communication channel, e.g. disfluencies, restarts, pauses, errors or other signals of miscommunication.

However, empirical investigation of dialogue has demonstrated that this "noise" consists of mechanisms that assist mutual intelligibility: interlocutors use filled pauses such as "umm" and "uhh" to signal the length of upcoming pauses in an utterance (Clark and Fox Tree 2002), and also to guide referent identification (Arnold, Kam and Tanenhaus, 2007). Moreover, interlocutors' use of feedback mechanisms for resolving miscommunication, such as "What?", "ok?" lead to the development of referring conventions that are more concise (Krauss and Weinheimer, 1967; Clark, 1996), more abstract (Schwartz, 1995; Healey 1997), more systematized (Galantucci, 2005; Mills and Healey, 2006), more stable and more arbitrary (Garrod, Fay et al., 2007). There is also evidence that clarification mechanisms play a role in language change (Healey, 1997).

A central feature of these dialogue mechanisms is that they place sequential constraints on interlocutors' contributions (Schegloff, 2007). However, although pre-existing sequential structures (e.g. adjacency pairs) have been studied in great detail, there has been a paucity of studies that directly investigate how sequential organization in dialogue is both established and sustained.

To address this issue, we report a collaborative task which presents participants with the recurrent co-ordination problem of ordering their actions and utterances into a single coherent sequence: Pairs of participants communicate via a text-based chat-tool (Healey and Mills 2006). Each participant's computer also displays a task window containing a list of randomly generated words. Solving the task requires participants to combine their lists of words into a single alphabetically ordered list. To select a word, participants type the word preceded with "/". To ensure collaboration, participants can only select words displayed on the other participant's screen and vice versa. Note that this task is trivial for an individual participant. However, for pairs of participants, this task presents the coordination problem of interleaving their selections correctly: participants cannot select each other's words, words can't be selected twice, and the words need to be selected in the correct order (See Mills, 2011, for a more detailed description of the task).

Despite the task only permitting a single logical solution (and being referentially transparent – the words are the referents), participants develop group-specific routines for both signalling and resolving instances of miscommunication. Importantly, we show how this development does not occur through explicit negotiation: in the initial trials, participants' attempts to explicitly negotiate these routines more often than not prove unsuccessful (cf. Pickering and Garrod 2004, who observed similar patterns in a series of maze game experiments).

Instead, we demonstrate how these routines emerge tacitly as a consequence of interlocutors' collaborative attempts to deal with the sequential co-ordination problem presented by the task. Drawing on how interlocutors engage in resolving these co-ordination problems, we argue that these collaborative routines operate normatively, having become conventionalized by the interlocutors.

References

Clark, H. H. (1996). Using language. Cambridge: Cambridge University Press.

Galantucci, B. (2005). An experimental study of the emergence of human communication systems. *Cognitive Science,* 29(5), 737-767

Garrod, S., Fay, N., Lee, J., Oberlander, J., & MacLeod, T. (2007). Foundations of Representation: Where Might Graphical Symbol Systems Come From? *Cognitive Science: A Multidisciplinary Journal*, 31(6), 961–987.

Healey, P.G.T. (1997). Expertise or expert-ese: The emergence of task-oriented sub-languages. In Proceedings of the 19th Conference of Cog Sci,. Stanford.

Healey, P. G. T. & Mills, G. (2006). Participation, precedence and co-ordination. In Proceedings of the 28th Conference of CogSci, Canada.

Krauss, R. M. and Weinheimer, S. (1966). Concurrent feedback, confirmation and the encoding of referents in verbal communication. JPSP, 4 (3), 343–346

Mills, G. J. (2011). The emergence of procedural conventions in dialogue. In Proceedings of the 33rd Annual Conference of Cog Sci.. Boston. USA

Pickering, M. J. and Garrod, S. (2004). Towards a mechanistic psychology of dialogue. Behavioural and Brain Sciences, 27(2), 169–190.

Schegloff, E. A. (2007). Sequence Organization in Interaction: Volume 1: A Primer in Conversation Analysis. Cambridge University Press.

THE GRICEAN INTENTIONAL STRUCTURE OF APE GESTURAL COMMUNICATION

RICHARD MOORE

Department of Developmental and Comparative Psychology, Max Planck Institute for Evolutionary Anthropology, Deutscher Platz 6, Leipzig, 04103, Germany

Tomasello (2008) claims that that, in contrast to human utterances, ape gestures are not Gricean in character. Against this account, I argue that there are good reasons for thinking that they are, and that recognising this enables the adoption of an elegant account of the evolutionary trajectory from early hominid gestures to human language.

1. The Claim and Arguments for it

In recent decades, a wealth of observational and empirical studies have informed our understanding of the gestural communication of great apes (many are summarised in Tomasello & Call, 2007). Interest in these gestures has been motivated, in part, by the hypothesis that early hominid gestures are a more plausible ancestor of human language than vocalisations (Tomasello, 2008). However, while it has been widely recognised that ape gestures are intentional – in a way that their vocalisations may not be – relatively little consideration has been given to the appropriate intentional framework for their characterisation.

Human communication possesses a distinctive, embedded intentional character that was first described by Paul Grice (1957): one not only intends (1) that one's interlocutor produces some response *r*, but also (2) that she recognise that this is one's intention. Since the cognition of Gricean intentions has been thought to require 'theory of mind' abilities that are beyond the ken of non-linguistic creatures, this model has not been extended to the explanation of ape gestures. Indeed, Tomasello (2008) explicitly argues that ape gestures are not Gricean - without offering an alternative model. However, if we are interested in the cognitive processes that support communication, its intentional structure cannot be overlooked; and by identifying a framework suitable for characterising ape gestures, a lacuna in our theorising about language evolution could be filled.

I argue that with only a few minor adjustments, the Gricean framework can be used for this purpose; and that reasons for thinking Gricean intentions too demanding for characterising ape gestures are largely based on intellectualised readings of what is required for their cognition. In particular, cognising Gricean intent requires neither the ability to pass a false belief test (contra Breheny, 2005), nor the ability to entertain fourth order meta-representations (contra Sperber, 2000). Consistent with Neale's (1992) account, I will argue that it is sufficient for acting with Gricean intent that one produce a combination of two actions, which I call *vehicles of content* and *acts of ostension*. While a vehicle of content (e.g., a sentence or gesture) expresses the speaker's communicative goal, an act of ostension (e.g., eye contact) guides an interlocutor's attention onto the speaker's production of that vehicle. When produced together, these actions enact, respectively, the first and second clauses of Grice's analysis of meaning.

Drawing on recent studies (including Liebal et al., 2004), I will argue that ape gestures contain aspects that are interpretable as both vehicles of content and acts of ostension; such that they are well modelled by a Gricean analysis. While human utterances may differ from ape gestures in a number of cognitively important respects – not least, their compositionality; the complexity of their messages; and the motives with which they are produced – these differences are not relevant to intentional structure. Moreover, by positing a Gricean intentional structure as a starting point for characterising the evolutionary trajectory from early hominid gestures to human language, we avail ourselves of an elegant tool against which to plot the emergence of these distinctively human traits.

References

Breheny, R. (2006). Communication and folk psychology. *Mind & Language, 21(1)*, 74-107.

Grice, P. (1957). Meaning. Reprinted in P. Grice (1991), *Studies in the Way of Words* (pp.213-223). London: Harvard University Press.

Liebal, K., Pika, S., Call, J. & Tomasello, M. (2004). To move or not to move: How apes adjust to the intentional states of others. *Interaction Studies*, 5(2), 119-219.

Neale, S. (1992). Paul Grice and the philosophy of language. *Linguistics & Philosophy, 15*, 509-559.

Sperber, D. (2000). Metarepresentations in an evolutionary perspective. In D. Sperber (ed.) *Metarepresentations: A Multidisciplinary Perspective* (pp.117-137). Oxford: Oxford University Press.

Tomasello, M. (2008). *Origins of Human Communication*. Cambridge, MA: MIT Press.

Tomasello, M. & Call, J. (2007). *The Gestural Communication of Apes and Monkeys*. NJ: Erlbaum.

CEREBRAL LATERALITY FOR PROSODY PROCESSING IN HUMAN NEONATES: EVIDENCE FROM MULTICHANNEL NEAR-INFRARED SPECTROSCOPY

NOZOMI NAOI, YUTAKA FUCHINO, MINORU SHIBATA

Japan Agency of Science and Technology, Honcho 4-1-8, Kawaguchi, Saitama 332-0012, Japan

MASAHIKO KAWAI

Department of Pediatrics, Kyoto University Hospital, 54 Shogoin Sakyo, Kyoto 606-8507, Japan

YUKUO KONISHI

Center for Baby Science, Doshisha University, Kizugawa-shi, Kyoto 619-0225, Japan

KAZUO OKANOYA

Department of Life Sciences, Graduate School of Arts and Sciences, The University of Tokyo, Tokyo 153-8902, Japan

MASAKO MYOWA-YAMAKOSHI

Graduate School of Education, Kyoto University, Yoshida-Honmachi, Sakyo-ku, Kyoto 606-8501, Japan

Infant-directed speech (IDS) is important for human caregiver-infant interactions and may have evolutionary roots (Falk, 2004). However, few studies have examined the neural substrates underlying processing IDS in human neonates. We examined cerebral responses of full-term human neonates to prosodic modifications in infant-directed speech (IDS) by direct comparison with adult-directed speech (ADS). Generally, IDS is higher in pitch and has a wider pitch range than ADS.

A recent developed non-invasive optical imaging technique, multichannel Near Infrared Spectroscopy (NIRS), allows us to measure higher temporal changes in hemoglobin concentration and oxygen saturation in multiple brain regions simultaneously. This method can be used to assess healthy newborn infants without sedation. Using, multichannel NIRS, we examined whether particular brain regions are specifically involved in the processing of prosodic modifications in IDS.

Thirty healthy full-term newborn infants participated. In NIRS measurement, two sets of 3 x 10 probes (94 recording channels) were used to record activations in the frontal, temporal, and occipital regions (Figure 1A). A block design was used, and the two experimental conditions (IDS and ADS) alternated with a control condition (pink noise).

The results showed that increased activations were observed predominantly in infants' right frontal-temporal area when they listened to IDS rather than to ADS (Figure 1B). This rightward activation to prosody in speech is consistent with previous imaging studies in older infants.

Prenatal exposure to auditory stimulation in utero may be one of the possible origins of the cerebral asymmetries in human neonates. Even in the uterus, preserved prosodic properties of speech are accessible to the fetus (e.g., Benzaquen et al., 1990). Thus, it is possible that substantial auditory experience in utero has already shaped cortical processes associated with prosodic processing. In addition, postnatal experience during the first few days after birth may also influence brain activity in response to IDS.

Our findings suggest that the localized region of the right hemisphere is involved in prosodic processing at a very early developmental stage.

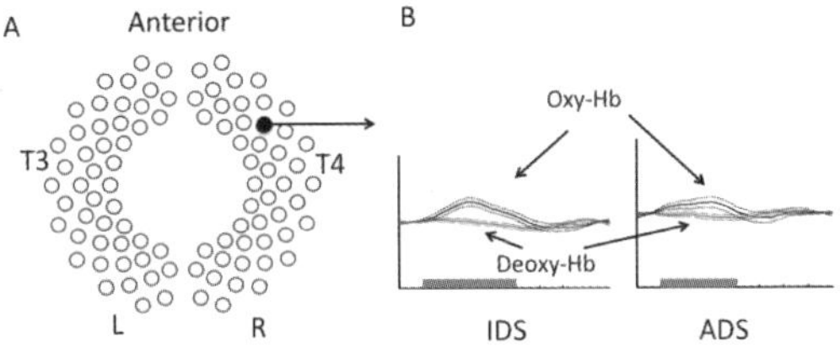

Figure 1. A. NIRS probe and channel settings, B. Grand averaged time courses of oxygenated-(Oxy-Hb) and deoxygenated-hemoglobin (Deoxy-Hb) changes in IDS and ADS condition.

Acknowledgements

This work was supported by Japan Agency of Science and Technology, ERATO, "Okanoya Emotional Information Project"

References

Benzaquen, S., Gagnon, R., Hunse, C., & Foreman, J. (1990). The intrauterine sound environment of the human fetus during labor. *American Journal of Obstetrics & Gynecology 163*, 484-490.

Cooper, R. P., & Aslin, R. N. (1990). Preference for infant-directed speech in the first month after birth. *Child Development, 61,* 1584-1595.

Falk, D. (2004). Prelinguistic evolution in early hominins: Whence motherese? *Behavioral and Brain Sciences 27*, 491-541.

THE IRREDUCIBLE SEMANTIC COMMUNICATIVE DRIVE: IMAGINATION AND CULTURE BEYOND THE HANDS

RAFAEL NÚÑEZ

Department of Cognitive Science, University of California, San Diego
9500 Gilman Drive , La Jolla, CA 92093, U.S.A.

In his critique of Theodosius Dobzhansky's influential work, the prominent evolutionary biologist Richard Lewontin wrote: "Dobzhansky's construction of the problem of speciation as solely the problem of reproductive isolation was a piece of scientific synecdoche, substituting the process of reproductive isolation for the speciation process in its entirety. It is a testimony to the influence that *Genetics and the Origin of Species* has wielded over 60 years that we continue to study the speciation process without reference to the world that organisms construct and occupy". With this remarkable passage, Lewontin addressed a crucial issue in the study of evolutionary biology, in particular, and science in general: The risks of *unwarranted* reductionism. Reductionism—the practice of studying a complex phenomenon in terms of simpler ones taken to stand for the former *without loss of explanatory power*—is an essential part of science. But, as Lewontin warns us, it can lead to profoundly misleading oversimplifications. Reductionism must be practiced with care, especially in the study of evolution, because most of the phenomena under scrutiny are multifactorial, and cannot be fully reproduced and tested under laboratory conditions.

The study of language evolution seems particularly at risk, since, unlike other domains in evolution research, the *practice* of language has neither left clear fossil records nor DNA data. Despite this, the field has been marked by unwarranted reductionism and a version of Lewontin's "scientific synecdoche"—taking "language" primarily to be syntax, lexicons and/or speech. Although convenient, such reductions can be misleading: phonation, for instance, is not necessary for language as there are many non-phonated languages around the world. As a consequence, meaning and communication have been largely underemphasized, doomed to a secondary status. Fortunately, some important proposals have partially remedied the situation. One line of research, focusing on the role of gesture, has suggested that early forms of communication may have moved from "simple gestures"—finger pointing and pantomimes—to conventionalized symbols. But even these gestures are not as "simple" as they seem, requiring a sophisticated coordination of cognitive mechanisms and bodily actions. A close inspection of contemporary speech-gesture co-production—a human universal—reveals subtle elements that, I argue, are crucial for addressing the question of language evolution in a non-reductionistic way. I defend this claim by drawing on relevant literature and studies we conducted in the lab and in fieldwork carried out in the remote mountains of Papua New Guinea and in the Andes.

As many reductionistic approaches have failed to address *actual linguistic practice*, critical multimodal phenomena have been left aside. Consider these facts: (1) children begin to produce intentional and communicative-rich deictic gestures before they produce even single words. The development of speech and gesture is tightly interconnected. (2) Despite the sophistication of contemporary language, some fully grammatical utterances demand—even today—a *synchronized obligatory bodily action* (SOBA). Such is the case with an ancient class of deictic words, demonstratives, which are universal and etymologically not analyzable. Utterances like *take this and put it over there* require a co-produced motor action (e.g., eye and/or face movement, manual pointing). (3) In real-world settings, such SOBAs—although co-produced with a restricted number of demonstrative words—do not have fixed morphology (unlike lexemes or emblematic gestures), and often opportunistically recruit many different parts of the body as articulators (e.g., head, feet). (4) SOBAs are culturally shaped. The so-called "canonical" (finger) pointing does not have a universal morphology: some cultures exhibit, in ordinary circumstances, lip- or nose-pointing, where the morphology is sometimes even modulated by grammatical roles. (5) And, crucially, pointings commonly do not refer to real-world referents but to (apparently simple) complex conceptual construals that, mediated culturally, make use of cognitive mechanisms for precise imagination such as conceptual metaphor (e.g., pointing at "tomorrow" in front of the speaker) and metonymy (pointing at someone's house while uttering "him"). This imaginative capacity—uniquely human—underlies much of symbol and convention production, and can generate infinitely many sharable stable outcomes. Since language most likely evolved in a scenario characterized by real-time, short-distance, and multimodal one-to-one/few interaction, these facts, taken together, point, beyond sequential discrete symbol processing, to the irreducibility of the semantic communicative drive in the co-evolutionary process that brought language into being.

STRUCTURAL REANALYSIS OF RESPONSES TO MUSICAL TONALITY: COMMONALITY WITH THE NEURAL PROCESSING OF EMOTION IN LANGUAGE

HIDEFUMI OHMURA[1, 2], TAKAYUKI HAMANO[1, 2], TOMASZ M. RUTKOWSKI[2, 3], HIROKO TERASAWA[3], KAZUO OKANOYA[1, 2, 4], KIYOSHI FURUKAWA[5]

1. Japan Science Technology Agency, ERATO, Okanoya Emotional Information Project, Wako, Saitama, 351-0198

2. RIKEN Brain Science Institute, Wako, Saitama, 351-0198, Japan

3. University of Tsukuba, Tsukuba, Ibaraki, 305-8577, Japan

4. The University of Tokyo, Meguro, Tokyo, 153-8902, Japan

5. Tokyo University of the Arts, Toride, Ibaraki, Japan

Background:

Music and language are both regarded as a communication tool with narrative and grammar, which can carry also emotional messages among people. Mithen (2006) and Rousseau (2000) formulated a hypothesis that language is evolved from music as a communication tool, since musical structures are similar in emotional aspects to metrical structures of language. In investigating this hypothesis, we focus on musical tonality (major/minor scale) that is one of the emotional grammatical elements in music. We analyze listener's ERPs while listening to major/minor monophonic melodies, which were composed for this experiment, and discuss the commonality in the neural processing of language and musical tonality.

Experiment:

Participants: N=5, who are professional or amateur musicians.

Musical Stimuli: Four types of monophonic melody; each type has two tonalities of C major and C minor scale. All of the melodies consist of eight bars by four beats. Each note is a quarter one and a second long. The timbre of the notes is composed based on simple sine waves.

Equipment: 32 channels active electrodes electroencephalograph manufactured by Brain Products.

Procedure: After the EEG electrodes setup on participants heads, they are requested to rest for three minutes. Next they then listen to musical stimuli one by one. The intervals between stimuli are 15 seconds. The orders of stimuli are random.

Analysis: (1) The recorded EEG is segmented into epochs from -200 to 800 ms based on the onsets of each tone. (2) The epochs are separated into two groups labeled as *diff* and *comm*. The *diff* tones are those that have the different pitch between major and minor scales. *comm* tones are those that have the same common pitch. (3) Finally ERPs in each group are averaged.
Results: We adopt a region of interest (ROI) approach that segments 32 channels into seven regions: #1 left anterior; #2 anterior; #3 right anterior; #4 center; #5 left posterior; #6 posterior; #7 right posterior. We compare the averaged responses between *diff* and *comm* at N1 (90 ms), P1 (180 ms), 400 ms and 600 ms ERP latencies using t-tests. As a result of the analysis a significant difference between *comm* and *diff* for N1 latency has been observed for ROI #3 and #7. For 600 ms latency significant difference in ROI #2, #3, #5 and #6 was elucidated.

Discussion:

It is known already that brain responses during language processing, especially ERP's 600 ms latency, indicates not only a reflection of syntactic deviance reanalysis and the structure, but also a load of an integrated syntax processing (Ueno & Kluender 2003). Similarly, in case of music, ERP's 600 ms latency difference is a sign of structural reanalysis and repair (Koelsch & Siebel 2006). Our experiment's results showed the significant differences between major and minor scale at 600 ms latency indicating participants' reanalysis of musical structures. A similar result may be obtained in a linguistic experiment, because the reanalysis has been confirmed as both linguistic and musical feature. This result shall account for linguistic prosody with musical tonality, such as a sigh-like contour represented in minor scale and a sign of cheerful greeting represented in major scale. With such contours and signs, emotional elements are embedded in musical tonality. Our experiment results suggest that there is a commonality in the neural processing of linguistic prosody and musical tonality, in decoding emotional expression. If these neural processing are primitive, this commonality suggests that a language and music may have a same origin. This experimental result may serve as a support for the hypothesis that language and music have a common origin in prosody and tonality.

References

Mithen, S. (2006), The Singing Neanderthals: The Origins of Music and Language, Mind and Body. Harvard University Press.

Rousseau, J.-J. (2000). Essai sur l'Origine des Langues. Nizet.

Ueno, M. & Kluender, R. (2003). Event-related brain indices of Japanese scrambling. *Brain and Language, Vol 86,* 243-271.

Koelsch, S & Siebel, W. A. (2005). Towads a neural basis of music perception. *TRENDS in Cognitive Sciences, Vol.9 No. 12*. 578-584.

FAILURE OF OPERANT DISCRIMINATION LEARNING OF SIMPLE ALGEBRIC CONCEPT IN A SONGBIRD

KAZUO OKANOYA, KENTA SUZUKI, YOSHIMASA SEKI

Department of Cognitive and Behavioral Science, The University of Tokyo, Komaba, Meguro-ku, Tokyo 153-0189, Japan; JST ERATO Okanoya Emotional Information Project, Wako, Saitama 351-0198 Japan

Several studies suggest that acquisition of sequential rules may be related with language learning. An artificial grammar of AAB versus ABB is readily acquired by children of 8 month (Marcus, Vijayan, Bandi Rao, & Vishton, 1999). We asked whether this faculty of simple sequential rule learning is related with language faculty or it represents more general faculty by examining this ability in songbirds.

The Bengalese finch is a species of songbirds with finite-state song phonological syntax (Okanoya, 2004). We trained Bengalese finches to respond when AAB was given but withhold responding when ABB was given (and vice-versa). In the first experiment, birds were trained by stimuli composed of male calls (M) and female calls (F). Birds were trained to peck the observation key when it is ready for discrimination task. When the key was pecked stimuli either composed of AAB pattern or ABB pattern was presented. Half of the birds were assigned so that pecking for AAB resulted in food reinforcement but pecking for ABB resulted in timeout. The remaining half was trained with the reversed contingency.

Probe tests examined whether the discrimination is based on sequential rule or phonology. For example, a bird was initially trained to peck a key for AAB=MMF (male, male, female) and not to peck for ABB=MFF. The bird was then examined with probe test comprising of MMF, MFF, FFM (=AAB), and FMM (=ABB). The bird should respond for FFM but not for FMM if it was attending the sequential rule. Result was that bird responded to FMM and FFM almost equally. Results suggest that the bird was responding to phonological similarity of the stimulus, but not the sequential rule.

The first experiment might have biased birds to respond for phonology, but not sequential rule. To overcome this, we designed next experiment in a different strategy. In the second experiment, AAB and ABB rules were substantiated in various combinations of song notes. Several songs recorded from male Bengalese finches were analyzed and 12 distinctive song notes were identified. These were combined to make AAB or ABB pattern.

Six birds were trained with GO/NOGO task, each with unique combinations of song notes. When one set of AAB and ABB discrimination was learned, we introduced another set with different song notes. We continued this to see whether birds acquire a concept of stimulus configuration and learning might take shorter as sessions progressed. This task is called as "learning set formation" in behavioral psychology (Harlow, 1949). Our aim was to examine whether birds can form learning set of ABB versus AAB pattern.

We set the criterion for learning to be more than 80% correct responses in two successive sessions. One session comprised of 30 GO and 30 NOGO trials. All birds acquired the discrimination of the initial set within 25-100 sessions and one of the birds progressed up to sixth set of stimuli. Nevertheless, number of sessions required for learning did not decrease in none of the six birds as experiment progressed with different set of stimuli. Results indicate that learning set was not formed in the subjects, suggesting that the algebraic concept of AAB versus ABB was not readily learned by birds.

The fist experiment asked whether the birds pay more attention to the phonological or the syntactical feature of the stimuli. The second experiment explicitly trained birds to acquire the algebraic concept. Both resulted in the failure of the concept formation for the sequential rule. While there remains a possibility that the use of natural vocal tokens might interfere the learning process, the present study cautions design of the artificial grammar learning experiments in animals. To discern that is truly based on the rule rather than phonology, stimuli should always be unique in test stimuli.

Acknowledgements

Work supported by Kakenhi (Kiban A), RIKEN BSI, and JST Okanoya Emotional Information Project all awarded to KO.

References

Harlow, H. F. (1949). The formation of learning sets. *Psychological review, 56*(1), 51.

Marcus, G. F., Vijayan, S., Bandi Rao, S., & Vishton, P. M. (1999). Rule learning by seven-month-old infants. *Science, 283*(5398), 77.

Okanoya, K. (2004). Song syntax in Bengalese finches: proximate and ultimate analyses. *Advances in the Study of Behaviour, 34*, 297-346.

RODENT ULTRASONIC VOCALIZATION AS A MODEL OF HUMAN SPEECH: A MOLECULAR AND CELLULAR VIEW

NORIKO OSUMI

Division of Developmental Neuroscience, Tohoku University School of Medicine, 2-1, Seiryo-machi, Aoba-ku, Sendai 980-8575, Japan

Each species has its own unique ways in communication, which is inevitably based on its biological features. It is thus difficult to consider commonality between the language of human and communication tools of other animals. Recently, more attention has been paid on ultrasonic vocalization (USV) in rodents as a communication tool in rodents. Mice and rats communicate using USV not only between mothers and pups, but also between males to females, and even between males to males (Wohr et al., 2011). A practical reason of measuring USV in rodents is to model autism and autism spectrum disorders (ASD), in which communication deficit is one of the core symptoms. Genetics of autism/ASD has recently been accelerated due to advancement of technologies (e.g., Autism Genome Project Consortium, et al, 2007). Among genes that are related to the risk for autism/ASD, we are focusing on *PAX6*, a major player in brain development (Osumi, 2001; Davis et al., 2008; Xu et al., 2008; Maekawa et al., 2009; Umeda et al., 2010). Pax6 gene encodes a transcription factor and regulates multiple target genes including those related with autism/ASD such as neuregulin3, protochadherin11, PTEN, and Foxp2 (Coutinho et al., 2011), a so-called "speech gene" identified from a large family of speech disorders (Vargha-Khadem et al., 1995; Lai et al., 2001; Pinker, 2001; Enard et al., 2002). Transcription factors, such as Pax6 and Foxp2, do not play "direct" roles in neuronal functions, but they can switch on/off other neuronal genes, thereby coordinating specific neuronal characters. Expression patterns of Pax6 and Foxp2 are regionally restricted but observed in various mouse brain regions. From literatures, they might be overlapped in specific regions such as the cerebellum and brain stem (Stoykova & Gruss, 1994: Osumi et al., 1997; Gray, 2008; Enard et al., 2009; Takahashi & Osumi, 2002, 2011). Interesting here is that these brain regions include nuclei for motor control and respiration that are crucial for regulation of USV/speech activities. Therefore, elucidating the mechanism how Pax6 and Foxp2 work in harmony during development of motor and repiratory neurons would shed light on understanding molecular and cellular features of USV in rodent toward elucidation of the origin of the human language.

References

Autism Genome Project Consortium, et al. (2007). Mapping autism risk loci using genetic linkage and chromosomal rearranfements. *Nature Genetics, 39,* 319-328.

Coutinho, P. et al. (2011). Discovery and assessment of conserved Pax6 target genes and enhacers. *Genome Research, 21,* 1349-1359.

Davis, L.K. et al. (2008). *PAX6* 3' deletion results in aniridia, autism and mental retardation. *Human Genetics, 123,* 371-378.

Enard, W. et al. (2002). Molecular evolution of *FOXP2*, a gene involved in speech and language. *Nature, 418,* 869-872.

Gray, P.A. (2008). Transcription factors and the genetic organization of brain stem respiratory neurons. *Journal of Applied Physiology, 104,* 1513-1531.

Lai, C.S. et al. (2001). A forkhead-domain gene is mutated in a severe speech and language disorder. *Nature, 413,* 519-523.

Maekawa, M. et al. (2009). A novel missense mutation (Leu46Val) of *PAX6* found in an autistic patient. *Neuroscience Letters, 462*, 267-271.

Osumi, N. (2001). The role of Pax6 in brain patterning. *Tohoku Journal of Experimental Medicine, 193,* 163-174.

Osumi, N. et al. (1997). Pax-6 is involved in the specification of hindbrain motor neuron subtype. *Development, 124,* 2961-2972.

Pinker, S. (2001). Talk of genetics and vice versa. *Nature, 413,* 456-466.

Stoykova A, & Gruss, P. (1994). Roles of Pax-genes in developing and adult brain as suggested by expression patterns. *Journal of Neuroscience, 14,* 1395-1412.

Takahashi, M. & Osumi, N. (2002). Pax6 regulates specification of ventral neuron subtypes in the hindbrain by establishing progenitor domains. *Development, 129,* 1327-1338.

Takahashi, M. & Osumi, N. (2010). Pax6 regulates boundary-cell specification in the rat hindbrain. *Mechanisms of Development, 128,* 289-302.

Umeda, T. et al. (2010). Evaluation of *Pax6* mutant rat as a model for autism. *PLoS ONE, 5*, e15500.

Vargha-Khadem, F. et al. (1995). Praxic and nonverbal cognitive deficits in a large family with a genetically transmitted speech and language disorder. *Proceedings of National Academy of Science USA, 92,* 930-933.

Wohr, M. et al. (2011). Communication impairments in mice lacking Shank1: reduced levels of ultrasonic vocalizations and sent marking behavior. *PLoS ONE, 6,* e20631.

Xu, S. et al. (2008). Characterization of 11p14-p12 deletion in WAGR syndrome by array CGH for identifying genes contributing to mental retardation and autism. *Cytogenetic and Genome Research, 122,* 181-187.

PARROTS AS MODELS FOR LANGUAGE EVOLUTION

IRENE M. PEPPERBERG

Department of Psychology, Harvard University, William James Hall, 33Kirkland Street, Cambridge, MA 02138, USA

Although most studies on language evolution focus on the primate lineage, many studies have also examined songbirds—creatures that, like humans but unlike nonhuman primates, engage in vocal learning. These birdsong studies have demonstrated striking parallels for the ontogeny and the neurological underpinnings of vocal communication in both songbirds and humans (e.g., Jarvis et al. 2005). Recently, after demonstrating psittacine vocal learning in the field, researchers have proposed that parrots might be even more appropriate models than songbirds for language evolution (e.g., Berg et al., 2011). Although interesting, the idea is not new. Over three decades of research on vocal learning, communicative capacities, and cognitive processing in parrots (e.g., reviewed in Pepperberg, 1999, 2010), both in the wild and in captivity, have provided extensive data that has mostly been ignored in terms of their value for research on language evolution. This paper provides a review of some of the relevant studies. Among the specific points that will be examined: (1) Although many researchers emphasize similarities between sensitive periods for language and song/call acquisition, in reality humans, like parrots, are open-ended learners, with the ability to acquire some new sounds and communication systems throughout life—for humans, often phonological but not usually communicative capacities may be affected by age; in contrast, few songbirds are open-ended learners. (2) Parrots, as well as songbirds and humans, engage in practice or babbling periods, wherein they experiment with the sounds that will ultimately become part of the repertoire; like children, they engage in sound play and spontaneous recombinations. Additionally, parrots, like humans, demonstrate phonological awareness and segmentation—they understand that a learned vocal code is made of individual units that can be recombined in various ways to form novel vocalizations (labels and sentence frames) to refer to novel objects/situations. (3) Furthermore, parrots, like humans, learn their vocal communication system best through extensive social interaction, during a relatively *protracted* juvenile period; and, like humans, learn the appropriate contextual, *referential* use of numerous vocalizations through social interactions with peers and adult members of their community, in which joint attention appears to play an extensive role. (4) Grey parrots, at least, demonstrate some cognitive capacities similar to those of 5-6 year old children, suggesting the existence of mental abilities needed to understand, learn, and produce complex communication (e.g., concepts such as physical exclusion that relate to linguistic mutual exclusivity; Pepperberg & Wilcox, 2000; Pepperberg et al. in prep). (5) Parrots, like both humans and songbirds, have specific brains structures that are devoted to vocal learning: Additional understanding of how any brain evolved to accommodate vocal learning might, in the future, be achieved by comparing brain structures and genetics not only of taxonomically-related avian vocal nonlearners and vocal learners but also by comparing brain structures and genetics of parrots having somewhat less capacity for *allospecific* vocal learning (e.g., keas) with those known for their large imitative repertoires (e.g., Greys).

References

Berg, K.S., Delgado, S., Cortopassi, K.A., Bessinger, S.R., & Bradbury, J.W. (2011) Vertical transmission of learned signature calls in a wild parrot. *Proceedings of the Royal Society B:* doi:10.1098/rspb.2011.0932.

Jarvis, J.D., Güntürkün, O., Bruce, L., Csillag, A., Karten, H., Kuenzel, W. et al. (2005). Avian brains and a new understanding of vertebrate evolution. *Nature Reviews Neuroscience, 6,* 151-159.

Pepperberg, I.M. (1999). *The Alex studies.* Cambridge, MA: Harvard University Press.

Pepperberg, I.M. (2010). Vocal learning in Grey parrots: A brief review of perception, production, and cross-species comparisons. *Brain & Language*, *115*, 81-91.

Pepperberg, I.M., & Wilcox, S.E. (2000). Evidence for a form of mutual exclusivity during label acquisition by Grey parrots (*Psittacus erithacus*)? *Journal of Comparative Psychology*, *114*, 219-231.

Pepperberg, I.M., Koepke, A., & Livingston, P. (in prep). Studies on exclusion in the Grey parrot (*Psittacus erithacus*).

A MODEL OF THE EVOLUTION OF FREQUENT SOCIAL COMMUNICATION

JUSTIN QUILLINAN
Language Evolution and Computation Research Unit
School of Philosophy, Psychology & Language Sciences
The University of Edinburgh
justin@ling.ed.ac.uk

Nonhuman primates monitor their social network through direct contact and observation, maintaining a model of their groups dominance hierarchy (Bergman et al., 2003). In dense populations this social monitoring may be the primary function of vigilance behaviour and should increase with group size and density (Hirsch, 2002). One widespread method of social monitoring involves individuals extracting social information from signalling interactions between conspecifics (*Social Eavesdropping*) (Peake, 2005). Information acquired in this way could reflect the group's social structure (Cheney & Seyfarth, 2005) and may also display many properties of human language (Seyfarth et al., 2005). Some species go further while eavesdropping by uttering specific vocalisations that may function as a comment on the interaction to other group members (Brumm et al., 2005).

"A crucial step in language evolution occurred when individuals came under strong selective pressure to communicate their thoughts, as opposed to simply extracting information from the calls of others" (Seyfarth et al., 2005). Language enables this further mechanism for social monitoring, allowing the exchange of social information beyond contact and observation, and may have evolved for this purpose (Dunbar, 1996). Human language use differs from the above accounts of nonhuman primate communication in certain ways: the ability to refer to individuals and events remote in space or time (*Displacement*) (Hockett, 1960); and, perhaps unique to humans (Tomasello, 1999), the tendency to frequently share thoughts and feelings with others (*Mitteilungsbedürfnis*) (Fitch, 2010).

Previous simulations have shown that larger group sizes can increase the probability of choosing to exchange social information (*Gossip*) over engaging in physical contact (*Grooming*) (Slingerland et al., 2009). They consider the trade-off between gossip and grooming in an unstructured population. I propose a computational model of communication in a structured, dynamic population of agents that monitor their social network, to show the conditions under which the frequent exchange of social information can evolve. The population consists of a number of agents embedded in a social network. Agents observe interaction events between other agents and can communicate these events to their neighbours with a certain variable probability. Agents receive fitness based on the number and quality of interactions they participate in, and knowledge of interactions that they have gained through observation or communication. In addition, this knowledge determines who the agents communicate and interact with. The model demonstrates the effect of group size and population structure on the probability of communication. Group size can be the selective pressure that drives the frequency of communication, where contact or observation is not sufficient to maintain a stable social network.

References

Bergman, T. J., Beehner, J. C., Cheney, D. L., & Seyfarth, R. M. (2003). Hierarchical Classification by Rank and Kinship in Baboons. *Science*, *302*(5648), 1234-1236.

Brumm, H., Kipper, S., Riechelmann, C., & Todt, D. (2005). Do barbary macaques comment on what they see? a first report on vocalizations accompanying interactions of third parties. *Primates*, *46*, 141-144.

Cheney, D. L., & Seyfarth, R. M. (2005). Social complexity and the information acquired during eavesdropping by primates and other animals. In P. McGregor (Ed.), *Animal communication networks* (pp. 583–603). Cambridge: Cambridge University Press.

Dunbar, R. (1996). *Grooming, gossip and the evolution of language.* London: Faber and Faber.

Fitch, W. T. (2010). *The evolution of language.* Cambridge University Press.

Hirsch, B. (2002). Social monitoring and vigilance behavior in brown capuchin monkeys (cebus apella). *Behavioral Ecology and Sociobiology*, *52*, 458-464.

Hockett, C. F. (1960). The origin of speech. *Scientific American*, *203*, 88-96.

Peake, T. M. (2005). Eavesdropping in communication networks. In P. McGregor (Ed.), *Animal communication networks* (pp. 13–37). Cambridge: Cambridge University Press.

Seyfarth, R., Cheney, D., & Bergman, T. (2005). Primate social cognition and the origins of language. *Trends in cognitive sciences*, *9*, 264–266.

Slingerland, I., Mulder, M., Van Der Vaart, E., & Rineke, V. (2009). A multi-agent systems approach to gossip and the evolution of language. In N. Taatgen & H. van Rijn (Eds.), *Proceedings of the 31st annual meeting of the cognitive science society.* Cognitive Science Society, Inc.

Tomasello, M. (1999). *The cultural origins of human cognition.* Harvard University Press.

RECURSIVITY IS A BY-PRODUCT OF ASSOCIATIVE LEARNING AND WORKING MEMORY CONSTRAINTS: EVIDENCE FROM BABOONS (*PAPIO PAPIO*)

ARNAUD REY[1], PIERRE PERRUCHET[2], JOEL FAGOT[1]
[1] *CNRS - Aix-Marseille Université, Marseille, France*
[2] *CNRS - Université de Bourgogne, Dijon, France*

1. Introduction

Recent hypotheses make the central claim that the ability to produce recursive structures is a critical cognitive feature distinguishing human language from any nonhuman communication system (Hauser, Chomsky, & Fitch, 2002). During the last decade, this critical claim has been highly debated and submitted to several empirical tests. In the present study, we provide an additional test by showing that after an intensive paired-associate training, baboons (*papio papio*) spontaneously produce recursive syntactic patterns.

2. Method

Using a newly developed operant conditioning device (Fagot & Bonté, 2010), eleven baboons were first trained to learn six different ordered pairs of visual shapes (noted a_1b_1, $a_2b_2 \ldots a_6b_6$) presented on a touch screen. Training consisted of five phases during which baboons learned in various conditions to sequentially touch the first, and then the second element of each pair, while ignoring visual distractors. The ability of baboons to produce recursive structures was then evaluated with two different testing procedures.

Tests 1-2 started with the same events. The first element of a pair (e.g., a_1) was presented with a first distractor. Baboons had to touch a_1 and to avoid the distractor. The first element of another pair (e.g., a_2) and a second distractor were then displayed. Again, they had to select a_2 and to avoid the distractor. The third resulting screen was different for Test 1 and 2. For Test 1, b_1, b_2, and a third visual distractor were displayed while for Test 2, b_1, b_2, and b_3 were presented on the screen. To be rewarded in Test 1, baboons had to touch both b_1 and b_2 with no constraint on order. To be rewarded in Test 2, they had to touch two of the three displayed shapes with no constraint on order.

3. Results

In Test 1 and 2, baboons spontaneously produced more recursive structures (i.e., *a1a2b2b1*) than non-recursive ones (i.e., *a1a2b1b2*) and that bias was present in all baboons. In Test 2, there was also a significant effect on the first selected item, b_2 being more selected than b_1, which was more selected than b_3. Finally, the difference between b_2b_1 and b_2b_3 was also statistically significant, indicating that after selecting b_2, baboons did not produce the next response at random but had a preference for b_1 (i.e., the last element of the recursive structure) over b_3.

4. Discussion

Contrary to the commonly accepted claim that recursion is human specific (Hauser, Chomsky, & Fitch, 2002), we found that at least one nonhuman species spontaneously produced recursive responses without such a structure being specifically reinforced. These results are consistent with the idea that recursive structures produced by humans could have their origins in associative and working memory processes already present in animals.

Although this explanation does not yet account for the richness of human language, it suggests that one of its presumably distinctive features (i.e., recursion) could in fact originate in elementary cognitive processes allowing the segmentation and the maintenance in working memory of previously associated elements. Following that explanation, the limited ability for recursion in animals should more likely be found in working memory limitations than in an inability to produce recursive structures *per se*.

A critical feature of human working memory is the development of phonological recoding processes that provide a crucial evolutionary advantage for maintaining information in working memory, computing long-distance dependencies, and producing complex forms of linguistic patterns. Future studies could gauge this alternative claim by testing the ability of nonhuman primates to learn minimal forms of phonological recoding and by evaluating its potentially strong impact on animal working memory capacities[1].

References

Fagot, J., and Bonté, E. (2010). Automated testing of cognitive performance in monkeys: Use of a battery of computerized test systems by a troop of semi-free ranging baboons (*Papio papio*). *Behavior, Research, Method, 42*, 507-516.

---

[1] For more details, see Rey, Perruchet, & Fagot (2012).

Hauser, M. D., Chomsky, N., and Fitch, W. T. (2002). The faculty of language: what is it, who has it, and how did it evolve? *Science*, *298*, 1569-1579.
Rey, A., Perruchet, P., & Fagot, J. (2012). Centre-embedded structures produced by non-humans primates. *Cognition*. DOI:10.1016/j.cognition.2011.12.005.

A BOTTOM-UP APPROACH TO LANGUAGE EVOLUTION

SEÁN G. ROBERTS

Language Evolution and Computation Research Unit

School of Philosophy, Psychology & Language Sciences, The University of Edinburgh

s.g.roberts@sms.ed.ac.uk

Computational models have been used to assess whether bilingualism can be maintained over generations and whether bilingualism was likely at early stages of language evolution(Castelló, Loureiro-Porto, Eguflíuz, & Miguel, 2007; Burkett & Griffiths, 2010). These models usually encode languages as discrete, static entities. The current model demonstrates that bilingualism can be studied by modelling languages as continuous, dynamic, context-dependent categories that emerge though interaction. It assumes that learners try to find structure in their input by conditioning the linguistic variation they receive on relevant semantic variables. The learning mechanism is domain general (e.g. statistical learning) and could learn multiple levels of linguistic structure. This allows a divergence in the importance of conditioning factors between populations. For example, for some languages, contrasts of intonation are important at a high level (questions versus statements), while in tonal languages they would be important at a lower level (words). Speaker identity may be an important conditioning factor in a society with two semi-isolated communities, but less important in a tight-knit society.

The evolution of linguistic diversity is modelled using an iterating learning process. A group of P learners try to explain the variation in a linguistic signal using a set of N semantic variables. Any semantic property may potentially become an important conditioning factor, including the identity of the speaker who produced the data. Learners receive a sub-sample of the linguistic and semantic data in the community, tagged with speaker identity. Learners fit a model to their sub-sample using stepwise regression. The learner's model is used to predict a new linguistic signal which becomes part of the input for the next generation. This process repeats for many generations with learners replaced at each generation. The probability of receiving a sample from a particular speaker depends on the structure of the community (fully integrated, isolated or partially overlapping).

Linguistic diversity is assessed using two bottom-up measures of intelligibility. The comprehensive intelligibility score I_c measures how similar the speakers' signals are, given the same semantic data as input (including a range of speaker identities). The functional intelligibility score I_f measures how similar the speak-

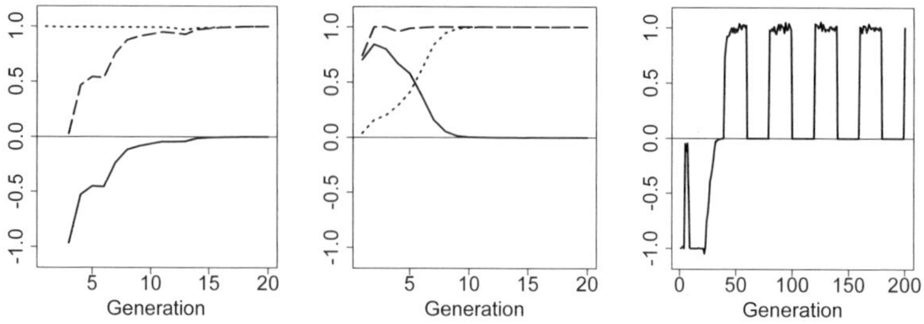

Figure 1. I_c (dotted), I_f (dashed) and B (solid line) for two semi-isolated communities (left) a minority situation where only one group receives data from both communities (middle) and for a community that flips between the two situations every 20 generations (right, B only). $P = 2$, $N = 4$.

ers' linguistic signals are when they try to design their utterances for each other (in pairs). We can now define a bottom-up measure of linguistic diversity at the language level, B, as $I_f - I_c$. A negative score suggests each community has a language with some amount of bilingualism (low I_f because speaker X produces Y's language and Y produces X's language but higher I_c because they both produce some amount of each language). A positive score suggests that one community may have two languages while the other has one (e.g. high I_f because both X and Y produce the mutual language but low I_c because X produces two languages and Y one). B near zero implies a single language (figure 1).

This bottom-up model leads to three important conclusions for language evolution. First, the linguistic signal will come to represent many features of meaning, but the ordering of conditioning factors for two isolated communities will diverge. Second, speaker identity can become a salient conditioning factor given the right social structures. Finally, bilingualism is able to emerge, given the right change in social structure, at any point and from any previous social structure. This means that a bottom-up approach, in contrast with top-down approaches, does not limit the scenarios for an early stage of language evolution.

References

Burkett, D., & Griffiths, T. (2010). Iterated learning of multiple languages from multiple teachers. In A. Smith, M. Schouwstra, B. de Boer, & K. Smith (Eds.), *The evolution of language: Proceedings of evolang 2010* (p. 58-65). World Scientific.

Castelló, X., Loureiro-Porto, L., Eguflíuz, V. M., & Miguel, M. S. (2007). The fate of bilingualism in a model of language competition. In S. Takahashi, D. Sallach, & J. Rouchier (Eds.), *Advancing social simulation: The first world conference* (pp. 83–94). Tokyo: Springer.

THE NATURE OF COORDINATION: EVIDENCE FROM RUSSIAN

TATIANA ROMANCHISHINA
KATHRYN H. THOMPSON

Department of Linguistics, University of Southern Maine, Portland, ME, 04104-9300, USA

Cowart and colleagues have proposed that coordination and subordination (Merge) are evolutionarily distinct functions (Cowart & Agupova 2009; Cowart & McDaniel 2008). They suggest that a derivative of a well-studied quantitative cognitive function known to be evolutionarily ancient and developmentally pre-linguistic (Carey 2009) led to the emergence of coordination some time after the human/chimpanzee split and before the emergence of Merge. According to this account, modern coordinate structures are linguistic fossils that are only apparently integrated with Merge structures.[1] Such accounts predict that coordinate and subordinate structures should manifest different behaviors under certain circumstances. The claim is that the coordinating mechanism is a set-forming function that applies a criterion of similarity when conjoining structures. We explore the implications of these proposals experimentally.

In our study, we investigated certain canonical and noncanonical agreement patterns of both coordinate and subordinate structures in Russian. The materials consisted of sentences whose subjects were either a coordinate NP or an NP containing a PP. We varied the grammatical number of both NPs making up the subject (e.g., *the star behind the clouds* vs. *the stars behind the cloud)*, the structural type (coordination vs. subordination, e.g., *the star behind the cloud* vs. *the star and the cloud*), and the grammatical number of the predicate, agreeing or disagreeing with the subject (e.g., *the star behind the clouds is …* vs. *the star behind the clouds are…*). Native adult Russian speakers judged such sentences on a seven-point scale.

---

[1] Progovac (2009) makes a somewhat similar proposal, though hers incorporates a gradualist account of Merge whereas the one considered here does not.

Our findings support the account of coordination as a set-making function, distinct from subordination. The subordinate cases show attraction effects (number on the non-head NP adjacent to the verb influences acceptability of both canonical and noncanonical agreement on the verb), which is consistent with findings in various languages, including Russian (Lorimor et al. 2008). In the coordinate cases, on the other hand, judgments of grammatical sentences (with a plural verb) significantly declined in acceptability when the conjuncts were mismatched in number, even where this produced superficial agreement between the second conjunct and the verb. That is, the latter pattern is the opposite of an attraction effect. This result differs from English where grammatical coordinates showed neither attraction effects nor the similarity effect. The model of coordination discussed above can account for these results. Set-formation requires similarity among the elements of the set. Assuming that this criterion applies at all levels (morphological as well as syntactic and semantic) accounts for the English pattern and the differences between English and Russian. The critical difference is in the richness of inflectional morphology. In English, the singular noun is a kind of default; it is unmarked and thus does not overtly clash with a plural on a conjoined NP. In Russian, however, both singular and plural are morphologically richly specified and thus conjoined NPs carrying differing number will always be relatively conspicuously unlike each other in this respect. Any contrast in number between the conjuncts in Russian will impair acceptability, as our results show.

References

Carey, S. (2009). *The Origin of Concepts*. Oxford University Press, Inc. New York, NY.

Cowart, W., & Agupova, T. (2009). On Homogeneity of Syntax: How similar do coordinates and subordinates look to the comprehension system? In *Time and Again*. (reprinted from *Linguistics Today*, 2008, 121-134).

Cowart, W., & McDaniel, D. (2008). The syntax of coordination and the evolution of syntax. In A. D. Smith et al. (Eds.), The Evolution of Language: Proceedings of the 7th International Conference.

Lorimor, H., Bock, K., Zalkind, E., & Sheyman, A. (2008). Agreement and Attraction in Russian. *Language and Cognitive Processes, 23(6),* 769-799.

Progovac, L. (2009) Sex and syntax: Subjacency revisited. *Biolinguistics*, *3*, pp. 305-336.

NO WORDS WITHOUT SYNTAX NO SYNTAX WITHOUT WORDS

J. ROSSELLÓ[1], C. ALBA[2], TX. MARTIN[3], O. BORREGA[1],
[1] *Dept. Lingüística General, Universitat de Barcelona, Barcelona, 08007, Spain*
[2]*Dept. Traducció/Ciències Llenguatge, Universitat Pompeu Fabra, Barcelona, 08018*
[3] *Dept. Linguistics, New York University, New York, NY, 10003, USA*

Whatever definition we adopt of linguistic recursion relates it to an unbounded combinatorial procedure to build sentences. That procedure operates on words (roots, stems, morphemes, depending on your framework). It is however often disregarded that the words that enter the recursive procedure have an internal structure that comes from a phonological unbounded combinatorial capacity that operates on meaningless units, and is responsible for the open-endedness of human lexicons. Our thesis here is that we are in front of two different implementations of a single underlying combinatorial mechanism that yields discrete infinities of sentences or words, and that they entail each other. Hence, there's no place for a lexical protolanguage stage (Bickerton 1990) nor for a phrase structure exapted from syllable structure (Carstairs-McCarthy 1999). The split in two implementations, syntax and phonology, results in a maximally optimal linguistic architecture that adapts internally to a dual memory, to the conceptual-intentional systems, and to our sensory-motor apparatus. This reflects itself in that we can have a phrase within a phrase, but we can't a syllable within a syllable. Now, the identity of the source of syntactic and phonological *Merge* can be argued for on a variety of factors including that (*i*) both implementations combine units to form meaningful structures; (*ii*) both implementations are unbounded and yield discrete entities; (*iii*) their unboundedness is not likely the result of any external adaptive necessity; and (*iv*) it is highly implausible that two independent evolutionary events created the two systems separately.

While the centrality of recursion goes undisputed in syntax, the combination of meaningless elements to yield words, i.e. *Duality of Patterning* (henceforth DP), is seen as unrelated to recursion, something we reject (Rosselló 2006). In addition, we address some problems with the concept of DP. Firstly, Hockett's (1958) original formulation is often misunderstood in the evolutionary literature (Hurford 2002; Pinker 2003; a.o.), in the sense that it is considered a mere restatement of the fact that languages have syntax and phonology. For Hockett, DP refers to the idea that minimal meaningful units are built out of meaningless elements, a definition in which syntax plays no role. Secondly, against Hockett we understand DP as an *unbounded* lexicalization technique that combines meaningless elements into minimal meaningful units. This thus turns DP into a basic design feature of the faculty of language, just like recursion, that is to say a property without which no language is possible.

Our thesis, however, contradicts the ideas in Everett (2005) on Pirahã, or Aronoff *et al.* (2010) and Sandler *et al.* (2011) on Al-Sayyid Bedouin Sign Language (ABSL), according to which Pirahã would lack recursion, while ABSL would not exhibit DP. We assume Nevins *et al.* (2009) with respect to recursion, and focus here on ABSL and DP. We address some conceptual problems in Aronoff *et al.* (2010), and then provide a reinterpretation of their empirical data. The main points we discuss include among others (*i*) their resort to current contingent glossogeny to shed light on phylogeny, (*ii*) their inconsistent use of E-language and I-language that makes of DP a property of E-language, (*iii*) their identification of iconicity and holism in ABSL, or (iv) their idea that social convention is a requirement for systematic phonology. We consider that convention accounts for uniformity among speakers, rather than for systematicity in grammar, which is strictly individual. In light of all that, we reinterpret several of the data offered in their paper, and show that they are better accounted for in our proposal. Our proposal is in accordance with the data put forward in Brentari *et al.* (2011), showing that homesigners exhibit a phonological system rather than holistic gestures. In doing all this we take issue with any theory stating that languages can lack basic design features, and we argue that no (proto)language is possible with words without syntax, or with syntax without words.

Selected References

Aronoff, M.; Meir, I.; Padden, C. A. & Sandler, W. (2010). The roots of linguistic organization in a new language. In M. Arbib and D. Bickerton (Eds.), *The Emergence of Protolanguage. Holophrasis vs. Compositionality* (pp. 133-152). Amsterdam/Philadelphia: John Benjamins.

Carstairs-McCarthy, A. (1999) *The Origins of Complex Language. An Inquiry into the Evolutionary Beginnings of Sentences, Syllables, and Truth*. Oxford: Oxford UP.

Brentari, D.; Coppola, M.; Mazzoni, L. & Goldin-Meadow, S. (to appear) When does a system become phonological? Handshape production in gesturers, signers, and homesigners. *NLLT* 30.

Rosselló, J. (2006). Combinatorial properties at the roots of language. In J. Rosselló & J. Martín (Eds.) *The Biolinguistic Turn. Issues on Language and Biology* (pp. 162-186). Barcelona: PPU.

Sandler, W.; Aronoff, M.; Meir, I. & Padden, C. (2011) The gradual emergence of phonological form in a new language. *NLLT* 29: 503-543.

OUT OF THE BRAINS OF BABES: DOMAIN-GENERAL LEARNING MECHANISMS & DOMAIN-SPECIFIC SYSTEMS

JENNY SAFFRAN

Department of Psychology, University of Wisconsin - Madison, 1202 W. Johnson St., Madison, WI, 53706, USA

1. Overview

In order to persist across generations, a language must be learnable. The primary agents of language learning and change are the infants and young children who are acquiring their first language(s). We all agree that language structure is shaped by language learnability; patterns that are learnable should be ubiquitous cross-linguistically relative to patterns that are not. What is more contentious is the nature of those learning mechanisms. In particular, are they domain-specific; that is, did they evolve solely to subserve language acquisition? Or are they domain-general: that is, used for the acquisition of complex sequential structure more generally? I will suggest that the answer, as usual, is both.

My research is focused on infant learning. This talk will link empirical results from infant studies to the question of why natural languages are structured the way they are. To do so, I will pursue the following line of argumentation.

1.1. *Infants possess powerful learning mechanisms*

Infants readily track the distribution of linguistic *tokens*, a process often termed "statistical learning" (e.g., Aslin, Saffran, & Newport, 1998; Pelucchi, Hay, & Saffran, 2009a, 2009b; Saffran, Aslin, & Newport, 1996). Infants also track the distribution of linguistic *types*, generalizing beyond the specific tokens presented in the input (e.g., Gomez & Gerken, 2000; Marcus et al., 1999).

1.2. *These mechanisms perform domain-general computations*

That is, they operate over structured sources of input – including language – but do not appear to be tailored specifically for language. Importantly, learning is gated by one's perception of the input; infants must be able to adequately represent input types and/or tokens as distinct primitives before they can enter into subsequent computations. Thus, for example, infants can track the distribution of non-linguistic tokens including tones (e.g., Saffran et al., 1999), objects (e.g., Fiser & Aslin, 2002), and actions (Roseberry et al., 2011). However, infants' statistical learning is affected by their representations of the input (e.g., Saffran & Griepentrog, 2001; Saffran et al., 2005). A similar story emerges when tracking and generalizing across types; infants' representations of the input affect the unfolding of the learning process (e.g., Frank et al., 2009; Johnson et al., 2009; Saffran, Pollak, Seibel, & Shkolnik, 2007).

1.3. *Patterns that are easier for infants and young children to acquire should be more prevalent cross-linguistically*

I will present two lines of work suggesting that infants find the types of patterns prevalent in natural languages easier to acquire. The first line of work concerns phonotactic patterns, and suggests that infants find novel featural regularities easier to acquire than patterns of mixed sets of phonemes (Saffran & Thiessen, 2003). The second set of studies suggests that infants are better able to acquire novel syntactic patterns that contain predictive dependencies (as found in natural language phrase structure) than equally complex patterns lacking predictive dependencies (Saffran et al., 2007). These results are consistent with the **constrained statistical learning framework** (Saffran, 2002), which suggests that language learning is one source of constraint on language structure (see also Christiansen & Chater, 2008). Cross-linguistic similarities arise (in part) because statistical learning is constrained such that some patterns are more easily learned than others. These constraints do not necessarily arise from language-specific knowledge. Instead, learning is constrained by domain-general factors such as memory, prior experience, and perception.

2. Further considerations

If this is all so, then why do only humans learn human languages? For example, Bengalese finches also learn better in the presence of predictive dependencies (Abe & Watanabe, 2011). It seems likely that part of the answer is that rather than simply tracking and discriminating between different patterns, human infants **make use** of the patterns they have tracked in fundamentally linguistic ways. Infants rapidly organize patterns acquired via these learning mechanisms into the building blocks of natural languages; other animals likely do not. For example, infants don't merely track the statistics of syllable tokens; they map emerging multi-syllabic units onto their referents to form words (e.g., Graf Estes et al., 2007; Hay et al., 2011). Similarly, as they discover word types, infants begin to map meanings onto lexical categories (e.g., Lany & Saffran, 2010). So while the learning mechanisms involved may be quite general (both across domains and across species), the system of knowledge that is human language is unlike anything else.

References

Abe, K. & Watanabe, D. (2011). Songbirds possess the spontaneous ability to discriminate syntactic rules. *Nature Neuroscience, 14,* 1067–1074.

Aslin, R. N., Saffran, J. R., & Newport, E. L. (1998). Computation of conditional probability statistics by 8-month-old infants. *Psychological Science, 9,* 321-324.

Christiansen, M. H., & Chater, N. (2008). Language as shaped by the brain. *Behavioral and Brain Sciences, 31,* 489–558.

Fiser, J., & Aslin, R. N. (2002). Statistical learning of new visual feature combinations by infants. *Proceedings of the National Academy of Science, 99*, 15822-15826.

Frank, M. C., Slemmer, J. A., Marcus, G. F., & Johnson, S. P. (2009). Information from multiple modalities helps 5-month-olds learn abstract rules. *Developmental Science*, *12*, 504-509.

Gómez, R. L., & Gerken L. (1999). Artificial grammar learning by 1-year-olds leads to specific and abstract knowledge. *Cognition, 70*, 109-135.

Graf Estes, K. M., Evans, J., Alibali, M. W., & Saffran, J. R. (2007). Can infants map meaning to newly segmented words? Statistical segmentation and word learning. *Psychological Science, 18,* 254-260.

Hay, J. F., Pelucchi, B., *Graf Estes, K.,* & Saffran, J. R. (2011). Linking sounds to meanings: Infant statistical learning in a natural language. *Cognitive Psychology, 63,* 93-106.

Johnson, S. P., Fernandes, K. J., Frank, M. C., Kirkham, N. Z., Marcus, G. F., Rabagliati, H., & Slemmer, J. A. (2009). Abstract rule learning for visual sequences in 8- and 11-month-olds. *Infancy*, *14*, 2-18.

Lany, J., & Saffran, J. R. (2010). From statistics to meanings: Infant acquisition of lexical categories. *Psychological Science, 21,* 284-291.

Marcus, G. F., Vijayan, S., Bandi Rao, S., & Vishton, P. M. (1999). Rule learning by seven-month-old infants. *Science*, *283*, 77-80.

Pelucchi, B., Hay, J. F., & Saffran, J. R. (2009). Statistical learning in a natural language by 8-month-old infants. *Child Development, 80,* 674-685.

Pelucchi, B., Hay, J. F., & Saffran, J. R. (2009). Learning in reverse: 8-month-old infants track backward transitional probabilities. *Cognition, 113,* 244-247.

Roseberry, S., Richie, R., Hirsh-Pasek, K., Golinkoff, M. R., & Shipley, T. F. (2011). Babies catch a break: 7- to 9-month-olds track statistical probabilities in continuous dynamic events. *Psychological Science, 22,* 1422-1424.

Saffran, J. R. (2002). Constraints on statistical language learning. *Journal of Memory and Language, 47,* 172-196.

Saffran, J. R., Aslin, R. N., & Newport, E. L. (1996). Statistical learning by 8-month-old infants. *Science, 274,* 1926-1928.

Saffran, J. R., & Griepentrog, G. J. (2001). Absolute pitch in infant auditory learning: Evidence for developmental reorganization. *Developmental Psychology, 37,* 74-85.

Saffran, J. R., Johnson, E. K., Aslin, R. N., & Newport, E. L. (1999). Statistical learning of tone sequences by human infants and adults. *Cognition, 70,* 27-52.

Saffran, J. R., Pollak, S. D., Seibel, R. L., & Shkolnik, A. (2007). Dog is a dog is a dog: Infant rule learning is not specific to language. *Cognition, 105,* 669-680.

Saffran, J. R., Reeck, K., Niehbur, A., & Wilson, D. P. (2005). Changing the tune: Absolute and relative pitch processing by adults and infants. *Developmental Science, 8,* 1-7.

Saffran, J. R., & Thiessen, E. D. (2003). Pattern induction by infant language learners. *Developmental Psychology, 39,* 484-494.

EVOLUTION OF 'SMALL-WORLD' BIRDSONG SYNTAX: AN IMPLICATION FOR LANGUAGE EVOLUTION

KAZUTOSHI SASAHARA[1], MARTIN L. CODY[2], AND CHARLES E. TALOR[2]

[1]*Graduate School of Arts and Sciences, University of Tokyo, 3-8-1 Komaba, Meguro-ku, Tokyo 153-8902, Japan*

[2]*Department of Ecology and Evolutionary Biology, University of California, Los Angeles, 621 Charles E. Young Drive South, Los Angeles, CA 90095, USA*

kazutoshi.sasahara@gmail.com

Birdsongs have been studied with increasing interest for language evolution; in particular, birds with relatively simple songs and several tens of song elements, such as Zebra finch and Bengalese finch, have been well-studied (Berwick, Okanoya, Beckers, & Bolhuis, 2011). It is, however, still unclear how birds with complex songs and a large repertoire learn and organize their songs, although there have been a number of qualitative studies (Todt & Hultsh, 1998).

We studied the structure of California Thrasher song using a network-based approach. We recorded spontaneous singing from a single male individual from his territory. Then we computed the sound spectrogram, identified 2897 phrases, and categorized them into 182 phrase types. The phrase sequences were converted into two types of song networks by examining each transition between different phrases along song sequences (the repetitions of same phrase were omitted). In these networks, nodes represent phrase types and links (not weighted) represent transitions between them. We quantified the global song structure using the song undirected network (SUN). The SUN represents the connection topology among different phrase types, characterized by average path length L, clustering coefficient C, and degree distribution $P(k)$. We then investigated the local song structure using the song directed network (SDN). The SDN is the SUN that includes directionality of transitions among phrase types. The transitions in the SDN can be characterized by five 'transition motifs,' defined by the combination of indegree and outdegree. One-way and Bottleneck are deterministic, in that one or more phrases transit to a specific phrase; Branch and Hourglass are non-deterministic, in that transitions through a specific phrase may transit to one or another of several different phrases. Furthermore, we quantified the singing dynamics in terms of the predictability of successive phrases using the information entropy.

Three findings emerges. First, the SUN has a 'small-world' architecture, in which subsets of phrases are highly grouped and linked with a short average path

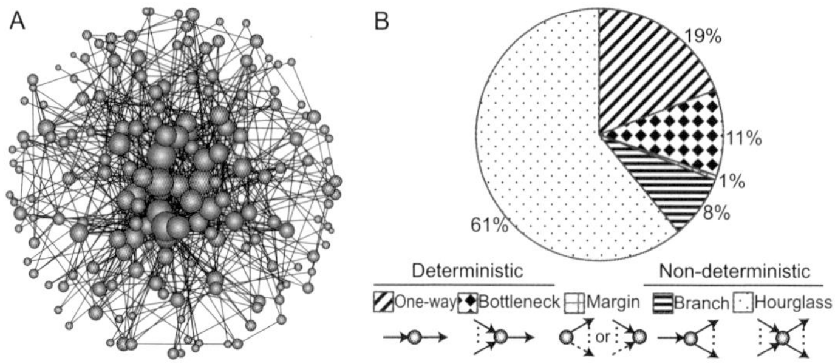

Figure 1. A, Song undirected network (SUN). Nodes are drawn with sizes proportional to their degree k. B, Transition motifs in the song directed network (SDN).

length (L=3.15 and C=0.21, while the values in comparable random networks are L=2.98 and C=0.03) (Fig.1A). Moreover, $P(k)$ of the SUN has a long tail to the right over higher k, in contrast to that of random networks where $P(k)$ is a bell-shaped curve. Small-worldness is a characteristic in common with human language; e.g., in written English, the network of word co-occurrence relationships also exhibits this property (Ferrer i Cancho & Sole, 2001). Second, the SDN shows a balanced transition diversity amongst phrases, in which deterministic and non-deterministic transitions are moderately mixed (Fig.1B), in contrast to random networks in which non-deterministic transitions dominate. Third, it appears that the singing dynamics can be attributed to a first-order Markov chain. These structural properties together facilitate an effective use of diverse phrases, generating song complexity with contexts that are locally predictable but globally unpredictable. This may be relevant to creating both familiarity and novelty for the signal receivers (female or male conspecifics); a balance between these two extremes may have evolved to establish both reliable singer identities as well as allowing development of individual virtuosity; with both aspects contributing to individual fitness. Complex birdsongs allows us to study how complex vocal signals evolve, contributing to a more unified understanding of language evolution.

References

Berwick, R. C., Okanoya, K., Beckers, G. J. L., & Bolhuis, J. J. (2011). Songs to syntax: the linguistics of birdsong. *Trends in Cognitive Sciences*, *15*, 113–121.

Ferrer i Cancho, R., & Sole, R. V. (2001). The small world of human language. *Proceedings of The Royal Society B*, *268*, 2261–2265.

Todt, D., & Hultsh, H. (1998). Hierarchical Learning, Development and Representation of Song. In R. P. Balda, I. M. Pepperberg, & A. C. Kamil (Eds.), (pp. 275–304). Academic Press.

HOW DO COMMUNICATION SYSTEMS EMERGE, AND WHAT DOES THIS TELL US ABOUT LANGUAGE?

THOMAS C. SCOTT-PHILLIPS

School of Philosophy, Psychology and Language Sciences, University of Edinburgh
3 Charles Street, Edinburgh, EH8 9AD

Communication is not a trait possessed by one or another individual. Rather, it is an interaction between two or more individuals (Krebs & Dawkins, 1984; Maynard Smith & Harper, 2003; Scott-Phillips, 2008). This is reflected in contemporary definitions of communication, which emphasise that whether a given behaviour is a signal depends on whether there is a corresponding response, and vice versa (Maynard Smith & Harper, 2003; Scott-Phillips, 2008). This suggests a chicken-and-egg problem: if signals and responses depend upon each other to explain their adaptive value, then how can communication emerge in the first place? The existing ethological literature provides two answers to this question: ritualization and sensory manipulation. In ritualization, signals evolve from behaviours that were originally only cues. For example, the use of urine to mark territory may have begun as a marker of fear, produced by animals leaving territory in which they felt safe, which other animals then used as the cue of the focal individual's presence (Maynard Smith & Harper, 2003). In sensory manipulation, signals evolve from behaviours that were originally only coercive. For example, many mating displays may have begun as scenarios in which a preference for objects of a certain colour allowed the behaviour of soon-to-be receivers to be manipulated by others (Bradbury & Vehrencamp, 2000).

These empirical observations raise a number of questions pertinent to the study of language origins. The most immediate is: does this framework apply to human intentional communication (of which language is the archetypal example), and if so, did it evolve by ritualization or by sensory manipulation? I will present both a mathematical and an agent-based model of the evolution of communication that directly addresses this question (Scott-Phillips et al., in press). In particular, I will show that there is in fact a third route to communication, separate to ritualization and sensory manipulation, but that this route requires that individual organisms are able to communicate their intention to communicate with one another. This ability overrides the dynamical constraints that otherwise ensure that communication emerges by one or the other of the two processes described above. Recent experimental work shows that humans are indeed able to communicate their communicative intent, even under quite demanding conditions (Scott-Phillips et al., 2009; de Ruiter et al., 2010). Consequently, the way in which communication systems emerge in human interaction is an exception to the empirical trends discussed above (see also Scott-Phillips, 2010). Moreover, it suggests that, with regards to the origins of language, comparative research on non-human primates should focus on the underlying cognitive capacities involved in intentional communication (e.g. Tomasello, 2008), rather than on structural similarities with language (e.g. Arnold & Zuberbühler, 2006; 2008).

References

Arnold, K., & Zuberbühler, K. (2006). Semantic combinations in primate calls. *Nature, 441*, 303.

Arnold, K., & Zuberbühler, K. (2008). Meaningful call combinations in a non-human primate. *Current Biology, 18*(5), R202-R203.

Bradbury, J. W., & Vehrencamp, S. L. (2000). Economic models of animal communication. *Animal Behaviour, 59*, 259-268.

de Ruiter, J. P., Noordzij, M. L., Newman-Norland, S., Newman-Norland, R., Hagoort, P., Levinson, S. C., & Toni, I. (2010). Exploring the cognitive infrastructure of communication. *Interaction Studies, 11*(1), 51-77.

Krebs, J. R., & Dawkins, R. (1984). Animal signals: Mind-reading and manipulation. In J. R. Krebs & N. B. Davies (Eds.), *Behavioural Ecology: An Evolutionary Approach* (2nd ed., pp. 380-402). Oxford: Blackwell.

Maynard Smith, J., & Harper, D. G. C. (2003). *Animal Signals*. Oxford: Oxford University Press.

Scott-Phillips, T. C. (2008). Defining biological communication. *Journal of Evolutionary Biology, 21*(2), 387-395.

Scott-Phillips, T. C., Kirby, S., & Ritchie, G. R. S. (2009). Signalling signalhood and the emergence of communication. *Cognition, 113*(2), 226-233.

Scott-Phillips, T. C. (2010). The evolution of communication: Humans may be exceptional. *Interaction Studies, 11*(1), 78-99.

Scott-Phillips, T. C., Blythe, R. A., Gardner, A., & West, S. A. (in press). How do communication systems emerge? *Proceedings of the Royal Society of London, B*.

Tomasello, M. (2003). *The Origins of Human Communication.* Cambridge, MA: MIT Press.

THE ORIGIN OF THE LEARNING SYSTEM OF SEQUENTIAL VOCALIZATIONS; NEURAL ACTIVITY OF BASAL-GANGLIA IN SINGING BEHAVIOR AND A COGNITIVE TASK IN SONGBIRDS

YOSHIMASA SEKI

ERATO, Japan Science and Technology Agency, 2-1 Hirosawa
Wako, 351-0198, Japan

NEAL A. HESSLER

Lab. for Vocal Behavior Mechanisms, RIKEN Brain Science Institute, 2-1 Hirosawa
Wako, 351-0198, Japan

KAZUO OKANOYA

Graduate School of Arts and Sciences, The University of Tokyo, 3-8-1 Komaba
Meguro-ku, Tokyo, 153-8901, Japan

It is well known that the basal ganglia are related to human speech. This means that the brain region is necessary for not only vocal motor-control but also operation of language itself. For example, in bilinguals, the left caudate plays an important role in monitoring and controlling the language in use (Clinion et al., 2006). Similarly, researchers have shown a cortico-basal ganglia circuit implicated for song learning and maintenance in songbirds, a model system of vocal learning. The basal ganglia nucleus of this pathway, Area X, has been well investigated in terms of singing behavior. The neurons in the nucleus have been categorized based upon the firing patterns and the connections; four classes of putative striatal neurons and two putative pallidal cell types. Area X receives dopaminergic projections from ventral tegmental area (VTA) and substantia nigra pars compacta (SNc). In mammals, dopamine neurons are activated in response to the delivery of rewards (Shultz et al., 1997). In songbirds, those neurons are active during courtship singing, and cause modulation of Area X activity (Hessler & Doupe, 1999). Thus, Area X may be involved in reinforcement learning as well as song learning, though song control system might be specialized for singing behavior.

To examine whether the activity of Area X neurons are modulated during a cognitive task as well as singing behavior, we trained a group of Bengalese finches (Lonchura striata var. domestica) to peck an LED key using an operant method. The key emitted green / red light at each trial. Different roles were assigned to each color. For example, pecking to the red light resulted in food delivery, while pecking to green light resulted in no-food but was required for the next trial.

Then, we obtained extracellular recordings with tungsten electrodes from Area X neurons of those birds during song production, which exhibited various firing patterns as shown in the previous studies; some of them were excited while some were inhibited as previously reported. We found some of those singing related neurons exhibited responses also in the key pecking task. The recordings showed a diversity of firing pattern. Some neurons exhibited different firing rate in response to each color while some did not. Some neurons activated in response to food / no-food presentation.

Our findings provide a new insight of ultimate and proximate causations of singing behavior. The results showed that the song learning system is not independent from other cognitive systems and partially overlaps with the general learning or reward system. This idea might be a key to clarify the origin of the vocal learning system in songbirds. Also, this knowledge might contribute to understand the origin of the neural system related to human language.

References

Crinion, J., Turner, R., Grogan, A., Hanakawa, T., Noppeney, U., Devlin, J. T., Aso, T., Urayama, S., Fukuyama, H., Stockton, K., Usui, K., Green, D.W., Price, C. J. (2006). Language control in the bilingual brain. *Science*, *312*, 1537.

Schultz, W, Dayan, P. & Montague, R. R. (1997). A neural substrate of prediction and reward. *Science*, *275*, 1593-1599.

Hessler, N. A. & Doupe, A. J. (1999). Singing-related neural activity in a dorsal forebrain-basal ganglia circuit of adult zebra finches. *Journal of Neuroscience*, *19*, 10461-10481.

SIMULATING LANGUAGE CONVERGENCE

LAN SHUAI

Department of Chinese, Translation and Linguistics, City University of Hong Kong
Tat Chee Avenue, Kowloon, Hong Kong

TAO GONG, & UMBERTO ANSALDO

Department of Linguistics, University of Hong Kong, Pokfulam Road, Hong Kong

Mathematical or behavioral simulations have been recently adopted to study language contact (e.g., Abrams & Strogatz, 2003; Minett & Wang, 2008). Many of them treat contacting languages as monolithic wholes and focus on the effect of language-external factors (e.g., social prestige or structure) on individuals' language choices. Besides death or bilingualism, language contact also leads to *language convergence* (merging linguistic features of original contacting languages, e.g., pidgins/creoles or mixed languages). During convergence, both language-internal (e.g., lexical/syntactic similarity of contacting languages) and language-external (e.g., frequency of inter-group communications) factors can take effect, but these effects have not been widely addressed by simulations.

Based on *the lexicon-syntax coevolution model* (Gong, 2011), we examine the roles of lexical/syntactic similarity and inter-/intra-group communications in the convergence of two contacting languages. Artificial individuals (agents) in the model use general learning mechanisms to acquire lexical items and word order during iterated communications. The model can simulate *language origin* (agents initially share no or limited linguistic knowledge) and *change* (agents initially share a full set of linguistic knowledge to encode a set of integrated meanings having simple predicate-argument structures) at the population level. We use *Inter-* and *Intra-rate* to denote ratios of inter- or intra-group communications, *lexical/syntactic similarity* (*similar lexicons*: contacting languages share 80% lexical items; *similar syntax*: they share 2 out of 3 local word orders) to control the linguistic knowledge of contacting languages, and UR_{mutual} (mutual understandability of contacting languages) and CT_{mutual} (number of communications for UR_{mutual} to be above 0.8) to trace convergence.

Language origin simulations and 1-way ANCOVA (covariate: number of communications) show a significant effect of the ratio of inter- and intra-group communications ($F(3, 8075) = 2995.79$, $p < .001$, $\eta_p^2 = .527$) on UR_{mutual}. Language change simulations and 2-way ANCOVA further reveal that besides the ratio of inter- and intra-group communications ($F(3, 32303) = 9796.165$, $p < .001$, $\eta_p^2 = .476$) (Fig. 1, middle panel), lexical ($F(1, 32303) = 15517.984$, $p < .001$, $\eta_p^2 = .325$) and syntactic similarities ($F(1, 32303) = 281.821$, $p < .001$, $\eta_p^2 = .009$) also have significant effects on UR_{mutual} (Fig. 1, right panel). Moreover, the effect of lexical similarity is more explicit than that of syntactic similarity (Fig. 1, right panel, the UR_{mutual} difference between the dash and solid lines is smaller than the UR_{mutual} difference between the Lex (L) conditions). This reflects a *lexical basis* of language contact: sharing lexical items makes syntactic features explicit, thus making convergence much easier than that in the situation of sharing syntactic features. Such a lexical basis has been observed in some contact situations such as grammatical borrowing or creolization (Atshogs, 2004; King, 2000), and it helps predict the outcome of convergence among languages having similar lexical or syntactic features, and explain why lexical items tend to play a leading role in creolization.

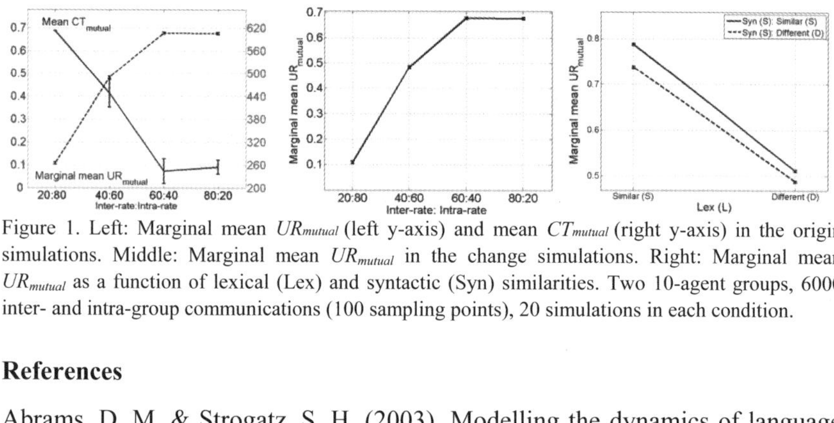

Figure 1. Left: Marginal mean UR_{mutual} (left y-axis) and mean CT_{mutual} (right y-axis) in the origin simulations. Middle: Marginal mean UR_{mutual} in the change simulations. Right: Marginal mean UR_{mutual} as a function of lexical (Lex) and syntactic (Syn) similarities. Two 10-agent groups, 6000 inter- and intra-group communications (100 sampling points), 20 simulations in each condition.

References

Abrams, D. M. & Strogatz, S. H. (2003). Modelling the dynamics of language death. *Nature*, 424, 900.

Atshogs, Y. V. (2004). *Research on Daohua*. Beijing: Ethnic Publishing House.

Gong, T. (2011). Simulating the coevolution of compositionality and word order regularity. *Interaction Studies*, 12(1), 63-106.

King, R. E. (2000). *The Lexical Basis of Grammatical Borrowing: A Prince Edward Island French Case Study*. Amsterdam: Benjamins.

Minett, J. W. & Wang, W. S-Y. (2008). Modelling endangered languages: The effects of bilingualism and social structure. *Lingua*, 118, 19-45.

LINGUISTIC REPLICATORS: A WILD GOOSE CHASE?

ANDREW D. M. SMITH

Literatures and Languages, School of Arts and Humanities, University of Stirling
andrew.smith@stir.ac.uk

Much recent research has sought to model language as a complex adaptive system, in which linguistic patterns emerge from the social and communicative interactions in which language is used (e.g. Beckner et al., 2009). Compelling cases have been made unifying language change and the development of complex linguistic structure from pre-language (Heine & Kuteva, 2007; Hoefler & Smith, 2009). Language is clearly adapted to its environment: a wealth of research has shown that constraints from cognitive biases in the human brain (Christiansen & Chater, 2008) to the mechanisms of cultural transmission (Kirby, Cornish, & Smith, 2008; Cornish, Tamariz, & Kirby, 2009) produce in language the appearance of design without an intentional designer, just as natural selection does in biological organisms. Formalising language evolution in Darwinian terms, therefore, appears an attractive proposition: linguistic correspondences should be found for genetic replicators, entities which survive long enough to make reliable copies of themselves, and contribute to their own chances of replication (Dawkins, 1989). Yet no wholly satisfactory account of linguistic replicators has gained acceptance, and I will argue that such an account is actually impossible, because of the ostensive-inferential nature of linguistic communication.

Thorough and considered treatments of linguistic replicators have been proposed by, e.g., Croft (2000) and Ritt (2004); both have been subsequently applied to modelling specific historical linguistic cases (Baxter, Blythe, Croft, & McKane, 2009; Ritt, 2004). Croft proposes as replicators linguemes, form-meaning constructions which replicate through interactive communication. Ritt's search leads him instead to mental phonetic tokens, possibly even the neuronal structures these may be encoded in. His reluctance to accept Croft's linguemes flows from an acceptance of the nature of linguistic communication, which is crucially based on ostension and inference (Sperber & Wilson, 1995). Meanings are 'replicated' through a process of inferential reconstruction by the hearer. Language users, however, have highly idiosyncratic collections of discourse world knowledge, and can construct arbitrarily complex models of the communicative context; it is correspondingly vanishingly unlikely for either two people's individual sets of knowledge, or their representations of the communicative context, to be identical (Hoefler & Smith, 2009), and thus every meaning reconstructed by the hearer is inevitably different from its source in the speaker. Meaning reconstruction, indeed, is characterised by uncertainty, approximation and constant re-analysis (Smith, 2008); it is an analogue system rather than a digital code, yielding levels of fidelity which are arguably more reminiscent of mutation than replication.

The problem, then, is that all potential linguistic replicators contain (or are paired with) semantic components which cannot be reliably replicated. While parallels between biology and language are seductive, language evolution is not the same as biological evolution. Frameworks such as that outlined by Price (1995), which can account for both genetic evolution and linguistic evolution as instances of a single more general phenomenon, are likely to be more fruitful than trying to insist that language should behave like genes in every respect.

References

Baxter, G., Blythe, R. A., Croft, W., & McKane, A. (2009). Modeling language change: an evaluation of Trudgill's theory of the emergence of New Zealand English. *Language Variation and Change*, *21*(2), 257–296.

Beckner, C., Blythe, R. A., Bybee, J. L., Christiansen, M. H., Croft, W., Ellis, N. C., Holland, J., Ke, J., Larsen-Freeman, D., & Schoenemann, T. (2009). Language is a complex adaptive system: Position paper. *Language Learning*, *59*(S1), 1–26.

Christiansen, M. H., & Chater, N. (2008). Language as shaped by the brain. *Behavioral and Brain Sciences*, *31*(5), 489–508.

Cornish, H., Tamariz, M., & Kirby, S. (2009). Complex adaptive systems and the origins of adaptive structure: What experiments can tell us. *Language Learning*, *59*(S1), 187–205.

Croft, W. (2000). *Explaining language change: an evolutionary approach.*

Dawkins, R. (1989). *The selfish gene.* Cambridge University Press.

Heine, B., & Kuteva, T. (2007). *The genesis of grammar: a reconstruction.* Oxford University Press.

Hoefler, S., & Smith, A. D. M. (2009). The pre-linguistic basis of grammaticalisation: a unified approach to metaphor and reanalysis. *Studies in Language*, *33*(4), 883–906.

Kirby, S., Cornish, H., & Smith, K. (2008). Cumulative cultural evolution in the lab: an experimental approach to the origins of structure in human language. *Proceedings of the National Academy of Sciences*, *105*(31), 10681–10686.

Price, G. R. (1995). The nature of selection. *Journal of Theoretical Biology*, *175*(3), 373–388.

Ritt, N. (2004). *Selfish sounds and linguistic evolution.* Cambridge.

Smith, A. D. M. (2008). Protolanguage reconstructed. *Interaction Studies*, *9*(1), 100–116.

Sperber, D., & Wilson, D. (1995). *Relevance: Communication and cognition.*

ITERATED LEARNING IN POPULATIONS: LEARNING AND EVOLVING EXPECTATIONS ABOUT LINGUISTIC HOMOGENEITY

KENNY SMITH, BILL THOMPSON

Language Evolution and Computation Research Unit, School of Philosophy, Psychology and Language Sciences, University of Edinburgh

Natural languages do not differ arbitrarily, but are constrained so that certain properties recur across the languages of the world. One theory argues that language universals are a direct reflection of constraints hard-wired into the language acquisition process (Chomsky, 1965). An alternative suggestion (e.g. Kirby, Dowman & Griffiths, 2007) is that the same universals could arise given only weak biases in individual learners, as a consequence of cultural transmission. This debate has profound implications for theories of the origins and evolution of language, because the culturally-mediated mapping between learner biases and language structure complicates the biological evolution of the language faculty (Smith & Kirby, 2008).

One technique for investigating the relationship between language structure and the prior expectations of language learners is to treat language acquisition as Bayesian inference, and model cultural transmission as the process of iterated learning. Using this framework, Burkett & Griffiths (2010) model the situation where learners learn one or more languages based on linguistic data produced by multiple teachers, where learners have a prior preference for languages of one structural type. Burkett & Griffiths identify two patterns of results, depending on the assumptions learners make about the linguistic homogeneity of their speech community. When learners expect their community to be relatively heterogeneous (i.e. they expect to learn to speak multiple languages), then populations converge to a situation where each language is spoken with a frequency given by its prior probability: in other words, the distribution of languages in a population (and within each individual in that population) accurately reflects the expectations of individual learners about language structure. However, when learners expect their speech community to be homogenous (i.e. they expect to learn one or a few languages), a single language type dominates the population: consequently, the distribution of languages does not just reflect the biases of learners regarding language structure, e.g. a priori less probable languages can dominate if initially frequent.

Burkett & Griffiths therefore show that learners' expectations regarding the homogeneity of their speech community mediate the relationship between properties of individual learners and language universals. We explore two explanations of how these expectations could be formed. In the first model, we assume that learners infer the homogeneity of their speech community from their linguistic data, at the same time as inferring the distribution over languages implied by that data. Under some conditions, the learner's inferences about the homogeneity of their linguistic input can be affected by the social structure of their population, which can in turn affect the types of languages that evolve in that population; however, the determining factor is generally the learner's prior expectations about the homogeneity of their speech community. In the second model, we explicitly evolve these prior expectations: this expectation is genetically transmitted, with reproduction depending on ability to coordinate on a shared language. Under this scenario, we see strong selection for learners who expect linguistic homogeneity, even in situations where such genotypes are rare; consequently, populations converge on languages which do not straightforwardly reflect the learners' expectations about linguistic structure.

This work indicates that there are plausible circumstances under which cultural transmission obscures the relationship between learner biases and their linguistic consequences. Evolutionary pressures acting on the language faculty therefore face an opaque mapping between the structure of languages (over which selection presumably acts) and the cognitive traits that produce those linguistic structures, rendering the evolution of the language faculty problematic.

References

Burkett, D., & Griffiths, T. L. (2010). Iterated learning of multiple languages from multiple teachers. In A. D. M. Smith, M. Schouwstra, B. de Boer, & K. Smith (Eds.), *The Evolution of Language* (pp. 58-65). Singapore: Word Scientific.

Chomsky, N. (1965). *Aspects of the theory of syntax*. Cambridge: MIT Press.

Kirby, S., Dowman, M., & Griffiths, T. L. (2007). Innateness and culture in the evolution of language. *PNAS, 104,* 5241–5245.

Smith, K., & Kirby, S. (2008). Cultural evolution: implications for understanding the human language faculty and its evolution. *Philosophical Transactions of the Royal Society B, 363*, 3591- 3603.

REGULARIZATION OF LINGUISTIC VARIATION IN POPULATIONS

KENNY SMITH

Language Evolution and Computation Research Unit, PPLS, University of Edinburgh

ELIZABETH WONNACOTT

Department of Experimental Psychology, University of Oxford

AMY PERFORS

School of Psychology, University of Adelaide

Natural languages do not differ arbitrarily, but are constrained so that certain properties recur across the languages of the world. These *language universals* presumably arise from the nature of the human brain, but the mapping from brain to language structure is unclear: linguistic universals may reflect hard constraints on language acquisition, or may arise given only weak biases in individual learners, as a consequence of cultural transmission in populations (e.g., Chater & Christiansen, 2010). Understanding this mapping from properties of learners to language structure has profound implications for theories of the origins and evolution of language, because the culturally-mediated mapping between learner biases and language structure potentially obscures those learner biases from selection and therefore influences the biological evolution of the language faculty (Smith & Kirby, 2008).

One universal (or near universal) feature of human languages is the *predictability of linguistic variation*: in general, no two linguistic forms will occur in precisely the same environments and perform precisely the same functions. In previous work, we demonstrated experimentally that an artificial language that exhibited unpredictability in plural marking became increasingly predictable over repeated episodes of transmission (Smith & Wonnacott, 2010). A classic diffusion chain design was used in which participants were organized into independent iterated learning chains, with the language produced by the first generation being used to train the second generation, and so on. This result demonstrates that regularity can arise via language transmission even if learners have weak rather than absolute biases.

One limitation of this work, however, is that each learner was only exposed to the output of a *single* participant. In real-world language learning, of course, learners are exposed to linguistic input generated by multiple individuals. To investigate the effects of this, a new experiment was conducted using the same input languages as in Smith & Wonnacott (2010) but with generations consisting of *two* individuals (each of the two participants per generation received input from the previous two participants, and so on). As a control comparison, ten additional *single-person* chains were also run.

Analyses revealed a significant main effect of generation number, indicative of cumulative regularization, but also a significant chain type x generation number interaction: languages in two-person chains regularize much more slowly than in one-person chains, but do still exhibit a (minimal) cumulative increase in predictability. In other words, scaling up to two-person chains attenuates the regularization seen in single-person chains. This effect was further explored using computational modeling. Participants were modeled as Bayesian learners who infer the distribution of plural markers based on the linguistic data presented to the first participants in each chain. The model suggests that the rate of regularization diminishes as population size increases, and also suggests a possible explanation for this effect: each additional learner per generation adds variability to the input. Together, these experimental and computational results imply that transmission alone may not be enough to engender predictability in natural languages, even if individual learners have a bias for regularity.

This work demonstrates that transmission in populations may mask learner biases and further complicate the mapping from properties of individuals to features of language. Evolutionary pressures acting on the language faculty face a similarly opaque mapping between the structure of the languages (over which selection presumably acts) and the cognitive traits that produce that structure.

References

Chater, N. & Christiansen, M.H. (2010). Language acquisition meets language evolution. *Cognitive Science, 34,* 1131-1157.

Smith, K., & Kirby, S. (2008). Cultural evolution: implications for understanding the human language faculty and its evolution. *Philosophical Transactions of the Royal Society B, 363*, 3591- 3603.

Smith, K., & Wonnacott, E. (2010). Eliminating unpredictable variation through iterated learning. *Cognition, 116,* 444-449.

ABDUCTIVE INFERENCE AND INSIGHT IN THE EVOLUTION OF SYMBOLIC COMMUNICATION

JUSTIN SULIK

Language Evolution and Computation Research Unit, School of Philosophy, Psychology & Language Sciences, The University of Edinburgh
j.w.b.sulik@sms.ed.ac.uk

Insight and inference are two key concepts in the evolution of symbolic communication. I propose that abductive inference (i.e. *novel* hypothesis generation), though not studied in language evolution and poorly understood generally, is vital in linking these key concepts in an account of how our pre-linguistic ancestors first came to learn novel symbols in complex communicative contexts.

Peirce (1934) considered abduction more fundamental to our cognition than his better known distinction between icons, indices and symbols. Both he and Chomsky (2006) claim that abduction is how we learn new words, but such claims have not been explored much: the focus has instead been on insight and induction.

On one hand, Deacon (1997) argues that our mental representations are reorganised in a flash of insight when we cross the threshold into symbolic communication. On the other hand, various authors treat symbol learning as a matter of Bayesian inductive inference, where we evaluate the probable truth of hypotheses concerning novel meanings. Though insight-based and inference-based approaches are not incompatible, there is little point of contact between them.

I argue that abduction fills this role as it is the starting point of the process that ends with induction, and since the cognitive mechanisms underlying abduction are related to those underlying insight. First I define abduction and outline predictions; then I review and present empirical data to support these predictions.

It is often assumed that inference falls into two categories: deduction (which is necessarily true) and induction (which is not). In this sense, induction is a broad category, covering a range of specific subtypes. Bayesian inference is one such subtype; category generalisation is another. Peirce argued, however, that there are three basic types of inference: abduction and induction are both non-deductive, but abduction is not a subtype of induction.

Abduction is the formation of novel hypotheses to explain data; deduction derives predictions from these hypotheses; induction decides which hypotheses best explain data. The crucial distinction is that induction evaluates a finite set of hypotheses, while abduction is what generates that finite set out of (sometimes countless) possible hypotheses *if* the hypotheses or the data are new. We rely on these to different extents in different circumstances. When doctors have learnt several possible causes of a symptom, they rely mainly on induction in deciding the most likely explanation from the learnt set for a specific case. However, the first person ever to think up germs performed an abduction: the information was new to that person's representation of the world. Hypotheses in response to novel symptoms are also abductive, as are hypotheses about the motivations behind novel co-specific behaviour. I will thus argue that an account of the evolution of symbolic behaviour in our pre-linguistic ancestors relies comparatively more heavily on abductive inference. Testable predictions of this approach include:

1. Hypothesis generation is independent of hypothesis evaluation
2. Abduction requires cognitive mechanisms associated with insight
3. Small-world hypothesis generation (with a given or learnt set of candidates) is distinct from large-world hypothesis generation (without such a set)
4. Learning a novel symbol system is more abductive/less inductive than learning a novel symbol in a known system
5. Animals are comparatively poor at abducing explanations

In this talk I focus on the first three of these. In a priming study, Bonawitz and Griffiths (2010) show that the probability of an hypothesis being generated is independent of the posterior probability of the hypothesis, and I discuss extensions to their study. Bowden and Jung-Beeman (2007) show how subjective reporting and brain imaging support the claim that insight problem solving is a distinct cognitive mechanism, and I show that abduction relies on similar mechanisms. Finally, I contrast word learning in small worlds and in large worlds.

I conclude that abduction is distinct from induction in that it is insightful and in that it is comparatively more important for hypothesis generation in communicative contexts like those facing our ancestors crossing the symbolic threshold.

References

Bonawitz, E. B., & Griffiths, T. L. (2010). Deconfounding hypothesis generation and evaluation in Bayesian models. In *Proceedings of the Thirty-second Cognitive Science Society.*

Bowden, E. M., & Jung-Beeman, M. (2007). Methods for investigating the neural components of insight. *Methods*, *42*, 87-99.

Chomsky, N. (2006). *Language and Mind* (3rd ed.). Cambridge: Cambridge University Press.

Deacon, T. W. (1997). *The Symbolic Species.* London: Penguin.

Peirce, C. S. (1934). *Collected Papers of Charles Sanders Peirce* (Vol. 5). Cambridge, MA: Harvard University Press.

GRAMMATICALIZATION, LIGHT VERBS, AND THE ORIGINS OF COMPLEX LANGUAGE

JOHN D. SUNDQUIST

Department of Foreign Languages and Literatures, Purdue University
West Lafayette, Indiana, 47907, USA

Previous proposals on the evolution of grammar have varied widely in their views on the origins of morphology and syntax (Tallerman 2007). On the one hand, Wray (2000) proposes that words first emerged in protolanguage as a string of formulaic language or holistic utterances. This view suggests that protolanguage resembled a system of primate vocalization in which holistic signals/calls were formulaic utterances that gradually became segmented into individual word-like subunits of the utterance. On the other hand, Bickerton (2003) proposes a synthetic model of protolanguage in which isolated vocabulary items that correspond to simple concepts were juxtaposed against each other to convey a message. Eventually, a more complex system arose as more frequent word combinations led to the emergence of semantic roles and hierarchical structure. As van Gelderen (2011) notes, presumably after the development of a system of combination such as Chomsky's (2005) Merge, the process of grammaticalization became responsible for subsequent developments of more complex grammatical marking.

Using evidence from the history of Swedish, I analyze examples of grammaticalization that lend support to a synthetic approach. I investigate the development of "light verbs" in a corpus of early Swedish texts written between 1300 and 1600 and discuss the importance of the grammaticalization data for theories on the origin of complex morphosyntax. Light verbs, such as English *have, take*, or *give,* often occur in pairings with different nominal complements that could be expressed by a single lexical verb (e.g., *take a drive=drive).* In the earliest Swedish texts, full lexical verbs such as *lofa* 'to praise' occur alongside light verb+nominal complements (*loff giva* 'give praise').

Results of the quantitative analysis of the study indicate that a wider range of light verb+noun collocations emerges in subsequent stages of the language, and a gradual increase in their frequency occurs at the same time as a decrease in the use of the single-verb equivalents. As semantically bleached verbs, light verbs exhibit some of the typical effects of grammaticalization, progressing from a full lexical verb to something with less semantic force and more grammatical function.

The Swedish data imply the opposite development that Wray (2000) suggests in the holistic model of protolanguage grammar. The change to light verbs in Swedish indicates that collocations are the end products of this change, that individual lexical items are semantically bleached, and that syntactic structures become simpler. In the holistic approach, on the other hand, units of formulaic language are the starting point for change; these collocations becomes more lexical as they are segmented into multiple meaning-bearing units, and more complex grammatical forms arise during subsequent stages. Moreover, the grammaticalization data here indicate that the assumptions of a synthetic approach are more on track. Isolated lexical items--and not formulaic phrases--are the building blocks that take on new grammatical functions. Furthermore, the relevance of the history of light verbs for a synthetic approach lies in the idea that whatever psychological, logical, or linguistic motivations lie behind the evolution of grammar, these motivations did not disappear with the advent of historical language. They remain present and at work in the history of all languages and operate cyclically.

References

Bickerton, D. (2003). Symbol and structure: a comprehensive framework for language evolution. In M. H. Christiansen and S. Kirby (Eds.), *Language evolution* (pp. 77-93). Oxford: Oxford University Press.

Chomsky, N. (2005). Three factors in language design. *Linguistic Inquiry,* 36, 1-22.

Gelderen, E. van. (2011). *The Linguistic Cycle.* Oxford: Oxford Univ. Press.

Tallerman, M. (2007). Did our ancestors speak a holistic protolanguage? *Lingua,* 117, 579–604.

Wray, A. (2000). Holistic utterances in protolanguage: the link from primates to humans. In C. Knight, M. Studdert-Kennedy, and J. R. Hurford, J.R. (Eds.), *The Evolutionary Emergence of Language* (pp. 285-302). Cambridge: Cambridge University Press.

DIVERGENCE AND CONVERGENCE IN VOCAL CULTURES

MIKI TAKAHASI[1, 2], HIROKO KAGAWA[1], KENTA SUZUKI[3, 4], OLGA FEHÉR[5] AND KAZUO OKANOYA[1, 3]

1 Graduates School of Arts and Sciences, The University of Tokyo, Komaba 3-8-1 Tokyo, 153-8902, Japan

2 JSPS Research Fellow, Chiyoda-ku, Tokyo, 102-8472, Japan

3 Japan Science Technology Agency, ERATO Okanoya Emotional Information Project, Wako, Saitama, 351-0198, Japan

4 Graduate School of Science and Engineering, Saitama University, Saitama, Saitama, 338-8570, Japan

5 Biology Department, The City College of New York, 138th St. at Convent Ave. New York, NY, 10031 USA

Vocal learning is considered to be guided by innate constraints. A preference for a specific class of sounds is one of such constraints. In human infants, speech sounds facilitate the extraction of rules from auditory tokens (Marcus et al. 2007). Songbirds learn their vocalization from adults and the innate preference for their own species song is documented in several species.

Bengalese finches (BF) have been domesticated for more than 250 years from wild White-rumped munias (WRM) living in East Asia. BFs have a different song type from their wild strain. They sing songs with acoustically clear sounds and complex syntax. WRMs sing stereotyped songs with noisy sounds. Cross-fostering studies show that WRMs have strong preference for their strain's songs and tend to make an exact copy of them. In BFs, this preference is relaxed. The relaxation of song preference would allow learning songs from other strains (Takahasi & Okanoya, 2010).

To investigate this, we conducted a "cultural evolution experiment" (Fehér et al. 2009) with three BF and three WRM colonies. An isolated male and three non-singing females were bred as founders of each colony. Songs of isolated birds would not reflect the innate preference because there are no models to be learned from. Prediction was that after several generations songs would be diverse in BF colonies, while they would converge to the strain-specific songs in WRM colonies.

Figure1 shows examples of songs which came from the cultural evolution experiment. In the BF founder song of this colony, there are three types of sounds: sounds with clear harmonic structure (single line), noisy sounds (dotted line), and long sounds with frequency modulation (double line). Fourteen tutees from 9 generations (clutches) in the BF colony had different combinations of these sounds and 5 types of songs came from this colony. Nine tutees from 2 generations in the WRM colony made an exact copy from the founder or copied a part from the founder song.

In BF colonies, the songs of tutees were diverse. On the other hand, WRM tutees tend to copy the founder song. These results suggest that differences in innate song preference lead to different song divergence in a colony, and that the relaxation of song preferences lead to rich variations. Species specific songs would be useful to avoid hybridization with other species. Bengalese finches were free from this pressure under domestication, and the song preference must be relaxed (Deacon 2003). The relaxation of innate preferences should also affect language evolution in humans to make complex syntactical rules.

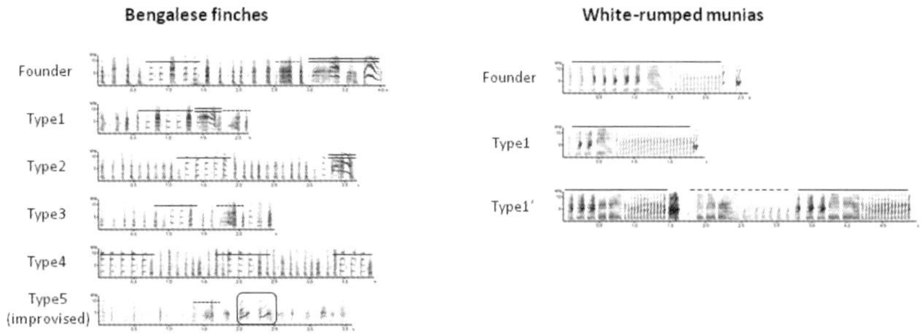

Figure 1. Examples of founder and tutees' songs in Bengalese finch and White-rumped munia colonies. Five types of song came from the founder song in the BF colony. In the WRM colony, tutees copied the founder song (Type 1, single line), and some tutees had an arranged part (dotted line) between copied part (Type 1').

References

Deacon, T. W. (2003). Universal grammar and semiotic constraints. In: M. H. Christiansen & S. Kirby (eds.) Evolution of Language, Oxford University Press, pp. 111-140.

Fehér, O., Wang, H., Saar. S., Mitra, P. P., & Tchernichovski, O. (2009). De novo establishment of wild-type song culture in the zebra finch. *Nature, 459*,564-568.

Marcus, G. F., Fernandes, K. J., & Johnson, S. P. (2007). Infant rule learning facilitated by speech. *Psychological Science, 18*,387-391.

Takahasi, M., & Okanoya, K. (2010). Song learning in wild and domesticated strains of white-rumped munia, *Lonchura striata*, compared by cross-fostering procedures: domestication increases song variability by decreasing strain-specific bias. *Ethology, 116*,396-405.

REPLICATION AND EMERGENCE PROCESSES IN LANGUAGE EVOLUTION

MÓNICA TAMARIZ

Language Evolution and Computation Research Unit, School of Philosophy, Psychology & Language Sciences, The University of Edinburgh monica@ling.ed.ac.uk.

Replication and emergence characterize many complex adaptive systems such as life or the immune system. In this paper I propose that the evolution of language structure over generations is best explained by a conjunction of replication and emergence processes at the level of linguistic utterances.

REPLICATION happens when a token of a type is produced, and it is (a) similar, (b) caused by and (c) has received information from other tokens of the same type (Sperber, 1996). EMERGENCE is a property of complex adaptive systems (Gell-Mann, 1994), which are sets of elements that interact with their environment following simple rules. As the system unravels, its behaviour is not reducible to its elements and rules: its new properties are emergent or self-organised.

Transmission involves a flow of linguistic information towards new generations of speakers. In their first year of life, infants learn the sound categories of their ambient language, and this involves production and perception reinforcement loops (e.g. Vihman et al., 2009) and statistical category learning (e.g. Maye et al. 2002). With sound categories in place, actual phonetic realizations of sounds behave to all effects as REPLICATORS (Wedel, 2006). Symbolic, referential function is not involved in this process, and the replicated information is purely formal.

Towards the end of their first year, infants begin to produce their first stable sound combinations, which may be words, prosodic patterns etc. learned by imitation. Stable sound combinations also REPLICATE: the production of a token of sound combination is caused by and receives the information from similar tokens previously heard or produced. Imitation learning in humans, but not in other apes, tends to be more dependent on intention than on function: children seem to copy behaviours that they perceive as intentional (Tomasello, 2003) even if they do not have a function (Horner & Whiten, 2005).

In contrast, morphosyntactic, semantic and pragmatic rules and categories cannot be replicated by imitation learning because they are not tokens in speech, but mental abstractions. I argue, *contra* the memetic position, but in agreement with e.g. Sperber (1996), that mental entities do not replicate: a linguistic rule or category in a speaker's head is not directly caused by tokens of the same rule or category in other speakers' brains and there is certainly no need for information transfer (e.g. by teaching) towards new speakers. Instead, rules and categories EMERGE from interactions between the replicated information (sounds and sound combinations) and their environment, which is rather complex. It includes other sounds and sound combinations; the referents they become symbolically associated with, which have their own set of categories, dependencies and frequency distributions; and the speakers' communicative needs and social interaction patterns.

The perspective of cultural transmission as replication plus emergence has two important consequences. Firstly, the replication of forms independently of their functions suggests that models of language evolution should not be based on units such as Saussurean signs or constructions, where form and function are inseparable. Secondly, this perspective focuses the study of the BIOLOGICAL evolution of language on cognitive mechanisms for the replication of sounds and stable sound combinations (such as vocal learning or form imitation) and for the emergence of complex utterances (such as symbolic association, inference, communication or categorization).

Acknowledgments

The author acknowledges support from UK AHRC Grant AH/F017677/1.

References

Gell-Mann, M. (1994) The Quark and the Jaguar: Adventures in the Simple and Complex. New York: Freeman

Horner, V. & Whiten, A. (2005). Causal knowledge and imitation/emulation switching in chimpanzees (*Pan troglodytes*) and children (*Homo sapiens*). *Animal Cognition*, 8: 164-181.

Maye, J., Werker, J. F. & Gerken, L. (2002). Infant sensitivity to distributional information can affect phonetic discrimination. *Cognition*, 82(3): B101-B111.

Sperber, D. (1996). *Explaining culture*. Oxford: Blackwell.

Vihman, M.M., DePaolis, R.A., & Keren-Portnoy, T. (2009). Babbling and word: A dynamic systems perspective on phonological development. In E. L. Bavin (ed.) *The Cambridge Handbook of Child Language*. Cambridge: CUP.

Tomasello, M. (2003). Constructing a Language: A Usage-Based Theory of Language Acquisition. Cambridge, MA: Harvard University Press.

Wedel, A. (2006). Exemplar models, evolution and language change. *Ling. Review*, 23: 247-274.

THE EFFECTS OF GENERATION TURNOVER AND INTERLOCUTOR NEGOTIATION ON LINGUISTIC STRUCTURE

MÓNICA TAMARIZ, HANNAH CORNISH, KENNY SMITH, SEÁN ROBERTS AND SIMON KIRBY

Language Evolution and Computation Research Unit, School of Philosophy, Psychology & Language Sciences, The University of Edinburgh
{monica,hannah,kenny,simon}@ling.ed.ac.uk, S.G.Roberts@sms.ed.ac.uk

Cultural transmission has a key impact on the evolution of linguistic structure (Kirby, Cornish & Smith, 2008). During transmission, new individuals learn the conventions of the language through observation and participation in communicative interactions in context. We present a series of experiments which disentangle the role of *generation turnover*, or new minds coming into the linguistic community (e.g. Kirby et al. 2008) from that of *negotiation* of shared form-meaning conventions during interlocutor interaction (studied in graphical, but not linguistic, systems by e.g. Fay et al. 2007, Galantucci 2005).

In the experimental task, two interlocutors played a communicative cooperative game using an artificial miniature language. Players were trained on a random language, which they then used to ask each other for specific objects; they scored a point for each successful interaction. The language produced by one (randomly selected) participant was then used as training data for the following training-and-usage round. We manipulated generation turnover: in *dyads*, two participants played six training-and-usage rounds; in *chains*, six different participant pairs played one round each. We also manipulated negotiation. In the *negotiation* condition there were two human players; in the *no-negotiation* condition, one of the players was replaced with a simulated computer *agent* who had perfect memory (i.e. it always used the training language without errors, and never offered or adopted suggestions during usage). The training languages in this condition came from the human player.

We examined the effects of generation turnover and negotiation on the *systematic structure* of the resulting languages (measured using the technique described in Kirby et al., 2008) and found a significant effect of both factors. Structure increased over the six rounds in chains, but not in dyads. Looking at chains only, the level of structure at the final round was markedly higher when there was negotiation between two interlocutors than when a single participant played with the non-responding agent. However, presence/absence of negotiation in dyads had no such effect.

We also examined the effects on *communicative success*, measured as the scores obtained during the communicative task. Dyads, where there was no generation turnover, scored more points, performing at ceiling level in the last few rounds, while chains did significantly worse. Looking at chains only, while negotiating player pairs improved their scores over rounds to approach optimal communicative success, non-negotiating player-agent pairs did not show any improvement.

These results indicate that both generation turnover and negotiation facilitate communicative success and the emergence and evolution of systematic structure. At *generation turnover*, a memory pressure (only so much can be learned during the brief training stage) and an expressivity pressure (to name all objects unambiguously in order to score points) operate. Structured languages are well adapted to both pressures because they are at the same time compressible (minimal amount of information to memorize) and expressive. At each individual *negotiation*, interlocutors need to make decisions (e.g. whether to adopt their interlocutor's suggestions or stick to their own, or what to say or understand when they cannot remember language items). If both interlocutors are under the same pressures for compressibility and expressivity, then the extra pressure of coordination – for finding a common language between interlocutors – may enhance the effects of the pressures for compressibility and expressivity: the decisions during negotiation constitute extra opportunities for competition between linguistic items that may accelerate evolution.

In conclusion, investigating cultural transmission at the level of communicative interactions can give us a richer understanding of the mechanisms underlying the cultural evolution of linguistic structure.

Acknowledgments

The authors acknowledge support from ESRC Grant Award RES-062-231537.

References

Fay N., Garrod S. & Swoboda N. (2010). The interactive evolution of human communicative systems. *Cognitive Science*, 34: 351-386.

Galantucci, B. (2005). An experimental study of the emergence of human communication systems. *Cognitive Science*, 29(5): 737-767.

Kirby, S., Cornish, H., & Smith, K. (2008). Cumulative cultural evolution in the lab: an experimental approach to the origins of structure in human language. *Proceedings of the National Academy of Sciences*, *105*(31): 10681–10686.

CULTURAL EVOLUTION RENDERS LINGUISTIC NATIVISM IMPLAUSIBLE

BILL THOMPSON, KENNY SMITH, SIMON KIRBY
Language Evolution & Computation Research Unit,
The University of Edinburgh, 3 Charles St., Edinburgh, EH8 9AD, UK
Bill@ling.ed.ac.uk, Kenny@ling.ed.ac.uk, Simon@ling.ed.ac.uk

A central issue of debate in linguistics is the nativist hypothesis: the proposal that universally observed features of languages can be explained by a universally shared and biologically determined cognitive substrate that strongly and transparently predicts these linguistic features (Chomsky, 1965). An evolutionary stance appears to provide support for this hypothesis (Pinker & Bloom, 1990). However, language is underpinned by social learning and cultural transmission alongside biological evolution, and the interactions between these three systems are relatively poorly understood. We set out a general model of these interactions that leads to a surprising conclusion: cultural transmission renders the biological evolution of strong domain-specific innate constraints unlikely, but we nonetheless witness strong universal tendencies in the cultural systems of these simulated populations. In this talk, we present the results of a simple implementation of this model. The details of our approach are as follows.

Our formalisation has a basis in three components: a rational framework for language acquisition, an iterated learning model of cultural transmission, and a representation of biological evolution. We assume language learners must identify which of two arbitrarily distinct language types, t_0 and t_1, is most likely to have generated the linguistic output of a learner from the previous generation: an observed set of b utterances, d. Each language type is associated with a diagnostic utterance class u, such that $P(u_y|t_y) = 1 - \epsilon$ and $P(u_y|t_{x \neq y}) = \epsilon$. Learners apply Bayes' rule to determine $P(t_y|d)$ on the basis of this likelihood function and a prior expectation for t_y given by a prior distribution over language types, which is characterised by the parameter p, where $P(t_1) = p$ and $P(t_0) = 1 - p$. A learner's prior expectations are given by an inherited genome, which is simply a set of n genes, where each gene in a genome $g^n = \{g_1, g_2, \ldots, g_n\}$ is a member of the set $G = \{0, 1\}$. We treat the prior as a polygenic quantitative trait determined by the additive effects of individual genes, so that $p = \frac{1}{n}\sum_{i=1}^{n} g_i$. Genetic transmission is subject to point mutation at rate μ, and under selection: each individual reproduces with a probability proportional to the accuracy with which it could communicate with the rest of the population. That is, we are selecting for learners who will converge on a shared language.

Previous work (Kirby, Dowman, & Griffiths, 2007) shows that iterated learning can amplify weak biases. The results of our model (Fig.1) show that, as tiny perturbations in initial gene frequencies move the population away from perfectly neutral priors, cultural transmission unmasks these weak biases in individuals, yielding large effects in the population's language. Natural selection then favours biases encoding the emerging majority language. However, iterated learning also masks relative strength of bias. Consequently, the combination of unmasking and masking leads to a balance of evolutionary forces: mutation pressure induces drift towards neutrality, but natural selection keeps biases away from perfect neutrality. We therefore witness rapid fixation of the weakest biases, and the concomitant emergence of linguistic universals that are facilitated, but not determined, by biology. Our results indicate that cultural transmission radically changes the evolution of learning constraints: the default explanation of arbitrary, universal aspects of language should be in terms of defeasible, weak innate biases.

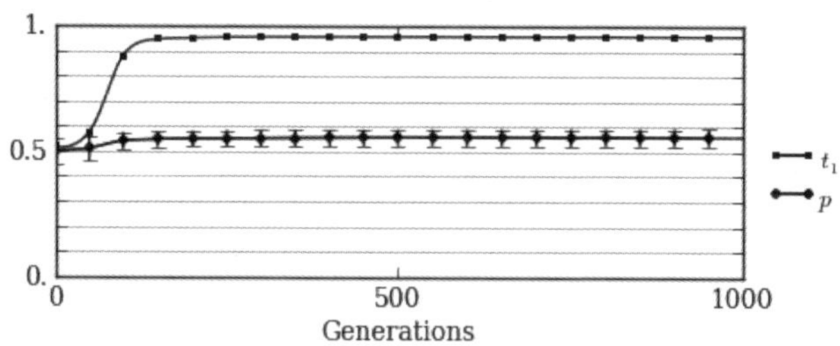

Figure 1. Numerical results for our model. Circles & error bars give the mean value and one standard deviation of the distribution of priors in the population at fifty intervals over 1000 generations. Squares give the corresponding proportion of the population speaking language type t_1. Results show rapid fixation of just-off-neutral biases towards t_1, which quickly becomes universal. $n = 100, \mu = .001, b = 2, \epsilon = .05$.

References

Chomsky, N. (1965). *Aspects of the theory of syntax* (Vol. 119). The MIT press.

Kirby, S., Dowman, M., & Griffiths, T. L. (2007). Innateness and culture in the evolution of language. *Proceedings of the National Academy of Sciences, USA*, *104*, 5241–5245.

Pinker, S., & Bloom, P. (1990). Natural language and natural selection. *Behavioral and Brain Sciences*, *13*(4), 707–784.

NAMING A STRUCTURED WORLD: A CULTURAL ROUTE TO DUALITY OF PATTERNING

FRANCESCA TRIA

Institute for Scientific Interchange (ISI),
Viale Settimio Severo 65, Torino, 10133, Italy
tria@isi.it

BRUNO GALANTUCCI

Dept. of Psychology, Yeshiva University
2495 Amsterdam Ave, New York, NY, 10033, USA
galantuc@yu.edu

VITTORIO LORETO

Physics Dept., Sapienza University of Rome
Piazzale Aldo Moro 5, 00185 Roma, Italy and
Institute for Scientific Interchange (ISI), Viale Settimio Severo 65, 10133 Torino, Italy
vittorio.loreto@roma1.infn.it

Shared by all human languages and absent in any animal's communication systems (Hockett, 1960), duality of patterning refers to the organization of the meaningful elements in a language (e.g., words) at two distinct levels. At a first combinatorial level, meaningless forms (referred to as phonemes) are combined into meaningful forms (e.g., in English lexicon /kat/, /akt/, and /tak/ are composed by /k/, /a/, and /t/). At a second compositional level, meaningful forms (referred to as morphemes) are composed into larger lexical units, the meaning of which is related to the meaning of the individual composing morphemes (e.g., 'bathroom', 'policeman', etc., or 'scientist', 'dancer', etc..). The question remains wide open regarding how and why such a structure did emerge. Here we address this question in the framework of multi-agents modeling, where a population of individuals plays elementary language games (Wittgenstein, 1953) aiming at a success in communication (Steels, 1995; Baronchelli, Felici, Caglioti, Loreto, & Steels, 2006; Puglisi, Baronchelli, & Loreto, 2008). We focus on lexicon, though the compositional level involves syntax as well. We introduce in particular a Blending Game in which we let an initially *blank slate* population of individuals to bootstrap a lexicon using an open-ended set of forms in a large meaning space modeled as a graph (Newman, 2003). We do not make use of any notion of predefined linguistic categories, predefined meanings or relations between objects and forms, letting the graph to account for the semantic structure which organizes our conceptual understanding.

The main result of this study is the identification of two main mechanisms leading to the emergence of duality of patterning. First, a minimal semantic mechanism for word coinage that exploits the structure of the world to compose individual forms into words. This mechanism (a) feeds the combinatorial level of the lexicon and (b) entails that part of the semantic structure percolates into the lexicon. Second, the existence of noise (Nowak, Krakauer, & Dress, 1999) in the message transmission and the possibility for individuals of progressively increasing their level of comprehension each time they are exposed to each particular form. This mechanism is essential for limiting the number of different forms in emerged lexicons, without any a priori constraints on it. We show that combinatoriality is enhanced when comprehension improves slowly, highlighting it as a good solution for message transmission in noisy environments. Compositionality is connected, on the other hand, with the level of structure detectable in the environment, being maximal when the networks representing semantic relations among the objects are neither too sparse nor too dense. Further, we find that the emergence of a shared lexicon in a population is faster when some structure of the world can be exploited. These results demonstrate that the two sides of duality of patterning can emerge simultaneously as a consequence of a pure cultural dynamics in a simulated environment which contains meaningful relations, when a simple constraint on message transmission fidelity is also considered.

References

Baronchelli, A., Felici, M., Caglioti, E., Loreto, V., & Steels, L. (2006). Sharp transition towards shared vocabularies in multi-agent systems. *Journal of Statistical Mechanics, P06014.*

Hockett, C. F. (1960). Logical considerations in the study of animal communication. In L. W & T. W. (Eds.), *Animal sounds and communications* (p. 392-430). Americal Institute of Biological Sciences.

Newman, M. E. J. (2003). The structure and function of complex networks. *SIAM Review*, *45*, 167–256.

Nowak, M. A., Krakauer, D., & Dress, A. (1999). An error limit for the evolution of language. *Proceedings of The Royal Society of London. Series B, Biological Sciences*, *266*(1433), 2131-2136.

Puglisi, A., Baronchelli, A., & Loreto, V. (2008). Cultural route to the emergence of linguistic categories. *Proc. Natl. Acad. Sci. USA*, *105*(23), 7936.

Steels, L. (1995). A self-organizing spatial vocabulary. *Artificial Life*, *2*(3), 319–332.

Wittgenstein, L. (1953). *Philosophical investigations. (translated by anscombe, g.e.m.).* Oxford, UK: Basil Blackwell.

NEURAL CORRELATES OF SONG PERCEPTION DURING ZEBRA FINCH SONG LEARNING AS SHOWN BY BOLD FMRI

ANNE VAN DER KANT
ANNEMIE VAN DER LINDEN
Bio Imaging Lab, University of Antwerp, Universiteitsplein 1
B-2060 Wilrijk (Antwerp), Belgium

Songbirds provide the best animal model currently available for the study of human speech acquisition, since both songbirds and human infants need to be exposed to adult vocalizations early in life in order to develop their own. Zebra finches exhibit a sensitive period for song acquisition and are thus particularly suitable for human speech acquisition research. In recent years an increasing number of studies have addressed the neural underpinnings of vocal learning in this species. However, no studies to date have been able to map the neural correlates of birdsong learning longitudinally in the same individual. Therefore it is yet unclear how perceptual changes related to opening and closing of the sensitive period are reflected in the brain.

In the present study we used whole-brain functional Magnetic Resonance Imaging (fMRI) to longitudinally study the neural correlates of song perception in juvenile male zebra finches (Taeniopygia guttata) during song learning. In order to monitor the development closely, the BOLD response elicited by song was measured in five anaesthetized male juvenile birds at 30, 40, 55 and 90-100 days post hatching (DPH). During the fMRI measurements, birds were presented with auditory stimuli consisting of their tutor's song, a conspecific song and a heterospecific song.

Our data show functional changes in the auditory forebrain both during the sensory and during the sensorimotor period. Specifically, between 40 DPH and song crystallization (90-100 DPH) neural activity induced by listening to song increased significantly and broadened in field L, the avian homologue of the primary auditory cortex and the caudomedial nidopallium (NCM), a secondary auditory area. Additionally, song induced activation increased significantly in the entopallium during the course of song learning. Finally, a selective response to the tutor song was shown in MLd, the auditory midbrain nucleus, throughout development (Figure 1).

Our findings show changes in the neural correlates of song perception of male zebra finches during the sensitive period for song learning. This confirms electrophysiological results obtained in different age groups (Gehr et al, 2000).

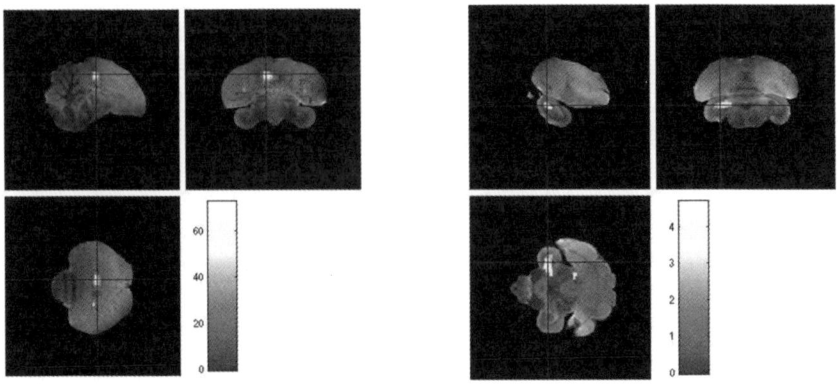

Figure 1. Left panel: Increase of the BOLD response in Field L, NCM and the Entopallium between 40 and 100 DPH. The color bar shows corresponding F-values. Right panel: Selective response to the tutor song in the left auditory midbrain. The color bar shows corresponding T-values.

The increased activation in the entopallium in response to song towards song crystallization is surprising as this structure is regarded part of the visual system. However, it has also been shown to be involved in pattern recognition (Wanatabe et al, 2011), which may play a role in song perception. Song selectivity in the auditory midbrain has been shown before (Poirier *et al*, 2009; van der Kant *et al*, in prep.) and has now been shown in juveniles. Our results thus suggest that the neural correlates of song perception are influenced by the progression of song learning during development. Furthermore, the present data not only support the hypothesis that the auditory midbrain is involved in memory and learning, but show that it is already involved during the sensitive period for song learning.

Studying the neural correlates of birdsong learning might show us to which extent the neural processes underlying vocal learning in humans and songbirds bear resemblance to each other. Ultimately, we might answer the question whether the difference between vocal learning in birds and humans is 'one of degree and not of kind', as Charles Darwin once proposed for the mind.

References

Gehr D.D., Hofer S.B., Marquardt D., Leppelsack H. (2000). Functional changes in field L complex during song development of juvenile male zebra finches. *Developmental Brain Research, 29*, 153-165.

Poirier C., Boumans T., Verhoye M., Balthazart J., Van der Linden A. (2009). Own-song recognition in the songbird auditory pathway: selectivity and lateralization. *Journal of Neuroscience, 18,* 2252-2258

Wanatabe S., Mayer U., Bischof H.J. (2011). Visual Wulst analyses "where" and Entopallium analyzes "what" in the zebra finch visual system. *Behavioural Brain Research, 12*, 51-56

HUMAN NON-LEXICAL VOCAL EVENTS AND PROSODY IN THE PERSPECTIVE OF LANGUAGE EVOLUTION

ANNE VANPÉ AND DIDIER DEMOLIN

GIPSA-Lab, Université Stendhal Grenoble
avanpe@yahoo.fr, didier.demolin@gipsa-lab.grenoble-inp.fr
Université Stendhal, Domaine universitaire BP25
38040 Grenoble Cedex 9, France

Humans produce non-lexical vocal micro-events; both vocal and not, with realizations ranging from physiological noises to phonological vocal productions (interjections). (We term these 'vocal events' in this paper, though some are not voiced.) Note that, as opposed to the term 'vocalization' as commonly used, these are acoustic speech events accompanying, and indispensable for, efficient communication. During the dynamic process of face-to-face interaction, subjects spontaneously and continuously express their varying mental/cognitive and affective states, even outside talk turns. We characterize such vocal events with terms from fillers, through grunts and bursts, to interjections. We present an annotation and description of the vocal events in a realistic emotionally induced French corpus (Aubergé et al., 2006). Their impressionistic phonetic/prosodic description is given and globally analyzed (Vanpé, 2011). Categorization (Table 1) shows that most frequent are mouth noises where production requires simple articulatory control or vocalic interjections, and wherein duration and airflow vary greatly. Overall, 46% of vocal events use ingressive airflow (e.g. inspiration, clicks, articulator slackening). We characterize these events as a continuum from grunts through interjections with increasing prosodic control, which we then present in phylogenetic perspective (see also Eklund 2008). The continuum Jackendoff discussed (2002) as fossils of language evolution shares some of our vocal events, but he focuses on the symbolic level of the elements. Burling (2005) also discusses non vocal communication in a language evolution perspective, but focuses mainly on evolutionary factors (e.g. sexual selection). We expect study of vocal events to illuminate various aspects of language evolution, and indeed to reveal certain necessary conditions for language emergence. It should likewise relate to some current linguistic concerns.

Ethologically; these events are essential for communication in modern humans. What is their role in non-human primate communication? What was it in the evolution of primate communication? Comparing our vocal event data with that addressing non-human primates will help clarify the possibilities.

Table 1. Inventory of vocal events from our corpus, ordered by frequency.

Vocal event type	*Number of occurrences*	*Percentage of the total*
inspiration	577	19,2%
articulator slackening	477	15,8%
expiration	393	13,1%
vocalic (V) interjection	316	10,5%
ingressive occlusion_inspiration	251	8,3%
swallowing	220	7,3%
plosion	151	5,0%
respiration releasing	127	4,2%
brutal expiration	126	4,2%
tongue-lips interaction	92	3,1%
tongue click	76	2,5%
VC interjection	58	1,9%
CV interjection	52	1,7%
consonantal (C) interjection	34	1,1%
combination[1] interjection	30	1,0%
friction	13	0,4%
clearing one's throat	10	0,3%
moan	8	0,3%
Total	**3011**	**100%**

References

Aubergé, V., Audibert, N., & Rilliard, A. (2006). De E-Wiz à C-Clone. Recueil, modélisation et synthèse d'expressions authentiques. *Revue d'Intelligence Artificielle-"Interactions émotionnelles"*, 20(4-5), 499-528.

Burling, R. (2005). *The talking ape: How language evolved.* New York: Oxford University Press.

Eklund, R. (2008). Pulmonic ingressive phonation: Diachronic and synchronic characteristics, distribution and function in animal and human sound production and in human speech. *Journal of the International Phonetic Association*, 38(3), 235-324. Cambridge University Press.

Jackendoff, R. (2002). An evolutionary perspective on the architecture. In *Foundations of Language: Brain, Meaning, Grammar, Evolution* (pp. 231-264). Oxford: Oxford University Press.

Vanpé, A. (2011). Expressions et micro-expressions spontanées de la face et de la voix en Interaction Homme-Machine : esquisse d'un modèle du "Feeling of Thinking". PhD Thesis. Grenoble University.

[1]When an interjection was composed of more than one consonantal or vocalic phoneme, it was labeled "combination".

BIASED COPYING IN THE EVOLUTION OF HUMAN COMMUNICATION SYSTEMS

BRADLEY WALKER, NICOLAS FAY, T MARK ELLISON

School of Psychology, University of Western Australia, 35 Stirling Highway Perth, 6009, Australia

1. Background & Aim

People copy one another's utterances during communication (Garrod & Anderson, 1987). In laboratory micro-societies this copying leads to the creation of shared communication systems (Fay, Garrod, Roberts, & Swoboda, 2010). If biased copying is seen in human communication, such that some individuals are more likely to be copied than others, certain individuals will have a disproportionate influence on the evolution of their communication system.

People copy others they perceive to be skilful, successful, prestigious or similar to themselves (Henrich & McElreath, 2003; Richerson & Boyd, 2005). The present study tested whether people exhibit biased copying in a communication task similar to the game Pictionary™. It is hypothesized that participants will copy the drawings of others more when told the drawer was skilful, successful, prestigious or similar to themselves (than when told the opposite).

2. Method

Participants (N = 244) first drew pictures of 8 concepts (from a list of 16), including items such as "Museum", "Brad Pitt" and "Poverty". Next they were shown drawings of the same concepts produced by another person who was described as being HIGH or LOW on Skill, Success, Prestige or Similarity (to the participant). Finally, participants drew the eight concepts again. Pairs of drawings were rated for similarity to measure how much participants had changed their drawings to copy those of the other drawer. The task was completed on a computer, drawing with a mouse.

3. Results & Discussion

Pairs of drawings were rated for similarity. Inter-rater reliability was high, $r = .78$, $p < .01$. Comparisons were made between the participants' first drawings and the other drawer's (Baseline), their second drawings and the other drawer's (Self-Other), and their first and second drawings (Self-Self).

Both conditions showed an increase from Baseline to Self-Other similarity, indicating a degree of copying. We found a statistically significant difference between the HIGH and LOW groups on Self-Other similarity, showing a tendency for participants to copy more of the other's drawings when they were identified with a HIGH trait value. While biased copying was observed, the degree of copying was small (reflected by a small effect size). A stronger tendency was for participants to retain large portions of their originals (showing high Self-Self similarity). Thus, participants behaved egocentrically, preferring their own productions to those produced by a skilful/successful/prestigious or similar model. In other words, participants preferred individual learning to social learning.

The study is limited by being non-interactive. In an interaction, the traits of a partner may be more salient, potentially increasing preferential copying, and a small bias may accumulate. Further research should examine this.

4. Conclusion

Participants, told that another drawer was highly skilled, successful, prestigious or similar to themselves, copied that drawer's pictures more than those told the opposite. This is evidence for biased copying in communication. In being copied more, individuals favoured by this bias may make greater contributions than others to the origins and evolution of their communication system, whether it is a laboratory exercise or a natural language.

References

Fay, N., Garrod, S., Roberts, L., & Swoboda, N. (2010). The interactive evolution of human communication systems. *Cognitive Science*, *34*, 351-386.

Garrod, S., & Anderson, A. (1987). Saying what you mean in dialogue: A study of conceptual and semantic coordination. *Cognition, 27*(2), *181-218.*

Henrich, J., & McElreath, R. (2003). The evolution of cultural evolution. *Evolutionary Anthropology, 12*(3), 123-135.

Richerson, P. J., & Boyd, R. (2005). *Not by Genes Alone: How Culture Transformed Human Evolution*. Chicago, IL: University of Chicago Press.

EMOTION, APPROACH-AVOIDANCE MOTIVATION, AND BLENDING IN THE EVOLUTION OF LANGUAGE

PAUL A. WILSON

Department of English Language & Applied Linguistics, University of Łódź, ul.Kosciuszki 65, 90-514, Łódź, Poland

BARBARA LEWANDOWSKA-TOMASZCZYK

Department of English Language & Applied Linguistics, University of Łódź, ul.Kosciuszki 65, 90-514, Łódź, Poland

It is argued in the present paper that an assessment of the relationship between language, emotion, approach-avoidance motivation, conceptual associations, and conceptual integration or blending may bring us a better understanding of the possible role played by emotion and approach-avoidance motivation in the first utterances of human beings.

Heightened emotional state has been identified as causing associations between previously weakly related concepts to become more salient. Lubart and Getz (1997) argue that this is based on the automatic resonance mechanism, which "propagates an emotional "wave" throughout the memory system" (p. 290). The strengthening of such conceptual associations is a fundamental feature underpinning metaphor, and one can therefore consider evidence showing that metaphor production is facilitated when an individual is in a heightened emotional state (e.g., Fainsilber and Ortony, 1987) as support for the role of emotion in these enhanced conceptual links. It is also important to note that these conceptual associations are also at the heart of the theory of conceptual integration or blending (Fauconnier & Turner, 2002).

Research suggests that it is positive rather than negative emotions that strengthen the connections between concepts that underlie blending, and there is some evidence that this is based on positive emotions being associated with approach motivation and negative emotions with withdrawal motivation. However, this clear-cut dichotomy has been challenged by the finding that anger, traditionally viewed as a negative emotion, is associated with approach motivation. This is based on the suggestion that anger, similar to happiness, is associated with optimistic expectations (Lerner, and Keltner, 2001), and leads to the possibility that the motivational direction of emotion should be considered as independent of the valence of emotion (Harmon-Jones et al., 2008). Further research is required to determine more precisely the relative influence of positive vs. negative emotions and approach vs. avoidance motivation on the strengthening of conceptual associations and blending.

The final point discussed in the paper is the place and function of the thesis of the embodied mind (Lakoff, 1987) in the development of abstract thinking and reasoning and its relevance to drawing associations between distant concepts and hence metaphor understanding and production, and blending.

The importance of the influence of emotion-based and motivation-based effects on the strength of distant associations between concepts extends beyond blending to language evolution. Fauconnier and Turner (2008) posit that when humans developed the most advanced form of conceptual integration, which they refer to as double-scope blending, perhaps 50 to 80 thousand years ago, language evolved. When juxtaposing this with the possible influence of emotional state and approach-avoidance motivation on blending, we can draw the conclusion that emotion and approach-avoidance motivation played a potentially important role in the genesis of language.

References

Fainsilber, L., & Ortony, A. (1987). Metaphorical uses of language in the expression of emotions. *Metaphor and Symbolic Activity, 2,* 239-250.

Fauconnier, G., & Turner, M. (2002). *Conceptual blending and the mind's hidden complexities.* New York: Basic Books.

Fauconnier, G., & Turner, M. (2008). The origin of language as a product of the evolution of double-scope blending. *Behavioral and Brain Sciences, 31,* 520-521.

Harmon-Jones, E., Peterson, C., Gable, P. A., & Harmon-Jones, C. (2008). Anger and approach-avoidance motivation. In A, J. Elliot (Ed.), *Handbook of approach and avoidance motivation* (pp. 399-413). New York, NY: Psychology Press.

Lakoff, G. (1987). *Women, fire, and dangerous things: What categories reveal about the mind.* Chicago: University of Chicago Press.

Lerner, J. S., & Keltner, D. (2001). Fear, anger, and risk. *Journal of Personality and Social Psychology, 81,* 146–159.

Lubart, T. I., & Getz, I. (1997). Emotion, metaphor, and the creative process. *Creativity Research Journal, 10 (4),* 285-301.

THE MYTH SURROUNDING THE BAN BY *SOCIÉTÉ DE LINGUISTIQUE DE PARIS*

HAJIME YAMAUCHI

TERRENCE W. DEACON

Department of Anthropology, University of California, Berkeley, Kroeber Hall, Berkeley, CA, 94720 USA
hoplite@berkeley.edu, deacon@berkeley.edu

KAZUO OKANOYA

Department of Cognitive and Behavioral Sciences, The University of Tokyo, 3-8-1 Komaba, Meguro-ku, Tokyo 153-8902 JAPAN
cokanoya@mail.ecc.u-tokyo.ac.jp

The Society will accept no communication dealing with either the origin of language or the creation of a universal language.

Translated from French by Stam (1976)

This is arguably the most important (and the most *in*famous) article in the study of language evolution: Inserted as the second article of "statuts de 1866", it is widely supposed that the *Société de linguistique de Paris (SLP)* officially killed the field of language evolution. Its impact was not confined within the society itself nor 19th century linguistics in general. Quite the contrary, as Fitch (2010) ironically points out, the ban practically remained in force almost over a century. Consequently, our knowledge of language from evolutionary perspectives has lagged behind other similar disciplines, such as evolutionary psychology.

Yet, there are surprisingly few details available about this historical fact. While almost all major books in this field published since 1990 have some reference to it, one could ask how many readers realize that the second article was simply abandoned by the society within a mere decade. Or, that the creation of the ban was deeply motivated by the fact that the conservative society was in the midst of a competition against a more politically-charged learned society "*Société d'Anthropologie de Paris* (SAP)", led by the hardcore positivist, P. Broca (Auroux, 1988)?

Indeed, the SLP had never been stable and autonomous. As a society that branched off from the *Société d'Ethnographie Américaine et Orientale* (SEAO), this learned society was privately formed by (both politically and religiously) highly conservative ethnologists/ethnographers around 1863 (Bergounioux, 2005). This is precisely the reason that the first article of SLP begins with "the Society of Linguistics has its object the study of languages, and legends, traditions, customs, and documents *which could clarify ethnographic science*"(translated by Stam, 1976, and emphasis by the authors). SLP was under the heavy influence of the authoritarian government: its first official president (É Egger) was successfully elected due support from French education ministry. As such, it was practically impossible to ignore the views of the Second Empire. Indeed, the sole reason that the society set its official articles was to transform the private society into an official one so that it could serve as an educational body for the fourth section of *Ecole Pratique des Hautes Études*.

This transformation allowed them to introduce young comparativists (e.g., M. Bréal) into the society, which, at the time, was thought to be a cutting-edge research program. However, this made the society a mishmash of original conservative members and young, somewhat more liberal members. This was in stark contrast to Broca's SAP, whose members had united to establish a positivistic program in the study of human beings, namely "the Science of Man." Some of its core members (most notably H. Chavée and Hovelacque) even established their own journal in linguistics, which was strongly influenced by German linguistics (such as A. Schleicher's). The time that positivism the sole privilege of Natural Science had been long gone: it was now eclipsing good, old, morally-rooted Humanities. For the pro-governments, the devouts, or the orthodoxies, monism, materialism and Darwinism were all hazardous ideologies. In the end, the situations surrounding SLP were a miniature version of revolution-inclined, turbulent French society.

In this presentation, we will first summarize the field of linguistics in 19th century France with considerations of political, religious and scholastic perspectives in Europe. Then we will argue that the second article was indeed the result of the political compromise whose primary intention was to avoid any positivist-flavored discussions in linguistics which would potentially dismantle the unity of SLP.

References

Auroux, S. (1988). La question de l'origine des langues: ordres et raisons du rejet institutionnel. In J. Gessinger & W. v. Rahden (Eds.), *Theorien vom ursprung der sprache* (Vol. 2, p. 122-150). de Gruyter.

Bergounioux, G. (2005). L'origine du langage: Mythes et théories. In J.-M. Hombert (Ed.), *Aux origines des langues et du langage* (p. 15-39). Fayard.

Fitch, W. T. (2010). *The evolution of language.* Cambridge University Press.

Stam, J. H. (1976). *Inquiries into the origin of language: The fate of a question.* Harper and Row.

WHY LANGUAGE EVOLVED ONLY ONCE

CHARLES YANG

Department of Linguistics, Computer Science & Psychology, Institute for Research in Cognitive Science, University of Pennsylvania, 619 Williams Hall, Philadelphia PA 19104, USA

It is easy, almost trivial, to claim the superiority of a combinatorial linguistic system over a finite repository of fixed expressions. The traditional problem has always been to explain how the finite-to-infinity transition might have taken place. For a gradualist approach to the origin of language, a common answer points to the recapitulation of phylogeny in ontology. The developmental stages in child language acquisition are said to trace similar steps in language evolution (Bickerton 1996, Studdert-Kennedy 1998, Wray 1998, Tomasello 2003), as both processes are envisioned to move from concrete utterances to increasingly abstract grammatical processes.

While we cannot directly examine our evolutionary past, we can indeed focus on the present. The presupposition that child language starts off as a system of limited productivity (Tomasello 1992, 2003) has been established on observations that the diversity of syntactic usage appears to be much more restricted than what a freely combinatorial system would entail. Yet it is worth noting that the usage-based approach has never been subject to rigorous empirical tests. That is, the (low) syntactic diversity of child language has not been compared to a combinatorial grammar resulting in its rejection, nor has it been tested to statistically confirm the predictions of usage-based learning, which has so far eluded formalization.

In this paper, we present two extensive studies of early child language to show that a non-productive or formulaic stage of grammar does not appear to exist. First, we propose a mathematically precise formulation of usage diversity (Yang

2011) building on well known distributional properties of language (Zipf 1949). Using the diversity in determiner-noun combination as a case study (Pine & Lievin 1997, Valian et al. 2008), we show that early child language is statistically indistinguishable from a productive rule that independently combines these two syntactic categories. Furthermore, the memory plus retrieval approach advocated in the usage based literature (Tomasello 2000) under-predicts usage diversity in child language.

Second, we present results from the largest empirical study of English past tense acquisition to date (Gorman & Yang 2011). The associative storage of irregular past tense forms has been accepted by both sides of the so-called Past Tense debate (Pinker & Ullman 2002, McClelland & Patterson 2002), and would constitute a prime example of directly paired linguistic expressions (e.g., *think-thought*). A mixed-effects analysis of children's over-egularization errors, however, show relatively minor effects of verb past tense frequencies, which has been consistently cited to support for the storage theory, but show much stronger effects of rule frequencies (Yang 2002), or the sum of past tense frequencies of verbs belonging to the same class (e.g., *thought, caught, bought, brought, taught* for the rule "-t suffixation and change Rime to *a*"). This finding provides strong support for the compositional approach to word formation as held in generative grammar (Chomsky & Halle 1968) as well as traditional descriptions (e.g., the Oxford English Dictionary), even for a very small number of arbitrary words.

These surveys of child language suggest that all stages of linguistic development can, and should, be characterized as a compositional system of linguistic generation. A gradualist account of language evolution thus loses its starting position never mind the transitional steps toward the terminal point. And we are left to contemplate the saltationist alternative, that the key component of Language evolved only once.

References

Bickerton, D. (1996). *Language and human behavior.* Seattle, WA: U. Washington Press.

Chomsky, N. & Halle, M. (1968). *The sound pattern of English.* Harper & Row.

Gorman, K. & Yang, C. (2011). Word vs. rule frequencies in irregular acquisition. Paper presented at the 2011 Boston University Conference on Language Development.

McClelland, J. & Patterson, K. (2002). Rules or connections in past-tense inflections: What does the evidence rule out? *Trends in Cognitive Sciences,* 6, 11, 465-472.
Pine, J. & Lieven, E. (1997). Slot and frame patterns in the development of the determiner category. *Applied Psycholinguistics*, 18, 123-138.
Pinker, S. & Ullman, M. (2002). The past and future of the past tense. *Trends in Cognitive Sciences,* 6:11, 456-463.
Studdert-Kennedy, M. (1998). The particulate origins of language generativity: from syllable to gestures. In Hurford, J. et al. (Eds.) *Approaches to the evolution of language: social and cognitive bases.* Cambridge University Press. 202-221.
Tomasello, M. (1992). *First verbs: A case study of early grammatical development.* Cambridge, MA: Harvard University Press.
Tomasello, M. (2000). First steps toward a usage-based theory of language acquisition. *Cognitive Linguistics*, 11, 61-82.
Tomasello, M. (2003). *Constructing a language.* Cambridge, MA: Harvard University Press.
Wray, A. (1998). Protolanguage as a holistic system for social interaction. *Language and Communication*, 18, 47-67.
Valian, V., Solt, S. & Stewart, J. (2008). Abstract categories or limited-scope formulae? The case of children's determiners. *Journal of Child Language*, 35, 1-36.
Yang, C. (2002). *Knowledge and language in natural language.* Oxford: Oxford University Press.
Yang, C. (2011). A statistical test for grammar. *Proceedings of ACL/HLT.* Portland, OR.
Zipf, G. (1949). *Human behavior and the principle of least effort: An introduction to human ecology.* Addison-Wesley.

INTERSUBJECTIVITY AS THE KEY PRECONDITION FOR LANGUAGE: ITS EVOLUTION (AND POSSIBLE DEVOLUTION)

JORDAN ZLATEV

Centre for Languages and Literature, Lund University, Box 201 Lund, 221 00, Sweden

Language is primarily about *sharing* – meanings, grammatical rules/constructions, conventions of use (different aspects of "knowing a language"), and putting these to use for communicating factual knowledge and fictive beliefs. Thus, human languages are essentially "socially shared symbolic systems" (Nelson and Shaw 2002). At the same time, "the cooperative sharing of information … remains a central puzzle in language evolution" (Fitch 2010: 417). Proposals to resolve this puzzle on the basis of factors such as reciprocal altruism, prestige, or kin selection have remained at best incomplete. The puzzle is not only to explain the evolution of "honest cheap signals", but of a way of life characterized by intentional mimesis (Donald 1991) and joint attention/action/commitment (Tomasello 2008), arguably serving as the "biocultural niche" for the evolution of language (Sinha 2010). Such a niche lacks parallels in the animal kingdom. This claim does not deny the existence of social learning and even "culture" in non-human animals, but points out that there are nevertheless key species differences. All attested cases of social learning in animals involve patterns of behavior that directly satisfy a biological need (e.g. nut cracking), while human cultures imply conformity to rules and practices that relate to individual or group survival only indirectly. From such a perspective, the key hurdle to explaining the evolution of language is to account for the uniquely human propensity for (symbolic) culture, a puzzle just as great as that of language. So we are back to square one.

A recent proposal, however, suggests a possible resolution to the puzzle. Hrdy (2009) builds her theory of the "evolutionary origins of mutual understanding" on the observation that we, uniquely among the great apes, extensively share food and infant care amongst individuals, not all of which are even closely biologically related. Hrdy's proposal that "cooperative breeding was the pre-existing condition" (ibid: 299) for the evolution of uniquely human sociality can be compared with alternative proposals such as that of Dunbar (1998): larger group size and the negative side effects of intra-group competition, and Deacon (1997): sexual division of labor and the origin of "marriage". I argue that Hrdy's theory fairs best on the basis of the following criteria: (1) "Why us and not them"? (2) Timing of anatomical changes according to fossil evidence; (3) Anthropological evidence from hunter-gather societies; (4) Developmental evidence, concerning infant intersubjectivity and attachment; and (5) Darwinian logic, e.g. differences in reproductive interests between mothers and fathers.

Perhaps most striking, however, are the implications of Hrdy's theory for our present day situation: "The modern emphasis on individualism and personal independence along with consumption-oriented economics, compartmentalized living arrangements in highrise apartments or suburban homes… combine to undermine social connectedness." (: 286). In particular, it offers a possible explanation for the "sobering statistics about the emotional well-being of children." (: 289): intersubjectivity develops in particular rearing condition, while "an ever-increasing proportion of the species fails to encounter those conditions but nevertheless survives to reproduce" (: 293). This would imply that the essence of what makes us human, and the essential precondition for language evolution and development, is in the process of devolution. This is staggering conclusion, but one that needs to be taken most seriously.

References

Deacon, T. (1997). *The Symbolic Species: The Co-evolution of Language and the Brain.* New York: Norton.

Donald, M. (1991). *Origins of the Modern Mind: Three Stages in the Evolution of Culture and Cognition.* Cambridge, Mass.: Harvard University Press.

Dunbar, R. (1998). *Grooming, Gossip and the Evolution of Language.* Cambridge, Mass.: Harvard University Press.

Fitch. T. (2010). *The Evolution of Language*. Oxford: Oxford University Press.

Hrdy, S.B. (2009). *Mothers and Others: The Evolutionary Origins of Mutual Understanding*. Cambridge, Mass.: Harvard University Press.

Nelson, K. and Shaw, L. K. (2002). Developing a socially shared symbolic system. In J. Byrnes and E. Amseli (Eds.) *Language, Literacy and Cognitive Development* (pp. 27-57). Mahwah, N.J.: Erlbaum.

Sinha, C. (2010). Language as a biocultural niche and social institution. In V. Evans and S. Pourcel (Eds.), *New Directions in Cognitive Linguistics.* Amsterdam: John Benjamins.

Tomasello, M. (2008). *Origins of Human Communication.* Cambridge, Mass.: MIT Press.

Author Index